second e

PHILOS-OPHY
OF RELIGION

Selected Readings

second edition

PHILOSOPHY OF RELIGION

Selected Readings

William L. Rowe
Purdue University

William J. Wainwright
University of Wisconsin—Milwaukee

Under the General Editorship of

Robert Ferm
Middlebury College

HARCOURT BRACE JOVANOVICH, PUBLISHERS

San Diego   New York   Chicago   Austin   Washington, D.C.

London   Sydney   Tokyo   Toronto

ISBN: 0-15-570581-4

Library of Congress Catalog Card Number: 88-80644

Printed in the United States of America

PREFACE

T he aim of this volume is to introduce students to the philosophy of religion by acquainting them with the writings of some of the thinkers who have made substantial contributions in this area. The book covers many topics that are central to the philosophy of religion, and, for each topic it considers, we have sought to provide readings that reflect various philosophical viewpoints and pursue them in some depth without a loss of clarity.

This new edition expands the range of topics by including an entirely new chapter on Death and Immortality and a new subsection on The Moral Argument. There is also some new material on Wittgenstein and Fideism, Religious Pluralism, and Faith and the Need for Evidence. In addition, almost every chapter has been changed by deletions or additions in order to update the selections and provide more material that is understandable to beginning students.

The editorial material includes new introductions to each major topic, with suggestions for further reading presented at the end of each chapter. The student may also benefit from the brief biographical footnotes about the authors of the selections.

We appreciate the help and encouragement given us by Bill McLane and the staff at Harcourt Brace Jovanovich. We also appreciate the helpful advice of Robert Ferm of Middlebury College. We thank Robert F. Brown, University of Delaware; Malcolm E. Munson, Our Lady of the Lake University of San Antonio; Georgette Sinkler, Washington University; and William J. Wood, Wheaton College, for their reviews of the manuscript. Finally, we wish to acknowledge and thank Jeff Jordan of Purdue University for his revision of the Suggestions for Further Reading and for other assistance in the preparation of the manuscript.

W. L. R.
W. J. W.

CONTENTS

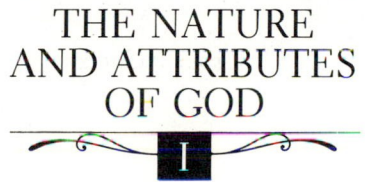

KNOWLEDGE   25

POWER   59

THE METAPHYSICAL ATTRIBUTES   77

ARGUMENTS
FOR THE EXISTENCE
OF GOD
II

THE PROBLEM OF EVIL

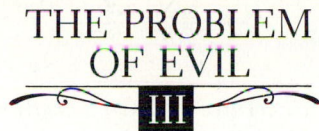

III

OBJECTIONS TO TRADITIONAL THEISM

IV

MEANING AND VERIFICATION   266

WITTGENSTEIN AND FIDEISM   275

RELIGIOUS PLURALISM   295

MYSTICISM AND RELIGIOUS EXPERIENCE
V

THE NATURE AND TYPES OF RELIGIOUS AND MYSTICAL EXPERIENCE   313

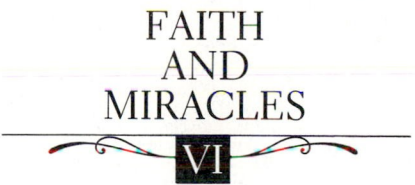

FAITH AND MIRACLES
VI

DEATH
AND
IMMORTALITY

THE NATURE AND ATTRIBUTES OF GOD

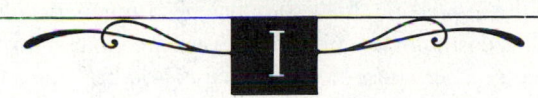

I

The theistic concept of God is the concept of a purely spiritual being who is perfectly good, omnipotent, and omniscient. A number of important theologians—Augustine, Anselm, and Aquinas—have held that the concept of God also requires that He be necessary, timeless, immutable, and simple (without parts). The readings in this section serve two general aims. First, they clarify and explain some of the very basic attributes of the theistic God. Second, they examine some of the fundamental problems that have arisen in connection with the theistic concept of God.

The idea that God is a necessary being is a fundamental theme of theism. But what is meant by the expression "necessary being"? Proponents of the eighteenth-century form of the cosmological argument used the expression to mean a *logically* necessary being, one whose nonexistence is a logical impossibility. Certain remarks by Anselm and Aquinas suggest that they had also thought of God as a logically necessary being. John Hick, however, challenges this interpretation of Anselm and Aquinas and points out—particularly in Aquinas—a different sense of "necessary being" according to which God is necessary provided that He is incorruptible, indestructible, without beginning or end, and not dependent on anything for His existence. In Hick's view, God is a *factually* necessary being, not a logically necessary being. Like other beings, God's nonexistence is a logical possibility, but unlike other beings, God has no beginning or end and does not depend for His existence on any other thing.

Hick accepts without criticism the view of many modern philosophers that logical necessity applies only to propositions and that no proposition affirming the existence of something can be logically necessary. But it is doubtful that either feature of this view is acceptable as it stands. For, in the first place, we can define the notion of a logically necessary being in terms of some proposition being logically necessary—for example, "God is a logically necessary being just in case some proposition affirming the existence of the being who is God is logically necessary." And, in the second place, it is not true that no proposition affirming the existence of something can be logically necessary. "There exists a prime number between 1 and 3" affirms the existence of something and is generally admitted to be logically necessary.

One traditional theistic belief is that God knows everything that has happened, everything that is now happening, and everything that will happen in the future. It is the last of these, the concept of Divine Foreknowledge, that has been thought to lead to a difficulty. For if God has foreknowledge of everything that happens, then it seems to follow that whatever happens happens of necessity, could not have failed to happen. Whatever we may believe about Divine Foreknowledge, most of us believe that not everything that happens happens of necessity. For example, consider such events as the election of Richard Nixon to the Presidency or the invasion of Cambodia. These events have happened, but they could have failed to happen. We think that at some time before their occurrence it was in the power of some person or group to have prevented them from happening— they were not bound to happen. It was, in the months preceding their occurrence,

2

possible for them to occur and possible for them not to occur. They were then what the medievals called future contingent events. They were then still in the future, and they were then contingent: it was possible for them to be and possible for them not to be. Of course, once they had occurred they were no longer future, nor were they any longer contingent—for it was no longer possible for them not to be. Thus to believe, as we do, that many events that occur are such that in the time preceding their occurrence it is equally possible for them to occur or not to occur, that their occurrence or nonoccurrence can be determined by some individual or group, is to believe that not everything that happens is bound to happen, happens of necessity. Most of us believe, in short, that there are future contingent events. But many people have thought that Divine Foreknowledge is inconsistent with future contingency. In their view, for example, if in the year 5000 B.C. God knew that Nixon would be elected in 1968, then it follows that in the months and years preceding the election, his election to the Presidency was future, but not contingent, for it was then not possible for it not to be. Given God's Foreknowledge, the election of Nixon was (in the months preceding the election) bound to happen; it was then (at that time) not possible for it not to happen.

Why should the fact that God knew in 5000 B.C. that Nixon would be elected in 1968 lead us to think in 1967 Nixon's election in 1968 was bound to happen, that in the months preceding the presidential election no person or group had the power to prevent Nixon's winning? Of course, given what God knew in 5000 B.C., it follows that in 1967 no one was to successfully exercise his power to prevent Nixon's election. But does it follow that in 1967 no one even had it in his power to do so? In support of the claim that it does follow, various reasons have been given, but the most forceful is the following: given the fact of what God knew in 5000 B.C.—namely, that Nixon would be elected in 1968—to say that in 1967 some person or group had the power to prevent Nixon's election seems to imply that some person or group had the power to alter a fact about the past—that is, the fact of what God knew in 5000 B.C. But surely no one ever has it in his power to alter a fact about the past. The past is beyond our power. God's foreknowledge, therefore, is inconsistent with the idea of the future being contingent.

Nelson Pike endeavors to establish that, given that God exists in time (and other relevant assumptions), the above reasoning is correct: God's foreknowledge and human freedom are incompatible. Boethius and Aquinas, however, endeavor to dissolve the problem by appealing to the idea that God is a timeless being. Since He is outside of time, it is not strictly true that God knows, at a time before you act, what you will do. Thus, for Boethius and Aquinas, there is no fact about some time past that you must have the power to alter if you are to act freely.

How are we to understand the attribute of omnipotence as applied to God? Suppose we say that

1. God is omnipotent = God can do anything.

But, as Aquinas points out, even God cannot create things that are absolutely impossible (contradictory)—for example, an object that is both perfectly round and perfectly square. God's power extends only to those things that are possible. Following Aquinas' suggestion we have

2. God is omnipotent = God can do anything that is logically possible.

Difficulties remain, however. Although making an object both round and square is impossible, self-destruction and evil are things that clearly can be done. But many theologians have denied that God's power extends to self-destruction and evil. For the doing of such things, as Samuel Clarke argues, is inconsistent with God's nature (His infinity and perfect goodness). It might be argued that God's perfections imply only that God will not destroy Himself or do evil, not that He cannot—He has the power to do evil, but because He is supremely perfect it is a power He will never exercise. What this objection overlooks is that to attribute to God the power to do evil is to attribute to Him the power to cease to have an attribute (perfection) that is part of His very essence or nature. For since "God does evil" entails "God is not supremely perfect," if God has the power to do evil then He has the power to become not supremely perfect. And it is doubtful that any being has the power to remove from itself an attribute essential to it. Perhaps, then, we should replace definition 2 with

3. God is omnipotent = God can do anything that is logically possible and that is not inconsistent with any of His essential attributes.

In his discussion, Peter Geach shows the inadequacy of several attempts to explicate the doctrine of divine omnipotence. Geach's objections to some naive accounts of omnipotence are compelling; his objections to more sophisticated accounts are, however, not fully convincing. In place of omnipotence, Geach advances the doctrine that God is almighty in the sense that He has power over all things.

Plato argued that God must be unchangeable, for to change is to change either for the worse or for the better. But God, being perfect, cannot change for the worse. Nor can He change for the better since only what is less than supremely perfect can be improved. In his discussion of God's unchangeableness (immutability), Anselm presupposes a distinction between essential and accidental attributes of a thing. An essential attribute is a quality that a thing cannot lose and remain the thing that it is—for example, being human is an essential attribute of Plato, whereas being a philosopher is accidental to Plato. Among accidental properties Anselm distinguishes those which, if lost, result in a real change in a thing and those which do not. If one thing has the property of being taller than a second and, as a result of a change in the second thing, comes to have the property of being shorter than the second, no change need have occurred in it; whereas if a thing is red, but later becomes blue, a real change has occurred in it. God's immutability, in Anselm's view, implies that no change whatever can occur in God, either accidental or essential. God may, however, acquire the property of being worshiped by someone without undergoing any change. The implication of the foregoing is that God cannot be subject to feelings and emotions—for if a being comes to feel joy and then remorse, it has undergone change. Finally, immutability, as Anselm understands it, relates closely to timelessness. A being in time changes in virtue of the fact that, with each passing moment, it becomes older. But, as Anselm claims, God is completely outside of time: He does not endure through any period of time nor is He located at any point in time.

The selection by Charles Hartshorne raises serious objections to the metaphysical attributes of God described by Anselm and Aquinas. In his view, these attributes, as traditionally understood, seem to render God indifferent to the sufferings of His creatures.

W. L. R.

NECESSARY BEING

ST. ANSELM
The Divine Nature Exists through Itself

CHAPTER IV.

. . . There is, therefore, a certain Nature, or Substance, or Essence, which is through itself good and great, and through itself is what it is; and through which exists whatever is truly good, or great, or has any existence at all; and which is the supreme good being, the supreme great being, being or subsisting as supreme, that is, the highest of all existing beings.

CHAPTER V.   JUST AS THIS NATURE EXISTS THROUGH ITSELF, AND OTHER BEINGS THROUGH IT, SO IT DERIVES EXISTENCE FROM ITSELF, AND OTHER BEINGS FROM IT.

Seeing, then, that the truth already discovered has been satisfactorily demonstrated, it is profitable to examine whether this Nature, and all things that have any existence, derive existence from no other source than it, just as they do not exist except through it.

But it is clear that one may say, that what derives existence from something exists through the same thing; and what exists through something also derives existence from it. For instance, what derives existence from matter, and exists through the artificer, may also be said to exist through matter, and to derive existence from the artificer, since it exists through both, and derives existence

St. Anselm (1033–1109), consecrated Archbishop of Canterbury in 1093, was the most important philosopher and theologian of the eleventh century. His major works include *Monologium*, *Proslogium*, and *Cur Deus Homo*.

THE DIVINE NATURE EXISTS THROUGH ITSELF   Reprinted from *Monologium* by St. Anselm, translated by Sidney N. Deane. By permission of The Open Court Publishing Co., La Salle, Illinois.

from both. That is, it is endowed with existence by both, although it exists through matter and from the artificer in another sense than that in which it exists through, and from, the artificer.

It follows, then, that just as all existing beings are what they are, through the supreme Nature, and as that Nature exists through itself, but other beings through another than themselves, so all existing beings derive existence from this supreme Nature. And therefore, this Nature derives existence from itself, but other beings from it.

CHAPTER VI.   THIS NATURE WAS NOT BROUGHT INTO EXISTENCE WITH THE HELP OF ANY EXTERNAL CAUSE, YET IT DOES NOT EXIST THROUGH NOTHING, OR DERIVE EXISTENCE FROM NOTHING.—HOW EXISTENCE THROUGH SELF, AND DERIVED FROM SELF, IS CONCEIVABLE.

Since the same meaning is not always attached to the phrase, "existence through" something, or, to the phrase, "existence derived from" something, very diligent inquiry must be made, in what way all existing beings exist through the supreme Nature, or derive existence from it. For, what exists through itself, and what exists through another, do not admit the same ground of existence. Let us first consider, separately, this supreme Nature, which exists through self; then these beings which exist through another.

Since it is evident, then, that this Nature is whatever it is, through itself, and all other beings are what they are, through it, how does it exist through itself? For, what is said to exist through anything apparently exists through an efficient agent, or through matter, or through some other external aid, as through some instrument. But, whatever exists in any of these three ways exists through another than itself, and it is of later existence, and, in some sort, less than that through which it obtains existence.

But, in no wise does the supreme Nature exist through another, nor is it later or less than itself or anything else. Therefore, the supreme Nature could be created neither by itself, nor by another; nor could itself or any other be the matter whence it should be created; nor did it assist itself in any way; nor did anything assist it to be what it was not before.

What is to be inferred? For that which cannot have come into existence by any creative agent, or from any matter, or with any external aids, seems either to be nothing, or, if it has any existence, to exist through nothing, and derive existence from nothing. And although, in accordance with the observations I have already made, in the light of reason, regarding the supreme Substance, I should think such propositions could in no wise be true in the case of the supreme Substance; yet, I would not neglect to give a connected demonstration of this matter.

For, seeing that this my meditation has suddenly brought me to an important and interesting point, I am unwilling to pass over carelessly even any simple or almost foolish objection that occurs to me, in my argument; in order that by leaving no ambiguity in my discussion up to this point, I may have the better assured strength to advance toward what follows; and in order that if, perchance,

I shall wish to convince any one of the truth of my speculations, even one of the slower minds, through the removal of every obstacle, however slight, may acquiesce in what it finds here.

That this Nature, then, without which no nature exists, is nothing, is as false as it would be absurd to say that whatever is is nothing. And, moreover, it does not exist through nothing, because it is utterly inconceivable that what is something should exist through nothing. But, if in any way it derives existence from nothing, it does so through itself, or through another, or through nothing. But it is evident that in no wise does anything exist through nothing. If, then, in any way it derives existence from nothing, it does so either through itself or through another.

But nothing can, through itself, derive existence from nothing, because if anything derives existence from nothing, through something, then that through which it exists must exist before it. Seeing that this Being, then, does not exist before itself, by no means does it derive existence from nothing.

But if it is supposed to have derived existence from some other nature, then it is not the supreme Nature, but some inferior one, nor is it what it is through itself, but through another.

Again: if Nature derives existence from nothing, through something, that through which it exists was a great good, since it was the cause of good. But no good can be understood as existing before that good, without which nothing is good; and it is sufficiently clear that this good, without which there is no good, is the supreme Nature which is under discussion. Therefore, it is not even conceivable that this Nature was preceded by any being, through which it derived existence from nothing.

Hence, if it has any existence through nothing, or derives existence from nothing, there is no doubt that either, whatever it is, it does not exist through itself, or derive existence from itself, or else it is itself nothing. It is unnecessary to show that both these suppositions are false. The supreme Substance, then, does not exist through any efficient agent, and does not derive existence from any matter, and was not aided in being brought into existence by any external causes. Nevertheless, it by no means exists through nothing, or derives existence from nothing; since, through itself and from itself, it is whatever it is.

Finally, as to how it should be understood to exist through itself, and to derive existence from itself: it did not create itself, nor did it spring up as its own matter, nor did it in any way assist itself to become what it was not before, unless, haply, it seems best to conceive of this subject in the way in which one says that *the light lights* or is *lucent*, through and from itself. For, as are the mutual relations of *the light* and *to light* and *lucent (lux, lucere, lucens)*, such are the relations of *essence*, and *to be* and *being*, that is, *existing* or *subsisting*. So the supreme *Being*, and *to be* in the highest degree, and *being* in the highest degree, bear much the same relations, one to another, as *the light* and *to light* and *lucent*.

ST. THOMAS AQUINAS
God's Nature Cannot Be Separated from His Existence

FIRST ARTICLE.   WHETHER THE EXISTENCE OF GOD IS SELF-EVIDENT?

. . . A thing can be self-evident in either of two ways: on the one hand, self-evident in itself, though not to us; on the other, self-evident in itself, and to us. A proposition is self-evident because the predicate is included in the essence of the subject: *e.g.*, *Man is an animal*, for animal is contained in the essence of man. If, therefore, the essence of the predicate and subject be known to all, the proposition will be self-evident to all; as is clear with regard to the first principles of demonstration, the terms of which are certain common notions that no one is ignorant of, such as being and non-being, whole and part, and the like. If, however, there are some to whom the essence of the predicate and subject is unknown, the proposition will be self-evident in itself, but not to those who do not know the meaning of the predicate and subject of the proposition. Therefore, it happens, as Boethius says, that there are some notions of the mind which are common and self-evident only to the learned, as that incorporeal substances are not in space.[1] Therefore I say that this proposition, *God exists*, of itself is self-evident, for the predicate is the same as the subject, because God is His own existence as will be hereafter shown.[2] Now because we do not know the essence of God, the proposition is not self-evident to us, but needs to be demonstrated by things that are more known to us, though less known in their nature—namely, by His effects. . . .

THIRD ARTICLE.   WHETHER GOD IS THE SAME AS HIS ESSENCE OR NATURE?

We proceed thus to the Third Article:—

Objection 1. It seems that God is not the same as His essence or nature. For nothing is in itself. But the essence or nature of God—*i.e.*, the Godhead—is said to be in God. Therefore it seems that God is not the same as His essence or nature.

Obj. 2. Further, the effect is assimilated to its cause; for every agent produces its like. But in created things the *suppositum* is not identical with its nature; for a

St. Thomas Aquinas (1225–1274) was a Dominican friar and, in the opinion of many, the greatest medieval philosopher and theologian. His writings, which attempt to adapt Aristotle's philosophy to a Christian setting, are the basis for modern Thomism and constitute the semiofficial philosophy of the Roman Catholic Church. His principal works are *Summa Theologica* and *Summa Contra Gentiles*.

GOD'S NATURE CANNOT BE SEPARATED FROM HIS EXISTENCE   From *Summa Theologica*, Part I, Questions 2 and 3, in *Basic Writings of Saint Thomas Aquinas*, edited by Anton C. Pegis. By permission of the A. C. Pegis estate.

[1] *De Hebdom.* (PL 64, 1311).

[2] Q. 3, a. 4 [in *Philosophy of Religion: Selected Readings*, 2nd ed., 10–12].

man is not the same as his humanity. Therefore God is not the same as His Godhead.

On the contrary, It is said of God that He is life itself, and not only that He is a living thing: *I am the way, the truth, and the life* (Jo. xiv. 6). Now the relation between Godhead and God is the same as the relation between life and a living thing. Therefore God is His very Godhead.

I answer that, God is the same as His essence or nature. To understand this, it must be noted that in things composed of matter and form, the nature or essence must differ from the *suppositum,* for the essence or nature includes only what falls within the definition of the species; as humanity includes all that falls within the definition of man, for it is by this that man is man, and it is this that humanity signifies, that, namely, whereby man is man. Now individual matter, with all the individuating accidents, does not fall within the definition of the species. For this particular flesh, these bones, this blackness or whiteness, etc., do not fall within the definition of a man. Therefore this flesh, these bones, and the accidental qualities designating this particular matter, are not included in humanity; and yet they are included in the reality which is a man. Hence, the reality which is a man has something in it that humanity does not have. Consequently, humanity and a man are not wholly identical, but humanity is taken to mean the formal part of a man, because the principles whereby a thing is defined function as the formal constituent in relation to individuating matter. The situation is different in things not composed of matter and form, in which individuation is not due to individual matter—it is to say, to *this* matter—but the forms themselves are individuated of themselves. Here it is necessary that the forms themselves should be subsisting *supposita.* Therefore *suppositum* and nature in them are identified. Since, then, God is not composed of matter and form, He must be His own Godhead, His own Life, and whatever else is so predicated of Him.

Reply Obj. 1. We can speak of simple things only as though they were like the composite things from which we derive our knowledge. Therefore, in speaking of God, we use concrete nouns to signify His subsistence, because with us only those things subsist which are composite, and we use abstract nouns to signify His simplicity. In speaking therefore of Godhead, or life, or the like as being in God, we indicate the composite way in which our intellect understands, but not that there is any composition in God.

Reply Obj. 2. The effects of God do not imitate Him perfectly, but only as far as they are able. It pertains to defect in imitation that what is simple and one can be represented only by a multiplicity. This is the source of composition in God's effects, and therefore in them *suppositum* is not the same as nature.

FOURTH ARTICLE.   WHETHER ESSENCE AND BEING ARE THE SAME IN GOD?

We proceed thus to the Fourth Article:—

Objection 1. It seems that essence and being [*esse*] are not the same in God. For if it be so, then the divine being has nothing added to it. Now being to which no addition is made is the being-in-general which is predicated of all things. Therefore it follows that God is being-in-general which can be predicated of everything. But this is false: *For men gave the incommunicable name to stones and wood* (*Wisd.* xiv. 21). Therefore God's being is not His essence.

Obj. 2. Further, we can know *whether* God exists, as was said above,[3] but we cannot now *what* He is. Therefore God's being is not the same as His essence—that is, as His quiddity or nature.

On the contrary, Hilary says: *In God being is not an accidental quality but subsisting truth.*[4] Therefore what subsists in God is His being.

I answer that, God is not only His own essence, as has been shown, but also His own being. This may be shown in several ways. First, whatever a thing has besides its essence must be caused either by the constituent principles of that essence (like a proper accident that necessarily accompanies the species—as the faculty of laughing is proper to a man—and is caused by the constituent principles of the species), or by some exterior agent,—as heat is caused in water by fire. Therefore, if the being of a thing differs from its essence, this being must be caused either by some exterior agent or by the essential principles of the thing itself. Now it is impossible for a thing's being to be caused only by its essential constituent principles, for nothing can be the sufficient cause of its own being, if its being is caused. Therefore that thing, whose being differs from its essence, must have its being caused by another. But this cannot be said of God, because we call God the first efficient cause. Therefore it is impossible that in God His being should differ from His essence.

Second, being is the actuality of every form or nature; for goodness and humanity are spoken of as actual, only because they are spoken of as being. Therefore, being must be compared to essence, if the latter is distinct from it, as actuality to potentiality. Therefore, since in God there is no potentiality, as shown above, it follows that in Him essence does not differ from being. Therefore His essence is His being. Third, just as that which has fire, but is not itself fire, is on fire by participation, so that which has being, but is not being, is a being by participation. But God is His own essence, as was shown above. If, therefore, He is not His own being, He will be not essential, but participated, being. He will not therefore be the first being—which is absurd. Therefore, God is His own being, and not merely His own essence.

Reply Obj. 1. A thing-that-has-nothing-added-to-it can be understood in two ways. Either its essence precludes any addition (thus, for example, it is of the essence of an irrational animal to be without reason), or we may understand a thing to have nothing added to it, inasmuch as its essence does not require that anything should be added to it (thus the genus animal is without reason, because it is not of the essence of animal in general to have reason; but neither is it of the essence of animal to lack reason). And so the divine being has nothing added to it in the first sense; whereas being-in-general has nothing added to it in the second sense.

Reply Obj. 2. To *be* can mean either of two things. It may mean the act of being, or it may mean the composition of a proposition effected by the mind in

[3] Q. 2, a. 2.

[4] *De Trin.*, VII (PL 10, 208).

joining a predicate to a subject. Taking *to be* in the first sense, we cannot understand God's being (or His essence); but only in the second sense. We know that
this proposition which we form about God when we say *God is*, is true; and this
we know from His effects, as was said above.[5]

JOHN HICK
Necessary Being

I

'Necessary being' is one of the terms by means of which Christian thought has
sought to define the difference between God and man. The notion of necessary
being, applied to God and withheld from man, indicates that God and man differ
not merely in the characteristics which they possess but more fundamentally, in
their modes of being, or in the fact that they exist in different senses of the
word 'exist.'

That such a distinction, however it may be best expressed, is essential to the
Christian concept of God is agreed virtually on all hands. Paul Tillich in our own
day emphasises the distinction to the extent of using different terms to refer to the
reality of God and of man respectively. Human beings and other created things
exist; God, on the other hand, does not exist, but is Being-itself. This is the most
recent way of formulating a discrimination which has been classically expressed
in the history of Christian thought by the idea of the necessary being of God in
contrast to the contingent being of man and of the whole created order.

There are, however, two importantly different concepts which may be, and
which have been, expressed by the phrase 'necessary being.' 'Necessity,' in a
philosophical context, usually means logical necessity, and gives rise in theology
to the concept of a being such that it is logically impossible that this being should
not exist. But this is not the only kind of necessity referred to in philosophical
literature. The non-logical concepts of causal, empirical and material necessity
can be grouped together as forms of *factual* necessity. The distinction between
logical and factual necessity first appears, so far as I know, in the *Critique of Pure*

John Hick (1922–   ) was educated at Edinburgh University and Oxford and Cambridge Universities.
Among his many influential writings are *Faith and Knowledge, Evil and the God of Love,* and *Argu-
ments for the Existence of God.* Hick has been Danforth Professor of Religion at Claremont Graduate
School, Claremont, California, since 1979.

NECESSARY BEING   From *Scottish Journal of Theology*, December 1961. Reprinted by permission of
the publisher, Scottish Academic Press (Journals) Limited.

[5]Q. 2, a. 2.

Reason, where Kant treats of the three modal categories of possibility, existence and necessity. The category of necessity is derived by him from the necessary or analytic proposition in formal logic. But its schema in time is the existence of an object throughout all time;[1] and the corresponding 'postulate of empirical thought' is called by Kant *die materiale Notwendigkeit* and is equivalent to what is often described as causal necessity, i.e., being part of the universal causal system of nature.[2] The schema of necessity as existence throughout all time suggests the notion of a temporally unlimited being, and this is an important part, though not the whole, of the concept of God as a factually necessary being. I shall argue that the notion of factual necessity, when appropriately spelled out, is an essential element in the Christian doctrine of God, but that the notion of logical necessity is both philosophically and religiously profitless, and indeed even dangerous, to theology.

It is important to distinguish explicitly between logical and factual necessity, not only for the elucidation of the doctrine of God within the Church, but also in the interests of apologetics. For a number of contemporary philosophers of the analytical school have assumed that Christian theology requires the notion of logically necessary being, and having noted that this idea is rendered meaningless by the modern understanding of the nature of logical necessity, have rejected what they suppose to be the Christian concept of God. They are, however, I believe, mistaken in their initial assumption. My thesis thus has a threefold bearing. I wish to suggest, as a matter of theology, that the idea of the divine being as factually necessary is more adequate to the data of Christian faith than the idea of God's being as logically necessary; and as a matter of philosophy, that the idea of factually necessary being is immune from the criticisms which have rightly been leveled against the notion of logically necessary being; and as a matter of history, that the notion of God's being as factually necessary has a stronger claim to be regarded as the normative Christian use of the term 'necessary being' than has its interpretation in terms of logical necessity.

Let us begin with the idea of logically necessary being. To say that God has logically necessary being, or that His existence is logically necessary, is to say that it is logically impossible that God should not exist; or that the concept of God is such that the proposition 'God exists' is a logical, analytic or *a priori* truth; or again that the proposition 'God does not exist' is a self-contradiction, a statement of such a kind that it is logically impossible for it to be true. Such a claim, however, contravenes one of the fundamental positions of empiricist philosophy— that an existential proposition (i.e., a proposition asserting existence) cannot be logically necessary. For modern empiricism is largely founded upon the distinction between, in Hume's phrases, 'the relations between ideas' on the one hand, and 'matters of fact and existence' on the other. Given this distinction, logical necessity clearly belongs exclusively to the sphere of the relations between ideas. The ideas of 'larger' and 'smaller' for example, are such that it is a logically necessary truth that if A is larger than B, then B is smaller than A, the necessity

[1] [Second Edition] 184.

[2] [Second Edition] 279–80.

arising from the meanings which we have given to the words 'larger' and 'smaller.' On the same principle, such propositions as 'God is omniscient' and 'God is omnipotent' express necessary truths, if 'God' has been defined as 'a being who is omniscient and omnipotent' or, compendiously, as 'unlimited Being.' Given this definition, it is not only a truth but an analytic truth that God is omniscient and omnipotent; for the definition renders it incorrect to call a Being 'God' who is other than omniscient and omnipotent. But, on the other hand, 'God exists' cannot be treated in the same way. God cannot be *defined* as existing. For, in the familiar slogan which has emerged from the critiques of the Ontological Argument, existence is not a predicate. To say that x exists is not to define, or to expand the definition of, the term 'x,' but is to assert that this term refers to some object. And whether a given description has a referent or, to use another terminology, whether a given term has denotation, is a question of fact which cannot be settled *a priori*.

The logical doctrine involved, which had been previously clearly delineated by Hume and Kant, has been formulated definitely in our own time by Bertrand Russell in his theory of descriptions.[3] Russell showed that the question 'Does x exist?' does not imply that in some prior sense the x of which we speak is, or subsists, or has being; and further, that the assertion that x exists is not an attribution to a subsisting x of the further characteristic of existence. It is rather the assertion, with regard to a certain description (or name as standing for a description) that this description has a referent. Thus 'horses exist' has the logical structure: 'there are x's such that "x is a horse" is true.' Such an analysis exorcises the puzzle which has tended since the time of Plato to haunt negative existential propositions. 'Unicorns do not exist' does not entail that unicorns must first in some mysterious sense *be* in order that we may then say of them that they do not exist; it means simply that 'there are no x's such that "x is a unicorn" is true.' And 'God exists' means 'there is one (and only one) x such that "x is omniscient, omnipotent, etc." is true.' This Russelian analysis makes plain the logical structure of propositions asserting existence. Their structure is such that they cannot be true by definition, nor therefore by *a priori* necessity. Hence the concept of a being such that the proposition asserting its existence is a logically necessary truth, is a self-contradictory concept. There cannot—logically cannot—be a being whose nonexistence is logically impossible. I conclude then that we must on philosophical grounds repudiate all talk of God as having necessary being, when the necessity in question is construed as logical necessity.

Granting then that the notion of God's existence as *logically* necessary has to be ruled out as untenable, it is perhaps worth asking, as a matter of history, whether this notion has in fact figured at all prominently in Christian thought.[4]

[3] *Introduction to Mathematical Philosophy*, 2nd edn. (1920), ch. 16.

[4] Whether or not this notion occurs prominently in Christian thought, it does apparently have a place in Muslim theology. Apparently the *pons asinorum* which the theological novice must cross is the distinction between the necessary, the possible and the impossible; and the necessary is defined as that the non-existence of which cannot be thought. (D. B. Macdonald, *Aspects of Islam* (London, 1911), p. 121.)

The first great thinker of the Church who comes to mind in this connexion is Anselm. The ontological argument, to the effect that the concept of God, as the concept of the greatest conceivable being, entails the existence of God, appears to be an attempt to show that the proposition 'God exists' is a logically necessary truth. Certainly Descartes' version of the ontological argument has this character. According to Descartes, as the concept of a triangle entails the truth that its internal angles as jointly equal to two right angles, so the concept of God entails the truth that God exists.[5] But in Anselm himself there is another line of thought which stands in conflict with such an interpretation. In the second formulation of the ontological argument, in the third chapter of the *Proslogium*, we read that 'it is possible to conceive of a being which cannot be conceived not to exist *(potest cogitari esse aliquid, quod non possit cogitari non esse).*' On the face of it this statement would seem to confirm the view that Anselm has in mind what we would today call the notion of logically necessary being. For the most natural interpretation of his words, at any rate by a twentieth-century reader, is that a being which cannot be conceived not to exist means a being whose non-existence is logically inconceivable, that is to say, logically impossible. However, when we turn to Anselm's reply to Gaunilo we find that he states explicitly what he means by the notion of beings which can and which cannot be conceived not to exist. 'All those objects, and those alone,' he says, 'can be conceived not to exist, which have a beginning or end or composition of parts: also . . . whatever at any place or at any time does not exist as a whole. That being alone, on the other hand, cannot be conceived not to exist, in which any conception discovers neither beginning nor end nor composition of parts *(nec initium nec finem nec partium conjunctionem),* and which any conception finds always and everywhere as a whole.'[6]

Here we have something quite different from the claim that 'God exists' is a logically necessary truth. We have instead the essence of the contrasting notion of factual necessity—the notion, that is, of God as sheer, ultimate, unconditioned reality, without origin or end. Another aspect of the concept of factual necessity, namely *aseity*, is contributed by Anselm in the *Monologion*, where he draws the distinction between existence *a se* and existence *ab alio*. He says of God: 'The supreme Substance, then, does not exist through any efficient agent, and does not derive existence from any matter, and was not aided in being brought into existence by any external causes. Nevertheless, it by no means exists through nothing, or derives existence from nothing; since, through itself and from itself, it is whatever it is *(per seipsam et ex seipsa est quidquid est).*'[7] The relation between this aspect of Anselm's thought and his ontological argument is another and difficult question into which I do not propose to enter; I only wish, for the present purpose, to point to the presence, often I think unnoticed, of the notion of factually necessary being in his discussions.

Let us now turn the centuries to Thomas Aquinas, who explicitly uses the term

[5] *Meditations*, V.

[6] *Responsio editoris*, ch. IV. Cf. *Proslogium*, ch. XXII.

[7] Ch. VI.

'necessary being.'[8] The conclusion of his Third Way argument is that 'there must exist something the existence of which is necessary' (oportet aliquid esse necessarium in rebus).[9] But he also, I believe, like Anselm, uses the idea of necessary existence in the sense of factually, and not logically, necessary existence. For in the Third Way passage the mark of contingency is transciency, or temporal finitude—having a beginning and an end in time. And by contrast the mark of non-contingency, or of the necessary being of God, must be not having a beginning or an end in time—in other words, *eternal* being.

Can we then perhaps equate contingent with transient existence, and necessary with eternal existence? The answer that must be given, which is also the answer implicit in Thomas, is No. Eternity is one of the ingredients of the necessary being of the Godhead, but is not by itself sufficient. For it is possible to conceive of something existing eternally, not because it is such that there is and could be no power capable of abolishing it, but only because, although there are powers capable of abolishing it, they always refrain from doing so. Such a being would be eternal by courtesy of the fact that it is never destroyed but not by the positive virtue or power of being indestructible. And it is surely integral to the Christian concept of God that God, as the ultimate Lord of all, is not capable of being destroyed.

We must add at this point that, as the ultimate Lord of all, God is also incorruptible, in the sense of being incapable of ceasing either to exist or to possess His divine characteristics by reason of an inner decay or discerption. God can neither be destroyed from without nor suffer dissolution from within.

Indestructibility and incorruptibility, however, even taken together, cannot replace but must supplement the notion of eternal being. For it is possible to conceive of something being both indestructible and incorruptible and yet not eternal in the sense of being without beginning or end. Such a being would exist only if created, but once created would be indissoluble and indestructible.

In Thomist theology angels and human souls are held to have precisely this character, on the ground that they are simple substances. They have a beginning by divine creation, but once created they exist for ever, unless of course destroyed by omnipotent divine action. As incorruptible, such beings are described as necessary beings, and it is presumably these, and perhaps especially angels, that Thomas has in mind when he distinguishes in the Third Way passage between necessary beings which have their necessary existence caused by another and ultimately necessary being which does not have its necessary existence caused by another, but which is uncreated and is God. Some Thomist theologians describe these two kinds of necessary being as, in the one case, intrinsically but not extrinsically necessary, and in the other case, both intrinsically and extrinsically necessary. These definitional refinements do not concern us here except as emphasising that in Thomist thought the notion of necessary being is not an all-or-nothing logical concept but is a factual notion, capable of degrees and qualifications; so that the distinction between necessary and contingent being is not to be correlated with

[8] *Summa Theologica*, bk. I, q. 2, art. 3.

[9] Cf. Norman Malcolm, 'Anselm's Ontological Arguments,' *Philosophical Review*, January 1960.

the distinction between logically necessary and contingent truths. Necessity is for Thomas a factual or ontic and not a logical characteristic.

I conclude then, concerning Thomas, that whilst he does not explicitly make the distinction between logical and factual necessity, in practice he cleaved so consistently to one side of the distinction that he was not led into any important ambiguity or confusion by the lack of an explicit separation of the two notions. However, some Thomist writers of our own day do fall into the ambiguity which their master avoided. M. Maritain, for example,[10] uses an instance of logical necessity to illustrate the idea of existence *a se*, thereby revealing that he is not conscious of the difference between these two notions. He first defines necessary existence in these terms: 'a thing is necessary when it *cannot* be prevented, contingent when it *can* be prevented. A thing is *absolutely necessary* when nothing can prevent it from being.' This is a clear enough account of the notion of existence *a se*. But in the next sentence Maritain offers an example from mathematics. 'Thus the properties of the sphere,' he says, 'are absolutely necessary.' Now the properties of a sphere—for example, the fact that every point on its surface is equidistant from the centre—are indeed absolutely necessary; that is to say, there could not possible be a sphere which lacked these properties. But the reason for this is not that there is nothing that can *prevent* a sphere from having these properties, but simply that these properties belong to the definition of 'sphere.' There is nothing to prevent there being objects which approximate in varying degrees to this particular set of properties, but such objects would not be called spheres for the simple reason that we have chosen to confine the name 'sphere' to objects which fit certain specifications, which thus constitute the defining and necessary properties of a sphere.

II

If a skilled theologian can suppose that the Christian concept of God requires the notion of logically necessary existence, we can hardly blame secular philosophers if they make the same assumption and proceed to draw damaging conclusions from it. I should like in this connexion to refer to the much discussed article by Professor J. N. Findlay of London University, entitled 'Can God's existence be disproved?'[11] in which he derives from the self-contradictory nature of the idea of logically necessary being what he regards as a strict disproof of divine existence. To see what is amiss with Findlay's argument is by contrast to see a little more clearly the outlines of a religiously and philosophically acceptable account of the unique mode of being of the Godhead.

Professor Findlay is, so far as I know, the first philosopher to have proposed an *a priori* proof of the non-existence of God. He puts the ontological argument into reverse by contending that the concept of deity, so far from guaranteeing the

---

[10] 'Necessity and Contingency' in *Essays in Thomism*, edited by Robert E. Brennan (New York, 1942).

[11] *Mind*, 1948. Reprinted in *New Essays in Philosophical Theology*, edited by Flew and MacIntyre (London, 1955).

existence of an object corresponding to it, is such as to guarantee that no object corresponds to it.

Findlay defines the concept of God as that of the adequate object of religious attitudes, a religious attitude being described as one in which we tend 'to abase ourselves before some object, to defer to it wholly, to devote ourselves to it with unquestioning enthusiasm, to bend the knee before it, whether literally or meta-phorically,'[12] such an attitude is rationally adopted only by one who believes that the object to which he relates himself as worshipper has certain very remarkable characteristics. Findlay lists the most important of these characteristics. First, an adequate object of religious attitudes must be conceived as being infinitely supe-rior to ourselves in value or worth. (Accordingly Findlay refers to this object as 'he' rather than as 'it.') Second, he must be conceived as being unique: God must not merely be one of a class of beings of the same kind, but stand in an asym-metrical relationship to all other objects as the source of whatever value they may have. Third, says Findlay, the adequate objects of religious attitudes must be conceived as not merely happening to exist, but as existing necessarily; if he merely happened to exist he would not be worthy of the full and unqualified attitude of worship. And fourth, this being must be conceived as not merely happening to possess his various characteristics, but as possessing them in some necessary man-ner. For our present purpose we may conflate these two necessities, necessary existence and the necessary possession of properties, and treat them as one. It should be borne in mind throughout that in Findlay's argument 'necessary' means 'logically necessary.'

It is the last two in his list of requirements that provide the ground for Findlay's ontological disproof of theism. 'For if God is to satisfy religious claims and needs, he must be a being in every way inescapable, One whose existence and whose possession of certain excellencies we cannot possibly conceive away. And modern views make it self-evidently absurd (if they don't make it ungrammatical) to speak of such a Being and attribute existence to him.'[13] For, as we have already noted, post-Humean empiricism can assign no meaning to the idea of necessary exis-tence, since nothing can be conceived to exist that cannot also be conceived not to exist. No propositions of the form 'x exists' can be analytically true. Hence, Findlay argues, the concept of an adequate object of religious attitudes, involving as it does the notion of a necessarily existent being who possesses his characteristic in some necessary manner, is a self-contradictory concept. We can know a priori, from inspection of the idea itself, that there is and can be no such thing.

We may distinguish in Findlay's argument a philosophical premise to the effect that no existential propositions can be necessary truths, and a theological premise to the effect that an adequate object of religious worship must be such that it is logically necessary that he exists. Of these two premises I wish to accept the for-mer and reject the latter. I deny, that is to say, the theological doctrine that God must be conceived, if at all, in such a way that 'God exists' is a logically necessary truth. I deny this for precisely the same reason as Findlay, namely that the de-mand that 'God exists' should be a necessary truth is, like the demand that a circle

[12] New Essays, p. 49.

[13] Op. cit., p. 55.

should be square, not a proper demand at all, but a misuse of language. Only, whereas Findlay concludes that the notion of an adequate object of religious attitude is an absurdity, I conclude that that of which the idea is an absurdity cannot be an adequate object of religious attitudes; it would on the contrary be an unqualifiedly *in*adequate object of worship.

Let us then ask the question, which seems highly appropriate at this point, as to how religious persons actually think of the Being whom they regard as the adequate object of their worship. What aspect of the Christian experience of God lies behind the idea of necessary being?

The concept of God held by the biblical writers was based upon their experience of God as awesome power and holy will confronting them and drawing them into the sphere of His ongoing purpose. God was known as a dynamic will interacting with their own wills; a sheer given reality, as inescapably to be reckoned with as destructive storm and life-giving sunshine, or the fixed contours of the land, or the hatred of their enemies and the friendship of their neighbors; indeed even more ineluctably so, as the Book of Jonah emphasises. God was not for them an inferred entity; He was an experienced reality. The biblical writers were (sometimes, though doubtless not at all times) as vividly conscious of being in God's presence as they were of living in a material environment. Their pages resound and vibrate with the sense of God's presence, as a building might resound and vibrate from the tread of some great being walking through it. They thought of this holy presence as unique—as the maker and ruler of the Universe, the sole rightful sovereign of men and angels, as eternal and infinite, and as the ultimate reality and determining power, in relation to whom His creatures have no standing except as the objects of His grace. But nowhere in the biblical thought about God is use made of the idea of logical necessity. The notion is quite foreign to the characteristically Hebraic and concrete utterances found in the Bible, and forms no part of the biblical concept or concepts of God.

But, it might be said, was it not to the biblical writers inconceivable that God should *not* exist, or that he should cease to exist, or should lose His divine powers and virtues? Would it not be inconceivable to them that God might one day go out of existence, or cease to be good and become evil? And does not this attitude involve an implicit belief that God exists necessarily, and possesses His divine characteristics in some necessary manner? The answer, I think, is that it was to the biblical writers psychologically inconceivable—as we say colloquially, unthinkable—that God might not exist, or that His nature might undergo change. They were so vividly conscious of God that they were unable to doubt His reality, and they were so firmly reliant upon His integrity and faithfulness that they could not contemplate His becoming other than they knew Him to be. They would have allowed as a verbal concession only that there might possibly be no God; for they were convinced that they were at many times directly aware of His presence and of His dealings with them. But the question whether the non-existence of God is *logically* inconceivable, or *logically* impossible, is a purely philosophical puzzle which could not be answered by the prophets and apostles out of their own first-hand religious experience. This does not of course represent any special limitation of the biblical figures. The logical concept of necessary being cannot be given in religious experience. It is an object of philosophical thought and not of religious experience. It is a product—as Findlay argues, a malformed product—of reflection. A religious person's reply to the question, Is God's existence logically necessary? will be determined by his view of the nature of logical necessity; and this is not part of his religion but of his system of logic. The biblical writers in point of fact display no view of the nature of logical necessity, and would doubtless have regarded the topic as of no religious significance. It cannot reasonably be claimed then, that necessary existence was part of their conception of the adequate object of human worship.

What, we must therefore ask, has led Findlay to hold so confidently that logically necessary existence is an essential element in the religious man's concept of God? His process of thought is revealed in these words: 'We can't help feeling that the worthy object of our worship can never be a thing that merely *happens* to exist, nor one on which all other objects merely *happen* to depend.'[14] The reasoning here is that if a being does not exist by logical necessity, He merely happens to exist; and in this case He ought not to be worshipped as God. But in presenting the dilemma, either God exists necessarily, or He merely happens to exist, Findlay makes the very mistake for which he has criticised the theologians. Findlay should be the last person to use this dichotomy, since he has himself rendered it inoperative by pointing out that one half of the dichotomy is meaningless. And to remove half a dichotomy is to remove the dichotomy. If for example it is said that all human beings are either witches or non-witches, and it is then discovered that there is no such thing as a witch, it becomes pointless, and indeed misleading, to describe everyone as a non-witch. Likewise, having concluded that the notion of necessary existence has no meaning, to continue to speak of things merely *happening* to exist, as though this stood in contrast to some other mode of existing, no longer has any validity, From an empiricist standpoint, there are not two different ways of existing, existing by logical necessity and merely happening to exist. A thing either exists or does not exist; or to be more exact a description either has or does not have a referent. But Findlay, after ruling out the notion of necessary existence, in relation to which alone the contrasting idea of 'merely happening to exist' has any meaning, continues to use the latter category, and what is more, to use it as a term of reproach! This is a very advanced form of the method of having it both ways.

Our conclusion must be that Findlay has only disproved the existence of God if we mean by God a being whose existence is a matter of logical necessity. Since, however, we do not mean this, we may take Findlay's argument instead as emphasizing that we must either abandon the traditional phrase 'necessary being,' or else be very clear that the necessary being of God is not to be construed as *logically* necessary being.

III

We have arrived thus far at an identification of the necessary being of the Godhead with incorruptible and indestructible being without beginning or end. These

---

[14] Ibid., p. 52.

characteristics, however, can properly be regarded as different aspects of the more fundamental characteristic which the Scholastics termed aseity, or being *a se*. The usual English translation, 'self-existence,' is strictly a meaningless phrase, but for the lack of a better we must continue to use it. The core of the notion of aseity is independent being. That God exists *a se* means that He is not dependent upon anything for His existence. In contrast to this the created Universe and everything in it exist *ab alio*. For it is true of each distinguishable item composing the Universe that its existence depends upon some factor or factors beyond itself. Only God exists in total non-dependence; He alone exists absolutely as sheer unconditioned, self-existent being.

From God's aseity, or ontic independence, His eternity, indestructibility and incorruptibility can be seen to follow. A self-existent being must be eternal, i.e. without temporal limitation. For if He had begun to exist, or should cease to exist, He must have been caused to exist, or to cease to exist, by some power other than Himself; and this would be inconsistent with His aseity. By the same token He must be indestructible, for to say that He exists in total ontic independence is to say that there is and could be no reality with the capacity to constitute or to destroy Him; and likewise He must be incorruptible, for otherwise His aseity would be qualified as regards its duration. The question might however be asked at this point: Although it is incompatible with the idea of a self-existent being that He should ever be destroyed from without, yet is there any contradiction in the thought of such a being destroying Himself? Is it not possible in principle that God might 'commit suicide'? The question perhaps deserves more than the brief discussion that is possible within the limits of this paper. I am inclined, however, to think that the query itself is as logically improper as it is obviously religiously improper; and this for three reasons. First, the expression 'commit suicide' is highly misleading in this context. The 'suicide' of the absolute self-existent being would not be like a human suicide though on a much grander scale. For the concept of divine death is not analogous to that of human death. The death of a human being means the destruction or the cessation of function of his physical body; but God has no physical body to be destroyed, whether by Himself or by another. We have to try to think instead of a purely 'mental suicide'; but so far as I can see this is a completely empty phrase, to which we are able to attach no positive meaning. Second, an absolute end is as inconceivable as is an absolute beginning. Third, there is an additional contradiction in the notion of sheer, unqualified *being* ceasing to exist. Specific modifications of being may alter or cease, but to speak of being itself ceasing to exist is apparently to speak without meaning. I cannot then accept the question as to whether God might commit suicide as a genuine question posing intelligible alternatives.

Finally, to refer back to Findlay's discussion, it is meaningless to say of the self-existent being that He might not have existed or that He merely happens to exist. For what could it mean to say of the eternal, uncreated Creator of everything other than Himself that He 'merely happens to exist'? When we assert of a dependent and temporally finite being, such as myself, that I only happen to exist, we mean that if such-and-such an event had occurred in the past, or if such-and-such another event had failed to occur, I should not now exist. But no such meaning can be given to the statement, 'A self-existent being only happens to exist,' or 'might not have existed.' There is no conceivable event such that if it had occurred, or failed to occur, a self-existent being would not have existed; for the concept of aseity is precisely the exclusion of such dependence. There is and could be nothing that would have prevented a self-existent being from coming to exist, for it is meaningless even to speak of a self-existent being as *coming* to exist.

What may properly be meant, then, by the statement that God is, or has, necessary as distinguished from contingent being is that God *is*, without beginning or end, and without origin, cause or ground of any kind whatsoever. He *is*, as the ultimate, unconditioned, absolute, unlimited being.

On the one hand, the fact that God is, is not a logically necessary truth; for no matter of fact can be logically necessary. The reality of God is a sheer datum. But on the other hand this is an utterly unique datum. That God is, is not one fact amongst others, but is related asymmetrically to all other facts as that which determines them. This is the ultimate given circumstance behind which it is not possible to go with either question or explanation. For to explain something means either to assign a cause to it or to show its place within some wider context in relation to which it is no longer puzzling to us. But the idea of the self-existent Creator of everything other than Himself is the idea of a reality which is beyond the scope of these explanatory procedures. As self-existent, such a being is uncaused, and is therefore not susceptible to the causal type of explanation; and as the Creator of all things other than Himself He stands in no wider context—on the contrary, His creative action constitutes the context in which all else stands. He is the ultimate reality, about which it is no longer meaningful to ask the questions which can be asked concerning other realities. For this reason God cannot but be mysterious to us. He is mysterious, not merely because there are questions about Him to which we do not know the answers, but because we frame questions about Him to which there are no answers since the questions themselves can have meaning only in relation to that which is not ultimate. As the final unconditioned, all-conditioning reality God cannot be included within any system of explanation. This is not to say that we cannot know any truths about Him, but that such truths are not logically deduced conclusions but sheer incorrigible facts disclosed within human experience. We may express this by saying that God has no characterising name; He is not of any kind, or for any reason, or from any cause He just *is*, and is what He is. When He reveals His nature to man He says to Moses 'I shall be what I shall be'[15]; and the fulfilment of that prolepsis is in the fact, the given historical fact, of Jesus Christ.

IV

A further step remains to be taken. For there are two respects in which the concept of aseity is less than adequate to the Christian understanding of God, or at least there are two dangers to be guarded against in speaking of God's aseity. One

[15] Exodus 3. and 14.

is the danger of understanding aseity in a purely static sense; and the other is the readiness of aseity to be construed in merely negative terms, simply as independence. The next major original treatment of the subject since Aquinas, that of Karl Barth in our own time, would appear to have been undertaken with these two dangers in mind; and it is accordingly to Barth that we now turn.

In his great dogmatic work Barth has a section on the *aseitas Dei* under the heading, *The Being of God in Freedom.*[16] As against any tendency to think of God as static, self-existent substance, the term 'freedom' reminds us that God is the living God, the Life which is the source of all life, and that He is Life not only as an Agent in human time, but also in His own hidden being, apart from and prior to that which is other than Himself. This is an important aspect of the Christian concept of God. The Scholastic *'actus purus,'* and the more biblical term 'life,' both point to it; and Paul Tillich, in his own theological system, seeks to introduce the same dynamic note when he refers to God as 'the power of Being.' All these terms—pure act, divine life, freedom, and power—are of course symbolic in Tillich's sense of being expressions whose ordinary meaning is partially negated by that to which they point. That is to say (speaking more prosaically) even as we use them we are conscious of certain respects in which they would be misleading if taken literally. However, granting the symbolic character of all these words, the term 'freedom,' as Barth uses it, does appear to have special appositeness as supplementing the notion of aseity.

Barth draws a distinction between what he calls the primary, or ontic, and the secondary, or neotic, absoluteness or freedom of God. The former refers to God's absoluteness in Himself, the latter to His absoluteness or Lordship in relation to His creation. This secondary absoluteness is characterised by Barth as total independence; God does not depend for His existence upon any factor external to Himself. From this point of view, He is 'the One who is free from all origination, conditioning or determination from without, by that which is not Himself.'[17] But, Barth insists, we must not think of God's unique mode of being only or even primarily in negative terms, as the absence of dependence upon His creation. God's absoluteness in relation to the world is secondary and derivative. Behind it there lies the primary absoluteness or freedom which is prior to and outside of all relations. God is free, says Barth, 'quite apart from His relation to another from whom He is free.'[18] God, in His own inner being, entirely apart from His creative action, is intrinsically free, and 'the freedom to exist which He exercises in His revelation is the same which He has in the depth of His eternal being, and which is proper to Him quite apart from His exercise of it ad extra.'[19] This insight of Barth's provides an important balancing note to the traditional discussion of aseity. Instead of being thought of primarily in His relation to the world, even though that relation be one of unqualified independence, God is to be conceived in the

[16]*Church Dogmatics*, vol. II, pt. I, ch. VI, § 28, 3.

[17]Op. cit., p. 307.

[18]Ibid., p. 307.

[19]Ibid., p. 305.

first instance as positive self-existence in infinite richness and plenitude. The ultimate Being should not be defined negatively as the One who does not depend upon other beings; on the contrary, His independence of the world is a corollary of His own sheer unique Godness, His infinite and absolute uncreated self-sustaining life.

Barth's doctrine of the primary absoluteness or freedom of God also provides the resonance for his response to the question, How can we think of the absolute, self-existent Being as creating a universe and bestowing upon it a relative autonomy over against Himself, and yet remaining unimpaired in His own absolute self-sufficiency and freedom?[20] This however is a distinct, though adjacent, topic which cannot be taken up in the present article.

Finally, a brief summary of conclusions. If we continue (as I think we properly may) to use the expression 'necessary being,' we must explicitly interpret it in terms of the concept of factual, as distinguished from logical, necessity.[21] So interpreted, the necessary being of the Godhead is His aseity, understood primarily, however, not as non-dependence upon His creation, but positively, as absolute and unlimited being in infinite plenitude and freedom.

---

[20] It should be noted that Barth has developed his position further, in IV/1, ch. XIV, § 59, 1, in the direction of holding that the self–other relationship is already present within the triune Godhead, so that creation does not involve the problem of the inherently unrelated entering into relations.

[21] Cf. Terrence Penelhum, 'Divine Necessity,' *Mind*, April 1960.

KNOWLEDGE

BOETHIUS
Divine Foreknowledge and Freedom of the Will

PROSE III

Boethius contends that divine foreknowledge and freedom of the human will are incompatible.

"Now I am confused by an even greater difficulty," I said.

"What is it?" Philosophy answered, "though I think I know what is bothering you."

"There seems to be a hopeless conflict between divine foreknowledge of all things and freedom of the human will. For if God sees everything in advance and cannot be deceived in any way, whatever his Providence foresees will happen, must happen. Therefore, if God foreknows eternally not only all the acts of men, but also their plans and wishes, there cannot be freedom of will; for nothing whatever can be done or even desired without its being known beforehand by the infallible Providence of God. If things could somehow be accomplished in some way other than that which God foresaw, his foreknowledge of the future would no longer be certain. Indeed, it would be merely uncertain opinion, and it would be wrong to think that of God.

"I cannot agree with the argument by which some people believe that they can solve this problem. They say that things do not happen because Providence foresees that they will happen, but, on the contrary, that Providence foresees what is to come because it will happen, and in this way they find the necessity to be in things, not in Providence. For, they say, it is not necessary that things should

Boethius (480–524) was a Roman scholar who translated into Latin a number of Aristotle's major works and wrote important commentaries on Aristotle and Cicero. He is the author of *The Consolation of Philosophy* and several books on logic.

happen because they are foreseen, but only that things which will happen be foreseen—as though the problem were whether divine Providence is the cause of the necessity of future events, or the necessity of future events is the cause of divine Providence. But our concern is to prove that the fulfillment of things which God has foreseen is necessary, whatever the order of causes, even if the divine foreknowledge does not seem to make the occurrence of future events necessary. For example, if a man sits down, the opinion that he is sitting must be true; and conversely, if the opinion that someone is sitting be true, then that person must necessarily be sitting. Therefore, there is necessity in both cases: the man must be sitting and the opinion must be true. But the man is not sitting because the opinion is true; the opinion is true because the sitting came before the opinion about it. Therefore, even though the cause of truth came from one side, necessity is common to both.

"A similar line of reasoning applies to divine foreknowledge and future events. For even though the events are foreseen because they will happen, they do not happen because they are foreseen. Nevertheless, it is necessary either that things which are going to happen be foreseen by God, or that what God foresees will in fact happen; and either way the freedom of the human will is destroyed. But of course it is preposterous to say that the outcome of temporal things is the cause of eternal foreknowledge. Yet to suppose that God foresees future events because they are going to happen is the same as supposing that things which happened long ago are the cause of divine Providence. Furthermore, just as when I know that a thing is, that thing must necessarily be; so when I know that something will happen, it is necessary that it happen. It follows, then, that the outcome of something known in advance must necessarily take place.

"Finally, if anyone thinks that a thing is other than it actually is, he does not have knowledge but merely a fallible opinion, and that is quite different from the truth of knowledge. So, if the outcome of some future event is either uncertain or unnecessary, no one can know in advance whether or not it will happen. For just as true knowledge is not tainted by falsity, so that which is known by it cannot be otherwise than as it is known. And that is the reason why knowledge never deceives; things must necessarily be as true knowledge knows them to be. If this is so, how does God foreknow future possibilities whose existence is uncertain? If He thinks that things will inevitably happen which possibly will not happen, He is deceived. But it is wrong to say that, or even to think it. And if He merely knows that they may or may not happen, that is, if He knows only their contingent possibilities, what is such knowledge worth, since it does not know with certainty? Such knowledge is no better than that expressed by the ridiculous prophecy of Tiresias: 'Whatever I say will either be or not be.'[1] Divine Providence would be no better than human opinion if God judges as men do and knows only that uncertain events are doubtful. But if nothing can be uncertain to Him who is the most certain source of all things, the outcome is certain of all things which He knows with certainty shall be.

"Therefore, there can be no freedom in human decisions and actions, since

---

[1] Horace, *Satires* II. 5. 59.

the divine mind, foreseeing everything without possibility of error, determines and forces the outcome of everything that is to happen. Once this is granted, it is clear that the structure of all human affairs must collapse. For it is pointless to assign rewards and punishment to the good and wicked since neither are deserved if the actions of men are not free and voluntary. Punishment of the wicked and recognition of the good, which are now considered just, will seem quite unjust since neither the good nor the wicked are governed by their own will but are forced by the inevitability of predetermination. Vice and virtue will be without meaning, and in their place there will be utter confusion about what is deserved. Finally, and this is the most blasphemous thought of all, it follows that the Author of all good must be made responsible for all human vice since the entire order of human events depends on Providence and nothing on man's intention.

"There is no use in hoping or praying for anything, for what is the point in hope or prayer when everything that man desires is determined by unalterable process? Thus man's only bonds with God, hope and prayer, are destroyed. We believe that our just humility may earn the priceless reward of divine grace, for this is the only way in which men seem able to communicate with God; we are joined to that inaccessible light by supplication before receiving what we ask. But if we hold that all future events are governed by necessity, and therefore that prayer has no value, what will be left to unite us to the sovereign Lord of all things? And so mankind must, as you said earlier, be cut off from its source and dwindle into nothing.[2]

POEM III

"What cause of discord breaks the ties which ought to bind this union of things? What God has set such conflict between these two truths? Separately each is certain, but put together they cannot be reconciled. Is there no discord between them? Can they exist side by side and be equally true?

"The human mind, overcome by the body's blindness, cannot discern by its dim light the delicate connections between things. But why does the mind burn with such desire to discover the hidden aspects of truth? Does it know what it is so eager to know? Then why does it go on laboriously trying to discover what it already knows? And if it does not know, why does it blindly continue the search? For who would want something of which he is unaware, or run after something he does not know? How can such a thing be found, or, if found, how would it be recognized by someone ignorant of its form?

"When the human mind knew the mind of God, did it know the whole and all its parts? Now the mind is shrouded in the clouds of the body, but it has not wholly forgotten itself; and, although it has lost its grasp of particulars, it still holds fast to the general truth. Therefore, whoever seeks the truth knows something: he is neither completely informed nor completely ignorant. He works with what he remembers of the highest truth, using what he saw on high in order to fill in the forgotten parts."

[2] See Book IV, Poem 6.

PROSE IV

> Philosophy begins her argument that divine Providence does not preclude freedom
> of the will by stressing the difference between divine and human knowledge.

"This is an old difficulty about Providence," Philosophy answered. "It was raised by Cicero in his book on divination,[3] and has for a long time been a subject of your own investigation, but so far none of you has treated it with enough care and conviction. The cause of the obscurity which still surrounds the problem is that the process of human reason cannot comprehend the simplicity of divine foreknowledge. If in any way we could understand that, no further doubt would remain. I shall try to make this clear after I have explained the things which trouble you.

"First, let me ask why you regard as inconclusive the reasoning of those who think that foreknowledge is no hindrance to free will because it is not the cause of the necessity of future things. For do you have any argument for the necessity of future events other than the principle that things which are known beforehand must happen? If, as you have just now conceded, foreknowledge does not impose necessity on future events, why must the voluntary outcome of things be bound to predetermined results? For the sake of argument, so that you may consider what follows from it, let us suppose that there is no foreknowledge. Then would the things which are done by free will be bound by necessity in this respect?"

"Not at all."

"Then, let us suppose that foreknowledge exists but imposes no necessity on things. The same independence and absolute freedom of will would remain.

"But you will say that even though foreknowledge does not impose necessity on future events, it is still a sign that they will necessarily happen. It must follow then that even if there were no foreknowledge the outcome of these future things would be necessary. For signs only show what is, they do not cause the things they point to. Therefore we must first prove that nothing happens other than by necessity, in order to demonstrate that foreknowledge is a sign of this necessity. Otherwise, if there is no necessity, then foreknowledge cannot be a sign of something that does not exist. Moreover, it is clear that firmly based proof does not rest on signs and extrinsic arguments but is deduced from suitable and necessary causes. But how can it be that things which are foreseen should not happen? We do not suppose that things will not happen, if Providence has foreknowledge that they will; rather we judge that, although they will happen, they have nothing in their natures which makes it necessary that they should happen. For we see many things in the process of happening before our eyes, just as the chariot driver sees the results of his actions as he guides his chariot; and this is true in many of our activities. Do you think that such things are compelled by necessity to happen as they do?"

"No. For the results of art would be vain if they were all brought about by compulsion."

"Then, since they come into being without necessity, these same things were not determined by necessity before they actually happened. Therefore, there are

---

[3] *De divinatione* II. 8ff.

some things destined to happen in the future whose outcome is free of any necessity. For everyone, I think, would say that things which are now happening were
going to happen before they actually came to pass. Thus, these things happen
without necessity even though they were known in advance. For just as knowledge
of things happening now does not imply necessity in their outcomes, so foreknowledge of future things imposes no necessity on their outcomes in the future.

"But, you will say, the point at issue is whether there can be any foreknowledge
of things whose outcomes are not necessary. For these things seem opposed to
each other, and you think that if things can be foreseen they must necessarily
happen, and that if the necessity is absent they cannot be foreseen, and that
nothing can be fully known unless it is certain. If uncertain things are foreseen as
certain, that is the weakness of opinion, not the truth of knowledge. You believe
that to judge that a thing is other than it is departs from the integrity of knowledge. Now the cause of this error lies in your assumption that whatever is known,
is known only by the force and nature of the things which are known; but the
opposite is true. Everything which is known is known not according to its own
power but rather according to the capacity of the knower.

"Let me illustrate with a brief example: the roundness of a body is known in
one way by the sense of touch and in another by the sight. The sight, remaining
at a distance, takes in the whole body at once by its reflected rays; but the touch
makes direct contact with the sphere and comprehends it piecemeal by moving
around its surface. A man himself is comprehended in different ways by the senses,
imagination, reason, and intelligence. The senses grasp the figure of the thing as
it is constituted in matter; the imagination, however, grasps the figure alone without the matter. Reason, on the other hand, goes beyond this and investigates by
universal consideration the species itself which is in particular things. The vision
of intelligence is higher yet, and it goes beyond the bounds of the universe and
sees with the clear eye of the mind the pure form itself.

"In all this we chiefly observe that the higher power of knowing includes the
lower, but the lower can in no way rise to the higher. For the senses achieve
nothing beyond the material, the imagination cannot grasp universal species, reason cannot know simple forms; but the intelligence, as though looking down from
on high, conceives the underlying forms and distinguishes among them all, but
in the same way in which it comprehends the form itself which cannot be known
to any other power. The intelligence knows the objects of the lower kinds of
knowledge: the universals of the reason, the figures of the imagination, the matter
of the senses, but not by using reason, or imagination, or senses. With a single
glance of the mind it formally, as it were, sees all things. Similarly, when reason
knows a universal nature, it comprehends all the objects of imagination and the
senses without using either. For reason defines the general nature of her conception as follows: man is a biped, rational animal. This is a universal idea, but no
one ignores the fact that man is also an imaginable and sensible object which
reason knows by rational conception rather than by the imagination and senses.
Similarly, although the imagination begins by seeing and forming figures with the
senses, nevertheless it can, without the aid of the senses, behold sensible objects
by an imaginative rather than a sensory mode of knowing.

"Do you see, then, how all these use their own power in knowing rather than the powers of the objects which are known? And this is proper, for since all judgment is in the act of the one judging, it is necessary that everyone should accomplish his own action by his own power, not by the power of something other than himself.

PROSE VI

>Philosophy solves the problem of Providence and free will by distinguishing between simple and conditional necessity.

"Since, as we have shown, whatever is known is known according to the nature of the knower, and not according to its own nature, let us now consider as far as is lawful the nature of the Divine Being, so that we may discover what its knowledge is. The common judgment of all rational creatures holds that God is eternal. Therefore let us consider what eternity is, for this will reveal both the divine nature and the divine knowledge.

"Eternity is the whole, perfect, and simultaneous possession of endless life. The meaning of this can be made clearer by comparison with temporal things. For whatever lives in time lives in the present, proceeding from past to future, and nothing is so constituted in time that it can embrace the whole span of its life at once. It has not yet arrived at tomorrow, and it has already lost yesterday; even the life of this day is lived only in each moving, passing moment. Therefore, whatever is subject to the condition of time, even that which—as Aristotle conceived the world to be—has no beginning and will have no end in a life coextensive with the infinity of time, is such that it cannot rightly be thought eternal. For it does not comprehend and include the whole of infinite life all at once, since it does not embrace the future which is yet to come. Therefore, only that which comprehends and possesses the whole plenitude of endless life together, from which no future thing nor any past thing is absent, can justly be called eternal. Moreover, it is necessary that such a being be in full possession of itself, always present to itself, and hold the infinity of moving time present before itself.

"Therefore, they are wrong who, having heard that Plato held that this world did not have a beginning in time and would never come to an end,[4] suppose that the created world is coeternal with its Creator. For it is one thing to live an endless life, which is what Plato ascribed to the world, and another for the whole of unending life to be embraced all at once as present, which is clearly proper to the divine mind. Nor should God be thought of as older than His creation in extent of time, but rather as prior to it by virtue of the simplicity of His nature. For the infinite motion of temporal things imitates the immediate present of His changeless life and, since it cannot reproduce or equal life, it sinks from immobility to motion and declines from the simplicity of the present into the infinite duration of future and past. And, since it cannot possess the whole fullness of its life at once, it seems to imitate to some extent that which it cannot completely express, and it does this by somehow never ceasing to be. It binds itself to a kind of present in this short and transitory period which, because it has a certain

___
[4] *Timaeus* 28ff.

likeness to that abiding, unchanging present, gives everything it touches a sem-
blance of existence. But, since this imitation cannot remain still, it hastens along
the infinite road of time, and so it extends by movement the life whose completeness it could not achieve by standing still. Therefore, if we wish to call things by
their proper names, we should follow Plato in saying that God indeed is eternal,
but the world is perpetual.[5]

"Since, then, every judgment comprehends the subjects presented to it according to its own nature, and since God lives in the eternal present, His knowledge
transcends all movement of time and abides in the simplicity of its immediate
present. It encompasses the infinite sweep of past and future, and regards all things
in its simple comprehension as if they were now taking place. Thus, if you will
think about the foreknowledge by which God distinguishes all things, you will
rightly consider it to be not a foreknowledge of future events, but knowledge of a
never-changing present. For this reason, divine knowledge is called providence,
rather than prevision, because it resides above all inferior things and looks out on
all things from their summit.

"Why then do you imagine that things are necessary which are illuminated by
this divine light, since even men do not impose necessity on the things they see?
Does your vision impose any necessity upon things which you see present before you?"

"Not at all," I answered.

"Then," Philosophy went on, "if we may aptly compare God's present vision
with man's, He sees all things in his eternal present as you see some things in
your temporal present. Therefore, this divine foreknowledge does not change the
nature and properties of things; it simply sees things present before it as they will
later turn out to be in what we regard as the future. His judgment is not confused;
with a single intuition of his mind He knows all things that are to come, whether
necessarily or not. Just as, when you happen to see simultaneously a man walking
on the street and the sun shining in the sky, even though you see both at once,
you can distinguish between them and realize that one action is voluntary, the
other necessary; so the divine mind, looking down on all things, does not disturb
the nature of the things which are present before it but are future with respect to
time. Therefore, when God knows that something will happen in the future, and
at the same time knows that it will not happen through necessity, this is not
opinion but knowledge based on truth.

"If you should reply that whatever God foresees as happening cannot help but
happen, and that whatever must happen is bound by necessity—if you pin me
down to this word 'necessity'—I grant that you state a solid truth, but one which
only a profound theologian can grasp. I would answer that the same future event
is necessary with respect to God's knowledge of it, but free and undetermined if
considered in its own nature. For there are two kinds of necessity: one is simple,
as the necessity by which all men are mortals; the other is conditional, as is the
case when, if you know that someone is walking, he must necessarily be walking.
For whatever is known, must be as it is known to be; but this condition does not

[5] *Timaeus* 37d ff.

involve that other, simple necessity. It is not caused by the peculiar nature of the person in question, but by an added condition. No necessity forces the man who is voluntarily walking to move forward; but as long as he is walking, he is necessarily moving forward. In the same way, if Providence sees anything as present, that thing must necessarily be, even though it may have no necessity by its nature. But God sees as present those future things which result from free will. Therefore, from the standpoint of divine knowledge, these things are necessary because of the condition of their being known by God; but, considered only in themselves, they lose nothing of the absolute freedom of their own natures.

"There is no doubt, then, that all things will happen which God knows will happen; but some of them happen as a result of free will. And, although they happen, they do not, by their existence, lose their proper natures by which, before they happened, they were able not to happen. But, you may ask, what does it mean to say that these events are not necessary, since by reason of the condition of divine knowledge they happen just as if they were necessary? The meaning is the same as in the example I used a while ago of the sun rising and the man walking. At the time they are happening, they must necessarily be happening; but the sun's rising is governed by necessity even before it happens, while the man's walking is not. Similarly, all the things God sees as present will undoubtedly come to pass; but some will happen by the necessity of their natures, others by the power of those who make them happen. Therefore, we quite properly said that these things are necessary if viewed from the standpoint of divine knowledge, but if they are considered in themselves, they are free of the bonds of necessity. In somewhat the same way, whatever is known by the senses is singular in itself, but universal as far as the reason is concerned.

"But, you may say, if I can change my mind about doing something, I can frustrate Providence, since by chance I may change something which Providence foresaw. My answer is this: you can indeed alter what you propose to do, but, because the present truth of Providence sees that you can, and whether or not you will, you cannot frustrate the divine knowledge any more than you can escape the eye of someone who is present and watching you, even though you may, by your free will, vary your actions. You may still wonder, however, whether God's knowledge is changed by your decisions, so that when you wish now one thing, now another, the divine knowledge undergoes corresponding changes. This is not the case. For divine Providence anticipates every future action and converts it to its own present knowledge. It does not change, as you imagine, foreknowing this or that in succession, but in a single instant, without being changed itself, anticipates and grasps your changes. God has this present comprehension and immediate vision of all things not from the outcome of future events, but from the simplicity of his own nature. In this way, the problem you raised a moment ago is settled. You observed that it would be unworthy of God if our future acts were said to be the cause of divine knowledge. Now you see that this power of divine knowledge, comprehending all things as present before it, itself constitutes the measure of all things and is in no way dependent on things that happen later.

"Since this is true, the freedom of the human will remains inviolate, and laws are just since they provide rewards and punishments to human wills which are not controlled by necessity. God looks down from above, knowing all things, and the eternal present of his vision concurs with the future character of our actions, distributing rewards to the good and punishments to the evil. Our hopes and prayers are not directed to God in vain, for if they are just they cannot fail. Therefore, stand firm against vice and cultivate virtue. Lift up your soul to worthy hopes, and offer humble prayers to heaven. If you will face it, the necessity of virtuous action imposed upon you is very great, since all your actions are done in the sight of a Judge who sees all things."

ST. THOMAS AQUINAS
The Knowledge of God

FIFTH ARTICLE.   WHETHER GOD KNOWS THINGS OTHER THAN HIMSELF?

We proceed thus to the Fifth Article:—

Objection 1. It seems that God does not know other things besides Himself. For all other things but God are outside of God. But Augustine says that *God does not behold anything out of Himself.*[1] Therefore He does not know things other than Himself.

Obj. 2. Further, the object understood is the perfection of the one who understands. If therefore God understands other things besides Himself, something else will be the perfection of God, and will be nobler than He; which is impossible.

Obj. 3. Further, the act of understanding is specified by the intelligible object, as is every other act from its own object. Hence the intellectual act is so much the nobler, the nobler the object understood. But God is His own intellectual act, as is clear from what has been said. If therefore God understands anything other than Himself, then God Himself is specified by something other than Himself; which cannot be. Therefore He does not understand things other than Himself.

On the contrary, It is written: *All things are naked and open to His eyes (Heb. iv. 13).*

I answer that, God necessarily knows things other than Himself. For it is manifest that He perfectly understands Himself; otherwise His being would not be perfect, since His being is His act of understanding. Now if anything is perfectly known, it follows of necessity that its power is perfectly known. But the power of

THE KNOWLEDGE OF GOD   From *Summa Theologica*, Part I, Question 14, in *Basic Writings of Saint Thomas Aquinas*, edited by Anton C. Pegis. By permission of the A. C. Pegis estate.

[1] *Lib. 83 Quaest.*, q. 46 (PL 40, 30).

anything can be perfectly known only by knowing to what that power extends. Since, therefore, the divine power extends to other things by the very fact that it is the first effective cause of all things, as is clear from the aforesaid,[2] God must necessarily know things other than Himself. And this appears still more plainly if we add that the very being of the first efficient cause—viz., God—is His own act of understanding. Hence whatever effects pre-exist in God, as in the first cause, must be in His act of understanding, and they must be there in an intelligible way: for everything which is in another is in it according to the mode of that in which it is.

Now in order to know how God knows things other than Himself, we must consider that a thing is known in two ways: in itself, and in another. A thing is known *in itself* when it is known by the proper species adequate to the knowable object itself; as when the eye sees a man through the species of a man. A thing is seen *in another* through the species of that which contains it; as when a part is seen in the whole through the species of the whole, or when a man is seen in a mirror through the species of the mirror, or by any other way by which one thing is seen in another.

So we say that God sees Himself in Himself, because He sees Himself through His essence; and He sees other things, not in themselves, but in Himself, inasmuch as His essence contains the likeness of things other than Himself.

Reply Obj. 1. The passage of Augustine in which it is said that God *sees nothing outside Himself* is not to be taken in such a way, as if God saw nothing that was outside Himself, but in the sense that what is outside Himself He does not see except in Himself, as was explained above.

Reply Obj. 2. The object understood is a perfection of the one understanding, not by its substance, but by its species, according to which it is in the intellect as its form and perfection. For, as is said, in *De Anima* iii,[3] *a stone is not in the soul, but its species*. Now those things which are other than God are understood by God inasmuch as the essence of God contains their species, as was explained above; and hence it does not follow that anything is the perfection of the divine intellect other than the divine essence.

Reply Obj. 3. The intellectual act is not specified by what is understood in another, but by the principal object understood in which other things are understood. For the intellectual act is specified by its object inasmuch as the intelligible form is the principle of the intellectual operation, since every operation is specified by the form which is its principle of operation, as heating by heat. Hence the intellectual operation is specified by that intelligible form which makes the intellect to be in act. And this is the species of the principal thing understood, which in God is nothing but His own essence in which all the species of things are comprehended. Hence it does not follow that the divine intellectual act, or rather God Himself, is specified by anything other than the divine essence itself.

[2] Q. 2 a. 3 [in *Philosophy of Religion: Selected Readings*, 2nd ed., 128–30].

[3] Aristotle, *De An.*, III, 8 (431b 29).

EIGHTH ARTICLE.   WHETHER THE KNOWLEDGE OF GOD IS THE CAUSE OF THINGS?

We proceed thus to the Eighth Article:—

Objection 1. It seems that the knowledge of God is not the cause of things. For Origen says (in *Rom.* viii. 30): *A thing will not happen, because God knows it as future, but because it is future, it is on that account known by God before it exists.*[4]

Obj. 2. Further, given the cause, the effect follows. But the knowledge of God is eternal. Therefore if the knowledge of God is the cause of created things, it seems that creatures are eternal.

Obj. 3. Further, *The knowable thing is prior to knowledge, and is its measure*, as the Philosopher says.[5] But what is posterior and measured cannot be a cause. Therefore the knowledge of God is not the cause of things.

On the contrary, Augustine says, *Not because they are, does God know all creatures spiritual and temporal, but because He knows them, therefore they are.*[6]

I answer that, The knowledge of God is the cause of things. For the knowledge of God is to all creatures what the knowledge of the artificer is to things made by his art. Now the knowledge of the artificer is the cause of the things made by his art from the fact that the artificer works through his intellect. Hence the form in the intellect must be the principle of action; as heat is the principle of heating. Nevertheless, we must observe that a natural form, being a form that remains in that to which it gives being, denotes a principle of action according only as it has an inclination to an effect; and likewise, the intelligible form does not denote a principle of action in so far as it resides in the one who understands unless there is added to it the inclination to an effect, which inclination is through the will. For since the intelligible form has a relation to contraries (inasmuch as the same knowledge relates to contraries), it would not produce a determinate effect unless it were determined to one thing by the appetite, as the Philosopher says.[7] Now it is manifest that God causes things by His intellect, since His being is His act of understanding; and hence His knowledge must be the cause of things, in so far as His will is joined to it. Hence the knowledge of God as the cause of things is usually called the *knowledge of approbation*.

Reply Obj. 1. Origen[8] spoke in reference to that aspect of knowledge to which the idea of causality does not belong unless the will is joined to it, as is said above.

But when he says that the reason why God foreknows some things is because they are future, this must be understood according to the cause of consequence, and not according to the cause of being. For if things are in the future, it follows

---

[4] *In Rom.*, VII, super VIII, 30 (PG 14, 1126).

[5] Aristotle, *Metaph.*, IX, 1 (1053a 33).

[6] *De Trin.*, XV, 13 (PL 42, 1076); VI, 10 (PL 42, 931).

[7] Aristotle, *Metaph.*, VIII, 5 (1048a 11).

[8] *In Rom.*, VII, super VIII, 30 (PG 14, 1126).

that God foreknows them; but the futurity of things is not the cause why God knows them.

Reply Obj. 2. The knowledge of God is the cause of things according as things are in His knowledge. But that things should be eternal was not in the knowledge of God; hence, although the knowledge of God is eternal, it does not follow that creatures are eternal.

Reply Obj. 3. Natural things are midway between the knowledge of God and our knowledge: for we receive knowledge from natural things, of which God is the cause by His knowledge. Hence, just as the natural things that can be known by us are prior to our knowledge, and are its measure, so the knowledge of God is prior to them, and is their measure; as, for instance, a house is midway between the knowledge of the builder who made it, and the knowledge of the one who gathers his knowledge of the house from the house already built.

NINTH ARTICLE.   WHETHER GOD HAS KNOWLEDGE OF THINGS THAT ARE NOT?

We proceed thus to the Ninth Article:—

Objection 1. It seems that God has not knowledge of things that are not. For the knowledge of God is of true things. But *truth* and *being* are convertible terms. Therefore the knowledge of God is not of things that are not.

Obj. 2. Further, knowledge requires likeness between the knower and the thing known. But those things that are not cannot have any likeness to God, Who is very being. Therefore what is not, cannot be known by God.

Obj. 3. Further, the knowledge of God is the cause of what is known by Him. But it is not the cause of things that are not, because a thing that is not has no cause. Therefore God has no knowledge of things that are not.

On the contrary, The Apostle says: *Who . . . calleth those things that are not as those that are* (Rom. iv. 17).

I answer that, God knows all things whatsoever that in any way are. Now it is possible that things that are not absolutely should be in a certain sense. For, absolutely speaking, those things are which are actual; whereas things, which are not actual, are in the power either of God Himself or of a creature, whether in active power, or passive; whether in the power of thought or of imagination, or of any other kind whatsoever. Whatever therefore can be made, or thought, or said by the creature, as also whatever He Himself can do, all are known to God, although they are not actual. And to this extent it can be said that He has knowledge even of things that are not.

Now, among the things that are not actual, a certain difference is to be noted. For though some of them may not be in act now, still they have been, or they will be; and God is said to know all these with the *knowledge of vision:* for since God's act of understanding, which is His being, is measured by eternity, and since eternity is without succession, comprehending all time, the present glance of God extends over all time, and to all things which exist in any time, as to objects present to Him. But there are other things in God's power, or the creature's, which nevertheless are not, nor will be, nor have been; and as regards these He is said to have the knowledge, not of vision, but of *simple intelligence*. This is so called because the things we see around us have distinct being outside the seer.

Reply Obj. 1. Those things that are not actual are true in so far as they are in potentiality, for it is true that they are in potentiality; and as such they are known by God.

Reply Obj. 2. Since God is very being, everything is in so far as it participates in the likeness of God; as everything is hot in so far as it participates in heat. So, things in potentiality are known by God, even though they are not in act.

Reply Obj. 3. The knowledge of God is the cause of things when the will is joined to it. Hence it is not necessary that whatever God knows shall be, or have been or is to be; but this is necessary only as regards what He wills to be, or permits to be. Further, it is not in the knowledge of God that these things be, but that they be possible.

ELEVENTH ARTICLE.   WHETHER GOD KNOWS SINGULAR THINGS?

We proceed thus to the Eleventh Article:—

Objection 1. It seems that God does not know singular things. For the divine intellect is more immaterial than the human intellect. Now the human intellect, by reason of its immateriality, does not know singular things; but as the Philosopher says, *reason has to do with universals, sense with singular things.*[9] Therefore God does not know singular things.

Obj. 2. Further, in us those powers alone know the singular, which receive the species not abstracted from material conditions. But in God things are in the highest degree abstracted from all materiality. Therefore God does not know singular things.

Obj. 3. Further, all knowledge comes about through some likeness. But the likeness of singular things, in so far as they are singular, does not seem to be in God; for the principle of singularity is matter, which, since it is in potentiality only, is altogether unlike God, Who is pure act. Therefore God cannot know singular things.

On the contrary, It is written (*Prov.* xvi. 2), *All the ways of a man are open to His eyes.*

I answer that, God knows singular things. For all perfections found in creatures pre-exist in God in a higher way, as is clear from the foregoing.[10] Now to know singular things is part of our perfection. Hence God must know singular things. Even the Philosopher considers it incongruous that anything known by us should be unknown to God; and thus against Empedocles he argues that *God would be most ignorant if He did not know discord.*[11] Now the perfections which are found divided among inferior beings exist simply and unitedly in God; hence, although

---

[9] *De An.*, II, 5 (417b 22).

[10] Q. 4, a. 2.

[11] *De An.*, I, 5 (410b 4); *Metaph.*, II, 4 (1000b 3).

by one power we know the universal and immaterial, and by another we know singular and material things, nevertheless God knows both by His simple intellect.

Now some, wishing to show how this can be, said that God knows singular things through universal causes.[12] For nothing exists in any singular thing that does not arise from some universal cause. They give the example of an astronomer who knows all the universal movements of the heavens, and can thence foretell all eclipses that are to come. This, however, is not enough; for from universal causes singular things acquire certain forms and powers which, however they may be joined together, are not individuated except by individual matter. Hence he who knows Socrates because he is white, or because he is the son of Sophroniscus, or because of something of that kind, would not know him in so far as he is this particular man. Hence, following the above explanation, God would not know singular things in their singularity.

On the other hand, others have said that God knows singular things by the application of universal causes to particular effects.[13] But this will not hold; for no one can apply a thing to another unless he first knows that other thing. Hence the said application cannot be the reason of knowing the particular; it rather presupposes the knowledge of singular things.

Therefore we must propose another explanation. Since God is the cause of things by His knowledge, as was stated above, His knowledge extends as far as His causality extends. Hence, as the active power of God extends not only to forms, which are the source of universality, but also to matter, as we shall prove further on, the knowledge of God must extend to singular things, which are individuated by matter.[14] For since He knows things other than Himself by His essence, as being the likeness of things, or as their active principle, His essence must be the sufficing principle of knowing all things made by Him, not only in the universal, but also in the singular. The same would apply to the knowledge of the artificer, if it were productive of the whole thing, and not only of the form.

Reply Obj. 1. Our intellect abstracts the intelligible species from the individuating principles; hence the intelligible species in our intellect cannot be the likeness of the individual principles, and on that account our intellect does not know the singular. But the intelligible species in the divine intellect, which is the essence of God, is immaterial not by abstraction, but of itself, being the principle of all the principles which enter into the composition of the thing, whether these be principles of the species or principles of the individual; hence by it God knows not only universals, but also singular things.

Reply Obj. 2. Although the species in the divine intellect has no material conditions in its being like the species received in the imagination and sense, yet it extends to both immaterial and material things through its power.

Reply Obj. 3. Although matter, because of its potentiality, recedes from likeness to God, yet, even in so far as it has being in this wise, it retains a certain likeness to the divine being.

[12]Cf. Avicenna, *Metaph.*, VIII, 6 (100rb).

[13]Cf. Averroes, *Destruct. Destruct.*, XI (IX, 47rb).

[14]Q. 44, a. 2.

TWELFTH ARTICLE.   WHETHER GOD CAN KNOW INFINITE THINGS?

We proceed thus to the Twelfth Article:—

Objection 1. It seems that God cannot know infinite things. For the infinite, as such, is unknown, since the infinite is that which, *to those who measure it, leaves always something more to be measured,* as the Philosopher says.[15] Moreover, Augustine says that *whatever is comprehended by knowledge is bounded by the comprehension of the knower.*[16] Now infinite things have no boundary. Therefore they cannot be comprehended by the knowledge of God.

Obj. 2. Further, if it be said that things infinite in themselves are finite in God's knowledge, against this it may be urged that the essence of the infinite is that it is untraversable, and of the finite that it is traversable, as is said in *Physics* iii.[17] But the infinite is not traversable either by the finite or by the infinite, as is proved in *Physics* vi.[18] Therefore the infinite cannot be bounded by the finite, not even by the infinite; and so the infinite cannot be finite in God's knowledge, which is infinite.

Obj. 3. Further, the knowledge of God is the measure of what is known. But it is contrary to the essence of the infinite that it be measured. Therefore infinite things cannot be known by God.

On the contrary, Augustine says, *Although we cannot number the infinite, nevertheless it can be comprehended by Him whose knowledge has no number.*[19]

I answer that, Since God knows not only things actual but also things possible to Himself or to created things, as was shown above, and since these must be infinite, it must be held that He knows infinite things. Although the *knowledge of vision,* which has relation only to things that are, or will be, or have been, is not of infinite things, as some say,[20] for we do not hold that the world is eternal, nor that generation and movement will go on for ever, so that individuals be infinitely multiplied; yet, if we consider more attentively, we must hold that God knows infinite things even by the knowledge of vision. For God knows even the thoughts and affections of hearts, which will be multiplied to infinity since rational creatures will endure forever.

The reason of this is to be found in the fact that the knowledge of every knower is measured by the mode of the form which is the principle of knowledge. For the sensible species in the sense is the likeness of only one individual thing, and can give the knowledge of only one individual. But the intelligible species in our intellect is the likeness of the things as regards its specific nature, which is participable by infinite particulars. Hence our intellect by the intelligible species of man in a certain way knows infinite men, not however as distinguished from each

---

[15]*Phys.*, III, 6 (207a 7).

[16]*De Civit. Dei*, XII, 18 (PL 41, 368).

[17]Aristotle, *Phys.*, III, 4 (204a 3).

[18]*Op. cit.*, VI, 7 (238b 17).

[19]*De Civit. Dei*, XII, 18 (PL 41, 368).

[20]Cf. q. 7, a. 4; q. 46, a. 2, ad 8.

other, but as communicating in the nature of the species; and the reason is because the intelligible species of our intellect is the likeness of man, not as to the individual principles, but as to the principles of the species. On the other hand, the divine essence, whereby the divine intellect understands, is a sufficing likeness of all things that are, or can be, not only as regards the universal principles, but also as regards the principles proper to each one, as was shown above. Hence it follows that the knowledge of God extends to infinite things, even according as they are distinct from each other.

Reply Obj. 1. The idea of the infinite pertains to quantity, as the Philosopher says.[21] But the idea of quantity implies an order of parts. Therefore to know the infinite according to the mode of the infinite is to know part after part; and in this way the infinite cannot be known, for whatever quantity of parts be taken, there will always remain something else outside. But God does not know the infinite, or infinite things, as if He enumerated part after part; since He knows all things simultaneously and not successively, as was said above. Hence there is nothing to prevent Him from knowing infinite things.

Reply Obj. 2. Transition imports a certain succession of parts; and hence it is that the infinite cannot be traversed by the finite, nor by the infinite. But equality suffices for comprehension, because that is said to be comprehended which has nothing outside the comprehender. Hence, it is not against the idea of the infinite to be comprehended by the infinite. And so, what is infinite in itself can be called finite to the knowledge of God as comprehended; but not as if it were traversable.

Reply Obj. 3. The knowledge of God is the measure of things, not quantitatively, for the infinite is not subject to this kind of measure, but because it measures the essence and truth of things. For everything has truth of nature according to the degree in which it imitates the knowledge of God, as the thing made by art agrees with the art. Granted, however, an actually infinite number of things (for instance, an infinitude of men, or an infinitude in continuous quantity, as an infinite air, as some of the ancients held),[22] yet it is manifest that these would have a determinate and finite being, because their being would be limited to certain determinate natures. Hence they would be measurable as regards the knowledge of God.

THIRTEENTH ARTICLE.   WHETHER THE KNOWLEDGE OF GOD IS OF FUTURE CONTINGENT THINGS?

We proceed thus to the Thirteenth Article:—

Objection 1. It seems that the knowledge of God is not of future contingent things. For from a necessary cause proceeds a necessary effect. But the knowledge of God is the cause of things known, as was said above. Since therefore that knowledge is necessary, what He knows must also be necessary. Therefore the knowledge of God is not of contingent things.

---

[21] *Phys.*, I, 2 (185a 33).

[22] Attributed to Anaximenes and Diogenes by Aristotle, *Phys.*, III, 4 (203a 18); *Metaph.*, I, 3 (984a 5).

Obj. 2. Further, every conditional proposition, of which the antecedent is absolutely necessary, must have an absolutely necessary consequent. For the antecedent is to the consequent as principles are to the conclusion: and from necessary principles only a necessary conclusion can follow, as is proved in *Poster.* i.[23] But this is a true conditional proposition, *If God knew that this thing will be, it will be,*[24] for the knowledge of God is only of true things. Now, the antecedent of this conditioned proposition is absolutely necessary, because it is eternal, and because it is signified as past. Therefore the consequent is also absolutely necessary. Therefore whatever God knows is necessary; and so the knowledge of God is not of contingent things.

Obj. 3. Further, everything known by God must necessarily be, because even what we ourselves know must necessarily be; and, of course, the knowledge of God is much more certain than ours. But no future contingent thing must necessarily be. Therefore no contingent future thing is known by God.

On the contrary, It is written (Ps. xxxii. 15), *He Who hath made the hearts of every one of them, Who understandeth all their works,* that is, of men. Now the works of men are contingent, being subject to free choice. Therefore God knows future contingent things.

I answer that, Since, as was shown above, God knows all things, not only things actual but also things possible to Him and to the creature, and since some of these are future contingent to us, it follows that God knows future contingent things.

In evidence of this, we must observe that a contingent thing can be considered in two ways. First, in itself, in so far as it is already in act, and in this sense it is not considered as future, but as present; neither is it considered as contingent to one of two terms, but as determined to one; and because of this it can be infallibly the object of certain knowledge, for instance to the sense of sight, as when I see that Socrates is sitting down. In another way, a contingent thing can be considered as it is in its cause, and in this way it is considered as future, and as a contingent thing not yet determined to one; for a contingent cause has relation to opposite things: and in this sense a contingent thing is not subject to any certain knowledge. Hence, whoever knows a contingent effect in its cause only, has merely a conjectural knowledge of it. Now God knows all contingent things not only as they are in their causes, but also as each one of them is actually in itself. And although contingent things become actual successively, nevertheless God knows contingent things not successively, as they are in their own being, as we do, but simultaneously. The reason is because His knowledge is measured by eternity, as is also His being; and eternity, being simultaneously whole, comprises all time, as we said above.[25] Hence, all things that are in time are present to God from eternity, not only because He has the essences of things present within Him, as

---

[23] Aristotle, *Post, Anal.*, I, 6 (75a 4).

[24] Cf. St. Anselm, *De Concord. Praesc. cum Lib. Arb.*, q. I, 1 (PL 158, 509); St. Augustine, *De Civit. Dei*, V, 9; XI, 21 (PL 41, 148; 334); *De Lib. Arb.*, III, 4 (PL 32, 1276); Boëthius, *De Consol.*, V, prose 3; prose 6 (PL 63, 840; 860); Peter Lombard, *Sent.*, I, xxxviii, 2 (I, 244).

[25] Q. 10, a. 2, ad 4.

some say, [26] but because His glance is carried from eternity over all things as they are in their presentiality. Hence it is manifest that contingent things are infallibly known by God, inasmuch as they are subject to the divine sight in their presentiality; and yet they are future contingent things in relation to their own causes.

Reply Obj. 1. Although the supreme cause is necessary, the effect may be contingent by reason of the proximate contingent cause; just as the germination of a plant is contingent by reason of the proximate contingent cause, although the movement of the sun, which is the first cause, is necessary. So, likewise, things known by God are contingent because of their proximate causes, while the knowledge of God, which is the first cause, is necessary.

Reply Obj. 2. Some say that this antecedent, *God knew this contingent to be future,* is not necessary, but contingent; because, although it is past, still it imports a relation to the future. [27] This, however, does not remove necessity from it, for whatever has had relation to the future, must have had it, even though the future sometimes is not realized. On the other hand, some say that this antecedent is contingent because it is a compound of the necessary and the contingent; [28] as this saying is contingent, *Socrates is a white man.* But this also is to no purpose; for when we say, *God knew this contingent to be future,* contingent is used here only as the matter of the proposition, and not as its principal part. Hence its contingency or necessity has no reference to the necessity or contingency of the proposition, or to its being true or false. For it may be just as true that I said a man is an ass, as that I said Socrates runs, or God is: and the same applies to necessary and contingent.

Hence it must be said that this antecedent is absolutely necessary. Nor does it follow, as some say, that the consequent is absolutely necessary because the antecedent is the remote cause of the consequent, which is contingent by reason of the proximate cause. [29] But this is to no purpose. For the conditional would be false were its antecedent the remote necessary cause, and the consequent a contingent effect; as, for example, if I said, *if the sun moves, the grass will grow.*

Therefore we must reply otherwise: when the antecedent contains anything belonging to an act of the soul, the consequent must be taken, not as it is in itself, but as it is in the soul; for the being of a thing in itself is other than the being of a thing in the soul. For example, when I say, *What the soul understands is immaterial,* the meaning is that it is immaterial as it is in the intellect, not as it is in itself. Likewise if I say, *If God knew anything, it will be,* the consequent must be understood as it is subject to the divine knowledge, that is, as it is in its presentiality. And thus it is necessary, as is also the antecedent; *for everything that is, while it is, must necessarily be,* as the Philosopher says in *Periherm* i. [30]

[26] Avicenna, *Metaph.,* VIII, 6 (100rb).

[27] St. Bonaventure, *In I Sent.,* d. xxxviii, a. 2, q. 2 (I, 678); St. Albert, *In I Sent.,* d. xxxviii, a. 4 (XXVI, 290).

[28] Robert Grosseteste, *De Lib. Arb.,* VI (p. 170).

[29] Alex of Hales, *Summa Theol.,* I, no. 171 (I, 255); no. 184 (I, 270); Alain of Lille, *Theol. Reg.,* LXVI (PL 210, 653).

[30] Aristotle, *Perih.,* I, 9 (19a 23).

Reply Obj. 3. Things reduced to actuality in time are known by us successively in time, but by God they are known in eternity, which is above time. Whence to us they cannot be certain, since we know future contingent things only as contingent futures; but they are certain to God alone, Whose understanding is in eternity above time. Just as he who goes along the road does not see those who come after him; whereas he who sees the whole road from a height sees at once all those traveling on it. Hence, what is known by us must be necessary, even as it is in itself; for what is in itself a future contingent cannot be known by us. But what is known by God must be necessary according to the mode in which it is subject to the divine knowledge, as we have already stated, but not absolutely as considered in its proper causes. Hence also this proposition, *Everything known by God must necessarily be,* is usually distinguished,[31] for it may refer to the thing or to the saying. If it refers to the thing, it is divided and false; for the sense is, *Everything which God knows is necessary.* If understood of the saying, it is composite and true, for the sense is, *This proposition, 'that which is known by God is' is necessary.*

Now some urge an objection and say that this distinction holds good with regard to forms that are separable from a subject.[32] Thus if I said, *It is possible for a white thing to be black,* it is false as applied to the saying, and true as applied to the thing: for a thing which is white can become black; whereas this saying, *a white thing is black,* can never be true. But in forms that are inseparable from a subject, this distinction does not hold: for instance, if I said, A *black crow can be white;* for in both senses it is false. Now to be known by God is inseparable from a thing; for what is known by God cannot be not known. This objection, however, would hold if these words *that which is known* implied any disposition inherent in the subject; but since they import an act of the knower, something can be attributed to the known thing in itself (even if it always be known) which is not attributed to it in so far as it falls under an act of knowledge. Thus, material being is attributed to a stone in itself, which is not attributed to it inasmuch as it is intelligible.

FIFTEENTH ARTICLE.   WHETHER THE KNOWLEDGE OF GOD IS VARIABLE?

We proceed thus to the Fifteenth Article:—

Objection 1. It seems that the knowledge of God is variable. For knowledge is related to what is knowable. But whatever imports relation to the creature is applied to God from time, and varies according to the variation of creatures. Therefore, the knowledge of God is variable according to the variation of creatures.

Obj. 2. Further, whatever God can make He can know. But God can make more things than He does. Therefore, He can know more than He knows. Thus, His knowledge can vary according to increase and diminution.

Obj. 3. Further, God knew that Christ would be born. But He does not know

---

[31] Cf. Wm. of Sherwood, *Introd. in Logicam* (p. 89); St. Albert, *In Prior. Anal.,* I, tr. 4, ch. 16 (I, 562).

[32] Cf. St. Thomas, *In 1 Sent.,* d. xxxviii, q. 1, a. 5, ad 5–6; *De Ver.,* II, 12, ad 4.

now that Christ will be born, because Christ is not to be born in the future. Therefore God does not know everything He once knew; and thus the knowledge of God is variable.

On the contrary, It is said, that in God *there is no change nor shadow of alteration* (*Jas.* i. 17).

I answer that, Since the knowledge of God is His substance, as is clear from the foregoing, just as His substance is altogether immutable, as was shown above,[33] so His knowledge likewise must be altogether invariable.

Reply Obj. 1. *Lord, Creator*, and the like, import relations to creatures in so far as they are in themselves. But the knowledge of God imports relation to creatures in so far as they are in God; because everything is actually understood according as it is in the one who understands. Now created things are in God in an invariable manner; while they exist variably in themselves.—Or we may say that *Lord, Creator*, and the like, import the relations consequent upon the acts which are understood as terminating in the creatures themselves as they are in themselves; and thus these relations are attributed to God variously, according to the variation of creatures. But *knowledge* and *love*, and the like, import relations consequent upon the acts which are understood to be in God; and therefore these are predicated of God in an invariable manner.

Reply Obj. 2. God knows also what He can make, and does not make. Hence from the fact that He can make more than He makes, it does not follow that He can know more than He knows, unless this be referred to the *knowledge of vision*, according to which He is said to know those things which actually exist in some period of time. But from the fact that He knows that some things can be which are not, or that some things can not-be which are, it does not follow that His knowledge is variable, but rather that He knows the variability of things. If, however, anything existed which God did not previously know, and afterwards knew, then His knowledge would be variable. But this is impossible, for whatever is, or can be in any period of time, is known by God in His eternity. Therefore, from the fact that a thing is said to exist in some period of time, we must say that it is known by God from all eternity. Therefore it cannot be granted that God can know more than He knows; because such a proposition implies that first of all He did not know, and then afterwards knew.

Reply Obj. 3. The ancient Nominalists said that it was the same thing to say *Christ is born* and *will be born*, and *was born*; because the same thing is signified by these three—viz., the nativity of Christ.[34] Therefore it follows, they said, that whatever God knew, He knows; because now He knows that Christ is born, which means the same thing as that Christ will be born. This opinion, however, is false, both because the diversity in the parts of a sentence causes a diversity in enunciations, and because it would follow that a proposition which is true once would always be true; which is contrary to what the Philosopher lays down when he says that this sentence, *Socrates sits*, is true when he is sitting, and false when he stands up.[35] Therefore, it must be conceded that this proposition, *Whatever God*

---

[33] Q. 9, a. 1.

[34] Cf. Abelard, *Introd. ad Theol.*, III, 5 (PL 178, 1102); Peter Lombard, *Sent.*, I, xli, 3 (I, 258).

[35] *Cat.*, V (4a 23).

knew He knows, is not true if referred to what is enunciated. But because of this, it does not follow that the knowledge of God is variable. For as it is without variation in the divine knowledge that God knows one and the same thing some-time to be, and sometime not, so it is without variation in the divine knowledge that God knows that an enunciation is sometime true, and sometime false. The knowledge of God, however, would be variable if He knew enunciations accord-ing to their own limitations, by composition and division, as occurs in our intel-lect. Hence our knowledge varies either as regards truth and falsity, for example, if when a thing is changed we retained the same opinion about it; or as regards diverse opinions, as if we first thought that someone was sitting, and afterwards thought that he was not sitting; neither of which can be in God.

NELSON PIKE
Divine Omniscience and Voluntary Action

In Part V, Section III of his *Consolatio Philosophiae*, Boethius entertained (though he later rejected) the claim that if God is omniscient, no human action is volun-tary. This claim seems intuitively false. Surely, given only a doctrine describing God's *knowledge*, nothing about the voluntary status of human actions will follow. Perhaps such a conclusion would follow from a doctrine of divine omnipotence or divine providence, but what connection could there be between the claim that God is *omniscient* and the claim that human actions are determined? Yet Boe-thius thought he saw a problem here. He thought that if one collected together just the right assumptions and principles regarding God's knowledge, one could derive the conclusion that if God exists, no human action is voluntary. Of course, Boethius did not think that all the assumptions and principles required to reach this conclusion are true (quite the contrary), but he thought it important to draw attention to them nonetheless. If a theologian is to construct a doctrine of God's knowledge which does not commit him to determinism, he must first understand that there is a way of thinking about God's knowledge which would so commit him.

In this paper, I shall argue that although his claim has a sharp counterintuitive ring, Boethius was right in thinking that there is a selection from among the various doctrines and principles clustering about the notions of knowledge, om-niscience, and God which, when brought together, demand the conclusion that if God exists, no human action is voluntary. Boethius, I think, did not succeed

Nelson Pike (1930–   ) is Professor of Philosophy at the University of California, Irvine. Pike received his Ph.D. from Harvard University in 1962. He has written many articles and is the author of *God and Timelessness*.

DIVINE OMNISCIENCE AND VOLUNTARY ACTION   FROM *The Philosophical Review*, Volume 74, No. 1, January 1965. Reprinted by permission of *The Philosophical Review* and the author.

in making explicit all of the ingredients in the problem. His suspicions were sound, but his discussion was incomplete. His argument needs to be developed. This is the task I shall undertake in the pages to follow. I should like to make clear at the outset that my purpose in rearguing this thesis is not to show that determinism is true, nor to show that God does not exist, nor to show that either determinism is true or God does not exist. Following Boethius, I shall not claim that the items needed to generate the problem are either philosophically or theologically adequate. I want to concentrate attention on the implications of a certain set of assumptions. Whether the assumptions are themselves acceptable is a question I shall not consider.

I

A. Many philosophers have held that if a statement of the form "A knows X" is true, then "A believes X" is true and "X" is true. As a first assumption, I shall take this partial analysis of "A knows X" to be correct. And I shall suppose that since this analysis holds for all knowledge claims, it will hold when speaking of God's knowledge. "God knows X" entails "God believes X" and " 'X' is true."

Secondly, Boethius said that with respect to the matter of knowledge, God "cannot in anything be mistaken."[1] I shall understand this doctrine as follows. Omniscient beings hold no false beliefs. Part of what is meant when we say that a person is omniscient is that the person in question believes nothing that is false. But, further, it is part of the "essence" of God to be omniscient. This is to say that any person who is not omniscient could not be the person we usually mean to be referring to when using the name "God." To put this last point a little differently: if the person we usually mean to be referring to when using the name "God" were suddenly to lose the quality of omniscience (suppose, for example, He came to believe something false), the resulting person would no longer be God. Although we might call this second person "God" (I might call my cat "God"), the absence of the quality of omniscience would be sufficient to guarantee that the person referred to was not the same as the person formerly called by that name. From this last doctrine it follows that the statement "If a given person is God, that person is omniscient" is an a priori truth. From this we may conclude that the statement "If a given person is God, that person holds no false beliefs" is also an a priori truth. It would be conceptually impossible for God to hold a false belief. " 'X' is true" follows from "God believes X." These are all ways of expressing the same principle—the principle expressed by Boethius in the formula "God cannot in anything be mistaken."

A second principle usually associated with the notion of divine omniscience has to do with the scope or range of God's intellectual gaze. To say that a being is omniscient is to say that he knows everything. "Everything" in this statement is usually taken to cover future, as well as present and past, events and circumstances. In fact, God is usually said to have had foreknowledge of everything that has ever happened. With respect to anything that was, is, or will be the case, God knew, *from eternity*, that it would be the case.

[1] *Consolatio Philosophiae*, Bk. V, sec. 3, par. 6.

The doctrine of God's knowing everything from eternity is very obscure. One particularly difficult question concerning this doctrine is whether it entails that with respect to everything that was, is, or will be the case, God knew *in advance* that it would be the case. In some traditional theological texts, we are told that God is *eternal* in the sense that He exists "outside of time," that is, in the sense that He bears no temporal relations to the events or circumstances of the natural world.[2] In a theology of this sort, God could not be said to have known that a given natural event was going to happen before it happened. If God knew that a given natural event was going to occur *before* it occurred, at least one of God's cognitions would then have occurred before some natural event. This, surely, would violate the idea that God bears no temporal relations to natural events.[3] On the other hand, in a considerable number of theological sources, we are told that God *has always* existed—that He existed long *before* the occurrence of any natural event. In a theology of this sort, to say that God is eternal is not to say that God exists "outside of time" (bears no temporal relations to natural events), it is to say, instead, God has existed (and will continue to exist) at each moment.[4] The doctrine of omniscience which goes with this second understanding of the notion of eternity is one in which it is affirmed that God *has always* known what was going to happen in the natural world. John Calvin wrote as follows:

> When we attribute foreknowledge to God, we mean that all things have ever been and perpetually remain before his eyes, so that to his knowledge nothing is future or past, but all things are present; and present in such manner, that he does not merely conceive of them from ideas formed in his mind, as things remembered by us appear to our minds, but really he holds and sees them as if (*tanquam*) actually placed before him.[5]

All things are "present" to God in the sense that He "sees" them as if (*tanquam*) they were actually before Him. Further, with respect to any given natural event, not only is that event "present" to God in the sense indicated, it has *ever been and has perpetually remained* "present" to Him in that sense. This latter is the point of special interest. Whatever one thinks of the idea that God "sees" things as if "actually placed before him," Calvin would appear to be committed to the idea that God has *always known* what was going to happen in the natural world. Choose an event (*E*) and a time (T_2) at which *E* occurred. For any time (T_1) prior to T_2 (say, five thousand, six hundred, or eighty years prior to T_2), God knew at T_1 that *E* would occur at T_2. It will follow from this doctrine, of course, that with respect to any human action, God knew well in advance of its performance that

[2] This position is particularly well formulated in St. Anselm's *Proslogium*, ch. xix and *Monologium*, chs. xxi–xxii; and in Frederick Schleiermacher's *The Christian Faith*, Pt. I, sec. 2, par. 51. It is also explicit in Boethius, *op. cit.*, secs. 4–6, and in St. Thomas' *Summa Theologica*, Pt. I, Q. 10.

[3] This point is explicit in Boethius, *op. cit.*, secs. 4–6.

[4] This position is particularly well expressed in William Paley's *Natural Theology*, ch. xxiv. It is also involved in John Calvin's discussion of predestination, *Institutes of the Christian Religion*, Bk. III, ch. xxi; and in some formulations of the first cause argument for the existence of God, e.g., John Locke's *Essay Concerning Human Understanding*, Bk. IV, ch. x.

[5] *Institutes of the Christian Religion*, Bk. III, ch. xxi; this passage trans. by John Allen (Philadelphia, 1813), II, 145.

the action would be performed. Calvin says, "when God created man, He foresaw what would happen concerning him." He adds, "little more than five thousand years have elapsed since the creation of the world."[6] Calvin seems to have thought that God foresaw the outcome of every human action well over five thousand years ago.

In the discussion to follow, I shall work only with this second interpretation of God's knowing everything *from eternity*. I shall assume that if a person is omniscient, that person has always known what was going to happen in the natural world—and, in particular, has always known what human actions were going to be performed. Thus, as above, assuming that the attribute of omniscience is part of the "essence" of God, the statement "For any natural event (including human actions), if a given person is God, that person would always have known that that event was going to occur at the time it occurred" must be treated as an a priori truth. This is just another way of stating a point admirably put by St. Augustine when he said: "For to confess that God exists and at the same time to deny that He has foreknowledge of future things is the most manifest folly. . . . One who is not prescient of all future things is not God."[7]

B. Last Saturday afternoon, Jones mowed his lawn. Assuming that God exists and is (essentially) omniscient in the sense outlined above, it follows that (let us say) eighty years prior to last Saturday afternoon, God knew (and thus believed) that Jones would mow his lawn at that time. But from this it follows, I think, that at the time of action (last Saturday afternoon) Jones was not *able*—that is, it was not *within Jones's power*—to refrain from mowing his lawn.[8] If at the time of action, Jones had been able to refrain from mowing his lawn, then (the most obvious conclusion would seem to be) at the time of action, Jones was able to do something which would have brought it about that God held a false belief eighty years earlier. But God cannot in anything be mistaken. It is not possible that some belief of His was false. Thus, last Saturday afternoon, Jones was not able to do something which would have brought it about that God held a false belief eighty years ago. To suppose that it was would be to suppose that, at the time of action, Jones was able to do something having a conceptually incoherent description, namely something that would have brought it about that one of God's beliefs was false. Hence, given that God believed eighty years ago that Jones would mow his

---

[6] *Ibid.*, p. 144.

[7] *City of God*, Bk. V, sec. 9.

[8] The notion of someone being *able* to do something and the notion of something being *within one's power* are essentially the same. Traditional formulations of the problem of divine foreknowledge (e.g., those of Boethius and Augustine) made use of the notion of what is (and what is not) *within one's power*. But the problem is the same when framed in terms of what one is (and one is not) *able* to do. Thus, I shall treat the statements "Jones was able to do X," "Jones had the ability to do X," and "It was within Jones's power to do X" as equivalent. Richard Taylor, in "I Can," *Philosophical Review*, LXIX (1960), 78–89, has argued that the notion of ability or power involved in these last three statements is incapable of philosophical analysis. Be this as it may, I shall not here attempt such an analysis. In what follows I shall, however, be careful to affirm only those statements about what is (or is not) within one's power that would have to be preserved on any analysis of this notion having even the most distant claim to adequacy.

lawn on Saturday, if we are to assign Jones the power on Saturday to refrain from mowing his lawn, this power must not be described as the power to do something that would have rendered one of God's beliefs false. How then should we describe it vis-à-vis God and His belief? So far as I can see, there are only two other alternatives. First, we might try describing it as the power to do something that would have brought it about that God believed otherwise than He did eighty years ago; or, secondly, we might try describing it as the power to do something that would have brought it about that God (Who, by hypothesis, existed eighty years earlier) did not exist eighty years earlier—that is, as the power to do something that would have brought it about that any person who believed eighty years ago that Jones would mow his lawn on Saturday (one of whom was, by hypothesis, God) held a false belief, and thus was not God. But again, neither of these latter can be accepted. Last Saturday afternoon, Jones was not able to do something that would have brought it about that God believed otherwise than He did eighty years ago. Even if we suppose (as was suggested by Calvin) that eighty years ago God knew Jones would mow his lawn on Saturday in the sense that He "saw" Jones mowing his lawn as if this action were occurring before Him, the fact remains that God knew (and thus believed) eighty years prior to Saturday that Jones would mow his lawn. And if God held such a belief eighty years prior to Saturday, Jones did not have the power on Saturday to do something that would have made it the case that God did not hold this belief eighty years earlier. No action performed at a given time can alter the fact that a given person held a certain belief at a time prior to the time in question. This last seems to be an a priori truth. For similar reasons, the last of the above alternatives must also be rejected. On the assumption that God existed eighty years prior to Saturday, Jones on Saturday was not able to do something that would have brought it about that God did not exist eighty years prior to that time. No action performed at a given time can alter the fact that a certain person existed at a time prior to the time in question. This, too, seems to me to be an a priori truth. But if these observations are correct, then, given that Jones mowed his lawn on Saturday, and given that God exists and is (essentially) omniscient, it seems to follow that at the time of action, Jones did not have the power to refrain from mowing his lawn. The upshot of these reflections would appear to be that Jones's mowing his lawn last Saturday cannot be counted as a voluntary action. Although I do not have an analysis of what it is for an action to be *voluntary*, it seems to me that a situation in which it would be wrong to assign Jones the *ability* or *power* to do *other* than he did would be a situation in which it would also be wrong to speak of his action as voluntary. As a general remark, if God exists and is (essentially) omniscient in the sense specified above, no human action is voluntary.[9]

---

[9] In Bk. II, ch xxi, secs. 8–11 of the *Essay*, John Locke says that an agent is not *free* with respect to a given action (i.e., that an action is done "under necessity") when it is not within the agent's power to do otherwise. Locke allows a special kind of case, however, in which an action may be *voluntary* though done under necessity. If a man chooses to do something without knowing that it is not within his power to do otherwise (e.g., if a man chooses to stay in a room without knowing that the room is locked), his action may be voluntary thought he is not free to forbear it. If Locke is right in this (and I shall not argue the point one way or the other), replace "voluntary" with (let us say) "free" in the above paragraph and throughout the remainder of this paper.

As the argument just presented is somewhat complex, perhaps the following schematic representation of it will be of some use.

1. "God existed at T_1" entails "If Jones did X at T_2, God believed at T_1 that Jones would do X at T_2."
2. "God believes X" entails " 'X' is true."
3. It is not within one's power at a given time to do something having a description that is logically contradictory.
4. It is not within one's power at a given time to do something that would bring it about that someone who held a certain belief at a time prior to the time in question did not hold that belief at the time prior to the time in question.
5. It is not within one's power at a given time to do something that would bring it about that a person who existed at an earlier time did not exist at that earlier time.
6. If God existed at T_1 and if God believed at T_1 that Jones would do X at T_2, then if it was within Jones's power at T_2 to refrain from doing X, then (1) it was within Jones's power at T_2 to do something that would have brought it about that God held a false belief at T_1, or (2) it was within Jones's power at T_2 to do something which would have brought it about that God did not hold the belief He held at T_1, or (3) it was within Jones's power at T_2, to do something that would have brought it about that any person who believed at T_1 that Jones would do X at T_2 (one of whom was, by hypothesis, God) held a false belief and thus was not God—that is, that God (who by hypothesis existed at T_1) did not exist at T_1.
7. Alternative 1 in the consequent of item 6 is false (from 2 and 3).
8. Alternative 2 in the consequent of item 6 if false (from 4).
9. Alternative 3 in the consequent of item 6 is false (from 5).
10. Therefore, if God existed at T_1, and if God believed at T_1 that Jones would do X at T_2, then it was not within Jones's power at T_2 to refrain from doing X (from 6 through 9).
11. Therefore, if God existed at T_1, and if Jones did X at T_2, it was not within Jones's power at T_2 to refrain from doing X (from 1 and 10).

In this argument, items 1 and 2 make explicit the doctrine of God's (essential) omniscience with which I am working. Items 3, 4, and 5 express what I take to be part of the logic of the concept of ability or power as it applies to human beings. Item 6 is offered as an analytic truth. If one assigns Jones the power to refrain from doing X at T_2 (given that God believed at T_1 that he would do X at T_2), so far as I can see, one would have to describe this power in one of the three ways listed in the consequent of item 6. I do not know how to argue that these are the only alternatives, but I have been unable to find another. Item 11, when generalized for all agents and actions, and when taken together with what seems to me to be a minimal condition for the application of "voluntary action," yields the conclusion that if God exists (and is essentially omniscient in the way I have described) no human action is voluntary.

C. It is important to notice that the argument given in the preceding paragraphs avoids use of two concepts that are often prominent in discussions of determinism.

In the first place, the argument makes no mention of the *causes* of Jones's action. Say (for example, with St. Thomas)[10] that God's foreknowledge of Jones's action was, itself, the cause of the action (though I am really not sure what this means). Say, instead, that natural events or circumstances caused Jones to act. Even say that Jones's action had no cause at all. The argument outlined above remains unaffected. If eighty years prior to Saturday, God believed that Jones would mow his lawn at that time, it was not within Jones's power at the time of action to refrain from mowing his lawn. The reasoning that justifies this assertion makes no mention of a causal series preceding Jones's action.

Secondly, consider the following line of thinking. Suppose Jones mowed his lawn last Saturday. It was then *true* eighty years ago that Jones would mow his lawn at that time. Hence, on Saturday, Jones was not able to refrain from mowing his lawn. To suppose that he was would be to suppose that he was able on Saturday to do something that would have made false a proposition that was *already true* eighty years earlier. This general kind of argument for determinism is usually associated with Leibniz, although it was anticipated in Chapter IX of Aristotle's *De Interpretatione*. It has been used since, with some modification, in Richard Taylor's article, "Fatalism."[11] This argument, like the one I have offered above, makes no use of the notion of causation. It turns, instead, on the notion of its being *true eighty years ago* that Jones would mow his lawn on Saturday.

I must confess that I share the misgivings of those contemporary philosophers who have wondered what (if any) sense can be attached to a statement of the form "It was true at T_1 that E would occur at T_2."[12] Does this statement mean that had someone believed, guessed, or asserted at T_1 that E would occur at T_2, he would have been right?[13] (I shall have something to say about this form of determinism later in this paper.) Perhaps it means that at T_1 there was sufficient

---

[10] *Summa Theologica*, Pt. I, Q. 14, a. 8.

[11] *Philosophical Review*, LXXI (1962), 56–66. Taylor argues that if an event E fails to occur at T_2, then at T_1 it was true that E would fail to occur at T_2. Thus, at T_1, a necessary condition of anyone's performing an action sufficient for the occurrence of E at T_2 is missing. Thus at T_1, no one could have the power to perform an action that would be sufficient for the occurrence of E at T_2. Hence, no one has the power at T_1 to do something sufficient for the occurrence of an event at T_2 that is not going to happen. The parallel between this argument and the one recited above can be seen very clearly if one reformulates Taylor's argument, pushing back the time at which it was true that E would not occur at T_2.

[12] For a helpful discussion of difficulties involved here, see Rogers Albritton's "Present Truth and Future Contingency," a reply to Richard Taylor's "The Problem of Future Contingency," both in the *Philosophical Review*, LXVI (1957), 1–28.

[13] Gilbert Ryle interprets it this way. See "It Was to Be," *Dilemmas* (Cambridge, 1954).

evidence upon which to predict that E would occur at T_2.[14] Maybe it means neither of these. Maybe it means nothing at all.[15] The argument presented above presupposes that it makes straightforward sense to suppose that God (or just anyone) held a true belief eighty years prior to Saturday. But this is not to suppose that *what* God believed *was true eighty years prior to Saturday*. Whether (or in what sense) it was true eighty years ago that Jones would mow his lawn on Saturday is a question I shall not discuss. As far as I can see, the argument in which I am interested requires nothing in the way of a decision on this issue.

II

I now want to consider three comments on the problem of divine foreknowledge which seem to be instructively incorrect.

A. Leibniz analyzed the problem as follows:

> They say that what is foreseen cannot fail to exist and they say so truly; but it follows not that what is foreseen is necessary. For necessary truth is that whereof the contrary is impossible or implies a contradiction. Now the truth which states that I shall write tomorrow is not of that nature, it is not necessary. Yet, supposing that God foresees it, it is necessary that it come to pass, that is, the consequence is necessary, namely that it exist, since it has been foreseen; for God is infallible. This is what is termed a *hypothetical necessity*. But our concern is not this necessity; it is an *absolute* necessity that is required, to be able to say that an action is necessary, that it is not contingent, that it is not the effect of free choice.[16]

The statement "God believed at T_1 that Jones would do X at T_2" (where the interval between T_1 and T_2 is, for example, eighty years) does not entail "Jones did X at T_2' is necessary." Leibniz is surely right about this. All that will follow from the first of these statements concerning "Jones did X at T_2" is that the latter is *true*, not that it is *necessarily true*. But this observation has no real bearing on the issue at hand. The following passage from St. Augustine's formulation of the problem may help to make this point clear.

> Your trouble is this. You wonder how it can be that these two propositions are not contradictory and incompatible, namely that God has foreknowledge of all future events, and that we sin voluntarily and not by necessity. For if, you say, God foreknows that a man will sin, he must necessarily sin. But if there is necessity there is no voluntary choice of sinning, but rather fixed and unavoidable necessity.[17]

[14] Richard Gale suggests this interpretation in "Endorsing Predictions," *Philosophical Review*, LXX (1961), 378–385.

[15] This view is held by John Turk Saunders in "Sea Fight Tomorrow?," *Philosophical Review*, LXVII (1958), 367–378.

[16] *Théodicée*, Pt. I, sec. 37. This passage trans. by E. M. Huggard (New Haven, 1952), p. 144.

[17] *De Libero Arbitrio*, Bk. III. This passage trans. by J. H. S. Burleigh, *Augustine's Earlier Writings* (Philadelphia, 1955).

In this passage, the term "necessity" (or the phrase "by necessity") is not used to express a modal-logical concept. The term "necessity" is here used in contrast with the term "voluntary," not (as in Leibniz) in contrast with the term "contingent." If one's action is necessary (or by necessity), this is to say that one's action is not voluntary. Augustine says that if God has foreknowledge of human actions, the actions are necessary. But the form of this conditional is *"P implies Q,"* not *"P implies N (Q)."* *"Q"* in the consequent of this conditional is the claim that human actions are not voluntary—that is, that one is not able, or does not have the power, to do other than he does.

Perhaps I can make this point clearer by reformulating the original problem in such a way as to make explicit the modal operators working within it. Let it be *contingently* true that Jones did X at T_2. Since God holds a belief about the outcome of each human action well in advance of its performance, it is then *contingently* true that God believed at T_1 that Jones would do X at T_2. But it follows from this that it is *contingently* true that at T_2 Jones was not able to refrain from doing X. Had he been (contingently) able to refrain from doing X at T_2, then either he was (contingently) able to do something at T_2 that would have brought it about that God held a false belief at T_1, or he was (contingently) able to do something at T_2 that would have brought it about that God believed otherwise than He did at T_1, or he was (contingently) able to do something at T_2 that would have brought it about that God did not exist at T_1. None of these latter is an acceptable alternative.

B. In *Concordia Liberti Arbitrii*, Luis de Molina wrote as follows:

> It was not that since He foreknew what would happen from those things which depend on the created will that it would happen; but, on the contrary, it was because such things would happen through the freedom of the will, that He foreknew it; and that He would foreknow the opposite if the opposite was to happen.[18]

Remarks similar to this one can be found in a great many traditional and contemporary theological texts. In fact, Molina assures us that the view expressed in this passage has always been "above controversy"—a matter of "common opinion" and "unanimous consent"—not only among the Church fathers, but also, as he says, "among all catholic men."

One claim made in the above passage seems to me to be truly "above controversy." With respect to any given action foreknown by God, God would have foreknown the opposite if the opposite was to happen. If we assume the notion of omniscience outlined in the first section of this paper, and if we agree that omniscience is part of the "essence" of God, this statement is a conceptual truth. I doubt if anyone would be inclined to dispute it. Also involved in this passage, however, is at least the suggestion of a doctrine that cannot be taken as an item of "common opinion" among *all* catholic men. Molina says it is not because God

---

[18]This passage trans. by John Mourant, *Readings in the Philosophy of Religion* (New York, 1954), p. 426.

foreknows what He foreknows that men act as they do: it is because men act as they do that God foreknows what He foreknows. Some theologians have rejected this claim. It seems to entail that men's actions determine God's cognitions. And this latter, I think, has been taken by some theologians to be a violation of the notion of God as self-sufficient and incapable of being affected by events of the natural world.[19] But I shall not develop this point further. Where the view put forward in the above passage seems to me to go wrong in an interesting and important way is in Molina's claim that God can have foreknowledge of things that will happen "through the freedom of the will." It is this claim that I here want to examine with care.

What exactly are we saying when we say that God can know in advance what will happen *through the freedom of the will?* I think that what Molina has in mind is this. God can know in advance that a given man is going to *choose* to perform a certain action sometime in the future. With respect to the case of Jones mowing his lawn, God knew at T_1 that Jones would *freely decide* to mow his lawn at T_2. Not only did God know at T_1 that Jones would mow his lawn at T_2, He also knew at T_1 that this action would be performed *freely*. In the words of Emil Brunner, "God knows that which will take place in freedom in the future as something which happens in freedom."[20] What God knew at T_1 is that Jones would *freely* mow his lawn at T_2.

I think that this doctrine is incoherent. If God knew (and thus believed) at T_1 that Jones would *do* X at T_2,[21] I think it follows that Jones was not able to do other than X at T_2, (for reasons already given). Thus, if God knew (and thus believed) at T_1 that Jones would *do* X at T_2, it would follow that Jones did X at T_2, but *not freely*. It does not seem to be possible that God could have believed at T_1 that Jones would freely do X at T_2. If God believed at T_1 that Jones would do X at T_2, Jones's action at T_2 was not free; and if God *also* believed at T_1 that Jones would freely act at T_2, it follows that God held a false belief at T_1—which is absurd.

C. Frederich Schleiermacher commented on the problem of divine foreknowledge as follows:

> In the same way, we estimate the intimacy between two persons by the foreknowledge one has of the actions of the other, without supposing that in either case, the one or the other's freedom is thereby endangered. So even the divine foreknowledge cannot endanger freedom.[22]

St. Augustine made this same point in *De Libero Arbitrio*. He said:

> Unless I am mistaken, you would not directly compel the man to sin, though you knew beforehand that he was going to sin. Nor does your prescience in itself compel

[19] Cf. Boethius' *Consolatio*, Bk. V, sec. 3, par. 2.

[20] *The Christian Doctrine of God*, trans. by Olive Wyon (Philadelphia, 1964), p. 262.

[21] Note: no comment here about *freely* doing X.

[22] *The Christian Faith*, Pt. I, sec. 2, par. 55. This passage trans. by W. R. Matthew (Edinburgh, 1928), p. 228.

him to sin even though he was certainly going to sin, as we must assume if you have real prescience. So there is no contradiction here. Simply you know beforehand what another is going to do with his own will. Similarly God compels no man to sin, though he sees beforehand those who are going to sin by their own will.[23]

If we suppose (with Schleiermacher and Augustine) that the case of an intimate friend having foreknowledge of another's action has the same implications for determinism as the case of God's foreknowledge of human actions, I can imagine two positions which might then be taken. First, one might hold (with Schleiermacher and Augustine) that God's foreknowledge of human actions cannot entail determinism—since it is clear that an intimate friend can have foreknowledge of another's voluntary actions. Or, secondly, one might hold that an intimate friend cannot have foreknowledge of another's voluntary actions—since it is clear that God cannot have foreknowledge of such actions. This second position could take either of two forms. One might hold that since an intimate friend *can* have foreknowledge of another's actions, the actions in question cannot be voluntary. Or, alternatively, one might hold that since the other's actions *are* voluntary, the intimate friend cannot have foreknowledge of them.[24] But what I propose to argue in the remaining pages of this paper is that Schleiermacher and Augustine were mistaken in supposing that the case of an intimate friend having foreknowledge of others' actions has the same implications for determinism as the case of God's foreknowledge of human actions. What I want to suggest is that the argument I used above to show that God cannot have foreknowledge of voluntary actions cannot be used to show that an intimate friend cannot have foreknowledge of another's actions. Even if one holds that an intimate friend *can* have foreknowledge of another's voluntary actions, one ought not to think that the case is the same when dealing with the problem of divine foreknowledge.

Let Smith be an ordinary man and an intimate friend of Jones. Now, let us start by supposing that Smith believed at T_1 that Jones would do X at T_2. We make no assumption concerning the truth or falsity of Smith's belief, but assume only that Smith held it. Given only this much, there appears to be no difficulty in supposing that at T_2 Jones was able to do X and that at T_2 Jones was able to do not-X. So far as the above description of the case is concerned, it might well have been within Jones's power at T_2 to do something (namely, X) which would have brought it about that Smith held a true belief at T_1, and it might well have been within Jones's power at T_2 to do something (namely, not-X) which would have brought it about that Smith held a false belief at T_1. So much seems apparent.

Now let us suppose that Smith *knew* at T_1 that Jones would do X at T_2. This is to suppose that Smith correctly believed (with evidence) at T_1 that Jones would do X at T_2. It follows, to be sure, that Jones *did* X at T_2. But now let us inquire about what Jones was *able* to do at T_2. I submit that there is nothing in the description of this case that requires the conclusion that it was not within Jones's

[23] *Loc. cit.*

[24] This last seems to be the position defended by Richard Taylor in "Deliberation and Foreknowledge," *American Philosophical Quarterly*, I (1964).

power at T_2 to refrain from doing X. By hypothesis, the belief held by Smith at T_1 was true. Thus, by hypothesis, Jones did X at T_2. But even if we assume that the belief held by Smith at T_1 was *in fact* true, we can add that the belief held by Smith at T_1 *might have* turned out to be false.[25] Thus, even if we say that Jones *in fact* did X at T_2, we can add that Jones *might not* have done X at T_2— meaning by this that it was within Jones's power at T_2 to refrain from doing X. Smith held a true belief which might have turned out to be false, and, correspondingly, Jones performed an action which he was able to refrain from performing. Given that Smith correctly believed at T_1 that Jones would do X at T_2, we can still assign Jones the *power* at T_2 to refrain from doing X. All we need add is that the power in question is one which Jones *did not exercise*.

These last reflections have no application, however, when dealing with God's foreknowledge. Assume that God (being essentially omniscient) existed at T_1, and assume that He believed at T_1 that Jones would do X at T_2. It follows, again, that Jones did X at T_2. God's beliefs are true. But now, as above, let us inquire into what Jones was *able* to do at T_2. We cannot claim now, as in the Smith case, that the belief held by God at T_1 was *in fact* true but *might have* turned out to be false. No sense of "might have" has application here. It is a conceptual truth that God's beliefs are true. Thus, we cannot claim, as in the Smith case, that Jones *in fact* acted in accordance with God's beliefs but had the *ability* to refrain from so doing. The ability to refrain from acting in accordance with one of God's beliefs would be the ability to do something that would bring it about that one of God's beliefs was false. And no one could have an ability of this description. Thus, in the case of God's foreknowledge of Jones's action at T_2, if we are to assign Jones the ability at T_2 to refrain from doing X, we must understand this ability in some way other than the way we understood it when dealing with Smith's foreknowledge. In this case, either we must say that it was the ability at T_2 to bring it about that God believed otherwise than He did at T_1; or we must say that it was the ability at T_2 to bring it about that any person who believed at T_1 that Jones would do X at T_2 (one of whom was, by hypothesis, God) held a false belief and thus was not God. But, as pointed out earlier, neither of these last alternatives can be accepted.

The important thing to be learned from the study of Smith's foreknowledge of Jones's action is that the problem of divine foreknowledge has as one of its pillars the claim that truth is *analytically* connected with God's *beliefs*. No problem of determinism arises when dealing with human knowledge of future actions. This is because truth is not analytically connected with human belief even when (as in the case of human knowledge) truth is contingently conjoined to belief. If we suppose that Smith knows at T_1 that Jones will do X at T_2, what we are supposing is that Smith believes at T_1 that Jones will do X at T_2 and (as an additional, contingent, fact) that the belief in question is true. Thus having supposed that Smith knows at T_1 that Jones will do X at T_2, when we turn to a consideration of

---

[25] The phrase "might have" as it occurs in this sentence does not express mere *logical* possibility. I am not sure how to analyze the notion of possibility involved here, but I think it is roughly the same notion as is involved when we say, "Jones might have been killed in the accident (had it not been for the fact that at the last minute he decided not to go)."

the situation of T_2 we can infer (1) that Jones *will* do X at T_2 (since Smith's belief is true); and (2) that Jones does not have the power at T_2 to do something that would bring it about that Jones did not *believe* as he did at T_1. But paradoxical though it may seem (and it seems paradoxical only at first sight), Jones can have the power at T_2 to do something that would bring it about that Smith did not have *knowledge* at T_1. This is simply to say that Jones can have the *power* at T_2 to do something that would bring it about that the belief held by Smith at T_1 (which was, in fact, true) was (instead) false. We are required only to add that since Smith's belief was in fact true (that is, was knowledge) Jones *did not* (in fact) *exercise* that power. But when we turn to a consideration of God's foreknowledge of Jones's action at T_2 the elbowroom between belief and truth disappears and, with it, the possibility of assigning Jones even the *power* of doing other than he does at T_2. We begin by supposing that God *knows* at T_1 that Jones will do X at T_2. As above, this is to suppose that God believes at T_1 that Jones will do X at T_2, and it is to suppose that this belief is true. But it is *not* an additional, contingent fact that the belief held by God is true. "God believes X" entails "X is true." Thus, having supposed that God knows (and thus believes) at T_1 that Jones will do X at T_2, we can infer (1) that Jones *will do* X at T_2 (since God's belief is true); (2) that Jones does not have the power at T_2 to do something that would bring it about that God did not hold the belief He held at T_1, and (3) that Jones does not have the power at T_2 to do something that would bring it about that the belief held by God at T_1 was false. This last is what we could *not* infer when truth and belief were only factually connected—as in the case of Smith's knowledge. To be sure, "Smith knows at T_1 that Jones will do X at T_2" and "God knows at T_1 that Jones will do X at T_2" both entail "Jones will do X at T_2" ("A knows X" entails " 'X' is true"). But this similarity between "Smith knows X" and "God knows X" is not a point of any special interest in the present discussion. As Schleiermacher and Augustine rightly insisted (and as we discovered in our study of Smith's foreknowledge) the mere fact that someone knows in advance how another will act in the future is not enough to yield a problem of the sort we have been discussing. We begin to get a glimmer of the knot involved in the problem of divine foreknowledge when we shift attention away from the *similarities* between "Smith knows X" and "God knows X" (in particular, that they both entail " 'X' is true") and concentrate instead on the logical *differences* which obtain between Smith's knowledge and God's knowledge. We get to the difference which makes the difference when, after analyzing the notion of knowledge as true belief (supported by evidence) we discover the radically dissimilar relations between truth and belief in the two cases. When truth is only factually connected with belief (as in Smith's knowledge) one can have the power (though, by hypothesis, one will not exercise it) to do something that would make the belief false. But when truth is analytically connected with belief (as in God's belief) no one can have the power to do something which would render the belief false.

   To conclude: I have assumed that any statement of the form "A knows X" entails a statement of the form "A believes X" as well as a statement of the form " 'X' is true." I have then supposed (as an analytic truth) that if a given person is omniscient, that person (1) holds no false beliefs, and (2) holds beliefs about the outcome of human actions in advance of their performance. In addition, I have assumed that the statement "If a given person is God that person is omniscient" is an a priori statement. (This last I have labeled the doctrine of God's essential omniscience.) Given these items (plus some premises concerning what is and what is not within one's power), I have argued that if God exists, it is not within one's power to do other than he does. I have inferred from this that if God exists, no human action is voluntary.

As emphasized earlier, I do not want to claim that the assumptions underpinning the argument are acceptable. In fact, is seems to me that a theologian interested in claiming both that God is omniscient and that men have free will could deny any one (or more) of them. For example, a theologian might deny that a statement of the form "A knows X" entails a statement of the form "A believes X" (some contemporary philosophers have denied this) or, alternatively, he might claim that this entailment holds in the case of human knowledge but fails in the case of God's knowledge. This latter would be to claim that when knowledge is attributed to God, the term "knowledge" bears a sense other than the one it has when knowledge is attributed to human beings. Then again, a theologian might object to the analysis of "omniscience" with which I have been working. Although I doubt if any Christian theologian would allow that an omniscient being could believe something false, he might claim that a given person could be omniscient although he did not hold beliefs about the outcome of human actions *in advance* of their performance. (This latter is the way Boethius escaped the problem.) Still again, a theologian might deny the doctrine of God's essential omniscience. He might admit that if a given person is God that person is omniscient, but he might deny that this statement formulates an a priori truth. This would be to say that although God is omniscient, He is not *essentially* omniscient. So far as I can see, within the conceptual framework of theology employing any one of these adjustments, the problem of divine foreknowledge outlined in this paper could not be formulated. There thus appears to be a rather wide range of alternatives open to the theologian at this point. It would be a mistake to think that commitment to determinism is an unavoidable implication of the Christian concept of divine omniscience.

But having arrived at this understanding, the importance of the preceding deliberations ought not to be overlooked. There is a pitfall in the doctrine of divine omniscience. That knowing involves believing (truly) is surely a tempting philosophical view (witness the many contemporary philosophers who have affirmed it). And the idea that God's attributes (including omniscience) are essentially connected to His nature, together with the idea that an omniscient being would hold no false beliefs and would hold beliefs about the outcome of human actions in advance of their performance, might be taken by some theologians as obvious candidates for inclusion in a finished Christian theology. Yet the theologian must approach these items critically. If they are embraced together, then if one affirms the existence of God, one is committed to the view that no human action is voluntary.

POWER

ST. THOMAS AQUINAS
The Omnipotence of God

THIRD ARTICLE.   WHETHER GOD IS OMNIPOTENT?

We proceed thus to the Third Article:—

Objection 1. It seems that God is not omnipotent. For movement and passiveness belong to everything. But this is impossible for God, since He is immovable, as was said above.[1] Therefore He is not omnipotent.

Obj. 2. Further, sin is an act of some kind. But God cannot sin, nor *deny Himself*, as it is said 2 *Tim.* ii. 13. Therefore He is not omnipotent.

Obj. 3. Further, it is said of God that He manifests His omnipotence *especially by sparing and having mercy.*[2] Therefore the greatest act possible to the divine power is to spare and have mercy. There are things much greater, however, than sparing and having mercy; for example, to create another world, and the like. Therefore God is not omnipotent.

Obj. 4. Further, upon the text, *God hath made foolish the wisdom of this world* (1 *Cor.* i. 20), the *Gloss* says: *God hath made the wisdom of this world foolish* by showing those things to be possible which it judges to be impossible.[3] Whence it seems that nothing is to be judged possible or impossible in reference to inferior causes, as the wisdom of this world judges them; but in reference to the divine power. If God, then, were omnipotent, all things would be possible; nothing, therefore, impossible. But if we take away the impossible, then we destroy also the necessary; for what necessarily exists cannot possibly not exist. Therefore, there

THE OMNIPOTENCE OF GOD   From *Summa Theologica*, Part I, Question 25, in *Basic Writings of Saint Thomas Aquinas*, edited by Anton C. Pegis. By permission of the A. C. Pegis estate.

[1] Q. 2, a. 3; q. 9, a. 1 [in *Philosophy of Religion: Selected Readings*, 2nd ed., pp. 128–30; 80–81].

[2] *Collect* of Tenth Sunday after Pentecost.

[3] *Glossa ordin., super I Cor.* I, 20 (VI, 34E).—Cf. St. Ambrose, *In I Cor.*, super I, 20 (PL 17, 199).

would be nothing at all that is necessary in things if God were omnipotent. But this is an impossibility. Therefore God is not omnipotent.

On the contrary, It is said: *No word shall be impossible with God (Luke* i. 37).

I answer that, All confess that God is omnipotent; but it seems difficult to explain in what His omnipotence precisely consists. For there may be a doubt as to the precise meaning of the word "all" when we say that God can do all things. If, however, we consider the matter aright, since power is said in reference to possible things, this phrase, *God can do all things,* is rightly understood to mean that God can do all things that are possible; and for this reason He is said to be omnipotent. Now according to the Philosopher a thing is said to be possible in two ways.[4] First, in relation to some power; thus whatever is subject to human power is said to be possible to man. Now God cannot be said to be omnipotent through being able to do all things that are possible to created nature; for the divine power extends farther than that. If, however, we were to say that God is omnipotent because He can do all things that are possible to His power, there would be a vicious circle in explaining the nature of His power. For this would be saying nothing else but that God is omnipotent because He can do all that He is able to do.

It remains, therefore, that God is called omnipotent because he can do all things that are possible absolutely; which is the second way of saying a thing is possible. For a thing is said to be possible or impossible absolutely, according to the relation in which the very terms stand to one another: possible, if the predicate is not incompatible with the subject, as that Socrates sits; and absolutely impossible when the predicate is altogether incompatible with the subject, as, for instance, that a man is an ass.

It must, however, be remembered that since every agent produces an effect like itself, to each active power there corresponds a thing possible as its proper object according to the nature of that act on which its active power is founded; for instance, the power of giving warmth is related, as to its proper object, to the being capable of being warmed. The divine being, however, upon which the nature of power in God is founded, is infinite; it is not limited to any class of being, but possesses within itself the perfection of all being. Whence, whatsoever has or can have the nature of being is numbered among the absolute possibles, in respect of which God is called omnipotent.

Now nothing is opposed to the notion of being except non-being. Therefore, that which at the same time implies being and non-being is repugnant to the notion of an absolute possible, which is subject to the divine omnipotence. For such cannot come under the divine omnipotence; not indeed because of any defect in the power of God, but because it has not the nature of a feasible or possible thing. Therefore, everything that does not imply a contradiction in terms is numbered among those possibles in respect of which God is called omnipotent; whereas whatever implies contradiction does not come within the scope of divine omnipotence, because it cannot have the aspect of possibility. Hence it is more

---

[4] *Metaph.,* IV, 12 (1019b 34).

appropriate to say that such things cannot be done, than that God cannot do them. Nor is this contrary to the word of the angel, saying: *No word shall be impossible with God (Luke* i. 37). For whatever implies a contradiction cannot be a word, because no intellect can possibly conceive such a thing.

Reply Obj. 1. God is said to be omnipotent in respect to active power, not to passive power, as was shown above. Whence the fact that He is immovable or impassible is not repugnant to His omnipotence.

Reply Obj. 2. To sin is to fall short of a perfect action; hence to be able to sin is to be able to fall short in action, which is repugnant to omnipotence. Therefore it is that God cannot sin, because of His omnipotence. Now it is true that the Philosopher says that *God can deliberately do what is evil.*[5] But this must be understood either on a condition, the antecedent of which is impossible—as, for instance, if we were to say that God can do evil things if He will. For there is no reason why a conditional proposition should not be true, though both the antecedent and consequent are impossible: as if one were to say: *If man is an ass, he has four feet.* Or he may be understood to mean that God can do some things which now seem to be evil: which, however, if He did them, would then be good. Or he is, perhaps, speaking after the common manner of the pagans, who thought that men became gods, like Jupiter or Mercury.

Reply Obj. 3. God's omnipotence is particularly shown in sharing and having mercy, because in this it is made manifest that God has supreme power, namely, that He freely forgives sin. For it is not for one who is bound by laws of a superior to forgive sins of his own free choice. Or, it is thus shown because by sparing and having mercy upon men, He leads them to the participation of an infinite good; which is the ultimate effect of the divine power. Or it is thus shown because, as was said above, the effect of the divine mercy is the foundation of all the divine works.[6] For nothing is due anyone, except because of something already given him gratuitously by God. In this way the divine omnipotence is particularly made manifest, because to it pertains the first foundation of all good things.

Reply Obj. 4. The absolute possible is not so called in reference either to higher causes, or to inferior causes, but in reference to itself. But that which is called possible in reference to some power is named possible in reference to its proximate cause. Hence those things which it belongs to God alone to do immediately—as, for example, to create, to justify, and the like—are said to be possible in reference to a higher cause. Those things, however, which are such as to be done by inferior causes, are said to be possible in reference to those inferior causes. For it is according to the condition of the proximate cause that the effect has contingency or necessity, as was shown above.[7] Thus it is that the wisdom of the world is deemed foolish, because what is impossible to nature it judges to be impossible to God. So it is clear that the omnipotence of God does not take away from things their impossibility and necessity.

[5] *Top.,* IV, 5 (126a 34).

[6] Q. 21, a. 4.

[7] Q. 14, a. 13, ad I [in *Philosophy of Religion: Selected Readings,* 2nd ed., pp. 40, 41].

SAMUEL CLARKE
Can God Do Evil?

. . . The self-existent being, the supreme cause of all things, must of necessity have infinite power. This proposition is evident and undeniable. For since nothing (as has been already proved) can possibly be self-existent besides himself, and consequently all things in the universe were made by him, and are entirely dependent upon him, and all the powers of all things are derived from him and must therefore be perfectly subject and subordinate to him; it is manifest that nothing can make any difficulty or resistance to the execution of his will, but he must of necessity have absolute power to do everything he pleases, with the perfect ease, and in the perfect manner, at once and in a moment, whenever he wills it. . . . The only question is, what the true meaning of what we call infinite power is, and to what things it must be understood to extend, or not to extend.

Now in determining this question, there are some propositions about which there is no dispute. Which therefore I shall but just mention. First, infinite power reaches to all possible things, but cannot be said to extend to the working of any thing which implies a *contradiction*: as that a thing should be and not be at the same time; that the same thing should be made and not be made, or have been and not have been; that twice two should not make four, or that that which is necessarily false should be true. The reason whereof is plain. Because the power of making a thing to be, at the same time that it is not, is only a power of doing that which is nothing, that is, no power at all. Second, infinite power cannot be said to extend to those things which imply *natural* imperfection in the being to whom such power is ascribed—as that it should destroy its own being, weaken itself, or the like. These things imply natural imperfection, and are by all men confessed to be such as cannot possibly belong to the necessary, self-existent being. There are also other things which imply imperfection in another kind, viz., *moral* imperfection.

. . . Though nothing, I say, is more certain than that God acts not necessarily, but voluntarily; yet it is nevertheless as truly and absolutely impossible for God not to do (or to do any thing contrary to) what his moral attributes require him to do, as if he was really not a free but a necessary agent. And the reason hereof is plain: because infinite knowledge, power, and goodness in conjunction may, notwithstanding the most perfect freedom and choice, act with altogether as much certainty and unalterable steadiness as even the necessity of fate can be supposed

Samuel Clarke (1675–1729) was an important exponent of rational theology as well as an early supporter of Newtonian physics. He is best known for his correspondence with Leibniz, in which he defended Newton's views on space and time. His principal philosophical works are A *Discourse Concerning the Being and Attributes of God* and *The Obligations of Natural Religion and the Truth and Certainty of the Christian Revelation*.

CAN GOD DO EVIL?   From *Discourse Concerning the Being and Attributes of God*, ninth edition. (Selections are from Propositions X and XII. Punctuation, use of capitals, etc. have been modernized by the editors.)

to do. Nay, these perfections cannot possibly but so act. Because free choice in a being of infinite knowledge, power and goodness can no more choose to act contrary to these perfections than knowledge can be ignorance, power be weakness, or goodness malice. So that free choice in such a being may be as certain and steady a principle of action as the necessity of fate. We may therefore as certainly and infallibly rely upon the moral, as upon the natural attributes of God—it being as absolutely impossible for him to act contrary to the one as to divest himself of the other; and as much a contradiction to suppose him choosing to do anything inconsistent with his justice, goodness and truth as to suppose him divested of infinity, power, or existence.

From hence it follows, that though God is both perfectly free and also infinitely powerful, yet he cannot possibly do anything that is evil. The reason of this is also evident. Because, as it is manifest infinite power cannot extend to natural contradictions which imply a destruction of that very power by which they must be supposed to be effected, so neither can it extend to moral contradictions which imply a destruction of some other attributes as necessarily belonging to the divine nature as power. I have already shown that justice, goodness and truth are necessarily in God, even as necessarily as power and understanding, and knowledge of the nature of things. It is, therefore, as impossible and contradictory to suppose his will should choose to do anything contrary to justice, goodness or truth as that his power should be able to do anything inconsistent with power. It is no diminution of power not to be able to do things which are no object of power. And it is in like manner no diminution either of power or liberty to have such a perfect and unalterable rectitude of will as never possibly to choose to do anything inconsistent with that rectitude.

P. T. GEACH
Omnipotence

It is fortunate for my purposes that English has the two words 'almighty' and 'omnipotent', and that apart from any stipulation by me the words have rather different associations and suggestions. 'Almighty' is the familiar word that comes

Peter Geach (1916–   ) is Professor of Logic at the University of Leeds. He was educated at Balliol College, Oxford. Among his publications are *Reason and Argument, The Virtues,* and *Providence and Evil.*

OMNIPOTENCE   From *Philosophy*, Volume 48, (April 1973). Copyright© The Royal Institute of Philosophy. Reprinted by permission of the author and Cambridge University Press. "Omnipotence" is also Chapter 1 of the author's *Providence and Evil* (Cambridge University Press, 1977).

in the creeds of the Church; 'omnipotent' is at home rather in formal theological discussions and controversies, e.g. about miracles and about the problem of evil. 'Almighty' derives by way of Latin 'omnipotens' from the Greek word '*pantokra-tōr*'; and both this Greek word, like the more classical '*pankratēs*', and 'almighty' itself suggest God's having power *over* all things. On the other hand the English word 'omnipotent' would ordinarily be taken to imply ability to *do* everything; the Latin word 'omnipotens' also predominantly has this meaning in Scholastic writers, even though in origin it is a Latinization of '*pantocrator*'. So there already is a tendency to distinguish the two words; and in this paper I shall make the distinction a strict one. I shall use the word 'almighty' to express God's power over all things, and I shall take 'omnipotence' to mean ability to do everything.

I think we can in a measure understand what God's almightiness implies, and I shall argue that almightiness so understood must be ascribed to God if we are to retain anything like traditional Christian belief in God. The position as regards omnipotence, or as regards the statement 'God can do everything', seems to me to be very different. Of course even 'God can do everything' may be understood simply as a way of magnifying God by contrast with the impotence of man. McTaggart described it as 'a piece of theological etiquette' to call God omnipotent: Thomas Hobbes, out of reverence for his Maker, would rather say that 'omnipotent' is an attribute of honour. But McTaggart and Hobbes would agree that 'God is omnipotent' or 'God can do everything' is not to be treated as a proposition that can figure as premise or conclusion in a serious theological argument. And I too wish to say this. I have no objection to such ways of speaking if they merely express a desire to give the best honour we can to God our Maker, whose Name only is excellent and whose praise is above heaven and earth. But theologians have tried *to prove* that God can do everything, or to derive conclusions from this thesis as a premise. I think such attempts have been wholly unsuccessful. When people have tried to read into 'God can do everything' a signification not of Pious Intention but of Philosophical Truth, they have only landed themselves in intractable problems and hopeless confusions; no graspable sense has ever been given to this sentence that did not lead to self-contradiction or at least to conclusions manifestly untenable from a Christian point of view.

I shall return to this; but I must first develop what I have to say about God's almightiness, or power over all things. God is not just more powerful than any creature; no creature can compete with God in power, even unsuccessfully. For God is also the source of all power; any power a creature has comes from God and is maintained only for such time as God wills. Nebuchadnezzar submitted to praise and adore the God of heaven because he was forced by experience to realize that only by God's favour did his wits hold together from one end of a blasphemous sentence to the other end. Nobody can deceive God or circumvent him or frustrate him; and there is no question of God's trying to do anything and failing. In Heaven and on Earth, God does whatever he will. We shall see that some propositions of the form 'God cannot do so-and-so' have to be accepted as true; but what God cannot be said to be able to do he likewise cannot will to do; we cannot drive a logical wedge between his power and his will, which are, as the

Scholastics said, really identical, and there is no application to God of the concept of trying but failing.

I shall not spend time on citations of Scripture and tradition to show that this doctrine of God's almightiness is authentically Christian; nor shall I here develop rational grounds for believing it is a true doctrine. But it is quite easy to show that this doctrine is indispensable for Christianity, not a bit of old metaphysical luggage that can be abandoned with relief. For Christianity requires an absolute faith in the promises of God: specifically, faith in the promise that some day the whole human race will be delivered and blessed by the establishment of the Kingdom of God. If God were not almighty, he might will and not do; sincerely promise, but find fulfilment beyond his power. Men might prove untamable and incorrigible, and might kill themselves through war or pollution before God's salvific plan for them could come into force. It is useless to say that after the end of this earthly life men would live again; for as I have argued elsewhere, only the promise of God can give us any confidence that there will be an after-life for men, and if God were not almighty, this promise too might fail. If God is true and just and unchangeable and almighty, we can have absolute confidence in his promises: otherwise we cannot—and there would be an end of Christianity.

A Christian must therefore believe that God is almighty; but he need not believe that God can do everything. Indeed, the very argument I have just used shows that a Christian must not believe that God can do everything: for he may not believe that God could possibly break his own word. Nor can a Christian even believe that God can do everything that is logically possible; for breaking one's word is certainly a logically possible feat.

It seems to me, therefore, that the tangles in which people have enmeshed themselves when trying to give the expression 'God can do everything' an intelligible and acceptable content are tangles that a Christian believer has no need to enmesh himself in; the spectacle of others enmeshed may sadden him, but need not cause him to stumble in the way of faith. The denial that God is omnipotent, or able to do everything, may seem dishonouring to God; but when we see where the contrary affirmation, in its various forms, has led, we may well cry out with Hobbes: 'Can any man think God is served with such absurdities? . . . As if it were an acknowledgment of the Divine Power, to say, that which is, is not; or that which has been, has not been.'

I shall consider four main theories of omnipotence. The first holds that God can do everything absolutely; everything that can be expressed in a string of words that makes sense; even if that sense can be shown to be self-contradictory, God is not bound in action, as we are in thought, by the laws of logic. I shall speak of this as the doctrine that God is *absolutely* omnipotent.

The second doctrine is that a proposition 'God can do so-and-so' is true when and only when 'so-and-so' represents a logically consistent description.

The third doctrine is that 'God *can* do so-and-so' is true just if 'God does so-and-so' is logically consistent. This is a weaker doctrine than the second; for 'God is doing so-and-so' is logically consistent only when 'so-and-so' represents a logically consistent description, but on the other hand there may be consistently describable feats which it would involve contradiction to suppose done *by God*.

The last and weakest view is that the realm of what can be done or brought about includes all future possibilities, and that whenever 'God *will* bring so-and-so about' is logically possible, 'God *can* bring so-and-so about' is true.

The first sense of 'omnipotent' in which people have believed God to be omnipotent implies precisely: ability to do absolutely everything, everything describable. You mention it, and God can do it. McTaggart insisted on using 'omnipotent' in this sense only; from an historical point of view we may of course say that he imposed on the word a sense which it, and the corresponding Latin word, have not always borne. But Broad seems to me clearly unjust to McTaggart when he implies that in demolishing this doctrine of omnipotence McTaggart was just knocking down a man of straw. As Broad must surely have known, at least one great philosopher, Descartes, deliberately adopted and defended this doctrine of omnipotence: what I shall call the doctrine of absolute omnipotence.

As Descartes himself remarked, nothing is too absurd for some philosopher to have said it some time; I once read an article about an Indian school of philosophers who were alleged to maintain that it is only a delusion, which the wise can overcome, that anything exists at all—so perhaps it would not matter all that much that a philosopher is found to defend absolute omnipotence. Perhaps it would not matter all that much that the philosopher in question was a very great one; for very great philosophers have maintained the most preposterous theses. What does make the denial of absolute omnipotence important is not that we are thereby denying what a philosopher, a very great philosopher, thought he must assert, but that this doctrine has a live influence on people's religious thought—I should of course say, a pernicious influence. Some naive Christians would explicitly assert the doctrine; and moreover, I think McTaggart was right in believing that in popular religious thought a covert appeal to the doctrine is sometimes made even by people who would deny it if it were explicitly stated to them and its manifest consequences pointed out.

McTaggart may well have come into contact with naive Protestant defenders of absolute omnipotence when he was defending his atheist faith at his public school. The opinion is certainly not dead, as I can testify from personal experience. For many years I used to teach the philosophy of Descartes in a special course for undergraduates reading French; year by year, there were always two or three of them who embraced Descartes' defence of absolute omnipotence *con amore* and protested indignantly when I described the doctrine as incoherent. It would of course have been no good to say I was following Doctors of the Church in rejecting the doctrine; I did in the end find a way of producing silence, though not, I fear, conviction, and going on to other topics of discussion; I cited the passages of the Epistle to the Hebrews which say explicitly that God cannot swear by anything greater than himself (vi. 13) or break his word (vi. 18). Fortunately none of them ever thought of resorting to the ultimate weapon which, as I believe George Mavrodes remarked, is available to the defender of absolute omnipotence; namely, he can always say: 'Well, you've stated a difficulty, but of course being omnipotent God can overcome that difficulty, though I don't see how.' But what

I may call, borrowing from C. S. Lewis's story, victory by the Deplorable Word is a barren one; as barren as a victory by an incessant demand that your adversary should prove his premises or define his terms.

Let us leave these naive defenders in their entrenched position and return for a moment to Descartes. Descartes held that the truths of logic and arithmetic are freely made to be true by God's will. To be sure we clearly and distinctly see that these truths are necessary; they are necessary in our world, and in giving us our mental endowments God gave us the right sort of clear and distinct ideas to see the necessity. But though they are necessary, they are not necessarily necessary; God could have freely chosen to make a different sort of world, in which other things would have been necessary truths. The possibility of such another world is something we cannot *comprehend*, but only dimly *apprehend*; Descartes uses the simile that we may girdle a tree-trunk with our arms but not a mountain—but we can *touch* the mountain. Proper understanding of the possibility would be possessed by God, or, no doubt, by creatures in the alternative world, who would be endowed by God with clear and distinct ideas corresponding to the necessities of their world.

In recent years, unsound philosophies have been defended by what I may call shyster logicians: some of the more dubious recent developments of modal logic could certainly be used to defend Descartes. A system in which 'possibly p' were a theorem—in which everything is possible—has indeed never been taken seriously; but modal logicians have taken seriously systems in which 'possibly possibly p', or again 'it is not necessary that necessarily p', would be a theorem for arbitrary interpretation of 'p'. What is more, some modern modal logicians notoriously take possible worlds very seriously indeed; some of them even go to the length of saying that what you and I vulgarly call the actual world is simply the world we happen to live in. People who take *both* things seriously—the axiom 'possibly possibly p' and the ontology of possible worlds—would say: You mention any impossibility, and there's a possible world in which that isn't impossible but possible. And this is even further away out than Descartes would wish to go; for he would certainly not wish to say that 'It is possible that God should not exist' is even *possibly* true. So *a fortiori* a shyster logician could fadge up a case for Descartes. But to my mind all that this shows is that modal logic is currently a rather disreputable discipline: not that I think modal notions are inadmissible—on the contrary, I think they are indispensable—but that current professional standards in the discipline are low, and technical ingenuity is mistaken for rigour. On that showing, astrology would be rigorous.

Descartes' motive for believing in absolute omnipotence was not contemptible: it seemed to him that otherwise God would be *subject to* the inexorable laws of logic as Jove was to the decrees of the Fates. The nature of logical truth is a very difficult problem, which I cannot discuss here. The easy conventionalist line, that it is our arbitrary way of using words that makes logical truth, seems to me untenable, for reasons that Quine among others has clearly spelled out. If I could follow Quine further in regarding logical laws as natural laws of very great generality—revisable in principle, though most unlikely to be revised, in a major theoretical reconstruction—then perhaps after all some rehabilitation of Descartes on this topic might be possible. But in the end I have to say that as we cannot say how a non-logical world would look, we cannot say how a supra-logical God would act or how he could communicate anything to us by way of revelation. So I end as I began: a Christian need not and cannot believe in absolute omnipotence.

It is important that Christians should clearly realize this, because otherwise a half-belief in absolute omnipotence may work in their minds subterraneously. As I said, I think McTaggart was absolutely right in drawing attention to this danger. One and the same man may deny the doctrine of absolute omnipotence when the doctrine is clearly put to him, and yet reassure himself that God can certainly do so-and-so by using *merely* the premise of God's omnipotence. And McTaggart is saying this is indefensible. At the very least this 'so-and-so' must represent a logically consistent description of a feat; and proofs of logical consistency are notoriously not always easy. Nor, as we shall see, are our troubles at an end if we assume that God *can* do anything whose description is logically consistent.

Logical consistency in the description of the feat is certainly a *necessary* condition for the truth of 'God can do so-and-so': if 'so-and-so' represents an inconsistent description of a feat, then 'God can do so-and-so' is certainly a false and impossible proposition, since it entails 'It could be the case that so-and-so came about'; so, by contraposition, if 'God can do so-and-so' is to be true, or even logically possible, then 'so-and-so' must represent a logically consistent description of a feat. And whereas only a minority of Christians have explicitly believed in absolute omnipotence, many have believed that a proposition of the form 'God can do so-and-so' is true whenever 'so-and-so' represents a description of a logically possible feat. This is our second doctrine of omnipotence. One classic statement of this comes in the *Summa Theologica* Ia q. xxv art. 3. Aquinas rightly says that we cannot explain 'God can do everything' in terms of what is within the power of some agent; for 'God can do everything any created agent can do', though true, is not a comprehensive enough account of God's power, which exceeds that of any created agent; and 'God can do everything God can do' runs uselessly in a circle. So he puts forward the view that if the description 'so-and-so' is in itself possible through the relation of the terms involved—if it does not involve contradictories' being true together—then 'God can do so-and-so' is true. Many Christian writers have followed Aquinas in saying this; but it is not a position consistently maintainable. As we shall see, Aquinas did not manage to stick to the position himself.

Before I raise the difficulties against this thesis, I wish to expose a common confusion that often leads people to accept it: the confusion between self-contradiction and gibberish. C. S. Lewis in *The Problem of Pain* says that meaningless combinations of words do not suddenly acquire meaning simply because we prefix to them the two other words 'God can', and Antony Flew has quoted this with just approval. But if we take Lewis's words strictly, his point is utterly trivial, and nothing to our purpose. For gibberish, syntactically incoherent combination of words, is quite different from self-contradictory sentences or descriptions; the latter certainly have an intelligible place in our language.

It is a common move in logic to argue that a set of premises A, B, C together yield a contradiction, and that therefore A and B as premises yield as conclusion the contradictory of C; some logicians have puritanical objections to this manoeuvre, but I cannot stop to consider them; I am confident, too, that neither Aquinas nor Lewis would share these objections to *reductio ad absurdum*. If, however, a contradictory formula were gibberish, *reductio ad absurdum* certainly would be an illegitimate procedure—indeed it would be a nonsensical one. So we have to say that when 'so-and-so' represents a self-contradictory description of a feat, 'God can do so-and-so' is likewise self-contradictory, but that being self-contradictory it is *not* gibberish, but merely false.

I am afraid the view of omnipotence presently under consideration owes part of its attractiveness to the idea that then 'God can do so-and-so' would never turn out *false*, so that there would be no genuine counterexamples to 'God can do everything'. Aquinas says, in the passage I just now cited: 'What implies contradiction cannot be a word, for no understanding can conceive it.' Aquinas, writing seven centuries ago, is excusable for not being clear about the difference between self-contradiction and gibberish; we are not excusable if we are not. It is not gibberish to say 'a God can bring it about that in Alcalá there lives a barber who shaves all those and only those living in Alcalá who do not shave themselves'; this is a perfectly well-formed sentence, and not on the face of it self-contradictory; all the same, the supposed feat notoriously is self-contradictory, so this statement of what God can do is not nonsense but false.

One instance of a description of a feat that is really but not overtly self-contradictory has some slight importance in the history of conceptions of omnipotence. It appeared obvious to Spinoza that *God can bring about everything that God can bring about*, and that to deny this would be flatly incompatible with God's omnipotence (*Ethics* I.17, scholium). Well, the italicized sentence is syntactically ambiguous. 'Everything that God can bring about God can bring about' is one possible reading of the sentence, and this is an obvious, indeed trivial predication about God, which must be true if there is a God at all. But the other way of taking the sentence relates to a supposed feat of *bringing about everything that God can bring about*—*all* of these bringable-about things *together*—and it says that God is capable of *this* feat. This is clearly the way Spinoza wishes us to take the sentence. But taken this way, it is not obvious at all; quite the contrary, it's obviously false. For among the things that are severally possible for God to bring about, there are going to be some pairs that are not *compossible*, pairs which it is logically impossible should both come about; and then it is beyond God's power to bring about such a pair together—let alone, to bring about all the things together which he can bring about severally.

This does not give us a description of a *logically possible* feat which God cannot accomplish. However, there is nothing easier than to mention feats which are logically possible but which God cannot do, if Christianity is true. Lying and promise-breaking are logically possible feats: but Christian faith, as I have said, collapses unless we are assured that God cannot lie and cannot break his promise.

This argument is an *ad hominem* argument addressed to Christians; but there are well-known logical arguments to show that on any view there must be some logically possible feats that are beyond God's power. One good example suffices:

making a thing which its maker cannot afterwards destroy. This is certainly a possible feat, a feat that some human beings have performed. Can God perform the feat or not? If he cannot there is already some logically possible feat which God cannot perform. If God can perform the feat, then let us suppose that he does: *ponatur in esse*, as medieval logicians say. Then we are supposing God to have brought about a situation in which he *has* made something he cannot destroy; and in that situation destroying this thing is a *logically* possible feat that God cannot accomplish, for we surely cannot admit the idea of a creature whose destruction is logically *im*possible.

There have been various attempts to meet this argument. The most interesting one is that the proposition 'God cannot make a thing that he cannot destroy' can be turned round to 'Any thing that God can make he can destroy'—which does not even look like an objection to God's being able to do everything logically possible. But this reply involves the very same bracketing fallacy that I exposed a moment ago in Spinoza. There, you will remember, we had to distinguish two ways of taking 'God can bring about everything that God can bring about':

A. Everything that God can bring about, God can bring about.
B. God can bring about the following feat: to bring about everything that God can bring about.

And we saw that A is trivially true, given that there *is* a God, and B certainly false. Here, similarly, we have to distinguish two senses of 'God cannot make a thing that its maker cannot destroy':

A. Anything that its maker cannot destroy, God cannot make.
B. God cannot bring about the following feat: to make something that its maker cannot destroy.

And here A does contrapose, as the objectors would have it, to 'Anything that God can make, its maker can destroy', which on the face of it says nothing against God's power to do anything logically possible. But just as in the Spinoza example, the B reading purports to describe a single feat, *bringing about everything that God can bring about* (this feat, I argued, is impossible for God, because logically impossible): so in our present case, the B reading purports to describe a single feat, *making something that its maker cannot destroy*. This, as I said, is a logically possible feat, a feat that men sometimes do perform; so we may press the question whether this is a feat God can accomplish or not; and either way there will be some *logically possible* feat God cannot accomplish. So this notion of omnipotence, like the Cartesian idea of absolute omnipotence, turns out to be obviously incompatible with Christian faith, and moreover logically untenable.

Let us see, then, if we fare any better with the third theory: the theory that the only condition for the truth of 'God can do so-and-so' is that 'God does so-and-so' or 'God is doing so-and-so' must be logically possible. As I said, this imposes a more restrictive condition than the second theory: for there are many feats that we can consistently suppose to be performed but cannot consistently suppose to be performed by God. This theory might thus get us out of the logical trouble that arose with the second theory about the feat: *making a thing that its maker cannot destroy*. For though this is a logically possible feat, a feat some creatures do perform, it might well be argued that 'God has made a thing that its maker cannot destroy' is a proposition with a buried inconsistency in it; and if so, then on the present account of omnipotence we need not say 'God *can* make a thing that its maker cannot destroy'.

This suggestion also, however, can easily be refuted by an example of great philosophical importance that I borrow from Aquinas. 'It comes about that Miss X never loses her virginity' is plainly a logically possible proposition: and so also is 'God brings it about that Miss X never loses her virginity'. All the same, if it so happens that Miss X already has lost her virginity, 'God *can* bring it about that Miss X never loses her virginity' is false (Ia q. xxv art. 4 ad 3 um). Before Miss X had lost her virginity, it would have been true to say this very thing; so what we can truly say about what God can do will be different at different times. This appears to imply a change in God, but Aquinas would certainly say, and I think rightly, that it doesn't really do so. It is just like the case of Socrates coming to be shorter than Theaetetus because Theaetetus grows up; here, the change is on the side of Theaetetus not of Socrates. So in our case, the change is really in Miss X not in God; something about her passes from the realm of possibility to the realm of *fait accompli*, and thus *no longer* comes under the concept of the accomplishable—*deficit a ratione possibilium* (Aquinas, *loc. cit.*, ad 2 um). I think Aquinas's position here is strongly defensible; but if he does defend it, he has abandoned the position that God can do everything that it is not *a priori* impossible *for God to do*, let alone the position that God can bring about everything describable in a logically consistent way.

Is it *a priori* impossible for God to do something wicked? And if not, *could* God do something wicked? There have been expressed serious doubts about this: I came across them in a favourite of modern moral philosophers, Richard Price. We must distinguish, he argues, between God's natural and his moral attributes: if God is a free moral being, even as we are, it must not be absolutely impossible for God to do something wicked. There must be just a chance that God should do something wicked: no doubt it will be a really infinitesimal chance—after all, God has persevered in ways of virtue on a vast scale for inconceivably long—but the chance must be there, or God isn't free and isn't therefore laudable for his goodness. The way this reverend gentleman commends his Maker's morals is so startling that you may suspect me of misrepresentation; I can only ask any sceptic to check in Daiches Raphael's edition of Price's work! Further comment on my part is I hope needless.

A much more restrained version of the same sort of thing is to be found in the Scholastic distinction between God's *potentia absoluta* and *potentia ordinata*. The former is God's power considered in abstraction from his wisdom and goodness, the latter is God's power considered as controlled in its exercise by his wisdom and goodness. Well, as regards a man it makes good sense to say: 'He has the bodily and mental power to do so-and-so, but he certainly will not, it would be pointlessly silly and wicked.' But does anything remotely like this make sense to say about Almighty God? If not, the Scholastic distinction I have cited is wholly frivolous.

Let us then consider our fourth try. Could it be said that the 'everything' in 'God can do everything' refers precisely to things that are not in the realm of *fait accompli* but of futurity? This will not do either. If God can promulgate promises to men, then as regards any promises that are not yet fulfilled we know that they certainly will be fulfilled: and in that case God clearly has not a *potentia ad utrumque*—a two-way power of either actualizing the event that will fulfil the promise or not actualizing it. God can then only do what will fulfil his promise. And if we try to evade this by denying that God can make promises known to men, then we have once more denied something essential to Christian faith, and we are still left with something that God cannot do.

I must here remove the appearance of a fallacy. God cannot but fulfil his promises, I argued; so he has not a two-way power, *potentia ad utrumque*, as regards these particular future events. This argument may have seemed to involve the fallacy made notorious in medieval logical treatises, of confusing the necessity by which something flows—*necessitas consequentiae*—with the necessity of that very thing which follows—*necessitas consequentis*. If it is impossible for God to promise and not perform, then if we know God has promised something we may infer with certainty that he will perform it. Surely, it may be urged, this is enough for Christian faith and hope; we need not go on to say that God *cannot not* bring about the future event in question. If we do that, are we not precisely committing the hoary modal fallacy I have just described?

I answer that there are various senses of 'necessary'. The future occurrence of such-and-such, when God has promised that such-and-such shall be, is of course not logically necessary; but it may be necessary in the sense of being, as Arthur Prior puts it, now unpreventable. If God *has* promised that Israel shall be saved, then there is nothing that anybody, even God, can do about that; this past state of affairs is now unpreventable. But it is also necessary in the same way that if God has promised then he will perform; God cannot do anything about that either—cannot make himself liable to break his word. So we have as premises 'Necessarily p' and 'Necessarily if p then q', in the same sense of 'necessarily'; and from these premises it not merely necessarily follows that q—the conclusion in the necessitated form, 'Necessarily q' with the same sense of 'necessarily', follows from the premises. So if God has promised that Israel shall be saved, the future salvation of Israel is not only certain but inevitable; God must save Israel, because he cannot not save Israel without breaking his word given in the past and he can neither alter the past nor break his word.

Again, in regard to this and other arguments, some people may have felt discomfort at my not drawing in relation to God the sort of distinction between various applications of 'can' that are made in human affairs: the 'can' of knowing how to, the 'can' of physical power to, the 'can' of opportunity, the 'can' of what fits in with one's plans. But of course the way we make these distinct applications of 'he can' to a human agent will not be open if we are talking about God. There is no question of God's knowing how but lacking the strength, or being physically able to but not knowing how; moreover (to make a distinction that comes in a logical example of Aristotle's) though there is a right time when God may bring something about, it is inept to speak of his then having the opportunity to do it. (To develop this distinction: if 'x' stands for a finite agent and 'so-and-so' for an act directly in x's power, there is little difference between 'At time t it is suitable for x to bring so-and-so about' and 'It is suitable for x to bring so-and-so about at time t'; but if 'x' means God, the temporal qualification 'at time t' can attach only to what is brought about; God does not live through successive times and find one more suitable than another.)

These distinct applications of 'can' are distinct only for finite and changeable agents, not for a God whose action is universal and whose mind and character and design are unchangeable. There is thus no ground for fear that in talking about God we may illicitly slip from one sort of 'can' to another. What we say God can do is always in respect of his changeless supreme power.

All the same, we have to assert different propositions at different times in order to say truly what God can do. What is past, as I said, ceases to be alterable even by God; and thus the truth-value of a proposition like 'God can bring it about that Miss X never loses her virginity' alters once she has lost it. Similarly, God's promise makes a difference to what we can thereafter truly say God can do; it is less obvious in this case that the real change involved is a change in creatures, not in God, than it was as regards Miss X's virginity, but a little thought should show that the promulgation or making known of God's intention, which is involved in a promise, is precisely a change in the creatures to whom the promise is made.

Thus all the four theories of omnipotence that I have considered break down. Only the first overtly flouts logic; but the other three all involve logical contradictions, or so it seems; and moreover, all these theories have consequences fatal to the truth of Christian faith. The last point really ought not to surprise us; for the absolute confidence a Christian must have in God's revelation and promises involves, as I said at the outset, both a belief that God is almighty, in the sense I explained, and a belief that there are certain describable things that God cannot do and therefore will not do.

If I were to end the discussion at this point, I should leave an impression of Aquinas's thought that would be seriously unfair to him; for although in the passage I cited Aquinas appears verbally committed to our second theory of omnipotence, it seems clear that this does not adequately represent his mind. Indeed, it was from Aquinas himself and from the *Summa Theologica* that I borrowed an example which refutes even the weaker third theory, let alone the second one. Moreover, in the other Summa (Book II, c. xxv) there is an instructive list of things that *Deus omnipotens* is rightly said not to be able to do. But the mere occurrence of this list makes me doubt whether Aquinas can be said to believe, in any reasonable interpretation, the thesis that God can do everything. That God is almighty in my sense Aquinas obviously did believe; I am suggesting that here his 'omnipotens' means 'almighty' rather than 'omnipotent'. Aquinas does not say or even imply that he has given an *exhaustive* list of kinds of case in which 'God can do so-and-so' or 'God can make so-and-so' turns out false; so what he says here does not commit him to 'God can do everything' even in the highly unnatural sense 'God can do everything that is not excluded under one or other of the following heads'.

I shall not explore Aquinas's list item by item, because I have made open or tacit use of his considerations at several points in the foregoing and do not wish to repeat myself. But one batch of items raises a specially serious problem. My attention was drawn to the problem by a contribution that the late Mr Michael Foster made orally during a discussion at the Socratic Club in Oxford. Aquinas tells us that if 'doing so-and-so' implies what he calls passive potentiality, then 'God can do so-and-so' is false. On this ground he excluded all of the following:

God can be a body or something of the sort.
God can be tired or oblivious.
God can be angry or sorrowful.
God can suffer violence or be overcome.
God can undergo corruption.

Foster pointed out that as a Christian Aquinas was committed to asserting the contradictory of all these theses. *Contra factum non valet ratio*; it's no good arguing that God cannot do what God has done, and in the Incarnation God did do all these things Aquinas said God cannot do. The Word that was God *was* made flesh (and the literal meaning of the Polish for this is: The Word became a body!); God the Son *was* tired and did sink into the oblivion of sleep; he *was* angry and sorrowful; he was bound like a thief, beaten, and crucified; and though we believe his Body did not decay, it suffered corruption and in the sense of becoming a corpse instead of a living body—Christ in the Apocalypse uses of himself the startling words 'I became a corpse', '*egenomēn nekros*', and the Church has always held that the dead Body of Christ during the *triduum mortis* was adorable with Divine worship for its union to the Divine Nature.

Foster's objection to Aquinas is the opposite kind of objection to the ones I have been raising against the various theories of omnipotence I have discussed. I have been saying that these theories say by implication that God *can* do certain things which Christian belief requires one to say God *cannot* do; Foster is objecting that Aquinas's account says God *cannot* do some things which according to Christian faith God *can* do and has in fact done.

It would take me too far to consider how Aquinas might have answered this objection. It would not of course be outside his intellectual milieu; it is the very sort of objection that a Jew or Moor might have used, accepting Aquinas's account of what God cannot do, in order to argue against the Incarnation. I shall simply mention one feature that Aquinas's reply would have had: it would have to make essential use of the particle 'as', or in Latin '*secundum quod*'. God did become man, so God can become man and have a human body; but God *as* God cannot be man or have a body.

The logic of these propositions with 'as' in them, reduplicative propositions as they are traditionally called, is a still unsolved problem, although as a matter of history it was a problem raised by Aristotle in the *Prior Analytics*. We must not forget that such propositions occur frequently in ordinary discourse; we use them there with an ill-founded confidence that we know our way around. Jones, we say, is Director of the Gnome Works and Mayor of Middletown; he gets a salary *as* Director and an expense allowance *as* Mayor; he signs one letter *as* Director, another *as* Mayor. We say all this, but how far do we understand the logical relations of what we say? Very little, I fear. One might have expected some light and leading from medieval logicians; the theological importance of reduplicative propositions did in fact lead to their figuring as a topic in medieval logical treatises. But I have not found much that is helpful in such treatments as I have read.

I hope to return to this topic later. Meanwhile, even though it has nothing directly to do with almightiness or omnipotence, I shall mention one important logical point that is already to be found in Aristotle. A superficial grammatical illusion may make us think that 'A as P is Q' attaches the predicate 'Q' to a complex subject 'A as P'. But Aristotle insists, to my mind rightly, on the analysis: 'A' subject, 'is, as P, Q' predicate—so that we have not a complex subject-term, but a complex predicate-term; clearly, this predicate entails the simple conjunctive predicate 'is both P and Q' but not conversely. This niggling point of logic has in fact some theological importance. When theologians are talking about Christ as God and Christ as Man, they may take the two phrases to be two logical subjects of predication, if they have failed to see the Aristotelian point; and then they are likely to think or half think that Christ as God is one entity or *Gegenstand* and Christ as Man is another. I am sure some theologians have yielded to this temptation, which puts them on a straight road to the Nestorian heresy.

What Aquinas would have done, I repeat, to meet Foster's objection in the mouth of a Jew or Moor is to distinguish between what we say God can do, *simpliciter*, and what we say God *as God* can do, using the reduplicative form of proposition. Now if we do make such a distinction, we are faced with considerable logical complications, particularly if we accept the Aristotelian point about the reduplicative construction. Let us go back to our friend Jones: there is a logical difference between:

1. Jones as Mayor can attend this committee meeting.
2. Jones can as Mayor attend this committee meeting

as we may see if we spell the two out a little:

1. Jones as Mayor has the opportunity of attending this committee meeting
2. Jones has the opportunity of (attending this committee meeting as Mayor).

We can easily see now that 1 and 2 are logically distinct: for one thing, if Jones is not yet Mayor but has an opportunity of becoming Mayor and *then* attending the committee meeting, 2 would be true and 1 false. And if we want to talk about what Jones as Mayor *cannot* do, the complexities pile up; for then we have to consider how the negation can be inserted at one or other position in a proposition of one of these forms, and how all the results are logically related.

All this is logical work to be done if we are to be clear about the implications of saying that God can or cannot do so-and-so, or again that God *as God* can or cannot do so-and-so. It is obvious, without my developing the matter further, that the logic of all this will not be simple. It's a far cry from the simple method of bringing our question 'Can God do so-and-so?' under a reassuring principle 'God can do *everything*'. But I hope I have made it clear that any reassurance we get that way is entirely spurious.

THE METAPHYSICAL ATTRIBUTES

ST. ANSELM
God Is Timeless, Immutable, and Impassible

CHAPTER XIX.   HE DOES NOT EXIST IN PLACE OR TIME, BUT ALL THINGS EXIST IN HIM.

But if through thine eternity thou hast been, and art, and wilt be; and to have been is not to be destined to be; and to be is not to have been, or to be destined to be; how does thine eternity exist as a whole forever? Or is it true that nothing of thy eternity passes away, so that it is not now; and that nothing of it is destined to be, as if it were not yet?

Thou wast not, then, yesterday, nor wilt thou be to-morrow; but yesterday and to-day and to-morrow thou art; or, rather, neither yesterday nor to-day nor to-morrow thou art; but simply, thou art, outside all time. For yesterday and to-day and to-morrow have no existence, except in time; but thou, although nothing exists without thee, nevertheless dost not exist in space or time, but all things exist in thee. For nothing contains thee, but thou containest all.

CHAPTER XXV.   IT CANNOT SUFFER CHANGE BY ANY ACCIDENTS.[1]

But does not this Being, which has been shown to exist as in every way substantially identical with itself, sometimes exist as different from itself, at any rate, accidentally? But how is it supremely immutable, if it can, I will not say, *be*, but, be conceived of, as variable by virtue of accidents? And, on the other hand, does

GOD IS TIMELESS, IMMUTABLE, AND IMPASSIBLE   Reprinted from *Proslogium* (Chapters VIII and XIX) and *Monologium* (Chapter XXV) by St. Anselm, translated by Sidney N. Deane. By permission of The Open Court Publishing Co., La Salle, Illinois.

[1] *Accidents*, as Anselm uses the term, are facts external to the essence of a being, which may yet be conceived to produce changes in a mutable being.

it not partake of accident, since even this very fact that it is greater than all other natures and that it is unlike them seems to be an accident in its case *(illi accidere)?* But what is the inconsistency between susceptibility to certain facts, called *accidents*, and natural immutability, if from the undergoing of these accidents the substance undergoes no change?

For, of all the facts, called accidents, some are understood not to be present or absent without some variation in the subject of the accident—all colors, for instance—while others are known not to effect any change in a thing either by occurring or not occurring—certain relations, for instance. For it is certain that I am neither older nor younger than a man who is not yet born, nor equal to him, nor like him. But I shall be able to sustain and to lose all these relations toward him, as soon as he shall have been born, according as he shall grow, or undergo change through divers qualities.

It is made clear, then, that of all those facts, called accidents, a part bring some degree of mutability in their train, while a part do not impair at all the immutability of that in whose case they occur. Hence, although the supreme Nature in its simplicity has never undergone such accidents as cause mutation, yet it does not disdain occasional expression in terms of those accidents which are in no wise inconsistent with supreme immutability; and yet there is no accident respecting its essence, whence it would be conceived of, as itself variable.

Whence this conclusion, also, may be reached, that it is susceptible of no accident; since, just as those accidents, which effect some change by their occurrence or non-occurrence, are by virtue of this very effect of theirs regarded as being true *accidents*, so those facts, which lack a like effect, are found to be improperly called accidents. Therefore, this Essence is always, in every way, substantially identical with itself; and it is never in any way different from itself, even accidentally. But, however it may be as to the proper signification of the term *accident*, this is undoubtedly true, that of the supremely immutable Nature no statement can be made, whence it shall be conceived of as mutable.

CHAPTER VIII.   HOW HE IS COMPASSIONATE AND PASSIONLESS. GOD IS COMPASSIONATE, IN TERMS OF OUR EXPERIENCE, BECAUSE WE EXPERIENCE THE EFFECT OF COMPASSION. GOD IS NOT COMPASSIONATE, IN TERMS OF HIS OWN BEING, BECAUSE HE DOES NOT EXPERIENCE THE FEELING *(AFFECTUS)* OF COMPASSION.

But how art thou compassionate, and, at the same time, passionless? For, if thou art passionless, thou dost not feel sympathy; and if thou dost not feel sympathy, thy heart is not wretched from sympathy for the wretched; but this it is to be compassionate. But if thou art not compassionate, whence cometh so great consolation to the wretched? How, then, art thou compassionate and not compassionate, O Lord, unless because thou art compassionate in terms of our experience, and not compassionate in terms of thy being.

Truly, thou art so in terms of our experience, but thou art not so in terms of thine own. For, when thou beholdest us in our wretchedness, we experience the effect of compassion, but thou dost not experience the feeling. Therefore, thou art both compassionate, because thou dost save the wretched, and spare those who sin against thee; and not compassionate, because thou art affected by no sympathy for wretchedness.

ST. THOMAS AQUINAS
The Simplicity and Immutability of God

SEVENTH ARTICLE.   WHETHER GOD IS ALTOGETHER SIMPLE?

We proceed thus to the Seventh Article:—

Objection 1. It seems that God is not altogether simple. For whatever is from God imitates Him. Thus from the first being are all beings, and from the first good are all goods. But in the things which God has made, nothing is altogether simple. Therefore neither is God altogether simple.

Obj. 2. Further, whatever is better must be attributed to God. But with us that which is composite is better than that which is simple; thus, chemical compounds are better than elements, and elements than the parts that compose them. Therefore it cannot be said that God is altogether simple.

On the contrary, Augustine says, *God is truly and absolutely simple.*[1]

I *answer* that, The absolute simplicity of God may be shown in many ways. First, from the previous articles of this question. For there is neither composition of quantitative parts in God, since He is not a body; nor composition of form and matter, nor does His nature differ from His *suppositum;* nor His essence from His being; neither is there in Him composition of genus and difference, nor of subject and accident. Therefore, it is clear that God is in no way composite, but is altogether simple. Secondly, because every composite is posterior to its component parts, and is dependent on them; but God is the first being, as has been shown above.[2] Thirdly, because every composite has a cause, for things in themselves diverse cannot unite unless something causes them to unite. But God is uncaused, as has been shown above,[3] since He is the first efficient cause. Fourthly, because in every composite there must be potentiality and actuality (this does not apply to God) for either one of the parts actualizes another, or at least all the parts

---

THE SIMPLICITY AND IMMUTABILITY OF GOD   From *Summa Theologica*, Part I, Questions 3 and 9, in *Basic Writings of Saint Thomas Aquinas*, edited by Anton C. Pegis. By permission of the A. C. Pegis estate.

[1] *De Trin.*, VI, 6 (PL 42, 928).

[2] Q. 2, a. 3 [in *Philosophy of Religion: Selected Readings*, 2nd ed., pp. 128–30].

[3] *Ibid.*

are as it were in potency with respect to the whole. Fifthly, because nothing composite can be predicated of any one of its parts. And this is evident in a whole made up of dissimilar parts; for no part of a man is a man, nor any of the parts of the foot, a foot. But in wholes made up of similar parts, although something which is predicated of the whole may be predicated of a part (as a part of the air is air, and a part of water, water), nevertheless certain things are predictable of the whole which cannot be predicated of any of the parts; for instance, if the whole volume of water is two cubits, no part of it can be two cubits. Thus in every composite there is something which is not itself. But, even if this could be said of whatever has a form, viz., that it has something which is not it itself, as in a white object there is something which does not belong to the essence of white, nevertheless, in the form itself there is nothing besides itself. And so, since God is absolute form, or rather absolute being, He can be in no way composite. Hilary touches upon this argument when he says: *God, Who is strength, is not made up of things that are weak; nor is He, Who is light, composed of things that are dark.*[4]

Reply Obj. 1. Whatever is from God imitates Him, as caused things imitate the first cause. But it is of the essence of a thing caused to be in some way composite; because at least its being differs from its essence, as will be shown hereafter.[5]

Reply Obj. 2. With us composite things are better than simple things, because the perfection of created goodness is not found in one simple thing, but in many things. But the perfection of divine goodness is found in one simple thing, as will be shown hereafter. . . .[6]

FIRST ARTICLE.   WHETHER GOD IS ALTOGETHER IMMUTABLE?

We proceed thus to the First Article:—

Objection 1. It seems that God is not altogether immutable. For whatever moves itself is in some way mutable. But, as Augustine says, *The Creator Spirit moves Himself neither by time, nor by place.*[7] Therefore God is in some way mutable.

Obj. 2. Further, it is said of Wisdom that *it is more mobile than all active things* (Wis. vii. 24). But God is wisdom itself, therefore God is movable.

Obj. 3. Further, to approach and to recede signify movement. But these are said of God in Scripture: *Draw nigh to God, and He will draw nigh to you* (Jas. iv. 8). Therefore God is mutable.

On the contrary, It is written, *I am the Lord, and I change not* (Mal. iii. 6).

I answer that, From what precedes, here is the proof that God is altogether immutable. First, because it was shown above that there is some first being, whom we call God,[8] and that this first being must be pure act, without the admixture of

---

[4] *De Trin.,* VII (PL 10, 223).

[5] Q. 50, a. 2.

[6] Q. 4, a. 1; Q. 6, a. 3.

[7] *De Genesis ad Litt.,* VIII, 20 (PL 34, 388).

[8] Q. 2, a. 3.

any potentiality, for the reason that, absolutely, potentiality is posterior to act.[9] Now everything which is in any way changed, is in some way in potentiality. Hence it is evident that it is impossible for God to change in any way. Secondly, because everything which is moved remains in part as it was, and in part passes away, as what is moved from whiteness to blackness remains the same as to substance; and thus in everything which is moved there is some kind of composition to be found. But it has been shown above that in God there is no composition, for He is altogether simple.[10] Hence it is manifest that God cannot be moved. Thirdly, because everything which is moved acquires something by its movement, and attains to what it had not attained previously. But since God is infinite, comprehending in Himself all the plenitude of the perfection of all being, He cannot acquire anything new, nor extend Himself to anything whereto He was not extended previously. Hence movement in no way belongs to Him. So it is that some of the ancients, constrained, as it were, by the truth, held that the first principle was immovable.[11]

Reply Obj. 1. Augustine there[12] speaks in a similar way to Plato, who said that the first mover moves Himself,[13] thus calling every operation a movement, according to which even the acts of understanding, and willing, and loving, are called movements. Therefore, because God understands and loves Himself, in that respect they said that God moves Himself; not, however, as movement and change belong to a thing existing in potentiality, as we now speak of change and movement.

Reply Obj. 2. Wisdom is called mobile by way of similitude, according as it diffuses its likeness even to the outermost of things, for nothing can exist which does not proceed from the divine wisdom, by way of some kind of imitation, as from the first effective and formal principle; as also works of art proceed from the wisdom of the artist. And so in the same way, inasmuch as the similitude of the divine wisdom proceeds in degrees from the highest things, which participate more fully of its likeness, to the lowest things which participate of it in a lesser degree, there is said to be a kind of procession and movement of the divine wisdom to things; as if we should say that the sun proceeds to the earth, inasmuch as a ray of its light reaches the earth. In this way Dionysius expounds the matter, saying that every procession of the divine manifestation comes to us from the movement of the Father of lights.[14]

Reply Obj. 3. These things are said of God in Scripture metaphorically. For as the sun is said to enter a house, or to go out, according as its rays reach the house, so God is said to approach to us, or to recede from us, when we receive the influx of His goodness or fall away from Him.

[9] Q. 3, a. 3.

[10] Q. 3, a. 7.

[11] Parmenides and Melissus, according to Aristotle, *Phys.*, I, 2 (184b 16).

[12] *De Genesi ad Litt.*, VIII, 20 (PL 34, 388).

[13] Aristotle, *Metaph.*, XI, 6 (1071b 37); cf. Plato, *Timaeus* (pp. 30a, 34b); *Phaedrus* (p. 245c).—Cf. also Averroes, *In Phys.*, VIII, comm. 40 (IV, 173r).

[14] *De Cael. Hier.*, I, 1 (PG 3, 120).

CHARLES HARTSHORNE
The Divine Relativity

RELIGIOUS MEANING OF ABSOLUTE

Why is it religiously significant that God be supposed absolute? The reason is at least suggested by the consideration that absoluteness is requisite for complete reliability. What is relative to conditions may fail us if the conditions happen to be unfavorable. Hence if there is to be anything that *cannot* fail, it must be nonrelative, absolute, in those respects to which "reliability" and "failure" have reference. But it is often not noted that this need not be every respect or aspect from which God's nature can be regarded. For there may be qualities in God whose relativity or variability would be neutral to his reliability. To say of a man that (as human affairs go) his reliability is established refers not to every quality of the man, but only to certain principles exhibited in his otherwise highly variable behavior. We do not mean that if something comes close to his eye he will not blink, or that if he is given bad-tasting food he will enjoy it as much as better fare. We mean that his fixed intention to act according to the requirements of the general welfare will not waver, and that his wisdom and skill in carrying out this aim will be constant. But in all this there is not only no implication that conditions will not have effect upon the man, but the very plain implication that they will have plenty of effect. Skill in one set of circumstances means one form of behavior, in another set another form, and the same is true of the intention to serve the general good. Of course, one may argue that complete fixity of good intention and complete constancy of skill imply every other sort of fixity as well. But this has never yet been definitely shown by careful, explicit reasoning, and anything less is inappropriate in as difficult a subject as we are dealing with. General hunches will not do.

A typically invalid argument in this connection is that unless God surveys at once the whole of time and thus is independent of change, he cannot be relied upon to arrange all events with due regard to their relations to all that has gone before and all that is to come after. This argument either rests on an equivocation or it destroys all religious meaning for the divine reliability. For, if it is meant in any clear sense, it implies that every event has been selected by deity as an element in the best of all possible worlds, the ideal total pattern of all time and all existence. But this ideal pattern includes all acts of sin and the most hideous suffering and catastrophe, all the tragedies of life. And what then becomes of the ideas of human responsibility and choice, and of the notion that some deeds ought not to have taken place? These are only the beginning of the absurdities

Charles Hartshorne (1897–   ), a Professor Emeritus of Philosophy at the University of Texas, is a leading advocate of the metaphysics of Alfred N. Whitehead. Among his important writings are *Reality as Social Process, Anselm's Discovery,* and *The Logic of Perfection.*

into which the view thrusts us. To mitigate these absurdities theologians introduce various more or less subtle equivocations. Would they not do better to take a fresh start (as indeed many have done) and admit that we have no good religious reason for positing the notion of providence as an absolute contriving of all events according to a completely detailed plan embracing all time? The religious value of such a notion is more negative than positive. It is the mother of no end of chicanery (see the book of Job for some examples), of much deep feeling of injustice (the poor unfortunate being assured that God has deliberately contrived everything as exactly the best way events could transpire), and of philosophical quagmires of paradox and unmeaning verbiage. The properly constituted man does not want to "rely" upon God to arrange all things, including our decisions, in accordance with a plan of all events which fixes every least detail with reference to every other that ever has happened or ever "is to" happen. How many atheists must have been needlessly produced by insistence upon this arbitrary notion, which after all is invariably softened by qualifications surreptitiously introduced *ad hoc* when certain problems are stressed! We shall see later that the really usable meaning of divine reliability is quite different and is entirely compatible with a profound relativity of God to conditions and to change. For the present, I suggest that all we can assert to have obvious religious value is the faith that God is to be relied upon to do for the world all that ought to be done for it, and with as much survey of the future as there ought to be or as is ideally desirable, leaving for the members of the world community to do for themselves and each other all that they ought to be left to do. We cannot assume that what ought to be done for the world by deity is everything that ought to be done at all, leaving the creatures with nothing to do for themselves and for each other. Nor can we assume that the ideal survey of what for us at least constitutes the future is one which fully defines it in every detail, leaving no open alternatives of possibility. So far from being self-evidently of religious value, these assumptions, viewed in the light of history, seem clearly of extreme disvalue. Yet they are often either asserted, or not unequivocally denied or avoided, in the intemperate insistence upon the total absoluteness of deity.

GOD AS SOCIAL

We have also to remember that if there is religious value in the absoluteness of God, as requisite for his reliability, there is equally manifest religious value in another trait which seems unequivocally to imply relativity rather than absoluteness. This is the social or personal nature of God. What is a person if not a being qualified and conditioned by social relations, relations to other persons? And what is God if not the supreme case of personality? Those who deny this have yet to succeed in distinguishing their position from atheism, as Hume pointedly noted. Either God really does love all beings, that is, is related to them by a sympathetic union surpassing any human sympathy, or religion seems a vast fraud. The common query Can the Absolute or Perfect Being be personal or social? should really run In what sense, if any, can a social being be absolute or perfect? For God is conceived socially before he is conceived absolutely or as perfect. God is the highest ruler, judge, benefactor; he knows, loves, and assists man; he has made the world with the design of sharing his bliss with lesser beings. The world is a vast society governed by laws instituted by the divine monarch—the supreme personal power to whom all other persons are subject. These are all, more or less clearly, social conceptions—if you like, metaphors (though aimed, as we shall see, at a literal, intuited meaning) drawn from the social life of man. They constitute the universal, popular meaning of "God," in relation to which descriptions such as "absolute," "perfect," "immutable," "impassive," "simple," and the like, are technical refinements aimed at logical precision. They seek to define the somewhat vague ideas of *highest* ruler, *supreme* power, or *author of all*, himself without author or origin. "Immutable," for example, is an attempted definition of the superiority of deity with respect to death and degeneration, and also with respect to vacillation of will due to fear, or other weakness. Earthly rulers are all brought low by death; and their promises and protection and execution of justice must always be discounted somewhat in anticipation of the effect upon them of changing circumstances and the development of their own motives, the growth of good and evil in their own hearts. God is not under sentence of death, cannot decay; and his convenant abides, nor is his wisdom ever clouded by storms of blind passion, the effects of strong drink or of disease.

The future of theology depends, I suggest, above all upon the answer to this question: can technically precise terms be found which express the supremacy of God, among social beings, without contradicting his social character? To say, on the one hand, that God is love, to continue to use popular religious terms like Lord, divine will, obedience to God, and on the other to speak of an absolute, infinite, immutable, simple, impassive deity, is either a gigantic hoax of priest-craft, or it is done with the belief that the social connotations of the popular language are ultimately in harmony with these descriptions. Merely to speak of the "mysteriousness" of God is not sufficient. If he escapes all the resources of our language and analysis, why be so insistent upon the obviously quite human concepts, absolute, infinite, perfect, immutable? These too are our conceptions, our terms, fragments of the English or Latin languages. Perhaps after all it is not correct to say God is absolute. How shall we know, if the subject is utterly mysterious and beyond our powers? . . .

COMPLETE INDEPENDENCE NOT ADMIRABLE

But, supposing that God is to be conceived worthy of utter respect, and in that sense "perfect," it may not follow that God is quite everything that has customarily been associated with this adjective. For it is entirely possible that theologians have sometimes respected things which, when more carefully considered, are seen not to be suitable objects of this respect. The being in the highest degree admirable will have, in the highest degree or manner, all properties that deserve admiration. But even tyrants and scoundrels have actually been admired and, it rather seems, admired sometimes for their very tyranny and rascality. To some of us, nothing is more deeply shocking than certain directions frequently taken by theological admiration. What is the ideal of the tyrant? Is it not that, while the fortunes of all should depend upon the tyrant's will, he should depend as little as possible, ideally not at all, upon the wills and fortunes of others? This one-sided independence, in ideally complete or "absolute" form, was held the crowning glory of deity! Sheer independence in every respect whatsoever, while all else in every respect depended upon him, was regarded as essential to God's perfection. There are those, including Berdyaev and many other good and wise men, who find no stimulus to admiration or respect in this doctrine.

Of course there are modes of independence which are admirable. But is it any less true that there are modes of dependence which we all admire, and of independence which we detest? The father that as little as possible depends upon the will and welfare of his child is an inhuman monster. Let the child—say, a daughter—be happy, let her be miserable, let her deeply desire this or deeply detest that, let her develop in a moral or in a vicious direction, it is all one to the independent parent, who goes his way in complete neutrality to all such alternatives (this neutrality being the exact meaning of absoluteness or independence) wholly uninfluenced by weal or woe, love or hate, preference or detestation, in the unlucky child that, in such a one-sided way, depends upon the parent. Is this really an ideal? Is not the correct ideal rather this, that the parent should be influenced in appropriate, and only in appropriate, ways by the child's desires and fortunes? One should not simply agree to every whim of the child, or strive always to save her from pain or furnish her with pleasure. Nor should one be sunk in misery with her every sorrow, or fantastically elated with her every triumph. But neither should one try to act and think and feel just as one would have acted or thought or felt had the child's joy been sorrow, or her sorrow joy, or her likes dislikes. Yet God, we are told, is impassive and immutable and without accidents, is just as he would be in his action and knowledge and being had we never existed, or had all our experiences been otherwise. Instead of attributing to God an eminently appropriate dependence upon us, the majority of theologians simply denied dependence of any and every sort. This seems plainly an idealization of the tyrant-subject relationship, as Whitehead, a critic as fair and moderate as he is profound, has reminded us.

THE INDEPENDENCE WHICH IS ADMIRABLE

Suppose as man says, I can be a good man, do my duty, only so long as a certain friend continues to live and to encourage me. Our feeling will surely be that, while it is natural and human to lean upon friends for moral assistance, still a man should do his duty whatever anyone else may do. In ethical character one should be as independent as possible of other contingent beings. Thus to depend for doing one's duty upon others is inappropriate, unadmirable dependence. God then, as object of piety, will be in highest degree, or utterly, independent of our actions and fortunes for the preservation of his holiness of will. That is, he will promote the highest cosmic good, come what may. But it does not in the least follow that what God will do to promote the cosmic good will be uninfluenced by our actions and fortunes, or that how he will think and feel about the world will in no way reflect what is going on in the world. The man who does his duty regardless of what happens will not have the same specific duties regardless of what happens. And with different duties he will perform different acts with different specific intentions, ideas, and feelings.

Suppose, on the other hand, a man says, I can be equally happy and serene and joyous regardless of how men and women suffer around me. Shall we admire this alleged independence? I think not. Why should we admire it when it is alleged of God? I have yet to learn a good answer to this question. On the other hand, if we see a person who is dragged down into helpless misery by the sight of suffering in others, we feel that this response is as inappropriate as the opposite one of gay serenity would be in the same circumstances. And there is no inconsistency in condemning both responses, for a clear logical principle can be applied to both. This is that we should respond to the total situation appropriately, not just to a part of it, or inappropriately. The suffering of the world is not the world; there is also the joy of the world. If the one should sadden us, the other should delight us. He who refuses to rejoice with the joy of others is as selfish as he who refuses to grieve with their sorrows. Indeed, as has been often remarked, it is if anything a rarer unselfishness to be really inspired by the happiness of our friends than to be saddened by their unhappiness. For the happiness of others may inspire us with envy instead of sympathetic pleasure. Such neutralization by envy of sympathetic dependence for our own happiness upon that of others is scarcely admirable!

PROPORTIONAL DEPENDENCE

The notion that total emotional independence is admirable seems, then, to be without foundation in experience. There *is* an admirable independence, but it is independence in basic ethical purpose, not in specific concrete experience and happiness. There is also admirable dependence, which is appropriate response, duly proportionate to the balance of factors in the world known to us, of sympathetic rejoicing and sorrowing. Why not attribute to the divine response the ideal of such appropriateness, or proportionality, of dependence? The requirement of piety seems entirely compatible with such attribution.

To depend upon others emotionally through sympathy is to change when they change—for example, to grow in joy when they do. But if God changes, it is often argued, then he changes either for the worse or for the better. If the former, how can we admire him without stint? If the latter, then it seems he must previously have lacked something, and been incomplete and imperfect. The first horn of the dilemma need not concern us, unless it can be proved that there is ever more sorrow than joy in the world. For if there is always more satisfaction than dissatisfaction, then God should always have more reason to rejoice than to grieve over the world, and since he can retain the consciousness of past joys, there will always be a *net increment* of value accruing to God at each moment. Now if life were not more satisfying than otherwise, could it go on? Is there anything to maintain the will to live save satisfaction in living? I do not see that there is. Hence I shall confine my attention to the second horn of the dilemma, that a God who increases in value must previously have lacked some value, and therefore have been imperfect. My reply is that, as we are here using the term, perfect means completely worthy of admiration and respect, and so the question becomes, is such complete admirableness infringed by the possibility of enrichment in total value? I say it is not. We do not admire a man less because we know he would be a happier man if his son, who is wretched, became well and happy, or because we anticipate that when a child is born to him it will enrich his life with many new joys. Admiration is not directed to happiness, except so far as we feel that a person does or does not attain the happiness appropriate to the state of the world as known to him. We admire not the amount but the appropriateness of the joy. We rejoice in another's happiness, we grieve over his misfortune, but we do not praise or blame or admire on this account, unless we think the good or bad fortune is the person's own doing. So far as it is due rather to the decisions of others, which were their responsibility, not his, then it determines not our respect, but only the tone of our sympathy or participatory feeling, toward the person. Why should it be otherwise in relation to God? If God rejoices less today than he will tomorrow, but ideally appropriately at both times, our reverence for him should in no way be affected by the increase in joy. Indeed, if he were incapable of responding to a better world with greater satisfaction, this should infringe upon our respect; for it would imply a lack of proportionality in the divine awareness of things.

Gratitude is the appropriate expression of genuine indebtedness, of really having received benefit from others. Conceited men would perhaps like to avoid occasions for gratitude, so that they might boast of their independence. But no good man blessed with a beloved wife is sorry to feel that without her he could not have been so happy. To God each of us is dearer than wife to husband, for no human being knows the inner experiences of another human being so intimately as they are known to God. And to know experiences is to appreciate them; for the value of experience is just the experience itself. As we are indebted to a few persons for the privilege of feeling something of the quality of their experiences, so God is indebted to *all* persons for the much fuller enjoyment of the same privilege. God is not conceited or envious; therefore he has no motive for wishing to escape or deny this indebtedness. It is envious men, priests, theologians, guardians—in some cases one could almost say watchdogs—of the divine majesty, who attribute such an attitude, such unbridled will to independence, to God. (No doubt God's sense of indebtedness to us lacks some of the connotations of "gratitude," such as the sense of a common moral frailty, almost miraculously overcome in a certain case.)

SYMPATHETIC DEPENDENCE

I have been contending that there are appropriate forms of dependence, in relation to certain terms. To this an opponent may object that the appropriateness is not determined solely by the nature of the entities toward which the dependence obtains, but involves also the nature of that which is thus made dependent. It is appropriate for man to depend upon man, not for the supreme being to depend upon anything. But my proposition is that the higher the being the more dependence of certain kinds will be appropriate for it. One does not expect an oyster to depend for its joy or sorrow upon my joy or sorrow, as such, or even upon that of other oysters to any great extent. Sympathetic dependence is a sign of excellence and waxes with every ascent in the scale of being. Joy calls for sympathetic joy, sorrow for sympathetic sorrow, as the most excellent possible forms of response to these states. The eminent form of sympathetic dependence can only apply to deity, for this form cannot be less than an omniscient sympathy, which depends upon and is exactly colored by every nuance of joy or sorrow anywhere in the world. It would certainly not be appropriate for man to even try to sympathize with all life. How could he hope to do such a thing? Thus I grant to the opponent that what is "appropriate dependence" varies with the subject as well as the object of the dependence relation. But I deny that zero dependence for happiness is ever appropriate, and I assert that the closest to such zero dependence would occur at the bottom, not the top of the scale of beings, while the top, the most eminent form of dependence for happiness, would be maximal dependence, dependence upon all life even to its least nuance for the exact happiness of the eminent individual.

I invite you to perform with me a mental experiment. Imagine someone to read aloud an eloquent poem, in the presence of: (A) a glass of water, (B) an ant, (C) a dog, (D) a human being unacquainted with the language of the poem, (E) a human being knowing the language but insensitive to poetry, (F) a person sensitive to poetry and familiar with the language. Now I submit that each member of this series is superior, in terms of the data, to its predecessors, and that each is more, not less, dependent upon or relative to the poem as such, including its meanings as well as its mere sounds. The molecules of water will be utterly "impassible" (the theological term) to the words of the poem as words, and not even much affected by the mere physical sounds. The ant, since it has hearing, will be affected by the physical sounds more drastically, it seems probable, than the water. The dog will not only hear and be influenced by the sound, as such, but will have some sense of the emotional tones of voice, and may be quite excited by these. It may also have a feeling of familiarity concerning some of the words. The human being not knowing the language will receive more varied influences of this kind and will enjoy some sense of the verbal music of the poem, which may furnish a rather absorbing experience. The insensitive, but comprehending, listener will be given a variety of images and ideas, even though without intense esthetic feeling or adequate integration. The adequate listener may go through a deep and thousandfold adventure of thought and feeling. Thus we see that the simple correlation of inferior with dependent or relative is anything but a report upon experience. The identification of "absolute" and "supreme" has to be proved, not blandly assumed, and it is in the teeth of the experiences without which we could not know what either absolute or supreme could reasonably mean.

Suggestions for Further Reading

A good collection of writings dealing with various concepts of God is Charles Hartshorne and William L. Reese, eds., *Philosophers Speak of God* (University of Chicago Press, 1953). For an excellent account of the traditional view of God's attributes see George H. Joyce, *Principles of Natural Theology* (AMS Press, 1972). H. P. Owen provides an interesting survey of the major views on God in *Concepts of Deity* (Herder and Herder, 1971). Anthony Kenny's *The God of the Philosophers* (Clarendon Press, 1979) is an important philosophical treatment of the major attributes of the theistic God. Another important treatment of the attributes is that of Richard Swinburne, *The Coherence of Theism* (Clarendon Press, 1978). Other notable works on the nature and attributes of God are Stephen Davies, *Logic and the Nature of God* (Eerdman's, 1984); Thomas V. Morris, *Anselmian Explorations* (University of Notre Dame Press, 1987); and Alvin Plantinga, *Does God Have a Nature?* (Marquette University Press, 1980).

Discussions of the notion of God as a necessary being can be found in Alvin Plantinga, *God and Other Minds* (Cornell University Press, 1967); James F. Ross, *Philosophical Theology* (Hackett Press, 1974); and William Rowe, *The Cosmological Argument* (Princeton University Press, 1975).

Important discussions of the problems of foreknowledge, future contingents, and omniscience include William Ockham, *Predestination, God's Foreknowledge and Future Contingents*, trans. M. A. Adams and N. Kretzmann (Hackett Press, 1983); and John C. Moskop, *Divine Omniscience and Human Freedom* (Mercer UP, 1984). See also Joseph Runzo, "Omniscience and Freedom for Evil," *International Journal for the Philosophy of Religion* 12 (1981); John M. Fischer, "Freedom and Foreknowledge," *Philosophical Review* 92 (1983); and Linda Zagzebski, "Divine Foreknowledge and Human Free Will," *Religious Studies* 21 (1985).

Notable recent discussions of omnipotence are George Mavrodes, "Some Puzzles Concerning Omnipotence," *Philosophical Review* 72 (1963); W. S. Anglin, "Can God Create A Being He Cannot Control?" *Analysis* 40 (1980); J. L. Cowan, "The Paradox of Omnipotence," in L. Urban and D. Walton, eds., *The Power of God* (Oxford University Press, 1978).

On the notion of eternality see Nelson Pike, *God and Timelessness* (Schocken, 1970); J. L. Tomkinson, "Divine Sempiternity and Atemporality," *Religious Studies* 18 (1982); and William Hasker, "Concerning the Intelligibility of 'God Is Timeless,' " *The New Scholasticism* 57 (1983).

ARGUMENTS FOR THE EXISTENCE OF GOD

II

For centuries, philosophers and theologians have sought to justify theism by advancing arguments for the existence of the theistic God. The most important of these arguments can be classified as ontological, cosmological, teleological, and moral. An ontological argument endeavors to show that, given our concept of God, it follows that God actually exists. An argument that is cosmological reasons for the existence of God in order to account for the fact that a world exists. A teleological argument reasons for the existence of God in order to account for the fact that a world that exhibits order and design exists. Finally, a moral argument reasons to the existence of God from certain moral facts and obligations.

The best known ontological argument is presented in Anselm's *Proslogium II*. Anselm understands the concept God to be the concept of a being than which none greater is possible. His argument that such a God actually exists goes as follows: If He did not exist—that is, if God were nonexistent like, for example, the Fountain of Youth—then, since He, like the Fountain of Youth, might (logically) have existed, He might (logically) have been greater than He in fact is. But, Anselm continues, this is impossible. For although there is no contradiction in thinking that the Fountain of Youth might have been a greater being than it is, there does seem to be a contradiction in the idea that the being than which none greater is possible is a being that might have been greater. Hence, given our concept of God, we are driven to the conclusion that He actually exists.

The fundamental idea on which Anselm's reasoning rests is that if a being does not exist, but might have existed, then it might have been greater than it in fact is. This idea implies that existence is a perfection, a quality that enhances the greatness of a being: a being that has existence is greater than it would have been had it lacked existence. Many philosophers object to this idea on the grounds that existence, unlike such qualities as wisdom and power, is not a quality a being may have or lack; it is not a real predicate. Others question Anselm's reasoning on the grounds that the concept of a being than which none greater is possible may be incoherent, like the concept of an integer than which none larger is possible. Yet another objection some philosophers make is that if the reasoning in the argument were correct, we could use it to prove the existence of things we know do not exist—for example, the island than which none greater is possible. These objections, and others, are presented in the selections from Kant and Gaunilo.

Alvin Plantinga's version of the ontological argument aims to demonstrate not merely that God exists, but that God exists necessarily. This so-called "modal version" assumes that necessary existence is a perfection. Given that assumption, a powerful argument is developed for God's necessary existence, an argument whose crucial premise asserts only that it is logically possible that there exists a being with the property of maximal greatness. (For some being to have *maximal greatness*, it is required that the being exist and be supremely excellent in *every possible world*.) The problem with the argument is that it is exceedingly difficult to establish its crucial premise. To see this, consider the property of being in less than perfect company, where it is understood that a person has that property provided every person (human and nonhuman) has some imperfection. It may be that we actually have this property. But even if we do not, it certainly seems logically possible that each person has some imperfection, however slight. But if it is possible, then Plantinga's premise is false: it is not possible that some being is maximally great. For, since a maximally great being would have to be a person, if it were possible that every person has some slight defect, then in some possible world no being is supremely excellent. But if in some world no being is supremely excellent, then in no possible world is there a being with maximal greatness—it is not logically possible that there exists a being with maximal greatness. The difficulty that remains for the proponent of the modal version, then, is to find some reason for believing its crucial premise to be true.

Cosmological arguments have been advanced since antiquity, but they received considerable attention in the thirteenth and eighteenth centuries. Among the following selections, the thirteenth-century form of the cosmological argument is presented by Aquinas and by Patterson Brown; the eighteenth-century form is presented by Samuel Clarke and by the character Demea in the selection from Hume. Criticisms of the eighteenth-century form of the argument are presented by the character Cleanthes in the selection from Hume. A defense of the argument against some of these criticisms is set forth by Rowe.

The eighteenth-century form of the argument is based on the Principle of Sufficient Reason, which maintains that there must be an explanation of the existence of any being and of any positive fact whatever. Using this principle, the argument endeavors to prove that there must exist a being whose existence is accounted for by its own nature.

We need to question this argument first by asking whether the idea of a being having the explanation of its existence within its own nature is a coherent idea. Some facts about a thing can, perhaps, be explained by referring to the thing's nature—for example, we might explain why a triangle has three angles by referring to the nature of a triangle, to what it is for something to be a triangle—but is the existence of a thing a fact about that thing, and even if it is, does it make sense to think of it being explained by the nature of that thing? Secondly, we need to question the Principle of Sufficient Reason itself. Do we have any reasons for thinking it to be true? Is it, as some philosophers have claimed, a principle that cannot be proved or disproved, one which is simply presupposed by us in our dealings with the world in which we live? Finally, we need to ask whether a necessary being, if there is one, would have to be God. As Hume's character Cleanthes suggests, why couldn't the necessary being be something less than God, such as matter?

In the teleological arguments for the existence of God, Paley compares the universe to a watch and Hume's character Cleanthes compares it to a machine. The point of these comparisons is to suggest an analogy between the universe and things known to be produced by intelligent beings, thereby to justify the conclusion that the universe probably was produced by an intelligent being. We may represent Cleanthes's version of the teleological argument as follows:

1. Machines are produced by intelligent design.
2. The universe is like a machine. Therefore—
3. Probably the universe was produced by intelligent design. Therefore—
4. Probably God exists and created the universe.

Concerning this argument, we need to ask first in what ways the entire universe can be said to resemble a machine. Paley assures us that every manifestation of design that exists in a watch also exists in the works of nature. And Cleanthes affirms that there is a "curious adapting of means to ends" throughout all nature. Apparently they hold that the parts of nature are related to one another in a manner similar to the way in which the parts of a machine are related to one another. If we introduce the idea of a *teleological system* to mean any system of parts in which the parts are so arranged that under proper conditions they work together to serve a certain end or purpose, it is clear that machines are teleological systems. For example, a watch is a system of parts in which the parts work together so that the watch will tell the time of day. Moreover, machines with complex parts, such as automobiles, are teleological systems and also systems of teleological systems—for many of their parts, like the carburetor in an automobile, are themselves teleological systems. It is also clear that many parts of living organisms are teleological systems. The human eye, for example, no less than a camera, is a teleological system. Can the same be said of the universe itself? Of course, if theism is true and God has created the universe and arranged its parts so that they work together for some far-off divine purpose, then the universe is indeed a teleological system. But, if we follow Cleanthes and limit ourselves to empirical observation of the universe and its parts, we cannot say with any degree of certainty that the universe is a teleological system. For we are not in a position to observe what the purpose of the universe is and how the parts of the universe are so arranged that they work together for the attainment of that purpose. Nevertheless, it may be reasonable to believe that the universe is a vast system of parts that are themselves teleological systems. And this concept may be all that is required to justify the conclusion that the universe probably was produced by intelligent design. But, as Hume has Philo point out, we observe at best only a small fraction of the total universe—perhaps elsewhere in the universe chaos reigns. Hence, we may be justified only in claiming that a small fraction of the universe contains a number of teleological systems. And if that is so, we may not be justified by empirical observation in thinking that the entire universe is, like a complex machine, a system of teleological systems. We must, then, seriously question whether the universe is sufficiently like a machine to warrant the conclusion that it was produced by intelligent design.

Even if the inference from points 1 and 2 of Cleanthes's argument to point 3 is acceptable, it is doubtful that the teleological argument can do much to establish theism. For there are several questions to be raised concerning the inference from point 3 to point 4. In the first place, since there are numerous instances of evil in the universe, the intelligent producer of the universe, for all we know, may be morally indifferent to his handiwork. Second, since many intricate teleological systems have resulted from the cooperative work of many architects, we cannot reasonably infer the unity of the Deity—many intelligent beings may have cooperated in the production of the universe. These and other objections are raised by Philo against Cleanthes's attempt to found theism on a teleological argument.

Versions of the moral argument center around the theme that our moral life makes sense only if there is a divine being. Some versions claim that moral laws require a lawgiver and argue that such a being would be divine. More sophisti-cated versions press three claims: (1) that we have moral obligations to achieve certain states of excellence, (2) that "ought" implies "can," and (3) that we can achieve certains states of excellence only if God exists. For example, Kant appears to argue that we have an obligation to achieve the highest good, something we can do only if there is a God who proportions happiness to virtue. Assessing Kant's argument is no easy matter. Indeed, as Mackie notes, it is very difficult to deter-mine exactly what argument Kant took himself to be giving. Mackie's chief objec-tion to Kant is that all the argument proves, at best, is that it must be possible that there is a God who proportions happiness to virtue. This objection is correct if we take Kant to be claiming only that it must be possible for us to attain the highest good. But if by "can" Kant means not just "possible" but also "in our power," then Kant's argument requires more than the mere possibility that there is a God. Perhaps the most interesting way to understand Kant's line of thought is to take him to be arguing that we can be rational in our moral life only if we suppose there is a God who so arranges things that we are able to attain the highest good.

W. L. R.

THE ONTOLOGICAL ARGUMENT

ST. ANSELM
The Ontological Argument

CHAPTER II.   TRULY THERE IS A GOD, ALTHOUGH THE FOOL HATH SAID IN HIS HEART, THERE IS NO GOD.

And so, Lord, do thou, who dost give understanding to faith, give me, so far as thou knowest it to be profitable, to understand that thou art as we believe; and that thou art that which we believe. And, indeed, we believe that thou art a being than which nothing greater can be conceived. Or is there no such nature, since the fool hath said in his heart, there is no God? (Psalms xiv. 1). But, at any rate, this very fool, when he hears of this being of which I speak—a being than which nothing greater can be conceived—understands what he hears, and what he understands is in his understanding; although he does not understand it to exist.

For, it is one thing for an object to be in the understanding, and another to understand that the object exists. When a painter first conceives of what he will afterwards perform, he has it in his understanding, but he does not yet understand it to be, because he has not yet performed it. But after he has made the painting, he both has it in his understanding, and he understands that it exists, because he has made it.

Hence, even the fool is convinced that something exists in the understanding, at least, than which nothing greater can be conceived. For, when he hears of this, he understands it. And whatever is understood, exists in the understanding. And assuredly that, than which nothing greater can be conceived, cannot exist in the understanding alone. For, suppose it exists in the understanding alone: then it can be conceived to exist in reality; which is greater.

Therefore, if that, than which nothing greater can be conceived, exists in the

THE ONTOLOGICAL ARGUMENT   Reprinted from *Proslogium* by St. Anselm, translated by Sidney N. Deane. By permission of The Open Court Publishing Co., La Salle, Illinois.

understanding alone, the very being, than which nothing greater can be conceived, is one, than which a greater can be conceived. But obviously this is impossible. Hence, there is no doubt that there exists a being, than which nothing greater can be conceived, and it exists both in the understanding and in reality.

CHAPTER III.   GOD CANNOT BE CONCEIVED NOT TO EXIST.—GOD IS THAT, THAN WHICH NOTHING GREATER CAN BE CONCEIVED.—THAT WHICH CAN BE CONCEIVED NOT TO EXIST IS NOT GOD.

And it assuredly exists so truly, that it cannot be conceived not to exist. For, it is possible to conceive of a being which cannot be conceived not to exist; and this is greater than one which can be conceived not to exist. Hence, if that, than which nothing greater can be conceived, can be conceived not to exist, it is not that, than which nothing greater can be conceived. But this is an irreconcilable contradiction. There is, then, so truly a being than which nothing greater can be conceived to exist, that it cannot even be conceived not to exist; and this being thou art, O Lord, our God.

So truly, therefore, dost thou exist, O Lord, my God, that thou canst not be conceived not to exist; and rightly. For, if a mind could conceive of a being better than thee, the creature would rise above the Creator; and this is most absurd. And, indeed, whatever else there is, except thee alone, can be conceived not to exist. To thee alone, therefore, it belongs to exist more truly than all other beings, and hence in a higher degree than all others. For, whatever else exists does not exist to truly, and hence in a less degree it belongs to it to exist. Why, then, has the fool said in his heart, there is no God (Psalms xiv. 1), since it is so evident, to a rational mind, that thou dost exist in the highest degree of all? Why, except that he is dull and a fool?

CHAPTER IV.   HOW THE FOOL HAS SAID IN HIS HEART WHAT CANNOT BE CONCEIVED.—A THING MAY BE CONCEIVED IN TWO WAYS: (1) WHEN THE WORD SIGNIFYING IT IS CONCEIVED; (2) WHEN THE THING ITSELF IS UNDERSTOOD. AS FAR AS THE WORD GOES, GOD CAN BE CONCEIVED NOT TO EXIST; IN REALITY HE CANNOT.

But how has the fool said in his heart what he could not conceive; or how is it that he could not conceive what he said in his heart? since it is the same to say in the heart, and to conceive.

But, if really, nay, since really, he both conceived, because he said in his heart; and did not say in his heart, because he could not conceive; there is more than one way in which a thing is said in the heart or conceived. For, in one sense, an object is conceived, when the word signifying it is conceived; and in another, when the very entity, which the object is, is understood.

In the former sense, then, God can be conceived not to exist; but in the latter, not at all. For no one who understands what fire and water are can conceive fire to be water, in accordance with the nature of the facts themselves, although this is possible according to the words. So, then, no one who understands what God is can conceive that God does not exist; although he says these words in his heart, either without any, or with some foreign, signification. For, God is that than which a greater cannot be conceived. And he who thoroughly understands this, assuredly understands that this being so truly exists, that not even in concept can it be non-existent. Therefore, he who understands that God so exists, cannot conceive that he does not exist.

I thank thee, gracious Lord, I thank thee; because what I formerly believed by thy bounty, I now so understand by thine illumination, that if I were unwilling to believe that thou dost exist, I should not be able not to understand this to be true.

GAUNILO
The Perfect Island Objection

. . . 5. But that this being must exist, not only in the understanding but also in reality, is thus proved to me:

If it did not exist, whatever exists in reality would be greater than it. And so the being which has been already proved to exist in my understanding, will not be greater than all other beings.

I still answer: if it should be said that a being which cannot be even conceived in terms of any fact, is in the understanding, I do not deny that this being is, accordingly, in my understanding. But since through this fact it can in no wise attain to real existence also, I do not yet concede to it that existence at all, until some certain proof of it shall be given.

For he who says that this being exists, because otherwise the being which is greater than all will not be greater than all, does not attend strictly enough to what he is saying. For I do not yet say, no, I even deny or doubt that this being is greater than any real object. Nor do I concede to it any other existence than this (if it should be called existence) which it has when the mind, according to a word merely heard, tries to form the image of an object absolutely unknown to it.

How, then, is the veritable existence of that being proved to me from the assumption, by hypothesis, that it is greater than all other beings? For I should still deny this, or doubt your demonstration of it, to this extent, that I should not admit that this being is in my understanding and concept even in the way in

Gaunilo, a monk, was a contemporary of St. Anselm. He is best known for his criticisms of Anselm's celebrated argument for the existence of God.

THE PERFECT ISLAND OBJECTION   Reprinted from "On Behalf of the Fool," in *St. Anselm: Basic Writings*, translated by Sidney N. Deane. By permission of The Open Court Publishing Co., La Salle, Illinois.

which many objects whose real existence is uncertain and doubtful, are in my understanding and concept. For it should be proved first that this being itself really exists somewhere; and then, from the fact that it is greater than all, we shall not hesitate to infer that it also subsists in itself.

6. For example: it is said that somewhere in the ocean is an island, which, because of the difficulty, or rather the impossibility, of discovering what does not exist, is called the lost island. And they say that this island has an inestimable wealth of all manner of riches and delicacies in greater abundance than is told of the Islands of the Blest; and that having no owner or inhabitant, it is more excellent than all other countries, which are inhabited by mankind, in the abundance with which it is stored.

Now if some one should tell me that there is such an island, I should easily understand his words, in which there is no difficulty. But suppose that he went on to say, as if by a logical inference: "You can no longer doubt that this island which is more excellent than all lands exists somewhere, since you have no doubt that it is in your understanding. And since it is more excellent not to be in the understanding alone, but to exist both in the understanding and in reality, for this reason it must exist. For if it does not exist, any land which really exists will be more excellent than it; and so the island already understood by you to be more excellent will not be more excellent."

If a man should try to prove to me by such reasoning that this island truly exists, and that its existence should no longer be doubted, either I should believe that he was jesting, or I know not which I ought to regard as the greater fool: myself, supposing that I should allow this proof; or him, if he should suppose that he had established with any certainty the existence of this island. For he ought to show first that the hypothetical excellence of this island exists as a real and indubitable fact, and in no wise as any unreal object, or one whose existence is uncertain, in my understanding. . . .

ST. ANSELM
Reply to Gaunilo

ANSELM'S APOLOGETIC.

IN REPLY TO GAUNILON'S ANSWER IN BEHALF OF THE FOOL.

It was a fool against whom the argument of my Proslogium was directed. Seeing, however, that the author of these objections is by no means a fool, and is a

REPLY TO GAUNILO   From "Reply to Gaunilo," in *St. Anselm: Basic Writings*, translated by Sydney N. Deane. Reprinted by permission of The Open Court Publishing Co., La Salle, Illinois.

Catholic, speaking in behalf of the fool, I think it sufficient that I answer the Catholic.

CHAPTER I.   A GENERAL REFUTATION OF GAUNILON'S ARGUMENT. IT IS SHOWN THAT A BEING THAN WHICH A GREATER CANNOT BE CONCEIVED EXISTS IN REALITY.

You say—whosoever you may be, who say that a fool is capable of making these statements—that a being than which a greater cannot be conceived is not in the understanding in any other sense than that in which a being that is altogether inconceivable in terms of reality, is in the understanding. You say that the inference that this being exists in reality, from the fact that it is in the understanding, is no more just than the inference that a lost island most certainly exists, from the fact that when it is described the hearer does not doubt that it is in his understanding.

But I say: if a being than which a greater is inconceivable is not understood or conceived, and is not in the understanding or in concept, certainly either God is not a being than which a greater is inconceivable, or else he is not understood or conceived, and is not in the understanding or in concept. But I call on your faith and conscience to attest that this is most false. Hence, that than which a greater cannot be conceived is truly understood and conceived, and is in the understanding and in concept. Therefore either the grounds on which you try to controvert me are not true, or else the inference which you think you base logically on those grounds is not justified.

But you hold, moreover, that supposing that a being than which a greater cannot be conceived is understood, it does not follow that this being is in the understanding; nor, if it is in the understanding, does it therefore exist in reality.

In answer to this, I maintain positively: if that being can be even conceived to be, it must exist in reality. For that than which a greater is inconceivable cannot be conceived except as without beginning. But whatever can be conceived to exist, and does not exist, can be conceived to exist through a beginning. Hence what can be conceived to exist, but does not exist, is not the being than which a greater cannot be conceived. Therefore, if such a being can be conceived to exist, necessarily it does exist.

Furthermore: if it can be conceived at all, it must exist. For no one who denies or doubts the existence of a being than which a greater is inconceivable, denies or doubts that if it did exist, its non-existence, either in reality or in the understanding, would be impossible. For otherwise it would not be a being than which a greater cannot be conceived. But as to whatever can be conceived, but does not exist—if there were such a being, its non-existence, either in reality or in the understanding, would be possible. Therefore if a being than which a greater is inconceivable can be even conceived, it cannot be non-existent.

But let us suppose that it does not exist, even if it can be conceived. Whatever can be conceived, but does not exist, if it existed, would not be a being than which a greater is inconceivable. If, then, there were a being a greater than which is inconceivable, it would not be a being than which a greater is inconceivable:

which is most absurd. Hence, it is false to deny that a being than which a greater cannot be conceived exists, if it can be even conceived; much the more, therefore, if it can be understood or can be in the understanding.

Moreover, I will venture to make this assertion: without doubt, whatever at any place or at any time does not exist—even if it does exist at some place or at some time—can be conceived to exist nowhere and never, as at some place and at some time it does not exist. For what did not exist yesterday, and exists to-day, as it is understood not to have existed yesterday, so it can be apprehended by the intelligence that it never exists. And what is not here, and is elsewhere, can be conceived to be nowhere, just as it is not here. So with regard to an object of which the individual parts do not exist at the same places or times: all its parts and therefore its very whole can be conceived to exist nowhere or never.

For, although time is said to exist always, and the world everywhere, yet time does not as a whole exist always, nor the world as a whole everywhere. And as individual parts of time do not exist when others exist, so they can be conceived never to exist. And so it can be apprehended by the intelligence that individual parts of the world exist nowhere, as they do not exist where other parts exist. Moreover, what is composed of parts can be dissolved in concept, and be non-existent. Therefore, whatever at any place or at any time does not exist as a whole, even if it is existent, can be conceived not to exist.

But that than which a greater cannot be conceived, if it exists, cannot be conceived not to exist. Otherwise, it is not a being than which a greater cannot be conceived: which is inconsistent. By no means, then, does it at any place or at any time fail to exist as a whole: but it exists as a whole everywhere and always.

Do you believe that this being can in some way be conceived or understood, or that the being with regard to which these things are understood can be in concept or in the understanding? For if it cannot, these things cannot be understood with reference to it. But if you say that it is not understood and that it is not in the understanding, because it is not thoroughly understood; you should say that a man who cannot face the direct rays of the sun does not see the light of day, which is none other than the sunlight. Assuredly a being than which a greater cannot be conceived exists, and is in the understanding, at least to this extent—that these statements regarding it are understood.

CHAPTER II.   THE ARGUMENT IS CONTINUED. IT IS SHOWN THAT A BEING
THAN WHICH A GREATER IS INCONCEIVABLE CAN BE CONCEIVED, AND ALSO, IN
SO FAR, EXISTS.

I have said, then, in the argument which you dispute, that when the fool hears mentioned a being than which a greater is inconceivable, he understands what he hears. Certainly a man who does not understand when a familiar language is spoken, has no understanding at all, or a very dull one. Moreover, I have said that if this being is understood, it is in the understanding. Is that in no understanding which has been proved necessarily to exist in the reality of fact?

But you will say that although it is in the understanding, it does not follow that it is understood. But observe that the fact of its being understood does necessitate its being in the understanding. For as what is conceived, is conceived by conception, and what is conceived by conception, as it is conceived, so is in conception; so what is understood, is understood by understanding, and what is understood by understanding, as it is understood, so is in the understanding. What can be more clear than this?

After this, I have said that if it is even in the understanding alone, it can be conceived also to exist in reality, which is greater. If, then, it is in the understanding alone, obviously the very being than which a greater cannot be conceived is one than which a greater can be conceived. What is more logical? For if it exists even in the understanding alone, can it not be conceived also to exist in reality? And if it can be so conceived, does not he who conceives of this conceive of a thing greater than that being, if it exists in the understanding alone? What more consistent inference, then, can be made than this: that if a being than which a greater cannot be conceived is in the understanding alone, it is not that than which a greater cannot be conceived?

But assuredly, in no understanding is a being than which a greater is conceivable a being than which a greater is inconceivable. Does it not follow, then, that if a being than which a greater cannot be conceived is in any understanding, it does not exist in the understanding alone? For if it is in the understanding alone, it is a being than which a greater can be conceived, which is inconsistent with the hypothesis.

CHAPTER III.   A CRITICISM OF GAUNILON'S EXAMPLE, IN WHICH HE TRIES TO SHOW THAT IN THIS WAY THE REAL EXISTENCE OF A LOST ISLAND MIGHT BE INFERRED FROM THE FACT OF ITS BEING CONCEIVED.

But, you say, it is as if one should suppose an island in the ocean, which surpasses all lands in its fertility, and which, because of the difficulty, or rather the impossibility, of discovering what does not exist, is called a lost island; and should say that there can be no doubt that this island truly exists in reality, for this reason, that one who hears it described easily understands what he hears.

Now I promise confidently that if any man shall devise anything existing either in reality or in concept alone except that than which a greater cannot be conceived to which he can adapt the sequence of my reasoning, I will discover that thing, and will give him his lost island, not to be lost again.

But it now appears that this being than which a greater is inconceivable cannot be conceived not to be, because it exists on so assured a ground of truth; for otherwise it would not exist at all.

Hence, if any one says that he conceives this being not to exist, I say that at the time when he conceives of this either he conceives of a being than which a greater is inconceivable, or he does not conceive at all. If he does not conceive, he does not conceive of the non-existence of that of which he does not conceive. But if he does conceive, he certainly conceives of a being which cannot be even conceived not to exist. For if it could be conceived not to exist, it could be conceived to have a beginning and an end. But this is impossible.

He, then, who conceives of this being conceives of a being which cannot be even conceived not to exist; but he who conceives of this being does not conceive that it does not exist; else he conceives what is inconceivable. The non-existence, then, of that than which a greater cannot be conceived is inconceivable.

RENÉ DESCARTES
The Supremely Perfect Being Must Exist

But now, if just because I can draw the idea of something from my thought, it follows that all which I know clearly and distinctly as pertaining to this object does really belong to it, may I not derive from this an argument demonstrating the existence of God? It is certain that I no less find the idea of God, that is to say, the idea of a supremely perfect Being, in me, than that of any figure or number whatever it is; and I do not know any less clearly and distinctly that an [actual and] eternal existence pertains to this nature than I know that all that which I am able to demonstrate of some figure or number truly pertains to the nature of this figure or number, and therefore, although all that I concluded in the preceding Meditations were found to be false, the existence of God would pass with me as at least as certain as I have ever held the truths of mathematics (which concern only numbers and figures) to be.

This indeed is not at first manifest, since it would seem to present some appearance of being a sophism. For being accustomed in all other things to make a distinction between existence and essence, I easily persuade myself that the existence can be separated from the essence of God, and that we can thus conceive God as not actually existing. But, nevertheless, when I think of it with more attention, I clearly see that existence can no more be separated from the essence of God than can its having its three angles equal to two right angles be separated from the essence of a [rectilinear] triangle, or the idea of a mountain from the idea of a valley; and so there is not any less repugnance to our conceiving a God (that is, a Being supremely perfect) to whom existence is lacking (that is to say, to whom a certain perfection is lacking), than to conceive of a mountain which has no valley.

René Descartes (1596–1650) marks the beginning of the modern period in philosophy and is also celebrated as a mathematician for his development of the principles of analytic geometry. He is best known in philosophy for seeking the foundation of knowledge in the certainty of one's own existence. Among his major writings are *Discourse on Method*, *Meditations on First Philosophy*, and *Principles of Philosophy*.

THE SUPREMELY PERFECT BEING MUST EXIST   From *Meditations on First Philosophy* by René Descartes, in *The Philosophical Works of Descartes*, translated by Elizabeth S. Haldane and G. R. T. Ross. Reprinted by permission of the publisher and copyright holder, Cambridge University Press.

But although I cannot really conceive of a God without existence any more than a mountain without a valley, still from the fact that I conceive of a mountain with a valley, it does not follow that there is such a mountain in the world; similarly although I conceive of God as possessing existence, it would seem that it does not follow that there is a God which exists; for my thought does not impose any necessity upon things, and just as I may imagine a winged horse, although no horse with wings exists, so I could perhaps attribute existence to God, although no God existed.

But a sophism is concealed in this objection; for from the fact that I cannot conceive a mountain without a valley, it does not follow that there is any mountain or any valley in existence, but only that the mountain and the valley, whether they exist or do not exist, cannot in any way be separated one from the other. While from the fact that I cannot conceive God without existence, it follows that existence is inseparable from Him, and hence that He really exists; not that my thought can bring this to pass, or impose any necessity on things, but, on the contrary, because the necessity which lies in the thing itself, i.e. the necessity of the existence of God determines me to think in this way. For it is not within my power to think of God without existence (that is of a supremely perfect Being devoid of a supreme perfection) though it is in my power to imagine a horse either with wings or without wings.

And we must not here object that it is in truth necessary for me to assert that God exists after having presupposed that He possesses every sort of perfection, since existence is one of these, but that as a matter of fact my original supposition was not necessary, just as it is not necessary to consider that all quadrilateral figures can be inscribed in the circle; for supposing I thought this, I should be constrained to admit that the rhombus might be inscribed in the circle since it is a quadrilateral figure, which, however, is manifestly false. [We must not, I say, make any such allegations because] although it is not necessary that I should at any time entertain the notion of God, nevertheless whenever it happens that I think of a first and a sovereign Being, and, so to speak, derive the idea of Him from the storehouse of my mind, it is necessary that I should attribute to Him every sort of perfection, although I do not get so far as to enumerate them all, or to apply my mind to each one in particular. And this necessity suffices to make me conclude (after having recognised that existence is a perfection) that this first and sovereign Being really exists; just as though it is not necessary for me ever to imagine any triangle, yet, whenever I wish to consider a rectilinear figure composed only of three angles, it is absolutely essential that I should attribute to it all those properties which serve to bring about the conclusion that its three angles are not greater than two right angles, even although I may not then be considering this point in particular. But when I consider which figures are capable of being inscribed in the circle, it is in no wise necessary that I should think that all quadrilateral figures are of this number; on the contrary, I cannot even pretend that this is the case, so long as I do not desire to accept anything which I cannot conceive clearly and distinctly. And in consequence there is a great difference between the false suppositions such as this, and the true ideas born within me, the first and principal of which is that of God. For really I discern in many ways that this idea is not something factitious, and depending solely on my thought, but that it is the image of a true and immutable nature; first of all, because I cannot conceive anything but God himself to whose essence existence [necessarily] pertains; in the second place because it is not possible for me to conceive two or more Gods in this same position; and, granted that there is one such God who now exists, I see clearly that it is necessary that He should have existed from all eternity, and that He must exist eternally; and finally, because I know an infinitude of other properties in God, none of which I can either diminish or change.

For the rest, whatever proof or argument I avail myself of, we must always return to the point that it is only those things which we conceive clearly and distinctly that have the power of persuading me entirely. And although amongst the matters which I conceive of in this way, some indeed are manifestly obvious to all, while others only manifest themselves to those who consider them closely and examine them attentively; still, after they have once been discovered, the latter are not esteemed as any less certain than the former. For example, in the case of every right-angled triangle, although it does not so manifestly appear that the square of the base is equal to the squares of the two other sides as that this base is opposite to the greatest angle; still, when this has once been apprehended, we are just as certain of its truth as of the truth of the other. And as regards God, if my mind were not pre-occupied with prejudices, and if my thought did not find itself on all hands diverted by the continual pressure of sensible things, there would be nothing which I could know more immediately and more easily than Him. For is there anything more manifest than that there is a God, that is to say, a Supreme Being, to whose essence alone existence pertains?[1]

IMMANUEL KANT
Of the Impossibility of an Ontological Proof

It is evident from what has been said, that the conception of an absolutely necessary being is a mere idea, the objective reality of which is far from being established by the mere fact that it is a need of reason. On the contrary, this idea serves merely to indicate a certain unattainable perfection, and rather limits the operations than, by the presentation of new objects, extends the sphere of the understanding. But a strange anomaly meets us at the very threshold; for the inference

Immanuel Kant (1724–1804) was born and lived all of his live in Königsberg, Prussia, where he taught at the University. In his enormously influential *Critique of Pure Reason*, he undertook to refute the ontological argument.

OF THE IMPOSSIBILITY OF AN ONTOLOGICAL PROOF   From *The Critique of Pure Reason*, second edition, translated by J. M. D. Meiklejohn, 1855.

[1] 'In the idea of whom alone necessary or external existence is comprised.' French version.

from a given existence in general to an absolutely necessary existence, seems to be correct and unavoidable, while the conditions of the *understanding* refuse to aid us in forming any conception of such a being.

Philosophers have always talked of an *absolutely necessary* being, and have nevertheless declined to take the trouble of conceiving, whether—and how—a being of this nature is even cogitable, not to mention that its existence is actually demonstrable. A verbal definition of the conception is certainly easy enough: it is something, the non-existence of which is impossible. But does this definition throw any light upon the conditions which render it impossible to cogitate the non-existence of a thing—conditions which we wish to ascertain, that we may discover whether we think anything in the conception of such a being or not? For the mere fact that I throw away, by means of the word *Unconditioned*, all the conditions which the understanding habitually requires in order to regard anything as necessary, is very far from making clear whether by means of the conception of the unconditionally necessary I think of something, or really of nothing at all.

Nay, more, this chance-conception, now become so current, many have endeavoured to explain by examples which seemed to render any inquiries regarding its intelligibility quite needless. Every geometrical proposition—a triangle has three angles—it was said, is absolutely necessary; and thus people talked of an object which lay out of the sphere of our understanding as if it were perfectly plain what the conception of such a being meant.

All the examples adduced have been drawn, without exception, from *judgments*, and not from *things*. But the unconditioned necessity of a judgment does not form the absolute necessity of a thing. On the contrary, the absolute necessity of a judgment is only a conditioned necessity of a thing, or of the predicate in a judgment. The proposition above-mentioned does not enounce that three angles necessarily exist, but, upon condition that a triangle exists, three angles must necessarily exist—in it. And thus this logical necessity has been the source of the greatest delusions. Having formed an *a priori* conception of a thing, the content of which was made to embrace existence, we believed ourselves safe in concluding that, because existence belongs necessarily to the object of the conception (that is, under the condition of my positing this thing is given), the existence of the thing is also posited necessarily, and that it is therefore absolutely necessary—merely because its existence has been cogitated in the conception.

If, in an identical judgment, I annihilate the predicate in thought, and retain the subject, a contradiction is the result; and hence I say, the former belongs necessarily to the latter. But if I suppress both subject and predicate in thought, no contradiction arises; and there *is nothing* at all, and therefore no means of forming a contradiction. To suppose the existence of a triangle and not that of its three angles, is self-contradictory; but to suppose the non-existence of both triangle and angles is perfectly admissable. And so is it with the conception of an absolutely necessary being. Annihilate its existence in thought, and you annihilate the thing itself with all its predicates; how then can there be any room for contradiction? Externally,[1] there is nothing to give rise to a contradiction, for a thing

---

[1] In relation to other things.—*Tr.*

cannot be necessary externally; nor internally, for, by the annihilation or suppression of the thing itself, its internal properties are also annihilated. God is omnipotent—that is a necessary judgment. His omnipotence cannot be denied, if the
existence of a Deity is posited—the existence, that is, of an infinite being, the two
conceptions being identical. But when you say, *God does not exist,* neither omnipotence nor any other predicate is affirmed; they must all disappear with the
subject, and in this judgment there cannot exist the least self-contradiction.

You have thus seen, that when the predicate of a judgment is annihilated in
thought along with the subject, no internal contradiction can arise, be the predicate what it may. There is no possibility of evading the conclusion—you find
yourselves compelled to declare: There are certain subjects which cannot be annihilated in thought. But this is nothing more than saying: There exists subjects
which are absolutely necessary—the very hypothesis which you are called upon to
establish. For I find myself unable to form the slightest conception of a thing
which, when annihilated in thought with all its predicates, leaves behind a contradiction; and contradiction is the only criterion of impossibility, in the sphere of
pure *a priori* conceptions.

Against these general considerations, the justice of which no one can dispute,
one argument is adduced, which is regarded as furnishing a satisfactory demonstration from the fact. It is affirmed, that there is one and only one conception,
in which the non-being or annihilation of the object is self-contradictory, and this
is the conception of an *ens realissimum.* It possesses, you say, all reality, and you
feel yourselves justified in admitting the possibility of such a being. (This I am
willing to grant for the present, although the existence of a conception which is
not self-contradictory is far from being sufficient to prove the possibility of an
object.[2] Now the notion of all reality embraces in it that of existence; the notion
of existence lies, therefore, in the conception of this possible thing. If this thing
is annihilated in thought, the internal possibility of the thing is also annihilated,
which is self-contradictory.

I answer: It is absurd to introduce—under whatever term disguised—into the
conception of a thing, which is to be cogitated solely in reference to its possibility,
the conception of its existence. If this is admitted, you will have apparently gained
the day, but in reality have enounced nothing but a mere tautology. I ask, is the
proposition, *this or that thing* (which I am admitting to be possible) *exists,* an
analytical or a synthetical proposition? If the former, there is no addition made to
the subject of your thought by the affirmation of its existence; but then the conception in your minds is identical with the thing itself, or you have supposed the
existence of a thing to be possible, and then inferred its existence from its internal
possibility—which is but a miserable tautology. The word *reality* in the conception of the thing, and the word *existence* in the conception of the predicate, will

---

[2]A conception is always possible, if it is not self-contradictory. This is the logical criterion of possibility, distinguishing the object of such a conception from the *nihil negativum.* But it may be, notwithstanding, an empty conception, unless the objective reality of this synthesis, by which it is generated,
is demonstrated; and a proof of this kind must be based upon principles of possible experience, and
not upon the principle of analysis or contradiction. This remark may be serviceable as a warning
against concluding, from the possibility of a conception—which is logical, the possibility of a thing—
which is real.

not help you out of the difficulty. For, supposing you were to term all positing of a thing, reality, you have thereby posited the thing with all its predicates in the conception of the subject and assumed its actual existence, and this you merely repeat in the predicate. But if you confess, as every reasonable person must, that every existential proposition is synthetical, how can it be maintained that the predicate of existence cannot be denied without contradiction?—a property which is the characteristic of analytical propositions, alone.

I should have a reasonable hope of putting an end for ever to this sophistical mode of argumentation, by a strict definition of the conception of existence, did not my own experience teach me that the illusion arising from our confounding a logical with a real predicate (a predicate which aids in the determination of a thing) resists almost all the endeavours of explanation and illustration. A *logical predicate* may be what you please, even the subject may be predicated of itself; for logic pays no regard to the content of a judgment. But the determination of a conception is a predicate, which adds to and enlarges the conception. It must not, therefore, be contained in the conception.

Being is evidently not a real predicate, that is, a conception of something which is added to the conception of some other thing. It is merely the positing of a thing, or of certain determinations in it. Logically, it is merely the copula of a judgment. The proposition, *God is omnipotent*, contains two conceptions, which have a certain object or content; the word *is*, is no additional predicate—it merely indicates the relation of the predicate to the subject. Now, if I take the subject (God) with all its predicates (omnipotence being one), and say: *God is*, or, *There is a God*, I add no new predicate to the conception of God, I merely posit or affirm the existence of the subject with all its predicates—I posit the *object* in relation to my *conception*. The content of both is the same; and there is no addition made to the conception, which expresses merely the possibility of the object, by my cogitating the object—in the expression, it *is*—as absolutely given or existing. Thus the real contains no more than the possible. A hundred real dollars contain no more than a hundred possible dollars. For, as the latter indicate the conception, and the former the object, on the supposition that the content of the former was greater than that of the latter, my conception would not be an expression of the whole object, and would consequently be an inadequate conception of it. But in reckoning my wealth there may be said to be more in a hundred real dollars than in a hundred possible dollars—that is, in the mere conception of them. For the real object—the dollars—is not analytically contained in my conception, but forms a synthetical addition to my conception (which is merely a determination of my mental state), although this objective reality—this existence—apart from my conceptions, does not in the least degree increase the aforesaid hundred dollars.

By whatever and by whatever number of predicates—even to the complete determination of it—I may cogitate a thing, I do not in the least augment the object of my conception by the addition of the statement, this thing exists. Otherwise, not exactly the same, but something more than what was cogitated in my conception, would exist, and I could not affirm that the exact object of my conception had real existence. If I cogitate a thing as containing all modes of reality except one, the mode of reality which is absent is not added to the conception of the thing by the affirmation that the thing exists; on the contrary, the thing exists—if it exist at all—with the same defect as that cogitated in its conception; otherwise not that which was cogitated, but something different, exists. Now, if I cogitate a being as the highest reality, without defect or imperfection, the question still remains—whether this being exists or not? For although no element is wanting in the possible real content of my conception, there is a defect in its relation to my mental state, that is, I am ignorant whether the cognition of the object indicated by the conception is possible *a posteriori*. And here the cause of the present difficulty becomes apparent. If the question regarded an object of sense merely, it would be impossible for me to confound the conception with the existence of a thing. For the conception merely enables me to cogitate an object as according with the general conditions of experience; while the existence of the object permits me to cogitate it as contained in the sphere of actual experience. At the same time, this connection with the world of experience does not in the least augment the conception, although a possible perception has been added to the experience of the mind. But if we cogitate existence by the pure category alone, it is not to be wondered at, that we should find ourselves unable to present any criterion sufficient to distinguish it from mere possibility.

Whatever be the content of our conception of an object, it is necessary to go beyond it, if we wish to predicate existence of the object. In the case of sensuous objects, this is attained by their connection according to empirical laws with some one of my perceptions; but there is no means of cognizing the existence of objects of pure thought, because it must be cognized completely *a priori*. But all our knowledge of existence (be it immediately by perception, or by inferences connecting some object with a perception) belongs entirely to the sphere of experience—which is in perfect unity with itself; and although an existence out of this sphere cannot be absolutely declared to be impossible, it is a hypothesis the truth of which we have no means of ascertaining.

The notion of a Supreme Being is in many respects a highly useful idea; but for the very reason that it is an idea, it is incapable of enlarging our cognition with regard to the existence of things. It is not even sufficient to instruct us as to the possibility of a being which we do not know to exist. The analytical criterion of possibility, which consists in the absence of contradiction in propositions, cannot be denied it. But the connection of real properties in a thing is a synthesis of the possibility of which an *a priori* judgment cannot be formed, because these realities are not presented to us specifically; and even if this were to happen, a judgment would still be impossible, because the criterion of the possibility of synthetical cognitions must be sought for in the world of experience, to which the object of an idea cannot belong. And thus the celebrated Leibnitz has utterly failed in his attempt to establish upon *a priori* grounds the possibility of this sublime ideal being.

The celebrated ontological or Cartesian argument for the existence of a Supreme Being is therefore insufficient; and we may as well hope to increase our stock of knowledge by the aid of mere ideas, as the merchant to augment his wealth by the addition of noughts to his cash-account.

ALVIN PLANTINGA
A Modal Version of the Ontological Argument

The . . . theistic argument I wish to discuss is the famous "ontological argument" first formulated by Anselm of Canterbury in the eleventh century. This argument for the existence of God has fascinated philosophers ever since Anselm first stated it. Few people, I should think, have been brought to belief in God by means of this argument; nor has it played much of a role in strengthening and confirming religious faith. At first sight Anselm's argument is remarkably unconvincing if not downright irritating; it looks too much like a parlor puzzle or word magic. And yet nearly every major philosopher from the time of Anselm to the present has had something to say about it; this argument has a long and illustrious line of defenders extending to the present. Indeed, the last few years have seen a remarkable flurry of interest in it among philosophers. What accounts for its fascination? Not, I think, its religious significance, although that can be underrated. Perhaps there are two reasons for it. First, many of the most knotty and difficult problems in philosophy meet in this argument. Is existence a property? Are existential propositions—propositions of the form *x exists*—ever necessarily true? Are existential propositions about what they seem to be about? Are there, in any respectable sense of "are," some objects that do not exist? If so, do they have any properties? Can they be compared with things that do exist? These issues and a hundred others arise in connection with Anselm's argument. And second, although the argument certainly looks at first sight as if it ought to be unsound, it is profoundly difficult to say what, exactly, is wrong with it. Indeed, I do not believe that any philosopher has ever given a cogent and conclusive refutation of the ontological argument in its various forms.

Anselm states his argument as follows:

> And so, Lord, do thou, who dost give understanding to faith, give me, so far as thou knowest to be profitable, to understand that thou art as we believe; and that thou art that which we believe. And indeed, we believe that thou art a being than which nothing greater can be conceived. Or is there no such nature, since the fool hath

Alvin Plantinga (1932–) is John A. O'Brien Professor of Philosophy at the University of Notre Dame. His works in philosophy of religion, modal logic, and philosophy of mind have been widely influential. These include *God and Other Minds* and *The Nature of Necessity*.

A MODAL VERSION OF THE ONTOLOGICAL ARGUMENT   From *God, Freedom and Evil* (Harper & Row, 1974). Reprinted by permission of the author.

said in his heart, there is no God? . . . But, at any rate, this very fool when he hears of this being of which I speak—a being than which nothing greater can be conceived—understands what he hears, and what he understands is in his understanding, although he does not understand it to exist.

For, it is one thing for any object to be in the understanding, and another to understand that the object exists. When a painter first conceives of what he will afterwards perform, he has it in his understanding, but he does not yet understand it to be, because he has not yet performed it. But after he has made the painting, he both has it in his understanding, and he understands that it exists, because he has made it.

Hence, even the fool is convinced that something exists in the understanding, at least, than which nothing greater can be conceived. For when he hears of this, he understands it. And whatever is understood, exists in the understanding. And assuredly that, than which nothing greater can be conceived, cannot exist in the understanding alone. For, suppose it exists in the understanding alone; then it can be conceived to exist in reality; which is greater.

Therefore, if that, than which nothing greater can be conceived, exists in the understanding alone, the very being, than which nothing greater can be conceived, is one, than which a greater can be conceived. But obviously this is impossible. Hence, there is no doubt that there exists a being, than which nothing greater can be conceived, and it exists both in the understanding and in reality.[1]

At first sight, this argument smacks of trumpery and deceit; but suppose we look at it a bit more closely. Its essentials are contained in these words:

> And assuredly that, than which nothing greater can be conceived, cannot exist in the understanding alone. For suppose it exists in the understanding alone; then it can be conceived to exist in reality; which is greater.

> Therefore, if that, than which nothing greater can be conceived, exists in the understanding alone, the very being, than which nothing greater can be conceived, is one, than which a greater can be conceived. But obviously this is impossible. Hence there is no doubt that there exists a being, than which nothing greater can be conceived, and it exists both in the understanding and in reality.[2]

How can we outline this argument? It is best construed, I think, as a *reductio ad absurdum* argument. In a *reductio* you prove a given proposition *p* by showing that its denial, *not-p*, leads to (or more strictly, entails) a contradiction or some other kind of absurdity. Anselm's argument can be seen as an attempt to deduce an absurdity from the proposition that there is no God. If we use the term "God" as an abbreviation for Anselm's phrase "the being than which nothing greater can be conceived," then the argument seems to go approximately as follows: Suppose

(1) God exists in the understanding but not in reality.

(2) Existence in reality is greater than existence in the understanding alone. (premise)

[1] St. Anselm, *Proslogium*, chapter 2, in *The Ontological Argument*, ed. A. Plantinga (New York: Doubleday Anchor, 1965), pp. 3–4.

[2] Ibid., pp. 4.

(3) God's existence in reality is conceivable. (premise)

(4) If God did exist in reality, then He would be greater than He is. [from (1) and (2)]

(5) It is conceivable that there is a being greater than God is. [(3) and (4)]

(6) It is conceivable that there be a being greater than the being than which nothing greater can be conceived. [(5) by the definition of "God"]

But surely (6) is absurd and self-contradictory; how could we conceive of a being greater than the being than which none greater can be conceived? So we may conclude that

(7) It is false that God exists in the understanding but not in reality.

It follows that if God exists in the understanding, He also exists in reality; but clearly enough He *does* exist in the understanding, as even the fool will testify; therefore, He exists in reality as well.

Now when Anselm says that a being *exists in the understanding*, we may take him, I think, as saying that someone has *thought of* or thought about that being. When he says that something *exists in reality*, on the other hand, he means to say simply that the thing in question really does exist. And when he says that a certain state of affairs is *conceivable*, he means to say, I believe, that this state of affairs is possible in our broadly logical sense . . . ; there is a possible world in which it obtains. This means that step (3) above may be put more perspicuously as

(3′) It is possible that God exists

and step (6) as

(6′) It is possible that there be a being greater than the being than which it is not possible that there be a greater.

An interesting feature of this argument is that all of its premises are *necessarily* true if true at all (1) is the assumption from which Anselm means to deduce a contradiction. (2) is a premise, and presumably necessarily true in Anselm's view; and (3) is the only remaining premise (the other items are consequences of preceding steps); it says of some *other* proposition (*God exists*) that it is possible. Propositions which thus ascribe a modality—possibility, necessity, contingency—to another proposition are themselves either necessarily true or necessarily false. So all the premises of the argument are, if true at all, necessarily true. And hence if the premises of this argument are true, then [provided that (6) is really inconsistent] a contradiction can be deduced from (1) together with necessary propositions; this means that (1) entails a contradiction and is, therefore, necessarily false. . . .

3.   KANT'S OBJECTION

The most famous and important objection to the ontological argument is contained in Immanuel Kant's *Critique of Pure Reason*.[3] Kant begins his criticism as follows:

> If, in an identical proposition, I reject the predicate while retaining the subject, contradiction results; and I therefore say that the former belongs necessarily to the latter. But if we reject the subject and predicate alike, there is no contradiction; for nothing is then left that can be contradicted. To posit a triangle, and yet to reject its three angles, is self-contradictory; but there is no contradiction in rejecting the triangle together with its three angles. The same holds true of the concept of an absolutely necessary being. If its existence is rejected, we reject the thing itself with all its predicates; and no question of contradiction can then arise. There is nothing outside it that would then be contradicted, since the necessity of the thing is not supposed to be derived from anything external; nor is there anything internal that would be contradicted, since in rejecting the thing itself we have at the same time rejected all its internal properties. "God is omnipotent" is a necessary judgment. The omnipotence cannot be rejected if we posit a Deity, that is, an infinite being; for the two concepts are identical. But if we say "There is no God," neither the omnipotence nor any other of its predicates is given; they are one and all rejected together with the subject, and there is therefore not the least contradiction in such a judgment. . . .
>
> For I cannot form the least concept of a thing which, should it be rejected with all its predicates, leaves behind a contradiction.[4]

One characteristic feature of Anselm's argument, as we have seen, is that if successful, it establishes that *God exists* is a *necessary* proposition. Here Kant is apparently arguing that no *existential* proposition—one that asserts the existence of something or other—is necessarily true; the reason, he says, is that no *contra-existential* (the denial of an existential) is contradictory or inconsistent. But in which of our several senses of inconsistent? What he means to say, I believe, is that no existential proposition is necessary in the broadly logical sense. And this claim has been popular with philosophers ever since. But why, exactly, does Kant think it's true? What is the argument? When we take a careful look at the purported reasoning, it looks pretty unimpressive; it's hard to make out an argument at all. The conclusion would apparently be this: if we deny the existence of something or other, we can't be contradicting ourselves; no existential proposition is necessary and no contra-existential is impossible. Why not? Well, if we say, for example, that God does not exist, then says Kant, "There is nothing outside it (i.e., God) that would then be contradicted, since the necessity of the thing is not supposed to be derived from anything external; nor is there anything internal that would be contradicted, since in rejecting the thing itself we have at the same time rejected all its internal properties."

[3]Immanuel Kant, *Critique of Pure Reason*, ed. Norman Kemp Smith (New York: Macmillan Co., 1929). Some relevant passages are reprinted in Plantinga, *The Ontological Argument*, pp. 57–64.

[4]Plantinga, *The Ontological Argument*, p. 59.

But how is this even *relevant?* The claim is that *God does not exist* can't be necessarily false. What could be meant, in this context, by saying that there's nothing "outside of" God that would be contradicted if we denied His existence? What would contradict a proposition like *God does not exist* is some other proposition—*God does exist*, for example. Kant seems to think that if the proposition in question *were* necessarily false, it would have to contradict, not a proposition, but some *object* external to God—or else contradict some internal part or aspect or property of God. But this certainly looks like confusion; it is *propositions* that contradict each other; they aren't contradicted by objects or parts, aspects or properties of objects. Does he mean instead to be speaking of *propositions* about things external to God, or about his aspects or parts or properties? But clearly many such propositions do contradict *God does not exist;* an example would be *the world was created by God.* Does he mean to say that no *true* proposition contradicts *God does not exist?* No, for that would be to affirm the *nonexistence* of God, an affirmation Kant is by no means prepared to make.

So this passage is an enigma. Either Kant was confused or else he expressed himself very badly indeed. And either way we don't have any argument for the claim that contra-existential propositions can't be inconsistent. This passage seems to be no more than an elaborate and confused way of *asserting* this claim.

The heart of Kant's objection to the ontological argument, however, is contained in the following passage:

> "Being" is obviously not a real predicate; that is, it is not a concept of something which could be added to the concept of a thing. It is merely the positing of a thing, or of certain determinations, as existing in themselves. Logically, it is merely the copula of a judgment. The proposition "God is omnipotent" contains two concepts, each of which has its object—God and omnipotence. The small word "is" adds no new predicate, but only serves to posit the predicate in its relation to the subject. If, now, we take the subject (God) with all its predicates (among which is omnipotence), and say "God is," or "There is a God," we attach no new predicate to the concept of God, but only posit it as an object that stands in relation to my concept. The content of both must be one and the same; nothing can have been added to the concept, which expresses merely what is possible, by my thinkings its object (through the expression "it is") as given absolutely. Otherwise stated, the real contains no more than the merely possible. A hundred real thalers does not contain the least coin more than a hundred possible thalers. For as the latter signify the concept and the former the object and the positing of the concept, should the former contain more than the latter, my concept would not, in that case, express the whole object, and would not therefore be an adequate concept of it. My financial position, however, is affected very differently by a hundred real thalers than it is by the mere concept of them (that is, of the possibility). For the object, as it actually exists, is not analytically contained in my concept, but is added to my concept (which is a determination of my state) synthetically; and yet the conceived hundred thalers are not themselves in the least increased through thus acquiring existence outside my concept.
>
> By whatever and by however many predicates we may think a thing—even if we completely determine it—we do not make the least addition to the thing when we further declare that this thing is. Otherwise it would not be exactly the same thing

that exists, but something more than we had thought in the concept: and we could not, therefore, say that the object of my concept exists. If we think in a thing every feature of reality except one, the missing reality is not added by my saying that this defective thing exists.[5]

Now how, exactly is all this relevant to Anselm's argument? Perhaps Kant means to make a point that we could put by saying that it's not possible to *define things into existence*. (People sometimes suggest that the ontological argument is just such an attempt to define *God* into existence.) And this claim is somehow connected with Kant's famous but perplexing *dictum* that *being* (or existence) is not a real predicate or property. But how shall we understand Kant here? What does it mean to say that existence isn't (or is) a real property?

Apparently Kant thinks this is equivalent to or follows from what he puts variously as "the real *contains* no more than the merely possible"; "the *content* of both (i.e., concept and object) must be one and the same"; "being is not the concept of something that could be *added to* the concept of a thing," and so on. But what does all this mean? And how does it bear on the ontological argument? Perhaps Kant is thinking along the following lines. In defining a concept—*bachelor*, let's say, or *prime number*—one lists a number of properties that are *severally necessary* and *jointly sufficient* for the concept's applying to something. That is, the concept applies to a given thing only if that thing has each of the listed properties, and if a thing does have them all, then the concept in question applies to it. So, for example, to define the concept *bachelor* we list such properties as *being unmarried, being male, being over the age of twenty-five*, and the like. Take any one of these properties: a thing is a bachelor only if it has it, and if a thing has all of them, then it follows that it is a bachelor.

Now suppose you have a concept C that has application *contingently* if at all. That is to say, it is not necessarily true that there are things to which this concept applies. The concept *bachelor* would be an example; the proposition *there are bachelors*, while *true*, is obviously not necessarily true. And suppose $P_1, P_2 \ldots ,$ P_n are the properties jointly sufficient and severally necessary for something's falling under C. Then C can be defined as follows:

A thing x is an instance of C (i.e., C applies to x) if and only if x has P_1, P_2 $\ldots , P_n.$

Perhaps Kant's point is this. There is a certain kind of mistake here we may be tempted to make. Suppose $P_1, \ldots , P_n$ are the defining properties for the concept *bachelor*. We might try to define a new concept *superbachelor* by adding *existence* to $P_1, \ldots , P_n$. That is, we might say

x is a superbachelor if and only if x has $P_1, P_2, \ldots , P_n$, and x exists.

Then (as we might mistakenly suppose) just as it is a necessary truth that bachelors are unmarried, so it is a necessary truth that superbachelors exist. And in this way it looks as if we've defined superbachelors into existence.

[5] Ibid., pp. 61–62.

But of course this is a mistake, and perhaps that is Kant's point. For while indeed it is a necessary truth that bachelors are unmarried, what this means is that the proposition

(8) Everything that is a bachelor is unmarried

is necessarily true. Similarly, then,

(9) Everything that is a superbachelor exists

will be necessarily true. But obviously it doesn't follow that there *are* any super-bachelors. All that follows is that

(10) All the superbachelors there are *exist*

which is not really very startling. If it is a contingent truth, furthermore, that there are bachelors, it will be equally contingent that there are superbachelors. We can see this by noting that the defining properties of the concept *bachelor* are included among those of *superbachelor*; it is a necessary truth, therefore, that every superbachelor is a bachelor. This means that

(11) There are some superbachelors

entails

(12) There are some bachelors.

But then if (12) is contingent, so is (11). Indeed, the concepts *bachelor* and *super-bachelor* are equivalent in the following sense: it is impossible that there exists an object to which one but not the other of these two concepts applies. We've just seen that every superbachelor must be a bachelor. Conversely, however, every bachelor is a superbachelor: for every bachelor exists and every existent bachelor is a superbachelor. Now perhaps we can put Kant's point more exactly. Suppose we say that a property or predicate P is *real* only if there is some list of properties P_1 to P_n such that the result of adding P to the list does not define a concept equivalent (in the above sense) to that defined by the list. It then follows, of course, that existence is not a real property or predicate. Kant's point, then, is that one cannot *define things into existence* because *existence* is not a real property or predicate in the explained sense.[6]

4.   THE IRRELEVANCE OF KANT'S OBJECTION

If this is what he means, he's certainly right. But is it relevant to the ontological argument? Couldn't Anselm thank Kant for this interesting point and proceed

[6] For a more detailed and extensive discussion of this argument, see Plantinga, *God and Other Minds*, pp. 29–38 and A. Plantinga, "Kant's Objection to the Ontological Argument," *Journal of Philosophy* 63 (1966): 537.

merrily on his way? Where did he try to define God into being by adding existence to a list of properties that defined some concept? According to the great German philosopher and pessimist Arthur Schopenhauer, the ontological argument arises when "someone excogitates a conception, composed out of all sorts of predicates, among which, however, he takes care to include the predicate actuality or existence, either openly or wrapped up for decency's sake in some other predicate, such as perfection, immensity, or something of the kind." If this were Anselm's procedure—if he had simply added existence to a concept that has application contingently if at all—then indeed his argument would be subject to the Kantian criticism. But he didn't, and it isn't.

The usual criticisms of Anselm's argument, then, leave much to be desired. Of course, this doesn't mean that the argument is successful, but it does mean that we shall have to take an independent look at it. What about Anselm's argument? Is it a good one? The first thing to recognize is that the ontological argument comes in an enormous variety of versions, some of which may be much more promising than others. Instead of speaking of *the* ontological argument, we must recognize that what we have here is a whole family of related arguments. (Having said this I shall violate my own directive and continue to speak of *the* ontological argument.)

5.   THE ARGUMENT RESTATED

Let's look once again at our initial schematization of the argument. I think perhaps it is step (2)

(2) Existence in reality is greater than existence in the understanding alone

that is most puzzling here. Earlier we spoke of the properties in virtue of which one being is greater, just as a being, than another. Suppose we call them *great-making properties*. Apparently Anselm means to suggest that *existence* is a great-making property. He seems to suggest that a nonexistent being would be greater than in fact it is, if it did exist. But how can we make sense of that? How could there be a nonexistent being anyway? Does that so much as make sense?

Perhaps we can put this perspicuously in terms of possible worlds. You recall that an object may exist in some possible worlds and not others. There are possible worlds in which you and I do not exist; these worlds are impoverished, no doubt, but are not on that account impossible. Furthermore, you recall that an object can have different properties in different worlds. In the actual world Paul J. Zwier is not a good tennis player; but surely there are worlds in which he wins the Wimbledon Open. Now if a person can have different properties in different worlds, then he can have different degrees of greatness in different worlds. In the actual world Raquel Welch has impressive assets; but there is a world RW_f in which she is fifty pounds overweight and mousy. Indeed, there are worlds in which she does not so much as exist. What Anselm means to be suggesting, I think, is that Raquel Welch enjoys very little greatness in those worlds in which she does not exist. But of course this condition is not restricted to Miss Welch.

What Anselm means to say, more generally, is that for any being x and worlds W and W', if x exists in W but not in W', then x's greatness in W exceeds x's greatness in W'. Or, more modestly, perhaps he means to say that if a being x does not exist in a world W (and there is a world in which x does exist), then *there is at least one world* in which the greatness of x exceeds the greatness of x in W. Suppose Raquel Welch does not exist in some world W. Anselm means to say that there is at least one possible world in which she has a degree of greatness that exceeds the degree of greatness she has in that world W. (It is plausible, indeed, to go much further and hold that she has *no greatness at all* in worlds in which she does not exist.)

But now perhaps we can restate the whole argument in a way that gives us more insight into its real structure. Once more, use the term "God" to abbreviate the phrase "the being than which it is not possible that there be a greater." Now suppose

(13) God does not exist in the actual world.

Add the new version of premise (2):

(14) For any being x and world W, if x does not exist in W, then there is a world W' such that the greatness of x in W' exceeds the greatness of x in W.

Restate premise (3) in terms of possible worlds:

(15) There is a possible world in which God exists.

And continue on:

(16) If God does not exist in the actual world, then there is a world W' such that the greatness of God in W' exceeds the greatness of God in the actual world. [from (14)]
(17) So there is a world W' such that the greatness of God in W' exceeds the greatness of God in the actual world. [(13) and (16)]
(18) So there is a possible being x and a world W' such that the greatness of x in W' exceeds the greatness of God in actuality. [(17)]
(19) Hence it's possible that there be a being greater than God is. [(18)]
(20) So it's possible that there be a being greater than the being than which it's not possible that there be a greater. (19), replacing "God" by what it abbreviates

But surely

(21) It's not possible that there be a being greater than the being than which it's not possible that there be a greater.

So (13) [with the help of premises (14) and (15)] appears to imply (20), which, according to (21), is necessarily false. Accordingly, (13) is false. So the actual world contains a being than which it's not possible that there be a greater—that is, God exists.

Now where, if anywhere, can we fault this argument? Step (13) is the hypothesis for *reductio*, the assumption to be reduced to absurdity, and is thus entirely above reproach. Steps (16) through (20) certainly look as if they follow from the items they are said to follow them. So that leaves only (14), (15), and (20). Step (14) says only that it is possible that God exists. Step (15) also certainly seems plausible: if a being doesn't even *exist* in a given world, it can't have much by way of greatness in that world. At the very least it can't have its *maximum* degree of greatness—a degree of greatness that it does not excel in any other world—in a world where it doesn't exist. And consider (20): surely it has the ring of truth. How could there be a being greater than the being than which it's not possible that there be a greater? Initially, the argument seems pretty formidable.

6.   ITS FATAL FLAW

But there is something puzzling about it. We can see this if we ask what sorts of things (14) is supposed to be *about*. It starts off boldly: "For any being x and world W, . . ." So (14) is talking about worlds and beings. It says something about each world-being pair. And (16) follows from it, because (16) asserts of *God* and *the actual world* something that according to (14) holds of every being and world. But then if (16) follows from (14), God must be a *being*. That is, (16) follows from (14) only with the help of the additional premise that God is a being. And doesn't this statement—that God is a being—imply that *there is* or *exists* a being than which it's not possible that there be a greater? But if so, the argument flagrantly begs the question; for then we can accept the inference from (14) to (16) only if we already know that the conclusion is true.

We can approach this same matter by a slightly different route. I asked earlier what sorts of things (14) was *about*; the answer was: beings and worlds. We can ask the same or nearly the same question by asking about the *range* of the *quantifiers*—"for any being," "for any world"—in (14). What do these quantifiers range over? If we reply that they range over possible worlds and beings—*actually existing beings*—then the inference to (16) requires the additional premise that God is an actually existing being, that there *really is* a being than which it is not possible that there be a greater. Since this is supposed to be our conclusion, we can't very gracefully add it as a *premise*. So perhaps the quantifiers don't range just over actually existing beings. But what else is there? Step (18) speaks of a *possible being*—a thing that may not in fact exist, but *could* exist. Or we could put it like this. A possible being is a thing that exists in some possible world or other; a thing x for which there is a world W, such that if W had been actual, x would have existed. So (18) is really about worlds and *possible beings*. And what it says is this: take any possible being x and any possible world W. If x does not exist in W, then there is a possible world W′ where x has a degree of greatness that surpasses the greatness that it has in W. And hence to make the argument complete perhaps we should add the affirmation that God is a *possible being*.

But *are* there any possible beings—that is, *merely* possible beings, beings that don't in fact exist? If so, what sorts of things are they? Do they have properties? How are we to think of them? What is their status? And what reasons are there for supposing that there are any such peculiar items at all?

These are knotty problems. Must we settle them in order even to consider this argument? No. For instead of speaking of *possible beings* and the worlds in which they do or don't exist, we can speak of *properties* and the worlds in which they do or don't *have instances*, are or are not *instantiated* or exemplified. Instead of speaking of a possible being named by the phrase, "the being than which it's not possible that there be a greater," we may speak of the property *having an unsurpassable degree of greatness—that is, having a degree of greatness such that it's not possible that there exist a being having more*. And then we can ask whether this property is instantiated in this or other possible worlds. Later on I shall show how to restate the argument this way. For the moment please take my word for the fact that we can speak as freely as we wish about possible objects; for we can always translate ostensible talk about such things into talk about properties and the worlds in which they are or are not instantiated.

The argument speaks, therefore, of an unsurpassably great being—of a being whose greatness is not excelled by any being in any world. This being has a degree of greatness so impressive that no other being in any world has more. But here we hit the question crucial for this version of the argument. *Where* does this being have that degree of greatness? I said above that the same being may have different degrees of greatness in different worlds; in which world does the possible being in question have the degree of greatness in question? All we are really told, in being told that God is a possible being, is this: among the possible beings there is one that in some world or other has a degree of greatness that is nowhere excelled.

And this fact is fatal to this version of the argument. I said earlier that (21) has the ring of truth; a closer look (listen?) reveals that it's more of a dull thud. For it is ambiguous as between

(21') It's not possible that there be a being whose greatness surpasses that enjoyed by the unsurpassably great being *in the worlds where its greatness is at a maximum*

and

(21") It's not possible that there be a being whose greatness surpasses that enjoyed by the unsurpassably great being *in the actual world*.

There is an important difference between these two. The greatest possible being may have different degrees of greatness in different worlds. Step (21') points to the worlds in which this being has its maximal greatness; and it says, quite properly, that the degree of greatness this being has in those worlds is nowhere excelled. Clearly this is so. The greatest possible being is a possible being who in some world or other has unsurpassable greatness. Unfortunately for the argument, however, (21') does not contradict (20). Or to put it another way, what follows from (13) [together with (14) and (15)] is not the denial of (21'). If that *did* follow, then the *reductio* would be complete and the argument successful. But what (20) says is not that there is a possible being whose greatness exceeds that enjoyed by the greatest possible being *in a world where the latter's greatness is at a maximum*; it says only that there is a possible being whose greatness exceeds that enjoyed by the greatest possible being *in the actual world*—where, for all we know, its greatness is *not* at a maximum. So if we read (21) as (21'), the *reductio* argument falls apart.

Suppose instead we read it as (21"). Then what it says is that there couldn't be a being whose greatness surpasses that enjoyed by the greatest possible being in Kronos, the actual world. So read, (21) does contradict (20). Unfortunately, however, we have no reason, so far, for thinking that (21") is true at all, let alone necessarily true. If, among the possible beings, there is one whose greatness *in some world or other* is absolutely maximal—such that no being in any world has a degree of greatness surpassing it—then indeed there couldn't be a being that was greater than *that*. But it doesn't follow that this being has that degree of greatness in the *actual* world. It has it *in some world or other* but not necessarily in Kronos, the actual world. And so the argument fails. If we take (21) as (21'), then it follows from the assertion that God is a possible being; but it is of no use to the argument. If we take it as (21"), on the other hand, then indeed it is useful in the argument, but we have no reason whatever to think it true. So this version of the argument fails.[7]

7.   A MODAL VERSION OF THE ARGUMENT

But of course there are many other versions; one of the argument's chief features is its many-sided diversity. The fact that *this* version is unsatisfactory does not show that *every* version is or must be. Professors Charles Hartshorne[8] and Norman Malcolm[9] claim to detect two quite different versions of the argument in Anselm's work. In the first of these versions *existence* is held to be a perfection or a great-making property; in the second it is *necessary existence*. But what could *that* amount to? Perhaps something like this. Consider a pair of beings A and B that both do in fact exist. And suppose that A exists in every other possible world as well—that is, if any other possible world has been actual, A would have existed. On the other hand, B exists in only some possible worlds; there are worlds W such that had any of *them* been actual, B would not have existed. Now according to the doctrine under consideration, A is so far greater than B. Of course, *on balance* it may be that A is not greater than B; I believe that the number seven, unlike Spiro Agnew, exists in every possible world; yet I should be hesitant to affirm on that

---

[7]This criticism of this version of the argument essentially follows David Lewis, "Anselm and Actuality," *Nous* 4 (1970): 175–188. See also Plantinga, *The Nature of Necessity*, pp. 202–205.

[8]Charles Hartshorne, *Man's Vision of God* (New York: Harper and Row, 1941). Portions reprinted in Plantinga, *The Ontological Argument*, pp. 123–135.

[9]Norman Malcolm, "Anselm's Ontological Arguments," *Philosophical Review* 69 (1960); reprinted in Plantinga, *The Ontological Argument*, pp. 136–159.

account that the number seven is greater than Agnew. Necessary existence is just one of several great-making properties, and no doubt Agnew has more of some of these others than does the number seven. Still, all this is compatible with saying that necessary existence is a great-making property. And given this notion, we can restate the argument as follows:

(22) It is possible that there is a greatest possible being.

(23) Therefore, there is a possible being that in some world W' or other has a maximum degree of greatness—a degree of greatness that is nowhere exceeded.

(24) A being B has the maximum degree of greatness in a given possible world W only if B *exists in every possible world*.

(22) and (24) are the premises of this argument; and what follows is that if W' had been actual, B would have existed in every possible world. That is, if W' had been actual, B's nonexistence would have been impossible. But logical possibilities and impossibilities do not vary from world to world. That is to say, if a given proposition or state of affairs is impossible in at least one possible world, then it is impossible in every possible world. There are no propositions that in fact are possible but could have been impossible; there are none that are in fact impossible but could have been possible.[10] Accordingly, B's nonexistence is impossible in every possible world; hence it is impossible in *this* world; hence B exists and exists necessarily.

8.   A FLAW IN THE OINTMENT

This is an interesting argument, but it suffers from at least one annoying defect. What it shows is that if it is possible that there be a greatest possible being (if the idea of a greatest possible being is coherent) and if that idea includes necessary existence, then in fact there is a being that exists in every world and in *some* world has a degree of greatness that is nowhere excelled. Unfortunately it doesn't follow that the being in question has the degree of greatness in question in Kronos, the actual world. For all the argument shows, this being might *exist* in the actual world but be pretty insignificant here. In some world or other it has maximal greatness; how does this show that it has such greatness in Kronos?

But perhaps we can repair the argument. J. N. Findlay once offered what can only be called an ontological *disproof* of the existence of God.[11] Findlay begins by pointing out that God, if He exists, is an "adequate object of religious worship." But such a being, he says, would have to be a *necessary* being; and, he adds, this idea is incredible "for all who share a contemporary outlook." "Those who believe in necessary truths which aren't merely tautological think that such

[10] See Plantinga, "World and Essence," *Philosophical Review* 79 (October 1970): 475; and Plantinga, *The Nature of Necessity*, chap. 4, sec. 6.

[11] J. N. Findlay, "Can God's Existence Be Disproved?" *Mind* 57 (1948): 176–183. Reprinted in ed., Plantinga, *The Ontological Argument*, pp. 111–122.

truths merely connect the *possible* instances of various characteristics with each other; they don't expect such truths to tell them whether there *will* be instances of any characteristics. This is the outcome of the whole medieval and Kantian criticism of the ontological proof." [12] I've argued above that "the whole medieval and Kantian criticism" of Anselm's argument may be taken with a grain or two of salt. And certainly most philosophers who believe that there are necessary truths, believe that *some* of them *do* tell us whether there will be instances of certain characteristics; the proposition *there are no married bachelors* is necessarily true, and it tells us that there will be no instances whatever of the characteristic *married bachelor*. Be that as it may what is presently relevant in Findlay's piece is this passage:

> Not only is it contrary to the demands and claims inherent in religious attitudes that their object should *exist* "accidentally"; it is also contrary to these demands that it should *possess its various excellences* in some merely adventitious manner. It would be quite unsatisfactory from the religious stand point, if an object merely *happened* to be wise, good, powerful, and so forth, even to a superlative degree. . . . And so we are led on irresistibly, by the demands inherent in religious reverence, to hold that an adequate object of our worship must possess its various excellences *in some necessary manner.* [13]

I think there is truth in these remarks. We could put the point as follows. In determining the greatness of a being *B* in a world *W*, what counts is not merely the qualities and properties possessed by *B in W*; what *B* is like in *other* worlds is also relevant. Most of us who believe in God think of Him as a being than whom it's not possible that there be a greater. But we don't think of Him as a being who, had things been different, would have been powerless or uninformed or of dubious moral character. God doesn't *just happen* to be a greatest possible being; He couldn't have been otherwise.

Perhaps we should make a distinction here between *greatness* and *excellence*. A being's excellence in a given world *W*, let us say, depends only upon the properties it has in *W*; its *greatness* in *W* depends upon these properties but also upon what it is like in other worlds. Those who are fond of the calculus might put it by saying that there is a function assigning to each being in each world a degree of excellence; and a being's *greatness* is to be computed (by someone unusually well informed) by integrating its excellence over all possible worlds. Then it is plausible to suppose that the maximal degree of greatness entails *maximal excellence in every world.* A being, then, has the maximal degree of *greatness* in a given world *W* only if it has *maximal excellence in every possible world.* But *maximal excellence* entails *omniscience, omnipotence,* and *moral perfection.* That is to say, a being *B* has maximal excellence in a world *W* only if *B* has omniscience, omnipotence, and moral perfection in *W*—only if *B* would have been omniscient, omnipotent, and morally perfect if *W* had been actual.

---

[12] P. 119. Mr. Findlay no longer endorses this sentiment. See the preface to his *Ascent to the Absolute* (1970).

[13] J. N. Findlay, "Can God's Existence Be Disproved?" p. 117.

9.   THE ARGUMENT RESTATED

Given these ideas, we can restate the present version of the argument in the following more explicit way.

(25) It is possible that there be a being that has maximal greatness.

(26) So there is a possible being that in some world W has maximal greatness.

(27) A Being has maximal greatness in a given world only if it has maximal excellence in every world.

(28) A being has maximal excellence in a given world only if it has omniscience, omnipotence, and moral perfection in that world.

And now we no longer need the supposition that necessary existence is a perfection; for obviously a being can't be omnipotent (or for that matter omniscient or morally perfect) in a given world unless it *exists* in that world. From (25), (27), and (28) it follows that there actually exists a being that is omnipotent, omniscient, and morally perfect; this being, furthermore, exists and has these qualities in every other world as well. For (26), which follows from (25), tells us that there is a possible world W', let's say, in which there exists a being with maximal greatness. That is, had W' been actual, there would have been a being with maximal greatness. But then according to (27) this being has maximal excellence in every world. What this means, according to (28), is that in W' this being has omniscience, omnipotence, and moral perfection *in every world*. That is to say, if W' had been actual, there would have existed a being who was omniscient and omnipotent and morally perfect and who would have had these properties in every possible world. So if W' had been actual, it would have been *impossible* that there be no omnipotent, omniscient, and morally perfect being. But (see above, p. 112) while *contingent* truths vary from world to world, what is logically impossible does not. Therefore, in every possible world W it is impossible that there be no such being; each possible world W is such that if it had been actual, it would have been impossible that there be no such being. And hence it is impossible in the *actual* world (which is one of the possible worlds) that there be no omniscient, omnipotent, and morally perfect being. Hence there really does exist a being who is omniscient, omnipotent, and morally perfect and who exists and has these properties in every possible world. Accordingly these premises, (25), (27), and (28), entail that God, so thought of, exists. Indeed, if we regard (27) and (28) as consequences of a *definition*—a definition of maximal greatness—then the only premise of the argument is (25).

But now for a last objection suggested earlier (p. 119). What about (26)? It says that there is a *possible being* having such and such characteristics. But what *are* possible beings? We know what *actual* beings are—the Taj Mahal, Socrates, you and I, the Grand Teton—these are among the more impressive examples of actually existing beings. But what is a *possible* being? Is there a possible mountain just like Mt. Rainier two miles directly south of the Grand Teton? If so, it is located at the same place as the Middle Teton. Does that matter? Is there another such possible mountain three miles east of the Grand Teton, where Jenny Lake is? Are there possible mountains like this all over the world? Are there also possible oceans at all the places where there are possible mountains? For any place you mention, of course, it is *possible* that there be a mountain there; does it follow that in fact *there is* a possible mountain there?

These are some questions that arise when we ask ourselves whether there are merely possible beings that don't in fact exist. And the version of the ontological argument we've been considering seems to make sense only on the assumption that there are such things. The earlier versions also depended on that assumption; consider, for example, this step of the first version we considered:

(18) So there is a possible being x and a world W' such that the greatness of x in W' exceeds the greatness of God in actuality.

This possible being, you recall, was God Himself, supposed not to exist in the actual world. We can make sense of (18), therefore, only if we are prepared to grant that there are possible beings who don't in fact exist. Such beings exist in other worlds, of course; had things been appropriately different, they would have existed. But in fact they don't exist, although nonetheless there *are* such things.

I am inclined to think the supposition that there are such things—things that are possible but don't in fact exist—is either unintelligible or necessarily false. But this doesn't mean that the present version of the ontological argument must be rejected. For we can restate the argument in a way that does not commit us to this questionable idea. Instead of speaking of *possible beings* that do or do not exist in various possible worlds, we may speak of *properties* and the worlds in which they are or are not *instantiated*. Instead of speaking of the possible fat man in the corner, noting that he doesn't exist, we may speak of the property *being a fat man in the corner*, noting that it isn't instantiated (although it could have been). Of course, the *property* in question, like the property *being a unicorn*, exists. It is a perfectly good property which exists with as much equanimity as the property of equininity, the property of being a horse. But it doesn't happen to apply to anything. That is, in *this* world it doesn't apply to anything; in other possible words it does.

10.   THE ARGUMENT TRIUMPHANT

Using this idea we can restate this last version of the ontological argument in such a way that it no longer matters whether there are any merely possible beings that do not exist. Instead of speaking of the possible being that has, in some world or other, a maximal degree of greatness, we may speak of *the property of being maximally great* or *maximal greatness*. The premise corresponding to (25) then says simply that maximal greatness is possibly instantiated, i.e., that

(29) There is a possible world in which maximal greatness is instantiated.

And the analogues of (27) and (28) spell out what is involved in maximal greatness:

(30) Necessarily, a being is maximally great only if it has maximal excellence in every world

and

(31) Necessarily, a being has maximal excellence in every world only if it has omniscience, omnipotence, and moral perfection in every world.

Notice that (30) and (31) do not imply that there are possible but nonexistent beings—any more than does, for example,

(32) Necessarily, a thing is a unicorn only if it has one horn.

But if (29) is true, then there is a possible world W such that if it had been actual, then there would have existed a being that was omnipotent, omniscient, and morally perfect; this being, furthermore, would have had these qualities in every possible world. So it follows that if W had been actual, it would have been *impossible* that there be no such being. That is, if W had been actual,

(33) There is no omnipotent, omniscient, and morally perfect being

would have been an impossible proposition. But if a proposition is impossible in at least one possible world, then it is impossible in every possible world; what is impossible does not vary from world to world. Accordingly (33) is impossible in the *actual* world, i.e., impossible *simpliciter*. But if it is impossible that there be no such being, then there actually exists a being that is omnipotent, omniscient, and morally perfect; this being, furthermore, has these qualities essentially and exists in every possible world.

What shall we say of this argument? It is certainly valid; given its premise, the conclusion follows. The only question of interest, it seems to me, is whether its main premise—that maximal greatness *is* possibly instantiated—is *true*. I think it *is* true; hence I think this version of the ontological argument is sound.

But here we must be careful; we must ask whether this argument is a successful piece of natural theology, whether it *proves* the existence of God. And the answer must be, I think, that it does not. An argument for God's existence may be *sound*, after all, without in any useful sense proving God's existence.[14] Since I believe in God, I think the following argument is sound:

Either God exists or $7 + 5 = 14$
It is false that $7 + 5 = 14$
Therefore God exists.

[14] See George Mavrodes, *Belief in God* (New York: Macmillan Co., 1970), pp. 22ff.

But obviously this isn't a *proof*; no one who didn't already accept the conclusion, would accept the first premise. The ontological argument we've been examining isn't just like this one, of course, but it must be conceded that not everyone who understands and reflects on its central premise—that the existence of a maximally great being is *possible*—will accept it. Still, it is evident, I think, that there is nothing *contrary* to *reason* or *irrational* in accepting this premise.[15] What I claim for this argument, therefore, is that it establishes, not the *truth* of theism, but its rational acceptability. And hence it accomplishes at least one of the aims of the tradition of natural theology.

[15] For more on this see Plantinga, *The Nature of Necessity*, chap. 10, sec. 8.

THE COSMOLOGICAL
ARGUMENT

ST. THOMAS AQUINAS
The Existence of God and the Beginning of the World

THIRD ARTICLE.   WHETHER GOD EXISTS?

We proceed thus to the Third Article:—

Objection 1. It seems that God does not exist; because if one of two contraries be infinite, the other would be altogether destroyed. But the name *God* means that He is infinite goodness. If, therefore, God existed, there would be no evil discoverable; but there is evil in the world. Therefore God does not exist.

Obj. 2. Further, it is superfluous to suppose that what can be accounted for by a few principles has been produced by many. But it seems that everything we see in the world can be accounted for by other principles, supposing God did not exist. For all natural things can be reduced to one principle, which is nature; and all voluntary things can be reduced to one principle, which is human reason, or will. Therefore there is no need to suppose God's existence.

On the contrary, It is said in the person of God: *I am Who am (Exod. iii. 14).*

I answer that, The existence of God can be proved in five ways.

The first and more manifest way is the argument from motion. It is certain, and evident to our senses, that in the world some things are in motion. Now whatever is moved is moved by another, for nothing can be moved except it is in potentiality to that towards which it is moved; whereas a thing moves inasmuch as it is in act. For motion is nothing else than the reduction of something from potentiality to actuality. But nothing can be reduced from potentiality to actuality, except by something in a state of actuality. Thus that which is actually hot, as fire, makes wood, which is potentially hot, to be actually hot, and thereby moves and changes it. Now it is not possible that the same thing should be at once in

THE EXISTENCE OF GOD AND THE BEGINNING OF THE WORLD   From *Summa Theologica*, Part I, Questions 2 and 46, in *Basic Writings of Saint Thomas Aquinas*, edited by Anton C. Pegis. By permission of the A. C. Pegis estate.

actuality and potentiality in the same respect, but only in different respects. For what is actually hot cannot simultaneously be potentially hot; but it is simultaneously potentially cold. It is therefore impossible that in the same respect and in the same way a thing should be both mover and moved, *i.e.*, that it should move itself. Therefore, whatever is moved must be moved by another. If that by which it is moved be itself moved, then this also must needs be moved by another, and that by another again. But this cannot go on to infinity, because then there would be no first mover, and, consequently, no other mover, seeing that subsequent movers move only inasmuch as they are moved by the first mover; as the staff moves only because it is moved by the hand. Therefore it is necessary to arrive at a first mover, moved by no other; and this everyone understands to be God.

The second way is from the nature of efficient cause. In the world of sensible things we find there is an order of efficient causes. There is no case known (neither is it, indeed, possible) in which a thing is found to be the efficient cause of itself; for so it would be prior to itself, which is impossible. Now in efficient causes it is not possible to go on to infinity, because in all efficient causes following in order, the first is the cause of the intermediate cause, and the intermediate is the cause of the ultimate cause, whether the intermediate cause be several, or one only. Now to take away the cause is to take away the effect. Therefore, if there be no first cause among efficient causes, there will be no ultimate, nor any intermediate, cause. But if in efficient causes it is possible to go on to infinity, there will be no first efficient cause, neither will there be an ultimate effect, nor any intermediate efficient causes; all of which is plainly false. Therefore it is necessary to admit a first efficient cause, to which everyone gives the name of God.

The third way is taken from possibility and necessity, and runs thus. We find in nature things that are possible to be and not to be, since they are found to be generated, and to be corrupted, and consequently, it is possible for them to be and not to be. But it is impossible for these always to exist, for that which can not-be at some time is not. Therefore, if everything can not-be, then at one time there was nothing in existence. Now if this were true, even now there would be nothing in existence, because that which does not exist begins to exist only through something already existing. Therefore, if at one time nothing was in existence, it would have been impossible for anything to have begun to exist; and thus even now nothing would be in existence—which is absurd. Therefore, not all beings are merely possible, but there must exist something the existence of which is necessary. But every necessary thing either has its necessity caused by another, or not. Now it is impossible to go on to infinity in necessary things which have their necessity caused by another, as has been already proved in regard to efficient causes. Therefore we cannot but admit the existence of some being having of itself its own necessity, and not receiving it from another, but rather causing in others their necessity. This all men speak of as God.

The fourth way is taken from the gradation to be found in things. Among beings there are some more and some less good, true, noble, and the like. But *more* and *less* are predicated of different things according as they resemble in their different ways something which is the maximum, as a thing is said to be hotter according as it more nearly resembles that which is hottest; so that there is something which is truest, something best, something noblest, and, consequently, something which is most being, for those things that are greatest in truth are greatest in being, as it is written in *Metaph*. ii.[1] Now the maximum in any genus is the cause of all in that genus, as fire, which is the maximum of heat, is the cause of all hot things, as is said in the same book.[2] Therefore there must also be something which is to all beings the cause of their being, goodness, and every other perfection; and this we call God.

The fifth way is taken from the governance of the world. We see that things which lack knowledge, such as natural bodies, act for an end, and this is evident from their acting always, or nearly always, in the same way, so as to obtain the best result. Hence it is plain that they achieve their end, not fortuitously, but designedly. Now whatever lacks knowledge cannot move towards an end, unless it be directed by some being endowed with knowledge and intelligence; as the arrow is directed by the archer. Therefore some intelligent being exists by whom all natural things are directed to their end; and this being we call God.

Reply Obj. 1. As Augustine says: *Since God is the highest good, He would not allow any evil to exist in His words, unless His omnipotence and goodness were such as to bring good even out of evil.*[3] This is part of the infinite goodness of God, that He should allow evil to exist, and out of it produce good.

Reply Obj. 2. Since nature works for a determinate end under the direction of a higher agent, whatever is done by nature must be traced back to God as to its first cause. So likewise whatever is done voluntarily must be traced back to some higher cause other than human reason and will, since these can change and fail; for all things that are changeable and capable of defect must be traced back to an immovable and self-necessary first principle, as has been shown. . . .

SECOND ARTICLE.   WHETHER IT IS AN ARTICLE OF FAITH THAT THE WORLD BEGAN?

We proceed thus to the Second Article:—

Objection 1. It would seem that it is not an article of faith but a demonstrable conclusion that the world began. For everything that is made has a beginning of its duration. But it can be proved demonstratively that God is the producing cause of the world; indeed this is asserted by the more approved philosophers. Therefore it can be demonstratively proved that the world began.[4]

Obj. 2. Further, if it is necessary to say that the world was made by God, it must have been made from nothing, or from something. But it was not made from something, or otherwise the matter of the world would have preceded the world; and against this are the arguments of Aristotle who held that the heavens are ungenerated. Therefore it must be said that the world was made from nothing;

---

[1] *Metaph*. Ia, 1 (993b 30).

[2] *Ibid.* (993b 25).

[3] *Enchir.*, XI (PL 40, 236).

[4] Alex. of Hales, *Summa Theol.*, I, no. 64 (I, 95); St. Bonaventure, *In II Sent.*, d. 1, pt. 1, a. 1, q. 3 (II, 22).

and thus it has been being after non-being. Therefore it must have begun to be, [5]

Obj. 3. Further, *everything which works by intellect works from some principle,* [6] as is revealed in all works of human art. But God acts by intellect, and therefore His work has a principle, from which to begin. The world, therefore, which is His effect, did not always exist.

Obj. 4. Further, it appears manifestly that certain arts have developed, and certain parts of the world have begun to be inhabited at some fixed time. But this would not be the case if the world had always been in existence. Therefore it is manifest that the world did not always exist.

Obj. 5. Further, it is certain that nothing can be equal to God. But if the world had always been, it would be equal to God in duration. Therefore it is certain that the world did not always exist. [7]

Obj. 6. Further, if the world always was, the consequence is that an infinite number of days preceded this present day. But it is impossible to traverse what is infinite. Therefore we should never have arrived at this present day; which is manifestly false. [8]

Obj. 7. Further, if the world was eternal, generation also was eternal. Therefore one man was begotten of another in an infinite series. But the father is the efficient cause of the son. [9] Therefore in efficient causes there could be an infinite series; which however is disproved in *Metaph.* ii. [10]

Obj. 8. Further, if the world and generation always were, there have been an infinite number of men. But man's soul is immortal. Therefore an infinite number of human souls would now actually exist, which is impossible. Therefore it can be known with certainty that the world began: it is not held by faith alone. [11]

On the contrary, The articles of faith cannot be proved demonstratively, because faith is of things *that appear not.* But that God is the Creator of the world in such a way that the world began to be is an article of faith; for we say, *I believe in one God,* etc. [12] And again, Gregory says that Moses prophesied of the past, saying, *In the beginning God created heaven and earth:* in which words the newness of the world is stated. [13] Therefore the newness of the world is known only by revelation, and hence it cannot be proved demonstratively.

I answer that, That the world did not always exist we hold by faith alone: it

---

[5] Alex. of Hales, *Summa Theol.,* I, no. 64 (I, 93).

[6] Aristotle, *Phys.,* III, 4 (203a 31).

[7] Alex. of Hales, *Summa Theol.,* I, no. 64 (I, 93).

[8] Argument of Algazel in Averroes, *Destruct. Destruct.,* I (IX, 9rb; 10rb); and of the Mutakallimin, found in Maimonides, *Guide,* I, 74 (p. 138).

[9] Aristotle, *Phys.,* II, 3 (194b 30).

[10] Aristotle, *Metaph.,* Ia, 2 (994a 5)—For the use of this argument, cf. the Mutakallimin in Averroes, *Destruct. Destruct.,* I (IX, 12vab).

[11] Argument of Algazel, found in Averroes, *Destruct. Destruct.,* I (IX, 12vab); and of the Mutakallimin in Maimonides, *Guide,* I, 73 (p. 132).

[12] *Symb. Nicaenum* (Denzinger, no. 54).

[13] *In Ezech.,* hom. 1, bk. 1 (PL 76, 786).

cannot be proved demonstratively; which is what was said above of the mystery of the Trinity.[14] The reason for this is that the newness of the world cannot be demonstrated from the world itself. For the principle of demonstration is the essence of a thing. Now everything, considered in its species, abstracts from *here* and *now*; which is why it is said that *universals are everywhere and always.*[15] Hence it cannot be demonstrated that man, or the heavens, or a stone did not always exist.

Likewise, neither can the newness of the world be demonstrated from the efficient cause, which acts by will. For the will of God cannot be investigated by reason, except as regards those things which God must will of necessity; and what He wills about creatures is not among these, as was said above.[16] But the divine will can be manifested by revelation, on which faith rests. Hence that the world began to exist is an object of faith, but not of demonstration or science. And it is useful to consider this, lest anyone, presuming to demonstrate what is of faith, should bring forward arguments that are not cogent; for this would give unbelievers the occasion to ridicule, thinking that on such grounds we believe the things that are of faith.

Reply Obj. 1. As Augustine says, the opinion of philosophers who asserted the eternity of the world was twofold.[17] For some said that the substance of the world was not from God, which is an intolerable error; and therefore it is refuted by proofs that are cogent. Some, however, said that the world was eternal, although made by God. *For they hold that the world has a beginning, not of time, but of creation; which means that, in a scarcely intelligible way, it was always made. And they try to explain their meaning thus: for just as, if a foot were always in the dust from eternity, there would always be a footprint which without doubt was caused by him who trod on it, so also the world always was, because its Maker always existed.*[18] To understand this we must consider that an efficient cause which acts by motion of necessity precedes its effect in time; for the effect exists only in the end of the action, and every agent must be the beginning of action. But if the action is instantaneous and not successive, it is not necessary for the maker to be prior in duration to the thing made, as appears in the case of illumination. Hence it is held that it does not follow necessarily that if God is the active cause of the world, He must be prior to the world in duration[19]; because creation, by which He produced the world, is not a successive change, as was said above.[20]

Reply Obj. 2. Those who would hold that the world was eternal, would say that the world was made by God from nothing; not that it was made after nothing,

[14]Q. 32, a. 1.

[15]Aristotle, *Post. Anal.*, I, 31 (87b 33).

[16]Q. 19, a. 3.

[17]De Civit. Dei, XI, 4 (PL 41, 319).

[18]Op. cit., X, 31 (PL 41, 311).

[19]Cf. Averroes, *Destruct. Destruct.*, I (IX, 13rb).

[20]Q. 45, a. 2, ad 3.

according to what we understand by the term *creation*, but that it was not made from anything. And so some of them even do not reject the term creation, as appears from Avicenna.[21]

Reply Obj. 3. This is the argument of Anaxagoras as reported in *Physics* iii.[22] But it does not lead to a necessary conclusion, except as to that intellect which deliberates in order to find out what should be done; which procedure is like movement. Such is the human intellect, but not the divine intellect.[23]

Reply Obj. 4. Those who hold the eternity of the world hold that some region was changed an infinite number of times from being uninhabitable to being inhabitable and *vice versa*.[24] They also hold that the arts, by reason of various corruptions and accidents, were subject to an infinite succession of discovery and decay.[25] Hence Aristotle says that it is absurd to base our opinion of the newness of the whole world on such particular changes.[26]

Reply Obj. 5. Even supposing that the world always was, it would not be equal to God in eternity, as Boethius says[27]; for the divine Being is all being simultaneously without succession, but with the world it is otherwise.

Reply Obj. 6. Passage is always understood as being from term to term. Whatever by-gone day we choose, from it to the present day there is a finite number of days which can be traversed. The objection is founded on the idea that, given two extremes, there is an infinite number of mean terms.

Reply Obj. 7. In efficient causes it is impossible to proceed to infinity *per se*. Thus, there cannot be an infinite number of causes that are *per se* required for a certain effect; for instance, that a stone be moved by a stick, the stick by the hand, and so on to infinity. But it is not impossible to proceed to infinity *accidentally* as regards efficient causes; for instance, if all the causes thus infinitely multiplied should have the order of only one cause, while their multiplication is accidental: *e.g.*, as an artificer acts by means of many hammers accidentally, because one after the other is broken. It is accidental, therefore, that one particular hammer should act after the action of another, and it is likewise accidental to this particular man as generator to be generated by another man; for he generates as a man, and not as the son of another man. For all men generating hold one grade in the order of efficient causes—viz., the grade of a particular generator. Hence it is not impossible for a man to be generated by man to infinity; but such a thing would be impossible if the generation of this man depended upon this man, and on an elementary body, and on the sun, and so on to infinity.

[21] *Metaph.*, IX, 4 (104va).

[22] Aristotle, *Phys.*, III, 4 (203a 31); VIII, 1 (250b 24).

[23] Q. 14, a. 7.

[24] Cf. St. Augustine, *De Civit. Dei*, XII, 10 (PL 41, 358); Aristotle, *Meteor.*, I, 14 (351a 19).

[25] Cf. St. Augustine, *De Civit. Dei*, XII, 10 (PL 41, 358); Averroes, *In Metaph.*, XII, comm. 50 (VIII, 156v).

[26] *Meteor.*, I, 14 (352a 26; 351b 8).

[27] *De Consol.*, V, prose 6 (PL 63, 859).

Reply Obj. 8. Those who hold the eternity of the world evade this argument in many ways. For some do not think it impossible for there to be an actual infinity of souls, as appears from the *Metaphysics* of Algazel, who says that such a thing is an accidental infinity.[28] But this was disproved above.[29] Some say that the soul is corrupted with the body.[30] And some say that of all souls only one remains.[31] But others, as Augustine says, asserted on this account a circulation of souls—viz., that souls separated from their bodies again return thither after a course of time.[32] A fuller consideration of this matter will be given later.[33] But be it noted that this argument considers only a particular case. Hence one might say that the world was eternal, or at least some creature, as an angel, but not man. But we are considering the question in general, namely, whether any creature can exist from eternity.

PATTERSON BROWN
Infinite Causal Regression

III

It is evident that we cannot hope to understand the argument against infinite causal regresses without first getting straight on the supposedly critical contrast between causal series ordered *per se* and those ordered *per accidens*. So let us examine the previously quoted explanation by Scotus that "in essentially ordered series, the second [that is, the posterior] depends upon the first [the prior] precisely in its act of causation." I assume that the entire argument would be laid bare if we fully understood this criterion and its application to the two paradigm cases, propulsion and genealogy.

The criterion delineated by Scotus seems straightforward enough; it is simply

Patterson Brown (1938–   ) has taught philosophy at the State University of New York at Binghamton. He is the author of several papers in the areas of philosophy of religion and medieval philosophy.

INFINITE CAUSAL REGRESSION   Sections III, V from *The Philosophical Review*, Volume LXXV, No. 4, October 1966. Reprinted by permission of *The Philosophical Review* and the author.

[28] *Metaph.*, I, tr. 1, div. 6 (p. 40).—Cf. Averroes, *Destruct. Destruct.*, I (IX, 12 vab).

[29] Q. 7, a. 4.

[30] Cf. Nemesius, *De Nat. Hom.*, II (PG 40, 537).

[31] Averroes, *Destruct. Destruct.*, I (IX, 10va).

[32] *Serm.* CCXLI, 4 (PL 38, 1135); *De Civit. Dei.* XII, 13 (PL 41, 361).—Cf. Plato *Timaeus* (p. 39a).

[33] Q. 75, a. 6; q. 76, a. 2; q. 118, a. 3.

that each member of an essential series (except of course the first and last *if* there be such) is causally dependent upon its predecessor for its own causal efficacy regarding its successor. The members are each intermediate (secondary, instrumental, dependent) in the sense discussed above. In an accidental series, however, each member is not dependent upon its predecessor for its own causal efficacy— though it may be dependent in some other regard. Thus a causal series is *per se* ordered if and only if it is throughout of the form: *w*'s being F causes x to be G, *x*'s being G causes y to be H, *y*'s being H causes z to be I, . . . (here $F\hat{x}$, $G\hat{x}$, $H\hat{x}$, and $I\hat{x}$ may be identical or differing functions). A causal series is ordered *per accidens*, however, if and only if it is throughout of the form: *w*'s being F causes x to be G, *x*'s being H causes y to be I, *y*'s being J causes z to be K, . . . (here $G\hat{x} \neq H\hat{x}$ and $I\hat{x} \neq J\hat{x}$, but otherwise $F\hat{x}$, $G\hat{x}$, $H\hat{x}$, $I\hat{x}$, $J\hat{x}$, and $K\hat{x}$ may be identical or differing functions). In other words, the two functions of each individual variable must be identical in the essential case, but must differ in the accidental case.

Consider the paradigm case where one's hand pushes a stick which in turn pushes a stone. This causal series is *per se* because it is the same function of the stick (namely, its locomotion) which both is caused by the movement of the hand and causes the movement of the stone. Again, a series where the fire heats the pot and the pot in turn heats the stew, causing it to boil, is also essentially ordered; for the warmth of the pot is both caused by the warmth of the fire and cause of the warmth of the stew, while the warmth of the stew is both caused by the warmth of the pot and cause of the stew's boiling.

On the other hand, consider the paradigm case of Abraham's begetting Isaac, who in turn begets Jacob. Here the series is accidentally ordered because the function of Isaac (namely, his copulating) which causes Jacob's birth is not caused by Abraham's copulation; the latter results in Isaac's *birth,* whereas it is Isaac's *copulation* which causes Jacob to be born. Genealogical series like the following are thus *per accidens*: Abraham's copulation causes Isaac's birth, Isaac's copulation causes Jacob's birth, Jacob's copulation causes Joseph's birth. Each member has one attribute qua effect (being born) and quite another attribute qua cause (copulating).

Now Aristotle and his followers held as a critically important thesis that the constituent relations in an essentially ordered series are *transitive*. This is, I suggest, the point of Aristotle's statement that "everything that is moved is moved by the movement that is further back in the series as well as by that which immediately moves it."[1] If, to use the standard example, the hand propels the stick and the stick in turn propels the stone, then the hand propels the stone by means of the stick. Again, if the fire heats the pot, which heats the stew, which causes the stew to boil, then the fire causes the stew to boil. St. Thomas makes this point in the following passage:

> If that which was given as moved locally is moved by the nearest mover which is increased, and that again is moved by something which is altered, and that again is moved by something which is moved in place, then that which is moved with respect

[1] *Physics,* 257a10–12. All quotations from Aristotle will be from R. McKeon (ed.), *The Basic Works of Aristotle* (New York, 1941).

to place will be moved more by the first thing which is moved with respect to place than by the second thing which is altered or by the third thing which is increased.[2]

Here we have an undisguised claim that "*x* moves *y*" is a transitive causal relation. . . .

V

I want now to suggest a reading of the argument against infinite causal regresses on the basis of our earlier understanding of the contrast between *per se* and *per accidens* ordering of causal series. I think that the substance of the proof was as follows, again using moving causation as our paradigmatic example. Parallel arguments could obviously be constructed regarding Aristotle's other types of cause, and also regarding Avicennian efficient causes.

The Aristotelian scientific model stipulates that all motions are to be given causal explanations, and that such explanations are to be of the form "*x* moves *y*." (Compare the analogous Newtonian stipulation that all accelerations are to be explained in terms of equations of the form "$F = ma$.") Suppose then that we observe something, *a*, to be moving, and we wish to explain this phenomenon by means of the Aristotelian physics. The explanation must be of the form "*x* moves *a*." Suppose further that *a* is moved by *b*, *b* is in turn moved by *c*, *c* in turn by *d*, and so on indefinitely. The issue is whether this series can continue ad infinitum. We now ask, what moves *a*? Well, it has already been stated that *b* moves *a*; so it may be suggested that "*b* moves *a*" is the desired explanation of *a*'s motion, the desired value of "*x* moves *a*." But this would be an inadequate account of the matter. For *b* is itself being moved by *c*, which—owing to the transitivity of "*x* moves *y*"—thus yields the implication that *a* is moved by *c*, with *b* serving merely as an instrument or intermediate. But in turn *d* moves *c*; and so *d* moves *a*. But *e* moves *d*; therefore *e* moves *a*. And so on indefinitely. Now, so long as this series continues, we have not found the real mover of *a*; that is to say, we have not found the *explaining* value of the function "*x* moves *a*." The regress is thus a vicious one, in that the required explanation of *a*'s motion is deferred so long as the series continues. With regard to any *x* which moves *a*, if there is a *y* such that *y* moves *x*, then we must infer that *y* moves *a*. And if for any *x* such that *x* moves *a* there were a *y* such that *y* moved *x* (and therefore moved *a* as well), then no explanation of *a*'s motion would be possible with the Aristotelian model. There would of course be any number of *true* statements of the form "*x* moves *a*"—namely, "*b* moves *a*," "*c* moves *a*," "*d* moves *a*," and so forth. But none of these is to count as the Aristotelian *explanation* of *a*'s motion. Nor, it must be noted, is any such explanation given merely by asserting that there is an infinite regress of movers of *a*. "An infinite regress of movers move *a*" is not a possible value of the function "*x* *moves a*," for the variable in the latter ranges over individuals, not classes (and a fortiori not over series, finite or infinite). An uncaused motion, however, is no motion at all; in other words, an inexplicable motion would be an unintelligible motion. There must be, therefore, an unmoved mover of *a*.

[2] *On Physics*, Bk. VIII, lec. 9, #1047.

The foregoing cause is to be contrasted with giving an explanation of, for example, Jacob's birth. Such an account is to be of the form "x begat Jacob." The complete and unique explanation of that form is that Isaac begat Jacob. We do not get a new value for the function on the grounds that Abraham in turn begat Isaac, since this does not imply that Abraham begat Jacob; on the contrary, it implies that he did not do so. So a full explanation of Jacob's birth can be given regardless of whether his family tree extends back to infinity. An explanation of Isaac's copulation is still required, of course; but that will center on his actions with Rebecca, rather than on his having been sired by Abraham. (The Aristotelians would contend that Isaac's copulation, being a locomotion, must be the termination of an essentially ordered *moving* series. This means that there indeed is a *per se* series which terminates in Jacob's birth, but it does not ascend through Isaac, Abraham, Terah, and so on; rather, it goes back through Isaac's copulation and thence instantaneously back through a series of contiguous movers reaching up to the celestial spheres. Aquinas writes that "whatever generates here below, moves to the production of the species as the instrument of a heavenly body. Thus the Philosopher says that 'man and the sun generate man.' "[3] God is then in turn causally responsible for the locomotion of the heavenly spheres—though not of course by himself changing.[4] In this way each man is supposed to be efficiently caused by God via an essentially ordered series of movers, regardless of whether he has an infinite regress of ancestors in an accidentally ordered genealogy series.)

SAMUEL CLARKE
The Cosmological Argument

I

First then, it is absolutely and undeniably certain that something has existed from all eternity. This is so evident and undeniable a proposition that no atheist in any age has ever presumed to assert the contrary; and therefore there is little need of being particular in the proof of it. For since something now is, it is evident that

THE COSMOLOGICAL ARGUMENT   From *Discourse Concerning the Being and Attributes of God*, ninth edition. (Selections are from Propositions I, II, and III. Punctuation, use of capitals, etc. have been modernized by the editors.)

[3] *ST*, I, Q. 115, Art. 3, Reply Obj. 2; the quotation from Aristotle is from *Physics*, 194b13. See also *ST*, I, Q. 118, Art. 1, Reply Obj. 3, where Aquinas asserts that the act of begetting is "concurrent with the power of a heavenly body."

[4] Aristotle held that God is merely the final cause of the celestial rotations; cf. *Metaphysics*, 1072a 19 ff. The medievals tended to abuse Avicenna's distinction (n. 2, *supra*) by saying that God is somehow the efficient cause of that locomotion, though perhaps with the intelligences (angels) as intermediates; see E. Gilson, *The Elements of Christian Philosophy* (New York, 1963), pp. 71–74.

something always was. Otherwise the things that now are must have been produced out of nothing, absolutely and without cause—which is a plain contradiction in terms. For, to say a thing is produced, and yet that there is no cause at all of that production, is to say that something is effected when it is effected by nothing; that is, at the same time when it is not effected at all. Whatever exists has a cause, a reason, a ground of its existence (a foundation on which its existence relies, a ground or reason why it does exist rather than not exist) either in the necessity of its own nature, and then it must have been of itself eternal, or in the will of some other being, and then that other being must, at least in the order of nature and causality, have existed before it.

That something therefore has really existed from eternity is one of the certain and most evident truths in the world, acknowledged by all men and disputed by none. Yet as to the manner how it can be, there is nothing in nature more difficult for the mind of man to conceive than this very first plain and self-evident truth. For, how anything can have existed eternally—that is, how an eternal duration can be now actually past—is a thing utterly as impossible for our narrow understandings to comprehend as anything that is not an explicit contradiction can be imagined to be; and yet to deny the truth of the proposition that an eternal duration is now actually past would be to assert something still far more unintelligible, even a real and explicit contradiction.

II

There has existed, from eternity, some one unchangeable and independent being. For since something must needs have been from eternity—as has been already proved and is granted on all hands—either there has always existed some one unchangeable and independent being, from which all other beings that are or ever were in the universe have received their original, or else there has been an infinite succession of changeable and dependent beings produced one from another in an endless progression, without any original cause at all. Now this latter supposition is so very absurd that though all atheism must in its account of most things (as shall be shown hereafter) terminate in it, yet I think very few atheists ever were so weak as openly and directly to defend it. For it is plainly impossible, and contradictory to itself. I shall not argue against it from the supposed impossibility of infinite succession, barely and absolutely considered in itself, for a reason which shall be mentioned hereafter. But, if we consider such an infinite progression as one entire endless series of dependent beings, it is plain this whole series of beings can have no cause from without of its existence, because in it are supposed to be included all things that are or ever were in the universe. And it is plain it can have no reason within itself of its existence, because no one being in this infinite succession is supposed to be self-existent or necessary (which is the only ground or reason of existence of any thing that can be imagined within the thing itself, as will presently more fully appear), but every one dependent on the foregoing. And where no part is necessary, it is manifest the whole cannot be necessary, absolute necessity of existence not being an extrinsic, relative, and accidental denomination but an inward and essential property of the nature of the thing which so exists. An infinite succession therefore of merely dependent beings, without any original independent cause, is a series of beings that has neither necessity, nor cause, nor any reason or ground at all of its existence, either within itself or from without. That is, it is an explicit contradiction and impossibility; it is supposing something to be caused (because it is granted, in every one of its stages of succession, not to be necessarily and of itself) and yet that, in the whole, it is caused absolutely by nothing, which every man knows is a contradiction to imagine done in time; and, because duration in this case makes no difference, it is equally a contradiction to suppose it done from eternity. And consequently there must, on the contrary, of necessity have existed from eternity some one immutable and independent being.

III

That unchangeable and independent being, which has existed from eternity without any external cause of its existence, must be self-existent, that is, necessarily existing. For whatever exists must either have come into being out of nothing, absolutely without cause, or it must have been produced by some external cause; or it must be self-existent. Now to arise out of nothing, absolutely without any cause, has been already shown to be a plain contradiction. To have been produced by some external cause cannot possibly be true of every thing; but something must have existed eternally and independently, as has likewise been shown already. It remains, therefore, that that being which has existed independently from eternity must of necessity be self-existent. Now to be self-existent is not to be produced by itself, for that is an explicit contradiction. But it is (which is the only idea we can frame of self-existence, and without which the word seems to have no signification at all), I say, to exist by an absolute necessity originally in the nature of the thing itself.

DAVID HUME
Some Objections to the Cosmological Argument

But if so many difficulties attend the argument *a posteriori*, said Demea, had we not better adhere to that simple and sublime argument *a priori*, which, by offering to us infallible demonstration, cuts off at once all doubt and difficulty? By this

David Hume (1711–1776), born in Scotland, was a philosopher and an historian and also served for several years as a member of the British diplomatic corps. Along with such philosophers as Locke and Berkeley, he is considered one of the major exponents of Empiricism. His philosophical works include *Treatise of Human Nature*, *Enquiry Concerning Human Understanding*, and *Enquiry Concerning the Principles of Morals*.

SOME OBJECTIONS TO THE COSMOLOGICAL ARGUMENT   From *Dialogues Concerning Natural Religion*, Part IX. *The Philosophical Works of David Hume*, Volume II. Edinburgh, Adam Black and William Tait; and Charles Tait, 1876.

argument, too, we may prove the INFINITY of the Divine attributes, which, I am afraid, can never be ascertained with certainty from any other topic. For how can an effect, which either is finite, or, for aught we know, may be so; how can such an effect, I say, prove an infinite cause? The unity too of the Divine Nature, it is very difficult, if not absolutely impossible, to deduce merely from contemplating the works of nature; nor will the uniformity alone of the plan, even were it allowed, give us any assurance of that attribute. Whereas the argument *a priori*. . . .

You seem to reason, Demea, interposed Cleanthes, as if those advantages and conveniences in the abstract argument were full proofs of its solidity. But it is first proper, in my opinion, to determine what argument of this nature you choose to insist on; and we shall afterwards, from itself, better than from its *useful* consequences, endeavour to determine what value we ought to put upon it.

The argument, replied Demea, which I would insist on, is the common one. Whatever exists must have a cause or reason of its existence; it being absolutely impossible for any thing to produce itself, or be the cause of its own existence. In mounting up, therefore, from effects to causes, we must either go on in tracing an infinite succession, without any ultimate cause at all; or must at least have recourse to some ultimate cause, that is *necessarily* existent: Now, that the first supposition is absurd, may be thus proved. In the infinite chain or succession of causes and effects, each single effect is determined to exist by the power and efficacy of that cause which immediately preceded; but the whole eternal chain or succession, taken together, is not determined or caused by any thing; and yet it is evident that it requires a cause or reason, as much as any particular object which begins to exist in time. The question is still reasonable, why this particular succession of causes existed from eternity, and not any other succession, or no succession at all. If there be no necessarily existent being, any supposition which can be formed is equally possible; nor is there any more absurdity in Nothing's having existed from eternity, than there is in that succession of causes which constitutes the universe. What was it, then, which determined Something to exist rather than Nothing, and bestowed being on a particular possibility, exclusive of the rest? *External causes*, there are supposed to be none. *Chance* is a word without a meaning. Was it *Nothing*? But that can never produce any thing. We must, therefore, have recourse to a necessarily existent Being, who carries the REASON of his existence in himself, and who cannot be supposed not to exist, without an express contradiction. There is, consequently, such a Being; that is, there is a Deity.

I shall not leave it to Philo, said Cleanthes, though I know that the starting objections is his chief delight, to point out the weakness of this metaphysical reasoning. It seems to me so obviously ill-grounded, and at the same time of so little consequence to the cause of true piety and religion, that I shall myself venture to show the fallacy of it.

I shall begin with observing, that there is an evident absurdity in pretending to demonstrate a matter of fact, or to prove it by any arguments *a priori*. Nothing is demonstrable, unless the contrary implies a contradiction. Nothing, that is distinctly conceivable, implies a contradiction. Whatever we conceive as existent, we can also conceive as non-existent. There is no being, therefore, whose non-existence implies a contradiction. Consequently there is no being, whose existence is demonstrable. I propose this argument as entirely decisive, and am willing to rest the whole controversy upon it.

It is pretended that the Deity is a necessarily existent being; and this necessity of his existence is attempted to be explained by asserting, that if we knew his whole essence or nature, we should perceive it to be as impossible for him not to exist, as for twice two not to be four. But it is evident that this can never happen, while our faculties remain the same as at present. It will still be possible for us, at any time, to conceive the non-existence of what we formerly conceived to exist; nor can the mind ever lie under a necessity of supposing any object to remain always in being; in the same manner as we lie under a necessity of always conceiving twice two to be four. The words, therefore, *necessary existence*, have no meaning; or, which is the same thing, none that is consistent.

But farther, why may not the material universe be the necessarily existent Being, according to this pretended explication of necessity? We dare not affirm that we know all the qualities of matter; and for aught we can determine, it may contain some qualities, which, were they known, would make its non-existence appear as great a contradiction as that twice two is five. I find only one argument employed to prove, that the material world is not the necessarily existent Being; and this argument is derived from the contingency both of the matter and the form of the world. 'Any particle of matter,' it is said,[1] 'may be *conceived* to be annihilated; and any form may be *conceived* to be altered. Such an annihilation or alteration, therefore, is not impossible.' But it seems a great partiality not to perceive, that the same argument extends equally to the Deity, so far as we have any conception of him; and that the mind can at least imagine him to be non-existent, or his attributes to be altered. It must be some unknown, inconceivable qualities, which can make his non-existence appear impossible, or his attributes unalterable: And no reason can be assigned, why these qualities may not belong to matter. As they are altogether unknown and inconceivable, they can never be proved incompatible with it.

Add to this, that in tracing an eternal succession of objects, it seems absurd to inquire for a general cause or first author. How can any thing, that exists from eternity, have a cause, since that relation implies a priority in time, and a beginning of existence?

In such a chain, too, or succession of objects, each part is caused by that which preceded it, and causes that which succeeds it. Where then is the difficulty? But the WHOLE, you say, wants a cause. I answer, that the uniting of these parts into a whole, like the uniting of several distinct countries into one kingdom, or several distinct members into one body, is performed merely by an arbitrary act of the mind, and has no influence on the nature of things. Did I show you the particular causes of each individual in a collection of twenty particles of matter, I should think it very unreasonable, should you afterwards ask me, what was the cause of the whole twenty. This is sufficiently explained in explaining the cause of the parts.

Though the reasonings which you have urged, Cleanthes, may well excuse me, said Philo, from starting any farther difficulties, yet I cannot forbear insisting still

[1] Dr Clarke.

upon another topic. It is observed by arithmeticians, that the products of 9 compose always either 9, or some lesser product of 9, if you add together all of the characters of which any of the former products is composed. Thus, of 18, 27, 36, which are products of 9, you make 9 by adding 1 to 8, 2 to 7, 3 to 6. Thus, 369 is a product also of 9; and if you add 3, 6, and 9, you make 18, a lesser product of 9.[2] To a superficial observer, so wonderful a regularity may be admired as the effect either of chance or design: but a skilful algebraist immediately concludes it to be the work of necessity, and demonstrates, that it must for ever result from the nature of these numbers. Is it not probable, I ask, that the whole economy of the universe is conducted by a like necessity, though no human albegra can furnish a key which solves the difficulty? And instead of admiring the order of natural beings, may it not happen, that, could we penetrate into the intimate nature of bodies, we should clearly see why it was absolutely impossible they could ever admit of any other disposition? So dangerous is it to introduce this idea of necessity into the present question! and so naturally does it afford an inference directly opposite to the religious hypothesis!

But dropping all these abstractions, continued Philo, and confining ourselves to more familiar topics, I shall venture to add an observation, that the argument *a priori* has seldom been found very convincing, except to people of a metaphysical head, who have accustomed themselves to abstract reasoning, and who, finding from mathematics, that the understanding frequently leads to truth through obscurity, and, contrary to the first appearances, have transferred the same habit of thinking to subjects where it ought not to have place. Other people, even of good sense and the best inclined to religion, feel always some deficiency in such arguments, though they are not perhaps able to explain distinctly where it lies; a certain proof that men ever did, and ever will derive their religion from other sources than from this species of reasoning.

WILLIAM L. ROWE
Two Criticisms of the Cosmological Argument

In this paper I wish to consider two major criticisms which have been advanced against the Cosmological Argument for the existence of God, criticisms which

William L. Rowe (1931–   ) is Professor of Philosophy at Purdue University. He is the author of *Religious Symbols and God: A Study of Tillich's Theology*, *The Cosmological Argument* and *Philosophy of Religion*.

TWO CRITICISMS OF THE COSMOLOGICAL ARGUMENT   From *The Monist*, vol. 54, no. 3 (1970). Copyright © 1970, *The Monist*, La Salle, Illinois 61301. Reprinted by permission of *The Monist* and the author.

[2] Republique des Lettres, Aout 1685.

many philosophers regard as constituting a decisive refutation of that argument. Before stating and examining these objections it will be helpful to have before us a version of the Cosmological Argument. The Cosmological Argument has two distinct parts. The first part is an argument to establish the existence of a necessary being. The second part is an argument to establish that this necessary being is God. The two objections I shall consider are directed against the first part of the Cosmological Argument. Using the expression "depending being" to mean "a being which has the reason for its existence in the causal efficacy or nature of some other being," and the expression "independent being" to mean "a being which has the reason for its existence within its own nature," we may state the argument for the existence of a necessary being as follows:

1. Every being is either a dependent being or an independent being; therefore,
2. Either there exists an independent being or every being is dependent;
3. It is false that every being is dependent; therefore,
4. There exists an independent being; therefore,
5. There exists a necessary being.

This argument consists of two premises—propositions (1) and (3)—and three inferences. The first inference is from (1) to (2), the second from (2) and (3) to (4), and the third inference is from (4) to (5). Of the premises neither is obviously true, and of the inferences only the first and second are above suspicion. Before discussing the main subject of this paper—the reasoning in support of proposition (3) and the two major objections which have been advanced against that reasoning—I want to say something about the other questionable parts of the argument; namely, proposition (1) and the inference from (4) and (5).

Proposition (1) expresses what we may call the strong form of the Principle of Sufficient Reason. It insists not only that those beings which begin to exist must have a cause or explanation (the weak form of the Principle of Sufficient Reason) but that absolutely every being must have an explanation of its existing rather than not existing—the explanation lying either within the causal efficacy of some other being or within the thing's own nature. In an earlier paper I examined this Principle in some detail.[1] The objections I wish to consider in this paper are, I believe, independent of the Principle of Sufficient Reason. That is, these objections are meant to refute the argument even if the first premise is true. This being so, it will facilitate our examination of these two objections if we take proposition (1) as an unquestioned premise throughout our discussion. Accordingly, in this paper proposition (1) will function as an axiom in our reasoning. This, of course, should not be taken as implying that I think the first premise of the argument is true.

The inference from proposition (4) to proposition (5) is not considered in this paper. Indeed, for purposes of this paper we could have ended the statement of the argument with proposition (4). I have included the inference from (4) to (5) simply because it is an important element in the first part of the Cosmological

[1] See "The Cosmological Argument and the Principle of Sufficient Reason," *Man and World*, I, No. 2 (1968).

Argument. Proposition (4) asserts the existence of a being which has the reason or explanation of its existence within its own nature. Proposition (5) asserts the existence of a necessary being. By "a necessary being" is meant a being whose non-existence is a logical impossibility.[2] Many philosophers have argued that it is logically impossible for there to be a necessary being in this sense of "necessary being." Hence, even if the two objections I shall examine in this paper can be met, the defender of the Cosmological Argument must still face objections not only to the inference from (4) to (5) but to (5) itself. But again, this is a matter which I shall not pursue in this paper. Unlike proposition (1), however, which I treat as an unquestioned assumption, neither proposition (5) nor the inference from (4) to (5) will be appealed to in this paper. In what follows we may simply ignore that part of the argument. Indeed, our attention will be focused entirely on proposition (3), the reasoning which supports it, and the two major criticisms which have been advanced against that reasoning.

Proposition (3) asserts that it is false that every being is dependent. For what reasons? Well, if every being which exists (or ever existed) is dependent, then the whole of existing things, it would seem, consists of a collection of dependent beings, that is, a collection of beings each member of which exists by reason of the causal efficacy of some other being. This collection would have to contain an infinite number of numbers. For suppose it contained a finite number, let us say three, *a*, *b*, and *c*. Now if in Scotus' phrase "a circle of causes is inadmissible" then if *c* is caused by *b* and *b* by *a*, *a* would exist without a cause, there being no other member of the collection that could be its cause. But in that case *a* would not be what by supposition it is, namely a *dependent* being. Hence, if we grant that a circle of causes is inadmissible it is important that the whole of existing things should consist of a collection of dependent beings *finite* in number.

Suppose, then, that the dependent beings making up the collection are infinite in number. Why is it impossible that the whole of existing things should consist of such a collection? The proponent of the Cosmological Argument answers as follows.[3] The finite collection *itself*, he argues, requires an explanation of its existence. For since it is true of each member of the collection that it might not have existed, it is true of the whole infinite collection that it might not have existed. But if the entire infinite collection might not have existed there must be

[2] Not all versions of the Cosmological Argument employ the notion of a logically necessary being. It seems likely, for example, that in Aquinas' Third Way the expression "necessary being" is not used to mean a logically necessary being. (See P. Brown, "St. Thomas' Doctrine of Necessary Being," *Philosophical Review*, 73 [1964], 76–90.) But in the version we are considering, it is clear that by "necessary being" is meant a being whose existence is logically necessary. Thus Samuel Clarke, from whose work our version has been adapted, remarks: ". . . the only true idea of a self-existent or necessarily existing being, is the idea of a being the supposition of whose not-existing is an express contradiction" (Samuel Clarke, A *Demonstration of the Being and Attributes of God*, 9th edition, p. 17). David Hume also understands the notion of a necessary being this way. Thus in his statement of the argument, which he adapted from Clarke, he has Demea conclude, "We must, therefore, have recourse to a necessarily existent being, who carries the reason of his existence in himself, and who cannot be supposed not to exist, without an express contradiction" (*Dialogues Concerning Natural Religion*, Part IX).

[3] See, for example, Samuel Clarke's discussion of Propositions II and III in his *Demonstration*. This discussion is summarized by Hume in Part IX of his *Dialogues*.

some explanation of why it exists rather than not. The explanation cannot lie in the causal efficacy of some being outside of the collection since by supposition the collection includes every being which is or ever was. Nor can the explanation of why there is an infinite collection be found within the collection itself, for since no member of the collection is independent, has the reason of its existence within itself, the collection as a whole cannot have the reason of its existence within itself. Thus the conception of an infinite collection of dependent beings is the conception of something whose existence has no explanation whatever. But since premise (1) tells us that whatever exists has an explanation for its existence, either within itself or in the causal efficacy of some other being, it cannot be that the whole of existing things consists of an infinite collection of dependent beings.

The reasoning developed here is exhibited as follows:

1. If every being is dependent then the whole of existing things consists of an infinite collection of dependent beings;
2. If the whole of existing things consists of an infinite collection of dependent beings then the infinite collection itself must have an explanation of its existence;
3. If the existence of the infinite collection of dependent beings has an explanation then the explanation must lie either in the causal efficacy of some being outside the collection or it must lie within the infinite collection itself;
4. The explanation of the existence of the infinite collection of dependent beings cannot lie in the causal efficacy of some being outside the collection;
5. The explanation of the existence of the infinite collection of dependent beings cannot lie within the collection itself; therefore,
6. There is no explanation of the infinite collection of dependent beings (from 3, 4, and 5); therefore,
7. It is false that the whole of existing things consists of an infinite collection of dependent beings (from 2 and 6); therefore,
8. It is false that every being is dependent (from 1 and 7).

Perhaps every premise in this argument is open to criticism. I propose here, however, to consider what I regard as the two major criticisms advanced against this reasoning in support of proposition (3) of the main argument. The first of these criticisms may be construed as directed against premise (2) of the above argument. According to this criticism it *makes no sense* to apply the notion of cause or explanation to the totality of things, and the arguments used to show that the whole of existing things must have a cause or explanation are *fallacious*. Thus in his B.B.C. debate with Father Copleston, Bertrand Russell took the view that the concept of cause is inapplicable to the universe conceived of as the total collection of things. When pressed by Copleston as to how he could rule out "the legitimacy of asking the question how the total, or anything at all comes to be there," Russell responded: "I can illustrate what seems to me your fallacy. Every man who exists has a mother, and it seems to me your argument is that therefore the human race must have a mother, but obviously the human race hasn't a mother—that's a different logical sphere."[4]

The second major criticism is directed at premise (5). According to this criticism it is *intelligible* to ask for an explanation of the existence of the infinite collection of dependent beings. But the answer to this question, so the criticism goes, is provided once we learn that each member of the infinite collection has an explanation of its existence. Thus Hume remarks: "Did I show you the particular causes of each individual in a collection of twenty particles of matter, I should think it very unreasonable, should you afterwards ask me, what was the cause of the whole twenty. This is sufficiently explained in explaining the cause of the parts."[5]

These two criticisms express the major reasons philosophers have given for rejecting what undoubtedly is the most important part of the Cosmological Argument—namely, that portion of the argument which seeks to establish that not every being can be a dependent being. In this paper my aim is to defend the Cosmological Argument against both of these criticisms. I shall endeavor to show that each of these criticisms rests on a philosophical mistake.

The first criticism draws attention to what appears to be a fatal flaw in the Cosmological Argument. It seems that the proponent of the argument *(i)* ascribes to the infinite collection itself a property (having a cause or explanation) which is applicable only to the members of that collection, and *(ii)* does so by means of a fallacious inference from a proposition about the members of the collection to a proposition about the collection itself. There are, then, two alleged mistakes committed here. The first error is, perhaps, a category mistake—the ascription to the collection of a property applicable only to the members of the collection. As Russell would say, the collection, in comparison with its members, belongs to a "different logical sphere." The second error is apparently what leads the proponent of the Cosmological Argument to make the first error. He ascribes the property of having an explanation to the infinite collection because he *infers* that the infinite collection must have a cause or explanation from the premise that each of its members has a cause. But to infer this, Russell suggests, is as fallacious as to infer that the human race must have a mother because each member of the human race has a mother.

That the proponent of the Cosmological Argument ascribes the property of having a cause or explanation to the infinite collection of dependent beings is certainly true. That to do so is a category mistake is, I think, questionable. But before pursuing this point I want to deal with the second charge. The main question we must consider in connection with the second charge is whether the Cosmological Argument involves the inference: Every member of the infinite collection has an explanation of its existence; therefore, the infinite collection itself has an

---

[4]"The Existence of God, A Debate between Bertrand Russell and Father F. C. Copleston," in John Hick (ed.), *The Existence of God* (New York: Macmillan, 1964), p. 175. The debate was originally broadcast by the British Broadcasting Corporation in 1948. References are to the debate as reprinted in *The Existence of God*.

[5]*Dialogues*, Part IX.

explanation of its existence. As we have seen, Russell thinks that Copleston has employed this inference in coming to the conclusion that there must be an explanation for the totality of things, and not simply for each of the things making up that totality.

Perhaps some proponents of the Cosmological Argument have used the argument which Russell regards as fallacious. But not all of them have.[6] Moreover, there is no need to employ such an inference since in its first premise the Cosmological Argument has available a principle from which it follows that the infinite collection of dependent beings must have an explanation of its existence. Thus one famous exponent of the argument—Samuel Clarke—reasons that the infinite collection of beings must have an explanation of its existence by appealing to the strong form of the Principle of Sufficient Reason. The principle assures us that whatever exists has an explanation of its existence. But if there exists an infinite succession or collection of dependent beings then that collection or succession, Clarke reasons, must have an explanation of its existence. Hence, we can, I think, safely dismiss the charge that the Cosmological Argument involves an erroneous inference from the premise that the members of a collection have a certain property to the conclusion that the collection itself must have that property.

We must now deal with the question whether it makes *sense* to ascribe the property of having an explanation or cause to the infinite collection of dependent beings. Clearly only if it does make sense is the reasoning in support of proposition (3) of the main argument acceptable. Our question, then, is whether it makes sense to ask for a cause or explanation of the entire universe, conceiving the universe as an infinite collection of dependent beings.

One recent critic of the Cosmological Argument, Ronald Hepburn, has stated our problem as follows:

> When we are seriously speaking of absolutely everything there is, are we speaking of something that requires a cause, in the way that events *in* the universe may require causes? What indeed can be safely said at all about the totality of things? For a great many remarks that one can make with perfect propriety about limited things quite obviously can*not* be made about the cosmos itself. It cannot, for instance, be said meaningfully to be "above" or "below" anything, although things-in-the-universe can be so related to one another. Whatever we might claim to be "*below* the universe" would turn out to be just some more *universe*. We should have been relating part to part, instead of relating the whole to something not-the-universe. The same applies to "outside the universe." We can readily imagine a boundary, a garden wall, shall we say, round something that we want to call the universe. But if we imagine ourselves boring a hole through that wall and pushing a stick out *beyond* it into a nameless zone "outside," we should still not in fact have given meaning to the phrase "outside the universe." For the place into which the stick was intruding would deserve to be called a part of the universe (even if consisting of empty space, no matter) just as much as the area within the walls. We should have demonstrated *not* that the universe has an outside, but that what we took to be the whole universe was not really the whole.

---

[6] Samuel Clarke did not. Nor do we find Hume appealing to this inference in the course of presenting the Cosmological Argument in Part IX of the *Dialogues*.

Our problem is this. Supposing we could draw up a list of questions that can be asked about objects in the universe, but cannot be asked about the *whole* universe: would the question, 'Has it a cause?' be on that list? One thing is clear. Whether or not this question is on the proscribed list, we are not entitled to argue as the Cosmological Argument does that *because* things in the world have causes, therefore the sum of things must also have *its* cause. No more (as we have just seen) can we argue from the fact that things in the world have tops and bottoms, insides and outsides, and are related to other things, to the belief that the universe has its top and bottom, inside and outside, and is related to a supra-cosmical something.[7]

In this passage Hepburn *(i)* points out that some properties (e.g., "above," "below," etc.) of things in the universe cannot properly be ascribed to the total universe, *(ii)* raises the question whether "having a cause" is such a property, and *(iii)* concludes that ". . . we are not entitled to argue as the Cosmological Argument does that *because* things in the world have causes, therefore, the sum of things must also have *its* cause." We noted earlier that the Cosmological Argument (i.e., the version we are examining) does not argue that the sum of things (the infinite collection of dependent beings) must have a cause *because* each being in the collection has a cause. Thus we may safely ignore Hepburn's main objection. However, his other two points are well taken. There certainly are properties which it makes sense to apply to things within a collection but which it makes no sense to apply to the collection itself. What assurance do we have that "having a cause" is not such a property?

Suppose we are holding in our hands a collection of ten marbles. Not only would each marble have a definite weight but the collection itself would have a weight. Indeed, from the premise that each marble weighs more than one ounce we could infer validly that the collection itself weighs more than an ounce. This example shows that it is not always fallacious to infer that a collection has a certain property from the premise that each member of the collection has that property.[8] But the collection in this example is, we might say, *concrete* rather than *abstract*. That is, we are here considering the collection as itself a physical entity, an aggregate of marbles. This, of course, is not a collection in the sense of a class or set of things. Holding several marbles in my hands I can consider the *set* whose members are those marbles. The set itself, being an *abstract* entity, rather than a physical heap, has no weight. Just as the set of human beings has no mother, so the set whose members are marbles in my hand has no weight. Therefore, in considering whether it makes sense to speak of the infinite collection of dependent beings as having a cause or explanation of its existence it is important to decide whether we are speaking of a collection as a *concrete* entity—for example, a physical whole or aggregate—or an *abstract* entity.

Suppose we view the infinite collection of dependent beings as itself a concrete entity. As far as the Cosmological Argument is concerned, one advantage of so

---

[7] Ronald W. Hepburn, *Christianity and Paradox* (London: Watts, 1958), pp. 167–168.

[8] For a consideration of inferences of this sort in connection with the fallacy of composition see my paper "The Fallacy of Composition," *Mind*, 71 (January 1962). For some needed corrections of my paper see Yehoshua Bar-Hillel, "More on the Fallacy of Composition," *Mind*, 73 (January 1964).

viewing it is that it is understandable why it might have the property of having a cause or explanation of its existence. For concrete entities—physical objects, events, physical heaps—can be caused. Thus if the infinite collection is a concrete entity it may well make sense to ascribe to it the property of having a cause or explanation.

But such a view of the infinite collection is implausible, if not plainly incorrect. Many collections of physical things cannot possibly be themselves concrete entities. Think, for example, of the collection whose members are the largest prehistoric beast, Socrates, and the Empire State Building. By any stretch of the imagination can we view this collection as itself a concrete thing? Clearly we cannot. Such a collection must be construed as an *abstract* entity, a class or set.[9] But if there are many collections of beings which cannot be concrete entities, what grounds have we for thinking that on the supposition that every being that is or ever was is dependent the collection of those beings would itself be a concrete thing such as a physical heap? At any rate our knowledge of the things (both past and present) comprising the universe and their interrelations would have to be much greater than it currently is before we would be entitled to view the *sum* of concrete things, past and present, as itself something *concrete*.

But if the infinite collection of dependent beings is to be understood as an abstract entity, say the set whose members include all the beings that are or ever were, haven't we conceded the point to Russell? A set or class conceived of as an abstract entity has no weight, is not below or above anything, and cannot be thought of as being caused or brought into being. Thus if the infinite collection is a set, an abstract entity, is not Russell right in charging that it makes no more sense to ascribe the property of having a cause or an explanation to the infinite collection than it does to ascribe the property of having a mother to the human race?

Suppose that every being that is or ever was is dependent. Suppose further that the number of such beings is infinite. Let A be the set consisting of these beings. Thus no being exists or ever existed which is not a member of A. Does it make *sense* to ask for an explanation of A's existence? We do, of course, ask questions about sets which are equivalent to questions about their members. For example, "Is set X included in set Y?" is equivalent to the question "Is every member of X a member of Y?" I suggest that the question "Why does A exist?" be taken to mean "Why does A have the members that it does rather than some other members or none at all?" Consider, for example, the set of men. Let M be this set. The question "Why does M exist?" is perhaps odd if we understand it as a request for an explanation of the existence of an abstract entity. But the question "Why does M exist?" may be taken to mean "Why does M have the members it has rather than some other members or none at all?" So understood the form of words "Why does M exist?" does, I think, ask an intelligible question. It is a contingent fact that Hitler existed. Indeed, it is a contingent fact that any men exist at all.

---

[9] Of course, the three members of this collection, unlike the members of the collection of dependent beings, presumably are causally related. But it is equally easy to think of collections which cannot possibly be concrete entities whose members are causally related—e.g., the collection whose members are the ancestors of a given man.

One of Leibniz' logically possible worlds is a world which includes some members of M, for example Socrates and Plato, but not others, say Hitler and Stalin. Another is a world in which the set of men is entirely empty and therefore identical with the null set. Why is it, then, that M exists? That is, why does M have just the members it has rather than some other members or none at all? Not only is this question intelligible but we seem to have some idea of what its answer is. Presumably, the theory of evolution might be a part of the explanation of why M is not equivalent to the null set and why its members have certain properties rather than others.

But if the question "Why does M exist?" makes sense, why should not the question "Why does A exist?" also make sense? A is the set of dependent beings. In asking why A exists we are not asking for an explanation of the existence of an abstract entity; we are asking why A has the members it has rather than some other members or none at all. I submit that this question does make sense. Moreover, I think that it is precisely this question which the proponents of the Cosmological Argument were asking when they asked for an explanation of the existence of the infinite collection or succession of dependent beings.[10] Of course, it is one thing for a question to make sense and another thing for there to be an answer to it.

The interpretation I have given to the question "Why does A exist?" is somewhat complex. For according to this interpretation what is being asked is not simply why does A have members rather than having none, but also why does A have just the members it has rather than having some other members. Although the proponents of the Cosmological Argument do seem to interpret the question in this way, it will facilitate our discussion if we simplify the interpretation somewhat by focusing our attention solely on the question why A has the members it has rather than having none. Hence, for purposes of simplification, in what follows I shall take the question "Why does A exist?" to mean "Why does A have the members it has rather than not having any?"

For any being to be a member of A it is necessary and sufficient that it have the reason of its existence in the causal efficacy of some other being. Imagine the following state of affairs. A has exactly three members: a_1, a_2, and a_3. a_3 exists by reason of the causal efficacy of a_2, and a_2 exists by reason of the causal efficacy of a_1. There exists an *eternal* being b which does not exist by reason of the causal efficacy of any other being. Since b is not a dependent being, b is not a member of A. At a certain time a_1 came into existence by reason of the causal efficacy of b. Clearly the question "Why does A exist?" when taken to mean "Why does A have the members it has rather than none at all?" makes sense when asked within the context of this imagined state of affairs. Indeed, part of the answer to the question would involve reference to b and its causal efficacy in bringing about the existence of one of the members of A, namely a_1.

What this case shows is that the question "Why does A exist?" is not always

---

[10] Thus in speaking of the infinite succession, Hume has Demea say: ". . . and yet it is evident that it requires a cause or reason, as much as any particular object which begins to exist in time. The question is still reasonable, *why this particular succession of causes existed from eternity, and not any other succession, or no succession at all*" (*Dialogues*, Part IX; italics mine).

(i.e., in every context) meaningless. If Russell holds that the question is meaningless, in the framework of the Cosmological Argument it must be because of some special assumption about A which forms part of the context of the Cosmological Argument. The assumption in question undoubtedly is that absolutely every being is dependent. On this assumption every being which is or ever was has membership in A and A has an infinite number of members.

Perhaps Russell's view is that within the context of the assumption that *every* being is dependent it makes no sense to ask why A has the members it has rather than none at all. It makes no sense, he might argue, for two reasons. First, on the assumption that every being is dependent there could not be such a thing as the *set* A whose members are all dependent beings. For the set A is, although abstract, presumably a being. But if every being is dependent then A would have to be dependent and therefore a member of itself. But apart from whatever difficulties arise when a set is said to be a member of itself, it would seem to make little sense to think of an abstract entity, such as a set, as being caused, as having the reason of its existence within the causal efficacy of some other being.

Second, Russell might argue that the assumption that every being is dependent and therefore a member of A rules out the possibility of any answer to the question why A has the members it has rather than none at all. For on that assumption our question about A is in effect a question about the totality of things. And, as Russell observes, "I see no reason whatsoever to suppose that the total has any cause whatsoever."[11]

Neither of these reasons suffices to show that our question about A is meaningless. The first reason does, however, point up the necessity of introducing some restriction of the assumption "Every being is dependent" in order that abstract entities like numbers and sets not fall within the scope of the expression "Every being." Such a restoration will obviate the difficulty that A is said to be both a member of itself and dependent. I propose the following rough restriction. In speaking of beings we shall restrict ourselves to beings that *could be caused* to exist by some other being or *could be causes* of the existence of other beings. God (if he exists), a man, the sun, a stone are beings of this sort. Presumably, numbers, sets, and the like are not. The assumption that every being is dependent is to be understood under this restriction. That is, we are here assuming that every being of the sort described by the restriction is *in fact* a being which exists by reason of the causal efficacy of some other being. The second reason given confuses the issue of whether a question makes sense, is meaningful, with the issue of whether a question has an answer. Of course, given the assumption that every being is a member of A we cannot expect to find the cause or reason of A's existence in some being which is not a member of A. If the explanation for A's existence cannot be found within A itself then we must conclude that there can be no explanation for the infinite collection of dependent beings. But this is to say only that on our assumption that every being is dependent there is no answer to the question "Why does A exist?" It is one thing for a question not to have an answer and quite another thing for the question to be *meaningless*.

[11] "Debate," p. 175.

We have been examining the first of the two major criticisms philosophers have directed at the reasoning the Cosmological Argument provides in support of the proposition that not every being is dependent. The heart of this criticism is that it *makes no sense* to ascribe the property of having a cause or explanation to the infinite collection of dependent beings. This criticism, I think, has been shown to be correct in one way, but incorrect in another. If we construe the infinite collection of dependent beings as an abstract entity, a set, it perhaps does not make sense to claim that something caused the existence of this abstract entity. But the question "Why does A exist?" may be interpreted to mean, "Why does A have the members it has rather than none at all?" I have argued that taken in this way the question "Why does A exist?" is a *meaningful* question.

According to the Principle of Sufficient Reason there must be an answer to the question "Why does A exist?," an explanation of the existence of the infinite collection of dependent beings. Moreover, the explanation either must lie in the causal efficacy of some being outside of the collection or it must lie within the collection itself. But since by supposition every being is dependent—and therefore in the collection—there is no being outside the collection whose causal efficacy might explain the existence of the collection. Therefore, either the collection has the explanation of its existence within itself *or* there can be no explanation of its existence. If the first alternative is rejected then, since the Principle of Sufficient Reason requires that everything has an explanation of its existence, we must reject the supposition that every being is dependent. For on that supposition there is no explanation for why there is an infinite collection of dependent beings.

The second major criticism argues that the proponent of the Cosmological Argument is mistaken in thinking that the explanation of the existence of the infinite collection cannot be found within the collection itself. The explanation of the existence of the collection is provided, so the criticism goes, once we learn what the explanation is of each of the members of the collection. As we noted earlier, this criticism was succinctly expressed by Hume in his remark: "Did I show you the particular causes of each individual in a collection of twenty particles of matter, I should think it very unreasonable, should you afterwards ask me, what was the cause of the whole twenty. This is sufficiently explained in explaining the cause of the parts." Applying this objection to the infinite collection of dependent beings, we obtain the result that to explain the existence of the infinite collection, A, amounts to no more than explaining the existence of each of its members. Now, of course, A is unlike Hume's collection of twenty particles in that we cannot give *individual* explanations for each of the members of A. For since A has an infinite number of members we would have to give an infinite number of explanations. But our inability to give a particular explanation for each of the members of A does not imply that there is any member of A for whose existence there is no explanation. Indeed, from the fact that each member of A is dependent (i.e., has the reason of its existence in the causal efficacy of some other being), we know that every member of A has an explanation of its existence; from the assumption that every being is a member of A we know that for each member of A the explanation lies in the causal efficacy of some other member of A. But, so the criticism goes, if every member of A has an explanation of its existence then the existence of A has been sufficiently explained. For to explain why a certain collection of things exists it is sufficient to explain the existence of each of its members. Hence, since we know that the existence of every one of A's members is explained we know that the existence of the collection A is explained.

This forceful criticism, originally advanced by Hume, has gained wide acceptance in contemporary philosophy. Indeed, the only remaining problem seems to be to explain why the proponents of the Cosmological Argument failed to see that to explain the existence of all the members of a collection is to explain the existence of the collection. In restating Hume's criticism, Paul Edwards suggests that perhaps they may have been misled by grammar.

> The demand to find the cause of the series as a whole rests on the erroneous assumption that the series is something over and above the members of which it is composed. It is tempting to suppose this, at least by implication, because the word "series" is a noun like "dog" or "man." Like the expression "this dog" or "this man" the phrase "this series" is easily taken to designate an individual object. But reflection shows this to be an error. If we have explained the individual members there is nothing additional left to be explained. Suppose I see a group of five Eskimos standing on the corner of Sixth Avenue and 50th Street and I wish to explain why the group came to New York. Investigation reveals the following stories:
> Eskimo No. 1 did not enjoy the extreme cold in the polar region and decided to move to a warmer climate.
> No. 2 is the husband of Eskimo No. 1. He loves her dearly and did not wish to live without her.
> No. 3 is the son of Eskimos 1 and 2. He is too small and too weak to oppose his parents.
> No. 4 saw an advertisement in the *New York Times* for an Eskimo to appear on television.
> No. 5 is a private detective engaged by the Pinkerton Agency to keep an eye on Eskimo No. 4.
> Let us assume that we have now explained in the case of each of the five Eskimos why he or she is in New York. Somebody then asks: "All right, but what about the group as a whole; why is *it* in New York?" This would plainly be an absurd question. There is no group over and above the five members, and if we have explained why each of the five members is in New York we have *ipso facto* explained why the group is there. It is just as absurd to ask for the cause of the series as a whole as distinct from asking for the causes of the individual members.[12]

The principle underlying the Hume–Edwards criticism may be stated as follows: *If the existence of every member of a set is explained the existence of that set is thereby explained.* This principle seems to be a corollary of our interpretation of the question "Why does this set exist?" For on our interpretation, once it is explained why the set has the members it has rather than none at all it is thereby explained why the set exists. And it would seem that if a set A has, say, three members, a_1, a_2, and a_3, then if we explain the existence of a_1, a_2, and a_3 we

---

[12] Paul Edwards, "The Cosmological Argument," in Donald R. Burrill (ed.), *The Cosmological Arguments* (New York: Doubleday, 1967), pp. 113–114. Edwards' paper was originally published in *The Rationalist Annual for the Year 1959*.

have explained why A has the members it has rather than none at all. Thus the principle which underlies the second major criticism seems to be implied by our conception of what is involved in explaining the existence of a set.

The principle underlying the Hume–Edwards criticism seems plausible enough when restricted to finite sets, i.e., sets with a finite number of members. But the principle is false, I believe, when extended to infinite sets in which the explanation of each member's existence is found in the causal efficacy of some other member. Consider M, the set of men. Suppose M consists of an infinite number of members, each member owing its existence to some other member which generated it. Suppose further that to explain the existence of a given man it is sufficient to note that he was begotten by some other man. That is, where x and y are men and x begat y we allow that the existence of y is explained by the causal efficacy of x. On these suppositions it is clear that the antecedent of the principle is satisfied with respect to M. For every member of M has an explanation of its existence. But does it follow that the existence of M has an explanation? I think not. We do not have an explanation of the existence of M until we have an explanation of why M has the members it has rather than none at all. But clearly if *all* we know is that there always have been men and that every man's existence is explained by the causal efficacy of some other man, we do not know *why* there always have been men rather than none at all. If I ask why M has the members it has rather than none, it is no answer to say that M always had members. We may, I suppose, answer the question "Why does M have the *currently existing* members it has?" by saying that M always had members and there were men who generated the currently existing men. But in asking why M has the members it has rather than none at all we are not asking why M has the currently existing members it has. To make this clear, we may rephrase our question as follows: "Why is it that M has now and always had members rather than never having had any members at all?" Surely we have not learned the answer to this question when we have learned that there always have been members of M and that each member's existence is explained by the causal efficacy of some other member.

What we have just seen is that from the fact that the existence of each member of a collection is explained it does not follow that the existence of the collection is thereby explained. It does not follow because when the collection (set) has an infinite number of members, each member's existence having its explanation in the causal efficacy of *some other member*, it is true that the existence of every member has an explanation, and yet it is still an open question whether the existence of the set has an explanation. To explain the existence of a set we must explain why it has the members it has rather than none. But clearly if every member's existence is explained by some other *member*, then although the existence of every member has an explanation it is still unexplained why the set has the members it has, rather than none at all.

Put somewhat differently, we have seen that the fact (assuming for the moment that it is a fact) that there always have been men, each man's existence brought about by some other man, is insufficient to explain *why* it is a fact that there always have been men rather than a fact that there never have been any men. If someone asks us to explain why there always have been men rather than never having been any it would not suffice for us to observe that there always have been men and each man has been brought into existence by some other man.

I have argued that the second major criticism rests on a false principle, namely, that if the existence of every member of a set is explained then the existence of that set is thereby explained. This principle, so far as I can determine, is true when restricted to sets with a *finite* number of members. For example, if a set A has two members, a_1 and a_2, and if we explain a_2 by a_1 and a_1 by some being b that caused a_1, then, I think, we have explained the existence of A. In any case we have explained why A has members rather than none at all. Thus I am not claiming that the principle underlying Hume's objection is always false. Indeed, as I have just indicated, it is easy to provide an example of a finite set of which the principle is true. And perhaps it is just this feature of the principle—i.e., its plausibility when applied to finite sets such as Hume's collection of twenty particles and Edwards' five Eskimos—which has led Hume and many philosophers since Hume to reject the Cosmological Argument's thesis that even if every member of the infinite succession of dependent beings has an explanation the infinite succession itself is not thereby explained. If so, then the mistake Hume and his successors have made is to assume that a principle which is true of all finite sets also is true of all infinite sets.

We know, for example, that if we have a set B consisting of five members and a set C consisting of three of the members of B, the members of C cannot be put in one-to-one correspondence with those of B. In reflecting on this fact, we are tempted to conclude that for *any* two sets X and Y, if all the members of X are members of Y but some members of Y are not members of X then the members of X cannot be put in one-to-one correspondence with those of Y. Indeed, so long as X and Y are restricted to *finite* sets the principle just stated is true. But if we let X be the set of *even* natural numbers—2, 4, 6, . . .—and Y be the set of natural numbers—1, 2, 3, . . .—the principle is shown to be false. For although all the members of X are members of Y and some members of Y—the odd integers—are not members of X, it is not true that the members of X cannot be put in one-to-one correspondence with those of Y. What this example illustrates is that a principle which holds of all finite sets may not hold of all infinite sets. The principle underlying the second major criticism is, I have argued, such a principle.

One final point concerning my reply to the second major criticism needs to be made clear. In rejecting the principle on which the criticism rests I have contended that when a set has an *infinite* number of members, every one of which has an explanation of its existence, it *does not follow* that the existence of the set is thereby explained. In saying this I do not mean to imply that in explaining the existence of every member of an infinite set we never thereby explain the existence of the set, only that we *sometimes* do not. Specifically, we do not, I think, when we explain the existence of each member of the set by some other member of *that set*. Recall our example of M, the set of men. If we think of the members of this set as forming a temporal series stretching infinitely back in time, each member's existence explained by the causal efficacy of the preceding member, we have an example, I think, in which an explanation of the existence of each member of M does not constitute an explanation of the existence of M. Let us suppose that each man is produced not by another man but by some superior being, say a god. What we are supposing is that M is described as before except that instead of every member having the explanation of its existence in some preceding member of M the explanation is found in the causal efficacy of some member of the set of gods. From eternity, then, gods have been producing men. There have always been members of M and every member has an explanation of its existence. Here it does seem true to say that in explaining the existence of every member of M we have thereby explained the existence of M. If someone asks why there now are and always have been men rather than never having been any, we can say in response that there always have been men because there always have been gods producing them. This, if true, would explain why M has always had members.

In this paper I have examined two criticisms which have been advanced against that part of the Cosmological Argument which seeks to establish that not every being can be a dependent being. I have argued that each of these criticisms is mistaken and, therefore, fails as a refutation of the Cosmological Argument. If my arguments are correct, it does not follow, of course, that the Cosmological Argument is a good argument for its conclusion. But it does follow that those philosophers who have rejected the argument for either of the two criticisms discussed in this paper need to re-examine the argument and, if they continue to reject it, provide some *good* reasons for doing so.

THE TELEOLOGICAL ARGUMENT

WILLIAM PALEY
The Evidence of Design

In crossing a heath, suppose I pitched my foot against a *stone*, and were asked how the stone came to be there, I might possibly answer, that, for any thing I knew to the contrary, it had lain there for ever: nor would it perhaps be very easy to shew the absurdity of this answer. But suppose I had found a *watch* upon the ground, and it should be enquired how the watch happened to be in that place, I should hardly think of the answer which I had before given, that, for any thing I knew, the watch might have always been there. Yet why should not this answer serve for the watch as well as for the stone? Why is it not as admissible in the second case, as in the first? For this reason, and for no other, viz. that, when we come to inspect the watch, we perceive (what we could not discover in the stone) that its several parts are framed and put together for a purpose, e.g. that they are so formed and adjusted as to produce motion, and that motion so regulated as to point out the hour of the day; that, if the several parts had been differently shaped from what they are, of a different size from what they are, or placed after any other manner, or in any other order, than that in which they are placed, either no motion at all would have been carried on in the machine, or none which would have answered the use that is now served by it. To reckon up a few of the plainest of these parts, and of their offices, all tending to one result:—We see a cyclindrical box containing a coiled, elastic spring, which, by its endeavour to relax itself, turns round the box. We next observe a flexible chain (artificially wrought for the sake of flexure) communicating the action of the spring from the box to the fusee. We then find a series of wheels, the teeth of which catch in, and apply to, each other, conducting the motion from the fusee to the balance,

William Paley (1743–1805) was an English theologian and a teacher of moral philosophy at Cambridge. His important writings include *Evidences of Christianity* and *Natural Theology*.

THE EVIDENCE OF DESIGN   From *Natural Theology* (ninth edition). London. Printed for R. Faulder, 1805.

and from the balance to the pointer; and at the same time, by the size and shape of those wheels, so regulating that motion, as to terminate in causing an index, by an equable and measured progression, to pass over a given space in a given time. We take notice that the wheels are made of brass, in order to keep them from rust; the springs of steel, no other metal being so elastic; that over the face of the watch there is placed a glass, a material employed in no other part of the work, but in the room of which, if there had been any other than a transparent substance, the hour could not be seen without opening the case. This mechanism being observed (it requires indeed an examination of the instrument, and perhaps some previous knowledge of the subject, to perceive and understand it; but being once, as we have said, observed and understood), the inference, we think, is inevitable, that the watch must have had a maker: that there must have existed, at some time and at some place or other, an artificer or artificers who formed it for the purpose which we find it actually to answer; who comprehended its construction, and designed its use.

I

Nor would it, I apprehend, weaken the conclusion, that we had never seen a watch made; that we had never known an artist capable of making one; that we were altogether incapable of executing such a piece of workmanship ourselves, or of understanding in what manner it was performed; all this being no more than what is true of some exquisite remains of ancient art, of some lost arts, and, to the generality of mankind, of the more curious productions of modern manufacture. Does one man in a million know how oval frames are turned? Ignorance of this kind exalts our opinion of the unseen and unknown, artist's skill, if he be unseen and unknown, but raises no doubt in our minds of the existence and agency of such an artist, at some former time, and in some place or other. Nor can I perceive that it varies at all the inference, whether the question arise concerning a human agent, or concerning an agent of a different species, or an agent possessing, in some respects, a different nature.

II

Neither, secondly, would it invalidate our conclusion, that the watch sometimes went wrong, or that it seldom went exactly right. The purpose of the machinery, the design, and the designer, might be evident, and in the case supposed would be evident, in whatever way we accounted for the irregularity of the movement, or whether we could account for it or not. It is not necessary that a machine be perfect, in order to shew with what design it was made: still less necessary, where the only question is, whether it were made with any design at all.

III

Nor, thirdly, would it bring any uncertainty into the argument, if there were a few parts of the watch, concerning which we could not discover, or had not yet discovered, in what manner they conduced to the general effect; or even some parts, concerning which we could not ascertain, whether they conduced to that effect in any manner whatever. For, as to the first branch of the case; if, by the loss, or disorder, or decay of the parts in question, the movement of the watch were found in fact to be stopped, or disturbed, or retarded, no doubt would remain in our minds as to the utility or intention of these parts, although we should be unable to investigate the manner according to which, or the connection by which, the ultimate effect depended upon their action, or assistance; and the more complex is the machine, the more likely is this obscurity to arise. Then, as to the second thing supposed, namely, that there were parts which might be spared, without prejudice to the movement of the watch, and that we had proved this by experiment,—these superfluous parts, even if we were completely assured that they were such, would not vacate the reasoning which we had instituted concerning other parts. The indication of contrivance remained, with respect to them, nearly as it was before.

IV

Nor, fourthly, would any man in his senses think the existence of the watch, with its various machinery, accounted for, by being told that it was one out of possible combinations of material forms; that whatever he had found in the place where he found the watch, must have contained some internal configuration or other; and that this configuration might be the structure now exhibited, viz. of the works of a watch, as well as a different structure.

V

Nor, fifthly, would it yield his enquiry more satisfaction to be answered, that there existed in things a principle of order, which had disposed the parts of the watch into their present form and situation. He never knew a watch made by the principle of order; nor can he even form to himself an idea of what is meant by a principle of order, distinct from the intelligence of the watch-maker.

VI

Sixthly, he would be surprised to hear, that the mechanism of the watch was no proof of contrivance, only a motive to induce the mind to think so.

VII

And not less surprised to be informed, that the watch in his hand was nothing more than the result of the laws of *metallic* nature. It is a perversion of language to assign any law, as the efficient, operative cause of any thing. A law presupposes an agent; for it is only the mode, according to which an agent proceeds: it implies a power; for it is the order, according to which that power acts. Without this agent, without this power, which are both distinct from itself, the *law* does nothing; is nothing. The expression, "the law of metallic nature," may sound strange and harsh to a philosophic ear, but it seems quite as justifiable as some others which are more familiar to him, such as "the law of vegetable nature"—"the law of animal nature," or indeed as "the law of nature" in general, when assigned as the cause of phænomena, in exclusion of agency and power; or when it is substituted into the place of these.

VIII

Neither, lastly, would our observer be driven out of his conclusion, or from his confidence in its truth, by being told that he knew nothing at all about the matter. He knows enough for his argument. He knows the utility of the end: he knows the subserviency and adaptation of the means to the end. These points being known, his ignorance of other points, his doubts concerning other points, affect not the certainty of his reasoning. The consciousness of knowing little, need not beget a distrust of that which he does know. . . .

Suppose, in the next place, that the person, who found the watch, should, after some time, discover, that, in addition to all the properties which he had hitherto observed in it, it possessed the unexpected property of producing, in the course of its movement, another watch like itself; (the thing is conceivable;) that it contained within it a mechanism, a system of parts, a mould for instance, or a complex adjustment of lathes, files, and other tools, evidently and separately calculated for this purpose; let us enquire, what effect ought such a discovery to have upon his former conclusion.

I

The first effect would be to increase his admiration of the contrivance, and his conviction of the consummate skill of the contriver. Whether he regarded the object of the contrivance, the distinct apparatus, the intricate, yet in many parts intelligible, mechanism, by which it was carried on, he would perceive, in his new observation, nothing but an additional reason for doing what he had already done; for referring the construction of the watch to design, and to supreme art. If that construction *without* this property, or, which is the same thing, before this property had been noticed, proved intention and art to have been employed about it; still more strong would the proof appear, when he came to the knowledge of this further property, the crown and perfection of all the rest.

II

He would reflect, that though the watch before him were, *in some sense*, the maker of the watch, which was fabricated in the course of its movements, yet it was in a very different sense from that, in which a carpenter, for instance, is the maker of a chair; the author of its contrivance, the cause of the relation of its parts to their use. With respect to these, the first watch was no cause at all to the second: in no such sense as this was it the author of the constitution and order, either of the parts which the new watch contained, or of the parts by the aid and instrumentality of which it was produced. We might possibly way, but with great latitude of expression, that a stream of water ground corn: but no latitude of expression would allow us to say, no stretch of conjecture could lead us to think, that the stream of water built the mill, though it were too ancient for us to know who the builder was. What the stream of water does in the affair is neither more nor less than this: by the application of an unintelligent impulse to a mechanism previously arranged, arranged independently of it, and arranged by intelligence, an effect is produced, viz. the corn is ground. But the effect results from the arrangement. The force of the stream cannot be said to be the cause or author of the effect, still less of the arrangement. Understanding and plan in the formation of the mill were not the less necessary, for any share which the water has in grinding the corn: yet is this share the same, as that which the watch would have contributed to the production of the new watch, upon the supposition assumed in the last section. Therefore,

III

Though it be now no longer probable, that the individual watch which our observer had found, was made immediately by the hand of an artificer, yet doth not this alteration in any wise affect the inference, that an artificer had been originally employed and concerned in the production. The argument from design remains as it was. Marks of design and contrivance are no more accounted for now, than they were before. In the same thing, we may ask for the cause of different properties. We may ask for the cause of the colour of a body, of its hardness, of its heat; and these causes may be all different. We are now asking for the cause of that subserviency to an use, that relation to an end, which we have remarked in the watch before us. No answer is given to this question by telling us that a preceding watch produced it. There cannot be design without a designer; contrivance without a contriver; order without choice; arrangement, without any thing capable of arranging; subserviency and relation to a purpose, without that which could intend a purpose; means suitable to an end, and executing their office in accomplishing that end, without the end ever having been contemplated, or the means accommodated to it. Arrangement, disposition of parts, subserviency of means to an end, relation of instruments to an use, imply the presence of intelligence and mind. No one, therefore, can rationally believe, that the insensible, inanimate watch, from which the watch before us issued, was the proper cause of the mechanism we so much admire in it; could be truly said to have constructed the instrument, disposed its parts, assigned their office, determined their order, action, and mutual dependency, combined their several motions into one result, and that also a result connected with the utilities of other beings. All these properties, therefore, are as much unaccounted for, as they were before.

IV

Nor is any thing gained by running the difficulty further back, i.e. by supposing the watch before us to have been produced from another watch, that from a former, and so on indefinitely. Our going back ever so far brings us no nearer to the least degree of satisfaction upon the subject. Contrivance is still unaccounted for. We still want a contriver. A designing mind is neither supplied by this supposition, nor dispensed with. If the difficulty were diminished the further we went back, by going back indefinitely we might exhaust it. And this is the only case to which this sort of reasoning applies. Where there is a tendency, or, as we increase the number of terms, a continual approach towards a limit, *there*, by supposing the number of terms to be what is called infinite, we may conceive the limit to be attained: but where there is no such tendency, or approach, nothing is effected by lengthening the series. There is no difference as to the point in question, (whatever there may be as to many points), between one series and another; between a series which is finite, and a series which is infinite. A chain, composed of an infinite number of links, can no more support itself, than a chain composed of a finite number of links. And of this we are assured, (though we never *can* have tried the experiment), because, by increasing the number of links, from ten for instance to a hundred, from a hundred to a thousand, &c. we make not the smallest approach, we observe not the smallest tendency, towards self-support. There is no difference in this respect (yet there may be a great difference in several respects), between a chain of a greater or less length, between one chain and another, between one that is finite and one that is infinite. This very much resembles the case before us. The machine, which we are inspecting, demonstrates, by its construction, contrivance and design. Contrivance must have had a contriver, design, a designer; whether the machine immediately proceeded from another machine or not. The circumstance alters not the case. That other machine may, in like manner, have proceeded from a former machine: nor does that alter the case: contrivance must have had a contriver. That former one from one preceding it: no alteration still: a contriver is still necessary. No tendency is perceived, no approach towards a diminution of this necessity. It is the same with any and every succession of these machines; a succession of ten, of a hundred, of a thousand; with one series as with another: a series which is finite, as with a series which is infinite. In whatever other respects they may differ, in this they do not. In all equally, contrivance and design are unaccounted for.

The question is not simply, How came the first watch into existence? which question, it may be pretended, is done away by supposing the series of watches thus produced from one another to have been infinite, and consequently to have had no such *first*, for which it was necessary to provide a cause. This, perhaps, would have been nearly the state of the question, if nothing had been before us but an unorganized, unmechanized, substance, without mark or indication of contrivance. It might be difficult to shew that such substance could not have existed from eternity, either in succession (if it were possible, which I think it is not, for unorganized bodies to spring from one another), or by individual perpetuity. But that is not the question now. To suppose it to be so, is to suppose that it made no difference whether we had found a watch or a stone. As it is, the metaphysics of that question have no place; for, in the watch which we are examining, are seen contrivance, design; an end, a purpose; means for the end, adaptation to the purpose. And the question, which irresistibly presses upon our thoughts, is, whence this contrivance and design. The thing required is the intending mind, the adapting hand, the intelligence by which that hand was directed. This question, this demand, is not shaken off, by increasing a number or succession of substances, destitute of these properties; nor the more, by increasing that number to infinity. If it be said, that, upon the supposition of one watch being produced from another in the course of that other's movements, and by means of the mechanism within it, we have a cause for the watch in my hand, viz. the watch from which it proceeded. I deny, that for the design, the contrivance, the suitableness of means to an end, the adaptation of instruments to an use (all which we discover in the watch), we have any cause whatever. It is in vain, therefore, to assign a series of such causes, or to allege that a series may be carried back to infinity; for I do not admit that we have yet any cause at all of the phænomena, still less any series of causes either finite or infinite. Here is contrivance, but no contriver; proofs of design, but no designer.

V

Our observer would further also reflect, that the maker of the watch before him, was, in truth and reality, the maker of every watch produced from it; there being no difference (except that the latter manifests a more exquisite skill) between the making of another watch with his own hands, by the mediation of files, lathes, chisels, &c. and the disposing, fixing, and inserting of these instruments, or of others equivalent to them, in the body of the watch already made, in such a manner, as to form a new watch in the course of the movements which he had given to the old one. It is only working by one set of tools, instead of another.

The conclusion which the *first* examination of the watch, of its works, construction, and movement, suggested, was, that it must have had, for the cause and author of that construction, an artificer, who understood its mechanism, and designed its use. This conclusion is invincible. A *second* examination presents us with a new discovery. The watch is found, in the course of its movement, to produce another watch, similar to itself: and not only so, but we perceive in it a system of organization, separately calculated for that purpose. What effect would this discovery have, or ought it to have, upon our former inference? What, as hath already been said, but to increase, beyond measure, our admiration of the skill, which had been employed in the formation of such a machine? Or shall it, instead of this, all at once turn us round to an opposite conclusion, viz. that no art or skill whatever has been concerned in the business, although all other evidences of art and skill remain as they were, and this last and supreme piece of art be now added to the rest? Can this be maintained without absurdity? Yet this is atheism.

This is atheism: for every indication of contrivance, every manifestation of design, which existed in the watch, exists in the works of nature; with the difference, on the side of nature, of being greater and more, and that in a degree which exceeds all computation. I mean that the contrivances of nature surpass the contrivances of art, in the complexity, subtility, and curiosity of the mechanism; and still more, if possible, do they go beyond them in number and variety: yet, in a multitude of cases, are not less evidently mechanical, not less evidently contrivances, not less evidently accommodated to their end, or suited to their office, than are the most perfect productions of human ingenuity. . . .

DAVID HUME
Design and the Teleological Argument

PART II

. . . Look round the world: contemplate the whole and every part of it: You will find it to be nothing but one great machine, subdivided into an infinite number of lesser machines, which again admit of subdivisions to a degree beyond what human senses and faculties can trace and explain. All these various machines, and even their most minute parts, are adjusted to each other with an accuracy which ravishes into admiration all men who have ever contemplated them. The curious adapting of means to ends, throughout all nature, resembles exactly, though it much exceeds, the productions of human contrivance; of human design, thought, wisdom, and intelligence. Since therefore the effects resemble each other, we are led to infer, by all the rules of analogy, that the causes also resemble; and that the Author of Nature is somewhat similar to the mind of man, though possessed of much larger faculties, proportioned to the grandeur of the work which he has executed. By this argument *a posteriori*, and by this argument alone, do we prove at once the existence of a Deity, and his similarity to human mind and intelligence.

I shall be so free, Cleanthes, said Demea, as to tell you, that from the beginning I could not approve of your conclusion concerning the similarity of the Deity to men; still less can I approve of the mediums by which you endeavour to establish it. What! No demonstration of the Being of God! No abstract arguments! No proofs *a priori*! Are these, which have hitherto been so much insisted on by philosophers, all fallacy, all sophism? Can we reach no farther in this subject than

DESIGN AND THE TELEOLOGICAL ARGUMENT　From *Dialogues Concerning Natural Religion*, Parts II, V, and VII. *The Philosophical Works of David Hume*, Volume II. Edinburgh, Adam Black and William Tait; and Charles Tait, 1876.

experience and probability? I will not say that this is betraying the cause of a Deity: But surely, by this affected candour, you give advantages to Atheists, which they never could obtain by the mere dint of argument and reasoning.

What I chiefly scruple in this subject, said Philo, is not so much that all religious arguments are by Cleanthes reduced to experience, as that they appear not to be even the most certain and irrefragable of that inferior kind. That a stone will fall, that fire will burn, that the earth has solidity, we have observed a thousand and a thousand times; and when any new instance of this nature is presented, we draw without hesitation the accustomed inference. The exact similarity of the cases gives us a perfect assurance of a similar event; and a stronger evidence is never desired nor sought after. But wherever you depart, in the least, from the similarity of the cases, you diminish proportionably the evidence; and may at last bring it to a very weak *analogy*, which is confessedly liable to error and uncertainty. After having experienced the circulation of the blood in human creatures, we make no doubt that it takes place in Titius and Mævius: But from its circulation in frogs and fishes, it is only a presumption, though a strong one, from analogy, that it takes place in men and other animals. The analogical reasoning is much weaker, when we infer the circulation of the sap in vegetables from our experience that the blood circulates in animals; and those, who hastily followed that imperfect analogy, are found, by more accurate experiments, to have been mistaken.

If we see a house, Cleanthes, we conclude, with the greatest certainty, that it had an architect or builder; because this is precisely that species of effect which we have experienced to proceed from that species of cause. But surely you will not affirm, that the universe bears such a resemblance to a house, that we can with the same certainty infer a similar cause, or that the analogy is here entire and perfect. The dissimilitude is so striking, that the utmost you can here pretend to is a guess, a conjecture, a presumption concerning a similar cause; and how that pretension will be received in the world, I leave you to consider.

It would surely be very ill received, replied Cleanthes; and I should be deservedly blamed and detested, did I allow, that the proofs of a Deity amounted to no more than a guess or conjecture. But is the whole adjustment of means to ends in a house and in the universe so slight a resemblance? The economy of final causes? The order, proportion, and arrangement of every part? Steps of a stair are plainly contrived, that human legs may use them in mounting; and this inference is certain and infallible. Human legs are also contrived for walking and mounting; and this inference, I allow, is not altogether so certain, because of the dissimilarity which you remark; but does it, therefore, deserve the name only of presumption or conjecture?

Good God! cried Demea, interrupting him, where are we? Zealous defenders of religion allow, that the proofs of a Deity fall short of perfect evidence! And you, Philo, on whose assistance I depended in proving the adorable mysteriousness of the Divine Nature, do you assent to all these extravagant opinions of Cleanthes? For what other name can I give them? or, why spare my censure, when such principles are advanced, supported by such an authority, before so young a man as Pamphilus?

You seem not to apprehend, replied Philo, that I argue with Cleanthes in his own way; and, by showing him the dangerous consequences of his tenets, hope at last to reduce him to our opinion. But what sticks most with you, I observe, is the representation which Cleanthes has made of the argument *a posteriori*; and finding that that argument is likely to escape your hold and vanish into air, you think it so disguised, that you can scarcely believe it to be set in its true light. Now, however, much I may dissent, in other respects, from the dangerous principles of Cleanthes, I must allow that he has fairly represented that argument; and I shall endeavour so to state the matter to you, that you will entertain no farther scruples with regard to it.

Were a man to abstract from every thing which he knows or has seen, he would be altogether incapable, merely from his own ideas, to determine what kind of scene the universe must be, or to give the preference to one state or situation of things above another. For as nothing which he clearly conceives could be esteemed impossible or implying a contradiction, every chimera of his fancy would be upon an equal footing; nor could he assign any just reason why he adheres to one idea or system, and rejects the others which are equally possible.

Again; after he opens his eyes, and contemplates the world as it really is, it would be impossible for him at first to assign the cause of any one event, much less of the whole of things, or of the universe. He might set his fancy a rambling; and she might bring him in an infinite variety of reports and representations. These would all be possible; but being all equally possible, he would never of himself give a satisfactory account for his preferring one of them to the rest. Experience alone can point out to him the true cause of any phenomenon.

Now, according to this method of reasoning, Demea, it follows (and is, indeed, tacitly allowed by Cleanthes himself), that order, arrangement, or the adjustment of final causes, is not of itself any proof of design; but only so far as it has been experienced to proceed from that principle. For aught we can know *a priori*, matter may contain the source or spring of order originally within itself, as well as mind does; and there is no more difficulty in conceiving, that the several elements, from an internal unknown cause, may fall into the most exquisite arrangement, than to conceive that their ideas, in the great universal mind, from a like internal unknown cause, fall into that arrangement. The equal possibility of both these suppositions is allowed. But, by experience, we find, (according to Cleanthes), that there is a difference between them. Throw several pieces of steel together, without shape or form; they will never arrange themselves so as to compose a watch. Stone, and mortar, and wood, without an architect, never erect a house. But the ideas in a human mind, we see, by an unknown, inexplicable economy, arrange themselves so as to form the plan of a watch or house. Experience, therefore, proves, that there is an original principle of order in mind, not in matter. From similar effects we infer similar causes. The adjustment of means to ends is alike in the universe, as in a machine of human contrivance. The causes, therefore, must be resembling.

I was from the beginning scandalized, I must own, with this resemblance, which is asserted, between the Deity and human creatures; and must conceive it to imply such a degradation of the Supreme Being as no sound Theist could endure. With your assistance, therefore, Demea, I shall endeavour to defend what you justly call the adorable mysteriousness of the Divine Nature, and shall refute this reasoning of Cleanthes, provided he allows that I have made a fair representation of it.

When Cleanthes had assented, Philo, after a short pause, proceeded in the following manner.

That all inferences, Cleanthes, concerning fact, are founded on experience; and that all experimental reasonings are founded on the supposition that similar causes prove similar effects, and similar effects similar causes; I shall not at present much dispute with you. But observe, I entreat you, with what extreme caution all just reasoners proceed in the transferring of experiments to similar cases. Unless the cases be exactly similar, they repose no perfect confidence in applying their past observation to any particular phenomenon. Every alteration of circumstances occasions a doubt concerning the event; and it requires new experiments to prove certainly, that the new circumstances are of no moment or importance. A change in bulk, situation, arrangement, age, disposition of the air, or surrounding bodies; any of these particulars may be attended with the most unexpected consequences: And unless the objects be quite familiar to us, it is the highest temerity to expect with assurance, after any of these changes, an event similar to that which before fell under our observation. The slow and deliberate steps of philosophers here, if any where, are distinguished from the precipitate march of the vulgar, who, hurried on by the smallest similitude, are incapable of all discernment or consideration.

But can you think, Cleanthes, that your usual phlegm and philosophy have been preserved in so wide a step as you have taken, when you compared to the universe houses, ships, furniture, machines, and, from their similarity in some circumstances, inferred a similarity in their causes? Thought, design, intelligence, such as we discover in men and other animals, is no more than one of the springs and principles of the universe, as well as heat or cold, attraction or repulsion, and a hundred others, which fall under daily observation. It is an active cause, by which some particular parts of nature, we find, produce alterations on other parts. But can a conclusion, with any propriety, be transferred from parts to the whole? Does not the great disproportion bar all comparison and inference? From observing the growth of a hair, can we learn any thing concerning the generation of a man? Would the manner of a leaf's blowing, even though perfectly known, afford us any instruction concerning the vegetation of a tree?

But, allowing that we were to take the *operations* of one part of nature upon another, for the foundation of our judgment concerning the *origin* of the whole, (which never can be admitted), yet why select so minute, so weak, so bounded a principle, as the reason and design of animals is found to be upon this planet? What peculiar privilege has this little agitation of the brain which we call *thought*, that we must thus make it the model of the whole universe? Our partiality in our own favour does indeed present it on all occasions; but sound philosophy ought carefully to guard against so natural an illusion.

So far from admitting, continued Philo, that the operations of a part can afford us any just conclusion concerning the origin of the whole, I will not allow any one part to form a rule for another part, if the latter be very remote from the former. Is there any reasonable ground to conclude, that the inhabitants of other planets possess thought, intelligence, reason, or any thing similar to these faculties in men? When nature has so extremely diversified her manner of operation in this small globe, can we imagine that she incessantly copies herself throughout so immense a universe? And if thought, as we may well suppose, be confined merely to this narrow corner, and has even there so limited a sphere of action, with what propriety can we assign it for the original cause of all things? The narrow views of a peasant, who makes his domestic economy the rule for the government of king-doms, is in comparison a pardonable sophism.

But were we ever so much assured, that a thought and reason, resembling the human, were to be found throughout the whole universe, and were its activity elsewhere vastly greater and more commanding than it appears in this globe; yet I cannot see, why the operations of a world constituted, arranged, adjusted, can with any propriety be extended to a world which is in its embryo-state, and is advancing towards that constitution and arrangement. By observation, we know somewhat of the economy, action, and nourishment of a finished animal; but we must transfer with great caution that observation to the growth of a fœtus in the womb, and still more to the formation of an animalcule in the loins of its male parent. Nature, we find, even from our limited experience, possesses an infinite number of springs and principles, which incessantly discover themselves on every change of her position and situation. And what new and unknown principles would actuate her in so new and unknown a situation as that of the formation of a universe, we cannot, without the utmost temerity, pretend to determine.

A very small part of this great system, during a very short time, is very imper-fectly discovered to us; and do we thence pronounce decisively concerning the origin of the whole?

Admirable conclusion! Stone, wood, brick, iron, brass, have not, at this time, in this minute globe of earth, an order or arrangement without human art and contrivance; therefore the universe could not originally attain its order and ar-rangement, without something similar to human art. But is a part of nature a rule for another part very wide of the former? Is it a rule for the whole? Is a very small part a rule for the universe? Is nature in one situation, a certain rule for nature in another situation vastly different from the former?

And can you blame me, Cleanthes, if I here imitate the prudent reserve of Simonides, who, according to the noted story, being asked by Hiero, *What God was?* desired a day to think of it, and then two days more; and after that manner continually prolonged the term, without ever bringing in his definition or descrip-tion? Could you even blame me, if I had answered at first, *that I did not know*, and was sensible that this subject lay vastly beyond the reach of my faculties? You might cry out sceptic and rallier, as much as you pleased: but having found, in so many other subjects much more familiar, the imperfections and even contra-dictions of human reason, I never should expect any success from its feeble con-jectures, in a subject so sublime, and so remote from the sphere of our observation. When two *species* of objects have always been observed to be conjoined together,

I can *infer*, by custom, the existence of one wherever I *see* the existence of the other; and this I call an argument from experience. But how this argument can have place, where the objects, as in the present case, are single, individual, without parallel, or specific resemblance, may be difficult to explain. And will any man tell me with a serious countenance, that an orderly universe must arise from some thought and art like the human, because we have experience of it? To ascertain this reasoning, it were requisite that we had experience of the origin of worlds; and it is not sufficient, surely, that we have seen ships and cities arise from human art and contrivance.

Philo was proceeding in this vehement manner, somewhat between jest and earnest, as it appeared to me, when he observed some signs of impatience in Cleanthes, and then immediately stopped short. What I had to suggest, said Cleanthes, is only that you would not abuse terms, or make use of popular expressions to subvert philosophical reasonings. You know, that the vulgar often distinguish reason from experience, even where the question relates only to matter of fact and existence; though it is found, where that *reason* is properly analyzed, that it is nothing but a species of experience. To prove by experience the origin of the universe from mind, is not more contrary to common speech, than to prove the motion of the earth from the same principle. And a caviller might raise all the same objections to the Copernican system, which you have urged against my reasonings. Have you other earths, might he say, which you have seen to move? Have . . . .

Yes! cried Philo, interrupting him, we have other earths. Is not the moon another earth, which we see to turn round its centre? Is not Venus another earth, where we observe the same phenomenon? Are not the revolutions of the sun also a confirmation, from analogy, of the same theory? All the planets, are they not earths, which revolve about the sun? Are not the satellites moons, which move round Jupiter and Saturn, and along with these primary planets round the sun? These analogies and resemblances, with others which I have not mentioned, are the sole proofs of the Copernican system; and to you it belongs to consider, whether you have any analogies of the same kind to support your theory.

In reality, Cleanthes, continued he, the modern system of astronomy is now so much received by all inquirers, and has become so essential a part even of our earliest education, that we are not commonly very scrupulous in examining the reasons upon which it is founded. It is now become a matter of mere curiosity to study the first writers on that subject, who had the full force of prejudice to encounter, and were obliged to turn their arguments on every side in order to render them popular and convincing. But if we peruse Galilæo's famous Dialogues concerning the system of the world, we shall find, that that great genius, one of the sublimest that ever existed, first bent all his endeavours to prove, that there was no foundation for the distinction commonly made between elementary and celestial substances. The schools, proceeding from the illusions of sense, had carried this distinction very far; and had established the latter substances to be ingenerable, incorruptible, unalterable, impassible; and had assigned all the opposite qualities to the former. But Galilæo, beginning with the moon, proved its similarity in every particular to the earth; its convex figure, its natural darkness when not illuminated, its density, its distinction into solid and liquid, the variations of its phases, the mutual illuminations of the earth and moon, their mutual eclipses, the inequalities of the lunar surface, &c. After many instances of this kind, with regard to all the planets, men plainly saw that these bodies became proper objects of experience; and that the similarity of their nature enabled us to extend the same arguments and phenomena from one to the other.

In this cautious proceeding of the astronomers, you may read your own condemnation, Cleanthes; or rather may see, that the subject in which you are engaged exceeds all human reason and inquiry. Can you pretend to show any such similarity between the fabric of a house, and the generation of a universe? Have you ever seen nature in any such situation as resembles the first arrangement of the elements? Have worlds ever been formed under your eye; and have you had leisure to observe the whole progress of the phenomenon, from the first appearance of order to its final consummation? If you have, then cite your experience, and deliver your theory. . . .

PART V

But to show you still more inconveniences, continued Philo, in your Anthropomorphism, please to take a new survey of your principles. *Like effects prove like causes.* This is the experimental argument; and this, you say too, is the sole theological argument. Now, it is certain, that the liker the effects are which are seen, and the liker the causes which are inferred, the stronger is the argument. Every departure on either side diminishes the probability, and renders the experiment less conclusive. You cannot doubt of the principle; neither ought you to reject its consequences.

All the new discoveries in astronomy, which prove the immense grandeur and magnificence of the works of Nature, are so many additional arguments for a Deity, according to the true system of Theism; but, according to your hypothesis of experimental Theism, they become so many objections, by removing the effect still farther from all resemblance to the effects of human art and contrivance. For, if Lucretius,[1] even following the old system of the world, could exclaim,

> Quis regere immensi summam, quis habere profundi
> Indu manu validas potis est moderanter habenas?
> Quis pariter cœlos omnes convertere? et omnes
> Ignibus ætheriis terras suffire feraces?
> Omnibus inque locis esse omni tempore præsto?

If Tully[2] esteemed this reasoning so natural, as to put it into the mouth of his Epicurean: 'Quibus enim oculis animi intueri potuit vester Plato fabricam illam tanti operis, qua construi a Deo atque ædificari mundum facit? quæ molito? quæ

[1] Lib. xi. 1094.

[2] De Nat. Deor. lib. i.

ferramenta? qui vectes? quæ machinæ? qui minstri tanti muneris fuerunt? que-madmodum autem obedire et parere voluntati architecti aer, ignis, aqua, terra potuerunt?' If this argument, I say, had any force in former ages, how much greater must it have at present, when the bounds of Nature are so infinitely en-larged, and such a magnificent scene is opened to us? It is still more unreasonable to form our idea of so unlimited a cause from our experience of the narrow productions of human design and invention.

The discoveries by microscopes, as they open a new universe in miniature, are still objections, according to you, arguments, according to me. The farther we push our researches of this kind, we are still led to infer the universal cause of all to be vastly different from mankind, or from any object of human experience and observation.

And what say you to the discoveries in anatomy, chemistry, botany?. . . . These surely are no objections, replied Cleanthes; they only discover new in-stances of art and contrivance. It is still the image of mind reflected on us from innumerable objects. Add, a mind *like the human*, said Philo. I know of no other, replied Cleanthes. And the liker the better, insisted Philo. To be sure, said Cleanthes.

Now, Cleanthes, said Philo, with an air of alacrity and triumph, mark the consequences. *First,* By this method of reasoning, you renounce all claim to infinity in any of the attributes of the Deity. For, as the cause ought only to be proportioned to the effect, and the effect, so far as it falls under our cognizance, is not infinite; what pretensions have we, upon your suppositions, to ascribe that attribute to the Divine Being? You will still insist, that, by removing him so much from all similarity to human creatures, we give in to the most arbitrary hypothesis, and at the same time weaken all proofs of his existence.

Secondly, You have no reason, on your theory, for ascribing perfection to the Deity, even in his finite capacity, or for supposing him free from every error, mistake, or incoherence, in his undertakings. There are many inexplicable diffi-culties in the works of Nature, which, if we allow a perfect author to be proved *a priori,* are easily solved, and become only seeming difficulties, from the narrow capacity of man, who cannot trace infinite relations. But according to your method of reasoning, these difficulties become all real; and perhaps will be insisted on, as new instances of likeness to human art and contrivance. At least, you must ac-knowledge, that it is impossible for us to tell, from our limited views, whether this system contains any great faults, or deserves any considerable praise, if compared to other possible, and even real systems. Could a peasant, if the Æneid were read to him, pronounce that poem to be absolutely faultless, or even assign to it its proper rank among the productions of human wit, he, who had never seen any other production?

But were this world ever so perfect a production, it must still remain uncertain, whether all the excellences of the work can justly be ascribed to the workman. If we survey a ship, what an exalted idea must we form of the ingenuity of the carpenter who framed so complicated, useful, and beautiful a machine? And what surprise must we feel, when we find him a stupid mechanic, who imitated others, and copied an art, which, through a long succession of ages, after multiplied trials, mistakes, corrections, deliberations, and controversies, had been gradually improving? Many worlds might have been botched and bungled, throughout an eternity, ere this system was struck out; much labour lost, many fruitless trials made; and a slow, but continued improvement carried on during infinite ages in the art of world-making. In such subjects, who can determine, where the truth; nay, who can conjecture where the probability lies, amidst a great number of hypotheses which may be proposed, and a still greater which may be imagined?

And what shadows of an argument, continued Philo, can you produce, from your hypothesis, to prove the unity of the Deity? A great number of men join in building a house or ship, in rearing a city, in framing a commonwealth; why may not several deities combine in contriving and framing a world? This is only so much greater similarity to human affairs. By sharing the work among several, we may so much farther limit the attributes of each, and get rid of that extensive power and knowledge, which must be supposed in one deity, and which, according to you, can only serve to weaken the proof of his existence. And if such foolish, such vicious creatures as man, can yet often unite in framing and executing one plan, how much more those deities or demons, whom we may suppose several degrees more perfect!

To multiply causes without necessity, is indeed contrary to true philosophy: but this principle applies not to the present case. Were one deity antecedently proved by your theory, who were possessed of every attribute requisite to the production of the universe; it would be needless, I own (though not absurd), to suppose any other deity existent. But while it is still a question, Whether all these attributes are united in one subject, or dispersed among several independent beings, by what phenomena in nature can we pretend to decide the controversy? Where we see a body raised in a scale, we are sure that there is in the opposite scale, however concealed from sight, some counterposing weight equal to it; but it is still allowed to doubt, whether that weight be an aggregate of several distinct bodies, or one uniform united mass. And if the weight requisite very much exceeds any thing which we have ever seen conjoined in any single body, the former supposition becomes still more probable and natural. An intelligent being of such vast power and capacity as is necessary to produce the universe, or, to speak in the language of ancient philosophy, so prodigious an animal exceeds all analogy, and even comprehension.

But farther, Cleanthes: Men are mortal, and renew their species by generation; and this is common to all living creatures. The two great sexes of male and female, says Milton, animate the world. Why must this circumstance, so universal, so essential, be excluded from those numerous and limited deities? Behold, then, the theogeny of ancient times brought back upon us.

And why not become a perfect Anthropomorphite? Why not assert the deity or deities to be corporeal, and to have eyes, a nose, mouth, ears, &c.? Epicurus maintained, that no man had ever seen reason but in a human figure; therefore the gods must have a human figure. And this argument, which is deservedly so much ridiculed by Cicero, becomes, according to you, solid and philosophical.

In a word, Cleanthes, a man who follows your hypothesis is able perhaps to assert, or conjecture, that the universe, sometime, arose from something like design: but beyond that position he cannot ascertain one single circumstance; and is left afterwards to fix every point of his theology by the utmost license of fancy and hypothesis. This world, for aught he knows, is very faulty and imperfect, compared to a superior standard; and was only the first rude essay of some infant deity, who afterwards abandoned it, ashamed of his lame performance: it is the work only of some dependent, inferior deity; and is the object of derision to his superiors: it is the production of old age and dotage in some superannuated deity; and ever since his death, has run on at adventures, from the first impulse and active force which it received from him. You justly give signs of horror, Demea, at these strange suppositions; but these, and a thousand more of the same kind, are Cleanthes's suppositions, not mine. From the moment the attributes of the Deity are supposed finite, all these have place. And I cannot, for my part, think that so wild and unsettled a system of theology is, in any respect, preferable to none at all.

These suppositions I absolutely disown, cried Cleanthes: they strike me, however, with no horror, especially when proposed in that rambling way in which they drop from you. On the contrary, they give me pleasure, when I see, that, by the utmost indulgence of your imagination, you never get rid of the hypothesis of design in the universe, but are obliged at every turn to have recourse to it. To this concession I adhere steadily; and this I regard as a sufficient foundation for religion.

PART VI

It must be a slight fabric, indeed, said Demea, which can be erected on so tottering a foundation. While we are uncertain whether there is one deity or many; whether the deity or deities, to whom we owe our existence, be perfect or imperfect, subordinate or supreme, dead or alive, what trust or confidence can we repose in them? What devotion or worship address to them? What veneration or obedience pay them? To all the purposes of life the theory of religion becomes altogether useless: and even with regard to speculative consequences, its uncertainty, according to you, must render it totally precarious and unsatisfactory.

To render it still more unsatisfactory, said Philo, there occurs to me another hypothesis, which must acquire an air of profitability from the method of reasoning so much insisted on by Cleanthes. That like effects arise from like causes: this principle he supposes the foundation of all religion. But there is another principle of the same kind, no less certain, and derived from the same source of experience; that where several known circumstances are observed to be similar, the unknown will also be found similar. Thus, if we see the limbs of a human body, we concluded that it is also attended with a human head, though hid from us. Thus, if we see, through a chink in a wall, a small part of the sum, we conclude, that, were the wall removed, we should see the whole body. In short, this method of reasoning is so obvious and familiar, that no scruple can ever be made with regard to its solidity.

Now, if we survey the universe, so far as it falls under our knowledge, it bears a great resemblance to an animal or organized body, and seems actuated with a like principle of life and motion. A continual circulation of matter in it produces no disorder: a continual waste in every part is incessantly repaired: the closest sympathy is perceived throughout the entire system: and each part or member, in performing its proper offices, operates both to its own preservation and to that of the whole. The world, therefore, I infer, is an animal; and the Deity is the SOUL of the world, actuating it, and actuated by it.

You have too much learning, Cleanthes, to be at all surprised at this opinion, which, you know, was maintained by almost all the Theists of antiquity, and chiefly prevails in their discourses and reasonings. For though, sometimes, the ancient philosophers reason from final causes, as if they thought the world the workmanship of God; yet it appears rather their favourite notion to consider it as his body, whose organization renders it subservient to him. And it must be confessed, that, as the universe resembles more a human body than it does the works of human art and contrivance, if our limited analogy could ever, with any propriety, be extended to the whole of nature, the inference seems juster in favour of the ancient than the modern theory.

There are many other advantages, too, in the former theory, which recommended it to the ancient theologians. Nothing [was] more repugnant to all their notions, because nothing [was] more repugnant to common experience, than mind without body; a mere spiritual substance, which fell not under their senses nor comprehension, and of which they had not observed one single instance throughout all nature. Mind and body they knew, because they felt both: an order, arrangement, organization, or internal machinery, in both, they likewise knew, after the same manner: and it could not but seem reasonable to transfer this experience to the universe; and to suppose the divine mind and body to be also coeval, and to have, both of them, order and arrangement naturally inherent in them, and inseparable from them.

Here, therefore, is a new species of *Anthropomorphism*, Cleanthes, on which you may deliberate; and a theory which seems not liable to any considerable difficulties. You are too much superior, surely, to *systematical prejudices*, to find any more difficulty in supposing an animal body to be, originally, of itself, or from unknown causes, possessed of order and organization, than in supposing a similar order to belong to mind. But the *vulgar prejudice*, that body and mind ought always to accompany each other, ought not, one should think, to be entirely neglected; since it is founded on *vulgar experience*, the only guide which you profess to follow in all these theological inquiries. And if you assert, that our limited experience is an unequal standard, by which to judge of the unlimited extent of nature; you entirely abandon your own hypothesis, and must thenceforward adopt our Mysticism, as you call it, and admit of the absolute incomprehensibility of the Divine Nature.

This theory, I own, replied Cleanthes, has never before occurred to me, though a pretty natural one; and I cannot readily, upon so short an examination and reflection, deliver any opinion with regard to it. You are very scrupulous, indeed, said Philo: were I to examine any system of yours, I should not have acted with half that caution and reserve, in starting objections and difficulties to it. However, if any thing occur to you, you will oblige us by proposing it.

Why then, replied Cleanthes, it seems to me, that, though the world does, in many circumstances, resemble an animal body; yet is the analogy also defective in many circumstances the most material: no organs of sense; no seat of thought or reason; no one precise origin of motion and action. In short, it seems to bear a stronger resemblance to a vegetable than to an animal, and your inference would be so far inconclusive in favour of the soul of the world.

THE MORAL ARGUMENT

IMMANUEL KANT
The Moral Argument

V. THE EXISTENCE OF GOD AS A POSTULATE OF PURE PRACTICAL REASON.

In the foregoing analysis the moral law led to a practical problem which is pre-scribed by pure reason alone, without the aid of any sensible motives, namely, that of the necessary completeness of the first and principal element of the *sum-mum bonum*, viz. Morality; and as this can be perfectly solved only in eternity, to the postulate of *immortality*. The same law must also lead us to affirm the possibility of the second element of the *summum bonum*, viz. Happiness propor-tioned to that morality, and this on grounds as disinterested as before, and solely from impartial reason; that is, it must lead to the supposition of the existence of a cause adequate to this effect; in other words, it must postulate the *existence of God*, as the necessary condition of the possibility of the *summum bonum* (an object of the will which is necessarily connected with the moral legislation of pure reason). We proceed to exhibit this connexion in a convincing manner.

Happiness is the condition of a rational being in the world with whom *every-thing goes according to his wish and will*; it rests, therefore, on the harmony of physical nature with his whole end, and likewise with the essential determining principle of his will. Now the moral law as a law of freedom commands by deter-mining principles, which ought to be quite independent on nature and on its harmony with our faculty of desire (as springs). But the acting rational being in the world is not the cause of the world and of nature itself. There is not the least ground, therefore, in the moral law for a necessary connexion between morality and proportionate happiness in a being that belongs to the world as part of it, and

THE MORAL ARGUMENT   From *Kant's Critique of Practical Reason and Other Works* (1788), translated by T. K. Abbott (Rept.; London: Longmans, Green, 1927).

therefore dependent on it, and which for that reason cannot by his will be a cause of this nature, nor by his own power, make it thoroughly harmonize, as far as his happiness is concerned, with his practical principles. Nevertheless, in the practical problem of pure reason, *i.e.* the necessary pursuit of the *summum bonum*, such a connexion is postulated as necessary: we ought to endeavour to promote the *summum bonum*, which, therefore, must be possible. Accordingly, the existence of a cause of all nature, distinct from nature itself, and containing the principle of this connexion, namely, of the exact harmony of happiness with morality, is also *postulated*. Now, this supreme cause must contain the principle of the harmony of nature, not merely with a law of the will of rational beings, but with the conception of this *law*, in so far as they make it the *supreme determining principle of the will*, and consequently not merely with the form of morals, but with their morality as their move, that is, with their moral character. Therefore, the *summum bonum* is possible in the world only on the supposition of a Supreme Being[1] having a causality corresponding to a moral character. Now a being that is capable of acting on the conception of laws is an *intelligence* (a rational being), and the causality of such a being according to the conception of laws is his *will*; therefore the supreme cause of nature, which must be presupposed as a condition of the *summum bonum* is a being which is the cause of nature by *intelligence* and *will*, consequently its author, that is God. It follows that the postulate of the possibility of the *highest derived good* (the best world) is likewise the postulate of the reality of a *highest original good*, that is to say, of the existence of God. Now it was seen to be a duty for us to promote the *summum bonum*; consequently it is not merely allowable, but it is a necessity connected with duty as a requisite, that we should presuppose the possibility of this *summum bonum*; and as this is possible only on condition of the existence of God, it inseparably connects the supposition of this with duty; that is, it is morally necessary to assume the existence of God.

It must be remarked here that this moral necessity is *subjective*, that is, it is a want, and not *objective*, that is, itself a duty, for there cannot be a duty to suppose the existence of anything (since this concerns only the theoretical employment of reason). Moreover, it is not meant by this that it is necessary to suppose the existence of God *as a basis of all obligation in general* (for this rests, as has been sufficiently proved, simply on the autonomy of reason itself). What belongs to duty here is only the endeavour to realize and promote the *summum bonum* in the world, the possibility of which can therefore be postulated; and as our reason finds it not conceivable except on the supposition of a supreme intelligence, the admission of this existence is therefore connected with the consciousness of our duty, although the admission itself belongs to the domain of speculative reason. Considered in respect of this alone, as a principle of explanation; it may be called a *hypothesis*, but in reference to the intelligibility of an object given us by the moral law (the *summum bonum*), and consequently of a requirement for practical purposes, it may be called *faith*, that is to say a pure *rational faith*, since pure

---

[1] [The original has "a Supreme Nature." "Natur," however, almost invariably means "physical nature"; therefore Hartenstein supplies the words "cause of" before "nature." More probably "Natur" is a slip for "Ursache," "cause."]

reason (both in its theoretical and its practical use) is the sole source from which it springs.

From this *deduction* it is now intelligible why the *Greek* schools could never attain the solution of their problem of the practical possibility of the *summum bonum*, because they made the rule of the use which the will of man makes of his freedom the sole and sufficient ground of this possibility, thinking that they had no need for that purpose of the existence of God. No doubt they were so far right that they established the principle of morals of itself independently on this postulate, from the relation of reason only to the will, and consequently made it the *supreme* practical condition of the *summum bonum*; but it was not therefore the *whole* condition of its possibility. The *Epicureans* had indeed assumed as the supreme principle of morality a wholly false one, namely, that of happiness, and had substituted for a law a maxim of arbitrary choice according to every man's inclination; they proceeded, however, *consistently* enough in this, that they degraded their *summum bonum* likewise just in proportion to the meanness of their fundamental principle, and looked for no greater happiness than can be attained by human prudence (including temperance and moderation of the inclinations), and this, as we know, would be scanty enough and would be very different according to circumstances; not to mention the exceptions that their maxims must perpetually admit and which make them incapable of being laws. The *Stoics*, on the contrary, had chosen their supreme practical principle quite rightly, making virtue the condition of the *summum bonum*; but when they represented the degree of virtue required by its pure law as fully attainable in this life, they not only strained the moral powers of the *man* whom they called *the wise* beyond all the limits of his nature, and assumed a thing that contradicts all our knowledge of men, but also and principally they would not allow the second *element* of the *summum bonum*, namely, happiness, to be properly a special object of human desire, but made their *wise man*, like a divinity in his consciousness of the excellence of his person, wholly independent on nature (as regards his own contentment); they exposed him indeed to the evils of life, but made him not subject to them (at the same time representing him also as free from moral evil). They thus, in fact, left out the second element of the *summum bonum*, namely personal happiness, placing it solely in action and satisfaction with one's own personal worth, thus including it in the consciousness of being morally minded, in which they might have been sufficiently refuted by the voice of their own nature.

The doctrine of Christianity,[2] even if we do not yet consider it as a religious

---

[2] It is commonly held that the Christian precept of morality has no advantage in respect of purity over the moral conceptions of the Stoics; the distinction between them is, however, very obvious. The Stoic system made the consciousness of strength of mind the pivot on which all moral dispositions should turn; and although its disciples spoke of duties and even defined them very well, yet they placed the spring and proper determining principle of the will in an elevation of the mind above the lower springs of the senses, which owe their power only to weakness of mind. With them, therefore, virtue was a sort of heroism in the *wise man* who, raising himself above the animal nature of man, is sufficient for himself, and while he prescribes duties to others is himself raised above them, and is not subject to any temptation to transgress the moral law. All this, however, they could not have done if they had conceived this law in all its purity and strictness, as the precept of the Gospel does. When I give the name *idea* to a perfection to which nothing adequate can be given in experience, it does not follow

doctrine, gives, touching this point, a conception of the *summum bonum* (the kingdom of God), which alone satisfies the strictest demand of practical reason. The moral law is holy (unyielding) and demands holiness of morals, although all the moral perfection to which man can attain is still only virtue, that is, a rightful disposition arising from *respect* for the law, implying consciousness of a constant propensity to transgression, or at least a want of purity, that is, a mixture of many spurious (not moral) motives of obedience to the law, consequently a self-esteem combined with humility. In respect, then, of the holiness which the Christian law requires, this leaves the creature nothing but a progress *in infinitum*, but for that very reason it justifies him in hoping for an endless duration of his existence. The *worth* of a character *perfectly* accordant with the moral law is infinite, since the only restriction on all possible happiness in the judgment of a wise and all-powerful distributor of it is the absence of conformity of rational beings to their duty. But the moral law of itself does not *promise* any happiness, for according to our conceptions of an order of nature in general, this is not necessarily connected with obedience to the law. Now Christian morality supplies this defect (of the second indispensable element of the *summum bonum*) by representing the world, in which rational beings devote themselves with all their soul to the moral law, as a *kingdom of God*, in which nature and morality are brought into a harmony foreign to each itself, by a holy Author who makes the derived *summum bonum* possible. *Holiness* of life is prescribed to them as a rule even in this life, while the welfare proportioned to it, namely, *bliss*, is represented as attainable only in an eternity; because the *former* must always be the pattern of their conduct in every state, and progress towards it is already possible and necessary in this life; while the *latter*, under the name of happiness, cannot be attained at all in this world (so far as our own power is concerned), and therefore is made simply an object of hope. Nevertheless, the Christian principle of *morality* itself is not theological (so as to be heteronomy), but is autonomy of pure practical reason, since it does not make the knowledge of God and His will the foundation of these laws, but only of the attainment of the *summum bonum*, on condition of following these laws, and it does not even place the proper *spring* of this obedience in the desired results, but solely in the conception of duty, as that of which the faithful observance alone constitutes the worthiness to obtain those happy consequences.

that the moral ideas are something transcendent, that is something of which we could not even determine the concept adequately, or of which it is uncertain whether there is any object corresponding to it at all, as is the case with the ideas of speculative reason; on the contrary, being types of practical perfection, they serve as the indispensable rule of conduct and likewise as the *standard of comparison*. Now if I consider *Christian morals* on their philosophical side, then compared with the ideas of the Greek schools they would appear as follows: the ideas of the *Cynics*, the *Epicureans*, the *Stoics*, and the *Christians* are: *simplicity of nature, prudence, wisdom*, and *holiness*. In respect of the way of attaining them, the Greek schools were distinguished from one another thus, that the Cynics only required *common sense*, the others the path of *science*, but both found the mere *use of natural powers* sufficient for the purpose. Christian morality, because its precept is framed (as a moral precept must be) so pure and unyielding, takes from man all confidence that he can be fully adequate to it, at least in this life, but again sets it up by enabling us to hope that if we act as well as it is in our *power to do*, then what is not in our power will come in to our aid from another source, whether we know how this may be or not. *Aristotle* and *Plato* differed only as to the *origin* of our moral conceptions. [See *Preface*, p. 115, *note*.]

In this manner the moral laws lead through the conception of the *summum bonum* as the object and final end of pure practical reason to *religion*, that is, to the *recognition of all duties as divine commands, not as sanctions,*[3] *that is to say, arbitrary ordinances of a foreign will and contingent in themselves*, but as essential *laws* of every free will in itself, which, nevertheless, must be regarded as commands of the Supreme Being, because it is only from a morally perfect (holy and good) and at the same time all-powerful will, and consequently only through harmony with this will, that we can hope to attain the *summum bonum* which the moral law makes it our duty to take as the object of our endeavours. Here again, then, all remains disinterested and founded merely on duty; neither fear nor hope being made the fundamental springs, which if taken as principles would destroy the whole moral worth of actions. The moral law commands me to make the highest possible good in a world the ultimate object of all my conduct. But I cannot hope to effect this otherwise than by the harmony of my will with that of a holy and good Author of the world; and although the conception of the *summum bonum* as a whole, in which the greatest happiness is conceived as combined in the most exact proportion with the highest degree of moral perfection (possible in creatures), includes *my own happiness*, yet it is not this that is the determining principle of the will which is enjoined to promote the *summum bonum*, but the moral law, which, on the contrary, limits by strict conditions my unbounded desire of happiness.

Hence also morality is not properly the doctrine how we should *make* ourselves happy, but how we should become *worthy* of happiness. It is only when religion is added that there also comes in the hope of participating some day in happiness in proportion as we have endeavoured to be not unworthy of it.

A man is *worthy* to possess a thing or a state when his possession of it is in harmony with the *summum bonum*. We can now easily see that all worthiness depends on moral conduct, since in the conception of the *summum bonum* this constitutes the condition of the rest (which belongs to one's state), namely, the participation of happiness. Now it follows from this that *morality* should never be treated as a *doctrine of happiness*, that is, an instruction of how to become happy; for it has to do simply with the rational condition (*conditio sine qua non*) of happiness, not with the means of attaining it. But when morality has been completely expounded (which merely imposes duties instead of providing rules for selfish desires), then first, after the moral desire to promote the *summum bonum* (to bring the kingdom of God to us) has been awakened, a desire founded on a law, and which could not previously arise in any selfish mind, and when for the behoof of this desire the step to religion has been taken, then this ethical doctrine may be also called a doctrine of happiness because the *hope* of happiness first begins with religion only.

We can also see from this that, when we ask what is God's *ultimate end* in creating the world, we must not name the *happiness* of the rational beings in it, but the *summum bonum*, which adds a further condition to that wish of such

---

[3] [The word 'sanction' is here used in the technical German sense, which is familiar to students of history in connexion with the 'Pragmatic Sanction.']

beings, namely, the condition of being worthy of happiness, that is, the *morality* of these same rational beings, a condition which alone contains the rule by which only they can hope to share in the former at the hand of a *wise* Author. For as *wisdom* theoretically considered signifies *the knowledge of the summum bonum*, and practically *the accordance of the will with the summum bonum*, we cannot attribute to a supreme independent wisdom an end based merely on *goodness*. For we cannot conceive the action of this goodness (in respect of the happiness of rational beings) as suitable to the highest original good, except under the restrictive conditions of harmony with the holiness of His will.[4] Therefore those who placed the end of creation in the glory of God (provided that this is not conceived anthropomorphically as a desire to be praised) have perhaps hit upon the best expression. For nothing glorifies God more than that which is the most estimable thing in the world, respect for His command, the observance of the holy duty that His law imposes on us, when there is added thereto His glorious plan of crowning such a beautiful order of things with corresponding happiness. If the latter (to speak humanly) makes Him worthy of love, by the *former* He is an object of adoration. Even men can never acquire respect by benevolence alone, though they may gain love, so that the greatest beneficence only procures them honour when it is regulated by worthiness.

That in the order of ends, man (and with him every rational being) is *an end in himself*, that is, that he can never be used merely as a means by any (not even by God) without being at the same time an end also himself, that therefore *humanity* in our person must be *holy* to ourselves, this follows now of itself because he is the *subject*[5] *of the moral law*, in other words, of that which is holy in itself, and on account of which and in agreement with which alone can anything be termed holy. For this moral law is founded on the autonomy of his will, as a free will which by its universal laws must necessarily be able to agree with that to which it is to submit itself.

VI.   OF THE POSTULATES OF PURE PRACTICAL REASON IN GENERAL.

They all proceed from the principle of morality, which is not a postulate but a law, by which reason determines the will directly, which will, because it is so determined as a pure will, requires these necessary conditions of obedience to its precept. These postulates are not theoretical dogmas but suppositions practically

---

[4] In order to make these characteristics of these conceptions clear, I add the remark that whilst we ascribe to God various attributes, the quality of which we also find applicable to creatures, only that in Him they are raised to the highest degree, *e.g.* power, knowledge, presence, goodness, &c., under the designations of omnipotence, omniscience, omnipresence, &c., there are three that are ascribed to God exclusively, and yet without the addition of greatness, and which are all moral. He is the *only holy*, the *only blessed*, the *only wise*, because these conceptions already imply the absence of limitation. In the order of these attributes he is also the *holy lawgiver* (and creator), the *good governor* (and preserver), and the *just judge*, three attributes which include everything by which God is the object of religion, and in conformity with which the metaphysical perfections are added of themselves in the reason.

[5] [That the ambiguity of the word *subject* may not mislead the reader, it may be remarked that it is here used in the psychological sense *subjectum legis*, not *subjectus legi*.]

necessary; while they do [not]⁶ extend our speculative knowledge, they give objective reality to the ideas of speculative reason in general (by means of their reference to what is practical), and give it a right to concepts, the possibility even of which it could not otherwise venture to affirm.

These postulates are those *of immorality, freedom* positively considered (as the causality of a being so far as he belongs to the intelligible world), and the *existence of God*. The *first* results from the practically necessary condition of a duration adequate to the complete fulfilment of the moral law; the *second* from the necessary supposition of independence on the sensible world, and of the faculty of determining one's will according to the law of an intelligible world, that is, of freedom; the *third* from the necessary condition of the existence of the *summum bonum* in such an intelligible world, by the supposition of the supreme independent good, that is, the existence of God.

Thus the fact that respect for the moral law necessarily makes the *summum bonum* an object of our endeavours, and the supposition thence resulting of its objective reality, lead through the postulates of practical reason to conceptions which speculative reason might indeed present as problems, but could never solve. Thus it leads—1. To that one in the solution of which the latter could do nothing but commit *paralogisms* (namely, that of immorality), because it could not lay hold of the character of permanence, by which to complete the psychological conception of an ultimate subject necessarily ascribed to the soul in self-consciousness, so as to make it the real conception of a substance, a character which practical reason furnishes by the postulate of a duration required for accordance with the moral law in the *summum bonum*, which is the whole end of practical reason. 2. It leads to that of which speculative reason contained nothing but *antinomy*, the solution of which it could only found on a notion problematically conceivable indeed, but whose objective reality it could not prove or determine, namely, the *cosmological* idea of an intelligible world and the consciousness of our existence in it, by means of the postulate of freedom (the reality of which it lays down by virtue of the moral law), and with it likewise the law of an intelligible world, to which speculative reason could only point, but could not define its conception. 3. What speculative reason was able to think, but was obliged to leave undetermined as a mere transcendental *ideal*, viz. the *theological* conception of the First Being, to this it gives significance (in a practical view, that is, as a condition of the possibility of the object of a will determined by that law), namely, as the supreme principle of the *summum bonum* in an intelligible world, by means of moral legislation in it invested with sovereign power.

Is our knowledge, however, actually extended in this way by pure practical reason, and is that *immanent* in practical reason which for the speculative was only *transcendent*? Certainly, but *only in a practical point of view*. For we do not thereby take knowledge of the nature of our souls, nor of the intelligible world, nor of the Supreme Being, with respect to what they are in themselves, but we have merely combined the conceptions of them in the *practical* concept of the *summum bonum* as the object of our will, and this altogether *à priori*, but only

---

⁶[Absent from the original text.]

by means of the moral law, and merely in reference to it, in respect of the object which it commands. But how freedom is possible, and how we are to conceive this kind of causality theoretically and positively, is not thereby discovered; but only that there is such a causality is postulated by the moral law and in its behoof. It is the same with the remaining ideas, the possibility of which no human intelligence will ever fathom, but the truth of which, on the other hand, no sophistry will ever wrest from the conviction even of the commonest man. . . .

VIII.   OF BELIEF FROM A REQUIREMENT OF PURE REASON.

A want or requirement of pure reason in its speculative use leads only to a *hypothesis*; that of pure practical reason to a *postulate*; for in the former case I ascend from the result as high as I please in the series of causes, not in order to give objective reality to the result (e.g. the causal connexion of things and changes in the world), but in order thoroughly to satisfy my inquiring reason in respect of it. Thus I see before me order and design in nature, and need not resort to speculation to assure myself of their *reality*, but to *explain* them I have *to pre-suppose a Deity* as their cause; and then since the inference from an effect to a definite cause is always uncertain and doubtful, especially to a cause so precise and so perfectly defined as we have to conceive in God, hence the highest degree of certainty to which this pre-supposition can be brought is, that it is the most rational opinion for us men.[7] On the other hand, a requirement of pure *practical* reason is based on a *duty*, that of making something (the *summum bonum*) the object of my will so as to promote it with all my powers; in which case I must suppose its possibility, and consequently also the conditions necessary thereto, namely, God, freedom, and immorality; since I cannot prove these by my speculative reason, although neither can I refute them. This duty is founded on something that is indeed quite independent on these suppositions, and is of itself apodictically certain, namely, the moral law; and so far it needs no further support by theoretical views as to the inner constitution of things, the secret final aim of the order of the world, or a presiding ruler thereof, in order to bind me in the most perfect manner to act in unconditional conformity to the law. But the subjective effect of this law, namely, the mental *disposition* conformed to it and made necessary by it, to promote the practically possible *summum bonum*, this presupposes at least that the latter is *possible*, for it would be practically impossible to strive after the object of a conception which at bottom was empty and had no object. Now the above-mentioned postulates concern only the physical or metaphysical conditions of the *possibility* of the *summum bonum*; in a word, those which lie in the nature of things; not, however, for the sake of an arbitrary

[7] But even here we should not be able to allege a requirement *of reason*, if we had not before our eyes a problematical, but yet inevitable, conception of reason, namely, that of an absolutely necessary being. This conception now seeks to be defined, and this, in addition to the tendency to extend itself, is the objective ground of a requirement of speculative reason, namely, to have a more precise definition of the conception of a necessary being which is to serve as the first cause of other beings, so as to make these* latter knowable by some means. Without such antecedent necessary problems there are no *requirements*—at least not of *pure reason*—the rest are requirements of *inclination*.

* I read 'diese' with the ed. of 1791. Rosenkranz and Hartenstein both read 'dieses,' 'this being.'

speculative purpose, but of a practically necessary end of a pure rational will, which in this case does not *choose*, but *obeys* an inexorable command of reason, the foundation of which is *objective*, in the constitution of things as they must be universally judged by pure reason, and is not based on *inclination*; for we are in nowise justified in assuming, on account of what we *wish* on merely *subjective* grounds, that the means thereto are possible or that its object is real. This, then, is an absolutely necessary requirement, and what it pre-supposes is not merely justified as an allowable hypothesis, but as a postulate in a practical point of view; and admitting that the pure moral law inexorably binds every man as a command (not as a rule of prudence), the righteous man may say: I *will* that there be a God, that my existence in this world be also an existence outside the chain of physical causes, and in a pure world of the understanding, and lastly, that my duration be endless; I firmly abide by this, and will not let this faith be taken from me; for in this instance alone my interest, because I *must* not relax anything of it, inevitably determines my judgment, without regarding sophistries, however unable I may be to answer them or to oppose them with others more plausible.[8]

.   .   .   .

In order to prevent misconception in the use of a notion as yet so unusual as that of a faith of pure practical reason, let me be permitted to add one more remark. It might almost seem as if this rational faith were here announced as itself a *command*, namely, that we should assume the *summum bonum* as possible. But a faith that is commanded is nonsense. Let the preceding analysis, however, be remembered of what is required to be supposed in the conception of the *summum bonum*, and it will be seen that it cannot be commanded to assume this possibility, and no practical disposition of mind is required to *admit* it; but that speculative reason must concede it without being asked, for no one can affirm that it is *impossible* in itself that rational beings in the world should at the same time be worthy of happiness in conformity with the moral law, and also possess this happiness proportionately. Now in respect of the first element of the *summum bonum*, namely, that which concerns morality, the moral law gives merely a command, and to doubt the possibility of that element would be the same as to call in question the moral law itself. But as regards the second element of that

---

[8] In the *Deutsches Museum*, February, 1787, there is a dissertation by a very subtle and clear-headed man, the late *Wizenmann*, whose early death is to be lamented, in which he disputes the right to argue from a want to the objective reality of its object, and illustrates the point by the example of *a man in love*, who, having fooled himself into an idea of beauty, which is merely a chimera of his own brain, would fain conclude that such an object really exists somewhere. I quite agree with him in this, in all cases where the want is founded on *inclination*, which cannot necessarily postulate the existence of its object even for the man that is affected by it, much less can it contain a demand valid for everyone, and therefore it is merely a *subjective* ground of the wish. But in the present case we have a want of reason springing from an objective determining principle of the will, namely, the moral law, which necessarily binds every rational being, and therefore justifies him in assuming *à priori* in nature the conditions proper for it, and makes the latter inseparable from the complete practical use of reason. It is a duty to realize the *summum bonum* to the utmost of our power, therefore it must be possible, consequently it is unavoidable for every rational being in the world to assume what is necessary for its objective possibility. The assumption is as necessary as the moral law, in connexion with which alone it is valid.

object, namely, happiness perfectly proportioned to that worthiness, it is true that there is no need of a command to admit its possibility in general, for theoretical reason has nothing to say against it; but *the manner* in which we have to conceive this harmony of the laws of nature with those of freedom has in it something in respect of which we have a *choice*, because theoretical reason decides nothing with apodictic certainty about it, and in respect of this there may be a moral interest which turns the scale.

I had said above that in a mere course of nature in the world an accurate correspondence between happiness and moral worth is not to be expected, and must be regarded as impossible and that therefore the possibility of the *summum bonum* cannot be admitted from this side except on the supposition of a moral Author of the world. I purposely reserved the restriction of this judgment to the *subjective* conditions of our reason, in order not to make use of it until the manner of this belief should be defined more precisely. The fact is that the impossibility referred to is *merely subjective*, that is, our reason finds it *impossible for it* to render conceivable in the way of a mere course of nature a connexion so exactly proportioned and so thoroughly adapted to an end, between two sets of events happening according to such distinct laws; although, as with everything else in nature that is adapted to an end, it cannot prove, that is, show by sufficient objective reasons, that it is not possible by universal laws of nature.

Now, however, a deciding principle of a different kind comes into play to turn the scale in this uncertainty of speculative reason. The command to promote the *summum bonum* is established on an objective basis (in practical reason); the possibility of the same in general is likewise established on an objective basis (in theoretical reason, which has nothing to say against it). But reason cannot decide objectively in what way we are to conceive this possibility; whether by universal laws of nature without a wise Author presiding over nature, or only on supposition of such an Author. Now here there comes in a *subjective* condition of reason the only way theoretically possible for it, of conceiving the exact harmony of the kingdom of nature with the kingdom of morals, which is the condition of the possibility of the *summum bonum*; and at the same time the only one conducive to morality (which depends on an objective law of reason). Now since the promotion of this *summum bonum*, and therefore the supposition of its possibility, are *objectively* necessary (though only as a result of practical reason), while at the same time the manner in which we would conceive it rests with our own choice, and in this choice a free interest of pure practical reason decides for the assumption of a wise Author of the world; it is clear that the principle that herein determines our judgment, though as a want it is *subjective*, yet at the same time being the means of promoting what is *objectively* (practically) necessary, is the foundation of a *maxim* of belief in a moral point of view, that is, a *faith of pure practical reason*. This, then, is not commanded, but being a voluntary determination of our judgment, conducive to the moral (commanded) purpose, and moreover harmonizing with the theoretical requirement of reason, to assume that existence and to make it the foundation of our further employment of reason, it has itself sprung from the moral disposition of mind; it may therefore at times waver even in the well-disposed, but can never be reduced to unbelief.

J. L. MACKIE
Kant on the Moral Argument

In the *Critique of Pure Reason* Kant argues that there is no sound speculative proof of the existence of a god. . . . But in the *Critique of Practical Reason* he suggests that moral reasoning can achieve what speculative reasoning cannot, and that the existence of a god, and also affirmative solutions to the other great metaphysical questions of the immorality of the soul and the freedom of the will, can be defended as being necessarily presupposed in moral consciousness.[1]

. . . What is morally right and obligatory is so, Kant holds, in itself, and can be rationally seen in itself to be so. Each rational being is, as such, competent to determine the moral law, to prescribe moral commands to himself, and therefore does not need God to command him—or even, it would seem, to advise him. 'Moreover, it is not meant by this that it is necessary to suppose the existence of God *as a basis of all obligation in general* (for this rests . . . simply on the autonomy of reason itself).' (267) Moral agents, or rational beings, are the citizens of an ideal commonwealth, making universal laws for themselves and one another. Morality is corrupted if it is derived from prudence and self-interest: divine rewards and punishments, therefore, far from supplying a necessary motive for morality, would introduce heteronomy, substituting an alien and morally worthless motive for the only genuinely valuable one of respect for the moral law.

However, Kant finds another and more appropriate place for a god in the moral universe. His positive argument starts from the notion of the *summum bonum*, the highest good, which, he says, is not merely moral rectitude but also includes happiness. Virtue and happiness together constitute the highest good for a person, and the distribution of happiness in proportion to morality constitutes the highest good for a possible world. Whereas the Epicureans made the mistake of reducing morality to the pursuit of happiness, the Stoics made the opposite mistake of either leaving happiness out of their conception of the highest good, or—what amounts to the same thing—identifying happiness simply with the consciousness of virtue. In contrast with both these mistakes, an adequate conception of the highest good must include both virtue and happiness, but each in its own right. Now since these two elements in the highest good are independent of one another, there is no logical necessity that they should go together, and hence no *a priori* guarantee that the realization of this highest good is even possible. Equally, there is no natural, causal, guarantee of this. Happiness (in this life) depends

John L. Mackie (1917–1981) was Reader in Philosophy at Oxford University and Fellow of University College since 1978. Mackie published influential works in such diverse areas as metaphysics, Hume Studies, and ethical theory as well as in philosophy of religion.

[1] I. Kant, *Critique of Practical Reason*, e.g. in T. K. Abbott, *Kant's Theory of Ethics* (Longmans, London, 1927), especially Part I, Book II, Chapter 2. References in the text to this work and to Kant's *Metaphysic of Morals* are to the pages in the German edition of Rosenkranz and Schubert, given at the top of each page in Abbott.

largely on what happens in the natural world, but the moral choices of rational beings are not to any great extent in control of this: our moral efforts cannot causally ensure that those who will and act rightly will be happy. Nor does nature as such conform to a moral standard. But, Kant says, moral thought tells us that we must take the highest good as a supreme end; that is, 'we ought to endeavour to promote the highest good, which must, therefore, be possible'. He infers that 'the existence of a cause of all nature, distinct from nature itself, and containing the principle . . . of the exact harmony of happiness with morality' is *postulated* in moral thought. 'The highest good is possible in the world only on the supposition of a Supreme Being having a causality corresponding to the moral character'—that is, a god. Since it is for us a duty to promote the highest good, there is 'a necessity connected with duty as a requisite, that we should presuppose the possibility of this *summum bonum*; and as this is possible only on condition of the existence of God . . . it is morally necessary to assume the existence of God.' But since happiness in this life is pretty plainly not proportioned to morality, it is also necessary to assume that individuals survive in a life after death; Kant has also argued separately for such immorality, again as a presupposition of moral thought, as being necessary to allow for an indefinite progress towards perfection which is involved in the first half of the highest good, complete virtue or 'the *perfect accordance* of the mind with the moral law.' (265–7)

It is not easy to decide just how Kant meant these conclusions to be interpreted. On the one hand he argues for 'the primacy of pure practical reason in its union with the speculative reason', saying that when certain propositions 'are *inseparably* attached *to the practical interest* of pure reason', theoretical reason must accept them, and 'must try to compare and connect them with everything that it has in its power as speculative reason' (261), and this is plainly intended to apply to the propositions asserting the immorality of the soul and the existence of a god, as well as the freedom of the will. But on the other hand, asking whether our knowledge is 'actually extended in this way by pure practical reason', and whether that is 'immanent in practical reason which for the speculative was only *transcendent*', Kant replies 'Certainly, but *only in a practical point of view*'—which seems to take away what it gives. We do not in this way gain knowledge of our souls or of the Supreme Being as they are in themselves. Theoretical reason 'is compelled to admit *that there are such objects*, although it is not able to define them more closely'; knowledge of them has been given 'only for practical use'. In fact speculative reason will work with regard to these objects only 'in a negative manner', to remove 'anthropomorphism, as the source of *superstition*, or seeming extension of these conceptions by supposed experience; and . . . *fanaticism*, which promises the same by means of supersensible intuition'. (276–9) He seems to be saying that the existence of a good and the immortality of the soul can be established as facts by the arguments from morality, but only in a highly indeterminate form. Yet he hints also at a more sceptical position, that the existence of a god, the freedom of the will, and the immortality of the soul cannot be established as facts, even by reasoning based on the moral consciousness, but can only be shown to be necessarily presupposed in that consciousness, to be, as it were, implicit in its content. In other words, we as rational beings cannot help thinking morally, and if we develop our moral thinking fully and coherently we cannot help supposing that there is a god; but whether in fact there is a god remains an open question. Kant says that 'the righteous man may say: I *will* that there be a God, that my existence in this world be also an existence outside the chain of physical causes, and in a pure world of the understanding, and lastly, that my duration be endless; I firmly abide by this, and will not let this faith be taken from me; for in this instance alone my interest, because I *must* not relax anything of it, inevitably determines my judgement', and he speaks of a *faith of pure practical reason*, which, he admits, is an 'unusual notion'. (289–92)

But in whichever of these ways we interpret his conclusion, Kant's argument is open to criticism. The most glaring weakness is in the step from the proposition that 'we ought to seek the highest good' to the claim that it 'must therefore be possible'. Even if, as Kant argues elsewhere, 'ought' implies 'can,' the thesis that we ought to seek to promote the highest good implies only that we can *seek to promote* it, and perhaps, since rational seeking could not be completely fruitless, that we can to some extent actually *promote* it. But this does not require that the full realization of the highest good should be possible. For example, it is thoroughly rational to try to improve the condition of human life, provided that some improvement is possible; there is no need to entertain vain hopes for its perfection. And even for the *possibility* of that full realization the most that would be needed is the possible existence of a wholly good and all-powerful governor of the world; the actual existence of such a governor would ensure not merely the possibility but the actuality of the highest good. Kant might say that we can and should aspire to the ultimate realization of the highest good, and that a *hope* for such ultimate realization is necessarily involved in moral thought. But he cannot claim that even its possible realization is a necessary postulate of moral thought in general; it is not even a necessary postulate of that particular sort of moral theory which Kant himself developed. The willing of universal laws by and for all rational beings as such could be a strictly autonomous activity.

There are, indeed, recurrent tensions between Kant's theism and his stress on the autonomy of morals. In sharp contrast with the popular view, and with Newman's, Kant holds that neither our knowledge of God and of his will, nor that will itself, is the foundation of the moral law. Yet because (as he thinks) we have to postulate a god who *also* wills these laws, as does every other free and rational will, he still calls them 'commands of the Supreme Being', but in a sense which is only a pale shadow of what is intended by most theological moralists. Again, Kant holds that no 'desired results' are 'the proper motive of obedience' to these laws, indeed that fear of punishment or hope of reward 'if taken as principles, would destroy the whole moral worth of actions'. Yet his belief that there is something appropriate about the *proportioning* of happiness to morality—a retributive thesis—again seems to be a pale shadow of the popular reliance on punishments and rewards. Is not this true also of his stress (after all) on happiness, whose conjunction with virtue we are to take not merely as a legitimate hope but as a *postulate* of moral thought? Would not a thoroughgoing recognition of the autonomy of morals lead rather to the Stoic view that morality needs no actual happiness beyond the consciousness of right action itself?

Suggestions for Further Reading

Notable recent works on the traditional theistic arguments for the existence of God include John Hick, *Arguments for the Existence of God* (Macmillan, 1970); J. L. Mackie, *The Miracle of Theism* (Clarendon Press, 1982); and Richard Swinburne, *The Existence of God* (Clarendon Press, 1979).

A useful treatment of the ontological argument can be found in Jonathan Barnes, *The Ontological Argument* (Macmillan, 1972). Helpful historical and contemporary essays on the ontological argument can be found in John Hick and Arthur McGill, eds., *The Many-Faced Argument: Recent Studies on the Ontological Argument for the Existence of God* (Macmillan, 1967). Gregory Schufreider's *An Introduction to Anselm's Argument* (Temple University Press, 1978) is a useful examination of Anselm's *Proslogium* argument. On modal versions of the proof see Clement Dore, *Theism* (D. Reidel, 1984).

William Rowe's *The Cosmological Argument* (Princeton University Press, 1975) is an extended examination of the eighteenth-century version of the cosmological argument. A good work on the thirteenth-century version is Anthony Kenny, *The Five Ways* (University of Notre Dame Press, 1982). Other works of interest are Bruce Reichenbach, *The Cosmological Argument: A Reassessment* (Charles C. Thomas, 1972); William Lane Craig, *The Cosmological Argument from Plato to Leibniz* (Macmillan, 1980); and Hugo Meynell, *The Intelligible Universe* (Barnes & Noble, 1982).

Concerning the teleological argument, one can begin at no better source than Thomas McPherson's *The Design Argument* (Macmillan, 1972). Three excellent articles dealing with the teleological argument are Bowman L. Clarke, "The Argument from Design," *American Journal of Theology and Philosophy* 1 (1980); Richard Swinburne, "The Argument from Design," *Philosophy* 43 (1968); and George Schlesinger, "Theism and Confirmation," *Pacific Philosophical Quarterly* 64 (1983). Another interesting work that concerns the question of design is Richard Dawkins, *The Blind Watchmaker* (W. W. Norton, 1986).

H. P. Owen's *The Moral Argument for Christian Theism* (Allen and Unwin, 1965) is a good treatment of the moral argument. One should also read R. M. Adam's "Moral Arguments for Theistic Belief," in C. F. Delaney, ed., *Rationality and Religious Belief* (University of Notre Dame Press, 1979).

THE PROBLEM OF EVIL

III

The problem of evil can be succinctly stated: If God is omnipotent and omniscient, He can prevent evil. If He is good, He wants to. It thus seems that, if God exists, there would not be any evil. But there is. Shouldn't we conclude, then, that God does not exist?

Critics like J. L. Mackie think that

(1) There is a God who is omnipotent, omniscient, and perfectly good

and

(2) Evil exists

are logically inconsistent. If the critics are right, theism should be rejected. Since (2) is clearly true, and logically inconsistent propositions cannot both be true, (1) must be false.

To defend the rationality of their position, theists must therefore show that (1) and (2) *are not* clearly inconsistent. There are several ways of doing this.

Since all true propositions are compatible, theists could establish the consistency of (1) and (2) by establishing the truth of (1). Even if (1) cannot be *fully* established, theists have reason to think (1) and (2) are consistent if they have reasons for believing that (1) is true.

Theists can also try to show that the inconsistency of (1) and (2) has not been proved. Alvin Plantinga, for example, thinks that Mackie's argument for their inconsistency is unsound. Mackie concedes that (1) and (2) aren't *obviously* inconsistent in the way that "John is a bachelor" and "John has a wife" or "Madison is the capital of Wisconsin" and "Madison is not the capital of Wisconsin" are obviously inconsistent. Nevertheless, he thinks their inconsistency becomes apparent when we conjoin them with such necessary truths as

(3) A good being always eliminates evil as far as it can.[1]

But as Plantinga points out, (3) *is not* necessarily true, because a good being may have morally sufficient reasons for not eliminating evil. A parent, for example, will not protect her child from all evil because an experience of some evils is necessary for the child's development.

What *may* be necessarily true is that

(4) An omnipotent, omniscient, and perfectly good being would not permit evil if it did not have a morally sufficient reason for doing so.

---

[1] Whatever is entailed by a set of propositions, s, and a necessary truth is entailed by s alone. Hence, if (1), (2), and (3) entail a logically impossible proposition (like "Evil exists and Evil does not exist") and (3) is necessarily true, then (1) and (2) entail a logically impossible proposition. If they do, they cannot both be true; i.e., they are not consistent.

The conjunction of (1), (2), and (4) will not entail a logically impossible proposition, however, unless we add that

(5) Some existing evils are such that an omnipotent, omniscient, and perfectly good being would not have a morally sufficient reason for permitting them,

and (5) does not seem to be necessarily true.

Theists have a third way of responding to the charge of inconsistency. Suppose there is a proposition, p, such that if p is true, (1) and (2) are true. Then, if p is *possibly* true, the conjunction of (1) and (2) together is possibly true; i.e., (1) and (2) are consistent. Plantinga, for example, describes a situation, s, in which God has a morally sufficient reason for creating free beings, even though He knows that any free being He can create would perform at least one evil action if He were to create it, and God creates free beings. If s were true, (1) and (2) would be true. Plantinga concludes that, because s is possible, (1) and (2) are consistent.

But even if the existence of God and the existence of evil are not inconsistent, doesn't evil *count against* God's existence? Suffering and wickedness are all too familiar. If God existed, He would have a morally sufficient reason for permitting these evils. But *could* an omnipotent and omniscient being have a morally sufficient reason for creating a world in which children sometimes suffer horribly and cruelty, exploitation, and betrayal are common occurrences? Most contemporary critics of theism concede the consistency of (1) and (2). They insist, however, that (2) provides a *conclusive reason* for disbelieving in God's existence. Even if the logical problem of evil (the problem of consistency) can be resolved, they think that the evidential problem of evil cannot. Theists respond to this challenge in two ways.

Some theists provide a "theodicy"—an account of the reasons God probably has for permitting evil. The two most popular theodicies are the Greater Goods Defense and the Free Will Defense.

The Greater Goods Defense attempts to show (roughly) that evil or its permission is (a) a logically necessary condition of some good that (b) outweighs it and (c) is at least as valuable as alternative goods not involving that evil. The first condition reflects that belief that while God is not bound by natural laws, He is bound by logical necessity. God can raise the dead, turn water into wine, reverse processes of illness, and so on. But God cannot create round squares or beings not created by Himself. The second and third conditions ensure that the good to which evil contributes is sufficient to justify its permission.

There are several versions of the Greater Goods Defense. One is the Aesthetic Defense. According to this view, evil contributes to the value of the universe in somewhat the same way an ugly daub of paint can contribute to the aesthetic effect of a picture or a dissonant chord to the beauty of a musical composition. This defense is often criticized on the ground that God alone can enjoy this good. To suppose that He permits evil so that this good can exist is thus to suppose that He permits it to secure His own selfish pleasure. However, this criticism ignores the theist's belief that the redeemed share in God's enjoyment. A second criticism is more telling, viz., that wickedness and suffering cannot be outweighed by any aesthetic good. This claim might not be self-evident but it is plausible, and most modern versions of the Greater Goods Defense concentrate on other goods. Two versions are especially popular.

The first tries to show that some evils are justified by moral goods. For example, evil may be a logically necessary condition of certain kinds of moral activity. Thus, some argue that compassionate or courageous activities are responses to suffering and evil, and hence are not possible if evil and suffering do not exist. Others argue that souls are morally and spiritually matured through suffering and their encounters with evil. The highest form of virtue and spirituality can be acquired only through struggle, and struggle presupposes real obstacles.

Another popular version of the Greater Goods Defense argues that evil is an unavoidable consequence of the operation of familiar natural laws and that the existence of a world governed by laws of this sort is a necessary condition of responsible and significant choices. We cannot choose responsibly if we cannot anticipate the consequences of our actions. But rational anticipation of the future is possible only if we can be confident that things will continue to behave in regular and lawlike ways. Nor would our choices be significant if we were protected from their evil consequences by frequent divine interventions.

For Greater Goods Defenses to be plausible, two conditions must be met. First, one must show that the evil or its permission really is entailed by the relevant good. Whether it is usually depends on precisely how the good is specified. For example, compassionate activity as such does not entail suffering, for we can compassionately respond to someone who we *mistakenly believe* is suffering. If the good is specified as a compassionate response to a situation about which one is adequately informed, however, the entailment may hold.

The second condition is that the good is great enough to justify the evil whose permission is required for its occurrence. For example, compassionate and fully informed responses justify the evils they entail only if illusion is a significant disvalue and only if compassion's value does not wholly consist in the relief of suffering. (If delusion is not a significant evil, compassionate responses to illusory evils seem better since no one really suffers. If compassion's only value is that it relieves suffering, it seems better not to have permitted suffering in the first place.)

The Free Will Defense contends that much, if not all, evil springs from our misuse of freedom. God need not create free beings. But if He does, He cannot both respect our freedom and determine our use of it. In particular, He cannot prevent us from choosing wickedly without destroying our freedom. Nevertheless, if the value of freedom and the goods to which it contributes outweighs the disvalue of our evil choices, God may be justified in creating us even though He foresees we will sometimes act badly.

The Free Will Defense assumes that God is not subject only to logical necessity. He is also limited by our freedom. This comes out clearly in Alvin Plantinga's discussion. Plantinga suggests that God's choices may be constrained by contingently true counterfactual conditionals such as "If Adam were created, he would freely sin." If creatures are genuinely free, God cannot determine which counterfactuals of this kind are true. Thus, He has no control over the fact that "If Adam were created, he would sin" is true and "If Adam were created, he would not sin" is false. The truth of counterfactuals like these is simply given and provides the framework within which God has to choose. If at least one of the creatures in any set of free beings worth creating would abuse its freedom, God cannot both create one of those sets and prevent all evil.[2]

The Free Will Defense has some problematic features. For example, it assumes that free actions cannot be fully determined by natural causes, God's decrees, or other causal antecedents. While this assumption is plausible, it is challenged by "compatibilists." Compatibilists argue that an action like going to the movies is free if (roughly) the agent chooses to go to the movies and would have refrained from doing so if he or she had not chosen to do so. An action can be free in this sense even if the choice is determined by God or natural causes.

The Free Will Defense is also incompatible with views held by a number of traditional theists—that God is limited only by logical constraints and that He determines every contingent state of affairs. If the Free Will Defense is sound, God's choices are constrained by contingent facts over which He has no control.

A theodicy is not the only possible response to the evidential problem of evil. Some theists admit that they cannot explain evil, but they deny that this counts against theism. Theism does not entail that we can explain evil by citing God's morally sufficient reasons for permitting it. Hence, the fact that we cannot do so is not evidence against God's existence.

The plausibility of this response depends on whether we should expect human beings to understand God's reasons for permitting evil if theism is true. There *are* reasons for thinking we could not *fully* understand them. Entailment relations between the world's goods and evils would be extraordinarily complex. Nor is it clear that we could fully appreciate the relevant goods. (Traditional theists believe that the principal good is a participation in God's own life and that this good is incommensurable with temporal goods and evils.) On the other hand, we should not exaggerate our ignorance of the relevant goods and evils and the entailments between them, for we understand at least some of them. Furthermore, God's goodness implies He would provide us with at least some understanding of His purposes. These considerations suggest that the theist should be able to provide fairly plausible accounts of at least some significant kinds of evil even if he or she cannot adequately explain all kinds (animal suffering, for example) or account for the quantity of evil.

How serious, then, is the problem of evil? The adequacy of theism's response depends on the success of its attempt to defend the consistency of "God exists" and "Evil exists," the strength of its grounds for believing in God's existence, and the scope and plausibility of its explanations of evil. Most contemporary

---

[2] Plantinga himself does not use the Free Will Defense as a theodicy; i.e., he does not try to show that it is a likely explanation of evil. He argues only that it *might* be true and that, if it were true, God's existence and the existence of evil would be consistent. In short, Plantinga uses the Free Will Defense to resolve only the *logical* problem of evil. Most of its advocates, however, believe that it also helps solve the *evidential* problem of evil.

philosophers of religion believe that the charge of inconsistency can be met. They differ over the strength of the grounds for theism and the adequacy of the theist's explanations. If there are good reasons for thinking theism is true, then fairly plausible explanations of some evils may be sufficient. If the reasons are weak, the theist's explanations should be more complete and their probability higher. If they are *very* weak, then the theist's inability to adequately account for the quantity of evil or explain certain important kinds of evil counts strongly against theism.

W. J. W.

THE PROBLEM OF EVIL

GOTTFRIED LEIBNIZ
The Argument Reduced to Syllogistic Form

Some persons of discernment have wished me to make this addition. I have the more readily deferred to their opinion, because of the opportunity thereby gained for meeting certain difficulties, and for making observations on certain matters which were not treated in sufficient detail in the work itself.

OBJECTION I

> Whoever does not choose the best course is lacking either in power, or knowledge, or goodness.
> God did not choose the best course in creating this world.
> Therefore God was lacking in power, or knowledge, or goodness.

ANSWER

I deny the minor, that is to say, the second premiss of this syllogism, and the opponent proves it by this.

PROSYLLOGISM

> Whoever makes things in which there is evil, and which could have been made without any evil, or need not have been made at all, does not choose the best course.

Gottfried Wilhelm Leibniz (1646–1716), a successful German jurist and diplomat, was also known as a logician and mathematician. He shares, with Newton, the honor of having discovered the calculus. His major philosophical works include the *Monadology* and the *Discourse on Metaphysics*.

THE ARGUMENT REDUCED TO SYLLOGISTIC FORM   From *Theodicy* by G. W. Leibniz, translated by E. M. Huggard, edited with an introduction by Austin Farrer. Reprinted by permission of Routledge & Kegan Paul Ltd.

God made a world wherein there is evil; a world, I say, which could have been made without any evil or which need not have been made at all.

Therefore God did not choose the best course.

ANSWER

I admit the minor of this prosyllogism: for one must confess that there is evil in this world which God has made, and that it would have been possible to make a world without evil or even not to create any world, since its creation depended upon the free will of God. But I deny the major, that is, the first of the two premisses of the prosyllogism, and I might content myself with asking for its proof. In order, however, to give a clearer exposition of the matter, I would justify this denial by pointing out that the best course is not always the one which tends towards avoiding evil, since it is possible that the evil may be accompanied by a greater good. For example, the general of an army will prefer a great victory with a slight wound to a state of affairs without wound and without victory. I have proved this in further detail in this work by pointing out, through instances taken from mathematics and elsewhere, that an imperfection in the part may be required for a greater perfection in the whole. I have followed therein the opinion of St. Augustine, who said a hundred times that God permitted evil in order to derive from it a good, that is to say, a greater good; and Thomas Aquinas says (in libr. 2, *Sent. Dist.* 32, qu. 1, art. 1) that the permission of evil tends towards the good of the universe. I have shown that among older writers the fall of Adam was termed *felix culpa*, a fortunate sin, because it had been expiated with immense benefit by the incarnation of the Son of God: for he gave to the universe something more noble than anything there would otherwise have been amongst created beings. For the better understanding of the matter I added, following the example of many good authors, that it was consistent with order and the general good for God to grant to certain of his creatures the opportunity to exercise their freedom, even when he foresaw that they would turn to evil: for God could easily correct the evil, and it was not fitting that in order to prevent sin he should always act in an extraordinary way. It will therefore sufficiently refute the objection to show that a world with evil may be better than a world without evil. But I have gone still further in the work, and have even shown that this universe must be indeed better than every other possible universe.

OBJECTION II

If there is more evil than good in intelligent creatures, there is more evil than good in all God's work.

Now there is more evil than good in intelligent creatures.

Therefore there is more evil than good in all God's work.

ANSWER

I deny the major and the minor of this conditional syllogism. As for the major, I do not admit it because this supposed inference from the part to the whole, from intelligent creatures to all creatures, assumes tacitly and without proof that creatures devoid of reason cannot be compared or taken into account with those that have reason. But why might not the surplus of good in the non-intelligent creatures that fill the world compensate for and even exceed incomparably the surplus of evil in rational creatures? It is true that the value of the latter is greater; but by way of compensation the others are incomparably greater in number; and it may be that the proportion of number and quantity surpasses that of value and quality.

The minor also I cannot admit, namely, that there is more evil than good in intelligent creatures. One need not even agree that there is more evil than good in the human kind. For it is possible, and even a very reasonable thing, that the glory and the perfection of the blessed may be incomparably greater than the misery and imperfection of the damned, and that here the excellence of the total good in the smaller number may exceed the total evil which is in the greater number. The blessed draw near to divinity through a divine Mediator, so far as can belong to these created beings, and make such progress in good as is impossible for the damned to make in evil, even though they should approach as nearly as may be the nature of demons. God is infinite, and the Devil is finite; good can and does go on *ad infinitum*, whereas evil has its bounds. It may be therefore, and it is probable, that there happens in the comparison between the blessed and the damned the opposite of what I said could happen in the comparison between the happy and the unhappy, namely that in the latter the proportion of degrees surpasses that of numbers, while in the comparison between intelligent and non-intelligent the proportion of numbers is greater than that of values. One is justified in assuming that a thing may be so as long as one does not prove that it is impossible, and indeed what is here put forward goes beyond assumption.

But secondly, even should one admit that there is more evil than good in the human kind, one still has every reason for not admitting that there is more evil than good in all intelligent creatures. For there is an inconceivable number of Spirits, and perhaps of other rational creatures besides: and an opponent cannot prove that in the whole City of God, composed as much of Spirits as of rational animals without number and of endless different kinds, the evil exceeds the good. Although one need not, in order to answer an objection, prove that a thing is, when its mere possibility suffices, I have nevertheless shown in this present work that it is a result of the supreme perfection of the Sovereign of the Universe that the kingdom of God should be the most perfect of all states or governments possible, and that in consequence what little evil there is should be required to provide the full measure of the vast good existing there.

OBJECTION III

If it is always impossible not to sin, it is always unjust to punish.
Now it is always impossible not to sin, or rather all sin is necessary.
Therefore it is always unjust to punish.
The minor of this is proved as follows.

FIRST PROSYLLOGISM

Everything predetermined is necessary.
Every event is predetermined.
Therefore every event (and consequently sin also) is necessary.
Again this second minor is proved thus.

SECOND PROSYLLOGISM

That which is future, that which is foreseen, that which is involved in causes
   is predetermined.
Every event is of this kind.
Therefore every event is predetermined.

ANSWER

I admit in a certain sense the conclusion of the second prosyllogism, which is the minor of the first; but I shall deny the major of the first prosyllogism, namely that everything predetermined is necessary; taking 'necessity', say the necessity to sin, or the impossibility of not sinning, or of not doing some action, in the sense relevant to the argument, that is, as a necessity essential and absolute, which destroys the morality of action and the justice of punishment. If anyone meant a different necessity or impossibility (that is, a necessity only moral or hypothetical, which will be explained presently) it is plain that we would deny him the major stated in the objection. We might content ourselves with this answer, and demand the proof of the proposition denied: but I am well pleased to justify my manner of procedure in the present work, in order to make the matter clear and to throw more light on this whole subject, by explaining the necessity that must be rejected and the determination that must be allowed. The truth is that the necessity contrary to morality, which must be avoided and which would render punishment unjust, is an insuperable necessity, which would render all opposition unavailing, even though one should wish with all one's heart to avoid the necessary action, and though one should make all possible efforts to that end. Now it is plain that this is not applicable to voluntary actions, since one would not do them if one did not so desire. Thus their prevision and predetermination is not absolute, but it presupposes will: if it is certain that one will do them, it is no less certain that one will will to do them. These voluntary actions and their results will not happen whatever one may do and whether one will them or not; but they will happen because one will do, and because one will will to do, that which leads to them. That is involved in prevision and predetermination, and forms the reason thereof. The necessity of such events is called conditional or hypothetical, or again necessity of consequence, because it presupposes the will and the other requisites. But the necessity which destroys morality, and renders punishment unjust and reward unavailing, is found in the things that will be whatever one may do and whatever one may will to do: in a word, it exists in that which is essential. This it is which is called an absolute necessity. Thus it avails nothing with regard to what is necessary absolutely to ordain interdicts or commandments, to propose penalties or prizes, to blame or to praise; it will come to pass no more and no less. In voluntary actions, on the contrary, and in what depends upon them, precepts, armed with power to punish and to reward, very often serve, and are included in the order of causes that make action exist. Thus it comes about that not only pains and effort but also prayers are effective, God having had even these prayers in mind before he ordered things, and having made due allowance for them. That is why the precept *Ora et labora* (Pray and work) remains intact. Thus not only those who (under the empty pretext of the necessity of events) maintain that one can spare oneself the pains demanded by affairs, but also those who argue against prayers, fall into that which the ancients even in their time called 'the Lazy Sophism'. So the predetermination of events by their causes is precisely what contributes to morality instead of destroying it, and the causes incline the will without necessitating it. For this reason the determination we are concerned with is not a neccessitation. It is certain (to him who knows all) that the effect will follow this inclination; but this effect does not follow thence by a consequence which is necessary, that is, whose contrary implies contradiction; and it is also by such an inward inclination that the will is determined, without the presence of necessity. Suppose that one has the greatest possible passion (for example, a great thirst), you will admit that the soul can find some reason for resisting it, even if it were only that of displaying its power. Thus though one may never have complete indifference of equipoise, and there is always a predominance of inclination for the course adopted, that predominance does not render absolutely necessary the resolution taken.

OBJECTION IV

> Whoever can prevent the sin of others and does not so, but rather contributes to it, although he be fully apprised of it, is accessary thereto.
> God can prevent the sin of intelligent creatures; but he does not so, and he rather contributes to it by his co-operation and by the opportunities he causes, although he is fully cognizant of it.
> Therefore, etc.

ANSWER

I deny the major of this syllogism. It may be that one can prevent the sin, but that one ought not to do so, because one could not do so without committing a sin oneself, or (when God is concerned) without acting unreasonably. I have given instances of that, and have applied them to God himself. It may be also that one contributes to the evil, and that one even opens the way to it sometimes, in doing things one is bound to do. And when one does one's duty, or (speaking of God) when, after full consideration, one does that which reason demands, one is not responsible for events, even when one foresees them. One does not will these evils; but one is willing to permit them for a greater good, which one cannot in reason help preferring to other considerations. This is a *consequent* will, resulting from acts of *antecedent* will, in which one wills the good. I know that some persons, in speaking of the antecedent and consequent will of God, have meant by the antecedent that which wills that all men be saved, and by the consequent that which wills, in consequence of persistent sin, that there be some damned, damnation being a result of sin. But these are only examples of a more general notion, and one may say with the same reason, that God wills by his antecedent will that men sin not, and that by his consequent or final and decretory will (which is always followed by its effect) he wills to permit that they sin, this permission being a result of superior reasons. One has indeed justification for saying, in general, that the antecedent will of God tends towards the production of good and the prevention of evil, each taken in itself, and as it were detached (*particulariter et secundum quid*: Thom., I, qu. 19, art. 6) according to the measure of the degree of each good or of each evil. Likewise one may say that the consequent, or final and total, divine will tends towards the production of as many goods as can be put together, whose combination thereby becomes determined, and involves also the permission of some evils and the exclusion of some goods, as the best possible plan of the universe demands. Arminius, in his *Antiperkinsus*, explained very well that the will of God can be called consequent not only in relation to the action of the creature considered beforehand in the divine understanding, but also in relation to other anterior acts of divine will. But it is enough to consider the passage cited from Thomas Aquinas, and that from Scotus (I, dist. 46, qu. 11), to see that they make this distinction as I have made it here. Nevertheless if anyone will not suffer this use of the terms, let him put 'previous' in place of 'antecedent' will, and 'final' or 'decretory' in place of 'consequent' will. For I do not wish to wrangle about words.

OBJECTION V

Whoever produces all that is real in a thing is its cause.
God produces all that is real in sin.
Therefore God is the cause of sin.

ANSWER

I might content myself with denying the major or the minor, because the term 'real' admits of interpretations capable of rendering these propositions false. But in order to give a better explanation I will make a distinction. 'Real' either signifies that which is positive only, or else it includes also privative beings: in the first case, I deny the major and I admit the minor; in the second case, I do the opposite. I might have confined myself to that; but I was willing to go further, in order to account for this distinction. I have therefore been well pleased to point out that every purely positive or absolute reality is a perfection, and that every imperfection comes from limitation, that is, from the privative: for to limit is to withhold extension, or the more beyond. Now God is the cause of all perfections, and consequently of all realities, when they are regarded as purely positive. But limitations or privations result from the original imperfection of creatures which restricts their receptivity. It is as with a laden boat, which the river carries along more slowly or less slowly in proportion to the weight that it bears: thus the speed comes from the river, but the retardation which restricts this speed comes from the load. Also I have shown in the present work how the creature, in causing sin, is a deficient cause; how errors and evil inclinations spring from privation; and how privation is efficacious accidentally. And I have justified the opinion of St. Augustine (lib. I, *Ad. Simpl.*, qu. 2) who explains (for example) how God hardens the soul, not in giving it something evil, but because the effect of the good he imprints is restricted by the resistance of the soul, and by the circumstances contributing to this resistance, so that he does not give it all the good that would overcome its evil. 'Nec *(inquit)* ab illo erogatur aliquid quo homo fit deterior, sed tantum quo fit melior non erogatur.' But if God had willed to do more here he must needs have produced either fresh natures in his creatures or fresh miracles to change their natures, and this the best plan did not allow. It is just as if the current of the river must needs be more rapid than its slope permits or the boats themselves be less laden, if they had to be impelled at a greater speed. So the limitation or original imperfection of creatures brings it about that even the best plan of the universe cannot admit more good, and cannot be exempted from certain evils, these, however, being only of such a kind as may tend towards a greater good. There are some disorders in the parts which wonderfully enhance the beauty of the whole, just as certain dissonances, appropriately used, render harmony more beautiful. But that depends upon the answer which I have already given to the first objection.

OBJECTION VI

Whoever punishes those who have done as well as it was in their power to do is unjust.
God does so.
Therefore, etc.

ANSWER

I deny the minor of this argument. And I believe that God always gives sufficient aid and grace to those who have good will, that is to say, who do not reject this grace by a fresh sin. Thus I do not admit the damnation of children dying unbaptized or outside the Church, or the damnation of adult persons who have acted according to the light that God has given them. And I believe that, *if anyone has followed the light he had,* he will undoubtedly receive thereof in greater measure as he has need, even as the late Herr Hulsemann, who was celebrated as a profound theologian at Leipzig, has somewhere observed; and if such a man had failed to receive light during his life, he would receive it at least in the hour of death.

OBJECTION VII

Whoever gives only to some, and not to all, the means of producing effectively in them good will and final saving faith has not enough goodness.
God does so.
Therefore, etc.

ANSWER

I deny the major. It is true that God could overcome the greatest resistance of the human heart, and indeed he sometimes does so, whether by an inward grace or by the outward circumstances that can greatly influence souls; but he does not always do so. Whence comes this distinction, someone will say, and wherefore does his goodness appear to be restricted? The truth is that it would not have been in order always to act in an extraordinary way and to derange the connexion of things, as I have observed already in answering the first objection. The reasons for this connexion, whereby the one is placed in more favourable circumstances than the other, are hidden in the depths of God's wisdom: they depend upon the universal harmony. The best plan of the universe, which God could not fail to choose, required this. One concludes thus from the event itself; since God made the universe, it was not possible to do better. Such management, far from being contrary to goodness, has rather been prompted by supreme goodness itself. This objection with its solution might have been inferred from what was said with regard to the first objection; but it seemed advisable to touch upon it separately.

OBJECTION VIII

> Whoever cannot fail to choose the best is not free.
> God cannot fail to choose the best.
> Therefore God is not free.

ANSWER

I deny the major of this argument. Rather is it true freedom, and the most perfect, to be able to make the best use of one's free will, and always to exercise this power, without being turned aside either by outward force or by inward passions, whereof the one enslaves our bodies and the other our souls. There is nothing less servile and more befitting the highest degree of freedom than to be always led towards the good, and always by one's own inclination, without any constraint and without any displeasure. And to object that God therefore had need of external things is only a sophism. He creates them freely: but when he had set before him an end, that of exercising his goodness, his wisdom determined him to choose the means most appropriate for obtaining this end. To call that a *need* is to take the term in a sense not usual, which clears it of all imperfection, somewhat as one does when speaking of the wrath of God.

Seneca says somewhere, that God commanded only once, but that he obeys always, because he obeys the laws that he willed to ordain for himself: *semel jussit, semper paret*. But he had better have said, that God always commands and that he is always obeyed: for in willing he always follows the tendency of his own nature, and all other things always follow his will. And as this will is always the same one cannot say that he obeys that will only which he formerly had. Nevertheless, although his will is always indefectible and always tends towards the best, the evil or the lesser good which he rejects will still be possible in itself. Otherwise the necessity of good would be geometrical (so to speak) or metaphysical, and altogether absolute; the contingency of things would be destroyed, and there would be no choice. But necessity of this kind, which does not destroy the possibility of the contrary, has the name by analogy only: it becomes effective not through the mere essence of things, but through that which is outside them and above them, that is, through the will of God. This necessity is called moral, because for the wise what is necessary and what is owing are equivalent things; and when it is always followed by its effect, as it indeed is in the perfectly wise, that is, in God, one can say that it is a happy necessity. The more nearly creatures approach this, the closer do they come to perfect felicity. Moreover, necessity of this kind is not the necessity one endeavors to avoid, and which destroys morality, reward and commendation. For that which it brings to pass does not happen whatever one may do and whatever one may will, but because one desires it. A will to which it is natural to choose well deserves most to be commended; and it carries with it its own reward, which is supreme happiness. And as this constitution of the divine nature gives an entire satisfaction to him who possesses it, it is also the best and the most desirable from the point of view of the creatures who are all dependent upon God. If the will of God had not as its rule the principle of the best, it would tend towards evil, which would be worst of all; or else it would be indifferent somehow to good and to evil, and guided by chance. But a will that would always drift along at random would scarcely be any better for the government of the universe than the fortuitous concourse of corpuscles, without the existence of divinity. And even though God should abandon himself to chance only in some cases, and in a certain way (as he would if he did not always tend entirely towards the best, and if he were capable of preferring a lesser good to a greater good, that is, an evil to a good, since that which prevents a greater good is an evil) he would be no less imperfect than the object of his choice. Then he would not deserve absolute trust; he would act without reason in such a case, and the government of the universe would be like certain games equally divided between reason and luck. This all proves that this objection which is made against the choice of the best perverts the notions of free and necessary, and represents the best to us actually as evil: but that is either malicious or absurd.

DAVID HUME
God and the Problem of Evil

PART X

. . . And is it possible, Cleanthes, said Philo, that after all these reflections, and infinitely more, which might be suggested, you can still persevere in your

GOD AND THE PROBLEM OF EVIL   From *Dialogues Concerning Natural Religion*, Parts X and XI. *The Philosophical Works of David Hume*, Volume II. Edinburgh, Adam Black and William Tait; and Charles Tait, 1876.

Anthropomorphism, and assert the moral attributes of the Deity, his justice, benevolence, mercy, and rectitude, to be of the same nature with these virtues in human creatures? His power we allow is infinite: whatever he wills is executed: but neither man nor any other animal is happy: therefore he does not will their happiness. His wisdom is infinite: he is never mistaken in choosing the means to any end: but the course of Nature tends not to human or animal felicity: therefore it is not established for that purpose. Through the whole compass of human knowledge, there are no inferences more certain and infallible than these. In what respect, then, do his benevolence and mercy resemble the benevolence and mercy of men?

Epicurus's old questions are yet unanswered.

Is he willing to prevent evil, but not able? then is he impotent. Is he able, but not willing? then is he malevolent. Is he both able and willing? whence then is evil?

You ascribe, Cleanthes (and I believe justly), a purpose and intention to Nature. But what, I beseech you, is the object of that curious artifice and machinery, which she has displayed in all animals? The preservation alone of individuals, and propagation of the species. It seems enough for her purpose, if such a rank be barely upheld in the universe, without any care or concern for the happiness of the members that compose it. No resource for this purpose: no machinery, in order merely to give pleasure or ease: no fund of pure joy and contentment: no indulgence, without some want or necessity accompanying it. At least, the few phenomena of this nature are overbalanced by opposite phenomena of still greater importance.

Our sense of music, harmony, and indeed beauty of all kinds, gives satisfaction, without being absolutely necessary to the preservation and propagation of the species. But what racking pains, on the other hand, arise from gouts, gravels, megrims, toothaches, rheumatisms, where the injury to the animal machinery is either small or incurable? Mirth, laughter, play, frolic, seem gratuitous satisfactions, which have no farther tendency: spleen, melancholy, discontent, superstition, are pains of the same nature. How then does the Divine benevolence display itself, in the sense of you Anthropomorphites? None but we Mystics, as you were pleased to call us, can account for this strange mixture of phenomena, by deriving it from attributes, infinitely perfect, but incomprehensible.

And have you at last, said Cleanthes smiling, betrayed your intentions, Philo? Your long agreement with Demea did indeed a little surprise me; but I find you were all the while erecting a concealed battery against me. And I must confess, that you have now fallen upon a subject worthy of your noble spirit of opposition and controversy. If you can make out the present point, and prove mankind to be unhappy or corrupted, there is an end at once of all religion. For to what purpose establish the natural attributes of the Deity, while the moral are still doubtful and uncertain?

You take umbrage very easily, replied Demea, at opinions the most innocent, and the most generally received, even amongst the religious and devout themselves: and nothing can be more surprising than to find a topic like this, concerning the wickedness and misery of man, charged with no less than Atheism and profaneness. Have not all pious divines and preachers, who have indulged their rhetoric on so fertile a subject; have they not easily, I say, given a solution of any difficulties which may attend it? This world is but a point in comparison of the universe; this life but a moment in comparison of eternity. The present evil phenomena, therefore, are rectified in other regions, and in some future period of existence. And the eyes of men, being then opened to larger views of things, see the whole connection of general laws; and trace with adoration, the benevolence and rectitude of the Deity, through all the mazes and intricacies of his providence.

No! replied Cleanthes, No! These arbitrary suppositions can never be admitted, contrary to matter of fact, visible and uncontroverted. Whence can any cause be known but from its known effects? Whence can any hypothesis be proved but from the apparent phenomena? To establish one hypothesis upon another, is building entirely in the air; and the utmost we ever attain, by these conjectures and fictions, is to ascertain the bare possibility of our opinion; but never can we, upon such terms, establish its reality.

The only method of supporting Divine benevolence, and it is what I willingly embrace, is to deny absolutely the misery and wickedness of man. Your representations are exaggerated; your melancholy views mostly fictitious; your inferences contrary to fact and experience. Health is more common than sickness; pleasure than pain; happiness than misery. And for one vexation which we meet with, we attain, upon computation, a hundred enjoyments.

Admitting your position, replied Philo, which yet is extremely doubtful, you must at the same time allow, that if pain be less frequent than pleasure, it is infinitely more violent and durable. One hour of it is often able to outweigh a day, a week, a month of our common insipid enjoyments; and how many days, weeks, and months, are passed by several in the most acute torments? Pleasure, scarcely in one instance, is ever able to reach ecstasy and rapture; and in no one instance can it continue for any time at its highest pitch and altitude. The spirits evaporate, the nerves relax, the fabric is disordered, and the enjoyment quickly degenerates into fatigue and uneasiness. But pain often, good God, how often! rises to torture and agony; and the longer it continues, it becomes still more genuine agony and torture. Patience is exhausted, courage languishes, melancholy seizes us, and nothing terminates our misery but the removal of its cause, or another event, which is the sole cure of all evil, but which, from our natural folly, we regard with still greater horror and consternation.

But not to insist upon these topics, continued Philo, though most obvious, certain, and important; I must use the freedom to admonish you, Cleanthes, that you have put the controversy upon a most dangerous issue, and are unawares introducing a total scepticism into the most essential articles of natural and revealed theology. What! no method of fixing a just foundation for religion, unless we allow the happiness of human life, and maintain a continued existence even in this world, with all our present pains, infirmities, vexations, and follies, to be eligible and desirable! But this is contrary to every one's feeling and experience: It is contrary to an authority so established as nothing can subvert. No decisive proofs can ever be produced against this authority; nor is it possible for you to compute, estimate and compare, all the pains and all the pleasures in the lives of all men and of all animals: And thus, by your resting the whole system of religion on a point, which, from its very nature, must for ever be uncertain, you tacitly confess, that that system is equally uncertain.

But allowing you what never will be believed, at least what you never possibly can prove, that animal, or at least human happiness, in this life, exceeds its misery, you have yet done nothing: For this is not, by any means, what we expect from infinite power, infinite wisdom, and infinite goodness. Why is there any misery at all in the world? Not by chance surely. From some cause then. Is it from the intention of the Deity? But he is perfectly benevolent. Is it contrary to his intention? But he is almighty. Nothing can shake the solidity of this reasoning, so short, so clear, so decisive; except we assert, that these subjects exceed all human capacity, and that our common measures of truth, and falsehood are not applicable to them; a topic which I have all along insisted on, but which you have, from the beginning, rejected with scorn and indignation.

But I will be contented to retire still from this intrenchment, for I deny that you can ever force me in it. I will allow, that pain or misery in man is *compatible* with infinite power and goodness in the Deity, even in your sense of these attributes: What are you advanced by all these concessions? A mere possible compatibility is not sufficient. You must *prove* these pure, unmixt, and uncontrollable attributes from the present mixt and confused phenomena, and from these alone. A hopeful undertaking! Were the phenomena ever so pure and unmixt, yet being finite, they would be insufficient for that purpose. How much more, where they are also so jarring and discordant!

Here, Cleanthes, I find myself at ease in my argument. Here I triumph. Formerly, when we argued concerning the natural attributes of intelligence and design, I needed all my sceptical and metaphysical subtilty to elude your grasp. In many views of the universe, and of its parts, particularly the latter, the beauty and fitness of final causes strike us with such irresistible force, that all objections appear (what I believe they really are) mere cavils and sophisms; nor can we then imagine how it was ever possible for us to repose any weight on them. But there is no view of human life, or of the condition of mankind, from which, without the greatest violence, we can infer the moral attributes, or learn that infinite benevolence, conjoined with infinite power and infinite wisdom, which we must discover by the eyes of faith alone. It is your turn now to tug the labouring oar, and to support your philosophical subtilties against the dictates of plain reason and experience.

PART XI

I scruple not to allow, said Cleanthes, that I have been apt to suspect the frequent repetition of the word *infinite*, which we meet with in all theological writers, to savour more of panegyric than of philosophy; and that any purposes of reasoning, and even of religion, would be better served, were we to rest contented with more accurate and more moderate expressions. The terms, *admirable, excellent, superlatively great, wise,* and *holy*; these sufficiently fill the imaginations of men; and any thing beyond, besides that it leads into absurdities, has no influence on the affections or sentiments. Thus, in the present subject, if we abandon all human analogy, as seems your intention, Demea, I am afraid we abandon all religion, and retain no conception of the great object of our adoration. If we preserve human analogy, we must for ever find it impossible to reconcile any mixture of evil in the universe with infinite attributes; much less can we ever prove the latter from the former. But supposing the Author of Nature to be finitely perfect, though far exceeding mankind, a satisfactory account may then be given of natural and moral evil, and every untoward phenomenon be explained and adjusted. A less evil may then be chosen, in order to avoid a greater; inconveniences be submitted to, in order to reach a desirable end; and in a word, benevolence, regulated by wisdom, and limited by necessity, may produce just such a world as the present. You, Philo, who are so prompt at starting views, and reflections, and analogies, I would gladly hear, at length, without interruption, your opinion of this new theory; and if it deserve our attention, we may afterwards, at more leisure, reduce it into form.

My sentiments, replied Philo, are not worth being made a mystery of; and therefore, without any ceremony, I shall deliver what occurs to me with regard to the present subject. It must, I think, be allowed, that if a very limited intelligence, whom we shall suppose utterly unacquainted with the universe, were assured, that it were the production of a very good, wise, and powerful Being, however finite, he would, from his conjectures, form *beforehand* a different notion of it from what we find it to be by experience; nor would he ever imagine, merely from these attributes of the cause, of which he is informed, that the effect could be so full of vice and misery and disorder, as it appears in this life. Supposing now, that this person were brought into the world, still assured that it was the workmanship of such a sublime and benevolent Being; he might, perhaps, be surprised at the disappointment; but would never retract his former belief, if founded on any very solid argument; since such a limited intelligence must be sensible of his own blindness and ignorance, and must allow, that there may be many solutions of those phenomena, which will for ever escape his comprehension. But supposing, which is the real case with regard to man, that this creature is not antecedently convinced of a supreme intelligence, benevolent, and powerful, but is left to gather such a belief from the appearances of things; this entirely alters the case, nor will he ever find any reason for such a conclusion. He may be fully convinced of the narrow limits of his understanding; but this will not help him in forming an inference concerning the goodness of superior powers, since he must form that inference from what he knows, not from what he is ignorant of. The more you exaggerate his weakness and ignorance, the more diffident you render him, and give him the greater suspicion that such subjects are beyond the reach of his faculties. You are obliged, therefore, to reason with him merely from the known phenomena, and to drop every arbitrary supposition or conjecture.

Did I show you a house or palace, where there was not one apartment convenient or agreeable; where the windows, doors, fires passages, stairs, and the whole economy of the building, were the source of noise, confusion, fatigue, darkness, and the extremes of heat and cold; you would certainly blame the contrivance, without any farther examination. The architect would in vain display his subtilty, and prove to you, that if this door or that window were altered, greater ills would ensue. What he says may be strictly true: The alteration of one particular, while the other parts of the building remain, may only augment the inconveniences. But still you would assert in general, that, if the architect had had skill and good intentions, he might have formed such a plan of the whole, and might have adjusted the parts in such a manner, as would have remedied all or most of these inconveniences. His ignorance, or even your own ignorance of such a plan, will never convince you of the impossibility of it. If you find any inconveniences and deformities in the building, you will always, without entering into any detail, condemn the architect.

In short, I repeat the question: Is the world, considered in general, and as it appears to us in this life, different from what a man, or such a limited being, would, *beforehand*, expect from a very powerful, wise, and benevolent Deity? It must be strange prejudice to assert the contrary. And from thence I conclude, that however consistent the world may be, allowing certain suppositions and conjectures, with the idea of such a Deity, it can never afford us an inference concerning his existence. The consistence is not absolutely denied, only the inference. Conjectures, especially where infinity is excluded from the Divine attributes, may perhaps be sufficient to prove a consistence, but can never be foundations for any inference.

There seem to be *four* circumstances, on which depend all, or the greatest part of the ills, that molest sensible creatures; and it is not impossible but all these circumstances may be necessary and unavoidable. We know so little beyond common life, or even of common life, that, with regard to the economy of a universe, there is no conjecture, however wild, which may not be just; nor any one, however plausible, which may not be erroneous. All that belongs to human understanding, in this deep ignorance and obscurity, is to be sceptical, or at least cautious, and not to admit of any hypothesis whatever, much less of any which is supported by no appearance of probability. Now, this I assert to be the case with regard to all the causes of evil, and the circumstances on which it depends. None of them appear to human reason in the least degree necessary or unavoidable; nor can we suppose them such, without the utmost license of imagination.

The *first* circumstance which introduces evil, is that contrivance or economy of the animal reaction, by which pains, as well as pleasures, are employed to excite all creatures to action, and make them vigilant in the great work of self-preservation. Now pleasure alone, in its various degrees, seems to human understanding sufficient for this purpose. All animals might be constantly in a state of enjoyment: but when urged by any of the necessities of nature, such as thirst, hunger, weariness; instead of pain, they might feel a diminution of pleasure, by which they might be prompted to seek that object which is necessary to their subsistence. Men pursue pleasure as eagerly as they avoid pain; at least, they might have been so constituted. It seems, therefore, plainly possible to carry on the business of life without any pain. Why then is any animal ever rendered susceptible of such a sensation? If animals can be free from it an hour, they might enjoy a perpetual exemption from it; and it required as particular a contrivance of their organs to produce that feeling, as to endow them with sight, hearing, or any of the senses. Shall we conjecture, that such a contrivance was necessary, without any appearance of reason? and shall we build on that conjecture as on the most certain truth?

But a capacity of pain would not alone produce pain, were it not for the *second* circumstance, viz. the conducting of the world by general laws; and this seems nowise necessary to a very perfect Being. It is true, if every thing were conducted by particular volitions, the course of nature would be perpetually broken, and no man could employ his reason in the conduct of life. But might not other particular volitions remedy this inconvenience? In short, might not the Deity exterminate all ill, wherever it were to be found; and produce all good, without any preparation, or long progress of causes and effects?

Besides, we must consider, that, according to the present economy of the world, the course of nature, though supposed exactly regular, yet to us appears not so, and many events are uncertain, and many disappoint our expectations. Health and sickness, calm and tempest, with an infinite number of other accidents, whose causes are unknown and variable, have a great influence both on the fortunes of particular persons and on the prosperity of public societies; and indeed all human life, in a manner, depends on such accidents. A being, therefore, who knows the secret springs of the universe, might easily, by particular volitions, turn all these accidents to the good of mankind, and render the whole world happy, without discovering himself in any operation. A fleet, whose purposes were salutary to society, might always meet with a fair wind. Good princes enjoy sound health and long life. Persons born to power and authority, be framed with good tempers and virtuous dispositions. A few such events as these, regularly and wisely conducted, would change the face of the world; and yet would no more seem to disturb the course of nature, or confound human conduct, than the present economy of things, where the causes are secret, and variable, and compounded. Some small touches given to Caligula's brain in his infancy, might have converted him into a Trajan. One wave, a little higher than the rest, by burying Caesar and his fortune in the bottom of the ocean, might have restored liberty to a considerable part of mankind. There may, for aught we know, be good reasons why Providence interposes not in this manner; but they are unknown to us; and though the mere supposition, that such reasons exist, may be sufficient to *save* the conclusion concerning the Divine attributes, yet surely it can never be sufficient to *establish* that conclusion.

If every thing in the universe be conducted by general laws, and if animals be rendered susceptible of pain, it scarcely seems possible but some ill must arise in the various shocks of matter, and the various concurrence and opposition of general laws; but this ill would be very rare, were it not for the *third* circumstance, which I proposed to mention, viz. the great frugality with which all powers and faculties are distributed to every particular being. So well adjusted are the organs and capacities of all animals, and so well fitted to their preservation, that, as far as history or tradition reaches, there appears not to be any single species which has yet been extinguished in the universe. Every animal has the requisite endowments; but these endowments are bestowed with so scrupulous an economy, that any considerable diminution must entirely destroy the creature. Wherever one power is increased, there is a proportional abatement in the others. Animals which excel in swiftness are commonly defective in force. Those which possess both are either imperfect in some of their senses, or are oppressed with the most craving wants. The human species, whose chief excellency is reason and sagacity, is of all others the most necessitous, and the most deficient in bodily advantages; without clothes, without arms, without food, without lodging, without any convenience of life, except what they owe to their own skill and industry. In short, nature seems to have formed an exact calculation of the necessities of her creatures; and, like a *rigid master*, has afforded them little more powers or endowments than what are strictly sufficient to supply those necessities. An *indulgent parent* would have bestowed a large stock, in order to guard against accidents, and secure the happiness and welfare of the creature in the most unfortunate concurrence of circumstances. Every course of life would not have been so surrounded with precipices, that the least departure from the true path, by mistake or necessity, must involve us in misery and ruin. Some reserve, some fund, would have been provided to ensure happiness; nor would the powers and the necessities have been adjusted with so rigid an economy. The Author of Nature is inconceivably powerful: his force is supposed great, if not altogether inexhaustible: nor is there any reason, as far as we can judge, to make him observe this strict frugality in his dealings with his creatures. It would have been better, were his power extremely limited, to have created fewer animals, and to have endowed these with more faculties for their happiness and preservation. A builder is never esteemed prudent, who undertakes a plan beyond what his stock will enable him to finish.

In order to cure most of the ills of human life, I require not that man should have the wings of the eagle, the swiftness of the stag, the force of the ox, the arms of the lion, the scales of the crocodile or rhinoceros; much less do I demand the sagacity of an angel or cherubim. I am contented to take an increase in one single power or faculty of his soul. Let him be endowed with a greater propensity to industry and labour; a more vigorous spring and activity of mind; a more constant bent to business and application. Let the whole species possess naturally an equal diligence with that which many individuals are able to attain by habit and reflection; and the most beneficial consequences, without any allay of ill, is the immediate and necessary result of this endowment. Almost all the moral, as well as natural evils of human life, arise from idleness; and were our species, by the original constitution of their frame, exempt from this vice or infirmity, the perfect cultivation of land, the improvement of arts and manufactures, the exact execution of every office and duty, immediately follow; and men at once may fully reach that state of society, which is so imperfectly attained by the best regulated government. But as industry is a power, and the most valuable of any, Nature seems determined, suitably to her usual maxims, to bestow it on men with a very sparing hand; and rather to punish him severely for his deficiency in it, than to reward him for his attainments. She has so contrived his frame, that nothing but the most violent necessity can oblige him to labour; and she employs all his other wants to overcome, at least in part, the want of diligence, and to endow him with some share of a faculty of which she has thought fit naturally to bereave him.

Here our demands may be allowed very humble, and therefore the more reasonable. If we required the endowments of superior penetration and judgment, of a more delicate taste of beauty, of a nicer sensibility to benevolence and friendship; we might be told, that we impiously pretend to break the order of Nature; that we want to exalt ourselves into a higher rank of being; that the presents which we require, not being suitable to our state and condition, would only be pernicious to us. But it is hard; I dare to repeat it, it is hard, that being placed in a world so full of wants and necessities, where almost every being and element is either our foe or refuses its assistance. . . . we should also have our own temper to struggle with, and should be deprived of that faculty which can alone fence against these multiplied evils.

The *fourth* circumstance, whence arises the misery and ill of the universe, is the inaccurate workmanship of all the springs and principles of the great machine of nature. It must be acknowledged, that there are few parts of the universe, which seem not to serve some purpose, and whose removal would not produce a visible defect and disorder in the whole. The parts hang all together; nor can one be touched without affecting the rest, in a greater or less degree. But at the same time, it must be observed, that none of these parts or principles, however useful, are so accurately adjusted, as to keep precisely within those bounds in which their utility consists; but they are, all of them, apt, on every occasion, to run into the one extreme or the other. One would imagine, that this grand production had not received the last hand of the maker; so little finished is every part, and so coarse are the strokes with which it is executed. Thus, the winds are requisite to convey the vapours along the surface of the globe, and to assist men in navigation: but how oft, rising up to tempests and hurricanes, do they become pernicious? Rains are necessary to nourish all the plants and animals of the earth: but how often are they defective? how often excessive? Heat is requisite to all life and vegetation; but is not always found in the due proportion. On the mixture and secretion of the humours and juices of the body depend the health and prosperity of the animal: but the parts perform not regularly their proper function. What more useful than all the passions of the mind, ambition, vanity, love, anger? But how oft do they break their bounds, and cause the greatest convulsions in society? There is nothing so advantageous in the universe, but what frequently becomes pernicious, by its excess or defect; nor has Nature guarded, with the requisite accuracy, against all disorder or confusion. The irregularity is never perhaps so great as to destroy any species; but is often sufficient to involve the individuals in ruin and misery.

On the concurrence, then, of these *four* circumstances, does all or the greatest part of natural evil depend. Were all living creatures incapable of pain, or were the world administered by particular volitions, evil never could have found access into the universe: and were animals endowed with a large stock of powers and faculties, beyond what strict necessity requires; or were the several springs and principles of the universe so accurately framed as to preserve always the just temperament and medium; there must have been very little ill in comparison of what we feel at present. What then shall we pronounce on this occasion? Shall we say that these circumstances are not necessary, and that they might easily have been altered in the contrivance of the universe? This decision seems too presumptuous for creatures so blind and ignorant. Let us be more modest in our conclusions. Let us allow, that, if the goodness of the Diety (I mean a goodness like the human) could be established on any tolerable reasons *a priori*, these phenomena, however untoward, would not be sufficient to subvert that principle; but might easily, in some unknown manner, be reconcileable to it. But let us still assert, that as this goodness is not antecedently established, but must be inferred from the phenomena, there can be no grounds for such an inference, while there are so many ills in the universe, and while these ills might so easily have been remedied, as far as human understanding can be allowed to judge on such a subject. I am Sceptic enough to allow, that the bad appearances, notwithstanding all my reasonings, may be compatible with such attributes as you suppose; but surely they can never prove these attributes. Such a conclusion cannot result from Scepticism, but must arise from the phenomena, and from our confidence in the reasonings which we deduce from these phenomena.

Look round this universe. What an immense profusion of beings, animated and organized, sensible and active! You admire this prodigious variety and fecundity. But inspect a little more narrowly these living existences, the only beings worth regarding. How hostile and destructive to each other! How insufficient all of them for their own happiness! How contemptible or odious to the spectator! The whole presents nothing but the idea of a blind Nature, impregnated by a great vivifying principle, and pouring forth from her lap, without discernment or parental care, her maimed and abortive children!

Here the Manichæan system occurs as a proper hypothesis to solve the difficulty: and no doubt, in some respects, it is very specious, and has more probability than the common hypothesis, by giving a plausible account of the strange mixture of good and ill which appears in life. But if we consider, on the other hand, the perfect uniformity and agreement of the parts of the universe, we shall not discover in it any marks of the combat of a malevolent with a benevolent being. There is indeed an opposition of pains and pleasure in the feelings of sensible creatures: but are not all the operations of Nature carried on by an opposition of principles, of hot and cold, moist and dry, light and heavy? The true conclusion is, that the original Source of all things is entirely indifferent to all these principles; and has no more regard to good above ill, than to heat above cold, or to drought above moisture, or to light above heavy.

There may *four* hypotheses be framed concerning the first causes of the universe: *that* they are endowed with perfect goodness; *that* they have perfect malice; *that* they are opposite, and have both goodness and malice; *that* they have neither goodness nor malice. Mixt phenomena can never prove the two former unmixt principles; and the uniformity and steadiness of general laws seem to oppose the third. The fourth, therefore, seems by far the most probable.

What I have said concerning natural evil will apply to moral, with little or no variation; and we have no more reason to infer, that the rectitude of the Supreme Being resembles human rectitude, than that his benevolence resembles the human. Nay, it will be thought, that we have still greater cause to exclude from him moral sentiments, such as we feel them; since moral evil, in the opinion of many, is much more predominant above moral good than natural evil above natural good.

But even though this should not be allowed, and though the virtue which is in mankind should be acknowledged much superior to the vice, yet so long as there is any vice at all in the universe, it will very much puzzle you Anthropomorphites, how to account for it. You must assign a cause for it, without having recourse to the first cause. But as every effect must have a cause, and that cause another, you must either carry on the progression *in infinitum*, or rest on that original principle, who is the ultimate cause of all things. . . .

FYODOR DOSTOEVSKY
Rebellion

"I must make you one confession," Ivan began. "I could never understand how one can love one's neighbours. It's just one's neighbours, to my mind, that one can't love, though one might love those at a distance. I once read somewhere of John the Merciful, a saint, that when a hungry, frozen beggar came to him, he took him into his bed, held him in his arms, and began breathing into his mouth, which was putrid and loathsome from some awful disease. I am convinced that he did that from 'self-laceration,' from the self-laceration of falsity, for the sake of the charity imposed by duty, as a penance laid on him. For any one to love a man, he must be hidden, for as soon as he shows his face, love is gone."

"Father Zossima has talked of that more than once," observed Alyosha; "he, too, said that the face of a man often hinders many people not practised in love, from loving him. But yet there's a great deal of love in mankind, and almost Christ-like love. I know that myself, Ivan."

"Well, I know nothing of it so far, and can't understand it, and the innumerable mass of mankind are with me there. The question is, whether that's due to men's bad qualities or whether it's inherent in their nature. To my thinking, Christ-like love for men is a miracle impossible on earth. He was God. But we are not gods. Suppose I, for instance, suffer intensely. Another can never know how much I suffer, because he is another and not I. And what's more, a man is rarely ready to admit another's suffering (as though it were a distinction). Why

Fyodor Dostoevsky (1821–1881), considered one of the greatest Russian novelists, was deeply concerned with theological questions and often presented philosophical arguments within his fictional works. Among his best known novels are *Crime and Punishment*, *The Idiot*, and *The Brothers Karamazov*.

REBELLION   Reprinted with permission of Macmillan Publishing Company from *The Brothers Karamazov* by Fyodor Dostoevsky, translated by Constance Garnett (New York: Macmillan, 1923).

won't he admit it, do you think? Because I smell unpleasant, because I have a stupid face, because I once trod on his foot. Besides there is suffering and suffering; degrading, humiliating suffering such as humbles me—hunger, for instance—my benefactor will perhaps allow me; but when you come to higher suffering—for an idea, for instance—he will very rarely admit that, perhaps because my face strikes him as not at all what he fancies a man should have who suffers for an idea. And so he deprives me instantly of his favour, and not at all from badness of heart. Beggars, especially genteel beggars, ought never to show themselves, but to ask for charity through the newspapers. One can love one's neighbours in the abstract, or even at a distance, but at close quarters it's almost impossible. If it were as on the stage, in the ballet, where if beggars come in, they wear silken rags and tattered lace and beg for alms dancing gracefully, then one might like looking at them. But even then we should not love them. But enough of that. I simply wanted to show you my point of view. I meant to speak of the suffering of mankind generally, but we had better confine ourselves to the sufferings of the children. That reduces the scope of my argument to a tenth of what it would be. Still we'd better keep to the children, though it does weaken my case. But, in the first place, children can be loved even at close quarters, even when they are dirty, even when they are ugly (I fancy, though, children never are ugly). The second reason why I won't speak of grown-up people is that, besides being disgusting and unworthy of love, they have a compensation—they've eaten the apple and know good and evil, and they have become 'like god.' They go on eating it still. But the children haven't eaten anything, and are so far innocent. Are you fond of children, Alyosha? I know you are, and you will understand why I prefer to speak of them. If they, too, suffer horribly on earth, they must suffer for their fathers' sins, they must be punished for their fathers, who have eaten the apple; but that reasoning is of the other world and is incomprehensible for the heart of man here on earth. The innocent must not suffer for another's sins, and especially such innocents! You may be surprised at me, Alyosha, but I am awfully fond of children, too. And observe, cruel people, the violent, the rapacious, the Karamazovs are sometimes very fond of children. Children while they are quite little—up to seven, for instance—are so remote from grown-up people; they are different creatures, as it were, of a different species. I knew a criminal in prison who had, in the course of his career as a burglar, murdered whole families, including several children. But when he was in prison, he had a strange affection for them. He spent all his time at his window, watching the children playing in the prison yard. He trained one little boy to come up to his window and made great friends with him. . . . You don't know why I am telling you all this, Alyosha? My head aches and I am sad."

"You speak with a strange air," observed Alyosha uneasily, "as though you were not quite yourself."

"By the way, a Bulgarian I met lately in Moscow," Ivan went on, seeming not to hear his brother's words, "told me about the crimes committed by Turks and Circassians in all parts of Bulgaria through fear of a general rising of the Slavs. They burn villages, murder, outrage women and children, they nail their prisoners by the ears to the fences, leave them so till morning, and in the morning they hang them—all sorts of things you can't imagine. People talk sometimes of bestial cruelty, but that's a great injustice and insult to the beasts; a beast can never be so cruel as a man, so artistically cruel. The tiger only tears and gnaws, that's all he can do. He would never think of nailing people by the ears, even if he were able to do it. These Turks took a pleasure in torturing children, too; cutting the unborn child from the mother's womb, and tossing babies up in the air and catching them on the points of their bayonets before their mother's eyes. Doing it before the mother's eyes was what gave zest to the amusement. Here is another scene that I thought very interesting. Imagine a trembling mother with her baby in her arms, a circle of invading Turks around her. They've planned a diversion; they pet the baby, laugh to make it laugh. They succeed, the baby laughs. At that moment a Turk points a pistol four inches from the baby's face. The baby laughs with glee, holds out its little hands to the pistol, and he pulls the trigger in the baby's face and blows out its brains. Artistic, wasn't it? By the way, Turks are particularly fond of sweet things, they say."

"Brother, what are you driving at?" asked Alyosha.

"I think if the devil doesn't exist, but man has created him, he has created him in his own image and likeness."

"Just as he did God, then?" observed Alyosha.

" 'It's wonderful how you can turn words,' as Polonius says in *Hamlet*," laughed Ivan. "You turn my words against me. Well, I am glad. Yours must be a fine God, if man created Him in His image and likeness. You asked just now what I was driving at. You see, I am fond of collecting certain facts, and, would you believe, I even copy anecdotes of a certain sort from newspapers and books, and I've already got a fine collection. The Turks, of course, have gone into it, but they are foreigners. I have specimens from home that are even better than the Turks. You know we prefer beating—rods and scourges—that's our national institution. Nailing ears is unthinkable for us, for we are, after all, Europeans. But the rod and the scourge we have always with us and they cannot be taken from us. Abroad now they scarcely do any beating. Manners are more humane, or laws have been passed, so that they don't dare to flog men now. But they make up for it in another way just as national as ours. And so national that it would be practically impossible among us, though I believe we are being inoculated with it, since the religious movement began in our aristocracy. I have a charming pamphlet, translated from the French, describing how, quite recently, five years ago, a murderer, Richard, was executed—a young man, I believe, of three and twenty, who repented and was converted to the Christian faith at the very scaffold. This Richard was an illegitimate child who was given as a child of six by his parents to some shepherds on the Swiss mountains. They brought him up to work for them. He grew up like a little wild beast among them. The shepherds taught him nothing, and scarcely fed or clothed him, but sent him out at seven to herd the flock in cold and wet, and no one hesitated or scrupled to treat him so. Quite the contrary, they thought they had every right, for Richard had been given to them as a chattel, and they did not even see the necessity of feeding him. Richard himself describes how in those years, like the Prodigal Son in the Gospel, he longed to eat of the mash given to the pigs, which were fattened for sale. But they wouldn't even give him that, and beat him when he stole from the pigs. And that was how he spent all his childhood and his youth, till he grew up and was strong enough to go away and be a thief. The savage began to earn his living as a day labourer in Geneva. He drank what he earned, he lived like a brute, and finished by killing and robbing an old man. He was caught, tried, and condemned to death. They are not sentimentalists there. And in prison he was immediately surrounded by pastors, members of Christian brotherhoods, philanthropic ladies, and the like. They taught him to read and write in prison, and expounded the Gospel to him. They exhorted him, worked upon him, drummed at him incessantly, till at last he solemnly confessed his crime. He was converted. He wrote to the court himself that he was a monster, but that in the end God had vouchsafed him light and shown grace. All Geneva was in excitement about him—all philanthropic and religious Geneva. All the aristocratic and well-bred society of the town rushed to the prison, kissed Richard and embraced him; 'You are our brother, you have found grace.' and Richard does nothing but weep with emotion, 'Yes, I've found grace! All my youth and childhood I was glad of pigs' food, but now even I have found grace. I am dying in the Lord.' 'Yes, Richard, die in the Lord; you have shed blood and must die. Though it's not your fault that you knew not the Lord, when you coveted the pig's food and were beaten for stealing it (which was very wrong of you, for stealing is forbidden); but you've shed blood and you must die.' And on the last day, Richard, perfectly limp, did nothing but cry and repeat every minute: 'This is my happiest day. I am going to the Lord.' 'Yes,' cry the pastors and the judges and philanthropic ladies. 'This is the happiest day of your life, for you are going to the Lord!' They all walk or drive to the scaffold in procession behind the prison van. At the scaffold they call to Richard: 'Die, brother, die in the Lord, for even thou hast found grace!' And so, covered with his brothers' kisses, Richard is dragged on to the scaffold, and led to the guillotine. And they chopped off his head in brotherly fashion, because he had found grace. Yes, that's characteristic. That pamphlet is translated into Russian by some Russian philanthropists of aristocratic rank and evangelical aspirations, and has been distributed gratis for the enlightenment of the people. The case of Richard is interesting because it's national. Though to us it's absurd to cut off a man's head, because he has become our brother and has found grace, yet we have our own specialty, which is all but worse. Our historical pastime is the direct satisfaction of inflicting pain. There are lines in Nekrassov describing how a peasant lashes a horse on the eyes, 'on its meek eyes,' every one must have seen it. It's peculiarly Russian. He describes how a feeble little nag had foundered under too heavy a load and cannot move. The peasant beats it, beats it savagely, beats it at last not knowing what he is doing in the intoxication of cruelty, thrashes it mercilessly over and over again. 'However weak you are, you must pull, if you die for it.' The nag strains, and then he begins lashing the poor defenceless creature on its weeping, on its 'meek eyes.' The frantic beast tugs and draws the load, trembling all over, gasping for breath, moving sideways, with a sort of unnatural spasmodic action—it's awful in Nekrassov. But that's only a horse, and God has given horses to be beaten. So the Tatars have taught us, and they left us the knout as a remembrance of it. But men, too, can be beaten. A well-educated, cultured gentleman and his wife beat their own child with a birch-rod, a girl of seven. I have an exact account of it. The papa was glad that the birch was covered with twigs. 'It stings more,' said he, and so he began stinging his daughter. I know for a fact there are people who at every blow are worked up to sensuality, to literal sensuality, which increases progressively at every blow they inflict. They beat for a minute, for five minutes, for ten minutes, more often and more savagely. The child screams. At last the child cannot scream, it gasps, 'Daddy! daddy!' By some diabolical unseemly chance the case was brought into court. A counsel is engaged. The Russian people have long called a barrister 'a conscience for hire.' The counsel protests in his client's defence. 'It's such a simple thing,' he says, 'an everyday domestic event. A father corrects his child. To our shame be it said, it is brought into court.' The jury, convinced by him, give a favourable verdict. The public roars with delight that the torturer is acquitted. Ah, pity I wasn't there! I would have proposed to raise a subscription in his honour! . . . Charming pictures.

"But I've still better things about children. I've collected a great, great deal about Russian children, Alyosha. There was a little girl of five who was hated by her father and mother, 'most worthy and respectable people, of good education and breeding.' You see, I must repeat again, it is a peculiar characteristic of many people, this love of torturing children, and children only. To all other types of humanity these torturers behave mildly and benevolently, like cultivated and humane Europeans; but they are very fond of tormenting children, even fond of children themselves in that sense. It's just their defencelessness that tempts the tormentor, just the angelic confidence of the child who has no refuge and no appeal, that sets his vile blood on fire. In every man, of course, a demon lies hidden—the demon of rage, the demon of lustful heat at the screams of the tortured victim, the demon of lawlessness let off the chain, the demon of diseases that follow on vice, gout, kidney disease, and so on.

"This poor child of five was subjected to every possible torture by those cultivated parents. They beat her, thrashed her, kicked her for no reason till her body was one bruise. Then, they went to greater refinements of cruelty—shut her up all night in the cold and frost in a privy, and because she didn't ask to be taken up at night (as though a child of five sleeping its angelic, sound sleep could be trained to wake and ask), they smeared her face and filled her mouth with excrement, and it was her mother, her mother did this. And that mother could sleep, hearing the poor child's groans! Can you understand why a little creature, who can't even understand what's done to her, should beat her little aching heart with her tiny fist in the dark and the cold, and weep her meek unresentful tears to dear, kind God to protect her? Do you understand that, friend and brother, you pious and humble novice? Do you understand why this infamy must be and is permitted? Without it, I am told, man could not have existed on earth, for he could not have known good and evil. Why should he know that diabolical good and evil when it costs so much? Why, the whole world of knowledge is not worth that child's prayer to 'dear, kind God'! I say nothing of the sufferings of grown-up people, they have eaten the apple, damn them, and the devil take them all! But these little ones! I am making you suffer, Alyosha, you are not yourself. I'll leave off if you like."

"Never mind. I want to suffer too," muttered Alyosha.

"One picture, only one more, because it's so curious, so characteristic, and I have only just read it in some collection of Russian antiquities. I've forgotten the name. I must look it up. It was in the darkest days of serfdom at the beginning of the century, and long live the Liberator of the People! There was in those days a general of aristocratic connections, the owner of great estates, one of those men— somewhat exceptional, I believe, even then—who, retiring from the service into a life of leisure, are convinced that they've earned absolute power over the lives of their subjects. There were such men then. So our general, settled on his property of two thousand souls, lives in pomp, and domineers over his poor neighbours as though they were dependents and buffoons. He has kennels of hundreds of hounds and nearly a hundred dog-boys—all mounted, and in uniform. One day a serf boy, a little child of eight, threw a stone in play and hurt the paw of the general's favourite hound. 'Why is my favourite dog lame?' He is told that the boy threw a stone that hurt the dog's paw. 'So you did it.' The general looked the child up and down. 'Take him.' He was taken—taken from his mother and kept shut up all night. Early that morning the general comes out on horseback, with the hounds, his dependents, dog-boys, and huntsmen, all mounted around him in full hunting parade. The servants are summoned for their edification, and in front of them all stands the mother of the child. The child is brought from the lock-up. It's a gloomy cold, foggy autumn day, a capital day for hunting. The general orders the child to be undressed; the child is stripped naked. He shivers, numb with terror not daring to cry. . . . 'Make him run,' commands the general. 'Run! run!' shout the dog-boys. The boy runs. . . . 'At him!' yells the general, and he sets the whole pack of hounds on the child. The hounds catch him, and tear him to pieces before his mother's eyes! . . . I believe the general was afterwards declared incapable of administering his estates. Well—what did he deserve? To be shot? To be shot for the satisfaction of our moral feelings? Speak, Alyosha!"

"To be shot," murmured Alyosha, lifting his eyes to Ivan with a pale, twisted smile.

"Bravo!" cried Ivan delighted. "If even you say so . . . You're a pretty monk! So there is a little devil sitting in your heart, Alyosha Karamazov!"

"What I said was absurd, but———"

"That's just the point, that 'but'!" cried Ivan. "Let me tell you, novice, that the absurd is only too necessary on earth. The world stands on absurdities, and perhaps nothing would have come to pass in it without them. We know what we know!"

"What do you know?"

"I understand nothing," Ivan went on, as though in delirium. "I don't want to understand anything now. I want to stick to the fact. I made up my mind long ago not to understand. If I try to understand anything, I shall be false to the fact and I have determined to stick to the fact."

"Why are you trying me?" Alyosha cried, with sudden distress. "Will you say what you mean at last?"

"Of course, I will; that's what I've been leading up to. You are dear to me, I don't want to let you go, and I won't give you up to your Zossima."

Ivan for a minute was silent, his face became all at once very sad.

"Listen! I took the case of children only to make my case clearer. Of the other tears of humanity with which the earth is soaked from its crust to its centre, I will say nothing. I have narrowed my subject on purpose. I am a bug, and I recognise in all humility that I cannot understand why the world is arranged as it is. Men are themselves to blame, I suppose; they were given paradise, they wanted free-dom, and stole fire from heaven, though they knew they would become unhappy, so there is no need to pity them. With my pitiful, earthly, Euclidian understand-ing, all I know is that there is suffering and that there are none guilty; that cause follows effect, simply and directly; that everything flows and finds its level—but that's only Euclidian nonsense, I know that, and I can't consent to live by it! What comfort is it to me that there are none guilty and that cause follows effect simply and directly, and that I know it—I must have justice, or I will destroy myself. And not justice in some remote infinite time and space, but here on earth, and that I could see myself. I have believed in it. I want to see it, and if I am dead by then, let me rise again, for if it all happens without me, it will be too unfair. Surely I haven't suffered, simply that I, my crimes and my sufferings, may manure the soil of the future harmony for somebody else. I want to see with my own eyes the hind lie down with the lion and the victim rise up and embrace his murderer. I want to be there when every one suddenly understands what it has all been for. All the religions of the world are built on this longing, and I am a believer. But then there are the children, and what am I to do about them? That's a question I can't answer. For the hundredth time I repeat, there are numbers of questions, but I've only taken the children, because in their case what I mean is so unanswerably clear. Listen! If all must suffer to pay for the eternal harmony, what have children to do with it, tell me, please? It's beyond all comprehension why they should suffer, and why they should pay for the harmony. Why should they, too, furnish material to enrich the soil for the harmony of the future? I understand solidarity in sin among men. I understand solidarity in retribution, too; but there can be no such solidarity with children. And if it is really true that they must share responsibility for all their fathers' crimes, such a truth is not of this world and is beyond my comprehension. Some jester will say, perhaps, that the child would have grown up and have sinned, but you see he didn't grow up, he was torn to pieces by the dogs, at eight years old. Oh, Alyosha, I am not blaspheming! I understand, of course, what an upheaval of the universe it will be, when everything in heaven and earth blends in one hymn of praise and everything that lives and has lived cries aloud: 'Thou art just, O Lord, for Thy ways are revealed.' When the mother embraces the fiend who threw her child to the dogs, and all three cry aloud with tears, 'Thou art just, O Lord!' then, of course, the crown of knowledge will be reached and all will be made clear. But what pulls me up here is that I can't accept that harmony. And while I am on earth, I make haste to take my own measures. You see, Alyosha, perhaps it really may happen that if I live to that moment, or rise again to see it, I, too, perhaps, may cry aloud with the rest, looking at the mother embracing the child's torturer. 'Thou art just. O Lord!' but I don't want to cry aloud then. While there is still time, I hasten to protect myself and so I renounce the higher harmony altogether. It's not worth the tears of that one tortured child who beat itself on the breast with its little fist and prayed in its stinking outhouse, with its unexpiated tears to 'dear, kind God'! It's not worth it, because those tears are unatoned for. They must be atoned for, or there can be no harmony. But how? How are you going to atone for them? Is it possible? By their being avenged? But what do I care for avenging them? What do I care for a hell for oppressors? What good can hell do, since those children have already been tortured? And what becomes of harmony, if there is hell? I want to forgive. I want to embrace. I don't want more suffering. And if the sufferings of children go to swell the sum of sufferings which was necessary to pay for truth, then I protest that the truth is not worth such a price. I don't want the mother to embrace the oppressor who threw her son to the dogs! She dare not forgive him! Let her forgive him for herself, if she will, let her forgive the torturer for the immeasurable suffering of her mother's heart. But the sufferings of her tortured child she has no right to forgive; she dare not forgive the torturer, even if the child were to forgive him! And if that is so, if they dare not forgive, what becomes of harmony? Is there in the whole world a being who would have the right to forgive and could forgive? I don't want harmony. From love for humanity I don't want it. I would rather be left with the unavenged suffering. I would rather remain with my unavenged suffering and unsatisfied indignation, *even if I were wrong*. Besides, too high a price is asked for harmony; it's beyond our means to pay so much to enter on it. And so I hasten to give back my entrance ticket, and if I am an honest man I am bound to give it back as soon as possible. And that I am doing. It's not God that I don't accept, Alyosha, only I most respectfully return Him the ticket."

"That's rebellion," murmured Alyosha, looking down.

"Rebellion? I am sorry you call it that," said Ivan earnestly. "One can hardly live in rebellion, and I want to live. Tell me yourself, I challenge you—answer. Imagine that you are creating a fabric of human destiny with the object of making men happy in the end, giving them peace and rest at last, but that it was essential and inevitable to torture to death only one tiny creature—that baby beating its breast with its fist, for instance—and to found that edifice on its unavenged tears, would you consent to be the architect on those conditions? Tell me, and tell the truth."

"No, I wouldn't consent," said Alyosha softly.

"And can you admit the idea that men for whom you are building it would agree to accept their happiness on the foundation of the unexpiated blood of a little victim? And accepting it would remain happy for ever?"

"No, I can't admit it. Brother," said Alyosha suddenly, with flashing eyes, "you said just now, is there a being in the whole world who would have the right to forgive and could forgive? But there is a Being and He can forgive everything, all and for all, because He gave His innocent blood for all and everything. You have forgotten Him, and on Him is built the edifice, and it is to Him they cry aloud, 'Thou art just, O Lord, for Thy ways are revealed!' "

"Ah! the One without sin and His blood! No, I have not forgotten Him; on the contrary I've been wondering all the time how it was you did not bring Him in before, for usually all arguments on your side put Him in the foreground. . . .

J. L. MACKIE
Evil and Omnipotence

The traditional arguments for the existence of God have been fairly thoroughly criticised by philosophers. But the theologian can, if he wishes, accept this criticism. He can admit that no rational proof of God's existence is possible. And he can still retain all that is essential to his position, by holding that God's existence is known in some other, non-rational way. I think, however, that a more telling criticism can be made by way of the traditional problem of evil. Here it can be shown, not that religious beliefs lack rational support, but that they are positively irrational, that the several parts of the essential theological doctrine are inconsistent with one another, so that the theologian can maintain his position as a whole only by a much more extreme rejection of reason than in the former case. He must now be prepared to believe, not merely what cannot be proved, but what can be *disproved* from other beliefs that he also holds.

The problem of evil, in the sense in which I shall be using the phrase, is a problem only for someone who believes that there is a God who is both omnipotent and wholly good. And it is a logical problem, the problem of clarifying and reconciling a number of beliefs: it is not a scientific problem that might be solved by further observations, or a practical problem that might be solved by a decision or an action. These points are obvious; I mention them only because they are sometimes ignored by theologians, who sometimes parry a statement of the problem with such remarks as "Well, can you solve the problem yourself?" or "This is a mystery which may be revealed to us later" or "Evil is something to be faced and overcome, not to be merely discussed".

In its simplest form the problem is this: God is omnipotent; God is wholly good; and yet evil exists. There seems to be some contradiction between these three propositions, so that if any two of them were true the third would be false. But at the same time all three are essential parts of most theological positions: the theologian, it seems, at once *must* adhere and *cannot consistently* adhere to all three. (The problem does not arise only for theists, but I shall discuss it in the form in which it presents itself for ordinary theism.)

EVIL AND OMNIPOTENCE   From *Mind*, Vol. LXIV, No. 254 (1955). Reprinted by permission of Oxford University Press.

However, the contradiction does not arise immediately; to show it we need some additional premises, or perhaps some quasi-logical rules connecting the terms 'good', 'evil', and 'omnipotent'. These additional principles are that good is opposed to evil, in such a way that a good thing always eliminates evil as far as it can, and that there are no limits to what an omnipotent thing can do. From these it follows that a good omnipotent thing eliminates evil completely, and then the propositions that a good omnipotent thing exists, and that evil exists, are incompatible.

A.   ADEQUATE SOLUTIONS

Now once the problem is fully stated it is clear that it can be solved, in the sense that the problem will not arise if one gives up at least one of the propositions that constitute it. If you are prepared to say that God is not wholly good, or not quite omnipotent, or that evil does not exist, or that good is not opposed to the kind of evil that exists, or that there are limits to what an omnipotent thing can do, then the problem of evil will not arise for you.

There are, then, quite a number of adequate solutions of the problem of evil, and some of these have been adopted, or almost adopted, by various thinkers. For example, a few have been prepared to deny God's omnipotence, and rather more have been prepared to keep the term 'omnipotence' but severely to restrict its meaning, recording quite a number of things that an omnipotent being cannot do. Some have said that evil is an illusion, perhaps because they held that the whole world of temporal, changing things is an illusion, and that what we call evil belongs only to this world, or perhaps because they held that although temporal things *are* much as we see them, those that we call evil are not really evil. Some have said that what we call evil is merely the privation of good, that evil in a positive sense, evil that would really be opposed to good, does not exist. Many have agreed with Pope that disorder is harmony not understood, and that partial evil is universal good. Whether any of these views is *true* is, of course, another question. But each of them gives an adequate solution of the problem of evil in the sense that if you accept it this problem does not arise for you, though you may, of course, have *other* problems to face.

But often enough these adequate solutions are only *almost* adopted. The thinkers who restrict God's power, but keep the term 'omnipotence', may reasonably be suspected of thinking, in other contexts, that his power is really unlimited. Those who say that evil is an illusion may also be thinking, inconsistently, that this illusion is itself an evil. Those who say that "evil" is merely privation of good may also be thinking, inconsistently, that privation of good is an evil. (The fallacy here is akin to some forms of the "naturalistic fallacy" in ethics, where some think, for example, that "good" is just what contributes to evolutionary progress, and that evolutionary progress is itself good.) If Pope meant what he said in the first line of his couplet, that "disorder" is only harmony not understood, the "partial evil" of the second line must, for consistency, mean "that which, taken in isolation, falsely appears to be evil", but it would more naturally mean "that which, in isolation, really is evil". The second line, in fact, hesitates between two views, that "partial evil" isn't really evil, since only the universal quality is real, and that "partial evil" is really an evil, but only a little one.

In addition, therefore, to adequate solutions, we must recognise unsatisfactory inconsistent solutions, in which there is only a half-hearted or temporary rejection of one of the propositions which together constitute the problem. In these, one of the constituent propositions is explicitly rejected, but it is covertly re-asserted or assumed elsewhere in the system.

B.   FALLACIOUS SOLUTIONS

Besides these half-hearted solutions, which explicitly reject but implicitly assert one of the constituent propositions, there are definitely fallacious solutions which explicitly maintain all the constituent propositions, but implicitly reject at least one of them in the course of the argument that explains away the problem of evil.

There are, in fact, many so-called solutions which purport to remove the contradiction without abandoning any of its constituent propositions. These must be fallacious, as we can see from the very statement of the problem, but it is not so easy to see in each case precisely where the fallacy lies. I suggest that in all cases the fallacy has the general form suggested above: in order to solve the problem one (or perhaps more) of its constituent propositions is given up, but in such a way that it appears to have been retained, and can therefore be asserted without qualification in other contexts. Sometimes there is a further complication: the supposed solution moves to and fro between, say, two of the constituent propositions, at one point asserting the first of these but covertly abandoning the second, at another point asserting the second but covertly abandoning the first. These fallacious solutions often turn upon some equivocation with the words 'good' and 'evil', or upon some vagueness about the way in which good and evil are opposed to one another, or about how much is meant by 'omnipotence'. I propose to examine some of these so-called solutions, and to exhibit their fallacies in detail. Incidentally, I shall also be considering whether an adequate solution could be reached by a minor modification of one or more of the constituent propositions, which would, however, still satisfy all the essential requirements of ordinary theism.

(1) "Good cannot exist without evil" or "Evil is necessary as a counterpart to good."

It is sometimes suggested that evil is necessary as a counterpart to good, that if there were no evil there could be no good either, and that this solves the problem of evil. It is true that it points to an answer to the question "Why should there be evil?" But it does so only by qualifying some of the propositions that constitute the problem.

First, it sets a limit to what God can do, saying that God *cannot* create good without simultaneously creating evil, and this means either that God is not omnipotent or that there are *some* limits to what an omnipotent thing can do. It may be replied that these limits are always presupposed, that omnipotence has never meant the power to do what is logically impossible, and on the present view the existence of good without evil would be a logical impossibility. This interpretation of omnipotence may, indeed, be accepted as a modification of our original account which does not reject anything that is essential to theism, and I shall in general assume it in the subsequent discussion. It is, perhaps, the most common theistic view, but I think that some theists at least have maintained that God can do what is logically impossible. Many theists, at any rate, have held that logic itself is created or laid down by God, that logic is the way in which God arbitrarily chooses to think. (This is, of course, parallel to the ethical view that morally right actions are those which God arbitrarily chooses to command, and the two views encounter similar difficulties.) And *this* account of logic is clearly inconsistent with the view that God is bound by logical necessities—unless it is possible for an omnipotent being to bind himself, an issue which we shall consider later, when we come to the Paradox of Omnipotence. This solution of the problem of evil cannot, therefore, be consistently adopted along with the view that logic is itself created by God.

But, secondly, this solution denies that evil is opposed to good in our original sense. If good and evil are counterparts, a good thing will not "eliminate evil as far as it can". Indeed, this view suggests that good and evil are not strictly qualities of things at all. Perhaps the suggestion is that good and evil are related in much the same way as great and small. Certainly, when the term 'great' is used relatively as a condensation of 'greater than so-and-so', and 'small' is used correspondingly, greatness and smallness are counterparts and cannot exist without each other. But in this sense greatness is not a quality, not an intrinsic feature of anything; and it would be absurd to think of a movement in favour of greatness and against smallness in this sense. Such a movement would be self-defeating, since relative greatness can be promoted only by a simultaneous promotion of relative smallness. I feel sure that no theists would be content to regard God's goodness as analogous to this—as if what he supports were not the *good* but the *better*, and if he had the paradoxical aim that all things should be better than other things.

This point is obscured by the fact that 'great' and 'small' seem to have an absolute as well as a relative sense. I cannot discuss here whether there is absolute magnitude or not, but if there is, there could be an absolute sense for 'great', it could mean of at least a certain size, and it would make sense to speak of all things getting bigger, of a universe that was expanding all over, and therefore it would make sense to speak of promoting greatness. But in *this* sense great and small are not logically necessary counterparts: either quality could exist without the other. There would be no logical impossibility in everything's being small or in everything's being great.

Neither in the absolute nor in the relative sense, then, of 'great' and 'small' do these terms provide an analogy of the sort that would be needed to support this solution of the problem of evil. In neither case are greatness and smallness *both* necessary counterparts *and* mutually opposed forces or possible objects for support and attack.

It may be replied that good and evil are necessary counterparts in the same way as any quality and its logical opposite: redness can occur, it is suggested, only if non-redness also occurs. But unless evil is merely the privation of good, they are not logical opposites, and some further argument would be needed to show that they are counterparts in the same way as genuine logical opposites. Let us assume that this could be given. There is still doubt of the correctness of the metaphysical principle that a quality must have a real opposite: I suggest that it is not really impossible that everything should be, say, red, that the truth is merely that if everything were red we should not notice redness, and so we should have no word 'red'; we observe and give names to qualities only if they have real opposites. If so, the principle that a term must have an opposite would belong only to our language or to our thought, and would not be an ontological principle, and, correspondingly, the rule that good cannot exist without evil would not state a logical necessity of a sort that God would just have to put up with. God might have made everything good, though *we* should not have noticed it if he had.

But, finally, even if we concede that this *is* an ontological principle, it will provide a solution for the problem of evil only if one is prepared to say, "Evil exists, but only just enough evil to serve as the counterpart of good". I doubt whether any theist will accept this. After all, the *ontological* requirement that non-redness should occur would be satisfied even if all the universe, except for a minute speck, were red, and, if there were a corresponding requirement for evil as a counterpart to good, a minute dose of evil would presumably do. But theists are not usually willing to say, in all contexts, that all the evil that occurs is a minute and necessary dose.

(2) "Evil is necessary as a means to good."

It is sometimes suggested that evil is necessary for good not as a counterpart but as a means. In its simple form this has little plausibility as a solution of the problem of evil, since it obviously implies a severe restriction of God's power. It would be a *causal* law that you cannot have a certain end without a certain means, so that if God has to introduce evil as a means to good, he must be subject to at least some causal laws. This certainly conflicts with what a theist normally means by omnipotence. This view of God as limited by causal laws also conflicts with the view that causal laws are themselves made by God, which is more widely held than the corresponding view about the laws of logic. This conflict would, indeed, be resolved if it were possible for an omnipotent being to bind himself, and this possibility has still to be considered. Unless a favourable answer can be given to this question, the suggestion that evil is necessary as a means to good solves the problem of evil only by denying one of its constituent propositions, either that God is omnipotent or that 'omnipotent' means what it says.

(3) "The universe is better with some evil in it than it could be if there were no evil."

Much more important is a solution which at first seems to be a mere variant of the previous one, that evil may contribute to the goodness of a whole in which it is found, so that the universe as a whole is better as it is, with some evil in it, than it would be if there were no evil. This solution may be developed in either of two ways. It may be supported by an aesthetic analogy, by the fact that contrasts heighten beauty, that in a musical work, for example, there may occur discords which somehow add to the beauty of the work as a whole. Alternatively, it may be worked out in connexion with the notion of progress, that the best possible organisation of the universe will not be static, but progressive, that the gradual overcoming of evil by good is really a finer thing than would be the eternal un-challenged supremacy of good.

In either case, this solution usually starts from the assumption that the evil whose existence gives rise to the problem of evil is primarily what is called physi-cal evil, that is to say, pain. In Hume's rather half-hearted presentation of the problem of evil, the evils that he stresses are pain and disease, and those who reply to him argue that the existence of pain and disease makes possible the exis-tence of sympathy, benevolence, heroism, and the gradually successful struggle of doctors and reformers to overcome these evils. In fact, theists often seize the op-portunity to accuse those who stress the problem of evil of taking a low, materi-alistic view of good and evil, equating these with pleasure and pain, and of ignoring the more spiritual goods which can arise in the struggle against evils.

But let us see exactly what is being done here. Let us call pain and misery 'first order evil' or 'evil (1)'. What contrasts with this, namely, pleasure and happiness, will be called 'first order good' or 'good (1)'. Distinct from this is 'second order good' or 'good (2)' which somehow emerges in a complex situation in which evil (1) is a necessary component—logically not merely causally, necessary. (Exactly *how* it emerges does not matter: in the crudest version of this solution good [2] is simply the heightening of happiness by the contrast with misery, in other versions it includes sympathy with suffering, heroism in facing danger, and the gradual decrease of first order evil and increase of first order good.) It is also being assumed that second order good is more important than first order good or evil, in partic-ular that it more than outweighs the first order evil it involves.

Now this is a particularly subtle attempt to solve the problem of evil. It defends God's goodness and omnipotence on the ground that (on a sufficiently long view) this is the best of all logically possible worlds, because it includes the important second order goods, and yet it admits that real evils, namely first order evils, exist. But does it still hold that good and evil are opposed? Not, clearly, in the sense that we set out originally: good does not tend to eliminate evil in general. Instead, we have a modified, a more complex pattern. First order good (*e.g.* happiness) *contrasts with* first order evil (*e.g.* misery): these two are opposed in a fairly me-chanical way; some second order goods (*e.g.* benevolence) try to maximise first order good and minimise first order evil; but God's goodness is not this, it is rather the will to maximise *second* order good. We might, therefore, call God's goodness an example of a third order goodness, or good (3). While this account is different from our original one, it might well be held to be an improvement on it, to give a more accurate description of the way in which good is opposed to evil, and to be consistent with the essential theist position.

There might, however, be several objections to this solution.

First, some might argue that such qualities as benevolence—and *a fortiori* the third order goodness which promotes benevolence—have a merely derivative value, that they are not higher sorts of good, but merely means to good (1), that is, to happiness, so that it would be absurd for God to keep misery in existence in order to make possible the virtues of benevolence, heroism, etc. The theist who adopts the present solution must, of course, deny this, but he can do so with some plausibility, so I should not press this objection.

Secondly, it follows from this solution that God is not in our sense benevolent or sympathetic: he is not concerned to minimise evil (1), but only to promote good (2); and this might be a disturbing conclusion for some theists.

But, thirdly, the fatal objection is this. Our analysis shows clearly the possibility of the existence of a *second* order evil, an evil (2) contrasting with good (2) as evil (1) contrasts with good (1). This would include malevolence, cruelty, callousness, cowardice, and states in which good (1) is decreasing and evil (1) increasing. And just as good (2) is held to be the important kind of good, the kind that God is concerned to promote, so evil (2) will, by analogy, be the important kind of evil, the kind which God, if he were wholly good and omnipotent, would eliminate. And yet evil (2) plainly exists, and indeed most theists (in other contexts) stress its existence more than that of evil (1). We should, therefore, state the problem of evil in terms of second order evil, and against this form of the problem the present solution is useless.

An attempt might be made to use this solution again, at a higher level, to explain the occurrence of evil (2); indeed the next main solution that we shall examine does just this, with the help of some new notions. Without any fresh notions, such a solution would have little plausibility: for example, we could hardly say that the really important good was a good (3), such as the increase of benevolence in proportion to cruelty, which logically required for its occurrence the occurrence of some second order evil. But even if evil (2) could be explained in this way, it is fairly clear that there would be third order evils contrasting with this third order good: and we should be well on the way to an infinite regress, where the solution of a problem of evil, stated in terms of evil (*n*), indicated the existence of an evil (*n* + 1), and a further problem to be solved.

(4) "Evil is due to human freewill."

Perhaps the most important proposed solution of the problem of evil is that evil is not to be ascribed to God at all, but to the independent actions of human beings, supposed to have been endowed by God with freedom of the will. This solution may be combined with the preceding one: first order evil (*e.g.* pain) may be justified as a logically necessary component in second order good (*e.g.* sympathy) while second order evil (*e.g.* cruelty) is not *justified*, but is so ascribed to human beings that God cannot be held responsible for it. This combination evades my third criticism of the preceding solution.

The freewill solution also involves the preceding solution at a higher level. To explain why a wholly good God gave men freewill although it would lead to some important evils, it must be argued that it is better on the whole that men should act freely, and sometimes err, than that they should be innocent automata, acting rightly in a wholly determined way. Freedom that is to say, is now treated as a third order good, and as being more valuable than second order goods (such as sympathy and heroism) would be if they were deterministically produced, and it is being assumed that second order evils, such as cruelty, are logically necessary accompaniments of freedom, just as pain is a logically necessary pre-condition of sympathy.

I think that this solution is unsatisfactory primarily because of the incoherence of the notion of freedom of the will: but I cannot discuss this topic adequately here, although some of my criticisms will touch upon it.

First I should query the assumption that second order evils are logically necessary accompaniments of freedom. I should ask this: if God has made men such that in their free choices they sometimes prefer what is good and sometimes what is evil, why could he not have made men such that they always freely choose the good? If there is no logical impossibility in a man's freely choosing the good on one, or on several, occasions, there cannot be a logical impossibility in his freely choosing the good on every occasion. God was not, then, faced with a choice between making innocent automata and making beings who, in acting freely, would sometimes go wrong: there was open to him the obviously better possibility of making beings who would act freely but always go right. Clearly, his failure to avail himself of this possibility is inconsistent with his being both omnipotent and wholly good.

If it is replied that this objection is absurd, that the making of some wrong choices is logically necessary for freedom, it would seem that 'freedom' must here mean complete randomness or indeterminacy, including randomness with regard to the alternatives good and evil, in other words that men's choices and consequent actions can be "free" only if they are not determined by their characters. Only on this assumption can God escape the responsibility for men's actions; for if he made them as they are, but did not determine their wrong choices, this can only be because the wrong choices are not determined by men as they are. But then if freedom is randomness, how can it be a characteristic of *will*? And, still more, how can it be the most important good? What value or merit would there be in free choices if these were random actions which were not determined by the nature of the agent?

I conclude that to make this solution plausible two different senses of 'freedom' must be confused, one sense which will justify the view that freedom is a third order good, more valuable than other goods would be without it, and another sense, sheer randomness, to prevent us from ascribing to God a decision to make men such that they sometimes go wrong when he might have made them such that they would always freely go right.

This criticism is sufficient to dispose of this solution. But besides this there is a fundamental difficulty in the notion of an omnipotent God creating men with free will, for if men's wills are really free this must mean that even God cannot control them, that is, that God is no longer omnipotent. It may be objected that God's gift of freedom to men does not mean that he *cannot* control their wills, but that he always *refrains* from controlling their wills. But why, we may ask, should God refrain from controlling evil wills? Why should he not leave men free to will rightly, but intervene when he sees them beginning to will wrongly? If God could do this, but does not, and if he is wholly good, the only explanation could be that even a wrong free act of will is not really evil, that its freedom is a value which outweighs its wrongness, so that there would be a loss of value if God took away the wrongness and the freedom together. But this is utterly opposed to what theists say about sin in other contexts. The present solution of the problem of evil, then, can be maintained only in the form that God has made men so free that he *cannot* control their wills.

This leads us to what I call the Paradox of Omnipotence: can an omnipotent being make things which he cannot subsequently control? Or, what is practically equivalent to this, can an omnipotent being make rules which then bind himself? (These are practically equivalent because any such rules could be regarded as setting certain things beyond his control, and *vice versa*.) The second of these formulations is relevant to the suggestions that we have already met, that an omnipotent God creates the rules of logic or causal laws, and is then bound by them.

It is clear that this is a paradox: the questions cannot be answered satisfactorily either in the affirmative or in the negative. If we answer "Yes", it follows that if God actually makes things which he cannot control, or makes rules which bind himself, he is not omnipotent once he has made them: there are *then* things which he cannot do. But if we answer "No", we are immediately asserting that there are things which he cannot do, that is to say that he is already not omnipotent.

It cannot be replied that the question which sets this paradox is not a proper question. It would make perfectly good sense to say that a human mechanic has made a machine which he cannot control: if there is any difficulty about the question it lies in the notion of omnipotence itself.

This, incidentally, shows that although we have approached this paradox from the free will theory, it is equally a problem for a theological determinist. No one thinks that machines have free will, yet they may well be beyond the control of their makers. The determinist might reply that anyone who makes anything determines its ways of acting, and so determines its subsequent behaviour: even the human mechanic does this by his *choice* of materials and structure for his machine, though he does not know all about either of these: the mechanic thus determines, though he may not foresee, his machine's actions. And since God is omniscient, and since his creation of things is total, he both determines and foresees the ways in which his creatures will act. We may grant this, but it is beside the point. The question is not whether God *originally* determined the future actions of his creatures, but whether he can *subsequently* control their actions, or whether he was able in his original creation to put things beyond his subsequent control. Even on determinist principles the answers "Yes" and "No" are equally irreconcilable with God's omnipotence.

Before suggesting a solution of this paradox, I would point out that there is a parallel Paradox of Sovereignty. Can a legal sovereign make a law restricting its own future legislative power? For example, could the British parliament make a law forbidding any future parliament to socialise banking, and also forbidding the future repeal of this law itself? Or could the British parliament, which was legally sovereign in Australia in, say, 1899, pass a valid law, or series of laws, which made it no longer sovereign in 1933? Again, neither the affirmative nor the negative answer is really satisfactory. If we were to answer "Yes", we should be admitting the validity of a law which, if it were actually made, would mean that parliament was no longer sovereign. If we were to answer "No", we should be admitting that there is a law, not logically absurd, which parliament cannot validly make, that is, that parliament is not now a legal sovereign. This paradox can be solved in the following way. We should distinguish between first order laws, that is laws governing the actions of individuals and bodies other than the legislature, and second order laws, that is laws about laws, laws governing the actions of the legislature itself. Correspondingly, we should distinguish two orders of sovereignty, first order sovereignty (sovereignty (1)) which is unlimited authority to make first order laws, and second order sovereignty (sovereignty (2)) which is unlimited authority to make second order laws. If we say that parliament is sovereign we might mean that any parliament at any time has sovereignty (1), or we might mean that parliament has both sovereignty (1) and sovereignty (2) at present, but we cannot without contradiction mean both that the present parliament has sovereignty (2) and that every parliament at every time has sovereignty (1), for if the present parliament has sovereignty (2) it may use it to take away the sovereignty (1) of later parliaments. What the paradox shows is that we cannot ascribe to any continuing institution legal sovereignty in an inclusive sense.

The analogy between omnipotence and sovereignty shows that the paradox of omnipotence can be solved in a similar way. We must distinguish between first order omnipotence (omnipotence (1)), that is unlimited power to act, and second order omnipotence (omnipotence (2)), that is unlimited power to determine what powers to act things shall have. Then we could consistently say that God all the time has omnipotence (1), but if so no beings at any time have powers to act independently of God. Or we could say that God at one time had omnipotence (2), and used it to assign independent powers to act to certain things, so that God thereafter did not have omnipotence (1). But what the paradox shows is that we cannot consistently ascribe to any continuing being omnipotence in an inclusive sense.

An alternative solution of this paradox would be simply to deny that God is a continuing being, that any times can be assigned to his actions at all. But on this assumption (which also has difficulties of its own) no meaning can be given to the assertion that God made men with wills so free that he could not control them. The paradox of omnipotence can be avoided by putting God outside time, but the freewill solution of the problem of evil cannot be saved in this way, and equally it remains impossible to hold that an omnipotent God *binds himself* by causal or logical laws.

CONCLUSION

Of the proposed solutions of the problem of evil which we have examined, none has stood up to criticism. There may be other solutions which require examination, but this study strongly suggests that there is no valid solution of the problem which does not modify at least one of the constituent propositions in a way which would seriously affect the essential core of the theistic position.

Quite apart from the problem of evil, the paradox of omnipotence has shown that God's omnipotence must in any case be restricted in one way or another, that unqualified omnipotence cannot be ascribed to any being that continues through time. And if God and his actions are not in time, can omnipotence, or power of any sort, be meaningfully ascribed to him?

ALVIN PLANTINGA
The Free Will Defense

In a widely discussed piece entitled "Evil and Omnipotence" John Mackie repeats this claim:

> I think, however, that a more telling criticism can be made by way of the traditional problem of evil. Here it can be shown, not that religious beliefs lack rational support, but that they are positively irrational, that the several parts of the essential theological doctrine are *inconsistent* with one another. . . .[1]

Is Mackie right? Does the theist contradict himself? But we must ask a prior question: just what is being claimed here? That theistic belief contains an inconsistency or contradiction, of course. But what, exactly, is an inconsistency or contradiction? There are several kinds. An *explicit* contradiction is a *proposition* of a certain sort—a conjunctive proposition, one conjunct of which is the denial or negation of the other conjunct. For example:

Paul is a good tennis player, and it's false that Paul is a good tennis player.

(People seldom assert explicit contradictions). Is Mackie charging the theist with accepting such a contradiction? Presumably not; what he says is:

> In its simplest form the problem is this: God is omnipotent; God is wholly good; yet evil exists. There seems to be some contradiction between these three propositions, so that if any two of them were true the third would be false. But at the same time all three are essential parts of most theological positions; the theologian, it seems, at once *must* adhere and *cannot consistently* adhere to all three.[2]

THE FREE WILL DEFENSE   From *God, Freedom, and Evil* by Alvin Plantinga (Harper & Row, 1974). Reprinted by permission of the author.

[1] John Mackie, "Evil and Omnipotence," in *The Philosophy of Religion*, ed. Basil Mitchell (London: Oxford University Press, 1971), p. 92. [*Philosophy of Religion: Selected Readings*, Second Edition, p. 223.]

[2] Ibid., pp. 92–93. [*Philosophy of Religion: Selected Readings*, Second Edition, p. 223.]

According to Mackie, then, the theist accepts a group or set of three propositions; this set is inconsistent. Its members, of course, are

(1) God is omnipotent
(2) God is wholly good

and

(3) Evil exists.

Call this set A; the claim is that A is an inconsistent set. But what is it for a *set* to be inconsistent or contradictory? Following our definition of an explicit contradiction, we might say that a set of propositions is explicitly contradictory if one of the members is the denial or negation of another member. But then, of course, it is evident that the set we are discussing is not explicitly contradictory; the denials of (1), (2), and (3), respectively, are

(1′) God is not omnipotent (or it's false that God is omnipotent)
(2′) God is not wholly good

and

(3′) There is no evil

none of which is in set A.

Of course many sets are pretty clearly contradictory, in an important way, but not *explicitly* contradictory. For example, set B:

(4) If all men are mortal, then Socrates is mortal
(5) All men are mortal
(6) Socrates is not mortal.

This set is not explicitly contradictory; yet surely *some* significant sense of that term applies to it. What is important here is that by using only the rules of ordinary logic—the laws of propositional logic and quantification theory found in any introductory text on the subject—we can deduce an explicit contradiction from the set. Or to put it differently, we can use the laws of logic to deduce a proposition from the set, which proposition, when added to the set, yields a new set that is explicitly contradictory. For by using the law *modus ponens* (if *p*, then *q*; *p*; therefore *q*) we can deduce

(7) Socrates is mortal

from (4) and (5). The result of adding (7) to B is the set {(4), (5), (6), (7)}. This set, of course, is explicitly contradictory in that (6) is the denial of (7). We might say that any set which shares this characteristic with set B is *formally* contradictory. So a formally contradictory set is one from whose members an explicit contradiction can be deduced by the laws of logic. Is Mackie claiming that set A is formally contradictory?

If he is, he's wrong. No laws of logic permit us to deduce the denial of one of the propositions in A from the other members. Set A isn't formally contradictory either.

But there is still another way in which a set of propositions can be contradictory or inconsistent. Consider set C, whose members are

(8) George is older than Paul
(9) Paul is older than Nick

and

(10) George is not older than Nick.

This set is neither explicitly nor formally contradictory; we can't, just by using the laws of logic, deduce the denial of any of these propositions from the others. And yet there is a good sense in which it is consistent or contradictory. For clearly it is *not possible* that its three members all be true. It is *necessarily true* that

(11) If George is older than Paul, and Paul is older than Nick, then George is older than Nick.

And if we add (11) to set C, we get a set that is formally contradictory; (8), (9), and (11) yield, by the laws of ordinary logic, the denial of (10).

I said that (11) is *necessarily true*; but what does *that* mean? Of course we might say that a proposition is necessarily true if it is impossible that it be false, or if its negation is not possibly true. This would be to explain necessity in terms of possibility. Chances are, however, that anyone who does not know what necessity is, will be equally at a loss about possibility; the explanation is not likely to be very successful. Perhaps all we can do by way of explanation is to give some examples and hope for the best. In the first place many propositions can be established by the laws of logic alone—for example,

(12) If all men are mortal and Socrates is a man, then Socrates is mortal.

Such propositions are truths of logic; and all of them are necessary in the sense of question. But truths of arithmetic and mathematics generally are also necessarily true. Still further, there is a host of propositions that are neither truths of logic nor truths of mathematics but are nonetheless necessarily true; (11) would be an example, as well as

(13) Nobody is taller than himself
(14) Red is a color

(15) No numbers are persons
(16) No prime number is a prime minister

and

(17) Bachelors are unmarried.

So here we have an important kind of necessity—let's call it "broadly logical necessity." Of course there is a correlative kind of *possibility*: a proposition *p* is possibly true (in the broadly logical sense) just in case its negation or denial is not necessarily true (in that same broadly logical sense). This sense of necessity and possibility must be distinguished from another that we may call *causal* or *natural* necessity and possibility. Consider

(18) Henry Kissinger has swum the Atlantic.

Although this proposition has an implausible ring, it is not necessarily false in the broadly logical sense (and its denial is not necessarily true in that sense). But there is a good sense in which it is impossible: it is *causally* or *naturally* impossible. Human beings, unlike dolphins, just don't have the physical equipment demanded for this feat. Unlike Superman, furthermore, the rest of us are incapable of leaping tall buildings at a single bound or (without auxiliary power of some kind) traveling faster than a speeding bullet. These things are *impossible* for us— but not *logically* impossible, even in the broad sense.

So there are several senses of necessity and possibility here. There are a number of propositions, furthermore, of which it's difficult to say whether they are or aren't possible in the broadly logical sense; some of these are subjects of philosophical controversy. Is it possible, for example, for a person never to be conscious during his entire existence? Is it possible for a (human) person to exist *disembodied*? If that's possible, is it possible that there be a person who *at no time at all* during his entire existence has a body? Is it possible to see without eyes? These are propositions about whose possibility in that broadly logical sense there is disagreement and dispute.

Now return to set C (p. 235). What is characteristic of it is the fact that the conjunction of its members—the proposition expressed by the result of putting "and's" between (8), (9), and (10)—is necessarily false. Or we might put it like this: what characterizes set C is the fact that we can get a formally contradictory set by adding a necessarily true proposition—namely (11). Suppose we say that a set is *implicitly contradictory* if it resembles C in this respect. That is, a set S of propositions is implicitly contradictory if there is a necessary proposition *p* such that the result of adding *p* to S is a formally contradictory set. Another way to put it: S is implicitly contradictory if there is some necessarily true proposition *p* such that by using just the laws of ordinary logic, we can deduce an explicit contradiction from *p* together with the members of S. And when Mackie says that set A is contradictory, we may properly take him, I think, as holding that it is implicitly contradictory in the explained sense. As he puts it:

> However, the contradiction does not arise immediately; to show it we need some additional premises, or perhaps some quasi-logical rules connecting the terms "good" and "evil" and "omnipotent." These additional principles are that good is opposed to evil, in such a way that a good thing always eliminates evil as far as it can, and that there are no limits to what an omnipotent thing can do. From these it follows that a good omnipotent thing eliminates evil completely, and then the propositions that a good omnipotent thing exists, and that evil exists, are incompatible.[3]

Here Mackie refers to "additional premises"; he also calls them "additional principles" and "quasi-logical rules"; he says we need them to show the contradiction. What he means, I think, is that to get a formally contradictory set we must add some more propositions to set A; and if we aim to show that set A is implicitly contradictory, these propositions must be necessary truths—"quasi-logical rules" as Mackie calls them. The two additional principles he suggests are

(19) A good thing always eliminates evil as far as it can

and

(20) There are no limits to what an omnipotent being can do.

And, of course, if Mackie means to show that set A is implicitly contradictory, then he must hold that (19) and (20) are not merely *true* but *necessarily true*.

But, are they? What about (20) first? What does it mean to say that a being is omnipotent? That he is *all-powerful*, or *almighty*, presumably. But are there no limits *at all* to the power of such a being? Could he create square circles, for example, or married bachelors? Most theologians and theistic philosophers who hold that God is omnipotent, do not hold that He can create round squares or bring it about that He both exists and does not exist. These theologians and philosophers may hold that there are no *nonlogical* limits to what an omnipotent being can do, but they concede that not even an omnipotent being can bring about logically impossible states of affairs or cause necessarily false propositions to be true. Some theists, on the other hand—Martin Luther and Descartes, perhaps—have apparently thought that God's power is unlimited even by the laws of logic. For these theists the question whether set A is contradictory will not be of much interest. As theists they believe (1) and (2), and they also, presumably, believe (3). But they remain undisturbed by the claim that (1), (2), and (3) are jointly inconsistent—because, as they say, God can do what is logically impossible. Hence He can bring it about that the members of set A are all true, even if that set is contradictory (concentrating very intensely upon this suggestion is likely to make you dizzy). So the theist who thinks that the power of God isn't limited *at all*, not even by the laws of logic, will be unimpressed by Mackie's argument and won't find any difficulty in the contradiction set A is alleged to contain. This view is not very popular, however, and for good reason; it is quite incoherent. What the theist typically means when he says that God is omnipotent is not that

[3] Ibid., p. 93. [*Philosophy of Religion: Selected Readings*, Second Edition, p. 224.]

there are *no* limits to God's power, but at most that there are no nonlogical limits to what He can do; and given this qualification, it is perhaps initially plausible to suppose that (20) is necessarily true.

But what about (19), the proposition that every good thing eliminates every evil state of affairs that it can eliminate? Is that necessarily true? Is it true at all? Suppose, first of all, that your friend Paul unwisely goes for a drive on a wintry day and runs out of gas on a deserted road. The temperature dips to $-10°$, and a miserably cold wind comes up. You are sitting comfortably at home (twenty-five miles from Paul) roasting chestnuts in a roaring blaze. Your car is in the garage; in the trunk there is the full five-gallon can of gasoline you always keep for emergencies. Paul's discomfort and danger are certainly an evil, and one which you could eliminate. You don't do so. But presumably you don't thereby forfeit your claim to being a "good thing"—you simply didn't know of Paul's plight. And so (19) does not appear to be necessary. It says that every good thing has a certain property—the property of eliminating every evil that it can. And if the case I described is possible—a good person's failing through ignorance to eliminate a certain evil he can eliminate—then (19) is by no means necessarily true.

But perhaps Mackie could sensibly claim that if you *didn't know* about Paul's plight, then in fact you were *not*, at the time in question, able to eliminate the evil in question; and perhaps he'd be right. In any event he could revise (19) to take into account the kind of case I mentioned:

> (19a) Every good thing always eliminates every evil that *it knows about* and can eliminate.

{(1), (2), (3), (20), (19a)}, you'll notice is not a formally contradictory set—to get a formal contradiction we must add a proposition specifying that God *knows about* every evil state of affairs. But most theists do believe that God is omniscient or all-knowing; so if this new set—the set that results when we add to set A the proposition that God is omniscient—is implicitly contradictory then Mackie should be satisfied and the theist confounded. (And, henceforth, set A will be the old set A together with the proposition that God is omniscient.)

But is (19a) necessary? Hardly. Suppose you know that Paul is marooned as in the previous example, and you also know another friend is similarly marooned fifty miles in the opposite direction. Suppose, furthermore, that while you can rescue one or the other, you simply can't rescue both. Then each of the two evils is such that it is within your power to eliminate it; and you know about them both. But you can't eliminate *both*; and you don't forfeit your claim to being a good person by eliminating only one—it wasn't within your power to do more. So the fact that you don't doesn't mean that you are not a good person. Therefore (19a) is false; it is not a necessary truth or even a truth that every good thing eliminates every evil it knows about and can eliminate.

We can see the same thing another way. You've been rock climbing. still something of a novice, you've acquired a few cuts and bruises by inelegantly using your knees rather than your feet. One of these bruises is fairly painful. You mention it to a physician friend, who predicts the pain will leave of its own accord in a day or two. Meanwhile, he says, there's nothing he can do, short of amputating your leg above the knee, to remove the pain. Now the pain in your knee is an evil state of affairs. All else being equal, it would be better if you had no such pain. And it is within the power of your friend to eliminate this evil state of affairs. Does his failure to do so mean that he is not a good person? Of course not; for he could eliminate this evil state of affairs only by bringing about another, much worse evil. And so it is once again evident that (19a) is false. It is entirely possible that a good person fail to eliminate an evil state of affairs that he knows about and can eliminate. This would take place, if, as in the present example, he couldn't eliminate the evil without bringing about a *greater* evil.

A slightly different kind of case shows the same thing. A really impressive good state of affairs G will *outweigh* a trivial E—that is, the conjunctive state of affairs G *and* E is itself a good state of affairs. And surely a good person would not be obligated to eliminate a given evil if he could do so only by eliminating a good that outweighed it. Therefore (19a) is not necessarily true; it can't be used to show that set A is implicitly contradictory.

These difficulties might suggest another revision of (19); we might try

(19b) A good being eliminates every evil E that it knows about and that it can eliminate without either bringing about a greater evil or eliminating a good state of affairs that outweighs E.

Is this necessarily true? It takes care of the second of the two difficulties afflicting (19a) but leaves the first untouched. We can see this as follows. First, suppose we say that a being *properly eliminates* an evil state of affairs if it eliminates that evil without either eliminating an outweighing good or bringing about a greater evil. It is then obviously possible that a person find himself in a situation where he could properly eliminate an evil E and could also properly eliminate another evil E', but couldn't properly eliminate them *both*. You're rock climbing again, this time on the dreaded north face of the Grand Teton. You and your party come upon Curt and Bob, two mountaineers stranded 125 feet apart on the face. They untied to reach their cigarettes and then carelessly dropped the rope while lighting up. A violent, dangerous thunderstorm is approaching. You have time to rescue one of the stranded climbers and retreat before the storm hits; if you rescue both, however, you and your party and the two climbers will be caught on the face during the thunderstorm, which will very likely destroy your entire party. In this case you can eliminate one evil (Curt's being stranded on the face) without causing more evil or eliminating a greater good; and you are also able to properly eliminate the other evil (Bob's being thus stranded). But you can't properly eliminate them *both*. And so the fact that you don't rescue Curt, say, even though you could have, doesn't show that you aren't a good person. Here, then, each of the evils is such that you can properly eliminate it; but you can't properly eliminate them both, and hence can't be blamed for failing to eliminate one of them.

So neither (19a) nor (19b) is necessarily true. You may be tempted to reply that the sort of counterexamples offered—examples where someone is able to eliminate an evil A and also able to eliminate a different evil B, but unable to eliminate them both—are irrelevant to the case of a being who, like God, is both omnipotent and omniscient. That is, you may think that if an omnipotent and omniscient being is able to eliminate *each* of two evils, it follows that he can eliminate them *both*. Perhaps this is so; but it is not strictly to the point. The fact is the counterexamples show that (19a) and (19b) are not necessarily true and hence can't be used to show that set A is implicitly inconsistent. What the reply does suggest is that perhaps the atheologian will have more success if he works the properties of omniscience and omnipotence into (19). Perhaps he could say something like

(19c) An omnipotent and omniscient good being eliminates every evil that it can properly eliminate.

And suppose, for purposes of argument, we concede the necessary truth of (19c). Will it serve Mackie's purposes? Not obviously. For we don't get a set that is formally contradictory by adding (20) and (19c) to set A. This set (call it A') contains the following six members:

(1) God is omnipotent
(2) God is wholly good
(2') God is omniscient
(3) Evil exists
(19c) An omnipotent and omniscient good being eliminates every evil that it can properly eliminate

and

(20) There are no nonlogical limits to what an omnipotent being can do.

Now if A' were formally contradictory, then from any five of its members we could deduce the denial of the sixth by the laws of ordinary logic. That is, any five would *formally entail* the denial of the sixth. So if A' were formally inconsistent, the denial of (3) would be formally entailed by the remaining five. That is, (1), (2), (2'), (19c), and (20) would formally entail

(3') There is no evil.

But they don't; what they formally entail is not that there is no evil *at all* but only that

(3″) There is no evil that God can properly eliminate.

So (19c) doesn't really help either—not because it is not necessarily true but because its addition [with (20)] to set A does not yield a formally contradictory set.
    Obviously, what the atheologian must add to get a formally contradictory set is

(21) If God is omniscient and omnipotent, then he can properly eliminate every evil state of affairs.

Suppose we agree that the set consisting in A plus (19c), (20), and (21) is formally contradictory. So if (19c), (20), and (21) are all necessarily true, then set A is implicitly contradictory. We've already conceded that (19c) and (20) are indeed necessary. So we must take a look at (21). Is this proposition necessarily true?

No. To see this let us ask the following question. Under what conditions would an omnipotent being be unable to eliminate a certain evil E without eliminating an outweighing good? Well, suppose that E is *included in* some good state of affairs that outweighs it. That is, suppose there is some good state of affairs G so related to E that it is impossible that G obtain or be actual and E fail to obtain. (Another way to put this: a state of affairs S includes S' if the conjunctive state of affairs S *but not* S' is impossible, or if it is necessary that S' obtains if S does.) Now suppose that some good state of affairs G includes an evil state of affairs E that it outweighs. Then not even an omnipotent being could eliminate E without eliminating G. But *are* there any cases where a good state of affairs includes, in this sense, an evil that it outweighs?[4] Indeed there are such states of affairs. To take an artificial example, let's suppose that E is Paul's suffering from a minor abrasion and G is your being deliriously happy. The conjunctive state of affairs, G *and* E—the state of affairs that obtains if and only if both G and E obtain—is then a good state of affairs: it is better, all else being equal, that you be intensely happy and Paul suffer a mildly annoying abrasion than that this state of affairs not obtain. So G *and* E is a good state of affairs. And clearly G *and* E includes E: obviously it is necessarily true that if you are deliriously happy and Paul is suffering from an abrasion, then Paul is suffering from an abrasion.

But perhaps you think this example trivial, tricky, slippery, and irrelevant. If so, take heart; other examples abound. Certain kinds of values, certain familiar kinds of good states of affairs, can't exist apart from evil of some sort. For example, there are people who display a sort of creative moral heroism in the face of suffering and adversity—a heroism that inspires others and creates a good situation out of a bad one. In a situation like this the evil, of course, remains evil; but the total state of affairs—someone's bearing pain magnificently, for example—may be good. If it is, then the good present must outweigh the evil; otherwise the total situation would not be *good*. But, of course, it is not possible that such a good state of affairs obtain unless some evil also obtain. It is a necessary truth that if someone bears pain magnificently, then someone is in pain.

The conclusion to be drawn, therefore, is that (21) is not necessarily true. And our discussion thus far shows at the very least that it is no easy matter to find necessarily true propositions that yield a formally contradictory set when added to set A.[5] One wonders, therefore, why the many atheologians who confidently assert

---

[4] More simply, the question is really just whether any good state of affairs includes an evil; a little reflection reveals that no good state of affairs can include an evil that it does *not* outweigh.

[5] In Plantinga, *God and Other Minds* (Ithaca, N.Y.: Cornell University Press, 1967), chap. 5, I explore further the project of finding such propositions.

that this set is contradictory make no attempt whatever to *show* that it is. For the most part they are content just to *assert* that there is a contradiction here. Even Mackie, who sees that some "additional premises" or "quasi-logical rules" are needed, makes scarcely a beginning towards finding some additional premises that are necessarily true and that together with the members of set A formally entail an explicit contradiction.

3.   CAN WE SHOW THAT THERE IS NO INCONSISTENCY HERE?

To summarize our conclusions so far: although many atheologians claim that the theist is involved in contradiction when he asserts the members of set A, this set, obviously, is neither *explicitly* nor *formally* contradictory; the claim, presumably, must be that it is *implicitly* contradictory. To make good this claim the atheologian must find some necessarily true proposition p (it could be a conjunction of several propositions) such that the addition of p to set A yields a set that is formally contradictory. No atheologian has produced even a plausible candidate for this role, and it certainly is not easy to see what such a proposition might be. Now we might think we should simply declare set A implicitly consistent on the principle that a proposition (or set) is to be presumed consistent or possible until proven otherwise. This course, however, leads to trouble. The same principle would impel us to declare the atheologian's claim—that set A is *in*consistent—possible or consistent. But the claim that a given set of propositions is implicitly contradictory, is itself either necessarily true or necessarily false; so if such a claim is *possible*, it is not necessarily false and is, therefore, true (in fact, necessarily true). If we followed the suggested principle, therefore, we should be obliged to declare set A implicitly consistent (since it hasn't been shown to be otherwise), but we should have to say the same thing about the atheologian's claim, since we haven't shown *that* claim to be inconsistent or impossible. The atheologian's claim, furthermore, is necessarily true if it is possible. Accordingly, if we accept the above principle, we shall have to declare set A both implicitly consistent and implicitly inconsistent. So all we can say at this point is that set A has not been shown to be implicitly inconsistent.

Can we go any further? One way to go on would be to try to *show* that set A is implicitly consistent or possible in the broadly logical sense. But what is involved in showing such a thing? Although there are various ways to approach this matter, they all resemble one another in an important respect. They all amount to this: to show that a set S is consistent you think of a *possible state of affairs* (it needn't *actually obtain*) which is such that if it were actual, then all of the members of S would be true. This procedure is sometimes called *giving a model of* S. For example, you might construct an axiom set and then show that it is consistent by giving a model of it; this is how it was shown that the denial of Euclid's parallel postulate is formally consistent with the rest of his postulates.

There are various special cases of this procedure to fit special circumstances. Suppose, for example, you have a pair of propositions p and q and wish to show them consistent. And suppose we say that a proposition p_1 *entails* a proposition

p_2 if it is impossible that p_1 be true and p_2 false—if the conjunctive proposition *p_1 and not p_2* is necessarily false. Then one way to show that p is consistent with q is to find some proposition r whose conjunction with p is both possible, in the broadly logical sense, and entails q. A rude and unlettered behaviorist, for example, might hold that thinking is really nothing but movements of the larynx; he might go on to hold that

P Jones did not move his larynx after April 30

is inconsistent (in the broadly logical sense) with

Q Jones did some thinking during May.

By way of rebuttal, we might point out that P appears to be consistent with

R While convalescing from an April 30 laryngotomy, Jones whiled away the idle hours by writing (in May) a splendid paper on Kant's *Critique of Pure Reason*.

So the conjunction of P and R appears to be consistent; but obviously it also entails Q (you can't write even a passable paper on Kant's *Critique of Pure Reason* without doing some thinking); so P and Q are consistent.

We can see that this is a special case of the procedure I mentioned above as follows. This proposition R is consistent with P; so the proposition *P and R* is possible, describes a possible state of affairs. But *P and R* entails Q; hence if *P and R* were true, Q would also be true, and hence both P and Q would be true. So this is really a case of producing a possible state of affairs such that, if it were actual, all the members of the set in question (in this case the pair set of P and Q) would be true.

How does this apply to the case before us? As follows, let us conjoin propositions (1), (2), and (2′) and henceforth call the result (1):

(1) God is omniscient, omnipotent, and wholly good.

The problem, then, is to show that (1) and (3) (evil exists) are consistent. This could be done, as we've seen, by finding a proposition r that is consistent with (1) and such that (1) and (r) together entail (3). One proposition that might do the trick is

(22) God creates a world containing evil and has a good reason for doing so.

If (22) is consistent with (1), then it follows that (1) and (3) (and hence set A) are consistent. Accordingly, one thing some theists have tried is to show that (22) and (1) are consistent.

One can attempt this in at least two ways. On the one hand, we could try to apply the same method again. Conceive of a possible state of affairs such that, if it obtained, an omnipotent, omniscient, and wholly good God would have a good reason for permitting evil. On the other, someone might try to specify *what God's reason is* for permitting evil and try to show, if it is not obvious, that it is a good reason. St. Augustine, for example, one of the greatest and most influential philosopher-theologians of the Christian Church, writes as follows:

> . . . some people see with perfect truth that a creature is better if, while possessing free will, it remains always fixed upon God and never sins; then, reflecting on men's sins, they are grieved, not because they continue to sin, but because they were created. They say: He should have made us such that we never willed to sin, but always to enjoy the unchangeable truth.
>
> They should not lament or be angry. God has not compelled men to sin just because He created them and gave them the power to choose between sinning and not sinning. There are angels who have never sinned and never will sin.
>
> Such is the generosity of God's goodness that He has not refrained from creating even that creature which He foreknew would not only sin, but remain in the will to sin. As a runaway horse is better than a stone which does not run away because it lacks self-movement and sense perception, so the creature is more excellent which sins by free will than that which does not sin only because it has no free will.[6]

In broadest terms Augustine claims that God could create a better, more perfect universe by permitting evil than He could by refusing to do so:

> Neither the sins nor the misery are necessary to the perfection of the universe, but souls as such are necessary, which have the power to sin if they so will, and become miserable if they sin. If misery persisted after their sins had been abolished, or if there were misery before there were sins, then it might be right to say that the order and government of the universe were at fault. Again, if there were sins but no consequent misery, that order is equally dishonored by lack of equity.[7]

Augustine tries to tell us *what God's reason is* for permitting evil. At bottom, he says, it's that God can create a more perfect universe by permitting evil. A really top-notch universe requires the existence of free, rational, and moral agents; and some of the free creatures He created went wrong. But the universe with the free creatures it contains and the evil they commit is better than it would have been had it contained neither the free creatures nor this evil. Such an attempt to specify God's reason for permitting evil is what I earlier called a *theodicy*; in the words of John Milton it is an attempt to "justify the ways of God to man," to show that God is just in permitting evil. Augustine's kind of theodicy might be called a Free Will Theodicy, since the idea of rational creatures with free will plays such a prominent role in it.

A theodicist, then, attempts to tell us why God permits evil. Quite distinct from a Free Will Theodicy is what I shall call a Free Will Defense. Here the aim is not to say what God's reason *is*, but at most what God's reason *might possibly be*. We could put the difference like this. The Free Will Theodicist and Free Will Defender are both trying to show that (1) is consistent with (22), and of course if

---

[6] *The Problem of Free Choice*, Vol. 22 of *Ancient Christian Writers* (Westminster, Md.: The Newman Press, 1955), bk. 2, pp. 14–15.

[7] Ibid., bk. 3, p. 9.

so, then set A is consistent. The Free Will Theodicist tries to do this by finding some proposition *r* which in conjunction with (1) entails (22); he claims, further-more, that this proposition is *true*, not just consistent with (1). He tries to tell us what God's reason for permitting evil *really is*. The Free Will Defender, on the other hand, though he also tries to find a proposition *r* that is consistent with (1) and in conjunction with it entails (22), does *not* claim to know or even believe that *r* is true. And here, of course, he is perfectly within his rights. His aim is to show that (1) is consistent with (22); all he need do then is find an *r* that is consistent with (1) and such that (1) and (*r*) entail (22); whether *r* is *true* is quite beside the point.

So there is a significant difference between a Free Will Theodicy and A Free Will Defense. The latter is sufficient (if successful) to show that set A is consistent; in a way a Free Will Theodicy goes beyond what is required. On the other hand, a theodicy would be much more satisfying, if possible to achieve. No doubt the theist would rather know what God's reason *is* for permitting evil than simply that it's possible that He has a good one. But in the present context (that of investigat-ing the consistency of set A), the latter is all that's needed. Neither a defense or a theodicy, of course, gives any hint to what God's reason for some *specific* evil—the death or suffering of someone close to you, for example—might be. And there is still another function—a sort of pastoral function[8]—in the neighborhood that neither serves. Confronted with evil in his own life or suddenly coming to realize more clearly than before the *extent* and *magnitude* of evil, a believer in God may undergo a crisis of faith. He may be tempted to follow the advice of Job's "friends"; he may be tempted to "curse God and die." Neither a Free Will Defense nor a Free Will Theodicy is designed to be of much help or comfort to one suffering from such a storm in the soul (although in a specific case, of course, one or the other could prove useful). Neither is to be thought of first of all as a means of pastoral counseling. Probably neither will enable someone to find peace with him-self and with God in the face of the evil the world contains. But then, of course, neither is intended for that purpose.

4.   THE FREE WILL DEFENSE

In what follows I shall focus attention upon the Free Will Defense. I shall ex-amine it more closely, state it more exactly, and consider objections to it; and I shall argue that in the end it is successful. Earlier we saw that among good states of affairs there are some that not even God can bring about without bringing about evil: those goods, namely, that *entail* or *include* evil states of affairs. The Free Will Defense can be looked upon as an effort to show that there may be a very different kind of good that God can't bring about without permitting evil. These are good states of affairs that don't include evil; they do not entail the existence of any evil whatever; nonetheless God Himself can't bring them about without permitting evil.

---

[8] I am indebted to Henry Schuurman (in conversation) for helpful discussion of the difference between this pastoral function and those served by a theodicy or a defense.

So how does the Free Will Defense work? And what does the Free Will Defender mean when he says that people are or may be free? What is relevant to the Free Will Defense is the idea of *being free with respect to an action*. If a person is free with respect to a given action, then he is free to perform that action and free to refrain from performing it; no antecedent conditions and/or causal laws determine that he will perform the action, or that he won't. It is within his power, at the time in question, to take or perform the action and within his power to refrain from it. Freedom so conceived is not to be confused with unpredictability. You might be able to predict what you will do in a given situation even if you are free, in that situation, to do something else. If I know you well, I may be able to predict what action you will take in response to a certain set of conditions; it does not follow that you are not free with respect to that action. Secondly, I shall say that an action is *morally significant*, for a given person, if it would be wrong for him to perform the action but right to refrain or *vice versa*. Keeping a promise, for example, would ordinarily be morally significant for a person, as would refusing induction into the army. On the other hand, having Cheerios for breakfast (instead of Wheaties) would not normally be morally significant. Further, suppose we say that a person is *significantly free*, on a given occasion, if he is then free with respect to a morally significant action. And finally we must distinguish between *moral evil* and *natural evil*. The former is evil that results from free human activity; natural evil is any other kind of evil.[9]

Given these definitions and distinctions, we can make a preliminary statement of the Free Will Defense as follows. A world containing creatures who are significantly free (and freely perform more good than evil actions) is more valuable, all else being equal, than a world containing no free creatures at all. Now God can create free creatures, but He can't *cause* or *determine* them to do only what is right. For if He does so, then they aren't significantly free after all; they do not do what is right *freely*. To create creatures capable of *moral good*, therefore, He must create creatures capable of moral evil; and He can't give these creatures the freedom to perform evil and at the same time prevent them from doing so. As it turned out, sadly enough, some of the free creatures God created went wrong in the exercise of their freedom; this is the source of moral evil. The fact that free creatures sometimes go wrong, however, counts neither against God's omnipotence nor against His goodness; for He could have forestalled the occurrence of moral evil only by removing the possibility of moral good.

I said earlier that the Free Will Defender tries to find a proposition that is consistent with

(1) God is omniscient, omnipotent, and wholly good

and together with (1) entails that there is evil. According to the Free Will Defense, we must find this proposition somewhere in the above story. The heart of the Free Will Defense is the claim that is is *possible* that God could not have

---

[9]This distinction is not very precise (how, exactly, are we to construe "results from"?), but perhaps it will serve our present purposes.

created a universe containing moral good (or as much moral good as this world contains) without creating one that also contained moral evil. And if so, then it is possible that God has a good reason for creating a world containing evil.

Now this defense has met with several kinds of objections. For example, some philosophers say that *causal determinism* and *freedom*, contrary to what we might have thought, are not really incompatible.[10] But if so, then God could have created free creatures who were free, and free to do what is wrong, but nevertheless were causally determined to do only what is right. Thus He could have created creatures who were free to do what was wrong, while nevertheless preventing them from ever performing any wrong actions—simply by seeing to it that they were causally determined to do only what is right. Of course this contradicts the Free Will Defense, according to which there is inconsistency in supposing that God determines free creatures to do only what is right. But is it really possible that all of a person's actions are causally determined while some of them are free? How could that be so? According to one version of the doctrine in question, to say that George acts freely on a given occasion is to say only this: *if George had chosen to do otherwise, he would have done otherwise.* Now George's action A is causally determined if some event *E*—some event beyond his control—has already occurred, where the state of affairs consisting in *E's* occurrence conjoined with George's *refraining* from performing A, is a causally impossible state of affairs. Then one can consistently hold both that all of a man's actions are causally determined and that some of them are free in the above sense. For suppose that all of a man's actions are causally determined and that he *couldn't*, on any occasion, have made any choice or performed any action different from the ones he did make and perform. It could still be true that if he *had* chosen to do otherwise, he would have done otherwise. Granted, he couldn't have chosen to do otherwise; but this is consistent with saying that *if* he had, things would have gone differently.

This objection to the Free Will Defense seems utterly implausible. One might as well claim that being in jail doesn't really limit one's freedom on the grounds that if one were *not* in jail, he'd be free to come and go as he pleased. So I shall say no more about this objection here.[11]

A second objection is more formidable. In essence it goes like this. Surely it is possible to do only what is right, even if one is free to do wrong. It is *possible*, in that broadly logical sense, that there would be a world containing free creatures who always do what is right. There is certainly no *contradiction* or *inconsistency* in this idea. But God is omnipotent; his power has no nonlogical limitations. So if it's possible that there be a world containing creatures who are free to do what is wrong but never in fact do so, then it follows that an omnipotent God could create such a world. If so, however, the Free Will Defense must be mistaken in its insistence upon the possibility that God is omnipotent but unable to create a world containing moral good without permitting moral evil. J. L. Mackie . . . states this objection:

[10] See, for example, A. Flew, "Divine Omnipotence and Human Freedom," in *New Essays in Philosophical Theology*, eds. A. Flew and A. MacIntyre (London: SCM, 1955), pp. 150–153.

[11] For further discussion of it see Plantinga, *God and Other Minds*, pp. 132–135.

> If God has made men such that in their free choices they sometimes prefer what is good and sometimes what is evil, why could he not have made men such that they always freely choose the good? If there is no logical impossibility in a man's freely choosing the good on one, or on several occasions, there cannot be a logical impossibility in his freely choosing the good on every occasion. God was not, then, faced with a choice between making innocent automata and making beings who, in acting freely, would sometimes go wrong; there was open to him the obviously better possibility of making beings who would act freely but always go right. Clearly, his failure to avail himself of this possibility is inconsistent with his being both omnipotent and wholly good.[12]

Now what, exactly, is Mackie's point here? This. According to the Free Will Defense, it is possible both that God is omnipotent and that He was unable to create a world containing moral good without creating one containing moral evil. But, replies Mackie, this limitation on His power to create is inconsistent with God's omnipotence. For surely it's *possible* that there be a world containing perfectly virtuous persons—persons who are significantly free but always do what is right. Surely there are *possible worlds* that contain moral good but no moral evil. But God, if He is omnipotent, can create any possible world He chooses. So it is *not* possible, contrary to the Free Will Defense, both that God is omnipotent and that He could create a world containing moral good only by creating one containing moral evil. If He is omnipotent, the only limitations of His power are *logical* limitations; in which case there are no possible worlds He could not have created.

This is a subtle and important point. According to the great German philosopher G. W. Leibniz, *this* world, the actual world, must be the best of all possible worlds. His reasoning goes as follows. Before God created anything at all, He was confronted with an enormous range of choices; He could create or bring into actuality any of the myriads of different possible worlds. Being perfectly good, He must have chosen to create the best world He could; being omnipotent, He was able to create any possible world He pleased. He must, therefore, have chosen the best of all possible worlds; and hence *this* world, the one He did create, must be the best possible. Now Mackie, of course, agrees with Leibniz that God, if omnipotent, could have created any world He pleased and would have created the best world he could. But while Leibniz draws the conclusion that this world, despite appearances, must be the best possible, Mackie concludes instead that there is no omnipotent, wholly good God. For, he says, it is obvious enough that this present world is not the best of all possible worlds.

The Free Will Defender disagrees with both Leibniz and Mackie. In the first place, he might say, what is the reason for supposing that *there is* such a thing as the best of all possible worlds? No matter how marvelous a world is—containing no matter how many persons enjoying unalloyed bliss—isn't it possible that there be an even better world containing even more persons enjoying even more unalloyed bliss? But what is really characteristic and central to the Free Will Defense is the claim that God, though omnipotent, could not have actualized just any possible world He pleased.

---

[12] Mackie, in *The Philosophy of Religion*, pp. 100–101.

5.   WAS IT WITHIN GOD'S POWER TO CREATE ANY POSSIBLE WORLD
HE PLEASED?

This is indeed the crucial question for the Free Will Defense. If we wish to
discuss it with insight and authority, we shall have to look into the idea of *possible
worlds*. And a sensible first question is this: what sort of thing is a possible world?
The basic idea is that a possible world is a *way things could have been*; it is a *state
of affairs* of some kind. Earlier we spoke of states of affairs, in particular of good
and evil states of affairs. Suppose we look at this idea in more detail. What sort
of thing is a state of affairs? The following would be examples:

Nixon's having won the 1972 election
7 + 5's being equal to 12
All men's being mortal

and

Gary, Indiana's, having a really nasty pollution problem.

These are *actual* states of affairs: states of affairs that do in fact *obtain*. And corresponding to each such actual state of affairs there is a true proposition—in the
above cases, the corresponding propositions would be *Nixon won the 1972 presidential election, 7 + 5 is equal to 12, all men are mortal, and Gary, Indiana,
has a really nasty pollution problem*. A proposition *p corresponds* to a state of
affairs *s*, in this sense, if it is impossible that *p* be true and *s* fail to obtain and
impossible that *s* obtain and *p* fail to be true.

But just as there are false propositions, so there are states of affairs that do *not*
obtain or are *not* actual. *Kissinger's having swum the Atlantic* and *Hubert Horatio
Humphrey's having run a mile in four minutes* would be examples. Some states
of affairs that do not obtain are *impossible*: e.g., *Hubert's having drawn a square
circle, 7 + 5's being equal to 75*, and *Agnew's having a brother who was an only
child*. The propositions corresponding to these states of affairs, of course, are necessarily false. So there are states of affairs that *obtain* or *are actual* and also states
of affairs that don't obtain. Among the latter some are *impossible* and others are
possible. And a possible world is a possible state of affairs. Of course not every
possible state of affairs is a possible world; *Hubert's having run a mile in four
minutes* is a possible state of affairs but not a possible world. No doubt it is an
element of many possible worlds, but it isn't itself inclusive enough to be one. To
be a possible world, a state of affairs must be very large—so large as to be *complete*
or *maximal*.

To get at this idea of completeness we need a couple of definitions. As we have
already seen (above, p. 241) a state of affairs A *includes* a state of affairs B if it is
not possible that A obtain and B not obtain or if the conjunctive state of affairs A
but not B—the state of affairs that obtains if and only if A obtains and B does
not—is not possible. For example, *Jim Whittaker's being the first American to
climb Mt. Everest* includes *Jim Whittaker's being an American*. It also includes
*Mt. Everest's being climbed, something's being climbed, no American's having climbed
Everest before Whittaker did*, and the like. *Inclusion* among states of affairs is like

entailment among propositions; and where a state of affairs A includes a state of affairs B, the proposition corresponding to A entails the one corresponding to B. Accordingly, *Jim Whittaker is the first American to climb Everest* entails *Mt. Everest has been climbed, something has been climbed,* and *no American climbed Everest before Whittaker did.* Now suppose we say further that a state of affairs A *precludes* a state of affairs B if it is not possible that *both* obtain, or if the conjunctive state of affairs A *and* B is impossible. Thus *Whittaker's being the first American to climb Mt. Everest* precludes *Luther Jerstad's being the first American to climb Everest,* as well as *Whittaker's never having climbed any mountains.* If A precludes B, then A's corresponding proposition entails the denial of the one corresponding to B. Still further, let's say that the *complement* of a state of affairs is the state of affairs that obtains just in case A does not obtain. [Or we might say that the complement (call it $\overline{A}$) of A is the state of affairs corresponding to the *denial* or *negation* of the proposition corresponding to A.] Given these definitions, we can say what it is for a state of affairs to be *complete:* A is a complete state of affairs if and only if for every state of affairs B, either A *includes* B or A *precludes* B. (We could express the same thing by saying that if A is a complete state of affairs, then for every state of affairs B, either A includes B or A includes $\overline{B}$, the complement of B.) And now we are able to say what a possible world is: a possible world is any possible state of affairs that is complete. If A is a possible world, then it says something about everything; every state of affairs S is either included in or precluded by it.

Corresponding to each possible world W, furthermore, there is a set of propositions that I'll call *the book on* W. A proposition is in the book on W just in case the state of affairs to which it corresponds is included in W. Or we might express it like this. Suppose we say that a proposition P *is true in a world* W if and only if P *would have been true if* W *had been actual*—if and only if, that is, it is not possible that W be actual and P be false. Then the book on W is the set of propositions true in W. Like possible worlds, books are *complete;* if B is a book, then for any proposition P, either P or the denial of P will be a member of B. A book is a *maximal consistent set* of propositions; it is so large that the addition of another proposition to it always yields an explicitly inconsistent set.

Of course, for each possible world there is exactly one book corresponding to it (that is, for a given world W there is just one book B such that each member of B is true in W); and for each book there is just one world to which it corresponds. So every world has its book.

It should be obvious that exactly one possible world is actual. At *least* one must be, since the set of true propositions is a maximal consistent set and hence a book. But then it corresponds to a possible world, and the possible world corresponding to this set of propositions (since it's the set of *true* propositions) will be actual. On the other hand there is at *most* one actual world. For suppose there were two: W and W'. These worlds cannot include all the very same states of affairs; if they did, they would be the very same world. So there must be at least one state of affairs S such that W includes S and W' does not. But a possible world is maximal; W', therefore, includes the complement $\overline{S}$ of S. So if both W and W' were actual, as we have supposed, then both S and $\overline{S}$ would be actual—which is impossible. So there can't be more than one possible world that is actual.

Leibniz pointed out that a proposition p is necessary if it is true in every possible world. We may add that p is possible if it is true in one world and impossible if true in none. Furthermore, p entails q if there is no possible world in which p is true and q is false, and p is consistent with q if there is at least one world in which both p and q are true.

A further feature of possible worlds is that people (and other things) *exist* in them. Each of us exists in the actual world, obviously; but a person also exists in many worlds distinct from the actual world. It would be a mistake, of course, to think of all of these worlds as somehow "going on" at the same time, with the same person reduplicated through these worlds and actually existing in a lot of different ways. This is not what is meant by saying that the same person exists in different possible worlds. What is meant, instead, is this: a person Paul exists in each of those possible worlds W which is such that, if W *had been actual*, Paul would have existed—actually existed. Suppose Paul had been an inch taller than he is, or a better tennis player. Then the world that does in fact obtain would not have been actual; some other world—W', let's say—would have obtained instead. If W' had been actual, Paul would have existed; so Paul exists in W'. (Of course there are still other possible worlds in which Paul does not exist—worlds, for example, in which there are no people at all.) Accordingly, when we say that Paul exists in a world W, what we mean is that Paul *would have* existed had W been actual. Or we could put it like this: Paul exists in each world W that includes the state of affairs consisting in Paul's existence. We can put this still more simply by saying that Paul exists in those worlds whose books contain the proposition *Paul exists*.

But isn't there a problem here? *Many* people are named "Paul": Paul the apostle, Paul J. Zwier, John Paul Jones, and many other famous Pauls. So who goes with "Paul exists"? Which Paul? The answer has to do with the fact that books contain *propositions*—not sentences. They contain the sort of thing sentences are used to express and assert. And the same sentence—"Aristotle is wise," for example—can be used to express many different propositions. When Plato used it, he asserted a proposition predicating wisdom of his famous pupil; when Jackie Onassis uses it, she asserts a proposition predicating wisdom of her wealthy husband. These are distinct propositions (we might even think they differ in truth value); but they are expressed by the same sentence. Normally (but not always) we don't have much trouble determining which of the several propositions expressed by a given sentence is relevant in the context at hand. So in this case a given person, Paul, exists in a world W if and only if W's book contains the proposition that says that *he*—that particular person—exists. The fact that the sentence we use to express this proposition can also be used to express *other* propositions is not relevant.

After this excursion into the nature of books and worlds we can return to our question. Could God have created just any world He chose? Before addressing the question, however, we must note that God does not, strictly speaking, *create* any possible worlds or states of affairs at all. What He creates are the heavens and the earth and all that they contain. But He has not created states of affairs. There are, for example, the state of affairs consisting in God's existence and the state of affairs consisting in His nonexistence. That is, there is such a thing as the state of affairs consisting in the existence of God, and there is also such a thing as the state of affairs consisting in the nonexistence of God, just as there are the two propositions *God exists* and *God does not exist*. The theist believes that the first state of affairs is actual and the first proposition true, the atheist believes that the second state of affairs is actual and the second proposition true. But, of course, both propositions *exist*, even though just one is true. Similarly, there are two states of affairs here, just one of which is actual. So both states of affairs *exist*, but only one *obtains*. And God has not created either one of them since there never was a time at which either did not exist. Nor has He created the state of affairs consisting in the earth's existence; there was a time when *the earth* did not exist, but none when the state of affairs consisting in the earth's existence didn't exist. Indeed, God did not bring into existence any states of affairs at all. What He did was to perform actions of a certain sort—creating the heavens and the earth, for example—which resulted in the *actuality* of certain states of affairs. God *actualizes* states of affairs. He actualizes the possible world that does in fact obtain; He does not create it. And while He has created Socrates, He did not create the state of affairs consisting in Socrates' existence.[13]

Bearing this in mind, let's finally return to our question. Is the atheologian right in holding that if God is omnipotent, then he could have actualized or created any possible world He pleased? Not obviously. First, we must ask ourselves whether God is a *necessary* or a *contingent* being. A *necessary* being is one that exists in every possible world—one that would have existed no matter which possible world had been actual; a contingent being exists only in some possible worlds. Now if God is not a necessary being (and many, perhaps most, theists think that He is not), then clearly enough there will be many possible worlds He could not have actualized—all those, for example, in which He does not exist. Clearly, God could not have created a world in which He doesn't even exist.

So, if God is a contingent being then there are many possible worlds beyond His power to create. But this is really irrelevant to our present concerns. For perhaps the atheologian can maintain his case if he revises his claim to avoid this difficulty; perhaps he will say something like this: if God is omnipotent, then He could have actualized any of those possible worlds *in which He exists*. So if He exists and is omnipotent, He could have actualized (contrary to the Free Will Defense) any of those possible worlds in which He exists and in which there exist free creatures who do no wrong. He could have actualized worlds containing moral good but no moral evil. Is this correct?

Let's begin with a trivial example. You and Paul have just returned from an Australian hunting expedition: your quarry was the elusive double-wattled cassowary. Paul captured an aardvark, mistaking it for a cassowary. The creature's

---

[13] Strict accuracy demands, therefore, that we speak of God as *actualizing* rather than creating possible worlds. I shall continue to use both locutions, thus sacrificing accuracy to familiarity. For more about possible worlds see my book *The Nature of Necessity* (Oxford: The Clarendon Press, 1974), chaps. 4–8.

disarming ways have won it a place in Paul's heart; he is deeply attached to it. Upon your return to the States you offer Paul $500 for his aardvark, only to be rudely turned down. Later you ask yourself, "What would he have done if I'd offered him $700?" Now what is it, exactly, that you are asking? What you're really asking in a way is whether, under a *specific set of conditions*, Paul would have sold it. These conditions include your having offered him $700 rather than $500 for the aardvark, everything else being as much as possible like the conditions that did in fact obtain. Let S' be this set of conditions or state of affairs. S' includes the state of affairs consisting in your offering Paul $700 (instead of the $500 you did offer him); of course it does not include his *accepting* your offer, and it does not include his *rejecting* it; for the rest, the conditions it includes are just like the ones that did obtain in the actual world. So, for example, S' includes Paul's being free to accept the offer and free to refrain; and if in fact the going rate for an aardvark was $650, then S' includes the state of affairs consisting in the going rate's being $650. So we might put your question by asking which of the following conditionals is true:

(23) If the state of affairs S' had obtained, Paul would have accepted the offer
(24) If the state of affairs S' had obtained, Paul would not have accepted the offer.

It seems clear that at least one of these conditionals is true, but naturally they can't both be; so exactly one is.

Now since S' includes neither Paul's accepting the offer nor his rejecting it, the antecedent of (23) and (24) does not entail the consequent of either. That is,

(25) S' obtains

does not entail either

(26) Paul accepts the offer

or

(27) Paul does not accept the offer.

So there are possible worlds in which both (25) and (26) are true, and other possible worlds in which both (25) and (27) are true.

We are now in a position to grasp an important fact. Either (23) or (24) is in fact true; and either way there are possible worlds God could not have actualized. Suppose, first of all, that (23) is true. Then it was beyond the power of God to create a world in which (1) Paul is free to sell his aardvark and free to refrain, and in which the other states of affairs included in S' obtain, and (2) Paul does not sell. That is, it was beyond His power to create a world in which (25) and (27) are both true. There is at least one possible world like this, but God, despite His omnipotence, could not have brought about its actuality. For let W be such a world. To actualize W, God must bring it about that Paul is free with respect to this action, and that the other states of affairs included in S' obtain. But (23), as we are supposing, is true; so if God had actualized S' and left Paul *free* with respect to this action, he would have sold: in which case W would not have been actual. If, on the other hand, God had *brought it about* that Paul didn't sell or had *caused him* to refrain from selling, then Paul would not have been free with respect to this action; then S' would not have been actual (since S' includes Paul's being free with respect to it), and W would not have been actual since W includes S'.

Of course if it is (24) rather than (23) that is true, then another class of worlds was beyond God's power to actualize—those, namely, in which S' obtains and Paul *sells* his aardvark. These are the worlds in which both (25) and (26) are true. But either (23) or (24) is true. Therefore, there are possible worlds God could not have actualized. If we consider whether or not God could have created a world in which, let's say, both (25) and (26) are true, we see that the answer depends upon a peculiar kind of fact; it depends upon what Paul would have freely chosen to do in a certain situation. So there are any number of possible worlds such that it is partly up to Paul whether God can create them.[14]

That was a past tense example. Perhaps it would be useful to consider a future tense case, since this might seem to correspond more closely to God's situation in choosing a possible world to actualize. At some time *t* in the near future Maurice will be free with respect to some insignificant action—having freeze-dried oatmeal for breakfast, let's say. That is, at time *t* Maurice will be free to have oatmeal but also free to take something else—shredded wheat, perhaps. Next, suppose we consider S', a state of affairs that is included in the actual world and includes Maurice's being free with respect to taking oatmeal at time *t*. That is, S' includes Maurice's being free at time *t* to take oatmeal and free to reject it. S' does not include Maurice's taking oatmeal, however; nor does it include his rejecting it. For the rest S' is as much as possible like the actual world. In particular there are many conditions that do in fact hold at time *t* and are *relevant* to his choice—such conditions, for example, as the fact that he hasn't had oatmeal lately, that his wife will be annoyed if he rejects it, and the like; and S' includes each of these conditions. Now God no doubt knows what Maurice will do at time *t*, if S obtains; He knows which action Maurice would freely perform if S were to be actual. That is, God knows that one of the following conditionals is true:

(28) If S' were to obtain, Maurice will freely take the oatmeal

or

(29) If S' were to obtain, Maurice will freely reject it.

We may not know which of these is true, and Maurice himself may not know; but presumably God does.

---

[14] For a fuller statement of this argument see Plantinga, *The Nature of Necessity*, chap. 9, secs. 4–6.

So either God knows that (28) is true, or else He knows that (29) is. Let's suppose it is (28). Then there is a possible world that God, though omnipotent, cannot create. For consider a possible world W' that shares S' with the actual world (which for ease of reference I'll name "Kronos") and in which Maurice does *not* take oatmeal. (We know there *is* such a world, since S' does not include Maurice's taking the oatmeal.) S' obtains in W' just as it does in Kronos. Indeed, everything in W' is just as it is in Kronos up to time t. But whereas in Kronos Maurice takes oatmeal at time t, in W' he does not. Now W' is a perfectly possible world; but it is not within God's power to create it or bring about its actuality. For to do so He must actualize S'. But (28) is in fact true. So if God actualizes S' (as He must to create W') and leaves Maurice free with respect to the action in question, then he will take the oatmeal; and then, of course, W' will not be actual. If, on the other hand, God causes Maurice to *refrain* from taking the oatmeal, then he is not *free* to take it. That means, once again, that W' is not actual; for in W' Maurice is free to take the oatmeal (even if he doesn't do so). So if (28) is true, then this world W' is one that God can't actualize, it is not within His power to actualize it even though He is omnipotent and it is a possible world.

Of course, if it is (29) that is true, we get a similar result; then too there are possible worlds that God can't actualize. These would be worlds which share S' with Kronos and in which Maurice *does* take oatmeal. But either (28) or (29) *is* true; so either way there is a possible world that God can't create. If we consider a world in which S' obtains and in which Maurice freely chooses oatmeal at time t, we see that whether or not it is within God's power to actualize it depends upon what Maurice would do if he were free in a certain situation. Accordingly, there are any number of possible worlds such that it is partly up to Maurice whether or not God can actualize them. It is, of course, up to God whether or not to create Maurice and also up to God whether or not to make him free with respect to the action of taking oatmeal at time t. (God could, if He chose, cause him to succumb to the dreaded *equine obsession*, a condition shared by some people and most horses, whose victims find it *psychologically impossible* to refuse oats or oat products.) But if He creates Maurice and creates him free with respect to this action, then whether or not he actually performs the action is up to Maurice—not God.[15]

Now we can return to the Free Will Defense and the problem of evil. The Free Will Defender, you recall, insists on the possibility that it is not within God's power to create a world containing moral good without creating one containing moral evil. His atheological opponent—Mackie, for example—agrees with Leibniz in insisting that *if* (as the theist holds) God is omnipotent, then it *follows* that He could have created any possible world He pleased. We now see that this contention—call it "Leibniz' Lapse"—is a mistake. The atheologian is right in holding that there are many possible worlds containing moral good but no moral evil; his mistake lies in endorsing Leibniz' Lapse. So one of his premises—that God, if omnipotent, could have actualized just any world He pleased—is false.

[15] For a more complete and more exact statement of this argument see Plantinga, *The Nature of Necessity*, chap. 9, secs. 4–6.

6.   COULD GOD HAVE CREATED A WORLD CONTAINING MORAL GOOD BUT NO
MORAL EVIL?

Now suppose we recapitulate the logic of the situation. The Free Will Defender
claims that the following is possible:

(30) God is omnipotent, and it was not within His power to create a
world containing moral good but no moral evil.

By way of retort the atheologian insists that there are possible worlds containing
moral good but no moral evil. He adds that an omnipotent being could have
actualized any possible world he chose. So if God is omnipotent, it follows that
He could have actualized a world containing moral good but no moral evil, hence
(30), contrary to the Free Will Defender's claim, is not possible. What we have
seen so far is that his second premise—Leibniz' Lapse—is false.

Of course, this does not settle the issue in the Free Will Defender's favor.
Leibniz' Lapse (appropriately enough for a lapse) is false; but this doesn't show
that (30) is possible. To show this latter we must demonstrate the possibility that
among the worlds God could not have actualized are all the worlds containing
moral good but no moral evil. How can we approach this question?

Instead of choosing oatmeal for breakfast or selling an aardvark, suppose we
think about a morally significant action such as taking a bribe. Curley Smith, the
mayor of Boston, is opposed to the proposed freeway route; it would require destruction of the Old North Church along with some other antiquated and struc-
turally unsound buildings. L. B. Smedes, the director of highways, asks him whether
he'd drop his opposition for $1 million. "Of course," he replies. "Would you do
it for $2?" asks Smedes. "What do you take me for?" comes the indignant reply.
"That's already established," smirks Smedes; "all that remains is to nail down your
price." Smedes then offers him a bribe of $35,000; unwilling to break with the
fine old traditions of Bay State politics, Curley accepts. Smedes then spends a
sleepless night wondering whether he could have bought Curley for $20,000.

Now suppose we assume that Curley was free with respect to the action of
taking the bribe—free to take it and free to refuse. And suppose, furthermore, that
he would have taken it. That is, let us suppose that

(31) If Smedes had offered Curley a bribe of $20,000, he would have
accepted it.

If (31) is true, then there is a state of affairs S' that (1) includes Curley's being
offered a bribe of $20,000; (2) does not include either his accepting the bribe or
his rejecting it; and (3) is otherwise as much as possible like the actual world. Just
to make sure S' includes every relevant circumstance, let us suppose that it is a
maximal world segment. That is, add to S' any state of affairs compatible with but
not included in it, and the result will be an entire possible world. We could think
of it roughly like this: S' is included in at least one world W in which Curley
takes the bribe and in at least one world W' in which he rejects it. If S' is a

maximal world segment, then S' is what remains of W when *Curley's taking the bribe* is deleted; it is also what remains of W' when *Curley's rejecting the bribe* is detected. More exactly, if S' is a maximal world segment, then every possible state of affairs that includes S', but isn't included by S', is a possible world. So if (31) is true, then there is a maximal world segment S' that (1) includes Curley's being offered a bribe of $20,000; (2) does not include either his accepting the bribe or his rejecting it; (3) is otherwise as much as possible like the actual world—in particular, it includes Curley's being free with respect to the bribe; and (4) is such that if it were actual then Curley would have taken the bribe. That is,

(32) if S' were actual, Curley would have accepted the bribe is true.

Now, of course, there is at least one possible world W' in which S' is actual and Curley does not take the bribe. But God could not have created W'; to do so, He would have been obliged to actualize S', leaving Curley free with respect to the action of taking the bribe. But under these conditions Curley, as (32) assures us, would have accepted the bribe, so that the world thus created would not have been S'.

Curley, as we see, is not above a bit of Watergating. But there may be worse to come. Of course, there are possible worlds in which he is significantly free (i.e., free with respect to a morally significant action) and never does what is wrong. But the sad truth about Curley may be this. Consider W', any of these worlds: in W' Curley is significantly free, so in W' there are some actions that are morally significant for him and with respect to which he is free. But at least one of these actions—call it A—has the following peculiar property. There is a maximal world segment S' that obtains in W' and is such that (1) S' includes Curley's being free *re* A but neither his performing A nor his refraining from A; (2) S' is otherwise as much as possible like W'; and (3) if S' had been actual, Curley would have gone wrong with respect to A.[16] (Notice that this third condition holds in fact, in the actual world; it does not hold in that world W'.)

This means, of course, that God could not have actualized W'. For to do so He'd have been obliged to bring it about that S' is actual; but then Curley would go wrong with respect to A. Since in W' he always does what is right, the world thus actualized would not be W'. On the other hand, if God *causes* Curley to go right with respect to A or *brings it about that* he does so, then Curley isn't free with respect to A; and so once more it isn't W' that is actual. Accordingly God cannot create W'. But W' was just any of the worlds in which Curley is significantly free but always does only what is right. It therefore follows that it was not within God's power to create a world in which Curley produces moral good but no moral evil. Every world God can actualize is such that if Curley is significantly free in it, he takes at least one wrong action.

Obviously Curley is in serious trouble. I shall call the malady from which he suffers *transworld depravity*. (I leave as homework the problem of comparing

---

[16] A person goes wrong with respect to an action if he either wrongfully performs it or wrongfully fails to perform it.

transworld depravity with what Calvinists call "total depravity.") By way of explicit definition:

> (33) A person P *suffers from transworld depravity* if and only if the following holds: for every world W such that P is significantly free in W and P does only what is right in W, there is an action A and a maximal world segment S' such that
> (1) S' includes A's being morally significant for P
> (2) S' includes P's being free with respect to A
> (3) S' is included in W and includes neither P's performing A nor P's refraining from performing A

and

> (4) If S' were actual, P would go wrong with respect to A.

(In thinking about this definition, remember that (4) is to be true in fact, in the actual world—not in that world W.)

What is important about the idea of transworld depravity is that if a person suffers from it, then it wasn't within God's power to actualize any world in which that person is significantly free but does no wrong—that is, a world in which he produces moral good but no moral evil.

We have been here considering a crucial contention of the Free Will Defender: the contention, namely, that

> (30) God is omnipotent, and it was not within His power to create a world containing moral good but no moral evil.

How is transworld depravity relevant to this? As follows. Obviously it is possible that there be persons who suffer from transworld depravity. More generally, it is possible that *everybody* suffers from it. And if this possibility were actual, then God, though omnipotent, could not have created any of the possible worlds containing just the persons who do in fact exist, and containing moral good but no moral evil. For to do so He'd have to create persons who were significantly free (otherwise there would be no moral good) but suffered from transworld depravity. Such persons go wrong with respect to at least one action in any world God could have actualized and in which they are free with respect to morally significant actions; so the price for creating a world in which they produce moral good is creating one in which they also produce moral evil.

Suggestions for Further Reading

A good general treatment—as both an historical survey and a philosophical critique of the problem of evil—is *Evil and the God of Love* (Harper, 1966) by John Hick. The work *Evil and the Concept of God* (Charles C. Thomas, 1968) by

Edward Madden and Peter Hare critically examines standard solutions to the problem of evil. For a traditional approach see C. S. Lewis, *The Problem of Pain* (Macmillan, 1943), and Charles Journet, *The Meaning of Evil* (P. J. Kennedy, 1963). For an interesting approach to the problem of evil see George Schlesinger, "The Problem of Evil and the Problem of Suffering," *American Philosophical Quarterly* 1 (1964).

On the logical problem of evil see M. B. Ahern's accessible work *The Problem of Evil* (Schocken, 1971) and Chapter Nine of J. L. Mackie's *The Miracle of Theism* (Clarendon Press, 1982). The article by Keith Yandell, "Ethics, Evils and Theism," *Sophia* 8 (1969), is also a good treatment.

The empirical problem of evil is examined in Chapter Six of William Rowe's *Philosophy of Religion: An Introduction* (Wadsworth, 1978) and in his "The Empirical Problem of Evil" in R. Audi and W. J. Wainwright, eds., *Rationality, Religious Belief and Moral Commitment* (Cornell University Press, 1986). A rigorous critique of the empirical problem of evil is Alvin Plantinga's "The Probabilistic Argument from Evil," *Philosophical Studies* 35 (1979). A simpler account can be found in Chapters Four and Five of *Evil and the Christian God* (Baker, 1982) by Michael Peterson.

OBJECTIONS TO
TRADITIONAL THEISM

IV

People often doubt the truth of religious assertions. Many think them false. But some modern analytic philosophers have issued a deeper challenge. In their opinion, utterances like "God loves us" or "God has a plan for the world" are not factual assertions. In spite of appearances, such expressions do not really say anything. Antony Flew is a philosopher of this sort. According to Flew, (1) utterances like "God loves us" are *intended* to be "vast cosmological assertions." (2) Factual assertions, however, are empirical, and (3) any empirical assertion is subject to decisive falsification—one can specify observable states of affairs that would decisively refute the assertion if they were to occur. But (4) religious believers are not able to specify an observable state of affairs that would decisively count against their statements. Flew concludes that (5) their utterances do not express factual claims.

There were two immediate reactions to this challenge. Some philosophers argued that Flew's criterion of factual significance *is* satisfied by religious assertions—that believers *can* specify observable states of affairs that would force them to withdraw their claims. An extraordinary amount of evil might be an example. Others maintained that assertions like "God loves us" are factually significant because they meet criteria relevantly similar to Flew's. For example, some argued that even though religious assertions are not decisively falsifiable, they *are* decisively verifiable. Christian assertions, for instance, would be decisively confirmed by the coming of Christ in glory. Still others suggested that decisive falsification or verification is too strict a standard.[1] Statements are factually significant if some observable states of affairs would count for or against them if they were to occur; it is not necessary that they do so decisively. A test of this sort, of course, is easily met. As Basil Mitchell points out, theists believe that evil counts against their assertions although they do not think that it does so decisively.

The second reaction to Flew's challenge was different. His conclusion was accepted: religious assertions do not express factual claims. Nevertheless, assertions like "God has a plan" are significant, and the people who make them think differently about the world than those who do not. For example, R. M. Hare argues that an utterance of this sort expresses a *blik* (a German word meaning "look" or "view"). Although *bliks* are not factual assertions, they deeply affect our attitudes and practices. Hare thinks that our belief in the uniformity of nature is an example. It is not factual, since nothing would count decisively against it. It is more like a way of looking at things. But how we look at things matters. The belief in the uniformity of nature, for example, guides the practice of science and everyday life. The behavior and attitudes of a person who shares the *blik* are very different from those of a person who does not.

Ludwig Wittgenstein's position is rather similar to Hare's. Wittgenstein, too,

---

[1] Many empirical assertions fail to meet it. For example, consider "There is a solvent for every substance." No finite set of observations could conclusively verify this assertion. Even if every known substance has a solvent, an as-yet-unknown substance might not. Nor will any finite set of observations conclusively falsify the statement. Even if some substance cannot be dissolved by any known solvent, an as-yet-undiscovered solvent might do the job. Scientific statements about electrons and other theoretical entities also fail the test because they cannot be conclusively verified or falsified in Flew's sense.

thought that a belief in God or Providence is not factual. Empirical evidence is irrelevant to the "truth" (appropriateness) of utterances like "There will be a Last Judgment." Sentences of this kind express not factual assertions but "pictures." A person who believes in the Last Judgment, for example, does not subscribe to a factual claim about the future but instead holds a certain picture before the mind's eye, bringing it to bear on his or her life as a whole. As a result, this person thinks, feels, and behaves differently from nonbelievers.

D. Z. Phillips has developed these suggestions of Wittgenstein's in a number of books and articles. In his opinion, it is "superstitious" to treat religious beliefs as factual assertions. A properly religious belief in immortality, for instance, is concerned with a quality of one's present life that is indicated by expressions like "living in God's presence." It is not concerned with literal survival. Phillips thinks that religious belief is a matter of "living by" certain pictures, "drawing sustenance from them, judging oneself in terms of them."[2]

Phillips is also influenced by other important Wittgensteinian theses—(1) that language is part of a "form of life" (a complicated and rule-governed pattern of feeling, thought, and behavior), (2) that different "language-games" (ways of using language) are associated with different forms of life, and (3) that these forms of life, and the language-games that belong to them, are relatively autonomous. Each "game" has its own rules for assessing truth or adequacy. Imposing the rules of one language game on moves made in another is the result of logical confusion.

Phillips applies these theses to religion and other areas like science. They are different forms of life. Religious utterances and scientific utterances, for example, belong to different language-games and can be assessed only by their own criteria. Religious utterances are not factual assertions, because they are not properly assessed by the criteria used in assessing the truth or falsity of scientific statements or ordinary empirical claims like "The oven is hot." But it does not follow that these utterances are meaningless or that they say nothing at all. They have their own kind of sense. They can only be assessed, however, by criteria that are themselves part of the religious way of life.[3]

All these positions are controversial. For example, each of the philosophers discussed assumes that assertions are not factually significant unless they can be confirmed or disconfirmed by empirical evidence. Many contemporary philosophers think this mistaken. In their opinion, broad metaphysical theses like "All substance is material" or "Every event has a sufficient causal condition" or "Numbers, propositions, and other abstract entities really exist" *are* factual assertions. Although their truth or falsity cannot be determined by observation or experiment, they play a role in explanation and say something significant about the world that is either true or false. Religious utterances such as "God has a plan" may be assertions of this type.

[2] D. Z. Phillips, *Death and Immortality* (New York: St. Martin's Press, 1970), pp. 68 and 71.

[3] Hence the term "Wittgensteinian Fideism." Fideists believe that a properly formed faith is not based on rational evidence and cannot be properly assessed by rational standards. Phillips's view is similar in that he thinks religious belief should not be assessed by the rational criteria used in science, traditional metaphysics, or our commonsense reflections about the world or by other external standards.

The autonomy thesis is also controversial. Is religious language as isolated from other areas of discourse as Wittgenstein and Phillips suggest? Is it really true that standard philosophical arguments and empirical findings have no bearing on the truth of a belief in God or an afterlife? On the face of it, Kai Nielsen appears to be right when he insists that the basic question is whether concepts like "God" or "immortality" have any grip on reality. Showing that the religious language-game or form of life is internally coherent, or has its own kind of sense, does not clearly answer this question.

Nor is it clear that Hare, Wittgenstein, and Phillips have correctly analyzed religious language. Flew is surely right in saying that "some theological utterances seem to, and are *intended* to, provide explanations or make assertions." (My italics.) Few believers think that they are only expressing *bliks* or pictures. Of course, they might be mistaken. Nevertheless, the burden of proof is on those who refuse to take utterances like "God loves us" at face value, i.e., as factual assertions. Until the burden is met, accounts like those of Hare and Phillips are best viewed as reinterpretations of traditional religious belief and not as analyses of it. The question thus becomes "Are their alternatives to traditional religious belief superior to it?"

William James asserts that religion involves three beliefs: "1. That the visible world is part of a more spiritual universe from which it draws its chief significance; 2. That union or harmonious relation with that higher universe is our true end; 3. That prayer or inner communion with the spirit thereof . . . is a process wherein work is really done, and spiritual energy flows in and produces effects, psychological or material, within the phenomenal world."[4]

Western philosophers have usually identified the "higher universe" with God. This ignores important alternatives. For example, Advaita Vedānta identifies it with the Nirguna Brahman, which is beyond space, time, causality, and the subject–object relationship. Although the Brahman can be characterized as "being–consciousness–bliss," it really has no properties. Hīnayāna Buddhists believe that the higher universe is Nirvāna. Nirvāna is the end of ignorant desire and of the suffering that is its consequence. Some positive terms are applied to it. "Peace," "Purity," "Safety," "The Refuge," "The Island," and "The Opposite Shore" are examples. But Nirvāna cannot really be described. In particular, we should not describe it as a transcendent substance like God or Brahman. (Trevor Ling suggests that it is best thought of as a transcendent condition or place.[5])

There are, then, nontheistic as well as theistic religions. How should a person respond to this diversity? One response is relativism: that there is no objective way of deciding between religions or between religious and nonreligious world-views. Others attempt to show that theism is rationally superior to Advaita Vedānta and other alternatives or vice versa.

John Hick provides a sophisticated version of another popular response. Many believe that the insights of the major religious traditions are genuine but partial.

---

[4]William James, *The Varieties of Religious Experience* (New York: The Modern Library, 1902), p. 475.

[5]Trevor Ling, "Buddhist Mysticism," *Religious Studies* 1 (1966), pp. 166–67.

In their opinion, an adequate world-view must do equal justice to the truths of each. Hick agrees. He thinks that a God of love would make Himself accessible to all cultures equally. He also thinks that the Divine is infinite and "transcends the grasp of the human mind"; encounters with it are inevitably partial. It is thus unlikely that one tradition has a monopoly on the truth.

How, then, should we think of the Divine? Two "basic concepts" govern human religious life—"deity" (God) and the nonpersonal "Absolute." The First takes concrete form as Yahweh, Allah, Shiva, Vishnu, and so on. Brahman, Nirvāna, and Śūnyatā (Emptiness) are "concretizations" of the second. Religion is the joint product of transforming encounters with the Infinite and concepts and symbols like these. Although the concepts and symbols are products of particular cultures, they express real insights into a single reality. Jews and Buddhists, for example, experience the same thing, although they do so "from different historical and cultural standpoints." Since each tradition expresses different "aspects of the same infinite reality," each should be equally respected. The different traditions should be retained, but theology (the intellectual aspect of religion) must become "global."[6]

Hick's proposal is attractive. It is also problematic. If the major traditions are equally true, then it is equally true that the Infinite is personal and that it is not. Is this coherent? It may be significant that classical traditions that distinguish between personal and nonpersonal aspects of the infinite always subordinate one to the other. Advaita Vedānta, for example, regards theism as a lower truth. Viśiṣtadvaita Vedānta, on the other hand, subordinates the nontheistic features of the Vedānta tradition to theism.

Hick believes that the particular traditions should be retained but that theology should become global. This, too, is problematic, because it is not clear that these recommendations are compatible. Hick recognizes, for example, that a global theology cannot be "Christocentric." But wouldn't a theology that removed Christ from its center deprive Christian worship and practice of much of its meaning? Symbols and devotional practices presuppose the theologies of their respective communities. Will they retain their "life" and "power to nourish" once these theologies have been devalued as partial truths?

There may also be another problem. While Hick's global theology incorporates insights from the various traditions, it is incompatible with them. Traditional Christians, for example, will reject global theology because it implies that "deity" is not the best concept for expressing the Infinite and because it is not Christocentric. Advaitins will condemn it for placing too much weight on the personal aspect of the Ultimate. Buddhists will not accept Hick's allegedly neutral description of ultimate reality as "eternal" and "self-existent," "the transcendent ground of all existence," because it implies that the Ultimate is some sort of substance. The point is that Hick has not really transcended religious pluralism. He has simply added one more alternative.

W. J. W.

---

[6]The quotations from Hick are drawn from *God Has Many Names* (Philadelphia: The Westminster Press, 1982), Chapters III and VI, and from "The New Map of the Universe of Faiths" (see *Philosophy of Religion: Selected Readings*, Second Edition, pp. 295–305).

MEANING AND VERIFICATION

ANTONY FLEW, R. M. HARE, AND BASIL MITCHELL
Theology and Falsification

Let us begin with a parable. It is a parable developed from a tale told by John Wisdom in his haunting and revelatory article 'Gods'.[1] Once upon a time two explorers came upon a clearing in the jungle. In the clearing were growing many flowers and many weeds. One explorer says, 'Some gardener must tend this plot'. The other disagrees, 'There is no gardener'. So they pitch their tents and set a watch. No gardener is ever seen. 'But perhaps he is an invisible gardener.' So they set up a barbed-wire fence. They electrify it. They patrol with bloodhounds. (For they remember how H. G. Wells's *The Invisible Man* could be both smelt and touched though he could not be seen.) But no shrieks ever suggest that some intruder has received a shock. No movements of the wire ever betray an invisible climber. The bloodhounds never give cry. Yet still the Believer is not convinced. 'But there is a gardener, invisible, intangible, insensible to electric shocks, a gardener who has no scent and makes no sound, a gardener who comes secretly to look after the garden which he loves.' At last the Sceptic despairs, 'But what remains of your original assertion? Just how does what you call an invisible, intangible, eternally elusive gardener differ from an imaginary gardener or even from no gardener at all?'

The contributors to this discussion represent the style of analytical philosophy that emerged in England following World War II. Antony Flew is a professor at the University of Keele, Staffordshire. R. M. Hare and Basil Mitchell teach at Oxford University.

THEOLOGY AND FALSIFICATION   Reprinted with permission of Macmillan Company from *New Essays in Philosophical Theology*, edited by Antony Flew and Alasdair MacIntyre (New York: Macmillan, 1955).

[1]*P.A.S.*, 1944–5, reprinted as Ch. X of *Logic and Language*, Vol. I (Blackwell, 1951), and in his *Philosophy and Psychoanalysis* (Blackwell, 1953).

In this parable we can see how what starts as an assertion, that something exists or that there is some analogy between certain complexes of phenomena, may be reduced step by step to an altogether different status, to an expression perhaps of a 'picture preference'.[2] The Sceptic says there is no gardener. The Believer says there is a gardener (but invisible, etc.). One man talks about sexual behaviour. Another man prefers to talk of Aphrodite (but knows that there is not really a superhuman person additional to, and somehow responsible for, all sexual phenomena).[3] The process of qualification may be checked at any point before the original assertion is completely withdrawn and something of that first assertion will remain (Tautology). Mr. Wells's invisible man could not, admittedly, be seen, but in all other respects he was a man like the rest of us. But though the process of qualification may be, and of course usually is, checked in time, it is not always judiciously so halted. Someone may dissipate his assertion completely without noticing that he has done so. A fine brash hypothesis may thus be killed by inches, the death by a thousand qualifications.

And in this, it seems to me, lies the peculiar danger, the endemic evil, of theological utterance. Take such utterances as 'God has a plan', 'God created the world', 'God loves us as a father loves his children'. They look at first sight very much like assertions, vast cosmological assertions. Of course, this is no sure sign that they either are, or are intended to be, assertions. But let us confine ourselves to the cases where those who utter such sentences intend them to express assertions. (Merely remarking parenthetically that those who intend or interpret such utterances as crypto-commands, expressions of wishes, disguised ejaculations, concealed ethics, or as anything else but assertions, are unlikely to succeed in making them either properly orthodox or practically effective.)

Now to assert that such and such is the case is necessarily equivalent to denying that such and such is not the case.[4] Suppose then that we are in doubt as to what someone who gives vent to an utterance is asserting, or suppose that, more radically, we are sceptical as to whether he is really asserting anything at all, one way of trying to understand (or perhaps it will be to expose) his utterance is to attempt to find what he would regard as counting against, or as being incompatible with, its truth. For if the utterance is indeed an assertion, it will necessarily be equivalent to a denial of the negation of that assertion. And anything which would count against the assertion, or which would induce the speaker to withdraw it and to admit that it had been mistaken, must be part of (or the whole of) the meaning of the negation of that assertion. And to know the meaning of the negation of an

---

[2] Cf. J. Wisdom, 'Other Minds', Mind, 1940; reprinted in his Other Minds (Blackwell, 1952).

[3] Cf. Lucretius, De Rerum Natura, II, 655–60,

> Hic siquis mare Neptunum Cereremque vocare
> Constituet fruges et Bacchi nomine abuti
> Mavolt quam laticis proprium proferre vocamen
> Concedamus ut hic terrarum dictitet orbem
> Esse deum matrem dum vera re tamen ipse
> Religione animum turpi contingere parcat.

[4] For those who prefer symbolism: $p \equiv \sim \sim p$.

assertion, is as near as makes no matter, to know the meaning of that assertion.[5] And if there is nothing which a putative assertion denies then there is nothing which it asserts either: and so it is not really an assertion. When the Sceptic in the parable asked the Believer, 'Just how does what you call an invisible, intangible, eternally elusive gardener differ from an imaginary gardener or even from no gardener at all?' he was suggesting that the Believer's earlier statement had been so eroded by qualification that it was no longer an assertion at all.

Now it often seems to people who are not religious as if there was no conceivable event or series of events the occurrence of which would be admitted by sophisticated religious people to be a sufficient reason for conceding 'There wasn't a God after all' or 'God does not really love us then'. Someone tells us that God loves us as a father loves his children. We are reassured. But then we see a child dying of inoperable cancer of the throat. His earthly father is driven frantic in his efforts to help, but his Heavenly Father reveals no obvious sign of concern. Some qualification is made—God's love is 'not a merely human love' or it is 'an inscrutable love', perhaps—and we realize that such sufferings are quite compatible with the truth of the assertion that 'God loves us as a father (but, of course, . . .)'. We are reassured again. But then perhaps we ask: what is this assurance of God's (appropriately qualified) love worth, what is this apparent guarantee really a guarantee against? Just what would have to happen not merely (morally and wrongly) to tempt but also (logically and rightly) to entitle us to say 'God does not love us' or even 'God does not exist'? I therefore put to the succeeding symposiasts the simple central questions, 'What would have to occur or to have occurred to constitute for you a disproof of the love of, or of the existence of, God?'

R. M. HARE

I wish to make it clear that I shall not try to defend Christianity in particular, but religion in general—not because I do not believe in Christianity, but because you cannot understand what Christianity is, until you have understood what religion is.

I must begin by confessing that, on the ground marked out by Flew, he seems to me to be completely victorious. I therefore shift my ground by relating another parable. A certain lunatic is convinced that all dons want to murder him. His friends introduce him to all the mildest and most respectable dons that they can find, and after each of them has retired, they say, 'You see, he doesn't really want to murder you; he spoke to you in a most cordial manner; surely you are convinced now?' But the lunatic replies 'Yes, but that was only his diabolical cunning; he's really plotting against me the whole time, like the rest of them; I know it I tell you'. However many kindly dons are produced, the reaction is still the same.

Now we say that such a person is deluded. But what is he deluded about? About the truth or falsity of an assertion? Let us apply Flew's test to him. There is no behaviour of dons that can be enacted which he will accept as counting

---

[5] For by simply negating $\sim p$ we get p: $\sim \sim p \equiv p$.

against his theory; and therefore his theory, on this test, asserts nothing. But it does not follow that there is no difference between what he thinks about dons and what most of us think about them—otherwise we should not call him a lunatic and ourselves sane, and dons would have no reason to feel uneasy about his presence in Oxford.

Let us call that in which we differ from this lunatic, our respective *bliks*. He has an insane *blik* about dons; we have a sane one. It is important to realize that we have a sane one, not no *blik* at all; for there must be two sides to any argument—if he has a wrong *blik*, then those who are right about dons must have a right one. Flew has shown that a *blik* does not consist in an assertion or system of them; but nevertheless it is very important to have the right *blik*.

Let us try to imagine what it would be like to have different *bliks* about other things than dons. When I am driving my car, it sometimes occurs to me to wonder whether my movements of the steering-wheel will always continue to be followed by corresponding alterations in the direction of the car. I have never had a steering failure, though I have had skids, which must be similar. Moreover, I know enough about how the steering of my car is made, to know the sort of thing that would have to go wrong for the steering to fail—steel joints would have to part, or steel rods break, or something—but how do I know that this won't happen? The truth is, I don't know; I just have a *blik* about steel and its properties, so that normally I trust the steering of my car; but I find it not at all difficult to imagine what it would be like to lose this *blik* and acquire the opposite one. People would say I was silly about steel; but there would be no mistaking the reality of the difference between our respective *bliks*—for example, I should never go in a motor-car. Yet I should hesitate to say that the difference between us was the difference between contradictory assertions. No amount of safe arrivals or bench-tests will remove my *blik* and restore the normal one; for my *blik* is compatible with any finite number of such tests.

It was Hume who taught us that our whole commerce with the world depends upon our *blik* about the world; and that differences between *bliks* about the world cannot be settled by observation of what happens in the world. That was why, having performed the interesting experiment of doubting the ordinary man's *blik* about the world, and showing that no proof could be given to make us adopt one *blik* rather than another, he turned to backgammon to take his mind off the problem. It seems, indeed, to be impossible even to formulate as an assertion the normal *blik* about the world which makes me put my confidence in the future reliability of steel joints, in the continued ability of the road to support my car, and not gape beneath it revealing nothing below; in the general non-homicidal tendencies of dons; in my own continued well-being (in some sense of that word that I may not now fully understand) if I continue to do what is right according to my lights; in the general likelihood of people like Hitler coming to a bad end. But perhaps a formulation less inadequate than most is to be found in the Psalms: 'The earth is weak and all the inhabiters thereof: I bear up the pillars of it'.

The mistake of the position which Flew selects for attack is to regard this kind of talk as some sort of *explanation*, as scientists are accustomed to use the word. As such, it would obviously be ludicrous. We no longer believe in God as an

Atlas—*nous n'avons pas besoin de cette hypothèse*. But it is nevertheless true to say that, as Hume saw, without a *blik* there can be no explanation; for it is by our *bliks* that we decide what is and what is not an explanation. Suppose we believed that everything that happened, happened by pure chance. This would not of course be an assertion; for it is compatible with anything happening or not happening, and so incidentally, is its contradictory. But if we had this belief, we should not be able to explain or predict or plan anything. Thus, although we should not be *asserting* anything different from those of a more normal belief, there would be a great difference between us; and this is the sort of difference that there is between those who really believe in God and those who really disbelieve in him.

The word 'really' is important, and may excite suspicion. I put it in, because when people have had a good Christian upbringing, as have most of those who now profess not to believe in any sort of religion, it is very hard to discover what they really believe. The reason why they find it so easy to think that they are not religious, is that they have never got into the frame of mind of one who suffers from the doubts to which religion is the answer. Not for them the terrors of the primitive jungle. Having abandoned some of the more picturesque fringes of religion, they think that they have abandoned the whole thing—whereas in fact they still have got, and could not live without, a religion of a comfortably substantial, albeit highly sophisticated, kind, which differs from that of many 'religious people' in little more than this, that 'religious people' like to sing Psalms about theirs—a very natural and proper thing to do. But nevertheless there may be a big difference lying behind—the difference between two people who, though side by side, are walking in different directions. I do not know in what direction Flew is walking; perhaps he does not know either. But we have had some examples recently of various ways in which one can walk away from Christianity, and there are any number of possibilities. After all, man has not changed biologically since primitive times; it is his religion that has changed, and it can easily change again. And if you do not think that such changes make a difference, get acquainted with some Sikhs and some Mussulmans of the same Punjabi stock; you will find them quite different sorts of people.

There is an important difference between Flew's parable and my own which we have not yet noticed. The explorers do not *mind* about their garden; they discuss it with interest, but not with concern. But my lunatic, poor fellow, minds about dons; and I mind about the steering of my car; it often has people in it that I care for. It is because I mind very much about what goes on in the garden in which I find myself, that I am unable to share the explorers' detachment.

BASIL MITCHELL

Flew's article is searching and perceptive, but there is, I think, something odd about his conduct of the theologian's case. The theologian surely would not deny that the fact of pain counts against the assertion that God loves men. This very incompatibility generates the most intractable of theological problems—the problem of evil. So the theologian *does* recognize the fact of pain as counting against Christian doctrine. But it is true that he will not allow it—or anything—to count decisively against it; for he is committed by his faith to trust in God. His attitude is not that of the detached observer, but of the believer.

Perhaps this can be brought out by yet another parable. In time of war in an occupied country, a member of the resistance meets one night a stranger who deeply impresses him. They spend that night together in conversation. The Stranger tells the partisan that he himself is on the side of the resistance—indeed he is in command of it, and urges the partisan to have faith in him no matter what happens. The partisan is utterly convinced at that meeting of the Stranger's sincerity and constancy and undertakes to trust him.

They never meet in conditions of intimacy again. But sometimes the Stranger is seen helping members of the resistance, and the partisan is grateful and says to his friends, 'He is on our side'.

Sometimes he is seen in the uniform of the police handing over patriots to the occupying power. On these occasions his friends murmur against him: but the partisan still says, 'He is on our side'. He still believes that, in spite of appearances, the Stranger did not deceive him. Sometimes he asks the Stranger for help and receives it. He is then thankful. Sometimes he asks and does not receive it. Then he says, 'The Stranger knows best'. Sometimes his friends, in exasperation, say 'Well, what *would* he have to do for you to admit that you were wrong and that he is not on our side?' But the partisan refuses to answer. He will not consent to put the Stranger to the test. And sometimes his friends complain, 'Well, if *that's* what you mean by his being on our side, the sooner he goes over to the other side the better'.

The partisan of the parable does not allow anything to count decisively against the proposition 'The Stranger is on our side'. This is because he has committed himself to trust the Stranger. But he of course recognizes that the Stranger's ambiguous behaviour *does* count against what he believes about him. It is precisely this situation which constitutes the trial of his faith.

When the partisan asks for help and doesn't get it, what can he do? He can (a) conclude that the Stranger is not on our side or; (b) maintain that he is on our side, but that he has reasons for withholding help.

The first he will refuse to do. How long can he uphold the second position without its becoming just silly?

I don't think one can say in advance. It will depend on the nature of the impression created by the Stranger in the first place. It will depend, too, on the manner in which he takes the Stranger's behaviour. If he blandly dismisses it as of no consequence, as having no bearing upon his belief, it will be assumed that he is thoughtless or insane. And it quite obviously won't do for him to say easily, 'Oh, when used of the Stranger the phrase "is on our side" *means* ambiguous behaviour of this sort'. In that case he would be like the religious man who says blandly of a terrible disaster 'It is God's will'. No, he will only be regarded as sane and reasonable in his belief, if he experiences in himself the full force of the conflict.

It is here that my parable differs from Hare's. The partisan admits that many things may and do count against his belief: whereas Hare's lunatic who has a *blik* about dons doesn't admit that anything counts against his *blik*. Nothing *can* count against *bliks*. Also the partisan has a reason for having in the first instance committed himself, viz. the character of the Stranger; whereas the lunatic has no reason for his *blik* about dons—because, of course, you can't have reasons for *bliks*.

This means that I agree with Flew that theological utterances must be assertions. The partisan is making an assertion when he says, 'The Stranger is on our side'.

Do I want to say that the partisan's belief about the Stranger is, in any sense, an explanation? I think I do. It explains and makes sense of the Stranger's behaviour: it helps to explain also the resistance movement in the context of which he appears. In each case it differs from the interpretation which the others put upon the same facts.

'God loves men' resembles 'the Stranger is on our side' (and many other significant statements, e.g. historical ones) in not being conclusively falsifiable. They can both be treated in at least three different ways: (1) As provisional hypotheses to be discarded if experience tells against them; (2) As significant articles of faith; (3) As vacuous formulae (expressing, perhaps, a desire for reassurance) to which experience makes no difference and which make no difference to life.

The Christian, once he had committed himself, is precluded by his faith from taking up the first attitude: 'Thou shalt not tempt the Lord thy God'. He is in constant danger, as Flew has observed, of slipping into the third. But he need not; and, if he does, it is a failure in faith as well as in logic.

ANTONY FLEW

It has been a good discussion: and I am glad to have helped to provoke it. But now—at least in *University*—it must come to an end: and the Editors of *University* have asked me to make some concluding remarks. Since it is impossible to deal with all the issues raised or to comment separately upon each contribution, I will concentrate on Mitchell and Hare, as representative of two very different kinds of response to the challenge made in 'Theology and Falsification'.

The challenge, it will be remembered, ran like this. Some theological utterances seem to, and are intended to, provide explanations or express assertions. Now an assertion, to be an assertion at all, must claim that things stand thus and thus; *and not otherwise*. Similarly an explanation, to be an explanation at all, must explain why this particular thing occurs; *and not something else*. Those last clauses are crucial. And yet sophisticated religious people—or so it seemed to me—are apt to overlook this, and tend to refuse to allow, not merely that anything actually does occur, but that anything conceivably could occur, which would count against their theological assertions and explanations. But in so far as they do this their supposed explanations are actually bogus, and their seeming assertions are really vacuous.

Mitchell's response to this challenge is admirably direct, straightforward, and understanding. He agrees 'that theological utterances must be assertions'. He agrees that if they are to be assertions, there must be something that would count against their truth. He agrees, too, that believers are in constant danger of transforming their would-be assertions into 'vacuous formulae'. But he takes me to task for an oddity in my 'conduct of the theologian's case. The theologian surely would not deny that the fact of pain counts against the assertion that God loves men. This very incompatibility generates the most intractable of theological problems, the problem of evil'. I think he is right. I should have made a distinction between two very different ways of dealing with what looks like evidence against the love of God: the way I stressed was the expedient of qualifying the original assertion; the way the theologian usually takes, at first, is to admit that it looks bad but to insist that there is—there must be—some explanation which will show that, in spite of appearances, there really is a God who loves us. His difficulty, it seems to me, is that he has given God attributes which rule out all possible saving explanations. In Mitchell's parable of the Stranger it is easy for the believer to find plausible excuses for ambiguous behaviour: for the Stranger is a man. But suppose the Stranger is God. We cannot say that he would like to help but cannot: God is omnipotent. We cannot say that he would help if he only knew: God is ominiscient. We cannot say that he is not responsible for the wickedness of others: God creates those others. Indeed an omnipotent, omniscient God must be an accessory before (and during) the fact to every human misdeed; as well as being responsible for every non-moral defect in the universe. So, though I entirely concede that Mitchell was absolutely right to insist against me that the theologian's first move is to look for an *explanation*, I still think that in the end, if relentlessly pursued, he will have to resort to the avoiding action of *qualification*. And there lies the danger of that death by a thousand qualifications, which would, I agree, constitute 'a failure in faith as well as in logic'.

Hare's approach is fresh and bold. He confesses that 'on the ground marked out by Flew, he seems to me to be completely victorious'. He therefore introduces the concept of *blik*. But while I think that there is room for some such concept in philosophy, and that philosophers should be grateful to Hare for his invention, I nevertheless want to insist that any attempt to analyse Christian religious utterances as expressions or affirmations of a *blik* rather than as (at least would-be) assertions about the cosmos is fundamentally misguided. *First*, because thus interpreted they would be entirely unorthodox. If Hare's religion really is a *blik*, involving no cosmological assertions about the nature and activities of a supposed personal creator, then surely he is not a Christian at all? *Second*, because thus interpreted, they could scarcely do the job they do. If they were not even intended as assertions then many religious activities would become fraudulent, or merely silly. If 'You ought *because* it is God's will' asserts no more than 'You ought', then the person who prefers the former phraseology is not really giving a reason, but a fraudulent substitute for one, a dialectical dud cheque. If 'My soul must be immortal *because* God loves his children, etc.' asserts no more than 'My soul must be immortal', then the man who reassures himself with theological arguments for immortality is being as silly as the man who tries to clear his overdraft by writing his bank a cheque on the same account. (Of course neither of these utterances would be distinctively Christian: but this discussion never pretended to be so confined.) Religious utterances may indeed express false or even bogus assertions: but I simply do not believe that they are not both intended and interpreted to be or at any rate to presuppose assertions, at least in the context of religious practice; whatever shifts may be demanded, in another context, by the exigencies of theological apologetic.

One final suggestion. The philosophers of religion might well draw upon George Orwell's last appalling nightmare *1984* for the concept of *doublethink*. '*Doublethink* means the power of holding two contradictory beliefs simultaneously, and accepting both of them. The party intellectual knows that he is playing tricks with reality, but by the exercise of *doublethink* he also satisfies himself that reality is not violated' (*1984*, p. 220). Perhaps religious intellectuals too are sometimes driven to doublethink in order to retain their faith in a loving God in face of the reality of a heartless and indifferent world. But of this more another time, perhaps.

WITTGENSTEIN AND FIDEISM

LUDWIG WITTGENSTEIN
Religious Belief

An Austrian general said to someone: "I shall think of you after my death, if that should be possible." We can imagine one group who would find this ludicrous, another who wouldn't.

(During the war, Wittgenstein saw consecrated bread being carried in chromium steel. This struck him as ludicrous.)

Suppose that someone believed in the Last Judgement, and I don't, does this mean that I believe the opposite to him, just that there won't be such a thing? I would say: "not at all, or not always."

Suppose I say that the body will rot, and another says "No. Particles will rejoin in a thousand years, and there will be a Resurrection of you."

If some said: "Wittgenstein, do you believe in this?" I'd say: "No." "Do you contradict the man?" I'd say: "No."

If you say this, the contradiction already lies in this.

Would you say: "I believe the opposite", or "There is no reason to suppose such a thing"? I'd say neither.

Suppose someone were a believer and said: "I believe in a Last Judgement," and I said: "Well, I'm not so sure. Possibly." You would say that there is an enormous gulf between us. If he said "There is a German aeroplane overhead," and I said "Possibly I'm not so sure," you'd say we were fairly near.

It isn't a question of my being anywhere near him, but on an entirely different plane, which you could express by saying: "You mean something altogether different, Wittgenstein."

Ludwig Wittgenstein (1889–1951), one of the major twentieth-century philosophers, studied with Russell at Cambridge. After serving in the Austrian army in World War I, he abandoned philosophy for a decade, not returning to Cambridge until 1929. His major works include *Tractatus Logico-Philosophicus* (1921) and the posthumous publication *Philosophical Investigations* (1953).

RELIGIOUS BELIEF   From *Lectures and Conversations*, ed. Cyril Barrett (University of California Press, 1966). Reprinted by permission of Basil Blackwell Limited and the editor.

The difference might not show up at all in any explanation of the meaning.

Why is it that in this case I seem to be missing the entire point?

Suppose somebody made this guidance for this life: believing in the Last Judgment. Whenever he does anything, this is before his mind. In a way, how are we to know whether to say he believes this will happen or not?

Asking him is not enough. He will probably say he has proof. But he has what you might call an unshakeable belief. It will show, not by reasoning or by appeal to ordinary grounds for belief, but rather by regulating for in all his life.

This is a very much stronger fact—foregoing pleasures, always appealing to this picture. This in one sense must be called the firmest of all beliefs, because the man risks things on account of it which he would not do on things which are by far better established for him. Although he distinguishes between things well-established and not well-established.

Lewy: Surely, he would say it is extremely well-established.

First, he may use "well-established" or not use it at all. He will treat this belief as extremely well-established, and in another way as not well-established at all.

If we have a belief, in certain cases we appeal again and again to certain grounds, and at the same time we risk pretty little—if it came to risking our lives on the ground of this belief.

There are instances where you have a faith—where you say "I believe"—and on the other hand this belief does not rest on the fact on which our ordinary everyday beliefs normally do rest.

How should we compare beliefs with each other? What would it mean to compare them?

You might say: 'We compare the states of mind."

How do we compare states of mind? This obviously won't do for all occasions. First, what you say won't be taken as the measure for the firmness of a belief? But, for instance, what risks you would take?

The strength of a belief is not comparable with the intensity of a pain.

An entirely different way of comparing beliefs is seeing what sorts of grounds he will give.

A belief isn't like a momentary state of mind. "At 5 o'clock he had very bad toothache."

Suppose you had two people, and one of them, when he had to decide which course to take, thought of retribution, and the other did not. One person might, for instance, be inclined to take everything that happened to him as a reward or punishment, and another person doesn't think of this at all.

If he is ill, he may think: "What have I done to deserve this?" This is one way of thinking of retribution. Another way is, he thinks in a general way whenever he is ashamed of himself: "This will be punished."

Take two people, one of whom talks of his behaviour and of what happens to him in terms of retribution, the other one does not. These people think entirely differently. Yet, so far, you can't say they believe different things.

Suppose someone is ill and he says: "This is a punishment," and I say: "If I'm ill, I don't think of punishment at all." If you say: "Do you believe the opposite?"—you can call it believing the opposite, but it is entirely different from what we would normally call believing the opposite.

I think differently, in a different way. I say different things to myself. I have different pictures.

It is this way: if someone said: "Wittgenstein, you don't take illness as punishment, so what do you believe?"—I'd say: "I don't have any thoughts of punishment."

There are, for instance, these entirely different ways of thinking first of all—which needn't be expressed by one person saying one thing, another person another thing.

What we call believing in a Judgment Day or not believing in a Judgment Day—The expression of belief may play an absolutely minor role.

If you ask me whether or not I believe in a Judgement Day, in the sense in which religious people have belief in it, I wouldn't say: "No. I don't believe there will be such a thing." It would seem to me utterly crazy to say this.

And then I give an explanation: "I don't believe in . . .", but then the religious person never believes what I describe.

I can't say. I can't contradict that person.

In one sense, I understand all he says—the English words "God", "separate", etc. I understood. I could say: "I don't believe in this," and this would be true, meaning I haven't got these thoughts or anything that hangs together with them. But not that I could contradict the thing.

You might say: "Well, if you can't contradict him, that means you don't understand him. If you did understand him, then you might." That again is Greek to me. My normal technique of language leaves me. I don't know whether to say they understand one another or not.

These controversies look quite different from any normal controversies. Reasons look entirely different from normal reasons.

They are, in a way, quite inconclusive.

The point is that if there were evidence, this would in fact destroy the whole business.

Anything that I normally call evidence wouldn't in the slightest influence me.

Suppose, for instance, we knew people who foresaw the future; make forecasts for years and years ahead; and they described some sort of a Judgement Day. Queerly enough, even if there were such a thing, and even if it were more convincing than I have described but, belief in this happening wouldn't be at all a religious belief.

Suppose that I would have to forego all pleasures because of such a forecast. If I do so and so, someone will put me in fires in a thousand years, etc. I wouldn't budge. The best scientific evidence is just nothing.

A religious belief might in fact fly in the face of such a forecast, and say "No. There it will break down."

As it were, the belief as formulated on the evidence can only be the last result—in which a number of ways of thinking and acting crystallize and come together.

A man would fight for his life not to be dragged into the fire. No induction. Terror. That is, as it were, part of the substance of the belief.

That is partly why you don't get in religious controversies, the form of controversy where one person is *sure* of the thing, and the other says: 'Well, possibly.'

You might be surprised that there hasn't been opposed to those who believe in Resurrection those who say "Well, possibly."

Here believing obviously plays much more this role: suppose we said that a certain picture might play the role of constantly admonishing me, or I always think of it. Here, an enormous difference would be between those people for whom the picture is constantly in the foreground, and the others who just didn't use it at all.

Those who said: "Well, possibly it may happen and possibly not" would be on an entirely different plane.

This is partly why one would be reluctant to say: "These people rigorously hold the opinion (or view) that there is a Last Judgement". "Opinion" sounds queer.

It is for this reason that different words are used: 'dogma', 'faith'.

We don't talk about hypothesis, or about high probability. Nor about knowing.

In a religious discourse we use such expressions as: "I believe that so and so will happen," and use them differently to the way in which we use them in science.

Although, there is a great temptation to think we do. Because we do talk of evidence, and do talk of evidence by experience.

We could even talk of historic events.

It has been said that Christianity rests on an historic basis.

It has been said a thousand times by intelligent people that indubitability is not enough in this case. Even if there is as much evidence as for Napoleon. Because the indubitability wouldn't be enough to make me change my whole life.

It doesn't rest on an historic basis in the sense that the ordinary belief in historic facts could serve as a foundation.

Here we have a belief in historic facts different from a belief in ordinary historic facts. Even, they are not treated as historical, empirical, propositions.

Those people who had faith didn't apply the doubt which would ordinarily apply to *any* historical propositions. Especially propositions of a time long past, etc.

What is the criterion of reliability, dependability? Suppose you give a general description as to when you say a proposition has a reasonable weight of probability. When you call it reasonable, is this *only* to say that for it you have such and such evidence, and for others you haven't?

For instance, we don't trust the account given of an event by a drunk man.

Father O'Hara[1] is one of those people who make it a question of science.

Here we have people who treat this evidence in a different way. They base things on evidence which taken in one way would seem exceedingly flimsy. They base enormous things on this evidence. Am I to say they are unreasonable? I wouldn't call them unreasonable.

[1] Contribution to a Symposium on *Science and Religion* (Lond: Gerald Howe, 1931, pp. 107–116).

I would say, they are certainly not *reasonable*, that's obvious.

'Unreasonable' implies, with everyone, rebuke.

I want to say: they don't treat this as a matter of reasonability.

Anyone who reads the Epistles will find it said: not only that it is not reasonable, but that it is folly.

Not only is it not reasonable, but it doesn't pretend to be.

What seems to me ludicrous about O'Hara is his making it appear to be *reasonable*.

Why shouldn't one form of life culminate in an utterance of belief in a Last Judgement? But I couldn't either say "Yes" or "No" to the statement that there will be such a thing. Nor "Perhaps," nor "I'm not sure."

It is a statement which may not allow of any such answer.

If Mr. Lewy is religious and says he believes in a Judgement Day, I won't even know whether to say I understand him or not. I've read the same things as he's read. In a most important sense, I know what he means.

If an atheist says: "There won't be a Judgement Day," and another person says there will, do they mean the same?—Not clear what criterion of meaning the same is. They might describe the same things. You might say, this already shows that they mean the same.

We come to an island and we find beliefs there, and certain beliefs we are inclined to call religious. What I'm driving at is, that religious beliefs will not . . . They have sentences, and there are also religious statements.

These statements would not just differ in respect to what they are about. Entirely different connections would make them into religious beliefs, and there can easily be imagined transitions where we wouldn't know for our life whether to call them religious beliefs or scientific beliefs.

You may say they reason wrongly.

In certain cases you would say they reason wrongly, meaning they contradict us. In other cases you would say they don't reason at all, or "It is an entirely different kind of reasoning." The first, you would say in the case in which they reason in a similar way to us, and make something corresponding to our blunders.

Whether a thing is a blunder or not—it is a blunder in a particular system. Just as something is a blunder in a particular game and not in another.

You could also say that where we are reasonable, they are not reasonable—meaning they don't use *reason* here.

If they do something very like one of our blunders, I would say, I don't know. It depends on further surroundings of it.

It is difficult to see, in cases in which it has all the appearances of trying to be reasonable.

I would definitely call O'Hara unreasonable. I would say, if this is religious belief, then it's all superstition.

But I would ridicule it, not by saying it is based on insufficient evidence. I would say: here is a man who is cheating himself. You can say: this man is ridiculous because he believes, and bases it on weak reasons.

D. Z. PHILLIPS
Philosophy, Theology and the Reality of God

What kind of philosophical and theological account does the concept of divine reality call for? To answer this question one must determine the grammar of the concept to be investigated. All too often in the case of the reality of God this requirement has been overlooked or taken for granted. Because the question of divine reality can be construed as 'Is God real or not?' it has often been assumed that the dispute between the believer and the unbeliever is over *a matter of fact*. The philosophical investigation of the reality of God then becomes the philosophical investigation appropriate to an assertion of a matter of fact. That this is a misrepresentation of the religious concept is made obvious by a brief comparison of talk about facts with talk about God.

When do we say, 'It is a fact that . . .' or ask, 'Is it a fact that . . . ?" ? Often, we do so where there is some uncertainty. For example, if the police hear that a wanted criminal has died in some remote part of the world, their reaction might be, 'Check the facts'. Again, we often say that something is a fact in order to rule out other possibilities. A student asks, 'Is the professor coming in today?' and receives the reply, 'No, as a matter of fact he never comes in on Monday.' A fact might not have been: it is conceivable that the wanted criminal had not died, just as it is conceivable that it had been the custom of the professor to come in on Mondays. On the other hand, the religious believer is not prepared to say that God might not exist. It is not that *as a matter of fact* God will always exist, but that it *makes no sense* to say that God might not exist.

We decide the truth or falsity of many matters of fact by taking account of the truth or falsity of other matters of fact. What is to count in deciding whether something is a fact or not is agreed upon in most cases. Refusal to admit that something is a fact in face of the maximum evidence might be cause for alarm, as in the case of someone who sees chairs in a room which in fact is empty. Is this akin to the dispute between the believer and the unbeliever; one sees God, but the other does not? The believer is not like someone who sees objects when they are not there, since his reaction to the absence of factual evidence is not at all like that of the man suffering from hallucinations. In the case of the chairs there is no dispute over *the kind of evidence* needed to settle the issue. When the positivist claims that there is no God because God cannot be located, the believer does not object on the grounds that the investigation has not been thorough enough, but on the grounds that the investigation fails to understand the grammar of what is being investigated—namely, the reality of God.

It makes as little sense to say, 'God's existence is not a fact' as it does to say,

Dewi Z. Phillips (1934–   ) is Professor of Philosophy at the University College, Swansea. Notable among his many publication are *The Concept of Prayer* (1965) and *Religion Without Explanation* (1976).

PHILOSOPHY, THEOLOGY AND THE REALITY OF GOD   From *The Philosophical Quarterly*, vol. 13 (1963), pp. 344–350. Reprinted by permission of the publisher Basil Blackwell Limited and the author.

'God's existence is a fact.' In saying that something either is or is not a fact, I am not describing the 'something' in question. To say that x is a fact is to say something about the grammar of x; it is to indicate what it would and would not be sensible to say or do in connection with it. To say that the concept of divine reality does not share this grammar is to reject the possibility of talking about God in the way in which one talks about matters of fact. I suggest that more can be gained if one compares the question, 'What kind of reality is divine reality?' not with the question, 'Is this physical object real or not?' but with the different question, 'What kind of reality is the reality of physical objects?'. To ask whether physical objects are real is not like asking whether this appearance is real or not where often one can find out. I can find out whether unicorns are real or not, but how can I find out whether the physical world is real or not? This latter question is not about the possibility of carrying out an investigation. It is a question of whether it is possible to speak of truth and falsity in the physical world; a question prior to that of determining the truth or falsity of any particular matter of fact. Similarly, the question of the reality of God is a question of the possibility of sense and nonsense, truth and falsity, in religion. When God's existence is construed as a matter of fact, it is taken for granted that the concept of God is at home within the conceptual framework of the reality of the physical world. It is as if we said, 'We know where the assertion of God's existence belongs, we understand what kind of assertion it is; all we need do is determine its truth or falsity.' But to ask a question about the reality of God is to ask a question about *a kind of reality*, not about the reality of *this* or *that*, in much the same way as asking a question about the reality of physical objects is not to ask about the reality of this or that physical object.

What then is the appropriate philosophical investigation of the reality of God? Suppose one asks, 'His reality as opposed to what?" The possibility of the unreality of God does not occur *within* any religion, but it might well arise in disputes *between* religious. A believer of one religion might say that the believers of other religions were not worshipping the same God. The question how he would decide the identity of God is connected in many ways with what it means to talk of divine reality.

In a dispute over whether two people are discussing the same person there are ways of removing the doubt, but the identity of a god is not like the identity of a human being. To say that one worships the same God as someone else is not to point to the same object or to be confronted with it. How did Paul, for example, know that the God he worshipped was also the God of Abraham? What enabled him to say this was not anything like an objective method of agreement as in the case of two astronomers who check whether they are talking of the same star? What enabled Paul to say that he worshipped the God of Abraham was the fact that although many changes had taken place in the concept of God, there was nevertheless a common religious tradition in which both he and Abraham stood. To say that a god is not the same as one's own God involves saying that those who believe in him are in a radically different religious tradition from one's own. The criteria of what can sensibly be said of God are to be found *within* the religious tradition. This conclusion has an important bearing on the question of what account of religion philosophy and theology can give. It follows from my argument that the criteria of meaningfulness cannot be found *outside* religion, since they are given by religious discourse itself. Theology can claim justifiably to show what is meaningful in religion only when it has an internal relation to religious discourse. Philosophy can make the same claim only if it is prepared to examine religious concepts in the contexts from which they derive their meaning.

Some theologians have claimed that theology gives a justification of religion. E. L. Mascall, for instance, says: 'The primary task of rational theology is to ask what grounds can be found for asserting the existence of God.'[1]

Mascall implies that theology is external to religion and seeks a rational justification of religious truth. This view differs sharply from what I claim to be the internal role of theology in religion. This role can be explained as follows.

One cannot have religion without religious discourse. This is taught to children through stories by which they become acquainted with the attributes of God. As a result of this teaching the child forms an idea of God. We have far less idea than we sometimes suppose of what the nature of the child's idea is, but for our purposes its content is irrelevant. What is relevant to note is that the child does not listen to the stories, observe religious practices, reflect on all this, and then form an idea of God out of the experience. The idea of God is being formed in the actual story-telling and religious services. To ask which came first, the story-telling or the idea of God, is to ask a senseless question. Once one has an idea of God, what one has is a primitive theology. This is in many ways far removed from the theology of the professional theologian, but what makes it far removed is a difference in complexity or maturity, not a difference in kind or function. In each case theology decides what it makes sense to say to God and about God. In short, theology is the grammar of religious discourse.

There is a limited analogy between the relation of theology to religious discourse and the relation of logic to language. One cannot have a language without a logic, although one can have a language without explicitly formulated logical principles. On the other hand, logical principles can have no meaning apart from the language in which they are found. This is not refuted by the fact that the meaning of a formal system can be explained in terms of the rules of that system. The question remains whether the possibility of any such system is dependent on the existence of language. The argument appears circular and contradictory if one thinks of either logic or language as being prior to the other. But as in the case the child's stories and the concept of God, to ask which came first is to ask a senseless question. As soon as one has language one has logic which determines what can and what cannot be said in that language without being prior to it. As soon as one has religious discourse one has a theology which determines what it will be sensible to say and what it will be nonsensical to say within that religious discourse without being prior to it.

The limited nature of the analogy is evident when we want to talk of alternative theologies. To understand the need for a new theology, the need for a revised

[1] *Existence and Analogy*, I.

grammar of religious discourse, it is more helpful to consider an analogy with the development of scientific laws. In the course of scientific experimentation, in order to account for new phenomena, scientific laws have to be modified or changed. One would not say that the old laws are wrong, or that the new ones are nearer the truth, but simply that they differ in their range of application. There is an analogy here with the way in which old ideas of God are supplanted and new ones take their place. This will not seem arbitrary if one remembers that the need for a new theology, for a different idea of God, does not occur *in vacuo*. The development of scientific laws can only be understood by reference to the tradition of scientific enquiry, and the changes in the idea of God can only be understood in terms of a developing religion. This is not to say that the role of the concept of God is akin to the role of a scientific model, for the analogy with developing scientific laws, like the analogy with logic and language, is a limited one. I use it simply to re-emphasize the internal relation of theology to religion.

Theology cannot impose criteria of meaningfulness on religion from without. Neither can philosophy. Mascall, on the other hand, maintains that like theology, philosophy has a special role to play, namely to seek rational grounds for asserting the existence of God. This view misrepresents the relation of philosophy to religion. The role of philosophy in this context is not to justify, but to understand. Mascall says of the Christian: 'He knows what he means by God because the Bible and the Church have told him. He can then institute a purely rational enquiry into the grounds for asserting that God exists.'[2]

Why not remain with an understanding of what the Bible and the Church teach? What extra is this rational enquiry supposed to achieve? This question might be answered by indicating the problems connected with the existence of a plurality of religions. If one accepts the internal relation of theology to religion and the religious tradition as the means of identifying God, what is one to say of the conflicting claims of different religions? In much the same spirit in which I have been talking about the relation of theology to religion, Peter Winch says:

> . . . criteria of logic are not a direct gift of God, but arise out of, and are only intelligible in the context of, ways of living or modes of social life. It follows that one cannot apply criteria of logic to modes of social life as such. For instance, science is one such mode and religion is another; and each has criteria of intelligibility peculiar to itself. So within science or religion actions can be logical or illogical . . . in religion it would be illogical to suppose that one could pit one's strength against God's . . . But we cannot sensibly say that either the practice of science itself or that of religion is either illogical or logical; both are non-logical.[3]

But can this thesis hold in face of a plurality of religions? The problem is brought out if one considers the way in which the analogy between theology, logic and scientific laws which we have considered breaks down. In the development of scientific laws there is eventual agreement that such development is desirable. The

[2] *Ibid.*, 17.

[3] *The Idea of a Social Science*, 90–1.

same could be said, roughly speaking, of the development of the idea of God in the Old Testament. But this need not be true of modern developments in theology: opposing theologians will stick to their respective positions and declare the others to be wrong. This brings up the question of authority or reference to an authoritative system. Both logic and science are *public* in so far as it can be decided whether a statement is logical or illogical, or whether a given practice is scientific or not. Illogical and non-scientific statements are refutable. But because of the nature of theology one may only say that a religious statement is refuted by *a* theology. There is no analogy here with either logic or science. This is due to what might be called *the personal element* in theology. In the formulation of logical and scientific principles there is no personal element involved. This is not true of theology.

As I have already said, the systematic theology is a sophistication of that theology which is necessarily present in so far as religious language is present. The theological system is often constructed to answer certain questions and problems which may arise. But the foundation of a theological system is based on the non-formalized theology which is within the religious way of life carried on by the person who is constructing the theological system. In so far as this is true, theology is personal, since it is based on one's own experience of God. Where the connection between theology and experience is missing, there is a danger of theology becoming an academic game.

It is extremely difficult to steer a course between the personal and the public in this whole question. Theology must be personal in so far as it is concerned with one's own idea of God, and in this context religion must always be personal. On the other hand, in so far as religious language must be learnt, religion is public. One cannot have *any* idea of God. Once one has embraced theology, one has established 'what can be said' in that particular religion, but what can be said does not depend on the fact that an *individual* is saying it.

Some philosophers have held that in face of theological differences *within* religions and the more pronounced theological differences *between* religions, philosophy itself must decide what are the meaningful religious assertions. This view is expressed in no uncertain terms by Peter Munz in his book, *Problems of Religious Knowledge*. In face of the plurality of religious traditions Munz thinks it foolish to identify the truth with any *one* of them. On the other hand, he also objects to saying that religious truth is *the sum* of religious traditions. One of Munz's aims is '. . . to enquire whether it is not possible to find a criterion of religious truth which would enable us to avoid the identification of religious truth with any one provincial or with the alleged cosmopolitan tradition.'[4]

Munz thinks that such a criterion can be found in philosophy: '. . . the philosophy of religion imposes its own criterion of what is good theological reasoning and what is bad theological reasoning. And in doing this, it ceases to be purely descriptive of religious knowledge and begins to be normative.'[5]

Munz's disagreement with Winch is obvious. He thinks that the norm of truth

[4] *Problems of Religious Knowledge*, 9.

[5] *Ibid.*, 28.

and falsity is not to be found within religion, but *outside* it. One reason why he thinks that philosophical criteria of theological reasoning are needed is the absence of real discussion between adherents of different religions. He describes the contact that does occur as follows: 'These arguments are therefore no more than affirmations of positions. They are monologues. A real argument must be a dialogue, an exchange of opinions and a weighing of evidence. Only a *real* argument can be more than an exercise in self-assertion. But to argue *really*, one must be clear as to the things one is arguing about.'[6]

Munz says more than he realizes in the last sentence of the above quotation. In order for adherents of different religions to talk to each other, they must have something to talk about! But this is a religious matter, not a philosophical one. Philosophical speculation may help to distinguish religion from superstition, but where *religions* are concerned, whether they have enough in common to promote discussion depends on the content of their beliefs. No general answer is possible. In some cases, for instance between Christians and Jews, a wealth of discussion is possible. Between others—Christians and Buddhists, say—discussion is more difficult. When one considers tribal religions, one wonders whether one is talking about the same thing at all; whether here religion has a different meaning. The possibility of discussion then depends, not as Munz suggests on the intervention of philosophy from without, but on the theologies of the religions in question. If there were a union of religions this would be because of changes within the religions united. One might object to my analysis on the grounds that it stresses religious meaning at the expense of religious truth. The analysis does not indicate which religion is the true one. But why should anyone suppose that philosophy can answer that question?

One final objection. An opponent of religion might claim that far from leaving the questions of religious truth unanswered, I have guaranteed that any possible answer is favourable to religion by insisting that the criteria of intelligibility in religious matters are to be found within religion. The objection confuses my epistemological thesis with an absurd religious doctrine. To say that the criteria of truth and falsity in religion are to be found within a religious tradition is to say nothing of the truth or falsity of the religion in question. On the contrary, my thesis is as necessary in explaining unbelief as it is in explaining belief. It is because many have seen religion for what it is that they have thought it important to rebel against it. The rebel sees what religion is and rejects it. What can this 'seeing' be? Obviously, he does not see the point of religion as the believer does, since for the believer seeing the point of religion is believing. Nevertheless, the rebel has knelt in the church even if he has not prayed. He has taken the sacrament of Communion even if he has not communed. He knows the story from the inside, but it is not a story that captivates him. Nevertheless, he can see what religion is supposed to do and what it is supposed to be. At times we stand afar off saying, 'I wish I could be like that.' We are not like that, but we know what it must be like. The rebel stands on the threshold of religion seeing what it must be

[6]*Ibid.*, 11.

like, but saying, 'I do not want to be like that. I rebel against it all.' It is in this context, as Camus has said, that 'every blasphemy is, ultimately, a participation in holiness'.

KAI NIELSEN
A Critique of Wittgensteinian Fideism

I

It is a fundamental religious belief of Jews and Christians that a human being's chief end is to glorify God and to enjoy Him forever. Human beings are not simply creatures who will rot and die, but they will survive the death of their present bodies. They will, after the Last Judgment, if they are saved, come into a blissful union with God, free finally of all sin, and they will be united in Heaven in human brotherhood and love. But for now, that is, in our "earthly" condition of life, we stand in division both inwardly as self-divided creatures and against each other as well; a kingdom of heaven on earth is far from being realized. We humans—or so Jews and Christians believe—are sinful creatures standing before the God of mercy and of love whose forgiveness we need and to whom everything is owed.

The thing to see here is that being a Jew or a Christian is not just the having of one framework-belief, namely a belief that there is a God. And it is not just, as some philosophers seem to assume, the having of that belief and the having of another, namely that we will survive the death of our bodies. Rather, as Wittgenstein and Malcolm stress, what we have with a religion is a system, or as I would prefer to call it, a cluster of interlocking beliefs, qualifying and giving each other sense and mutual support.[1] We have here a world-picture which not only tells us, or purports to tell us, what is the case but orients and guides our lives and can touch profoundly—if we can accept such a world-picture—our hopes and expectations as well. To be a Jew or a Christian is to be a person whose sense of self and sense of the meaningfulness of life is tied up with that world-picture.

Kai Nielsen (1925–   ) is Professor of Philosophy at the University of Calgary. Among his works in philosophy of religion are *Scepticism* (1973) and *Philosophy and Atheism* (1985).

A CRITIQUE OF WITTGENSTEINIAN FIDEISM   From *The Autonomy of Religious Belief: A Critical Inquiry*, edited by Frederick Crosson. © 1981 by University of Notre Dame Press. Reprinted by permission.

[1] Ludwig Wittgenstein, *On Certainty*, trans. Denis Paul and G. E. M. Anscombe (Oxford: Basil Blackwell, 1969) and Norman Malcolm, "The Groundlessness of Belief," in Stuart C. Brown, ed., *Reason and Religion* (Ithaca, N.Y.: Cornell University Press, 1977), pp. 143–57.

It has seemed to many philosophers, believers and nonbelievers alike, that key concepts in this world-picture—God, heaven, hell, sin, the Last Judgment, a human being's chief end, being resurrected and coming to be a new man with a new body—are all in one degree or another problematic concepts whose very intelligibility or rational acceptability are not beyond reasonable doubt. Yet it is just this skeptical thrust—or so at least it would appear—that Wittgenstein and certain Wittgensteinians oppose as itself a product of *philosophical* confusion.[2] In the systemic home of various ongoing and deeply entrenched language-games, these concepts have a place, and in that context they are, and must be, perfectly in order as they are. Within those language-games no genuine questions of their intelligibility or rational acceptability can arise and criticisms from the outside—from the vantage point of some other language-game—are always irrelevant, for the criteria of intelligibility or rational acceptability are always in part dependent on a particular language-game.[3] It might be thought that the phrase "genuine question" in the above is a tip-off marking what in effect is a *persuasive* definition and showing, as clearly as can be, that such questions can and do arise over such general criteria within the parameters of such language-games. But the response would be that no one who commanded a clear view of what she or he was saying and doing would try to make such a challenge or search for such general criteria of intelligibility or rationality, for she would be perfectly aware that she had no place to stand in trying to gain such a critical vantage point. There just are no criteria of intelligibility or rationality *Überhaupt*.[4] Such a person has and can have no Archimedian point in accordance with which she could carry out such a critique.

Genuine criticism, such Wittgensteinians argue, will have to proceed piece-meal and within the parameters of these different but often interlocking language-games. Critique, if it is to cut deep and be to the point, must be concrete (specific) and involve an extended examination of the forms of life from *within*. For such a criticism to be a genuine possibility the critics must have a sensitive participant's or participant-like understanding of these forms of life as they are exhibited in the language-games with which they are matched. (Perhaps it is more adequate to say the language-games are embedded in forms of life!)

[2] Wittgenstein in *On Certainty* and again in a somewhat different way in his *Philosophical Investigations*. See Rush Rhees, *Without Answers* (London: Routledge and Kegan Paul, 1969); the article cited in the previous note from Malcolm; D. Z. Phillips, *The Concept of Prayer* (London: Routledge and Kegan Paul, 1965), *Death and Immortality* (New York: St. Martin's Press, 1970), *Faith and Philosophical Enquiry* (London: Routledge and Kegan Paul, 1970) and *Religion Without Explanation* (Oxford: Basil Blackwell, 1976); Ilham Dilman, "Wisdom's Philosophy of Religion," *Canadian Journal of Philosophy*, vol. V, no. 4 (December, 1975) and "Wittgenstein on the Soul," in G. Vesey, ed., *Understanding Wittgenstein* (London: Macmillan, 1974).

[3] In addition to the above references, note as well Peter Winch, "Understanding a Primitive Society," in Bryan R. Wilson, ed., *Rationality* (Oxford: Basil Blackwell, 1970) and "Meaning and Religious Language," in Stuart Brown, ed., *Reason and Religion*.

[4] See the above references to Phillips and Winch and, most centrally, Wittgenstein, *On Certainty*. I discuss further facets of this in my "Reasonable Belief Without Justification," in *Body, Mind and Method: Essays in Honor of Virgil C. Aldrich*, Donald Gustafson and Bangs L. Tapscott, eds. (Dordrecht, Holland: D. Reidel, 1979).

In such a context criticism is in order and is an indispensable tool in the *development* of a tradition, but there is—so the claim goes—no genuinely relevant criticism possible of language-games as a whole or of forms of life. There is no coherent sense, such Wittgensteinians argue, in which we can speak of a confused language-game or an irrational form of life or of a full-fledged, conceptually distinct practice which is irrational or incoherent.[5] Our language-games are rooted in these practices and are not in need of justification or of a foundation. In fact the whole idea of foundations or grounds or justification here is without sense. Foundationalism is a philosophical mythology. There is no logic which can give us the *a priori* order of the world. Rather our logical distinctions are found in or become a codification of distinctions found in our various language-games. But the sense—the intelligibility—of our language-games cannot be coherently questioned. There is, they claim, no coherent sense to the phrase "a confused language-game" or "a confused but conceptually distinct practice" or "an irrational form of life." We indeed have a deep philosophical penchant to go on to question, to ask for foundations for, to try to justify such practices, language-games, or forms of life. But it is just here that we fall into transcendental illusions. We do not recognize the import of Wittgenstein's full stop and we dream of justification where none exists or even could exist.

Both understanding and genuine criticism must, initially at least, proceed by seeing how the various concepts interlock and how in the form of a whole system—a cluster of concepts—they make sense. There is no understanding them in isolation. We come to understand their use by coming to see their place—their various roles—in the system. There is no understanding "the chief end of man" outside of something like a religious context and there is no understanding the distinctive end of man envisioned by Christianity without understanding its concept of God. And there is no, so the claim goes, even tolerable understanding of Christianity's concept of God without understanding the Christian concept of the end of man and man's highest good. And in turn to understand that, it is necessary to make sense of a man's surviving the death of his present body and coming to have a resurrection body in a resurrection world. There is no more breaking away the Christian conception of the end of man or man's highest good from such cosmological conceptions than there is a way of breaking away the conception of the Last Judgment from them. And in turn the concepts of heaven, blissful union with God, human brotherhood, love, and sin do not stand on their own feet but gain their distinctively Christian sense from their interlocking with these other concepts of Christian life. These concepts and many others like them cluster together, and we cannot understand them in isolation. Moreover, they stand and fall together.

II

Yet, these crucial Wittgensteinian points notwithstanding, there is a certain probing of those concepts which is quite natural and which can—or so it at least

---

[5] Most of the above references are pertinent here but note, as well, D. Z. Phillips, "Philosophers, Religion and Conceptual Change," in John King-Farlow, ed., *The Challenge of Religion Today* (New York: Neale Watson Academic Publications, 1976), pp. 190–200.

appears—be carried out in relative isolation from the examination of the other concepts of the cluster, provided we have something like a participant's grasp of the whole cluster. We, in wondering about the resurrection body in the resurrection world, naturally wonder how identity is preserved in the switch or in the resurrection or reconstitution of the body. Who is it that is me in the interim between the decay of the "old body" and the emergence of the "new" one, and in what space and in what world in relation to our present familiar world of everyday life and physics is this resurrection world? Is it even logically or conceptually possible for a rocket to be shot up to it? Somehow this all seems fatuous— a plain getting of it wrong—but what then is a getting of it right, what is it that we are talking about, and does it make sense? Does it help our understanding at all to say that we must just understand it in its own terms? Does it help particularly the perplexities we feel at this juncture to relate such conceptions to the other conceptions in our religious language-game? It is not at all clear to me that, about these particular worries, it does help much, if at all, to relate these philosophically perplexing conceptions to other religious conceptions.

Even more important is the role of the concept of God here. While gaining its meaning in a certain determinate context in a cluster of concepts, the concept of God can still have, in relative isolation, certain questions addressed to it. We glorify God and find our chief joy in Him, but *who* or *what* is this God we enjoy and how appropriate is the use of personal pronouns in such talk? We have the word 'God' but is it a proper name, an abbreviated definite description, a special kind of descriptive predicable or what? It surely appears to be some kind of referring expression, but what does it refer to? How could we be acquainted with, or could we be acquainted with or otherwise come to know, what it stands for or characterizes? How do we—or do we—identify God, how do we individuate God, what are we talking about when we talk of God, do we succeed in making any successful reference when we speak of God? What or who is this God we pray to, love, find our security in, make sense of our lives in terms of, and the like? Our cluster of religious concepts will help us somewhat here. We know He is the God of love who transcends in His might and mystery our paltry understanding. *Some* Jews and Christians believe He is that being whom we will somehow meet face to face when we are resurrected and our sins are washed away, and we know that He is a being of infinite mercy and love with whom we may somehow, someday, be in blissful union in a world without division, strife, or alienation, where love and brotherhood (sisterhood) prevail. This helps to some extent to locate God in *conceptual* space but only to some extent, for still the nagging question persists: *what* is it or *who* is it that is this being of infinite love, mercy, power, and understanding of whom we stand in need? What literally are we talking about when we speak of this being or what kind of reality or putative reality do we speak of when we speak of or even talk to God? (If we have no conception of what it is to speak literally here, then we can have no understanding of the possibility of speaking metaphorically or analogically either, for the possibility of the latter is parasitic on the possibility of the former.) Suppose someone says there is no reality here and 'God' answers to nothing at all—stands for, makes reference to, nothing at all. How are we to answer him and show he is mistaken? And how are we to answer the other chap who looks on the scene and says he does not know how to decide such an issue? He does not understand what it would be like to succeed in making reference with 'God', but not knowing that, he also does not know—indeed cannot know—that 'God' does *not* stand for anything either. If we don't understand what could count as success, how could we understand what could count as failure? All these people can play Jewish or Christian language-games with such a cluster of concepts, but they remain thoroughly perplexed about what, if anything, they are talking about in speaking of God. If that is so, how can we possibly be justified in saying that the concepts in question are unproblematic and are in order as they are? We know what it is religious people do with such words; we can do similar things with words as well, and we understand full well the uses of language involved. We could do it all quite competently in a play if necessary. But though we can speak and act and at least seem to share a common understanding, we cannot decide whether 'God' does, or even could (given its meaning), secure reference—stand for something, refer to something actually real, and we do not agree about or understand how to go about settling or resolving or even dissolving that issue. But how then can these key concepts or conceptions be unproblematic?

III

Some, whom I have called—perhaps tendentiously—Wittgensteinian Fideists, would respond that the core mistake in what I have been arguing is that I continue to construe God as an object or a thing or entity of some sort. That this is a governing assumption for me, as it is for Flew as well, is revealed in my and his repeated request for a specification of the referent (denotation) of 'God', in our asking repeatedly *who* or *what* is God.[6] We both are, it could be argued, looking for the substance answering to the substantive and sometimes at least that is a mistake of such an order as to show a fundamental confusion about the logic of God. It confuses the surface grammar of the concept with its depth grammar.

There is no more question, they claim, of finding out whether God exists than there is of finding out whether physical objects exist. The putative question "Is God real?" makes no more sense than does the question-form "Do material objects exist?" It is true that a man who rejects religious belief and does not believe in God is not cut off from reason—is not thereby shown to be irrational—as is the man who does not believe there are any physical objects. Indeed we would not know what to make of a child's doubting the reality of physical objects, but we would understand very well a child's not believing in God or an adult's coming not to believe in God. The kind of unquestionable propositions that Moore and Wittgenstein take to be bedrock unquestionable propositions may, in their normal employments in normal contexts, very well be propositions it really makes no sense to question. They are framework beliefs. Whatever other differences they may exhibit, they are propositions which are not, or at least so these Wittgensteinians claim, *testable empirically* and thus are, in that way, not grounded in

[6] See my *Contemporary Critiques of Religion* (New York: Herder and Herder, 1971) and my *Scepticism* (New York: St. Martin's, 1973), and see A. G. N. Flew's *God and Philosophy* (London: Hutchinson, 1966) and A. G. N. Flew's *The Presumption of Atheism* (New York: Barnes and Noble, 1976).

experience.[7] There is no finding out whether they are true or false. The fact that the basic teachings of religion cannot properly be called knowledge should cease to be paradoxical, shocking, or perplexing when we reflect on this and on the fact that these various framework beliefs—certain of them as we are—are still not bits of knowledge. Moreover, that is not distinctive of religion and ideology but is a feature, as Wittgenstein shows, of many quite unproblematic domains as well.[8] All language-games have their framework propositions and, as they are something we cannot be mistaken about or in any way test or establish, they are not bits of knowledge. Doubting, establishing, believing, finding out, and knowing are activities which only make sense within the confines of language-games, and they require each other for any such single activity to be possible. But such contrastive conceptions cannot be applied to the framework propositions themselves. And while it is perfectly true that cultural changes can and do bring about changes in what we do and do not regard as reasonable, what realism requires, Wittgenstein argues, is a recognition that we do not have and cannot come to have a historical vantage point which will tell us what, such historical contexts apart, is "really reasonable."[9] (Indeed such talk may very well have no coherent sense.) What we have in various areas are different and often incommensurable beliefs which are, for many at least, unshakable beliefs which regulate their lives. But there is no finding out, which, if any of them, are really true. There is, such Wittgensteinians argue, no establishing "philosophical foundations" which show that some or all of them have a rational underpinning. Such rationalist hopes are utterly misguided.[10]

To understand what we mean by 'God', to grasp its role in the stream of life, is to come to understand its role in such religious activities as worship, prayer, and the praise of God. That is where we come to understand what it is that we believe in when we believe in God. That is where the experience of God will have some reality, and it is in those surroundings that "Thou art God" has a clear sense. There God becomes a reality in our lives, and it is there where it becomes clear to us that the existence of God is neither a theoretical nor a quasi-theoretical nor even a metaphysical question. We respond, if we are religious, to religious talk, and on certain appropriate occasions some of us even sing out "God is our God above all other Gods." Some Wittgensteinians have even claimed that "God exists" in its actual logical form (its depth grammar) is not something which actually is, as it appears to be, in the indicative mood. Most definitely, such Wittgensteinians claim, it is not a statement of fact or even a putative statement of fact. 'God', they also claim, is not a term concerning which it makes any sense at all to look for its referent. In Christian and Jewish language-games "God is real" is a grammatical truth.

[7]Norman Malcolm, "The Groundlessness of Belief."

[8]Ludwig Wittgenstein, *On Certainty* and G. H. von Wright, "Wittgenstein On Certainty," in G. H. von Wright, ed., *Problems in the Theory of Knowledge* (The Hague: Martinus Nijhoff, 1972), pp. 47–60.

[9]Wittgenstein, *On Certainty*, pp. 43 and 80.

[10]Again, *On Certainty* seems to me a crucial reference here. See also Stanley Cavell, *Must We Mean What We Say?* (New York: Charles Scribner's Sons, 1969).

IV

These claims deserve a critical reception. "God is unreal. God is but a figment of our imaginations borne of our deepest needs" are not deviant English sentences. There are a number of language-games in which such talk is quite at home. But as believers don't speak that way, it will be claimed that the above skeptical utterances are not at home in religious language-games. (But again, believers could act in a play and speak that way or write novels, as Dostoevsky did, in which characters say such things.) At least some believers understand such talk and there are many ex-believers and doubting Thomases and people struggling in various ways with religious belief. In their struggles and in their expectable and understandable wrestlings with faith, such talk has a home. Questions about whether God is really a figment of our imagination quite naturally arise. Moreover, their typical contexts are not the bizarre and metaphysical contexts in which we can ask whether physical objects are real or whether memory beliefs are even reliable. In our lives, that is, they are, for believer and nonbeliever alike, not idling questions like "Is time real?"

It might be responded that it is necessary to recognize that for a medieval man asking "Is God real?" would be such an idling metaphysical question. Perhaps that is so—though that would have to be shown; after all, Machiavelli was a late medieval man—but, whatever we should say for the medievals, what is true in cultures such as ours is that such questions repeatedly arise in nonphilosophical contexts where the engine is not idling. Why are they not in order in those contexts? What grounds have we for saying they are not real doubts or that they would never be asked by anyone who understood what he was asking? That some people—even that many people—do not question these propositions does not show they are "unquestionable propositions." That they are plainly not *just* theoretical questions does not show that they are not theoretical at all. Perhaps changes over time and, in our culture, about what is taken to be reasonable and what is not, have changed our responses to these questions and our attitudes toward worship, praise, and prayer? But then we need to recognize just that and consider what that involves and what philosophical significance it has.

It is indeed true that we need an understanding of God-talk to understand the sense of sentences such as "I take my illness as a punishment," "Your sins are forgiven," "God is merciful to sinners," and "He has experienced God's mercy," but we also need, to understand them properly, to see how they fit into a system. (We can speak of a "system of salvation" and we need not think of it as a theoretical system.) But none of this precludes or makes unnecessary asking about the referent (alleged referent) of 'God'. Granted 'God' does not stand for an object among objects, but still what does 'God' stand for? None of the above has shown that to be a pseudoquestion.

V

Wittgensteinians—as is most evident in the work of Winch, Dilman, and Phillips—try very hard to avoid facing that issue. Indeed they struggle to show that in reality there is no such issue at all.[11] I have tried to expose the nerve of some of the issues here and to maintain against them that there appears at least to be a real issue here.

Wittgensteinians will contend that language-games and forms of life are neither well-founded nor ill-founded. They are just there like our lives. Our understanding of them and assurance concerning them is shown by the way we go on—by how we employ them—whether we claim, in our philosophical moments, to understand them or not. There is no showing that the evaluative conceptions and norms, including the norms of reasonability embedded in them, require a justification, a foundation, or even an explanation. Indeed, if they are right, the first two are impossible and even the third (i.e., that they require explanation) may be impossible as well, but, impossible or not, such things are unnecessary. The urge to attempt such justifications and explanations is very deep—as deep as the very subject that has traditionally been called "philosophy." But Wittgenstein schools us to resist this urge. If he is near to the mark, reason—the use by human beings of the various canons of rationality—requires that we resist it. Such general inquiries about religion and reality are senseless. There neither is nor can be a *philosophical* underpinning of religion or anything else. But such philosophical foundationalism is not needed. It is not something the loss of which undermines our capacity to make sense of our lives. Bad philosophy gives us the illusion that religion requires such a foundation and sometimes succeeds in so infiltrating religious conceptions that they do come to have incoherent elements which should not be accepted. Good philosophy will help us spot and excise those nonsensical, metaphysical elements. But when purified of such extraneous metaphysical elements, religious belief is both foundationless and not in the slightest need of foundations or of some philosophical justification.

I do not intend here to rise to the fundamental metaphilosophical issues raised by this Wittgensteinian rejection of the search for "philosophical foundations." Such a way of viewing things is plainly less popular now than when Wittgenstein and some of his followers first pressed it home. Yet it seems to me that philosophers have not so much answered it, or shown it to be a pointless lament, as simply to have ignored it. I think that this is a mistake and that a philosophical practice that survives taking this challenge seriously will look very different indeed from the practices that went before it.

However, I don't want to speak of that grand issue here but only to face some of its implications for religion, if one takes to heart Wittgenstein's critique of the pretensions of philosophy. I agree, of course, that religion can have no such philosophical or metaphysical foundations. I do not even have a tolerably clear sense of what it means to say that there is some *distinctive philosophical* knowledge that would give us "the true grounds" of religious belief. I am no more concerned than are the Wittgensteinians to defend such a metaphysical religiosity and I am

---

[11] Such accounts have been powerfully criticized by Robert C. Coburn, "Animadversions on a Wittgensteinian Apologetic," *Perkins Journal*, Spring 1971, pp. 25–36, and by Michael Durrant, "Is the Justification of Religious Belief a Possible Enterprise?" *Religious Studies*, vol. 9 (1971), pp. 440–54 and in his "Some Comments on 'Meaning and Religious Language,' " in Stuart Brown, ed., *Reason and Religion*, pp. 222–32.

not concerned to replace it with some distinctive atheological *"philosophical knowledge."*

However, our perplexities and difficulties about God and religion are not just in a second-order context where the engine is idling. Most of them are not like perplexities about how we can know whether there is an external world or whether induction is justified or whether our memory beliefs are ever reliable. It is not just the talk about God-talk that perplexes us but certain central bits of the first-order talk itself. People with a common culture and a common set of language-games are very much at odds over whether we can know or justifiably believe that there is a God and this can be, and often is, linked for some with an intense desire to believe in God or, for that matter (though much less frequently), not to believe in God. It is common ground between myself and Wittgensteinian Fideists that we do not think that there is any metaphysical Santa Claus that is going to provide us with answers here, to wit with some distinctively "metaphysical knowledge" which will assure us that there is or is not, must or cannot be, that putative reality for which 'God' is the English term.

Using their own procedures, procedures I take within a certain scope to be perfectly proper, I started by looking at religious language-games we all can play and concerning which we at least have a knowledge by *wont*. When we look at certain religious language-games and—indeed from inside them—put questions which are perfectly natural, questions that plain people ask, and ask without suffering from metaphysical hunger, we will see that perplexities *arise* about to whom or to what we could be praying, supplicating, or even denying when we talk in this manner. Where 'God' is construed nonanthropomorphically, as we must construe 'God' if our conception is not to betray our belief as a superstition, it appears at least to be the case that we do not understand who or what it is we believe in when we speak of believing in God. It is not just that we do not understand these matters very well—that is certainly to be expected and is quite tolerable—but that we are utterly at sea here.

Such considerations make skepticism about the reality of such a conception very real indeed. And that very skepticism—as Dostoevsky teaches us—can even come from someone who has a genuine need or at least a desire to believe. That skepticism is common enough and, if I am near to my mark, could be well-founded, even in complete innocence of or in utter irony about philosophical foundations for or against religious belief.

RELIGIOUS PLURALISM

JOHN HICK
The New Map of the Universe of Faiths

Let me begin this chapter by proposing a working definition of religion as an understanding of the universe, together with an appropriate way of living within it, which involves reference beyond the natural world to God or gods or to the Absolute or to a transcendent order or process. Such a definition includes such theistic faiths as Judaism, Christianity, Islam, Sikhism; the theistic Hinduism of the Bhagavad Gītā; the semi-theistic faith of Mahayana Buddhism and the non-theistic faiths of Theravada Buddhism and non-theistic Hinduism. It does not however include purely naturalistic systems of belief, such as communism and humanism, immensely important though these are today as alternatives to religious faith.

When we look back into the past we find that religion has been a virtually universal dimension of human life—so much so that man has been defined as the religious animal. For he has displayed an innate tendency to experience his environment as being religiously as well as naturally significant, and to feel required to live in it as such. To quote the anthropologist, Raymond Firth, 'religion is universal in human societies'.[1] 'In every human community on earth today', says Wilfred Cantwell Smith, 'there exists something that we, as sophisticated observers, may term religion, or a religion. And we are able to see it in each case as the latest development in a continuous tradition that goes back, we can now affirm, for at least one hundred thousand years.'[2] In the life of primitive man this religious tendency is expressed in a belief in sacred objects, endowed with *mana*, and in a multitude of nature and ancestral spirits needing to be carefully propitiated. The divine was here crudely apprehended as a plurality of quasianimal forces which could to some extent be controlled by ritualistic and magical procedures.

THE NEW MAP OF THE UNIVERSE OF FAITHS   From *God and the Universe of Faiths* by John Hick (St. Martin's Press, 1973). Reprinted by permission of Macmillan, London and Basingstoke.

[1] *Elements of Social Organisation*, 3rd ed. (London: Tavistock Publications, 1969), p. 216.

[2] *The Meaning and End of Religion* (New York: Mentor Books, 1963) p. 22.

This represents the simplest beginning of man's awareness of the transcendent in the infancy of the human race—an infancy which is also to some extent still available for study in the life of primitive tribes today.

The development of religion and religions begins to emerge into the light of recorded history as the third millennium B.C. moves towards the period around 2000 B.C. There are two main regions of the earth in which civilisation seems first to have arisen and in which religions first took a shape that is at least dimly discernible to us as we peer back through the mists of time—these being Meso-potamia in the Near East and the Indus valley of northern India. In Mesopotamia men lived in nomadic shepherd tribes, each worshipping its own god. Then the tribes gradually coalesced into nation states, the former tribal gods becoming ranked in hierarchies (some however being lost by amalgamation in the process) domi-nated by great national deities such as Marduk of Babylon, the Sumerian Ishtar, Amon of Thebes, Jahweh of Israel, the Greek Zeus, and so on. Further east in the Indus valley there was likewise a wealth of gods and goddesses, though appar-ently not so much tribal or national in character as expressive of the basic forces of nature, above all fertility. The many deities of the Near East and of India expressed man's awareness of the divine at the dawn of documentary history, some four thousand years ago. It is perhaps worth stressing that the picture was by no means a wholly pleasant one. The tribal and national gods were often martial and cruel, sometimes requiring human sacrifices. And although rather little is known about the very early, pre-Aryan Indian deities, it is certain that later Indian deities have vividly symbolised the cruel and destructive as well as the beneficent aspects of nature.

These early developments in the two cradles of civilisation, Mesopotamia and the Indus valley, can be described as the growth of natural religion, prior to any special intrusions of divine revelation or illumination. Primitive spirit-worship ex-pressed man's fears of unknown forces; his reverence for nature deities expressed his sense of dependence upon realities greater than himself; and his tribal gods expressed the unity and continuity of his group over against other groups. One can in fact discern all sorts of causal connections between the forms which early religion took and the material circumstances of man's life, indicating the large part played by the human element within the history of religion. For example, Trevor Ling points out that life in ancient India (apart from the Punjab immedi-ately prior to the Aryan invasions) was agricultural and was organised in small village units; and suggests that 'among agricultural peoples, aware of the fertile earth which brings forth from itself and nourishes its progeny upon its broad bosom, it is the motherprinciple which seems important.'[3] Accordingly God the Mother, and a variety of more specialised female deities, have always held a prominent place in Indian religious thought and mythology. This contrasts with the charac-teristically male expression of deity in the Semitic religions, which had their origins among nomadic, pastoral, herd-keeping peoples in the Near East. The divine was known to the desert-dwelling herdsmen who founded the Israelite tradition as God the King and Father; and this conception has continued both in later Judaism and

[3] A *History of Religion East and West* (London: Macmillan and New York: St. Martin's Press, 1968), p. 27.

in Christianity, and was renewed out of the desert experience of Mohammed in the islamic religion. Such regional variations in our human ways of conceiving the divine have persisted through time into the developed world faiths that we know today. The typical western conception of God is still predominantly in terms of the male principle of power and authority; and in the typical Indian conceptions of deity the female principle still plays a distinctly larger part than in the west.

Here then was the natural condition of man's religious life: religion without revelation. But sometime around 800 B.C. there began what has been called the golden age of religious creativity. This consisted in a remarkable series of revelatory experiences occurring during the next five hundred or so years in different parts of the world, experiences which deepened and purified men's conceptions of the ultimate, and which religious faith can only attribute to the pressure of the divine Spirit upon the human spirit. First came the early Jewish prophets, Amos, Hosea and first Isaiah, declaring that they had heard the Word of the Lord claiming their obedience and demanding a new level of righteousness and justice in the life of Israel. Then in Persia the great prophet Zoroaster appeared; China produced Lao-tzu and then Confucius; in India the Upanishads were written, and Gotama the Buddha lived, and Mahavira, the founder of the Jain religion and, probably about the end of this period, the writing of the Bhagavad Gītā;[4] and Greece produced Pythagoras and then, ending this golden age, Socrates and Plato. Then after the gap of some three hundred years came Jesus of Nazareth and the emergence of Christianity; and after another gap the prophet Mohammed and the rise of Islam.

The suggestion that we must consider is that these were all moments of divine revelation. But let us ask, in order to test this thought, whether we should not expect God to make his revelation in a single mighty act, rather than to produce a number of different, and therefore presumably partial, revelations at different times and places? I think that in seeing the answer to this question we receive an important clue to the place of the religions of the world in the divine purpose. For when we remember the facts of history and geography we realise that in the period we are speaking of, between two and three thousand years ago, it was not possible for God to reveal himself through any human mediation to all mankind. A world-wide revelation might be possible today, thanks to the inventions of printing, and even more of radio, TV and communication satellites. But in the technology of the ancient world this was not possible. Although on a time scale of centuries and millennia there has been a slow diffusion and interaction of cultures, particularly within the vast Euro-Asian land mass, yet the more striking fact for our present purpose is the fragmented character of the ancient world. Communications between the different groups of humanity was then so limited and slow that for all practical purposes men inhabited different worlds. For the most part people in Europe, in India, in Arabia, in Africa, in China were unaware of the others' existence. And as the world was fragmented, so was its religious life. If

---

[4]The dating of the Bhagavad Gītā has been a matter of much debate; but R. C. Zaehner in his recent monumental critical edition says that 'One would probably not be going far wrong if one dated it at some time between the fifth and second centuries B.C.' *The Bhagavad Gītā* (Oxford: Clarendon Press, 1969) p. 7.

there was to be revelation of the divine reality to mankind it had to be a pluriform revelation, a series of revealing experiences occurring independently within the different streams of human history. And since religion and culture were one, the great creative moments of revelation and illumination have influenced the development of the various cultures, giving them the coherence and impetus to expand into larger units, thus creating the vast, many-sided historical entities which we call the world religions.

Each of these religio-cultural complexes has expanded until it touched the boundaries of another such complex spreading out from another centre. Thus each major occasion of divine revelation has slowly transformed the primitive and national religions within the sphere of its influence into what we now know as the world faiths. The early Dravidian and Aryan polytheisms of India were drawn through the religious experience and thought of the Brahmins into what the west calls Hinduism. The national and mystery cults of the mediterranean world and then of northern Europe were drawn by influences stemming from the life and teaching of Christ into what has become Christianity. The early polytheism of the Arab peoples has been transformed under the influence of Mohammed and his message into Islam. Great areas of South-East Asia, of China, Tibet and Japan were drawn into the spreading Buddhist movement. None of these expansions from different centres of revelation has of course been simple and uncontested, and a number of alternatives which proved less durable have perished or been absorbed in the process—for example, Mithraism has disappeared altogether; and Zoroastrianism, whilst it greatly influenced the development of the judaic-christian tradition, and has to that extent been absorbed, only survives directly today on a small scale in Parseeism.

Seen in this historical context these movements of faith—the judaic-christian, the Buddhist, the Hindu, the Muslim—are not essentially rivals. They began at different times and in different places, and each expanded outwards into the surrounding world of primitive natural religion until most of the world was drawn up into one or other of the great revealed faiths. And once this global pattern had become established it has ever since remained fairly stable. It is true that the process of establishment involved conflict in the case of Islam's entry into India and the virtual expulsion of Buddhism from India in the medieval period, and in the case of Islam's advance into Europe and then its retreat at the end of the medieval period. But since the frontiers of the different world faiths became more or less fixed there has been little penetration of one faith into societies moulded by another. The most successful missionary efforts of the great faiths continue to this day to be 'downwards' into the remaining world of relatively primitive religions rather than 'sideways' into territories dominated by another world faith. For example, as between Christianity and Islam there has been little more than rather rare individual conversions; but both faiths have successful missions in Africa. Again, the christian population of the Indian subcontinent, after more than two centuries of missionary effort, is only about 2.7 per cent; but on the other hand the christian missions in the South Pacific are fairly successful. Thus the general picture, so far as the great world religions is concerned, is that each has gone through an early period of geographical expansion, converting a region of the world from its more primitive religious state, and has thereafter continued in a comparatively settled condition within more or less stable boundaries.

Now it is of course possible to see this entire development from the primitive forms of religion up to and including the great world faiths as the history of man's most persistent illusion, growing from crude fantasies into sophisticated metaphysical speculations. But from the standpoint of religious faith the only reasonable hypothesis is that this historical picture represents a movement of divine self-revelation to mankind. This hypothesis offers a general answer to the question of the relation between the different world religions and of the truths which they embody. It suggests to us that the same divine reality has always been self-revealingly active towards mankind, and that the differences of human response are related to different human circumstances. These circumstances—ethnic, geographical, climatic, ecnomic, sociological, historical—have produced the existing differentiations of human culture, and within each main cultural region the response to the divine has taken its own characteristic forms. In each case the post-primitive response has been initiated by some spiritually outstanding individual or succession of individuals, developing in the course of time into one of the great religio-cultural phenomena which we call the world religions. Thus Islam embodies the main response of the arabic peoples to the divine reality; Hinduism, the main (though not the only) response of the peoples of India; Buddhism, the main response of the peoples of South-East Asia and parts of northern Asia; Christianity, the main response of the european peoples, both within Europe itself and in their emigrations to the Americas and Australasia.

Thus it is, I think, intelligible historically why the revelation of the divine reality to man, and the disclosure of the divine will for human life, had to occur separately within the different streams of human life. We can see how these revelations took different forms related to the different mentalities of the peoples to whom they came, and developed within these different cultures into the vast and many-sided historical phenomena of the world religions.

But let us now ask whether this is intelligible theologically. What about the conflicting truth-claims of the different faiths? Is the divine nature personal or non-personal; does deity become incarnate in the world; are human beings born again and again on earth; is the Bible, or the Koran, or the Bhagavad Gītā the Word of God? If what Christianity says in answer to these questions is true, must not what Hinduism says be to a large extent false? If what Buddhism says is true, must not what Islam says be largely false?

Let us begin with the recognition, which is made in all the main religious traditions, that the ultimate divine reality is infinite and as such transcends the grasp of the human mind. God, to use our christian term, is infinite. He is not a thing, a part of the universe, existing alongside other things; nor is he a being falling under a certain kind. And therefore he cannot be defined or encompassed by human thought. We cannot draw boundaries round his nature and say that he is this and no more. If we could fully define God, describing his inner being and his outer limits, this would not be God. The God whom our minds can penetrate and whom our thoughts can circumnavigate is merely a finite and partial image of God.

From this it follows that the different encounters with the transcendent within the different religious traditions may all be encounters with the one infinite reality, though with partially different and overlapping aspects of that reality. This is a very familiar thought in Indian religious literature. We read, for example, in the ancient Rig-Vedas, dating back to perhaps as much as a thousand years before Christ:

> They call it Indra, Mitra, Varuna, and Agni
> And also heavenly, beautiful Garutman:
> The real is one, though sages name it variously.[5]

We might translate this thought into the terms of the faiths represented today in Britain:

> They call it Jahweh, Allah, Krishna, Param Atma,
> And also holy, blessed Trinity:
> The real is one, though sages name it differently.

And in the Bhagavad Gītā the Lord Krishna, the personal God of love, says, 'Howsoever men approach me, even so do I accept them; for, on all sides, whatever path they may choose is mine.'[6]

Again, there is the parable of the blind men and the elephant, said to have been told by the Buddha. An elephant was brought to a group of blind men who had never encountered such an animal before. One felt a leg and reported that an elephant is a great living pillar. Another felt the trunk and reported that an elephant is a great snake. Another felt a tusk and reported that an elephant is like a sharp ploughshare. And so on. And then they all quarrelled together, each claiming that his own account was the truth and therefore all the others false. In fact of course they were all true, but each referring only to one aspect of the total reality and all expressed in very imperfect analogies.

Now the possibility, indeed the probability, that we have seriously to consider is that many different accounts of the divine reality may be true, though all expressed in imperfect human analogies, but that none is 'the truth, the whole truth, and nothing but the truth'. May it not be that the different concepts of God, as Jahweh, Allah, Krishna, Param Atma, Holy Trinity, and so on; and likewise the different concepts of the hidden structure of reality, as the eternal emanation of Brahman or as an immense cosmic process culminating in Nirvana, are all images of the divine, each expressing some aspect or range of aspects and yet none by itself fully and exhaustively corresponding to the infinite nature of the ultimate reality?

Two immediate qualifications however to this hypothesis. First, the idea that we are considering is not that any and every conception of God or of the transcendent is valid, still less all equally valid; but that every conception of the divine which has come out of a great revelatory religious experience and has been tested through a long tradition of worship, and has sustained human faith over centuries of time and in millions of lives, is likely to represent a genuine encounter with the divine reality. And second, the parable of the blind men and the elephant is

[5] I 164.

[6] IV 11.

of course only a parable, and like most parables it is designed to make one point and must not be pressed as an analogy at other points. The suggestion is not that the different encounters with the divine which lie at the basis of the great religious traditions are responses to different *parts* of the divine. They are rather encounters from different historical and cultural standpoints with the same infinite divine reality and as such they lead to differently focused awarenesses of that reality. The indications of this are most evident in worship and prayer. What is said about God in the theological treatises of the different faiths is indeed often widely different. But it is in prayer that a belief in God comes alive and does its main work. And when we turn from abstract theology to the living stuff of worship we meet again and again the overlap and confluence of faiths.

Here, for example, is a Muslim prayer at the feast of Ramadan:

> Praise be to God, Lord of creation, Source of all livelihood, who orders the morning, Lord of majesty and honour, of grace and beneficence. He who is so far that he may not be seen and so near that he witnesses the secret things. Blessed be he and for ever exalted.[7]

And here is a Sikh creed used at the morning prayer:

> There is but one God. He is all that is.
> He is the Creator of all things and He is all-pervasive.
> He is without fear and without enmity.
> He is timeless, unborn and self-existent.
> He is the Enlightener
> And can be realised by grace of Himself alone.
> He was in the beginning; He was in all ages.
> The True One is, was, O Nanak, and shall forever be.[8]

And here again is a verse from the Koran:

> To God belongs the praise, Lord of the heavens and Lord of the earth, the Lord of all being. His is the dominion in the heavens and in the earth: he is the Almighty, the All-wise.[9]

Turning now to the Hindu idea of the many incarnations of God, here is a verse from the Rāmāyana:

> Seers and sages, saints and hermits, fix on Him their reverent gaze,
> And in faint and trembling accents, holy scripture hymns His praise.
> He the omnipresent spirit, lord of heaven and earth and hell,
> To redeem His people, freely has vouchsafed with men to dwell.[10]

And from the rich literature of devotional song here is a Bhakti hymn of the Vaishnavite branch of Hinduism:

[7] Kenneth Cragg, *Alive to God: Muslim and Christian Prayer* (London and New York: Oxford University Press, 1970) p. 65.

[8] Harbans Singh, *Guru Nanak and Origins of the Sikh Faith* (Bombay, London and New York: Asia Publishing House, 1969) pp. 96–7.

[9] *Alive to God*, p. 61 (Surah of the Kneeling, v. 35).

[10] *Sacred Books of the World* edited by A. C. Bouquet (London: Pelican Books, 1954) p. 226 (The Rāmāyana of Tulsi Das, Canto I, Chandha 2, translated by F. S. Growse).

Now all my days with joy I'll fill, full to the brim
With all my heart to Vitthal cling, and only Him.

He will sweep utterly away all dole and care;
And all in sunder shall I rend illusion's snare.

O altogether dear is He, and He alone,
For all my burden He will take to be His own.

Lo, all the sorrow of the world will straightaway, cease,
And all unending now shall be the reign of peace.[11]

And a Muslim mystical verse:

Love came a guest
Within my breast,
My soul was spread,
Love banqueted.[12]

And finally another Hindu (Vaishnavite) devotional hymn:

O save me, save me, Mightiest,
    Save me and set me free.
O let the love that fills my breast
    Cling to thee lovingly.
Grant me to taste how sweet thou art;
    Grant me but this, I pray,
And never shall my love depart
    Or turn from thee away.
Then I thy name shall magnify
    And tell thy praise abroad,
For very love and gladness I
    Shall dance before my God.[13]

Such prayers and hymns as these must express, surely, diverse encounters with the same divine reality. These encounters have taken place within different human cultures by people of different ways of thought and feeling, with different histories and different frameworks of philosophical thought, and have developed into different systems of theology embodied in different religious structures and organisations. These resulting large-scale religiocultural phenomena are what we call the religions of the world. But must there not lie behind them the same infinite divine reality, and may not our divisions into Christian, Hindu, Muslim, Jew, and so on, and all that goes with them, accordingly represent secondary, human, historical developments?

There is a further problem, however, which now arises. I have been speaking so far of the ultimate reality in a variety of terms—the Father, Son and Spirit of Christianity, the Jahweh of Judaism, the Allah of Islam, and so on—but always thus far in theistic terms, as a personal God under one name or another. But

---

[11] Ibid., p. 245 (A Hymn of Namdev, translated by Nicol MacNicol).

[12] *Alive to God*, p. 79 (From Ibn Hazm, 'The Ring of the Dove').

[13] *Sacred Books of the World*, p. 246 (A Hymn of Tukaram).

what of the non-theistic religions? What of the non-theistic Hinduism according to which the ultimate reality, Brahman, is not He but It; and what about Buddhism, which in one form is agnostic concerning the existence of God even though in another form it has come to worship the Buddha himself? Can these nontheistic faiths be seen as encounters with the same divine reality that is encountered in theistic religion?

Speaking very tentatively, I think it *is* possible that the sense of the divine as non-personal may indeed reflect an aspect of the same infinite reality that is encountered as personal in theistic religious experience. The question can be pursued both as a matter of pure theology and in relation to religious experience. Theologically, the Hindu distinction between Nirguna Brahman and Saguna Brahman is important and should be adopted into western religious thought. Detaching the distinction, then, from its Hindu context we may say that Nirguna God is the eternal self-existent divine reality, beyond the scope of all human categories, including personality; and Saguna God is God in relation to his creation and with the attributes which express this relationship, such as personality, omnipotence, goodness, love and omniscience. Thus the one ultimate reality is both Nirguna and non-personal, and Saguna and personal, in a duality which is in principle acceptable to human understanding. When we turn to men's religious awareness of God we are speaking of Saguna God, God in relation to man. And here the larger traditions of both east and west report a dual experience of the divine as personal and as other than personal. It will be a sufficient reminder of the strand of personal relationship with the divine in Hinduism to mention Iswara, the personal God who represents the Absolute as known and worshipped by finite persons. It should also be remembered that the characterisation of Brahman as *satcitananda*, absolute being, consciousness and bliss, is not far from the conception of infinitely transcendent personal life. Thus there is both the thought and the experience of the personal divine within Hinduism. But there is likewise the thought and the experience of God as other than personal within Christianity. Rudolph Otto describes this strand in the mysticism of Meister Eckhart. He says:

> The divine, which on the one hand is conceived in symbols taken from the social sphere, as Lord, King, Father, Judge—a person in relation to persons—is on the other hand denoted in dynamic symbols as the power of life, as light and life, as spirit ebbing and flowing, as truth, knowledge, essential justice and holiness, a glowing fire that penetrates and pervades. It is characterized as the principle of a renewed, supernatural Life, mediating and giving itself, breaking forth in the living man as his nova vita, as the content of his life and being. What is here insisted upon is not so much an 'immanent' God, as an 'experienced' God, known as an inward principle of the power of new being and life. Eckhart knows this *deuteros theos* besides the personal God. . . .[14]

Let me now try to draw the threads together and to project them into the future. I have been suggesting that Christianity is a way of salvation which, beginning some two thousand years ago, has become the principal way of salvation in three continents. The other great world faiths are likewise ways of salvation, providing

[14]Rudolph Otto, *Mysticism East and West*, trans. Bertha L. Bracey and Richenda C. Payne (New York: Meridian Books, 1957) p. 131.

the principal path to the divine reality for other large sections of humanity. I have also suggested that the idea that Jesus proclaimed himself as God incarnate, and as the sole point of saving contact between God and man, is without adequate historical foundation and represents a doctrine developed by the church. We should therefore not infer, from the christian experience of redemption through Christ, that salvation cannot be experienced in any other way. The alternative possibility is that the ultimate divine reality—in our christian terms, God—has always been pressing in upon the human spirit, but always in ways which leave men free to open or close themselves to the divine presence. Human life has developed along characteristically different lines in the main areas of civilisation, and these differences have naturally entered into the ways in which men have apprehended and responded to God. For the great religious figures through whose experience divine revelation has come have each been conditioned by a particular history and culture. One can hardly imagine Gotama the Buddha except in the setting of the India of his time, or Jesus the Christ except against the background of Old Testament Judaism, or Mohammed except in the setting of Arabia. And human history and culture have likewise shaped the development of the webs of religious creeds, practices and organisations which we know as the great world faiths.

It is thus possible to consider the hypothesis that they are all, at their experiential roots, in contact with the same ultimate reality, but that their differing experiences of that reality, interacting over the centuries with the different thought-forms of different cultures, have led to increasing differentiation and contrasting elaboration—so that Hinduism, for example, is a very different phenomenon from Christianity, and very different ways of conceiving and experiencing the divine occur within them.

However, now that the religious traditions are consciously interacting with each other in the 'one world' of today, in mutual observation and dialogue, it is possible that their future developments may be on gradually converging courses. For during the next few centuries they will no doubt continue to change, and it may be that they will grow closer together, and even that one day such names as 'Christianity', 'Buddhism', 'Islam', 'Hinduism', will no longer describe the then current configurations of men's religious experience and belief. I am not here thinking of the extinction of human religiousness in a universal wave of secularisation. This is of course a possible future; and indeed many think it the most likely future to come about. But if man is an indelibly religious animal he will always, even in his secular cultures, experience a sense of the transcendent by which he will be both troubled and uplifted. The future I am thinking of is accordingly one in which what we now call the different religions will constitute the past history of different emphases and variations within a global religious life. I do not mean that all men everywhere will be overtly religious, any more than they are today. I mean rather that the discoveries now taking place by men of different faiths of central common ground, hitherto largely concealed by the variety of cultural forms in which it was expressed, may eventually render obsolete the sense of belonging to rival ideological communities. Not that all religious men will think alike, or worship in the same way or experience the divine identically. On the contrary, so long as there is a rich variety of human cultures—and let us hope there will always be this—we should expect there to be correspondingly different forms of religious cult, ritual and organisation, conceptualised in different theological doctrines. And so long as there is a wide spectrum of human psychological types—and again let us hope that there will always be this—we should expect there to be correspondingly different emphases between, for example, the sense of the divine as just and as merciful, between *karma* and *bhakti*; or between worship as formal and communal and worship as free and personal. Thus we may expect the different world faiths to continue as religiocultural phenomena, though phenomena which are increasingly influencing one another's development. The relation between them will then perhaps be somewhat like that now obtaining between the different denominations of Christianity in Europe or the United States. That is to say, there will in most countries be a dominant religious tradition, with other traditions present in varying strengths, but with considerable awareness on all hands of what they have in common; with some degree of osmosis of membership through their institutional walls; with a large degree of practical co-operations; and even conceivably with some interchange of ministry.

Beyond this the ultimate unity of faiths will be an eschatological unity in which each is both fulfilled and transcended—fulfilled in so far as it is true, transcended in so far as it is less than the whole truth. And indeed even such fulfilling must be a transcending; for the function of a religion is to bring us to a right relationship with the ultimate divine reality, to awareness of our true nature and our place in the Whole, into the presence of God. In the eternal life there is no longer any place for religions; the pilgrim has no need of a way after he has finally arrived. In St John's vision of the heavenly city at the end of our christian scriptures it is said that there is no temple—no christian church or chapel, no jewish synagogue, no hindu or buddhist temple, no muslim mosque, no sikh gurdwara. . . . For all these exist in time, as ways through time to eternity.

Suggestions for Further Reading

James Thrower's *A Short History of Western Atheism* (Pemberton Books, 1971) is a readable survey of the rejection of religious belief up to the logical positivist movement of this century. See also the biographical essays on various religious sceptics and atheists in Jim Herrick, *Against the Faith: Essays on Deists, Skeptics and Atheists* (Prometheus Books, 1986). On philosophical accounts of atheism see Kai Nielsen, *Philosophy and Atheism* (Prometheus Books, 1981) and George Smith's easily read *Atheism: The Case Against God* (Prometheus Books, 1979).

A philosophical critique of Wittgensteinian Fideism can be found in Chapters Three, Four, and Five of Kai Nielsen's *An Introduction to the Philosophy of Religion* (St. Martin's Press, 1982). D. Z. Phillips's *Concept of Prayer* (Routledge & Kegan Paul, 1965) and *Death and Immortality* (Macmillan, 1970) are both good examples of the Wittgensteinian Fideistic approach.

On the religious rejection of classical theism see Germain Griseg, *Beyond the New Theism: A Philosophy of Religion* (University of Notre Dame Press, 1975). On religious pluralism see Ninian Smart, *A Dialogue of Religions* (SCM Press, 1960); Wilfred Cantwell Smith, *Towards a World Theology* (Westminster Press, 1981); and the collection of essays by John Hick, *Problems of Religious Pluralism* (St. Martin's Press, 1986).

MYSTICISM
AND
RELIGIOUS EXPERIENCE

V

William James expressed the opinion of many thoughtful people when he asserted that "myths, superstitions, dogmas, creeds, and metaphysical theologies" are spontaneously engendered by religious experience. "Feeling," he said, "is the deeper source of religion . . . philosophic and theological formulas are secondary."[1]

There are a variety of religious experiences. Visions and voices are common. Some Christians, for example, have visions of Jesus or seem to hear him speaking. Buddhists sometimes seek visions of celestial Buddhas and Bodhisattvas. Early Jewish mystics cultivated visions of God's throne-chariot.

"Numinous" encounters are important in the theistic traditions. These experiences include (1) awe or dread, "the feeling of 'something uncanny,' 'eerie,' or 'weird,' " and (2) a sense of "impotence and general nothingness, as over against overpowering might." They also involve (3) a conviction of being confronted with something alive, vital, and active and (4) a sense of mystery and wonder, of being in the presence of something we cannot express in ordinary categories. Finally, these experiences include (5) "fascination" or attraction, since their object seems so splendid that other values appear worthless in comparison.[2] Numinous experiences are sometimes focused on ordinary objects—an oddly shaped stone, for example, or a mountain or a human being. In other cases, their apparent object is sharply distinguished from ordinary things. In these latter cases, one seems to encounter a transcendent, sovereign will that thrusts itself into our lives and concerns and cannot be identified with any ordinary reality.

Mystical experiences should be distinguished from numinous experiences. Numinous experiences involve a sense of distance or otherness; a gulf seems to separate the experiencer and the awesome mystery that he or she confronts. Mystical consciousness, on the other hand, is "unitive." Distinctions are transcended or overcome (although the *way* in which they are overcome varies from one type of mystical experience to another).

Most earlier writers believed that mysticism is everywhere the same. In their view, Christian, Buddhist, and Jewish mystics have identical *experiences*; they merely *interpret* them differently.

This opinion is no longer widely accepted. For example, Walter Stace distinguishes two broad categories of mysticism—extrovertive and introvertive. Extrovertive mysticism is focused on the external world. Its object is nature, although nature is experienced in a new and different way. In introvertive mysticism, awareness of the space–time world becomes peripheral or vanishes altogether.

Most recent writers believe that Stace's two categories should themselves be subdivided. For example, there are several types of extrovertive experience. In one of the most common, the mystic has a sense of the identity of ordinary objects—stars, planets, trees, earth, sky, and so on. Hard and fast distinctions between these things vanish. They are no longer clearly differentiated, and the mystic may

---

[1] William James, *The Varieties of Religious Experience* (New York: The Modern Library, c. 1902), p. 423.

[2] Rudolf Otto, *The Idea of the Holy* (New York: Oxford University Press, 1958), Chapters III–VI.

exclaim with the medieval Christian Eckhart, "Here all blades of grass, wood and stone, all things are one. This is the deepest depth and thereby am I completely captivated."[3] The sense of fusion or union includes the person having the experience. Sometimes the mystic has a sense of "expanding," of growing larger and larger until he or she encompasses all things. As one of them said, "The seer sees only the all, he penetrates the all everywhere, He is simple, He is three fold, yea, he is twenty-thousand fold."[4] At other times, the mystic has a sense of "dissolution"—of dissolving or flowing into all things. In either case, the mystic no longer feels distinct from the natural phenomena that are the object of his or her experience.

In another form of extrovertive mysticism, nature seems alive, vital, imbued with life or soul. This mode of consciousness is also focused on nature. But in this case "blades of grass, wood and stone" are experienced as external manifestations of a living force or vital power that fills them and expresses itself through them.

Buddhists cultivate yet another form of extrovertive consciousness in which ordinary things are perceived as "empty." The experience of emptiness is achieved by viewing the world without attempting to conceptualize it and without feeling aversion or attachment to it.

Whether introvertive mysticism should be subdivided is more controversial. R. C. Zaehner identifies two distinct types. "Monistic" or "soul" mysticism occurs when the mystic empties his or her mind of percepts, images, and concepts until nothing remains but consciousness itself—joyous and empty, without object or content. "Theistic" mystics, too, purge their minds of percepts, mental images, and all but the most abstract and general concepts (such as "being," "presence," "love"). Nevertheless, theistic mystical experiences have an object, although this object cannot be identified with any spatio-temporal thing or with the space–time world as a whole. Theistic mysticism is a love mysticism. The tone and character of theistic mystical consciousness is indicated by the fact that theistic mystics invariably use erotic imagery to express the nature of their experiences. These mystics feel that a deeply passionate mutual love is the best symbol of their relation to the reality they seem to experience.

Walter Stace and Ninian Smart think Zaehner's distinction is spurious. In their opinion, "monistic" and "theistic" mystics are only offering different interpretations of the same experience. More and more students of mysticism, however, are embracing Zaehner' distinction. Indeed, many of them believe that Zaehner's classification is itself too simplified.

Why should these experiences interest a philosopher of religion? They are important because they are "noetic." That is, visionary, numinous, and mystical experiences are "apparent cognitions." They include a conviction that one is directly apprehending or perceiving some truth or reality. In this respect, the experiences we are discussing resemble sense experiences, memories, and our sense of the self-evidence of propositions like "$2 + 3 = 5$." Mystics, for example, typically

---

[3] Quoted in Rudolf Otto, *Mysticism East and West* (New York: Meridian Books, 1957), p. 61.

[4] Quoted in *Mysticism East and West*, p. 58.

compare their experiences with ordinary perception and speak of "seeing," "hearing," or even "touching" and "tasting" God.

How seriously should we take these claims? Richard Swinburne has suggested we should employ the "Principle of Credulity."[5] Roughly speaking, it states that apparent cognitions are innocent until proven guilty. That is, they should be taken at face value unless there is some special reason for discounting them. Thus, my seeming to remember having toast for breakfast is a sufficient reason for thinking I had toast for breakfast, unless there is some reason to distrust my memory. My seeming to see a badger behind my garage is a sufficient reason for believing I do see it, if there isn't any reason to think I am misperceiving. The apparent obviousness of "$2 + 3 = 5$" is a sufficient reason for believing it, in the absence of good reasons for thinking it false.

The principle is controversial. Nevertheless, it is plausible since some principle of this kind is needed to explain how we can know anything. If *every* apparent cognition has to be justified by other apparent cognitions, then *no* apparent cognition is justified. Either the chain of justifications ends in a circle or we are involved in an infinite regress. But circular justifications are not legitimate, and finite minds cannot encompass an infinite chain of justifications. In either case, none of our apparent cognitions is justified.

But if *any* apparent cognition is innocent until proven guilty, then surely *all* are, for it seems arbitrary to privilege some apparent cognitions and not others. In particular, there does not seem to be any convincing reason for thinking that memory experiences and sense experiences are innocent until proven guilty while religious experiences are guilty until proven innocent. Critics sometimes argue, for example, that religious experiences are inherently more suspect than memory or sense experiences because they are not reliable bases for predicting the future. But this is not compelling. If religious experiences really are what they purport to be (perceptions of God or some other *divine* reality), then there is no reason to expect them to furnish a basis for reliably predicting the course of *temporal* events. The difference in question thus seems irrelevant.

But, of course, *presumptive* innocence is not innocence. In our legal system, the accused is presumed innocent until proven guilty. Nevertheless, many accused people *are* guilty, and their guilt can often be established beyond reasonable doubt. Even if religious experiences should be accepted at face value in the absence of special reasons for discounting them, there may *be* good reasons for doing so.

Consider an obvious but important point. If someone *perceives* God, or Brahman, or the Tao (and does not merely mistakenly *think* he or she does so), then God, or Brahman, or the Tao really exists. Hence, if we have good reasons for thinking that these things *do not* exist, we can dismiss experiences of them as illusory.

Again, apparent cognitions activate "belief-producing mechanisms." For example, memory experiences dispose us to form beliefs about the past. Sense experiences dispose us to form beliefs about the existence and character of physical objects in our immediate vicinity. Our sense of self-evidence disposes us to believe

[5] Richard Swinburne, *The Existence of God* (Oxford: Oxford University Press, 1979), Chapter 13.

simple truths of logic and mathematics. Now reliable belief-producing mecha-nisms do not systematically produce inconsistent beliefs. Why not? Belief-produc-ing mechanisms are reliable only if they lead to significantly more true than false beliefs. Since two inconsistent beliefs cannot both be true, a belief-producing mechanism that results in massive inconsistencies cannot be reliable. But religious experiences seem to support incompatible claims. Some mystics, for example, claim to perceive the triune God of Christianity. Others think they taste Nirvāna. Still others believe they experience the impersonal Brahman. Yet surely these claims are not consistent. The mystics' conflicting claims, then, provide a reason for discounting their experiences, unless it can be shown that the conflicts are only apparent. Wainwright thinks they are. He also thinks that conflicts between mystical and numinous experience are only apparent. But even if he is right, the conflict between visionaries may be irreducible. If visions of Christ in majesty are veridical, then visions of celestial Buddhas are not (and vice versa), for the reli-gious import of these visions seems inconsistent. There may, then, be good rea-sons for discounting visionary experiences.

We also discount apparent cognitions when we have reasons for thinking that the causes that produced them typically lead to false beliefs. For example, we discount the visual experiences of someone who has taken a drug that distorts perception, or the memories of a person subject to psychosis.

The discovery of natural causes of religious experience is not itself sufficient to discount the experience. Suppose, for example, that theism is true. If it is, God is the immediate cause of everything (with the possible exception of free actions). Hence, the fact that a religious experience has natural causes no more shows that God is not its cause than the fact that a struck match bursts into flame shows that God does not maintain both this cause and its effect in being.

But suppose it could be shown that religious experiences are not produced by simply natural causes but by natural causes that systematically produce false be-liefs. In that case, the experiences *should* be discounted. If religious experiences are produced by psychosis or wish fulfillment, for example, we have good reasons for distrusting them.

In short, religious experiences may be innocent until proven guilty. Neverthe-less, reasons *have* been offered for discounting them. If the reasons are good, we should conclude that these apparent cognitions are not genuine. But the Principle of Credulity is not innocuous. If it is sound, and applies to religious experiences, the burden of proof is on those who refuse to accept their cognitive validity.

In thinking about these matters, it is useful to remember that attempts to ground religious belief in religious experience are quite recent. (The first to seriously undertake the task was Friedrich Schleiermacher [1768–1834].) Traditional mys-tics, and those who had numinous encounters, undoubtedly thought that their experiences *confirmed* their Christian, or Jewish, or Hindu beliefs. Nevertheless, their beliefs did not rest on these experiences but on scripture, tradition, and sometimes reason.

It is doubtful whether the whole weight of religious belief can be supported by religious experience. Even if religious experience is valid, it may entitle us to only some very general (though significant) conclusions—"That the visible world is part of a more spiritual universe,"[6] for example, or that the ordinary empirical personality is not the whole self, or that a transcendent, overwhelming, loving consciousness is real. Furthermore, if we abstract from all the other considerations supporting religious belief, then the case for taking religious experiences at face value depends entirely on some version of the Principle of Credulity and the success of attempts to defuse relevant objections. While many find this case persuasive, others do not. Religious experiences may support religious belief. Nevertheless, the support is not as strong as Schleiermacher and others thought.

But even if religious experiences cannot bear the whole weight of a robust structure of religious beliefs, they may significantly strengthen the case for them. If there are independent reasons for a system of religious metaphysics, then claims to perceive a supernatural reality are not only more credible; the experiences also provide additional support for what one already has some basis for believing on other grounds.

W. J. W.

[6] James, *op. cit.*, p. 475.

THE NATURE AND TYPES OF RELIGIOUS AND MYSTICAL EXPERIENCE

WALTER STACE
The Nature of Mysticism

I.   TERMINOLOGICAL

In these pages I shall often use the expressions "mysticism," "mystic," "mystical experience," "mystical consciousness," "mystical idea." "Mysticism," of course, is the general name of our entire subject, and its meaning will be gradually developed. By the word "mystic" I shall always mean a person who himself has had mystical experience. Often the word is used in a much wider and looser way. Anyone who is sympathetic to mysticism is apt to be labeled a mystic. But I shall use the word always in a stricter sense. However sympathetic toward mysticism a man may be, however deeply interested, involved, enthusiastic, or learned in the subject, he will not be called a mystic unless he has, or has had, mystical experience. The phrases "mystical experience" and "mystical consciousness" will be used as synonymous with each other. But "mystical consciousness" is the better term, the word "experience" being misleading in certain respects. It will be seen that both "mysticism" and "mystic" are defined in terms of mystical experience or consciousness. This is therefore the basic thing on which we have to fasten attention and in terms of which we have to understand the whole subject. Our question "What is mysticism?" really means "What is mystical experience?"

Walter Stace (1886–1967) served for twenty-two years in the British Civil Service, occupying various government posts in Ceylon. During this period he produced several books, including a study of the German philosopher Hegel. He became a member of the Department of Philosophy at Princeton in 1932 and remained at that university until his retirement in 1955. An empiricist in the tradition of Hume, he was nonetheless deeply sympathetic to mysticism. Among his many works are *Religion and the Modern Mind*, *Time and Eternity*, and *Mysticism and Philosophy*.

THE NATURE OF MYSTICISM   *From The Teachings of the Mystics* by Walter T. Stace. Reprinted by permission of Mrs. Walter T. Stace.

The phrase "mystical idea" has also to be defined in terms of mystical experience. It means an idea, belief, opinion, or proposition which was originally based on mystical experience, although the connection between the experience and the opinion may have been quite forgotten. The point is that a mystical idea is a product of the conceptual intellect, whereas a mystical experience is a nonintellectual mode of consciousness. The proposition that "time is unreal" is an example of a mystical idea. It must have arisen because mystics usually feel (a) that their experience is timeless and (b) it is more "real" (in some sense) than any other experience. But many philosophers who have never had any mystical experience, nor any knowledge of how the idea originated, yet come to adopt it in their philosophies and treat it as if it were a product of a process of reasoning. A mystical idea may be either true or false, though it must have originated in a genuine mystical experience.

II.   EXPERIENCE AND INTERPRETATION

On a dark night out of doors one may see something glimmering white. One person may think it is a ghost. A second person may take it for a sheet hung out on a clothesline. A third person may suppose that it is a white-painted rock. Here we have a single experience with three different interpretations. The experience is genuine, but the interpretations may be either true or false. If we are to understand anything at all about mysticism, it is essential that we should make a similar distinction between a mystical experience and the interpretations which may be put upon it either by mystics themselves or by nonmystics. For instance, the same mystical experience may be interpreted by a Christian in terms of Christian beliefs and by a Buddhist in terms of Buddhistic beliefs.

III.   SOME THINGS WHICH MYSTICISM IS NOT

The word "mysticism" is popularly used in a variety of loose and inaccurate ways. Sometimes anything is called "mystical" which is misty, foggy, vague, or sloppy. It is absurd that "mysticism" should be associated with what is "misty" because of the similar sound of the words. And there is nothing misty, foggy, vague, or sloppy about mysticism.

A second absurd association is to suppose that mysticism is sort of mystery-mongering. There is, of course, an etymological connection between "mysticism" and "mystery." But mysticism is not any sort of hocus-pocus such as we commonly associate with claims to the elucidation of sensational mysteries. Mysticism is not the same as what is commonly called the "occult"—whatever that may mean. Nor has it anything to do with spiritualism, or ghosts, or table-turning. Nor does it include what are commonly called parapsychological phenomena such as telepathy, telekinesis, clairvoyance, precognition. These are not mystical phenomena. It is perhaps true that mystics may sometimes claim to possess such special powers, but even when they do so they are well aware that such powers are not part of, and are to be clearly distinguished from, their mystical experience. Such powers, if they exist—as to which I express no opinion—may be possessed by persons who are not mystics. And conversely, even the greatest mystics may be devoid of them and know nothing about them. The closest connection one can admit will be to say that it may be the case that the sort of persons who are mystics also tend to be the sort of persons who have parapsychological powers.

Finally, it is most important to realize that visions and voices are not mystical phenomena, though here again it seems to be the case that the sort of persons who are mystics may often be the sort of persons who see visions and hear voices. A few years ago it was reported that certain persons in Italy saw a vision of the Virgin Mary in the clouds. Even if we suppose that these persons really did have this vision, it must be emphatically asserted that this was not a mystical experience and had nothing to do with mysticism. Nor are the voices which certain persons in history, such as Socrates, Mohammed, and Joan of Arc, are supposed to have heard to be classed as mystical experiences. Socrates, Mohammed, and Joan of Arc may have been mystics for all I know, but they are not to be classed as such because of these voices. Returning for a moment to the subject of visions, it is well known that certain mystics saw visions but that they did not themselves regard these visions as mystical experiences. A case in point is St. Teresa of Avila. She had frequent visions, but she knew that they were not the experiences she desired. Some of them, she thought, may have been sent to her by God to comfort and encourage her in trying to attain the mystical consciousness. Others, she supposed, might have been sent by the devil in order to confuse her and distract her from the true mystic quest.

The reader may perhaps suppose that the exclusion of visions and voices from the class of mystical phenomena is a matter of arbitrary choice on the part of the present writer. Of course, one is logically entitled to define his terms as he pleases. Therefore if anyone says that he intends to use the phrase "mystical experience" so as to include visions and voices, spiritualism, telepathy, and the like, we do not say that he is wrong. But we say that his usage does not conform to that which has been usual with those who have been recognized as the great mystics of the world. The case of St. Teresa has just been mentioned. St. John of the Cross specifically warns his readers not to seek visions, not to be misled by them, and not to mistake them for the true mystical union. And there are, one must add, good reasons for this. What mystics say is that a genuine mystical experience is nonsensuous. It is formless, shapeless, colorless, odorless, soundless. But a vision is a piece of visual imagery having color and shape. A voice is an auditory image. Visions and voices are sensuous experiences.

IV.   A NEW KIND OF CONSCIOUSNESS

In his book *The Varieties of Religious Experience* William James suggests, as a result of his psychological researches, that "our normal consciousness, rational consciousness as we call it, is but one special type of consciousness whilst all about it, parted from it by the filmiest of screens, there lie potential forms of consciousness entirely different." This statement exactly fits mystical consciousness. It is entirely unlike our everyday consciousness and is wholly incommensurable with it. What are the fundamental characteristics or elements of our ordinary consciousness? We may think of it as being like a building with three floors. The ground floor consists of physical sensations—sights, sounds, smells, tastes, touch sensations, and organic sensations. The second floor consist of images, which we tend to think of as mental copies of sensations. The third floor is the level of the intellect, which is the faculty of concepts. On this floor we find abstract thinking and reasoning processes. This account of the mind may be open to cavil. Some philosophers think that colors, sounds, and so on, are not properly called "sensations"; others that images are not "copies" of sensations. These fine points, however, need not seriously concern us. Our account is sufficiently clear to indicate what we are referring to when we speak of sensations, images, and concepts as being the fundamental elements of the cognitive aspects of our ordinary consciousness. Arising out of these basic cognitive elements and dependent upon them are emotions, desires, and volitions. In order to have a name for it we may call this whole structure—including sensations, images, concepts, and their attendant desires, emotions, and volitions—our *sensory-intellectual consciousness*.

Now the mystical consciousness is quite different from this. It is not merely that it involves different kinds of sensation, thought, or feeling. We are told that some insects or animals can perceive ultraviolet color and infrared color; and that some animals can hear sounds which are inaudible to us; even that some creatures may have a sixth sense quite different from any of our five senses. These are all, no doubt, kinds of sensations different from any we have. But they are still sensations. And the mystical consciousness is destitute of any sensations at all. Nor does it contain any concepts or thoughts. It is not a sensory-intellectual consciousness at all. Accordingly, it cannot be described or analyzed in terms of any of the elements of the sensory-intellectual consciousness, with which it is wholly incommensurable.

This is the reason why mystics always say that their experiences are "ineffable." All words in all languages are the products of our sensory-intellectual consciousness and express or describe its elements or some combination of them. But as these elements (with the doubtful exception of emotions) are not found in the mystical consciousness, it is felt to be impossible to describe it in any words whatever. In spite of this the mystics do describe their experiences in roundabout ways, at the same time telling us that the words they use are inadequate. This raises a serious problem for the philosophy of mysticism, but it is not possible for us to dwell on it here.

The incommensurability of the mystical with the sensory-intellectual consciousness is also the ultimate reason why we have to exclude visions and voices, telepathy, precognition, and clairvoyance from the category of the mystical. Suppose someone sees a vision of the Virgin Mary. What he sees has shape, the shape of a woman, and color—white skin, blue raiment, a golden halo, and so on. But these are all images or sensations. They are therefore composed of elements of our sensory-intellectual consciousness. The same is true of voices. Or suppose one has a precognition of a neighbor's death. The components one is aware of— a dead man, a coffin, etc.—are composed of elements of our sensory-intellectual consciousness. The only difference is that these ordinary elements are arranged in unfamiliar patterns which we have come to think cannot occur, so that if they do occur they seem supernormal. Or the fact that such elements are combined in an unusual way so as to constitute the figure of a woman up in the clouds, perhaps surrounded by other humanlike figures with wings added to them—all this does not constitute a different *kind* of consciousness at all. And just as sensory elements of any sort are excluded from the mystical consciousness, so are conceptual elements. It is not that the thoughts in the mystical consciousness are different from those we are accustomed to. It does not include any thoughts at all. The mystic, of course, expresses thoughts about his experience after that experience is over, and he remembers it when he is back again in his sensory-intellectual consciousness. But there are no thoughts *in* the experience itself.

If anyone thinks that a kind of consciousness without either sensations, images, or thoughts, because it is totally unimaginable and inconceivable to most of us, cannot exist, he is surely being very stupid. He supposes that the possibilities of this vast universe are confined to what can be imagined and understood by the brains of average human insects who crawl on a minute speck of dust floating in illimitable space.

On the other hand, there is not the least reason to suppose that the mystical consciousness is miraculous or supernatural. No doubt it has, like our ordinary consciousness, been produced by the natural processes of evolution. Its existence in a few rare men is a psychological fact of which there is abundant evidence. To deny or doubt that it exists as a psychological fact is not a reputable opinion. It is ignorance. Whether it has any value or significance beyond itself, and if so what—these, of course, are matters regarding which there can be legitimate differences of opinion. Owing to the comparative rarity of this kind of consciousness, it should no doubt be assigned to the sphere of abnormal psychology.

V.   THE CORE OF MYSTICISM

I shall, for the present, treat it as an hypothesis that although mystical experiences may in certain respects have different characteristics in different parts of the world, in different ages, and in different cultures, there are nevertheless a number of fundamental common characteristics. I shall also assume that the agreements are more basic and important, the differences more superficial and relatively less important. This hypothesis can only be fully justified by an elaborate empirical survey of the descriptions of their experiences given by mystics and collected from all over the world. But I believe that enough of the evidence for it will appear in the following pages to convince any reasonable person.

The most important, the central characteristic in which all *fully developed* mystical experiences agree, and which in the last analysis is definitive of them and serves to mark them off from other kinds of experiences, is that they involve the apprehension of *an ultimate nonsensuous unity in all things*, a oneness or a One to which neither the senses nor the reason can penetrate. In other words, it entirely transcends our sensory-intellectual consciousness.

It should be carefully noted that only fully developed mystical experiences are necessarily apprehensive of the One. Many experiences have been recorded which lack this central feature but yet possess other mystical characteristics. These are borderline cases, which may be said to shade off from the central core of cases.

They have to the central core the relation which some philosophers like to call "family resemblance."

We should also note that although at this stage of our exposition we speak of mystical experience as an apprehension *of* the Unity, the mystics of the Hindu and Buddhist cultures, as well as Plotinus and many others, generally insist that this is incorrect since it supposes a division between subject and object. We should rather say that the experience *is* the One. Thus Plotinus writes: "We should not speak of seeing, but instead of seen and seer, speak boldly of a simple Unity for in this seeing we neither distinguish, nor are there two." But we will leave the development of this point till later. And often for convenience' sake we shall speak of the experience *of* the unity.

VI.   EXTROVERTIVE MYSTICISM

There appear to be two main distinguishable types of mystical experience, both of which may be found in all the higher cultures. One may be called extrovertive mystical experience, the other introvertive mystical experience. Both are apprehensions of the One, but they reach it in different ways. The extrovertive way looks outward and through the physical senses into the external world and finds the One there. The introvertive way turns inward, introspectively, and finds the One at the bottom of the self, at the bottom of the human personality. The latter far outweighs the former in importance both in the history of mysticism and in the history of human thought generally. The introvertive way is the major strand in the history of mysticism, the extrovertive way a minor strand. I shall only briefly refer to extrovertive mysticism and then pass on, and shall take introvertive mysticism as the main subject of this book.

The extrovertive mystic with his physical senses continues to perceive the same world of trees and hills and tables and chairs as the rest of us. But he sees these objects transfigured in such manner that the Unity shines through them. Because it includes ordinary sense perceptions, it only partially realizes the description given in section (4). For the full realization of this we have to wait for the introvertive experience. I will give two brief historical instances of extrovertive experience. The great Catholic mystic Meister Eckhart (circa 1260–1329) wrote as follows: "Here [i.e., in this experience] all blades of grass, wood, and stone, all things are One. . . . When is a man in mere understanding? When he sees one thing separated from another. And when is he above mere understanding? When he sees all in all, then a man stands above mere understanding."

In this quotation we note that according to Eckhart seeing a number of things as separate and distinct, seeing the grass and the wood and the stone as three different things, is the mark of the sensory-intellectual consciousness. For Eckhart's word "understanding" means the conceptual intellect. But if one passes beyond the sensory-intellectual consciousness into the mystical consciousness, then one sees these three things as being "all one." However, it is evident that in this extrovertive experience the distinctions between things have not wholly disappeared. There is no doubt that what Eckhart means is that he sees the three things as distinct and separate and yet at the same time as not distinct but identical. The grass is identical with the stone, and the stone with the wood, although they are all different. Rudolph Otto, commenting on this, observes that it is as if one said that black is the same as white, white the same as black, although at the same time white remains white and black remains black. Of course this is a complete paradox. It is in fact contradictory. But we shall find that paradoxicality is one of the common characteristics of all mysticism. And it is no use saying that this is all logically impossible, and that no consciousness of this kind can exist, unless we wish, on these a priori grounds, to refuse to study the evidence—which is overwhelming.

What some mystics simply call the One other mystics often identify with God. Hence we find Jakob Böhme (1575–1624) saying much the same thing about the grass and the trees and the stones as Eckhart does, but saying that they are all God instead of just all One. The following is a statement of one of his experiences: "In this light my spirit saw through all things and into all creatures and I recognized God in grass and plants."

It is suggested that the extrovertive type of experience is a kind of halfway house to the introvertive. For the introvertive experience is wholly nonsensuous and nonintellectual. But the extrovertive experience is sensory-intellectual in so far as it still perceives physical objects but is nonsensuous and nonintellectual in so far as it perceives them as "all one."

We may sum up this short account of the extrovertive consciousness by saying that it is a perception of the world as transfigured and unified in one ultimate being. In some cultures the one being is identified with God; and since God is then perceived as the inner essence of all objects, this type of experience tends toward pantheism. But in some cultures—for example, Buddhism—the unity is not interpreted as God at all.

VII.   INTROVERTIVE MYSTICISM

Suppose that one could shut all physical sensations out of one's consciousness. It may be thought that this would be easy as regards some of the senses, namely sight, hearing, taste, and smell. One can shut one's eyes, stop up one's ears, and hold one's nose. One can avoid taste sensations by keeping one's mouth empty. But one cannot shut off tactual sensations in any simple way of this kind. And it would be even more difficult to get rid of organic sensations. However, one can perhaps suppose it possible somehow to thrust tactual and organic sensations out of conscious awareness—perhaps into the unconscious. Mystics do not, as far as I know, descend to the ignominious level of holding their noses and stopping their ears. My only point is that it is possible to conceive of getting rid of all sensations, and in one way or other mystics claim that they do this.

Suppose now, after this has been done, we next try to get rid of all sensuous *images* from our minds. This is very difficult. Most people, try as they will not to picture anything at all, will find vague images floating about in consciousness. Suppose, however, that it is possible to suppress all images. And suppose finally that we manage to stop all thinking and reasoning. Having got rid of the whole empirical content of sensations, images, and thoughts, presumably all emotions and desires and volitions would also disappear, since they normally exist only as attachments to the cognitive content. What, then, would be left of consciousness?

What would happen? It is natural to suppose that with all the elements of consciousness gone consciousness itself would lapse and the subject would fall asleep or become *un*conscious.

Now it happens to be the case that this total suppression of the whole empirical content of consciousness is precisely what the introvertive mystic claims to achieve. And he claims that what happens is not that all consciousness disappears but that only the ordinary sensory-intellectual consciousness disappears and is replaced by an entirely new kind of consciousness, the mystical consciousness. Naturally we now ask whether any description of this new consciousness can be given. But before trying to answer that difficult question, I propose to turn aside for a brief space to speak about the methods which mystics use to suppress sensuous images, and thinking, so as to get rid of their sensory-intellectual consciousness. There are the Yoga techniques of India; and Christian mystics in Catholic monasteries also evolved their own methods. The latter usually call their techniques "prayers," but they are not prayers in the vulgar sense of asking God for things; they are much more like the "meditation" and "concentration" of Yogis than may be commonly supposed. This is too vast a subject to be discussed in detail here. But I will give two elementary illustrations.

Everyone has heard of the breathing exercises undertaken by the yogins of India seeking samadhi—samadhi being the Indian name for mystical consciousness. What is this special method of breathing, and what is it supposed to accomplish? The theory of the matter is, I understand, something like this: It is practically impossible, or at least very difficult, to stop all sensing, imaging, and thinking by a forcible act of the will. What comes very near to it, however, is to concentrate one's attention on some single point or object so that all other mental content falls away and there is left nothing but the single point of consciousness. If this can be done, then ultimately that single point will itself disappear because contrast is necessary for our ordinary consciousness, and if there is only one point of consciousness left, there is nothing to form a contrast to it.

The question then is: On what single thing should one concentrate? A simple way is to concentrate on the stream of one's own breath. Simple instructions which I have heard given are those. One first adopts a suitable physical position with spine and neck perfectly erect. Then breathe in and out slowly, evenly, and smoothly. Concentrate your attention on this and nothing else. Some aspirants, I believe, count their breaths, 1, 2, 3, . . . up to 10, and then begin the count again. Continue this procedure till you attain the desired results.

A second method is to keep repeating in one's mind some short formula of words over and over again till the words lose all meaning. So long as they carry meaning, of course the mind is still occupied with the thought of this meaning. But when the words become meaningless there is nothing left of consciousness except the monotonous sound image, and that too, like the consciousness of one's breath, will in the end disappear. There is an interesting connection between this method and a remark made by the poet Tennyson. From childhood up Tennyson had frequent mystical experiences. They came to him spontaneously, without effort, and unsought. But he mentions the curious fact that he could induce them at will by the odd procedure of repeating his own name over and over again to himself. I know of no evidence that he studied mysticism enough to understand the theory of his own procedure, which would presumably be that the constantly repeated sound image served as the focus of the required one-pointed attention.

This leads to another curious reflection. Mystics who follow the procedure of constantly repeating a verbal formula often, I believe, tend to choose some religious set of words, for instance a part of the Lord's Prayer or a psalm. They probably imagine that these uplifting and inspirational words will carry them upwards toward the divine. But Tennyson's procedure suggests that any nonsense words would probably do as well. And this seems to agree with the general theory of concentration. It doesn't seem to matter what is chosen as the single point of concentration, whether it be one's breathing, or the sound of one's own name, or one's navel, or anything else, provided only it serves to shut off all other mental content.

Another point on which mystics usually insist in regard to spiritual training is what they call "detachment." Emphasis on this is found just as much in Hinduism and Buddhism as in Christianity. What is sought is detachment from desire, the uprooting of desire, or at any rate of all self-centered desires. The exact psychology of the matter presents great difficulties. In Christian mysticism the idea of detachment is usually given a religious and moral twist by insisting that it means the destruction of self-will or any kind of self-assertiveness, especially the rooting out of pride and the attainment of absolute humility. In non-Christian mysticism detachment does not usually get this special slant. But in the mysticism of all cultures detachment from desires for sensations and sensory images is emphasized.

We will now return to the main question. Supposing that the sensory-intellectual consciousness has been successfully supplanted by the mystical consciousness, can we find in the literatures of the subject any descriptions of this consciousness that will give us any idea of what it is like? The answer is that although mystics frequently say that their experiences are ineffable and indescribable, they nevertheless do often in fact describe them, and one can find plenty of such descriptive statements in the literature. They are usually extremely short—perhaps only three or four lines. And frequently they are indirect and not in the first person singular. Mystics more often then not avoid direct references to themselves.

I will give here a famous description which occurs in the Mandukya Upanishad. The Upanishads are supposed to have been the work of anonymous forest seers in India who lived between three thousand and twenty-five hundred years ago. They are among the oldest records of mysticism in the world. But they are of an unsurpassable depth of spirituality. For long ages and for countless millions of men in the East they have been, and they remain, the supreme source of the spiritual life. Of the introvertive mystical consciousness the Mandukya says that it is "beyond the senses, beyond the understanding, beyond all expression. . . . It is the pure unitary consciousness, wherein awareness of the world and of multiplicity is completely obliterated. It is ineffable peace. It is the Supreme Good. It is One without a second. It is the Self."

It will repay us, not to just slur over this passage, but to examine it carefully clause by clause. The first sentence is negative, telling us only what the experience is *not*. It is "beyond the senses, beyond the understanding." That is to say, it is beyond the sensory-intellectual consciousness; and there are in it no elements of sensation or sensuous imagery and no elements of conceptual thought. After these negatives there comes the statement that "it is the unitary consciousness, wherein all awareness of multiplicity has been obliterated." The core of the experience is thus described as an undifferentiated unity—a oneness or unity in which there is no internal division, no multiplicity.

I happen to have quoted a Hindu source. But one can find exactly the same thing in Christian mysticism. For instance the great Flemish mystic Jan van Ruysbroeck (1293–1381) says of what he calls "the God-seeing man" that "his spirit is undifferentiated and without distinction, and therefore it feels nothing but the unity." We see that the very words of the faithful Catholic are almost identical with those of the ancient Hindu, and I do not see how it can be doubted that they are describing the same experience. Not only in Christianity and Hinduism but everywhere else we find that the essence of the experience is that it is an *undifferentiated unity*, though each culture and each religion interprets this undifferentiated unity in terms of its own creeds or dogmas.

It may be objected that "undifferentiated unity" is a conceptual thought, and this is inconsistent with our statement that the experience is wholly nonintellectual. The answer is that concepts such as "one," "unity," "undifferentiated," "God," "Nirvana," etc., are only applied to the experience *after* it has passed and when it is being *remembered*. None can be applied during the experience itself.

The passage of the Upanishad goes on to say that the undifferentiated unity "is the Self." Why is this? Why is the unity now identified with the Self? The answer is plain. We started with the full self or mind of our ordinary everyday consciousness. What was it full of? It was full of the multiplicity of sensations, thoughts, desires, and the rest. But the mind was not merely this multiplicity. These disparate elements were held together in a unity, the unity of the single mind or self. A multiplicity without a unity in which the multiple elements are together is inconceivable—e.g., many objects in one space. Now when we emptied all the multiple contents out of this unity of the self what is left, according to the Upanishad, is the unity of the self, the original unity minus its contents. And this is the self. The Upanishads go further than this. They always identify this individual self with the Universal Self, the soul of the world. We will consider this in Chapter 2 [of *Teachings of the Mystics*]. For the moment we may continue to think in terms of the individual self, the pure ego of you or me. The undifferentiated unity is thought to be the pure ego.

I must draw the reader's attention to several facts about this situation. In the first place it flatly contradicts what David Hume said in a famous passage about the self. He said that when he looked introspectively into himself and searched for the I, the self, the ego, all he could ever introspect was the multiplicity of the sensations, images, thoughts, and feelings. He could never observe any I, any pure self apart from its contents, and he inferred that the I is a fiction and does not really exist. But now a vast body of empirical evidence, that of the mystics from all over the world, affirms that Hume was simply mistaken on a question of psychological fact, and that it is possible to get rid of all the mental contents and find the pure self left over and to experience this. This evidence need not mean that the self is a thing or a "substance," but can be taken as implying that it is a pure unity, the sort of being which Kant called the "transcendental unity" of the self.

The next thing to note is that the assertion of this new kind of consciousness is completely paradoxical. One way of bringing out the paradox is to point out that what we are left with here, when the contents of consciousness are gone, is a kind of consciousness which has no objects. It is not a consciousness *of* anything, but yet it is still consciousness. For the contents of our ordinary daily consciousness, the colors, sounds, wishes, thoughts are the same as the objects of consciousness, so that when the contents are gone the objects are gone. This consciousness of the mystics is not even a consciousness of consciousness, for then there would be a duality which is incompatible with the idea of an undifferentiated unity. In India it is called *pure* consciousness. The word "pure" is used in somewhat the same sense as Kant used it—meaning "without any empirical contents."

Another aspect of the paradox is that this pure consciousness is simultaneously both positive and negative, something and nothing, a fullness and an emptiness. The positive side is that it is an actual and positive consciousness. Moreover, all mystics affirm that it is pure peace, beatitude, joy, bliss, so that it has a positive affective tone. The Christians call it "the peace of God which passeth all understanding." The Buddhists call it Nirvana. But although it has this positive character, it is quite correct to say also that when we empty out all objects and contents of the mind *there is nothing whatever left*. That is the negative side of the paradox. What is left is sheer Emptiness. This is fully recognized in all mystical literature. In Mahayana Buddhism this total emptiness of the mystical consciousness is called the Void. In Christian mysticism the experience is identified with God. And this causes Eckhart and others to say that God, or the Godhead, is pure Nothingness, is a "desert," or "wilderness," and so on. Usually the two sides of the paradox are expressed in metaphors. The commonest metaphor for the positive side is light and for the negative side darkness. This is the darkness of God. It is called darkness because all distinctions disappear in it just as all distinctions disappear in a physical darkness.

We must not say that what we have here is a light *in* the darkness. For that would be no paradox. The paradox is that the light *is* the darkness, and the darkness *is* the light. This statement can be well documented from the literature of different cultures. I will give two examples, one from Christianity, one from Buddhism—and from the Buddhism of Tibet of all places in the world. Dionysius the Areopagite, a Christian, speaks of God as "the dazzling obscurity which outshines all brilliance with the intensity of its darkness." And the Tibetan Book of the Dead puts the same paradox in the words, "the clear light of the Void." In Dionysius we see that the obscurity, or the darkness, *is* the brilliance, and in the Tibetan book we see that the Void itself *is* a clear light.

VIII.   MYSTICISM AND RELIGION

Most writers on mysticism seem to take it for granted that mystical experience is a religious experience, and that mysticism is necessarily a religious phenomenon.

They seem to think that mysticism and religious mysticism are one and the same thing. But this is far from being correct. It is true that there is an important connection between mysticism and religion, but it is not nearly so direct and immediate as most writers have seemed to think, nor can it be simply taken for granted as an obvious fact.

There are several grounds for insisting that intrinsically and in itself mystical experience is not a religious phenomenon at all and that its connection with religions is subsequent and even adventitious. In the first place, it seems to be clear that if we strip the mystical experience of all intellectual interpretation such as that which identifies it with God, or with the Absolute, or with the soul of the world, what is left is simply the undifferentiated unity. Now what is there that is religious about an undifferentiated unity? The answer seems to be, in the first instance, "Nothing at all." There seems to be nothing religious about an undifferentiated unity as such.

In the theistic religions of the West, in Christianity, Judaism, and Islam, the experience of the undifferentiated unity is interpreted as "union with God." But this is an interpretation and is not the experience itself. It is true that some Christian mystics, such as St. Teresa of Avila, invariably speak simply of having experienced "union with God," and do not talk about an undifferentiated unity. St. Teresa did not have a sufficiently analytical mind to distinguish between the experience and its interpretation. But other Christian mystics who are more analytically minded, such as Eckhart and Ruysbroeck, do speak of the undifferentiated unity.

These considerations are further underlined by the fact that quite different interpretations of the same experience are given in different cultures. The undifferentiated unity is interpreted by Eckhart and Ruysbroeck in terms of the Trinitarian conception of God, but by Islamic mystics as the unitarian God of Islam, and by the leading school of the Vedantists as a more impersonal Absolute. And when we come to Buddhism we find that the experience is not interpreted as any kind of God at all. For the Buddhist it becomes the Void or Nirvana. Buddha denied the existence of a Supreme Being altogether. It is often said that Buddhism is atheistic. And whether this description of Buddhism is true or not, it is certainly the case that there can exist an atheistic mysticism, a mystical experience naked and not clothed in any religious garb.

In view of these facts, we have a problem on our hands. Why is it that, in spite of exceptions, mysticism *usually* takes on some religious form and is usually found in connection with a definitely religious culture and as being a part of some definite religion? The following are, I think, the main reasons.

First, there is a very important feature of the introvertive mystical experience which I have not mentioned yet. I refer to the experience of the "melting away" into the Infinite of one's own individuality. Such phrases as "melting away," "fading away," "passing away" are found in the mystical literature of Christianity, Islam, Hinduism, and Buddhism. Among the Sufis of Islam there is a special technical term for it. It is called fanā. It must be insisted that this is not an inference or an interpretation or a theory or a speculation. It is an actual experience. The individual, as it were, directly experiences the disappearance of his own individuality, its fading away into the Infinite. To document this, one could quote from Eckhart, or from the Upanishads or the Sufis. But I believe I can bring home the point to a modern reader better by quoting a modern author. I referred earlier to the fact that Tennyson had frequent mystical experiences. His account of them is quoted by William James in his *The Varieties of Religious Experience.* Tennyson wrote, "All at once, as it were out of the intensity of the consciousness of individuality, individuality itself seemed to dissolve and fade away into boundless being. . . . the loss of personality, if such it were, seeming no extinction but the only true life." "Boundless being" seems to have the same meaning as "the Infinite." The Infinite is in most minds identified with the idea of God. We are finite beings, God is the only Infinite Being. One can see at once, therefore, how this experience of the dissolution of one's own individuality, its being merged into the Infinite, takes on a religious meaning. In theistic cultures the experience of melting away into boundless being is interpreted as union with God.

A second reason for the connection between mysticism and religion is that the undifferentiated unity is necessarily thought of by the mystics as being *beyond space and beyond time.* For it is without any internal division or multiplicity of parts whereas the essence of time is its division into an endless multitude of successive parts, and the essence of space is its division into a multitude of parts lying side by side. Therefore the undifferentiated unity being without any multiplicity of parts, is necessarily spaceless and timeless. Being timeless is the same as being eternal. Hence Eckhart is constantly telling us that the mystical experience transcends time and is an experience of "the Eternal Now." But in religious minds the Eternal, like the Infinite, is another name for God. Hence the mystical experience is thought of as an experience of God.

A third reason for this identification of the undifferentiated unity with God lies in the emotional side of the experience. It is the universal testimony of the mystics that their kind of consciousness brings feelings of an exalted peace, blessedness, and joy. It becomes identified with the peace of God, the gateway of the Divine, the gateway of salvation. This is also why in Buddhism, though the experience is not personified or called God, it nevertheless becomes Nirvana which is the supreme goal of the Buddhist religious life.

Thus we see that mysticism naturally, though not necessarily, becomes intimately associated with whatever is the religion of the culture in which it appears. It is, however, important to realize that it does not favor any particular religion. Mystical experience in itself does not have any tendency to make a man a Christian or a Buddhist. Into the framework of what creed he will fit his experience will tend to depend mostly on the culture in which he lives. In a Buddhist country the mystic interprets his experience as a glimpse of Nirvana, in a Christian country he may interpret it as union with God or even (as in Eckhart) as penetrating into the Godhead which is beyond God. Or if he is a highly sophisticated modern individual, who has been turned by his education into a religious skeptic, he may remain a skeptic as regards the dogmas of the different religions; he may allow his mystical experience to remain naked without any clothing of creeds or dogmas; but he is likely at the same time to feel that in that experience he has found something *sacred.* And this feeling of the sacred may quite properly be called "religious" feeling though it does not clothe itself in any dogmas. And this alone may be enough to uplift his ideals and to revolutionize his life and to give it meaning and purpose.

IX.   THE ETHICAL ASPECTS OF MYSTICISM

It is sometimes asserted that mysticism is merely an escape from life and from its duties and responsibilities. The mystic, it is said, retreats into a private ecstasy of bliss, turns his back on the world, and forgets not only his own sorrows but the needs and sorrows of his fellow-men. In short, his life is essentially selfish.

It is possible that there have been mystics who deserved this kind of condemnation. To treat the bliss of the mystical consciousness as an end in itself is certainly a psychological possibility. And no doubt there have been men who have succumbed to this temptation. But this attitude is not the mystic ideal, and it is severely condemned by those who are most representative of the mystics themselves. For instance, St. John of the Cross condemns it as "spiritual gluttony." Eckhart tells us that if a man were in mystical ecstasy and knew of a poor man who needed his help, he should leave his ecstasy in order to go and serve the poor man. The Christian mystics especially have always emphasized that mystical union with God brings with it an intense and burning love of God which must needs overflow into the world in the form of love for our fellow-men; and that this must show itself in deeds of charity, mercy, and self-sacrifice, and not merely in words.

Some mystics have gone beyond this and have insisted that the mystical consciousness is the secret fountain of all love, human as well as divine; and that since love in the end is the only source of true moral activity, therefore mysticism is the source from which ethical values ultimately flow. For all selfishness and cruelty and evil result from the separateness of one human being from another. This separateness of individuals breeds egoism and the war of all against all. But in the mystical consciousness all distinctions disappear and therefore the distinction between "I" and "you" and "he" and "she." This is the mystical and metaphysical basis of love, namely the realization that my brother and I are one, and that therefore his sufferings are my sufferings and his happiness is my happiness. This reveals itself dimly in the psychological phenomena of sympathy and more positively in actual love. For one who had no touch of the mystical vision all men would be islands. And in the end it is because of mysticism that it is possible to say that "no man is an island" and that on the contrary every man is "a part of the main."

X.   ALTERNATIVE INTERPRETATIONS OF MYSTICISM

We have seen that the same experience may be interpreted in terms of different religious creeds. There is also another set of alternative interpretations which we ought to mention. We may believe that the mystic really is in touch, as he usually claims, with some being greater than himself, some spiritual Infinite which transcends the temporal flux of things. Or we may, on the other hand, adopt the alternative solution of the skeptic who will think that the mystical consciousness is entirely subjective and imports nothing outside itself. My own vote would be cast for the former solution. I would agree with the words of Arthur Koestler which are quoted in the final selection printed in this [Stace's] book. He speaks of a higher order of reality which for us is like a text written in invisible ink. "I also liked to think," he says, "that the founders of religions, prophets, saints and seers had at moments been able to read a fragment of the invisible text; after which they had so much padded, dramatised and ornamented it, that they themselves could no longer tell what parts of it were authentic."[1]

But I wish to point out that even if one should choose the skeptical alternative and suppose that the mystical consciousness reveals no reality outside its owner's brain, one is far from having disposed of mysticism as some worthless delusion which ought to be got rid of. Even if it is wholly subjective, it still reveals something which is supremely great in human life. It is still the peace which passeth all understanding. It is still the gateway to salvation—not, I mean, in a future life, but as the highest beatitude that a man can reach in this life, and out of which the greatest deeds of love can flow. But it must be added, of course, that it belongs among those things of which Spinoza wrote in those famous words: "If the road which I have shown is very difficult, it yet can be discovered. And clearly it must be very hard if it is so rarely found. For how could it be that it is neglected by practically all, if salvation . . . could be found without difficulty. But all excellent things are as difficult as they are rare."

R. C. ZAEHNER
Nature Mysticism, Soul Mysticism and Theistic Mysticism

Thus Śankara maintains that the highest Brahman, the One without a second, can only be attained by *sannyāsins*, men who renounce everything but their Selves, refuse to take part in religious ceremonies or to accept the grace of any God, and who abandon all works, whether good or evil.[2] 'By ceasing to do good to one's friends or evil to one's enemies (the *sannyāsin*) attains to the eternal Brahman by the *yoga* of meditation.'[3]

R. C. Zaehner (1913–1974) was educated at both Oxford and Cambridge and later taught for many years at Oxford University. His many works include *The Comparison of Religions, Hindu and Muslim Mysticism*, and *Concordant Discord: the Interdependence of Faiths*.

NATURE MYSTICISM, SOUL MYSTICISM AND THEISTIC MYSTICISM   From *Mysticism: Sacred and Profane* by R. C. Zaehner. Reprinted by permission of the Clarendon Press, Oxford.

[1] See p. 235 [in *Teachings of the Mystics*. The quotation from Arthur Koestler's *The Invisible Writing*, copyright 1954 by Arthur Koestler, is reproduced by permission of The Macmillan Company and A. D. Peters and Co.].

[2] See *Māndūkya Up.*, *Kārikā*, 2. 35.

[3] *Nārada Upaniṣad*, Schrader, p. 145; 'priyeṣu sveṣu sukṛtam apriyeṣu ca duṣkṛtam visṛjya dhyānayogena brahmāpyeti sanātanam.'

Now just as Rāmānuja and the other theistic philosophers in India attack Śankara and his followers for their extreme monism and for precisely this type of
conduct which is its logical sequel, so did Ruysbroeck and Suso attack the Beghards
in the European Middle Ages, for the latter held similar views and indulged in a
similar quietism, believing themselves to be perfect and incapable of sin. In his
Spiritual Espousals Ruysbroeck attacks those who seek to find perfect tranquillity
in themselves. This passage is extraordinarily relevant to our theme and must be
extensively quoted.

'Now observe', Ruysbroeck writes, 'that whenever man is empty and undistracted in his senses by images, and free and unoccupied in his highest powers,
he attains rest by purely natural means. And all men can find and possess this rest
in themselves by their mere nature, without the grace of God, if they are able to
empty themselves of sensual images and of all actions.'[3] Though he had obviously
never heard of Vedāntin monism and could never have done so, Ruysbroeck
seems not only to know exactly what this state of 'oneness without a second' is,
but he describes it so accurately that one cannot but conclude that he is writing
from actual experience. 'Whenever man is empty and undistracted in his senses
by images, and free and unoccupied in his highest powers', such a man, we might
continue, achieves the highest Brahman: for herein, precisely, lies the essence of
the non-dualist Vedānta.

However, as Ruysbroeck rightly saw, such an emptying of the human person
can only be the beginning of the mystical life for those who have experienced the
grace of a personal God; for according to Christianity God is Love, and the Muslim mystics, particularly in Persia, were later to make this idea their own. It is
present too in the tenth and thirteenth chapters of the Bhagavad-Gītā and in all
the devotional, as opposed to the philosophical, writing of the Hindus. Just as
Śankara despises his fellow countrymen who continue to worship 'illusory' gods
for being on a lower level than himself, so does Ruysbroeck fulminate against
contemporary European quietists. There are two states of tranquillity, Ruysbroeck
maintains, two types of *śānti*,—the rest one takes in one's self, purged as it has
been of all affections and desires, and the rest in God when the living flame
kindled by the fire of God is reunited with the divine fire. Thus Ruysbroeck has
no patience with those who are content to rest in the self or Self,—and it can
make no difference whether we spell this word with a capital letter or not since,
in Sanskrit, there are no capital letters,—for this state, blissful though it undoubtedly is, is not union with God. It is the eternal spirit of the individual man
contemplating itself in itself, as it issued from the mind of God but, because of
original sin, separated from God, though otherwise sinless.

These men, says Ruysbroeck, 'are, as it seems to them, occupied in the contemplation of God, and they believe themselves to be the holiest men alive. Yet they
live in opposition and dissimilarity to God and all saints and all good men. . . .

'Through the natural rest which they feel and have in themselves in emptiness,
they maintain that they are free, and united with God without mean, and that
they are advanced beyond all the exercises of Holy Church, and beyond the

---

[3] Blessed Jan van Ruysbroeck, *The Spiritual Espousals*, tr. Eric Colledge, London, Faber and Faber,
1952, pp. 166–7.

commandments of God, and beyond the law, and beyond all the virtuous works which one can in any way practise.' Here one calls to mind Śankara's contempt for those who perform the duties laid down by their religion and his preference for the perfect Yogin's withdrawal from all works. 'For', Ruysbroeck goes on to say, 'this emptiness seems to them to be so great that no-one ought to hinder them with the performance of any work, however good it be, for their emptiness is of greater excellence than are all virtues. And therefore they remain in mere passivity without the performance of any work directed up towards God or down towards man, just like the instrument which is itself passive and awaits the time when its owner wishes to work.'[4] Such men are indeed suspended between heaven and earth, isolated from man and Nature because they have severed all attachments, and isolated from God because the oneness of isolation is their end and goal, and because a conviction that they are the Absolute constitutes the toughest possible barrier between them and a possible irruption of grace: they 'maintain that they cannot advance, for they have achieved a life of unity and emptiness beyond which one cannot advance and in which there is no exercise'.[5]

It will be remembered that Christ said, 'No man cometh to the Father, but by me'.[6] It is, of course, possible to take this saying in an absolutely literal sense and thereby to dismiss all non-Christian religions as being merely false. It is, however, legitimate and certainly more charitable to interpret this saying, so far as it applies to mysticism, to mean that unless one approaches the Father through the Son and as a son with the trust and helplessness of a child, there is very little chance of finding Him,—none at all, it would appear, if you insist either that you are identical with the Father or that the Father is an illusion. Hence a sharp distinction must be drawn between those forms of religion in which love or charity plays a predominant part and those in which it does not. In Christian mysticism love is all-important, and it must be so, since God Himself is defined as Love. In Islam too, because the Muslims inherited more than they knew from the Christians, it assumes ever-increasing importance despite the predominantly terrifying picture of God we find in the Qur'ān. In Hinduism this religion of love breaks through in the Gītā and in the cults of both Viṣṇu and Śiva, and, of course, in the worship of Rāma and Krishna as incarnations of Viṣṇu. 'I am the origin of all,' says Krishna in the Bhagavad-Gītā, 'from me all things evolve. Thinking thus do wisemen, immersed in love (bhāva), worship Me. Thinking of Me, devoting their lives to Me, enlightening each other, and speaking of Me always, they are contented and rejoice. To these worshippers of Mine, always controlled, I give a steady mind by which they may approach Me, for I loved them first.'[7] This and very much else that is similar will be found in Hindu literature, yet always the shadow of a self-satisfied monism stalks behind it.

[4]Ibid., pp. 170–1.

[5]Ibid., p. 173.

[6]John xiv. 6.

[7]BhagG. 10. 8–10: 'aham sarvasya prabhavo, mattaḥ sarvaṃ pravartate; / iti matvā bhajante mām budhā bhāvasamanvitāḥ. / mac-cittā mad-gata-prāṇā bodhayantaḥ parasparam, / kathayantaśca mām nityaṃ tuṣyantica ramantica. / teṣāṃ satata-yuktānāṃ bhajatāṃ prīti-pūrvakam / dadāmi buddhi-yogaṃ taṃ yena mām upayānti te.'

And in monism there can be no love,—there is ecstasy and trance and deep peace, what Ruysbroeck calls 'rest', but there cannot be the ecstasy of union nor the loss of self in God which is the goal of Christian, Muslim, and all theistic mysticism.

> 'And therefore', says Ruysbroeck, 'all those men are deceived whose intention it is to sink themselves in natural rest, and who do not seek God with desire nor find Him in delectable love. For the rest which they possess consists in an emptying of themselves, to which they are inclined by nature and by habit. And in this natural rest men cannot find God. But it brings man indeed into an emptiness which heathens and Jews are able to find, and all men, however evil they may be, if they live in their sins with untroubled conscience, and are able to empty themselves of all images and all action. In this emptiness rest is sufficient and great, and it is in itself no sin, for it is in all men by nature, if they knew how to make themselves empty.'[8]

All mystics, including Ruysbroeck, agree that no progress in the inner life is possible without detachment from all things worldly, from all that comes to be and passes away, and above all from the individual ego or self. They are agreed that the 'second self', as Proust calls it, must be discovered and brought out into the open. The temptation is that with the finding of this second self the aspirant after spiritual perfection should think that he has reached his goal and that the 'second self', the *ātman* of the Vedānta, is God. . . .

In this book our investigations have led to the tentative conclusion that what goes by the name of mysticism, so far from being an identical expression of the selfsame Universal Spirit, falls into three distinct categories. Under the general heading of mysticism we have not included those experiences that are sometimes associated with it,—clairvoyance, clair-audition, telepathy, thought-reading, levitation, bi-location, and the rest: we have confined ourselves to praeternatural experiences in which sense perception and discursive thought are transcended in an immediate apperception of a unity or union which is apprehended as lying beyond and transcending the multiplicity of the world as we know it. Because these experiences are recorded at all times and from all parts of the world, it is fatally easy to assume that because they are, one and all, praeternatural, that is, not explicable in the present state of our knowledge, and because the keynote of all of them is 'union', they must necessarily be the same. It is not realized often enough that once these experiences are assumed to be identical and of identical provenance, the conclusion that the transports of the saint and the ecstasies of the manic are identical cannot be escaped. If this were really so, and if these praeternatural experiences were what religion is principally concerned with, then the only sensible course to adopt would be that which Rimbaud followed: we should all attempt to induce in ourselves an attack of acute mania; and this is in fact the solution that Mr. Huxley seems to propound in *The Doors of Perception*.

That 'nature mysticism' exists and is widely attested is not open to serious doubt. How the experience is to be explained is quite another matter. To identify it with the experience of Christian or Muslim saints, however, is hardly admissible, as I hope to have shown, however inadequately, in the course of this work. In this

[8]Op. cit., p. 167.

connexion it is significant that though Mr. Custance christened his familiar spirit Tyche-Teresa in recognition of the supposed fact that the Saint of Avila's experiences were comparable to, or even identical with, his own, he never quotes from her works though the words of Plotinus come readily enough to his lips.

Though it is easy enough to dismiss the experiences of the nature mystic as mere hallucination, this is really begging the question; for, in all cases of this experience, the impression of *reality* they leave behind is quite overwhelming. In every case,—whether the experience comes unheralded or whether it is produced by drugs or Yoga techniques,— the result is the same;—the person who has had the experience feels that he has gone through something of tremendous significance beside which the ordinary world of sense perception and discursive thought is almost the shadow of a shade. Huxley expresses this with the German word *Istigkeit*, and he has thereby fully caught the mood. The experience seems overpoweringly *real*; its authority obtrudes itself and will not be denied. It is this quality in it, I believe, which makes those who have been the subject of such a visitation assume that this must be identical with what the mystical saints have experienced. The Ṣūfīs reply to their critics by saying that their criticism is about as valid as that of a teetotaller who vainly tries to understand the pleasures of drunkenness without ever having tasted wine. It will not help him to know that wine is the fermented juice of the grape or what its chemical constituents are: until he has actually drunk deeply, he will never understand the exhilaration of the drinker. Similarly no child who has not reached the age of adolescence can understand what pleasure there can possibly be in the sexual act which seems to him revolting. So with the nature mystics,—it is extremely difficult for the purely rational man to understand in what the excitement and the joy consist, or why it should be that the sensation of losing one's individuality should be so intensely prized. No comparison is adequate: the nearest, perhaps, as Huxley saw, is an intense absorption in music or painting, or in dancing, for all these can be used as aids to produce such a condition, and the Ṣūfīs introduced song and dance, and the contemplation of beautiful boys, very early as aids to the attainment of praeternatural states. Yet even so, they can serve only as the faintest adumbrations, they can scarcely claim even to approximate to the real thing.

Ṣūfism is, in this respect, perhaps more instructive than either Christian or Indian mysticism. The distinction that Qushayrī drew between *bast*, or the sense of one's personality expanding indefinitely, and actual communion with God, is rarely met with again, and the opposition of the conservatives to the use of song and dance as stimulants broke down all too soon, because as Ṣūfism degenerated, the achievement of ecstasy as such became the Ṣūfī's goal regardless of whether such ecstasies proceeded from the hand of God or not. The later Ṣūfīs came to assume that all ecstasy was divine, and thereby put a ready weapon into the hands of the orthodox: for whereas sanctity is its own argument, mania is not, and no genuinely religious person is likely to be impressed by one who claims either to be in direct communion with God or actually to be identical with Him, if his conduct is, in fact, sub-human. Thus the confusion that is popularly made between nature mysticism and the mysticism of the Christian saints can only discredit the latter. By making the confusion one is forced into the position that God is simply another term for Nature; and it is an observable fact that in Nature there is neither morality nor charity nor even common decency. God, then, is reduced to the sum-total of natural impulses in which the terms 'good' and 'evil' have no meaning. Such a god is subhuman, a god fit for animals, not for rational creatures; and to experience such a god has rightly been termed 'downward transcendence' by Mr. Huxley.

However, if there is a God, and if it is true that our relations with Him will be very much more intimate after death, then 'it is not enough to know only that He exists, but one must know His nature and His will'.[9] This is even more important for the mystic than it is for the ordinary man, for the mystic is in fact the man who has a foretaste in this life of life after death; and just as the experiences of those who have taken mescalin have, to a certain extent, varied according to their beliefs, so will the experiences of persons who tame their senses and discipline their minds with a view to reaching a higher reality.

Indian religion is right in describing the object of religious disciplines as being *mokṣa* or liberation. By this they mean liberation from what St. Paul calls 'the flesh', that is, the life of blind instinct, the animal in man. Beyond this they also seek liberation from the third of Avicenna's three components of the lower soul, 'imagination' or distracting thought. As their final goal the Sāṃkhya-Yogins seek their own immortal soul in its nakedness and isolation. Having no clear idea of God, they cannot seek union with Him, nor do they claim to.

The Vedāntins are in a different case. The Upaniṣads teach that Brahman is both the source of all things and that he includes all things. Greater than all the universe, he is yet the fine point without magnitude which is the deep centre of the human heart. In so far as they teach this, they are fully at one with the mystical teaching of the Catholic Church. However, they also teach that Brahman *is* the universe and that he *is* the human soul. Rāmānuja and his followers interpret this as being a metaphor and as meaning that the universe and human souls are what he calls the 'body' of God whereas God or Brahman remains distinct from them though they are wholly dependent on him. Here again there is full agreement between Rāmānuja and Catholic mystical tradition. Whether Rāmānuja or Śankara more accurately represents the general trend of Upaniṣadic teaching must be left to the Hindus to decide. It is, however, fair to point out that the concept of *māyā*, the cosmic illusion, is only adumbrated and never formulated in the classical Upaniṣads themselves. Śankara and his followers, by establishing complete identity between the human soul and the Absolute, do in fact accept the Sāṃkhya-Yoga view *in practice*, for self-realization means for them, no less than for the Sāṃkhya-Yogin, the isolation of the immortal soul from all that is not itself. As we have tried to point out in another chapter there is much in the Vedānta philosophy which fits in with what Mr. Custance says when in a manic state, particularly the claim that the 'released' individual must make to be identical with the creator (of an imaginary universe). Precisely these views were attacked by Ruysbroeck who rightly saw that all people who firmly held them, must think that they had reached the highest possible mystical state, what the Hindus call the *paramā gatiḥ*, whereas they had only reached the stage of

[9] *Śkand-Gumānīk Vicār*, ed. Menasce, Fribourg, 1945, p. 117 (ch. 10, § 37).

self-isolation, of rest and 'emptiness' within themselves. Believing this to be union with God, they were prevented from taking any further step because they believed there was no further step to take. This, for Ruysbroeck, as for any Christian, was manifestly absurd, for how, as Abū Yazīd once said,[10] could one ever come to the end of the Godhead?

Here, then, are two distinct and mutually opposed types of mysticism,—the monist and the theistic. This is not a question of Christianity and Islam *versus* Hinduism and Buddhism: it is an unbridgeable gulf between all those who see God as incomparably greater than oneself, though He is, at the same time, the root and ground of one's being, and those who maintain that soul and God are one and the same and that all else is pure illusion. For them Christian mysticism is simply *bhakti* or devotion to a personal god carried to ludicrous extremes, whereas for the theist the monist's idea of 'liberation' is simply the realization of his immortal soul in separation from God, and is only, as Junayd pointed out, a stage in the path of the beginner. He is still in the bondage of original sin.

Hinduism has its theists as well as its monists; and the Bhagavad-Gītā as well as Rāmānuja stand nearer to St. John of the Cross than they do to Śankara. This is a quarrel that cuts clean across the conventional distinctions of creeds. In each of the great religions there have been upholders of both doctrines. Even Christianity has not completely avoided the monistic extreme even though it makes nonsense of its basic doctrine that God is Love. Meister Eckhart, for instance, at times adopted a fully monistic position, and Angelus Silesius could well be interpreted monistically though a literal interpretation of the *Cherubinischer Wandersmann*, taken out of the context of his other work, is scarcely permissible since mystics, when writing in verse, allow themselves, like all poets, the boldest figures of speech. . . .

NINIAN SMART
Numinous Experience and Mystical Experience

. . . It's primarily in the *numinous* experience—the experience which grows out of worship and the submission of oneself to God—that the notion of His Otherness arises. It's the contrast between the unholy, unclean, puny sinner and the terrible, holy, pure, majestic Godhead that gives us an inkling of His

Ninian Smart (1927–   ) is a Professor of Religious Studies at the University of California, Santa Barbara. His works include *Reasons and Faiths, Doctrine and Argument in Indian Philosophy*, and *Philosophers and Religious Truth*.

NUMINOUS EXPERIENCE AND MYSTICAL EXPERIENCE   From A *Dialogue of Religions* by Ninian Smart. Copyright 1960 by SCM Press Ltd. Reprinted by their permission.

[10] See p. 165 [in *Mysticism: Scared and Profane*].

transcendence. Now if this Being whom we encounter in worship and prostration appears to have personal characteristics (and don't the great prophets and teachers speak thus?), it's not surprising that theists ascribe to Him such personal attributes! But my main point is that the notion of Otherness is yielded by this kind of experience—the sort that Job had when he wished to clothe himself in dust and ashes and which one of your Hindu saints had when he cried that he was a cur and that it was sinful to think of any creature as Viṣṇu. . . .

. . . It's indeed typical of the mystical experience that there should be difficulty in distinguishing between subject and object (as the matter is often put), and so there arises a sense of merging with God or the Absolute. This is a special kind of religious experience which is different, I think, from the numinous experience of the worshipper. I know this is a very crude way of describing the situation, but perhaps you understand what I'm getting at. I'd like to propose the working hypothesis, which we can discuss later if you like, that the mystical experience has a distinctive connection with the more 'impersonalist' doctrines, such as those of Advaita Vedānta and of certain forms of Buddhism. . . .

. . . I suppose that the Brahman-Ātman doctrine is a way of bringing together the religion of sacrifice on the one hand with the inner contemplative quest towards insight and knowledge on the other. And certainly the identification of the Self with Brahman, the Power pervading and sustaining the cosmos, presents its difficulties, as also the Ṣūfī teachings created tensions within Islam. Assuredly it is a little surprising that the great God who rules the cosmos can be found within the heart 'tinier than a mustard-seed', as the Upaniṣad says. And it's difficult sometimes to resist the impression that the mystics' tendency to speak of deification is unorthodox and even perhaps blasphemous. All this I grant. But if one believes in a personal God it is hard not to allow that there is a way to Him through mysticism, through contemplation. This may lead to complications of doctrine, absurdities, difficulties; but the result is a marvellous welding together of the insights of different types of religious practice. And history may be on my side in these remarks. For, on my reading of the situation, early Islam was understood in its early days simply as a religion of worship of and obedience to Allah, and yet it flowered also, through the Ṣūfīs, into a faith where the profound and beautiful interior visions were also seen as a kind of contact with God. Then, conversely, isn't it significant that Buddhism itself became proliferated, in the Mahāyāna, in such a way that the intuitions of the numinous were given a central place? . . .

THE COGNITIVE STATUS
OF RELIGIOUS
AND MYSTICAL EXPERIENCE

C. B. MARTIN
"Seeing" God

Religious people may feel impatient with the harshness of argument in the last chapter [see Martin's *Religious Belief*]. They may feel confident that they have something that nonreligious people lack, namely, a direct experience or apprehension of God. They may claim that such religious experience is a way of knowing God's existence. This claim must now be examined.

We shall first consider accounts of religious experience that seem to sacrifice an existential claim for the security of the feeling of the moment. There is an influential and subtle group of religious thinkers who would not insist upon any existential claim. My remarks are largely irrelevant to this group. It would be hasty to describe their religious belief as "subjective" or to employ any other such general descriptive term. For example, the "call," in even the most liberal and "subjective" Quaker sects, could not be reduced to statements about feelings. The "call," among other things, implies a mission or intricate pattern of behavior. The nonsubjective element of the "call" is evident, because insofar as one failed to live in accordance with a mission just so far would the genuineness of the "call" be questioned. It will be seen that this verification procedure is necessarily not available in the religious way of knowing to be examined.

In the second part of the chapter we shall consider accounts of religious experience that are not so easily reduced to mere subjectivity.

C. B. Martin (1924–   ) taught for many years in Australia. He is currently a Professor of Philosophy at the University of Calgary. His philosophical writings are in the analytic tradition.

SEEING GOD   Reprinted from *Religious Belief*, C. B. Martin, Cornell University Press, 1959. Reprinted with permission of C. B. Martin.

I

> We are rejecting logical argument of any kind as the first chapter of our theology or as representing the process by which God comes to be known. We are holding that our knowledge of God rests rather on the revelation of His personal Presence as Father, Son, and Holy Spirit. . . . Of such a Presence it must be true that to those who have ever been confronted with it argument is useless, while to those who have it is superfluous.[1]

> It is not as the result of an inference of any kind, whether explicit or implicit, whether laboriously excogitated or swiftly intuited, that the knowledge of God's reality comes to us. It comes rather through our direct, personal encounter with Him in the Person of Jesus Christ His Son our Lord.[2]

> It will not be possible to describe the compelling touch of God otherwise than as the compelling touch of God. To anyone who has no such awareness of God, leading as it does to the typically religious attitudes of obeisance and worship, it will be quite impossible to indicate what is meant; one can only hope to evoke it, on the assumption that the capacity to become aware of God is part of normal human nature like the capacity to see light or to hear sound.[3]

The arguments of the theologians quoted have been taken out of context. The quotations by themselves do not give a faithful or complete impression of their total argument. The following quotations from Professor Farmer indicate two further lines of argument which cannot be discussed here.

> For what we have now in mind is not demonstrative proofs *from* the world, but rather confirmatory considerations which present themselves to us when we bring belief in God with us *to* the world. It is a matter of the coherence of the belief with other facts. If we find that the religious intuition which has arisen from other sources provides the mind with a thought in terms of which much else can without forcing be construed, then that is an intellectual satisfaction, and a legitimate confirmation of belief, which it would be absurd to despise.[4]

> We shall first speak in general terms of what may be called the human situation and need, and thereafter we shall try to show how belief in God, as particularized in its Christian form (though still broadly set forth), fits on to this situation and need.[5]

The alleged theological way of knowing may be described as follows: I have direct experience (knowledge, acquaintance, apprehension) of God; therefore I have valid reason to believe that God exists. By this it may be meant that the statement "I have had direct experience of God, but God does not exist" is contradictory. If so, the assertion that "I have had direct experience of God" commits

---

[1] John Baillie, *Our Knowledge of God* (London: Oxford University Press, 1949), p. 132.

[2] *Ibid.*, p. 143.

[3] H. H. Farmer, *Towards Belief in God* (London: SCM. Press, 1942), Pt. II, p. 40.

[4] *Ibid.*, p. 113.

[5] *Ibid.*, p. 62.

one to the assertion that God exists. From this it follows that "I have had direct experience of God" is more than a psychological statement, because it claims more than the fact that I have certain experiences—it claims that God exists. On this interpretation the argument is deductively valid. The assertion "I have direct experience of God" includes the assertion "God exists." Thus, the conclusion "Therefore, God exists" follows tautologically.

Unfortunately, this deduction is useless. If the deduction were to be useful, the addition of the existential claim "God exists" to the psychological claim of having religious experiences would have to be shown to be warrantable, and this cannot be done.

Consider the following propositions: (1) I feel as if an unseen person were interested in (willed) my welfare. (2) I feel an elation quite unlike any I have ever felt before. (3) I have feelings of guilt and shame at my sinfulness. (4) I feel as if I were committed to bending all my efforts to living in a certain way. These propositions state only that I have certain complex feelings and experiences. Nothing else follows deductively. The only thing that I can establish beyond possible correction on the basis of having certain feelings and experiences is that I have these feelings and sensations. No matter how unique people may think their experience to be, it cannot do the impossible.

Neither is the addition of the existential claim "God exists" to the psychological claim made good by any inductive argument. There are no tests agreed upon to establish genuine experience of God and distinguish it decisively from the non-genuine.[6] Indeed, many theologians deny the possibility of any such test or set of tests.

The believer may persuade us that something extraordinary has happened by saying, "I am a changed man since 6:37 P.M., May 6, 1939." This is a straightforward empirical statement. We can test it by noticing whether or not he has given up his bad habits. We may allow the truth of the statement even if he has not given up his bad habits, because we may find evidence of bad conscience, self-searchings and remorse that had not been present before that date.

However, if the believer says, "I had a direct experience of God at 6:37 P.M., May 6, 1939," this is not an empirical statement in the way that the other statement is. How could we check its truth? No matter how much or how little his subsequent behavior, such as giving up bad habits and so on, is affected, it could never prove or disprove his statement.

An important point to note is that theologians tend to discourage any detailed description of the required experience ("apprehension of God").[7] The more naturalistic and detailed the description of the required experience becomes, the easier would it become to deny the existential claim. One could say, "Yes, I had those very experiences, but they certainly did not convince me of God's existence." The only sure defense here would be for the theologian to make the claim analytic: "You couldn't have those experiences and at the same time sincerely deny God's existence."

[6]This will be qualified in the second part of this chapter.

[7]The detailed descriptions of the Catholic mystics will be discussed later.

The way in which many theologians talk would seem to show that they think of knowing God as something requiring a kind of sixth sense. The Divine Light is not of a color usually visible only to eagles, and the Voice of God is not of a pitch usually audible only to dogs. No matter how much more keen our senses became, we should be no better off than before. The sixth sense, therefore, must be very different from the other five.

This supposed religious sense has no vocabulary of its own but depends upon metaphors drawn from the other senses. There are no terms which apply to it and it alone. There is a vocabulary for what is sensed but not for the sense. We "see" the Holy, the Numinous, the Divine. In a similar way we often speak of "hearing" the voice of conscience and "seeing" logical connections. By using this metaphor we emphasize the fact that often we come to understand the point of an argument or problem in logic suddenly. We mark this occurrence by such phrases as "the light dawned," "understood it in a flash." Such events are usually described in terms of a complete assurance that one's interpretation is correct and a confidence that one will tend to be able to reproduce or recognize the argument or problem in various contexts in the future. But a vitally important distinction between this "seeing" and the religious "seeing" is that there is a checking procedure for the former but not for the latter. If, while doing a problem in geometry you "see" that one angle is equal to another and then on checking over your proof find that they are not equal after all, you say "I didn't really 'see,' I only thought I did."

The religious way of knowing is described as being unique. No one can deny the existence of feelings and experiences which the believer calls "religious," and no one can deny their power. Because of this and because the way of knowing by direct experience is neither inductive nor deductive, theologians have tried to give this way of knowing a special status. One way of doing this is to claim that religious experience is unique and incommunicable.

Professor Baillie, in likening our knowledge of God to our knowledge of other minds, says that it is "like our knowledge of tridimensional space and all other primary modes of knowledge, something that cannot be imagined by one who does not already possess it, since it cannot be described to him in terms of anything else than itself."[8] This kind of comparison is stated in the two sentences following, and we shall now examine the similarities and dissimilarities between them. (1) You don't know what the experience of God is until you have had it. (2) You don't know what the color blue is until you have seen it. Farmer says, "All the basic elements in our experience are incommunicable. Who could describe light and colour to one who has known nothing but darkness?"[9] All that Farmer proves is that a description of one group of sensations A in terms of another set of sensations B is never sufficient for knowing group A. According to this definition of "know," in order to know one must have those sensations. Thus, all that is proved is that, in order to know what religious experience is, one must have a religious experience. This helps in no way at all to prove that such

[8] Baillie, *Our Knowledge of God*, p. 217.

[9] Farmer, *Towards Belief in God*, p. 41.

experience is direct apprehension of God and helps in no way to support the existential claim "God exists."

Farmer makes the point that describing the experience of God to an unbeliever is like describing color to a man blind from birth. So it is, in the sense that the believer has usually had experiences which the unbeliever has not. However, it is also very much unlike. The analogy breaks down at some vital points.

The blind man may have genuine, though incomplete knowledge of color. He may have an instrument for detecting wave lengths, and the like. Indeed, he may even increase our knowledge of color. More important still, the blind man may realize the differences in powers of prediction between himself and the man of normal eyesight. He is well aware of the fact that, unlike himself, the man of normal eyesight does not have to wait to hear the rush of the bull in order to be warned.

This point concerning differences in powers of prediction is connected with the problem of how we are to know when someone has the direct experience of God or even when we ourselves have the direct experience of God. It was shown above how the situation is easier in the case of the blind man knowing about color. It is only when one comes to such a case as knowing God that the society of tests and checkup procedures, which surround other instances of knowing, completely vanishes. What is put in the place of these tests and checking procedures is an immediacy of knowledge that is supposed to carry its own guarantee. This feature will be examined later.

It is true that the man of normal vision has a way of knowing color which the blind man does not have, that is, he can see colored objects. However, as we have seen, it would be wrong to insist that this is the only way of knowing color and that the blind man has *no* way of knowing color. Perhaps Farmer has this in mind when he tries to make an analogy between the incommunicability of the believer's direct knowledge of God to the unbeliever and the incommunicability of the normal man's knowledge of color to the blind man. The analogy is justified if "knowing color" is made synonymous with "having color sensations." On this account, no matter how good his hearing, reliable his color-detecting instruments, and so on, the blind man could not know color, and the man of normal vision could not communicate to him just what this knowledge would be like.

The believer has had certain unusual experiences, which, presumably, the unbeliever has not had. If "having direct experience of God" is made synonymous with "having certain religious experiences," and the believer has had these and the unbeliever has not, then we may say that the believer's knowledge is incommunicable to the unbeliever in that it has already been legislated that in order to know what the direct experience of God is one must have had certain religious experiences. "To anyone who has no such awareness of God, leading as it does to the typically religious attitudes of obeisance and worship, it will be quite impossible to indicate what is meant; one can only hope to evoke it."[10] Reading theological textbooks and watching the behavior of believers is not sufficient.

The theologian has made the analogy above hold at the cost of endangering

[10] *Ibid.*, p. 40.

the existential claim about God which he hoped to establish. If "knowing color" is made synonymous with "having color sensations" and "having direct experience of God" is made synonymous with "having certain religious experiences," then it is certainly true that a blind man cannot "know color" and that a nonreligious man cannot "have direct experience of God." By definition, also, it is true that the blind man and the nonreligious man cannot know the meaning of the phrases "knowing color" and "having direct experience of God," because it has been previously legislated that one cannot know their meaning without having the relevant experiences.

If this analogy is kept, the phrases "knowing color" and "having direct experience of God" seem to make no claim beyond the psychological claims about one's color sensations and religious feelings.

If this analogy is not kept, there is no sense in the comparison of the incommunicability between the man of normal vision and the blind man with the incommunicability between the believer and the unbeliever.

If "knowing color" is to be shaken loose from its purely psychological implications and made to have an existential reference concerning features of the world, then a whole society of tests and checkup procedures, which would be wholly irrelevant to the support of the psychological claim about one's own color sensations, become relevant. For example, what other people see, the existence of light waves, and the description of their characteristics, which needs the testimony of research workers and scientific instruments, all must be taken into account.

Because "having direct experience of God" does not admit the relevance of a society of tests and checking procedures, it tends to place itself in the company of the other ways of knowing which preserve their self-sufficiency, "uniqueness," and "incommunicability" by making a psychological and not an existential claim. For example, "I seem to see a piece of blue paper,"[11] requires no further test or checking procedure in order to be considered true. Indeed, if Jones says, "I seem to see a piece of blue paper," he not only needs no further corroboration but cannot be shown to have been mistaken. If Smith says to Jones, "It does not seem to me as if I were seeing a piece of blue paper," this cannot rightly raise any doubts in Jones's mind, though it may express Smith's doubts. That is, Smith may feel that Jones is lying. However, if Jones had said, "I see a piece of blue paper," and Smith, in the same place and at the same time, had replied, "I do not see a piece of blue paper," or, "It does not seem to me as if I were now seeing a piece of blue paper," then Smith's remarks can rightly raise doubts in Jones's mind. Further investigation will then be proper, and if no piece of paper can be felt and other investigators cannot see or feel the paper and photographs reveal nothing, then Jones's statement will be shown to have been false. Jones's only refuge will be to say, "Well, I certainly seem to see a piece of blue paper." This is a perfect refuge, because no one can prove him wrong, but its unassailability has been bought at the price of making no claim about the world beyond the claim about his own experience of the moment.

The closeness of the religious statement to the psychological statement can be

[11] I shall call such statements "low-claim assertions."

brought out in another way, as follows. When one wishes to support the assertion that a certain physical object exists, the tests and checking procedures made by Jones himself are not the only things relevant to the truth of his assertion. Testimony of what others see, hear, and so on is also relevant. That is, if Jones wanted to know whether it was really a star that he saw, he could not only take photographs, look through a telescope, and the like but also ask others if they saw the star. If a large proportion of a large number of people denied seeing the star, Jones's claim about the star's existence would be weakened. Of course, he might still trust his telescope. However, let us now imagine that Jones does not make use of the tests and checking procedures (photographs and telescopes) but is left with the testimony of what he sees and the testimony of others concerning what they see. In this case, it is so much to the point if a large number of people deny seeing the star that Jones will be considered irrational or mad if he goes on asserting its existence. His only irrefutable position is to reduce his physical object claim to an announcement concerning his own sensations. Then the testimony of men and angels cannot disturb his certitude. These sensations of the moment he knows directly and immediately, and the indirect and nonimmediate testimony of men and angels is irrelevant. Absolute confidence and absolute indifference to the majority judgment is bought at the price of reducing the existential to the nonexistential.

The religious claim is similar to, though not identical with, the case above in certain important features. We have seen that there are no tests or checking procedures open to the believer to support his existential claim about God. Thus, he is left with the testimony of his own experience and the similar testimony of the experience of others. And, of course, he is not left wanting for such testimony, for religious communities seem to serve just this sort of function.

Let us imagine a case comparable to the one concerning the existence of a physical object. In this case Brown is a professor of divinity, and he believes that he has come to know of the existence of God through direct experience of God. In order to understand the intricate character of what Professor Brown is asserting we must imagine a highly unusual situation. The other members of the faculty and the members of Professor Brown's religious community suddenly begin sincerely to deny his, and what has been their own, assertion. Perhaps they still attend church services and pray as often as they used to do, and perhaps they claim to have the same sort of experiences as they had when they were believers, but they refuse to accept the conclusion that God exists. Whether they give a Freudian explanation or some other explanation or no explanation of their experiences, they are agreed in refusing to accept the existential claim (about God) made by Professor Brown. How does this affect Professor Brown and his claim? It may affect Professor Brown very deeply—indeed, he may die of broken-hearted disappointment at the loss of his fellow believers. However, the loss of fellow believers may not weaken his confidence in the truth of his assertion or in the testimony of his experience. In this matter his experience may be all that ultimately counts for him in establishing his confidence in the truth of his claim about the existence of God. It has been said that religious experience carries its own guarantee, and perhaps the account above describes what is meant by this.

It is quite obvious from these examples that the religious statement "I have direct experience of God" is of a different status from the physical-object statement "I see a star" and shows a distressing similarity to the low-claim assertion "I seem to see a star." The bulk of this chapter has so far been devoted to showing some of the many forms this similarity takes. Does this mean then that the religious statement and its existential claim concerning God amount to no more than a reference to the complex feelings and experiences of the believer?

Perhaps the best way to answer this question is to take a typical low-claim assertion and see if there is anything which must be said of it and all other low-claim assertions which cannot be said of the religious statement. One way of differentiating a physical object statement from a low-claim assertion is by means of prefixing the phrase "I seem."[12] For instance, the statement "I see a star" may be transformed into a statement concerning my sensations by translating it into the form "I seem to see a star." The first statement involves a claim about the existence of an object as well as an announcement concerning my sensations and therefore subjects itself to the risk of being wrong concerning that further claim. Whether one is wrong in this case is determined by a society of tests and checking procedures such as taking photographs and looking through telescopes and by the testimony of others that they see or do not see a star. The second statement involves no claim about the existence of an object and so requires no such tests and no testimony of others; indeed, the final judge of the truth of the statement is the person making it. If no existential claim is lost by the addition of this phrase to a statement then the assertion is low-claim. For instance, the statement "I feel pain" loses nothing by the addition "I seem to feel pain."

In the case of the religious statement "I have direct experience of God" the addition of the phrase is fatal to all that the believer wants to assert. "I seem to be having direct experience of God" is a statement concerning my feelings and sensations of the moment, and as such it makes no claim about the existence of God. Thus, the original statement "I have direct experience of God" is not a low-claim assertion. This should not surprise us. We should have known it all along, for is it not an assertion that one comes to know something, namely God, by means of one's feelings and sensations and this something is not reducible to them? The statement is not a low-claim one just because it is used to assert the existence of something. Whether this assertion is warranted and what exactly it amounts to is quite another question.

We are tempted to think that the religious statement must be of one sort or another. The truth is that *per impossible* it is both at once. The theologian must use it in both ways, and which way he is to emphasize at a particular time depends upon the circumstances of its use and most particularly the direction of our probings.

The statement "I seem to be having direct experience of God" is an eccentric one. It is eccentric not only because introspective announcements are unusual and because statements about God have a peculiar obscurity but for a further and

---

[12]This, clearly, is a superficial and mechanical move, for the prefixing of this phrase ordinarily would result in a qualified and hedging physical object statement. I shall just have to plead that the possibility that such a prefixing should result in a low-claim assertion is here realized.

more important reason. This eccentricity may be brought out by comparing this statement with others having the same form. A first formulation of this may be put in the following way. In reference to things other than our sensations of the moment knowledge is prior to seeming as if.

The statement "I seem to be looking directly at a chair" has a meaning only insofar as I already *know* what it is like to look directly at a chair. The statement "I seem to be listening to a choir," has a meaning only insofar as I already *know* what it is like to be listening to a choir. The assumption of knowledge in both these cases is one which all normal people are expected to be able to make and do in fact make.

The statement "I seem to be having direct experience of God" does not lend itself so easily to the criterion for meaning exemplified above, because if this statement has meaning only insofar as one already *knows* what it is like to have direct experience of God, the assumption of such knowledge is certainly not one which all normal people may be expected to be able to make or do in fact make. However, it may be said that the assumption of such knowledge as knowledge of what it is like to see a gorgon may not be made of all normal people and, therefore, the case of religious knowledge is in no peculiar position. This objection can be answered when we ask the question "How do we come to learn what it would be like to look directly at a chair, hear a choir, see a gorgon, have direct experience of God?"

It is not that there are no answers to the question concerning how we come to learn what it would be like to have direct experience of God. We are not left completely in the dark. Instead, the point is that the answers to this question are quite different from the answers to the questions concerning how we come to learn what it would be like to look directly at a chair, hear a choir, and see a gorgon. No one in our society has seen a gorgon, yet there are people who, by means of their specialized knowledge of mythical literature, may claim in a perfectly meaningful way that it now seems to them as if they were seeing a gorgon.

Let us imagine a society in which there are no chairs and no one knows anything at all about chairs. If we were to try to teach one of the members of this society what it would be like to see a chair and if we were not allowed to construct a chair, what might we do? We might look around at the furniture and say, "A chair is a kind of narrow settee. it is used to sit on." This would be a beginning. Then we might compare different settees as to which are more chairlike. We might draw pictures of chairs, make gestures with our hands showing the general shape and size of different sorts of chairs. If, on the following day, the person being instructed said, "I had a most unusual dream last night—I seemed to be looking directly at a chair," we should admit that his statement was closer in meaning to a similar one which we who have seen chairs might make than it would be to a similar one which another member might make who had no information or instruction or experience of chairs. We would insist that we had better knowledge of what it is to see a chair than has the instructed member of society who has still actually to see a chair. However, to know pictures of chairs is to know about chairs in a legitimate sense.

But let us now imagine a utopian society in which none of the members has ever been in the least sad or unhappy. If we were to try to teach one of the members of this society what it would be like to feel sad, how would we go about it? It can be said that giving definitions, no matter how ingenious would be no help; drawing pictures of unhappy faces, no matter how well drawn, would be no help, so long as these measures failed to evoke a feeling of sadness in this person. Comparing the emotion of sadness with other emotions would be no help, because no matter how like other emotions (weariness and the like) are to sadness they fail just because they are not sadness. No, sadness is unique and incomparable.

To anyone who has no such awareness of sadness, leading, as it does, to the typically unhappy behavior of tears and drawn faces, it will be quite impossible to indicate what is meant. One can only hope to evoke it on the assumption that the capacity to become aware of sadness is part of normal human nature like the capacity to see light or to hear sound.

This last paragraph is a play upon a quotation given at the very beginning of this chapter. The following is the original version.

> To anyone who has no such awareness of God, leading as it does to the typically religious attitudes of obeisance and worship, it will be quite impossible to indicate what is meant; one can only hope to evoke it, on the assumption that the capacity to become aware of God is part of normal human nature like the capacity to see light or to hear sound.[13]

Consider the following statements:

(1) We are rejecting logical argument of any kind as the first chapter of our epistemology of aesthetics, or as representing the process by which beauty comes to be known.

(2) It is not as the result of an inference of any kind, whether explicit or implicit, whether laboriously excogitated or swiftly intuited, that the knowledge of beauty comes to us.

(3) To those who have never been confronted with the experience of seeing the beauty of something, argument is useless.

As these statements stand, they are plainly false. Professors of aesthetics and professional art critics often do help us to come to "knowledge of beauty" by all kinds of inference and arguments. They may, and often do, help us to come to a finer appreciation of beautiful things. Knowledge of the rules of perspective and understanding of an artist's departure from them is relevant to an aesthetic appreciation of his work.

However, it is possible to interpret these statements as true, and this is more important for our purpose. There is sense in saying that an art critic, who has vastly increased our aesthetic sensitivity and whose books of art criticism are the very best, may never have known beauty. If there are no signs of this critic ever having been stirred by any work of art, then no matter how subtle his analyses,

---

[13] Farmer, *Towards Belief in God*, p. 40.

there is sense in claiming that he has never been confronted with the experience of seeing the beauty of something. This sense just is that we may be determined not to say that a person has seen the beauty of something or has knowledge of beauty if he does not at some time have certain complex emotions and feelings which are typically associated with looking at paintings, hearing music, and reading poetry. To "know beauty" or to "see the beauty of something" here means, among other things, to have certain sorts of emotions and feelings.

The statements on aesthetics given above are a play on a quotation given at the beginning of this chapter. The following is the original version with the appropriate omissions and transpositions.

> We are rejecting logical argument of any kind as the first chapter of our theology or as representing the process by which God comes to be known. . . .
>
> It is not as the result of an inference of any kind, whether explicit or implicit, whether laboriously excogitated or swiftly intuited, that the knowledge of God's reality comes to us.
>
> . . . To those who have never been confronted with it [direct, personal encounter with God] argument is useless.[14]

As these statements stand they are plainly false. Professors of divinity and clergymen are expected to do what Baillie claims cannot be done.

However, it is possible to interpret these statements as true, and this is more important for our purpose. There is sense in saying that a theologian (who has vastly increased our religious sensitivity and whose books of theology are the very best) may never have known God. If there are no signs of this theologian's ever having been stirred by a religious ritual or act of worship, then, no matter how subtle his analyses, there is sense in claiming that he has never been confronted with God's personal Presence. This sense just is that we are determined not to say that a person has knowledge of God if he does not at some time have certain complex emotions and feelings which are associated with attending religious services, praying, and reading the Bible. To "know God" or to be confronted with God's "personal Presence" means, of necessity, having certain sorts of emotions and feelings.

In this section the analogy between seeing blue and experiencing God has been examined and found to be misleading. I shall not deal in this chapter with the connexion between what the believer expects from immortality and his religious belief. This peculiar kind of test or verification has special difficulties which will be treated in another chapter.

So far I have tried to indicate how statements concerning a certain alleged religious way of knowing betray a logic extraordinarily like that of statements concerning introspective and subjective ways of knowing. It is not my wish to go from a correct suggestion that the logic is *very, very* like to an incorrect suggestion that their logic is *just* like that of introspective and subjective statements, for, after all, such statements are logically in order.

I have argued that one cannot read off the existence of God from the existence

---

[14] Baillie, *Our Knowledge of God,* pp. 132, 143.

of religious experience. Now, I must insist, in all charity, that *neither* can one read off the *non*-existence of God from the existence of religious experience.

In criticizing some of the foregoing argument, Mr. W. D. Glasgow claims,

> It is essential here for the defender of the religious way of knowing to assert that there are cases where a man *knows* himself to be experiencing an objective Deity, just as there are cases where he knows himself to be experiencing a subjective pain. Unless it is insisted that there is such a thing as *cognitive experience* in religion, Martin's assimilation of all religious existential statements to psychological statements (or what ought to be called psychological statements) becomes highly plausible. Indeed, even the phrase "*may* be objective" has no meaning, probably, for Martin, unless theoretically at least it is possible to find out or test whether religious experience *is* objective. The position is only saved, again, if we say that is some cases the agent himself anyhow *does* know.[15]

Glasgow cannot mean "a man *knows* himself to be experiencing an objective Deity" *in just the same way as* "he knows himself to be experiencing a subjective pain." One's pain is not a thing that exists independently of one's experience. I do not establish the existence of my pain on the basis of experience. There is nothing to establish beyond the experience. Presumably there is something to establish on the basis of religious experience, namely, the presence of God. When Glasgow says "there is such a thing as *cognitive experience* in religion" and "in some cases the agent himself anyhow *does* know," he must be read as saying that the presence of God is known on the basis of religious experience. That is, the presence of God is something over and above the experience itself. The model that Glasgow implies is that a cognitive experience is rather like a photograph of a friend: one can read off from the photograph that it is of that friend: and though this is a misleading model, there is something in it. If I am sitting at my desk and someone asks me if there is an ash tray on my desk, *all* that I have to do is have a look and say "Yes" or "No." But whether or not I know there is an ash tray on my desk is not to be read off simply from what my eyes at that moment told me. For if my eyes can tell me the truth they can tell me a lie, and the difference here would not be decided by what they tell. For me really to have seen and known there was an ash tray, other people must have been able to have seen it if they had looked. If I have only the testimony of my eyes and discount all else, then that testimony is mute concerning the existence of what is external. My eyes can tell me (in an hallucination) of the presence of an ash tray when there is no ash tray.

When someone uses the sentence "I see an ash tray" in such a way that he counts as relevant to its truth *only* his visual experience at the time, he is talking *only* about that experience, though the sentence has the form of making a statement about an ash tray. It does not help if he calls it a "cognitive experience" or if he says that he "anyhow *does* know" or if he says that his experience is "self-authenticating" or is a "direct encounter." We cannot allow a speaker any final

---

[15] W. D. Glasgow, "Knowledge of God," *Philosophy*, XXXII (1957), 236. This article is a criticism of my article "A Religious Way of Knowing," printed in Flew and MacIntyre, *New Essays in Philosophical Theology* (London: SCM Press, 1955), pp. 76–95.

authority in the account of how he is using his sentences. If such special dispen-
sation were allowable, conceptual confusion would be rare indeed.

Similarly, I have argued, when someone uses the sentence "I have or have had
direct experience of God" in such a way that he counts as relevant to its truth
only his experience at the time, he is talking *only* about that experience, though
the sentence has the form of making a statement about the presence of God, and
neither does it help if he calls it a "cognitive experience."

From the fact that someone uses the sentence "I see an ash tray" so that he is
talking *only* about his visual experience, nothing at all follows about whether or
not he is actually seeing an ash tray in front of him. His *statement* may be only
about his visual experience itself, and his actual *situation* may be that of seeing
that ash tray. Also, from the fact that someone uses the sentence "I have or have
had direct experience of God" in such a way that he is talking *only* about his
experience at the time, nothing at all follows about whether or not he is actually
experiencing the presense of a supernatural being. His *statement* may be only
about his experience itself, and his actual *situation* may be that of experiencing
the presence of a supernatural being.

The religious person will want, in what he says, to be able to distinguish between a "delusive" and a "veridical" experience of God. The experience should
be due to the actual presence of God and not due only to a drug or to self-
deception or to the action of Satan. Therefore he must use his sentence to refer
to more than an experience that is, in principle, compatible with these and other
similar causes.

What makes a form of experience a way of knowing? It is often suggested that
the mystic who "sees" God is like a man (in a society of blind men) who sees
colors. It is claimed that each has a form of experience and a way of knowing that
others lack. Let us now work out this analogy. A society of blind men is told by
one of its members that he has come to have a form of experience and a way of
knowing by means of which he has been able to discover the existence of things
not discoverable by ordinary experience. He says that these things have a *kind* of
size (not just like size as it is felt by the blind) and a *kind* of shape (not just like
shape as it is felt by the blind); he further says that these things are somehow
"everywhere" and that they cannot expect to understand what these things are like
and what he means by experiencing them unless they themselves have these experiences. He then tells them of a procedure by which they will be able to discover for themselves the existence of these things. He warns them that these things
do not always reveal themselves when the procedure is carried out, but, if a person
is sufficiently diligent and believes strongly enough in their existence, he will
probably come to know by means of unique and incomparable experiences of the
existence of these things.

Some people, with faith and diligence, submit themselves to the required procedure, and some of these are rewarded by a kind of experience they have not
known before. Color shapes float before them—things that they cannot touch or
feel and that are beyond the reach of their senses, and things that may be present
to one of their group and not experienced by the others, things that may as well
be everywhere as anywhere, since they are locatable only in the sense of being

"before" each observer to whom they appear. These people cannot correlate this new form of experience with the rest of experience, they cannot touch or smell these "things." Indeed, they "see" visions, not things. Or rather these people have no way of *knowing* the existence of the things that may or may not exist over and above the momentary experiences. May these experiences all the same be "cognitive"? Yes and no. Yes, there may be something, they know not what, responsible for their having these experiences. No, their experiences are not a way of *knowing* about this something. For the experience of a colored shape that needs no corroboration by the experience of others similarly placed, and that is not related to one's other senses, is not in itself a way of knowing what in the world is responsible for this experience even if there is something beyond the condition of the "observer" that is so responsible. So far, even the people concerned have no *way of knowing* what more is involved than the fact of their experiencing momentary "visions."

I have not denied that the religious mystic may have experiences that others do not. Neither have I denied that there might be some external agency responsible for these experiences. What I have denied is that the mystic's possession of these experiences is in itself a way of knowing the existence or nature of such an agency.

The argument of this chapter lies in an area in which confusion is common. I shall consider two cases of such confusion especially relevant to what I have been saying.

> You are acquainted with the distinction between feeling and emotion. Feeling, such as pleasure or pain, is in itself a purely subjective experience; emotion implies an objective situation within which there is something which arouses the emotion, and towards which the emotion is directed. The Divine is, it would seem, first experienced in such a situation; and is initially apprehended solely and exclusively as that which arouses certain types of emotion. If the emotion be awe, then the Divine is so far apprehended as the awesome, what Otto has so helpfully entitled the numinous.[16]

There are two questionable assumptions here: first, that whether or not an experience refers to an objective state of affairs can be read off from the experience itself; second, that emotions *must* do so.

The second claim that an emotion as such implies an objective situation can be refuted very simply. My feeling of pleasure while watching a game of football is related to something in my environment, but my feeling of pleasure at a tune running through my head is not. My emotion of awe in the presence of a particularly magnificent race horse is related to something in my environment, but my emotion of awe during a dream of a coronation service is not. Some people have aesthetic emotions aroused by the contemplation of mathematical proofs and theorems, and others have the emotion of fear toward ghosts and goblins.

In a criticism of the argument of the first part of this chapter (as originally

---

[16]N. Kemp Smith, *Is Divine Existence Credible?*, British Academy Lecture (London: British *Academy*, 1931), p. 23.

published in "A Religious Way of Knowing," in *Mind*, October, 1952) Professor H. D. Lewis seems to be making the first claim, that a reference to an objective state of affairs can be read off from the experience itself.

> He [Martin] seems to think that the only claim to objectivity which an experience may have is that which is established by tests and checking procedures. A man's statement that he "seems to see a blue piece of paper" is thus said to be unassailable only because it is a "claim about his own state of mind." This I would doubt, for the colour expanse which we only seem to see is neither a mere appearance nor a state of mind. It is "out there before me" and real enough while I seem to see it, however many problems may be involved in distinguishing between it and physical entities. . . . "Having been stirred" by a religious ritual or act of worship, or having "certain sorts of emotions and feelings," is not the essential thing in religious experience; it is what we apprehend that comes first.[17]

However, "what we apprehend," if anything, is the whole problem and cannot "come first." Certainly, people have had special sorts of experience which incline them to claim with the greatest confidence that their experiences are of God. But whether the experiences are or are not of God is not to be decided by describing or having those experiences. For whether anything or nothing is apprehended by experiences is not to be read off from the experiences themselves. The presence of a piece of blue paper is not to be read off from my experience as of a piece of blue paper. Other things are relevant: What would a photograph reveal? Can I touch it? What do others see? It is only when I admit the relevance of such checking procedures that I can lay claim to apprehending the paper, and, indeed, the admission of the relevance of such procedures is what gives meaning to the assertion that I am apprehending the paper. *What I apprehend is the sort of thing that can be photographed, touched, and seen by others.*

It does not help when Lewis says,

> The colour expanse which we only seem to see is neither a mere appearance nor a state of mind. It is "out there before me" and real enough while I seem to see it, however many problems may be involved in distinguishing between it and physical entities.

Think now of a man who claims to see a blue piece of paper, and when we complain that we cannot, he replies, "Oh, it isn't the sort of thing that can be photographed, touched, or see by others, but all the same, it is out there before me." Are we to think that he has come upon a special sort of object that is nevertheless "out there" as are desks and tables and the rest of the furniture of the world? No, ontological reference is something to be earned. We earn the designation "out there" of a thing by allowing its presence to be determined by the procedures we all know. We cannot just *say* "out there" of it, and we cannot just *say* "apprehended" of God.

---

[17] H. D. Lewis, "Philosophical Surveys X, The Philosophy of Religion, 1945–1952," *Philosophical Quarterly*, IV (July, 1954), p. 263.

It can be objected, "But God is different, and we never meant that our experiences of God should be checked by procedures relevant to physical objects." Of course not, but what *sort* of checks are there then, so that we are left with more than the mere experiences whose existence even the atheist need not deny?

II

Yet checking procedures are not on all accounts in all ways irrelevant. As in all theological discourse concerning the status of religious experience there are many, many voices, and so far we have listened to too few.

A religious experience is not just an ineffable, indescribable something that comes and goes unbidden and amenable to no criteria of identity. At least, the mystics seldom describe it in this way. There are certain steps one can take to bring about such experiences, and the experiences are describable within limits, and they leave certain kinds of identifiable aftereffects.

Alvarez de Paz and other mystics have emphasized the importance of practicing austerities, conquering the flesh, and mortifying the body.

Of course, this training of the body is not sufficient. The mind must be trained as well. To have a vision of the Holy Virgin one must be acquainted with the basic facts of "Christ's birth and life and death." To have the highest mystical apprehension of the Trinity, as did St. Teresa, one must have some elementary theological training.

Nor is bodily and intellectual training enough, for there must be moral and emotional training as well. The commandment to love one another was given not only to lead us to peace and brotherhood on earth but also to change our hearts so that we might see God.

Yet all of these may not be enough, for it is possible one should train oneself most assiduously in all of these ways and still not have truly religious experience. This possibility is characterized by saying that finally the favor and grace of God are required.

The paradoxical and negative ways in which mystics most often describe their experiences may seem, at first, unsatisfactory. But it helps to consider how similar sorts of descriptions are employed outside the religious context. One might say of one's emotion at a particular time that one felt both love and hate toward someone. This would be understood as a description of a complex emotion that most of us have experienced. And the paradoxical expression is not reducible to "in some ways love, in other ways hate," because it refers not only to different patterns of behaving and feeling but also to a particular feeling at a particular moment.

Alvarez de Paz gives a particularly sharp description that must strike even the most sceptical reader as in no way obscure or evasive.

> One perceives no representation of the face or the body, yet one knows with greater certainty than if one saw it with one's eyes that the person (Jesus Christ or the Blessed Virgin) is present on one's right hand or in one's heart. . . . It is as if, in darkness, one should feel at once that someone is at one's side, knowing that he has

goodwill and not enmity towards you; while one remains absolutely ignorant whether it is a man or a woman, young or old, handsome or ugly, standing or seated.[18]

It would be wrong for us to legislate against the mystic's claim that his experience is not sensory. For in a nonreligious context there may be a parallel. Many of us have felt or experienced the presence of some loved one dead or living but distant. (Of course, we do not tend to think that the person is in any way *actually* present unless the person is dead.) Certainly in such cases we do not see or hear the person. It is not even *as if* we heard or saw the person. Making the parallel even closer to the mystical, we do not even have to have any kind of mental image of the loved one. Neither is the presence felt as being in any specific place. The very subtle feelings and emotions typically directed to this one person and no other are now aroused as once they were by this person alone. The unique love and regard this person showed us, we, as it were, receive again. And we can feel ashamed at having done things of which the loved one would disapprove. And so we can feel guided where there is no guide and loved where the lover is dead. The emotion is in shadow felt but is no less real for that.

A child may read of a fairy-story giant who eats the children who do not think he is real and even some who do. He is described in detail (perhaps there is even a picture), and his hatred of children is made too clear. The child may have a bad dream about the giant. Or he may, as in the case above, just feel the giant's presence in no very localized place yet somewhere near. That is, the child reads the story, comes to feel a kind of fear toward the giant, and hates him in a way that others do not. Then the child, hearing and seeing nothing, may, in the dark, feel that fear and sense that hate so strongly that he will claim, even when the light is turned on and in spite of the most tender parental reassurance, that the giant had been in the room. That is, the experience of the child is such that he is left with a certitude which he considers the giant alone could give.

In order to have such an experience, then, with all of the sense of reality and conviction that it carries, it is not necessary that the being whose presence is so felt should ever have existed.

As children we are taught to love Christ in a very special way, and we are taught of Christ's very special love for us. Christ, as a person, is made extremely real to us. That we cannot see or hear him takes very little from his reality. He was once seen and heard, and we are told so much of his life and actions and visible love that we are apt to feel that we know him more clearly than we do any other historical person. As children (or, indeed, as adults) we are encouraged in this feeling by being told that he is somehow, if not actually somewhere, alive. We are told that God loves us as Christ loves us, and we learn that Christ and God are somehow One. So we know roughly how we *should* feel in God's presence. We have as reference countless stories of how others have felt. These experiences are very different, but they form a kind of family. At one extreme

---

[18] Quoted in Joseph Marechal, *Studies in the Psychology of the Mystics* (London: Burns Oates & Washbourne, 1927), p. 110.

there is a visible vision, and at the other extreme there is almost a kind of unconscious trance.

> Let us now speak of the sign which proves the prayer of union to have been genuine. As you have seen, God then deprives the soul of all its senses that he may the better imprint in it true wisdom; it neither sees, hears, nor understands anything while this state lasts. . . . God visits the soul in a manner which prevents its doubting, on returning to itself, that it dwelt in him and that he was within it. . . . But you may ask, how can a person who is incapable of sight and hearing see or know these things? I do not say that she saw it at the time, but that she perceives it clearly afterwards, not by any vision but by a certitude which remains in the heart which God alone could give. . . . If we did not see it, how can we feel so sure of it? That I do not know: it is the work of the Almighty and I am certain that what I say is the fact. I maintain that a soul which does not feel this assurance has not been united to God entirely, but only by one of its powers, or has received one of the many other favours God is accustomed to bestow on men.[19]

Yet, with all of this, it could be argued that all that has been accomplished is a description of a class of experiences and of methods of obtaining and recognizing them. Their ontological reference has still to be established. It could be dogmatically asserted that these experiences by definition come only through the grace of God, but this would be no more than a way of stamping one's foot and insisting on, rather than arguing for, that reference. St. Teresa once again is of help. She was plagued during her lifetime not by doubts about the character of her experiences but about their source. Was she perhaps being subtly deceived by Satan? She was not at a loss to provide a kind of settlement procedure.

> I could not believe that Satan, if he wished to deceive me, could have recourse to means so adverse to his purpose as this, of rooting out my faults and implanting virtues and spiritual strength: for I saw clearly that I had become another person by means of these visions. . . . Neither the imagination nor the evil one could represent what leaves such peace, calm, and good fruits in the soul, and particularly the following three graces of a very high order. The first of these is a perception of the greatness of God, which becomes clearer to us as we witness more of it. Secondly, we gain selfknowledge and humility as we see how creatures so base as ourselves in comparison with the Creator of such wonders, have dared to offend Him in the past or venture to gaze on Him now. The third grace is a contempt of all earthly things unless they are consecrated to the service of so great a God.[20]

But now, what more has really been accomplished by this? To say that the source of these experiences is God and not Satan in the absence of further criteria reduces to saying that these experiences have certain sorts of profound effects upon one's character, attitudes, and behavior. And why should an atheist deny any of this? If there is more that cannot be so reduced and if it is inconsistent with the claims of an atheist, it still remains to be said.

Unlike the first section of this chapter, this section has been concerned with views (those of the great Catholic mystics) in which statements about religious

---

[19] St. Teresa, *Interior Castle* (London: Thomas Baker, 1930), pp. 91–93.

[20] *Ibid.*, p. 171.

experience are not employed as in any way arguments for, or evidence of, the existence of God. The mystics are convinced on other grounds of the existence of God. Religious experience, then, is conceived by them as a way of coming to know better the object of their worship, whose existence is proved or assumed independent of that experience.

This conservative estimate of the status of religious experience in theology is not, however, necessarily safe from censure. The conceptual weight is shifted from the experience to the previously established or assumed notion of the object of the experience. In the previous chapter difficulties were found in typical notions of the qualities of God. No Catholic theologian and few Protestant theologians would claim that religious experience could resolve problems of this conceptual sort.

C. D. BROAD
The Appeal to Religious Experience

. . . Founders of religions and saints, e.g., often claim to have been in direct contact with God, to have seen and spoken with Him, and so on. An ordinary religious man would certainly not make any such claim, though he might say that he had had experiences which assured him of the existence and presence of God. So the first thing that we have to notice is that capacity for religious experience is in certain respects like an ear for music. There are a few people who are unable to recognize and distinguish the simplest tune. But they are in a minority, like the people who have absolutely no kind of religious experience. Most people have some slight appreciation of music. But the differences of degree in this respect are enormous, and those who have not much gift for music have to take the statements of accomplished musicians very largely on trust. Let us, then, compare tonedeaf persons to those who have no recognizable religious experience at all; the ordinary followers of a religion to men who have some taste for music but can neither appreciate the more difficult kinds nor compose; highly religious men and saints to persons with an exceptionally fine ear for music who may yet be unable to compose it; and the founders of religions to great musical composers, such as Bach and Beethoven.

This analogy is, of course, incomplete in certain important respects. Religious

C. D. Broad (1887–1971) was for many years a Professor of Moral Philosophy at Cambridge University. He is noted for his careful analyses of philosophical problems and for his contributions to psychical research. His major works include *The Mind and Its Place in Nature* and *Five Types of Ethical Theory*.

THE APPEAL TO RELIGIOUS EXPERIENCE   From *Religion, Philosophy and Psychical Research* by C. D. Broad. Reprinted by permission of Routledge & Kegan Paul Ltd.

experience raises three problems, which are different though closely interconnected. (i) What is the *psychological analysis* of religious experience? Does it contain factors which are present also in certain experiences which are not religious? Does it contain any factor which never occurs in any other kind of experience? If it contains no such factor, but is a blend of elements each of which can occur separately or in non-religious experiences, its psychological peculiarity must consist in the characteristic way in which these elements are blended in it. Can this peculiar structural feature of religious experience be indicated and described? (ii) What are the *genetic and causal conditions* of the existence of religious experience? Can we trace the origin and development of the disposition to have religious experiences *(a)* in the human race, and *(b)* in each individual? Granted that the disposition is present in nearly all individuals at the present time, can we discover and state the variable conditions which call it into activity on certain occasions and leave it in abeyance on others? (iii) Part of the content of religious experience is alleged knowledge or well-founded belief about the nature of reality, e.g., that we are dependent on a being who loves us and whom we ought to worship, that values are somehow conserved in spite of the chances and changes of the material world at the mercy of which they seem *prima facie* to be, and so on. Therefore there is a third problem. Granted that religious experience exists, that it has such-and-such a history and conditions, that it seems vitally important to those who have it, and that it produces all kinds of effects which would not otherwise happen, is it *veridical?* Are the claims to knowledge or well-founded belief about the nature of reality, which are an integral part of the experience, *true or probable?* Now, in the case of musical experience, there are analogies to the psychological problem and to the genetic or causal problem, but there is no analogy to the epistemological problem of validity. For, so far as I am aware, no part of the content of musical experience is alleged knowledge about the nature of reality; and therefore no question of its being veridical or delusive can arise.

Since both musical experience and religious experience certainly exist, any theory of the universe which was incompatible with their existence would be false, and any theory which failed to show the connexion between their existence, and the other facts about reality would be inadequate. So far the two kinds of experience are in exactly the same position. But a theory which answers to the condition that it allows of the *existence* of religious experience and indicates the *connexion* between its existence and other facts about reality may leave the question as to its *validity* quite unanswered. Or, alternatively, it may throw grave doubt on its cognitive claims, or else it may tend to support them. Suppose, e.g., that it could be shown that religious experience contains no elements which are not factors in other kinds of experience. Suppose further it could be shown that this particular combination of factors tends to originate and to be activated only under certain conditions which are known to be very commonly productive of false beliefs held with strong conviction. Then a satisfactory answer to the questions of psychological analysis and causal antecedents would have tended to answer the epistemological question of validity in the negative. On the other hand, it might be that the only theory which would satisfactorily account for the origin of the religious disposition and for the occurrence of actual religious experiences under certain conditions was a theory which allowed some of the cognitive claims made by religious experience to be true or probable. Thus the three problems, though entirely distinct from each other, may be very closely connected; and it is the existence of the third problem in connexion with religious experience which puts it, for the present purpose, in a different category from musical experience.

In spite of this essential difference the analogy is not to be despised, for it brings out at least one important point. If a man who had no ear for music were to give himself airs on that account, and were to talk *de haut en bas* about those who can appreciate music and think it highly important, we should regard him, not as an advanced thinker, but as a self-satisfied Philistine. And, even if he did not do this but only propounded theories about the nature and causation of musical experience, we might think it reasonable to feel very doubtful whether his theories would be adequate or correct. In the same way, when persons without religious experience regard themselves as being *on that ground* superior to those who have it, their attitude must be treated as merely silly and offensive. Similarly, any theories about religious experience constructed by persons who have little or none of their own should be regarded with grave suspicion. (For that reason it would be unwise to attach very much weight to anything that the present writer may say on this subject.)

On the other hand, we must remember that the possession of a great capacity for religious experience, like the possession of a great capacity for musical appreciation and composition, is no guarantee of high general intelligence. A man may be a saint or a magnificent musician and yet have very little common sense, very little power of accurate introspection or of seeing causal connexions, and scarcely any capacity for logical criticism. He may also be almost as ignorant about other aspects of reality as the nonmusical or non-religious man is about musical or religious experience. If such a man starts to theorize about music or religion, his theories may be quite as absurd, though in a different way, as those made by persons who are devoid of musical or religious experience. Fortunately it happens that some religious mystics of a high order have been extremely good at introspecting and describing their own experiences. And some highly religious persons have had very great critical and philosophical abilities. St. Teresa is an example of the first, and St. Thomas Aquinas of the second.

Now I think it must be admitted that, if we compare and contrast the statements made by religious mystics of various times, races, and religions, we find a common nucleus combined with very great differences of detail. Of course the interpretations which they have put on their experiences are much more varied than the experiences themselves. It is obvious that the interpretations will depend in a large measure on the traditional religious beliefs in which various mystics have been brought up. I think that such traditions probably act in two different ways.

(i) The tradition no doubt affects the theoretical interpretation of experiences which would have taken place even if the mystic had been brought up in a different tradition. A feeling of unity with the rest of the universe will be interpreted very differently by a Christian who has been brought up to believe in a personal God and by a Hindu mystic who has been trained in a quite different metaphysical tradition.

(ii) The traditional beliefs, on the other hand, probably determine many of the details of the experience itself. A Roman Catholic mystic may have visions of the Virgin and the saints, whilst a Protestant mystic pretty certainly will not.

Thus the relations between the experiences and the traditional beliefs are highly complex. Presumably the outlines of the belief are determined by the experience. Then the details of the belief are fixed for a certain place and period by the special peculiarities of the experiences had by the founder of a certain religion. These beliefs then become traditional in that religion. Thenceforth they in part determine the details of the experiences had by subsequent mystics of that religion, and still more do they determine the interpretations which these mystics will put upon their experiences. Therefore, when a set of religious beliefs has once been established, it no doubt tends to produce experiences which can plausibly be taken as evidence for it. If it is a tradition in a certain religion that one can communicate with saints, mystics of that religion will seem to see and to talk with saints in their mystical visions; and this fact will be taken as further evidence for the belief that one can communicate with saints.

Much the same double process of causation takes place in sense-perception. On the one hand, the beliefs and expectations which we have at any moment largely determine what *interpretation* we shall put on a certain sensation which we should in any case have had then. On the other hand, our beliefs and expectations do to some extent determine and modify some of the sensible characteristics of the *sensa themselves*. When I am thinking only of diagrams a certain visual stimulus may produce a sensation of a sensibly flat sensum; but a precisely similar stimulus may produce a sensation of a sensibly solid sensum when I am thinking of solid objects.

Such explanations, however, plainly do not account for the first origin of religious beliefs, or for the features which are common to the religious experiences of persons of widely different times, races, and traditions.

Now, when we find that there are certain experiences which, though never very frequent in a high degree of intensity, have happened in a high degree among a few men at all times and places; and when we find that, in spite of differences in detail which we can explain, they involve certain fundamental conditions which are common and peculiar to them; two alternatives are open to us. (i) We may suppose that these men are in contact with an aspect of reality which is not revealed to ordinary persons in their everyday experience. And we may suppose that the characteristics which they agree in ascribing to reality on the basis of these experiences probably do belong to it. Or (ii) we may suppose that they are all subject to a delusion from which other men are free. In order to illustrate these alternatives it will be useful to consider three partly analogous cases, two of which are real and the third imaginary.

(*a*) Most of the detailed facts which biologists tell us about the minute structure and changes in cells can be perceived only by persons who have had a long training in the use of the microscope. In this case we believe that the agreement among trained microscopists really does correspond to facts which untrained persons cannot perceive. *(b)* Persons of all races who habitually drink alcohol to excess eventually have perceptual experiences in which they seem to themselves to see snakes or rats crawling about their rooms or beds. In this case we believe that this agreement among drunkards is merely a uniform hallucination. *(c)* Let us now imagine a race of beings who can walk about and touch things but cannot see. Suppose that eventually a few of them developed the power of sight. All that they might tell their still blind friends about colour would be wholly unintelligible to and unverifiable by the latter. But they would also be able to tell their blind friends a great deal about what the latter would feel if they were to walk in certain directions. These statements would be verified. This would not, of course, *prove* to the blind ones that the unintelligible statements about colour correspond to certain aspects of the world which they cannot perceive. But it would show that the seeing persons had a source of additional information about matters which the blind ones could understand and test for themselves. It would not be unreasonable then for the blind ones to believe that probably the seeing ones are also able to perceive other aspects of reality which they are describing correctly when they make their unintelligible statements containing colour-names. The question then is whether it is reasonable to regard the agreement between the experiences of religious mystics as more like the agreement among trained microscopists about the minute structure of cells, or as more like the agreement among habitual drunkards about the infestation of their rooms by pink rats or snakes, or as more like the agreement about colours which the seeing men would express in their statements to the blind men.

Why do we commonly believe that habitual excess of alcohol is a cause of a uniform delusion and not a source of additional information? The main reason is as follows. The things which drunkards claim to perceive are not fundamentally different in kind from the things that other people perceive. We have all seen rats and snakes, though the rats have generally been grey or brown and not pink. Moreover the drunkard claims that the rats and snakes which he sees are literally present in his room and on his bed, in the same sense in which his bed is in his room and his quilt is on his bed. Now we may fairly argue as follows. Since these are the sort of things which we could see if they were there, the fact that we cannot see them makes it highly probable that they are not there. Again, we know what kinds of perceptible effect would generally follow from the presence in a room of such things as rats or snakes. We should expect fox-terriers or mongooses to show traces of excitement, cheese to be nibbled, corn to disappear from bins, and so on. We find that no such effects are observed in the bedrooms of persons suffering from *delirium tremens*. It therefore seems reasonable to conclude that the agreement among drunkards is a sign, not of a revelation, but of a delusion.

Now the assertions in which religious mystics agree are not such that they conflict with what we can perceive with our senses. They are about the structure and organization of the world as a whole and about the relations of men to the rest of it. And they have so little in common with the facts of daily life that there is not much chance of direct collision. I think that there is only one important point on which there is conflict. Nearly all mystics seem to be agreed that time and change and unchanging duration are unreal or extremely superficial, whilst these seem to plain men to be the most fundamental features of the world. But we must admit, on the one hand, that these temporal characteristics present very great philosophical difficulties and puzzles when we reflect upon them. On the other hand, we may well suppose that the mystic finds it impossible to state clearly in ordinary language what it is that he experiences about the facts which underlie the appearance of time and change and duration. Therefore it is not difficult to allow that what we experience as the temporal aspect of reality corresponds in some sense to certain facts, and yet that these facts appear to us in so distorted a form in our ordinary experience that a person who sees them more accurately and directly might refuse to apply temporal names to them.

Let us next consider why we feel fairly certain that the agreement among trained microscopists about the minute structure of cells expresses an objective fact, although we cannot get similar experiences. One reason is that we have learned enough, from simpler cases of visual perception, about the laws of optics to know that the arrangement of lenses in a microscope is such that it will reveal minute structure, which is otherwise invisible, and will not simply create optical delusions. Another reason is that we know of other cases in which trained persons can detect things which untrained people will overlook, and that in many cases the existence of these things can be verified by indirect methods. Probably most of us have experienced such results of training in our own lives.

Now religious experience is not in nearly such a strong position as this. We do not know much about the laws which govern its occurrence and determine its variations. No doubt there are certain standard methods of training and meditation which tend to produce mystical experiences. These have been elaborated to some extent by certain Western mystics and to a very much greater extent by Eastern Yogis. But I do not think that we can see here, as we can in the case of microscopes and the training which is required to make the best use of them, any conclusive reason why these methods should produce veridical rather than delusive experiences. Uniform methods of training and meditation would be likely to produce more or less similar experiences, whether these experiences were largely veridical or wholly delusive.

Is there any analogy between the facts about religious experience and the fable about the blind men some of whom gained the power of sight? It might be said that many ideals of conduct and ways of life, which we can all recognize now to be good and useful, have been introduced into human history by the founders of religions. These persons have made actual ethical discoveries which others can afterwards recognize to be true. It might be said that this is at least roughly analogous to the case of the seeing men telling the still blind men of facts which the latter could and did verify for themselves. And it might be said that this makes it reasonable for us to attach some weight to what founders of religions tell us about things which we cannot understand or verify for ourselves; just as it would have been reasonable for the blind men to attach some weight to the unintelligible statements which the seeing men made to them about colours.

I think that this argument deserves a certain amount of respect, though I should find it hard to estimate how much weight to attach to it. I should be inclined to sum up as follows. When there is a nucleus of agreement between the experiences of men in different places, times, and traditions, and when they all tend to put much the same kind of interpretation on the cognitive content of these experiences, it is reasonable to ascribe this agreement to their all being in contact with a certain objective aspect of reality *unless* there be some positive reason to think otherwise. The practical postulate which we go upon everywhere else is to treat cognitive claims as veridical unless there be some positive reason to think them delusive. This, after all, is our only guarantee for believing that ordinary sense-perception is veridical. We cannot *prove* that what people agree in perceiving really exists independently of them; but we do always assume that ordinary waking sense-perception is veridical unless we can produce some positive ground for thinking that it is delusive in any given case. I think it would be inconsistent to treat the experiences of religious mystics on different principles. So far as they agree they should be provisionally accepted as veridical unless there be some positive ground for thinking that they are not. So the next question is whether there is any positive ground for holding that they are delusive.

There are two circumstances which have been commonly held to cast doubt on the cognitive claims of religious and mystical experience. (i) It is alleged that founders of religions and saints have nearly always had certain neuropathic symptoms or certain bodily weaknesses, and that these would be likely to produce delusions. Even if we accept the premisses, I do not think that this is a very strong argument. (*a*) It is equally true that many founders of religions and saints have exhibited great endurance and great power of organization and business capacity which would have made them extremely successful and competent in secular affairs. There are very few offices in the cabinet or in the highest branches of the civil service which St. Thomas Aquinas could not have held with conspicuous success. I do not, of course, regard this as a positive reason *for* accepting the metaphysical doctrines which saints and founders of religions have based on their experiences; but it is relevant as a *rebuttal* of the argument which we are considering. (*b*) Probably very few people of extreme genius in science or art are perfectly normal mentally or physically, and some of them are very crazy and eccentric indeed. Therefore it would be rather surprising if persons of religious genius were completely normal, whether their experiences be veridical or delusive. (*c*) Suppose, for the sake of argument, that there is an aspect of the world which remains altogether outside the ken of ordinary persons in their daily life. Then it seems very likely that some degree of mental and physical abnormality would be a necessary condition for getting sufficiently loosened from the objects of ordinary sense-perception to come into cognitive contact with this aspect of reality. Therefore the fact that those persons who claim to have this peculiar kind of cognition generally exhibit certain mental and physical abnormalities is rather what might be anticipated if their claims were true. One might need to be slightly 'cracked' in order to have some peep-holes into the super-sensible world. (*d*) If mystical experience were veridical, it seems quite likely that it would *produce* abnormalities of behaviour in those who had it strongly. Let us suppose, for the sake of argument, that those who have religious experience are in frequent contact with an aspect of reality of which most men get only rare and faint glimpses. Then such persons are, as it were, living in two worlds, while the ordinary man is living in only one of them. Or, again, they might be compared to a man who has to conduct his life with one ordinary eye and another of a telescopic kind. Their behaviour may be appropriate to the aspect of reality which they alone perceive and think all-important; but, for that very reason, it may be inappropriate to those other aspects of reality which are all that most men perceive or judge to be important and on which all our social institutions and conventions are built.

(ii) A second reason which is commonly alleged for doubt about the claims of religious experience is the following. It is said that such experience always originates from and remains mixed with certain other factors, e.g., sexual emotion, which are such that experiences and beliefs that arise from them are very likely to be delusive. I think that there are a good many confusions on this point, and it will be worth while to begin by indicating some of them.

When people say that B 'originated from' A, they are liable to confuse at least three different kinds of connexion between A and B. (i) It might be that A is a necessary but insufficient condition of the existence of B. (ii) It might be that A is a necessary and sufficient condition of the existence of B. Or (iii) it might be that B simply *is* A in a more complex and disguised form. Now, when there is in fact evidence only for the first kind of connexion, people are very liable to jump to the conclusion that there is the third kind of connexion. It may well be the case, e.g., that no one who was incapable of strong sexual desires and emotions could have anything worth calling religious experience. But it is plain that the possession of a strong capacity for sexual experience is not a *sufficient* condition of having religious experience; for we know that the former quite often exists in persons who show hardly any trace of the latter. But, even if it could be shown that a strong capacity for sexual desire and emotion is *both* necessary and sufficient to produce religious experience, it would not follow that the latter is just the former in disguise. In the first place, it is not at all easy to discover the exact meaning of this metaphorical phrase when it is applied to psychological topics. And, if we make use of physical analogies, we are not much helped. A mixture of oxygen and hydrogen in the presence of a spark is necessary and sufficient to produce water accompanied by an explosion. But water accompanied by an explosion is not a mixture of oxygen and hydrogen and a spark 'in a disguised form', whatever that may mean.

Now I think that the present rather vaguely formulated objection to the validity of the claims of relgious experience might be stated somewhat as follows. 'In the individual religious experience originates from, and always remains mixed with, sexual desires and emotions. The other generative factor of it is the religious tradition of the society in which he lives, the teachings of his parents, nurses, school-mates, etc. In the race religious experience originated from a mixture of false beliefs about nature and man, irrational fears and other impulses, and so on. Thus the religious tradition arose from beliefs which we now recognize to have been false and from emotions which we now recognize to have been irrelevant and misleading. It is now drilled into children by those who are in authority over them at a time of life when they are intellectually and emotionally at much the same stage as the primitive savages among whom it originated. It is, therefore, readily accepted, and it determines beliefs and emotional dispositions which persist long after the child has grown up and acquired more adequate knowledge of nature and of himself.'

Persons who use this argument might admit that it does not definitely *prove* that religious beliefs are false and groundless. False beliefs and irrational fears in our remote ancestors *might* conceivably be the origin of true beliefs and of an appropriate feeling of awe and reverence in ourselves. And, if sexual desires and emotions be an essential condition and constituent of religious experience, the experience *may* nevertheless be veridical in important respects. We might merely have to rewrite one of the beatitudes and say 'Blessed are the *impure* in heart, for they shall see God'. But, although it is logically possible that such causes should produce such effects, it would be said that they are most unlikely to do so. They seem much more likely to produce false beliefs and misplaced emotions.

It is plain that this argument has considerable plausibility. But it is worth while to remember that modern science has almost as humble an ancestry as contemporary religion. If the primitive witch-smeller is the spiritual progenitor of the Archbishop of Canterbury, the primitive rain-maker is equally the spiritual progenitor of the Cavendish Professor of Physics. There has obviously been a gradual refinement and purification of religious beliefs and concepts in the course of history, just as there has been in the beliefs and concepts of science. Certain persons of religious genius, such as some of the Hebrew prophets and the founders of Christianity and of Buddhism, do seem to have introduced new ethico-religious concepts and beliefs which have won wide acceptance, just as certain men of scientific genius, such as Galileo, Newton, and Einstein, have done in the sphere of science. It seems somewhat arbitrary to count this process as a continual approximation to true knowledge of the material aspect of the world in the case of science, and to refuse to regard it as at all similar in the case of religion. Lastly, we must remember that all of us have accepted the current common-sense and scientific view of the material world on the authority of our parents, nurses, masters, and companions at a time when we had neither the power nor the inclination to criticize it. And most of us accept, without even understanding, the more recondite doctrines of contemporary physics simply on the authority of those whom we have been taught to regard as experts.

On the whole, then, I do not think that what we know of the conditions under which religious beliefs and emotions have arisen in the life of the individual and the race makes it reasonable to think that they are *specially* likely to be delusive or misdirected. At any rate any argument which starts from that basis and claims to reach such a conclusion will need to be very carefully handled if its destructive effects are to be confined within the range contemplated by its users. It is reasonable to think that the concepts and beliefs of even the most perfect religions known to us are extremely inadequate to the facts which they express; that they are highly confused and are mixed up with a great deal of positive error and sheer nonsense; and that, if the human race goes on and continues to have religious experiences and to reflect on them, they will be altered and improved almost out of recognition. But all this could be said, *mutatis mutandis*, of scientific concepts and theories. The claim of any particular religion or sect to have complete or final truth on these subjects seems to me to be too ridiculous to be worth a moment's consideration. But the opposite extreme of holding that the whole religious experience of mankind is a gigantic system of pure delusion seems to me to be almost (though not quite) as far-fetched.

WILLIAM J. WAINWRIGHT
The Cognitive Status of Mystical Experience

I

Mystical experience is often said to involve a kind of 'seeing' or 'tasting' or 'touching'. We are told that mystical experience is an 'experimental knowledge' of the divine. Mystical experiences are believed to involve a direct or immediate awareness of reality or some aspect of reality which is normally hidden from us. It is clear that an analogy with sense experience is intended and that part of what is implied in ascribing cognitive value to mystical experience is that these experiences are, in some important respects, like ordinary perceptual experience. In the opposite camp we find critics like C. B. Martin who assume that ordinary perceptual experiences provide us with the paradigm of a cognitive or perceptual experience and go on to argue that religious experiences cannot be cognitive or perceptual because they deviate in certain important ways from that paradigm.

The analogy (or lack of it) between mystical experience and sense experience appears, then, to be critically important both to those who ascribe cognitive value to mystical experiences and to those who refuse to do so.

A

Mystical experiences and sense experiences are alike in two important respects. (1) Both types of experience are noetic. (2) On the basis of both types of experience claims are made about something other than the experience itself. These claims are corrigible and independently checkable. In each case there are tests for determining whether or not the object of the experience is real and tests for determining whether or not an apparent perception of that object is a genuine one.

(1) Sense experiences (whether veridical or not) have a noetic quality. This involves two things. (a) The experiences have an object, i.e. they are experiences of something (real or imagined). In this respect sense experiences are unlike pains,

William J. Wainwright (1935–   ) is Professor of Philosophy at the University of Wisconsin, Milwaukee. He is the author of *Philosophy of Religion: An Annotated Bibliography of Twentieth-Century Writings in English* and *Mysticism: A Study of Its Nature, Cognitive Value, and Moral Implications.* He is coeditor, with Robert Audi, of *Rationality, Religious Belief, and Moral Commitment.*

THE COGNITIVE STATUS OF MYSTICAL EXPERIENCE   From *Mysticism: A Study of Its Nature, Cognitive Value, and Moral Implications* (Madison: University of Wisconsin Press, 1981). Reprinted by permission of the University of Wisconsin Press.

feelings of depression and so on. The latter may have causes. They may be aroused or occasioned by certain kinds of events or objects but (in spite of certain continental philosophers) they are not experiences *of* those events or objects. (To the question 'What is the object of a visual [auditory] experience?' we can reply 'Colours and shapes [sounds]'. The question 'What is the object of a dull pain [a feeling of depression]?' cannot be answered so easily.) (b) Sense experience typically involves the conviction that the object on which the experience is focused is 'really there', that it exists and that one 'experimentally' apprehends it. To use Berkeley's language, the experience has 'outness'. This conviction is not an interpretation which is placed upon the experience, but part of the experience itself.

In spite of the fact that some mystics speak as if their experiences transcended the subject-object structure of ordinary perceptual experience, many mystical experiences (and perhaps all of them) are noetic in this sense. (For example, monistic mystics by and large agree that they experience something which transcends space and time, is devoid of distinctions and is supremely valuable. Theistic mystics believe that they experimentally perceive God.)

(2) No type of experience can be called cognitive if it induces those who have it to make false claims. Thus, the experience of a mirage or the experiences one obtains by pressing one's eyeball and seeing double are called delusive because they are inherently misleading—the very nature of these experiences is such that (until one learns better) one is likely to base false claims upon them, (that water is really present or that there are two candles rather than one). There is no conclusive reason to suppose that mystical experiences are delusive in this sense. The mystic does not make false empirical statements on the basis of his experiences because he does not make empirical statements. Rather he claims to know, on the basis of his experience, that God is real and present to him or that there is an 'uncreated, imperishable Beyond', or something of the sort. It would therefore seem that we are entitled to assert that these experiences are delusive only if we have good independent reasons for believing that claims of this kind are false. It is by no means clear that we do.

But the fact that experiences are not delusive does not imply that they are cognitive. Pains are not delusive, but they are not cognitive either. One of the reasons for calling sense experiences cognitive is that not only do they not induce *false* claims, they also provide a basis for making *true* claims about something other than the experience itself. This involves two things. First, sense experiences are means of apprehending (some aspect of) reality. Those who have them are more likely to discern certain truths than those who do not, or can at least discern them more easily. Second, sense experiences can be appealed to, to justify the truths which have been made out by their means. For example, people with normal vision are more likely to discern truths about colours and shapes, and can do so more easily, than those who are blind, and they are entitled to appeal to their visual experiences to justify their claims.

Are mystical experiences like sense experiences in this respect? We can at least say this: on the basis of their experiences, mystics make claims about something other than their own experiences. They believe that they have directly apprehended a reality which others accept on faith, or on the basis of certain arguments, and they appeal to their experiences to justify their claims. Furthermore (assuming that there is no disproof of God's existence, or of the reality of the One, etc.) these claims are not known to be false. We seem therefore to have found a respect in which sense experiences and mystical experiences are like each other and unlike pains.

The analogy extends further. When a person claims to see, hear or touch something, his claim is not self-certifying. Things other than his own experience are relevant to a determination of the truth or falsity of his claim. C. B. Martin and others have asserted that sense experiences are radically unlike mystical experiences in this respect, for (they say) when the mystic claims to experience God or the Brahman, his claims are not corrigible—there are (to use Martin's phrase) no independent tests and check-up procedures which he and others would regard as relevant to a determination of the truth or falsity of the claims he makes. His claims are therefore private (like first person psychological reports), not public (like ordinary perceptual claims).

This is simply false. Misled by the fact that certain familiar tests (for example, the appeal to the agreement of others) play at most a minor role in the evaluation of mystical experiences, critics like Martin have illicitly concluded that mystics, therefore, dismiss all tests and check-up procedures as irrelevant and regard their claims as incorrigible.

Suppose someone claims to have seen an elephant in his backyard. There are at least two ways in which his claim might be attacked. One might try to show that no elephant was there at all, or one might try to show that he could not have seen it because, for example, he was not in a position to observe it, or his sensory equipment was defective. When we turn to mystical experience we find both sorts of test and check-up procedure (at least in a rough and ready way), that is, we find independent procedures for determining whether its object is real and we find independent procedures for determining whether the experience is a genuine perception of its object.

Even when claims about such things as God or Nibbāna are grounded in mystical consciousness, they are not self-certifying. Things other than the experience itself are relevant to an evaluation of their truth. For example, considerations of logic are relevant. *Pace* Stace, these claims cannot be true if the concepts of God or Nibbāna are self-contradictory. Again, considerations adduced in arguments for and against the existence of God have some bearing on the truth of the claims made by theistic mystics. Even the statement that there is a One beyond distinctions does not appear to be self-certifying though, since what is claimed is relatively minimal, it would be harder to disprove. (Considerations of logic, and considerations adduced by positivists and naturalists, might count against it.) When the mystic asserts that he has experienced God (or Nibbāna, or Brahman) he implies that what he has experienced is real. He should therefore recognise that things besides his own experience are relevant to an evaluation of his claim. It is true that mystics are usually certain of the truth of the claims that they make, but this is no more incompatible with their corrigibility than the fact that I am certain that there is a red pen in front of me is incompatible with the fact that that claim is corrigible. In short, claims about God, or Nibbāna and other things of that kind are not self-certifying, and we have some idea of the sorts of things which count for and against them.

There are, then, independent tests for determining whether the object of mystical experience is real. There are also independent tests for determining whether an experience of this object is a genuine perception of it. Consider theistic mystical experiences, for example. Even if God exists and a direct experience of Him is possible, it does not follow that every claim to be immediately aware of God is justified. How, though, do we distinguish experiences of God which are veridical from those which are not? If we turn our attention to the communities in which theistic mysticism has flourished we find that various tests have been used to distinguish the experiences which genuinely involve a perception of God from those which do not. Each of the following six criteria is employed in the Christian (particularly the Catholic) community. Similar criteria are used in other communities.

(1) The consequences of the experience must be good for the mystic. The experience must lead to, produce, or reinforce, a new life marked by such virtues as wisdom, humility and charity. (Sanity should be subsumed under this criterion. A genuine experience of God is believed to have a tendency to produce a life of rather extraordinary goodness. It seems reasonable to suppose that sanity is a necessary condition of such a life.) This criterion helps to explain why people are bothered by the presence of certain kinds of causes. Many people find it impossible to believe that the use of drugs, nervous and physical disorders and so on, can play a part in the best sort of life. Consequently, if they find that these things play a major role in the life of a mystic, they will tend to discount his experience.

(2) One must consider the effect which the experience has on others. For instance, one should ask whether the mystic's words, actions and example tend to build up the community or weaken it.

(3) The depth, the profundity and the 'sweetness' (Jonathan Edwards) of what the mystic says on the basis of his experience counts in favour of the genuineness of that experience. On the other hand, the insignificance, or the silliness, of what he says counts against it. (On the basis of this criterion many would reject the claims of Margery Kempe.)

(4) We must examine what the mystic says on the basis of his experience and see whether it agrees or disagrees with orthodox talk. (It should be noted that this test is not circular. The statement being tested is a statement like 'Teresa saw God', or 'John received heavenly consolations'. Statements of this kind are not Christian dogmas.)

(5) It will be helpful to determine whether the experience in question resembles other mystical experiences regarded as paradigmatic by the religious community. (In the Roman Catholic church, experiences are often compared with the experiences of Teresa of Avila or of John of the Cross.)

(6) We must also consider the pronouncements of authority. In some communities (for example, Zen) the word of the spiritual director, guru or master is final. In other religious communities, the voice of the spiritual director is important though not conclusive. In some cases the relevant authority may be the community as a whole, or some special organ of it. (For example, the standing enjoyed by the experiences of John of the Cross and Teresa in the Roman Catholic community is largely a consequence of their acceptance by that community and its official representatives.) In some cases all of these authorities may be relevant.

If I am correct, these criteria are similar to the tests which we employ in ordinary perceptual cases to determine whether an apparent perception of an object is a genuine perception of it, that is, they are similar to the tests which take things into account like the position of the observer and the condition of his sensory equipment. Of course, the *nature* of the tests is not much alike. Nevertheless, the point of them is, viz, to show not that the object of the experience is real or unreal but that there is or is not a genuine perception of it. (One would not expect the nature of the tests to be much alike. For example, in the case of introvertive mystical experience there is no sensory equipment which can go awry because sense organs are not involved. Nor does there appear to be anything which clearly corresponds to the position of the observer in sense experience.)

B

Among the more important tests and check-up procedures which are used to evaluate ordinary perceptual claims are (1) the agreement and disagreement of others occupying similar positions, and (2) the success or failure of predictions which have been based upon the experience whose claims are in question. Are similar tests used to assess the cognitive status of mystical experience?

(1) The claim that mystical experience is cognitive is frequently supported by appealing to the rather surprising amount of agreement that exists. Extrovertive mystics, monistic mystics and theistic mystics can be found in radically different cultures, in places which have had little or no contact with each other, and in all periods of history. Not only are their experiences alike, they base remarkably similar claims upon them. But some kinds of agreement are irrelevant. The visual and auditory experiences of persons from different cultures, with diverse social backgrounds and different psychological makeups, are often quite similar. Analogously mystics from different cultures, with diverse social backgrounds and different psychological makeups often have similar experiences. It is also the case that people suffering from migraines or indigestion undergo similar experiences in spite of differences in culture, social background, psychological makeup and many other factors. Sense experiences are widespread and so are mystical experiences, but so also are migraines and stomachaches. Since migraines and stomachaches are paradigm cases of non-cognitive experience, the presence of this sort of agreement has little tendency to show that a mode of experience is cognitive.

There are other sorts of agreement. People who make visual (or auditory or tactual) observations are normally able to describe conditions under which others can make similar observations. ('If you go into the room on the left, you will see the body.' 'If the telescope is trained on such and such a place at such and such a time, you will obtain a sighting of the moons of Jupiter.') Now mystics are able to do something like this. For example, they can prescribe procedures which are likely to lead to introvertive experiences. (These include special postures, breathing techniques, a deliberate withdrawal of the attention from sense objects, mental concentration and so on. Sometimes these procedures are specified in detail. Furthermore, in spite of some variation—particularly in the emphasis placed upon physical techniques—there is a great deal of agreement as to just what these procedures involve.)

Now the only agreement or disagreement which is directly relevant to the cognitive value of a sense experience, is agreement or disagreement among those who use the procedures associated with that type of experience, and try to make the relevant observation under the prescribed conditions. Agreement among people who fail to follow these procedures is not expected, and its absence is therefore regarded as beside the point. If sense experience provides the model for all cognitive modes of experience, then the fact that most of us have never had a mystical experience is irrelevant, for most of us have made no attempt to use the mystic's techniques.

Nevertheless, agreement among those who employ a set of prescribed techniques is not decisive. This kind of agreement is characteristic of sense experience, but it is also characteristic of subjective experiences. (For example, it can be safely asserted that people eating ten *bratwurst* sandwiches within twenty minutes will undergo strikingly similar and equally unpleasant digestive experiences.) What sort of agreement, then, is relevant? People who see, hear and touch, base claims about the world upon their experiences, and a lack of agreement among those following the appropriate procedures is believed to have an important bearing on the truth of their claims. People suffering from headaches or indigestion, on the other hand, do not base claims about the world upon their experiences and hence do not consider the agreement or disagreement of others to be relevant to the *truth* of such claims.

Mystics base claims about 'objective' reality upon their experiences. They differ in this respect from people suffering from headaches and indigestion. But do they believe that the agreement or disagreement of others is relevant to the truth of their claims? Do they take the fact that some people have similar experiences when following the appropriate procedures as counting *for* their claims? And do they take the fact that there are others who do not have similar experiences when following these procedures as counting *against* their claims? If they do, then we have discovered what may be an important analogy between mystical experience and sense experience. If they do not, we have uncovered what many would regard as a significant disanalogy. Unfortunately, the situation is ambiguous.

I am inclined to think that at least some mystics believe that the fact that others have had similar experiences, and have made similar claims, supports the claims which they base upon their own experiences, and that because of this agreement these mystics are more confident of the cognitive value of their experiences than they would otherwise be. However, no distinction appears to be made between those experiences which are obtained by employing techniques of prayer and meditation and those which occur spontaneously. *All* similar experiences are thought to confirm (equally) the claims which are made or (which comes to more or less the same thing) the cognitive value of the experiences upon which those claims are based.

It is not clear whether mystics believe that disagreement has any bearing upon the cognitive value of their experiences. Mystics are clearly not disturbed by the fact that most people never enjoy mystical experiences. Nor do they seem to be bothered by the fact that some people earnestly employ the appropriate techniques but never achieve illumination or union. These points are not decisive, however, for it might nonetheless be true that if there *was* more disagreement than in fact obtains, the mystic would withdraw or qualify his claim. The mystic regards disagreement as relevant if there is *any* degree of disagreement which *would* be taken as counting against his claim if it *were* to occur. Suppose, for example, that the mystic were to discover that those whom he thought had achieved a unitive experience by employing the standard techniques had not really done so. Would he regard this discovery as counting against the cognitive value of his own experiences? Of course he might (particularly if he had used these techniques himself) but he might only conclude that the techniques were not as effective as he had believed them to be. Suppose, however, the mystic stood alone. While it is by no means clear that the mystic would (or should) repudiate his experience under these conditions (it is, perhaps, too impressive for that) he might nevertheless be bothered by the absence of supporting claims. (There is some evidence that those who believe that their religious experiences are comparatively unique are more suspicious of them than those who are aware of the fact that others have had similar experiences.) If he would, then perhaps the mystic does regard disagreement as having at least *some* relevance to the evaluation of his experiences.

What emerges from these considerations is this. The mystic bases ontological statements upon his experiences and seems to believe that the fact that others have similar experiences confirms those claims (or the veridical character of his own experience). It is *possible* that if others were to fail altogether to have similar experience, he would take this fact as counting against the veridical character of his own experience. In these respects mystical experience appears to be more like sense experience than like feelings of nausea or depression.

On the other hand there are significant disanalogies. (i) *All* similar experiences are believed to confirm the mystic's claim. The fact that some of these experiences were not obtained by employing the appropriate procedures but occurred spontaneously is ignored. (ii) Furthermore, it is not clear that a breakdown of the procedures for obtaining these experiences would induce the mystic to hedge his claims. In both respects mystical experience differs from sense experience. In the case of the latter, the only *relevant* agreement is that which is found among those who satisfy certain appropriate conditions, and a failure to obtain similar experiences after meeting those conditions casts serious doubts upon the experience's validity.

What is perhaps most significant is the fact that the presence of agreement or disagreement is not regarded as a crucial consideration by those who have had mystical experiences. It is not even clear that it is considered to be important. In the case of sense experience, on the other hand, the presence or absence of agreement (among those who employ the appropriate procedures) is always important, and often crucial.

(2) In evaluating a particular instance of sense experience, we consider predictions which have been based upon that experience. Successful predictions count for its verdicality and unsuccessful predictions count against it. Furthermore, if anyone were to attempt to justify the claim that sense experience in general is a cognitive mode of experience, he would undoubtedly appeal to the fact that a very large number of successful predictions about the course of external events have been based upon experiences of that type.

A few predictions do appear to be based upon mystical experience. On the basis of their experience mystics frequently assert that the soul is immortal and, of course, this involves a prediction. Furthermore, mystics occasionally claim that their experiences confirm theological systems which include certain predictions as an integral part. Thus, Christian mystics have sometimes regarded their experiences as confirmations of the truth of Christian dogma, and Christian dogma includes a belief in the general resurrection and the transfiguration of heaven and earth. A mystic may also, on the basis of his experience, predict that if one subjects oneself to the appropriate discipline (for example, practises the Jesus prayer or follows the noble eight-fold path) he will obtain a vision of God or pass into Nibbāna or something of the sort.

Now many, perhaps most, of the predictions made by those who can see or hear (etc.) can be checked *both* by others who can see or hear *and* by those who cannot. Suppose, for example, that I see thunderclouds approaching and predict it will rain. A blind man cannot do this (though he might predict rain on the basis of other factors). He can, however, *check* this prediction. If it rains he will not see it, but he will (if suitably situated) feel, hear, and perhaps even taste the rain. If he does not, he is entitled to conclude that my prediction was a failure.

The claim that we are immortal and the claim that human beings will be resurrected are, I think, verifiable (though not falsifiable). However, the experiences which would justify them are (in the first case) post-mortem experiences, and (in the second case) post-Advent experiences. Neither mystics nor non-mystics can verify these claims in this life, or before the second Advent. If one verified the third prediction one would be a mystic. The conclusion then is that none of these predictions can be checked in this life by the non-mystic, and the first two predictions cannot be checked in this life by anyone.

Since these predictions cannot be checked, they cannot be appealed to in order to establish the cognitive value of mystical experience as such, or to establish the cognitive value of a particular instance of mystical experience. It would thus appear that a blind man may have a reason for ascribing cognitive value to visual experience (*qua* mode of experience) or to a particular visual experience, which the non-mystic does not have for ascribing cognitive value to mystical experience (*qua* mode of experience) or to a particular mystical experience, viz, that the blind man knows that visual experiences in general, or a particular visual experience, have led to successful predictions, whereas the non-mystic does not know that mystical experiences in general, or a particular mystical experience, have led to successful predictions. This difference is striking and perhaps significant.

(3) A consideration of the presence of agreement or disagreement, and of the success or failure of predictions which have been based upon the experience play an important role in the evaluation of the cognitive status of sense consciousness but not in the evaluation of the cognitive status of mystical consciousness. These differences are intelligible if sense experiences are cognitive and mystical experiences are not. However, there is another way to account for them. The differences can be explained by the fact that the *objects* of these two kinds of experience are radically different.

Suppose[1] that God is the object of a mystical experience (rather than Nibbāna

---

[1] I am indebted to William Alston for the main point of the next three paragraphs. (See his *Religious Belief and Philosophical Thought*, New York, 1963, pp 124–5.)

or the Ātman, etc.). If God is what He is supposed to be (omnipotent, omniscient, mysterious, other, transcendent and so on), then whether or not one has an experience of Him will, in the last analysis, depend upon His will; there will be no set of procedures the correct use of which invariably results in illumination or union. Hence, while these experiences may be repeatable in the weak sense that given *exactly* the same conditions (including God's gracious activity), the same experience will occur, there is no reason to suppose that they will be repeatable in the strong sense, viz, that certain procedures or methods can be described which are such that (almost) all who correctly employ them will obtain the experience in question.

God is radically unlike physical objects in this respect. Physical objects exhibit spatio-temporal continuity, are relatively accessible and behave in law-like and regular ways. Given the nature of physical objects, one reasonably supposes that if one's experience of the object is veridical, others will enjoy similar experiences under similar conditions. One expects experiences of these objects to cohere and mutually support one another in certain familiar ways. If the nature of physical objects were different, however, these expectations would not be reasonable; experiences of these objects would not be repeatable in the strong sense, *even though the objects were real and experiences of them were veridical*. Suppose, for example, that mountains jumped about in a discontinuous fashion, randomly appeared and disappeared, and behaved in other lawless and unpredictable ways. If these conditions obtained, observation under similar conditions would not normally yield similar results even if mountains were real and experiences of them were veridical. There would be no reason to expect experiences in this area to cohere and support one another in the way they do.

The general point is this. The nature of an object should (at least partly) determine the tests for its presence. Given the nature of *physical* objects it is reasonable to suppose that genuine experiences of those objects can be confirmed by employing appropriate procedures and obtaining similar experiences, and that non-genuine experiences can be disconfirmed by employing the same procedures and obtaining different experiences. God's nature, on the other hand, is radically different from the nature of physical objects. It is therefore not clearly reasonable to suppose that (apparent) experiences of God can be confirmed or disconfirmed in the same fashion.

The difference in the nature of their respective objects thus explains why the presence or absence of agreement is an important test in the one case, but not in the other. This difference also explains other disanalogies. (1) God bestows His grace upon whom he pleases and is therefore not bound by our techniques. One person may employ mental prayer and fail to obtain the desired experience, while another who does not practise contemplation may experience (some degree) of illumination. It is therefore only to be expected that little distinction is made between similar experiences which are obtained by these techniques and similar experiences which occur spontaneously. In so far as agreement is considered to be relevant, *both* are regarded as confirmatory. (2) Since God freely bestows the experience upon whom He will, we have no idea of how many of these experiences to expect. Hence it is not clear at just what point (if any) a mystic should begin

to be bothered by the absence of agreement. We should, therefore, not be surprised if we find it difficult to specify a degree of disagreement which is so great
that in the face of it a mystic would or should withdraw his claim.

Similar considerations show that, in the case of theistic mystical experiences,
the demand for successful predictions may be inappropriate. It is reasonable to
insist on successful predictions when the type of experience which is involved is
supposed to provide access to ordinary empirical objects—objects which exhibit
spatial-temporal continuity, which are accessible, and which behave in law-like
and regular ways—for the nature of these objects is such that testable predictions
can be made about them. However, it is not clear that the demand for successful
predictions is reasonable when the object in question is (like God) a-spatial, a-
temporal (?), and neither accessible in the way in which ordinary objects are
accessible nor law-like and regular in its behaviour.

In short, there is no reason to believe that genuine experiences of God will be
supported by the experience of others in the way in which veridical sense experiences are supported by the experience of others, or that veridical experiences of
God will provide data which can be used to predict the future. The fact that
mystical experiences are not supported by the agreement of others in the way in
which veridical sense experiences are supported by the agreement of others, and
that they afford no glimpse of the future, is therefore not decisive.

But suppose that the object of a mystical experience is Nibbāna, the nirguṇa
Brahman, or one's own puruṣa rather than God. These realities do not dispense
favours, but are impersonal and inactive. Since they do not act, their 'behaviour'
cannot be irregular and unpredictable. Nor do they appear to have any other
features which would make it unreasonable to include agreement and disagreement among the tests and check-up procedures that are used to assess experiences
of them. However, there is a reason for disregarding the lack of successful predictions. By definition, predictions are concerned with the temporal order; their content is the future. Nibbāna, the nirguṇa Brahman, and one's puruṣa are non-
temporal realities. They are neither in time nor do they intervene in the temporal
order. There is thus no reason to suppose that veridical experiences of these things
will lead to successful predictions.

C

For a mode of experience to be accepted as cognitive, it is not sufficient that there
be tests for evaluating the cognitive character of instances of that type of experience. It is necessary that these tests be relevant to the cognitive status of these
experiences, and that they are satisfied by many (most?) instances of that type
of experience. We would dismiss a test which specified that valid experiences
occur only in months the English name of which contains the letter r, on the
ground that whether or not an experience occurs in those months has nothing to
do with its cognitive status. Furthermore, if in most instances the relevant tests
yielded negative results, we would not regard experiences of that type as cognitive.
(For example, we would not regard visual experiences as cognitive if they normally conflicted with one another and were an unreliable guide to future experience.)

Two significant sorts of disagreement are thus possible. People may disagree as to the relevance of the tests which are used to evaluate instances of an experience whose cognitive status is in question, or they may disagree as to whether the appropriate tests are met in a significant number of instances.

Whether the appropriate tests are met depends, of course, upon just what the appropriate tests are. The six tests considered earlier are met in many instances. On the other hand, while mystical experiences do not lead to patently false predictions, the few predictions which are based upon them are not *known* to be true. Nor is it clear that mystical experiences agree and cohere in the way in which sense experiences agree and cohere. We have seen however that neither of the last two tests is especially relevant to the evaluation of certain types of mystical experience. Therefore, the fact that they fail to satisfy them, or satisfy them very imperfectly, is of no particular importance. Or at least it is not crucial.

But are the tests relevant? As we have seen, there are two kinds of tests for evaluating mystical experiences—tests which are used to determine the reality of the *object* of mystical experience, and tests which are used to determine the genuineness of an *experience* of that object.

In determining the truth of the claim that God is real, one would address oneself to considerations of logic, review the more telling points made by theists and atheists, and so on. (One would do similar, though not identical things, in order to determine the reality of the Brahman or Nibbāna.) It would be generally agreed that this procedure is legitimate and that these considerations do bear upon the reality of the object of mystical experience. It is the other set of tests—the procedures which are used to determine the genuineness of an experience of the object—which create suspicion. Nevertheless, there are good reasons to believe that, at least under certain conditions, these tests too are relevant.

(1 and 2) The first two tests are moral tests. A veridical experience is one which is fruitful and edifying both for the mystic himself and for others. If the (apparent) object of a mystical experience is God, then these tests are relevant. For, if God is good and cares for His creatures (things analytically connected with the notion of God), then one would expect a direct experience of Him to be fruitful and edifying, to result in spiritual beauty and goodness, in holiness and in wisdom.

(3) The third test is also relevant when God is the (apparent) object of an experience; for if God is perfect goodness, omniscient, omnipotent, necessary, the 'mysterium tremendum,' holy, numinous, etc. (attributes which are once again analytically connected with the notion of God), then one would not expect a vision of Him to lead to twaddle. Quite the contrary.

(4) The fourth test is relevant to an evaluation of experiences which seem to involve a direct awareness of God provided that (a) God is not a deceiver, and that (b) orthodox beliefs are true. If God is a God of truth and orthodox beliefs are true, one would not expect a genuine experience of God to lead to (very much) non-orthodox talk.

(5 and 6) The relevance of the fifth and sixth tests depends upon the truth of doctrines concerning the holiness and authoritative character of the individual or community in question. For example, the claims of the Christian community and its representatives would be supported by an appeal to the notion that the Church is the body of Christ and the temple of the Holy Spirit, to the claim that its bishops possess teaching authority, and so on.

The relevance of the first three tests depends upon the truth of certain *conditional* propositions (viz, that *if* God is good and cares for His creatures, then genuine experiences of Him will be fruitful and edifying for the mystic and for others, etc.). One may be uncertain that God exists and yet admit that if an experience really *is* an experience of God, it will be fruitful and significant, and that there is therefore good reason to examine a mystic's verbal and non-verbal behaviour and its consequences. One need not be a theist to admit the relevance of these tests. The last three tests, on the other hand, are relevant only if the specific tenets of some particular religious community are true. One would have no reason to compare the talk of a mystic with orthodox Christian talk, or to stress the ways in which his experience is like and unlike the experience of John of the Cross (rather than some Sufi or Theravādin mystic), or to appeal to the concensus of the Church, if one were not a Christian.

These tests are therefore relevant to an evaluation of experiences that purport to be experiences of God. Are they relevant to the evaluation of extrovertive and monistic experiences? They are relevant to their evaluation when the person who has them claims they are perceptions of God (as they sometimes do. Although Eckhart's experiences appear to have been monistic, he thought they were experiences of God.) Suppose, though, that the object of an extrovertive experience is alleged to be nature's unity, or its inner life or soul. Or that the 'object' of a monistic experience is alleged to be an undifferentiated One, or one's own 'naked essence.'

Because nature embraces both good and evil and because an undifferentiated unity (or the essence of one's own soul?) transcends good and evil, there is no reason to suppose that the first two tests are relevant. One would not expect a vision of these things to promote righteousness and active charity. On the other hand, *other* behavioural tests may be relevant. One might, for example, expect that a vision of an undifferentiated unity transcending time and space would produce detachment and inner peace, or that a vision of nature's unity would lead to empathy with other creatures.

The other four tests may still be relevant. A vision of nature's unity or of an undifferentiated One should not lead to twaddle. If some kind of orthodox talk is true, then, since veridical experiences do not lead to (many) false claims, no veridical experience of *any* kind will lead to (very much) unorthodox talk. If some community or its representatives are authoritative, then the fifth and sixth tests are also relevant.

A minor problem remains. If I am correct, agreement is a test, although an unimportant one. Now we have seen that, because of the peculiar nature of its object, there is no reason to expect that veridical, theistic experiences will be confirmed by the experiences of others in the way in which veridical sense experiences are confirmed by the experiences of others, and having seen this, we may wonder whether there is any logical connection between the presence of agreement and a genuine perception of God. True, agreement seems to be implicitly appealed to, and the mystic might feel uncomfortable in the absence of any agreement, but this does not imply that agreement and disagreement have any *logical* significance. (Most of us take comfort in numbers and are uneasy when we find ourselves alone.)

Two considerations suggest that agreement and disagreement have some logical bearing upon the cognitive status of these experiences. If God's behaviour were completely erratic and unpredictable, then agreement and disagreement would not count at all. But it is not. Although God's behaviour does not possess the regularity and law-like character which belongs to the behaviour of physical objects, it is not thought to be completely erratic and lawless either.

The second consideration is this. Other things being equal, it *may* be reasonable to expect instances of a genuinely cognitive mode of experience to occur under radically different social and psychological conditions. (Similar visual experiences are of course, enjoyed by people with radically different natures and radically different backgrounds.) The presence of widespread agreement shows that this expectation is satisfied.

D

Are there, then, reasons for supposing that mystical experiences are cognitive? I believe that there are. Consider the following argument:

(1) If the analogy between mystical experience and sense experience is very close, then we are entitled to regard mystical experience as a mode of cognitive experience.
(2) The analogy is very close. (Both experiences are noetic. Both are the basis of corrigible and independently checkable claims about something other than the experience itself. In both cases there are tests for determining the reality of the object of experience as well as tests for determining the genuineness of an apparent perception of that object. [The tests are different in the two cases, but the differences can be explained by differences in the nature of the objects of the two experiences.] The tests are relevant in both cases, and their application yields positive results in a large number of instances.)
(3) Therefore, we are entitled to regard mystical experience as a mode of cognitive experience.

A variant of this argument may be more persuasive:

(4) The analogy between mystical experience and sense experience is close enough to warrant the conclusion that mystical experiences are cognitive *provided that* we have independent reasons for believing mystics when they assert that they have directly experienced some transcendent aspect of reality.
(5) We have independent reasons for believing mystics when they assert that they have experienced a transcendent aspect of reality. (For example, arguments for God's existence, and for the sanity, sanctity and intelligence of the great mystics.)
(6) We are therefore warranted in concluding that mystical experiences are cognitive.

Sense experience is the paradigm case of cognitive experience. (1) therefore seems plausible. The plausibility of (5) largely depends upon the success or failure of natural theology, and here opinions can and do differ. (2) and (4) involve the same problem. One's opinion of these premises will be determined not only by one's estimate of the number of respects in which sense experience and mystical experience are like and unlike each other, but also by one's judgment as to the relative importance of these resemblances and differences. (Thus, when evaluating sense experiences the presence or absence of agreement is regarded as vitally important; when evaluating mystical experiences, as relatively unimportant. One's assessment of the significance of this fact will depend upon whether or not one believes that the appeal to the presence or absence of agreement is an appropriate test for the evaluation of mystical experience, upon whether or not one thinks that this test *must* be among the tests used to determine the cognitive value of an experience, and so on.) No mechanical decision procedures are available which can be used to determine the truth value of these premises, just as there are no mechanical decision procedures which can be appealed to, to determine what one should do when moral obligations conflict, or how one should appraise a new style of art, or the general plausibility of a world view. These cases call for judgment and reasonable people may differ. (There are criteria, but it is sometimes difficult to see whether or not they have been applied correctly. For example, in choosing a world view, we should attempt to determine which view has the most explanatory power. But this itself calls for judgment.) In spite of these considerations, I submit that, if the argument of the preceding sections has been correct, the analogy between mystical experience and sense experience is sufficiently striking to justify (4) and, somewhat less clearly, (2).

Although I believe that the two arguments being considered in this section are good arguments, their failure would not show that mystical experiences are non-cognitive. It is often assumed that no experience can be cognitive which is unlike sense experience in very many important respects. This is, of course, quite vague. (What deviations are *important* and how many deviations are *very many*?) More significantly, it is not clear that the assumption is true. As far as I can see, all that we *mean* when we say that an experience is cognitive or perceptual is that through this experience we come to know something which we could not know, or could not know as easily, in other ways, and (probably) that the knowledge in question is non-inferential. If this is even roughly correct, then 'x is a cognitive experience' does not entail 'x is very much like sense experiences.' Of course sense experiences clearly are cognitive experiences. Therefore, if we can show that mystical experience is very much like sense experience, we have provided a good (if not conclusive) reason for supposing that mystical experience is cognitive. On the other hand, if the analysis I have provided is correct, then, even if mystical experience and sense experience were radically dissimilar, this dissimilarity, would not be decisive. (Even if mystical experiences were radically unlike such objective experiences as seeing or hearing, it would not follow that they were like paradigmatic subjective experiences. They might—as Stace suggests—be like neither.)

II

But the conclusion that mystical experiences are cognitive, may be premature. There are several substantial objections to mysticism's cognitive pretensions. These must be shown to be inconclusive before we are entitled to assert that mystical consciousness is a means of knowledge.

A

Antony Flew, Paul Schmidt and Ronald Hepburn maintain that the cognitive claims which are made for praeternatural experiences must be certified by independent checks.[2] Schmidt's argument is typical. He asks us to look at a case in which we judge that we have a cavity because we have a toothache. He suggests that this judgment is warranted only because we have independent criteria (criteria other than the toothache) by which we can establish the existence of a cavity and because we know (on the basis of past experience) that toothaches and cavities are correlated. Schmidt concludes that, in general, we can move from a first person psychological report about feelings (or some other kind of private experience) to a claim about a non-psychological entity or event only if we have independent criteria for determining the truth or falsity of the claim and have discovered by experience that a correlation exists between the occurrence of that sort of feeling and the existence of that type of entity or event.

The implication, of course, is that the mystic is only entitled to base religious and metaphysical claims upon his experience if he has independent criteria for establishing the existence (or presence) of the alleged object of his experience, and if he can show that experiences of that type and objects of that type are correlated.

What exactly is being demanded? We must distinguish (1) the demand that independent checks be provided for claims based on an instance of mystical experience from (2), the demand that one be given an independent certification of the claim that mystical experience as such provides an adequate basis for cognitive claims of a certain kind. In the latter case one is asking for a justification of the cognitive validity of an entire mode of experience.

The first demand is rather easily met. Just as there are tests other than the visual experiences of a person who bases a cognitive claim upon one of those experiences (for example, his own auditory and tactual experience, the sense experiences of others, etc.) so there are tests other than the mystical experiences of a person who bases cognitive claims on *those* particular experiences (for example, his sanity, the similarity of his experiences to those of other mystics, etc.). But this is clearly not what is at issue. What is at issue is the cognitive status of mystical experience in general. It is the second demand which is being made rather than the first, and Schmidt's argument is designed to show that this demand cannot be met.

Is Schmidt's argument convincing? There are reasons for thinking that it is not. (1) It is wrong to suppose that 'having certain feelings and sensations' is an adequate description of the subjective side of mystical experience. No description of these experiences is adequate which neglects their intentional character. As we have seen, these experiences are noetic. They have an object and incorporate the

[2] Antony Flew, *God and Philosophy*, London, New York, 1966, chapter 6; Paul Schmidt, *Religious Knowledge*, Glencoe, Illinois, 1961, chapter 8; Ronald Hepburn, *Christianity and Paradox*, London, 1958, p 37.

conviction that one is in the presence of that object. Having a mystical experience is not like feeling pain or being depressed.

(2) In the second place there may be independent reasons for thinking that (for example) God exists and that there is a correlation between the presence of God and the occurrence of certain kinds of religious experience. (These reasons might be provided by natural theology, tradition or authority.) Critics like Schmidt would not accept these reasons but it is not clear that this is significant. Again (though this is obviously not what Schmidt is looking for) one might suppose that a kind of independent certification of the cognitive character of mystical experience is provided by the arguments of the last section.

(3) Perhaps some other kind of experience can be used to confirm the claims made for mystical experience (by showing that judgments based on mystical experience cohere with judgments based on this other sort of experience). For example, it might be suggested that numinous experience corroborates theistic mystical experience in the way in which auditory and tactual experience corroborates visual experience, or (and this is essentially the same point) that theistic mystical experiences and numinous experiences support and reinforce one another in the way in which the various kinds of sense experience support and reinforce one another. Of course Schmidt would not accept this. In his view numinous and mystical experiences are equally suspect. What Schmidt is demanding is that we justify the claim that religious experience of any kind involves an awareness of the presence of God (or some transcendent being or state) in precisely the same way in which we would justify the claim that toothaches are a sign of cavities.

(4) It is not clear that this demand is reasonable. Suppose we were asked to justify the claim that sense experiences involve an awareness of something distinct from those experiences, viz, physical objects. It is not clear that we would know how to satisfy this request. In particular, it should be noticed that we cannot independently (of those experiences) establish the existence of physical objects and the occurrence of sense experiences, and observe that the two are correlated. (To suppose that we could, would be to suppose that there are tests for ascertaining the presence of physical objects which neither directly nor indirectly appeal to our own sense experiences, or the sense experiences of other people, and there are no tests of this kind.) In short, while the connection between mystical experiences and a transcendental object cannot be justified in the manner which Schmidt demands, the connection between sense experiences and physical objects cannot be justified in that manner either. Since the latter hardly entitles us to conclude that sense experiences do not provide cognitive access to physical objects, it is unclear why the former should entitle us to conclude that mystical experiences do not provide cognitive access to a transcendent object. Schmidt's demand *might* be in order when we are dealing with experiences which are not 'perception-like,' for example, toothaches, twinges, depression, etc. It is not clear that it is in order when the experiences in question are 'perception-like,' for example, visual experiences and mystical experiences.

One might object, however, that the two cases differ in the following important respect. When we learn the meaning of a physical object word like 'tree' we learn what trees look like, what they feel like, what they sound like when the wind blows through their branches, etc. That is, in learning the meaning of the word 'tree' we learn the connection between the presence of trees and experiences of this type. On the other hand numinous and mystical experiences are not connected in this way with the meaning of 'God' or 'Brahman.' A person who has never had numinous or mystical experiences and has no idea of what they are like can learn the meaning of 'God' or 'Brahman.' On the basis of these considerations it might seem reasonable to conclude that tree experiences and trees are analytically connected, whereas mystical or numinous experiences and God (or Brahman) are not, and that therefore while some kind of independent justification must be provided to connect mystical or numinous experiences and God (or Brahman), no such justification is needed to connect tree experiences and trees.

This move would be plausible if statements about trees and other physical objects could be translated into statements about sense experiences (i.e. if phenomenalism were true) and if statements about God (or Brahman) could not be translated into statements about mystical and numinous experiences. It is reasonably clear that statements about God (or Brahman) cannot be translated into statements about religious experience. A number of good philosophers have thought that statements about physical objects could be translated into statements about sense experiences but it is by no means clear that they are correct.

Consider the following: (1) There is a gap between the phenomenological object of mystical experience and its apparent object. For example, although the phenomenological object of theistic mystical experience is a loving will, theistic mystics typically experience or interpret this object as God. But there is also a gap between the phenomenological object of sense experience and its apparent object. When I look at my desk, the phenomenological object of my experience is a desk-like surface seen from a particular point of view. However, its apparent object is the desk itself. There is another gap between the claim that one appears to be confronted with a loving will and the claim that this loving will is real but, similarly, there is a gap between the claim that one is appeared to in a desk-like way and the claim that there really is something which appears to one in that fashion.

(2) It is logically possible for physical objects to exist and for no one to have sense experiences, just as it is logically possible for God (or Brahman) to exist and for there to be no mystical or numinous experiences. As far as I can see, it is also logically possible for there to be sense experiences even though independent physical objects do not exist just as it is logically possible for there to be religious experiences even though God (or Brahman) does not exist.

(3) Nevertheless, while there is no necessary connection between the existence of physical objects and the occurrence of sense experiences, there may be a necessary connection between the existence of physical objects and the *possibility* of sense experiences, e.g. it may be necessarily true that if a tree exists, then, if a normal observer is present under standard conditions, he will enjoy sense experiences of a certain type. But it should be noticed that a similar claim can be made about God and mystical experiences, viz, that it is necessarily true that, if God exists, then if there is an adequately prepared mystic whom God chooses to visit, he will enjoy mystical experiences.

The point is this. It is by no means clear that the logical relations between sense experiences and physical objects are significantly different from the logical relations between mystical or numinous experiences and an object like God. It is thus not clear that some sort of special justification is needed in the one case which is not needed in the other. If a special justification is not needed in the case of sense experience, and it does not seem to be, then it is not needed in the case of mystical experience. I conclude therefore that the first objection is unsuccessful.

B

It is sometimes argued that religious experiences cannot be cognitively valid because they support conflicting claims (about Allah, Jesus, Nibbāna, etc.).[3] As it stands, this argument is unconvincing. 'Religious experience' is an umbrella term covering many different types of experience—charismatic phenomena, numinous feeling, possession, conversion experiences, mystical consciousness, visions, voices, and so on. Religious experience in general may indeed support conflicting claims, but the most that follows is that not all of these experiences or types of experience can be cognitive. In particular, it does not follow that mystical consciousness (or numinous feeling) is delusive.

But even if we were to restrict our attention to types of experience which are not known to be delusive, and thus have some legitimate cognitive pretensions, the argument would still be unsound. Visual experiences support conflicting claims, for people hallucinate and misperceive in other ways, but it is surely wrong to conclude that visual experience is not cognitive. Our attention should be confined not only to types of experience with legitimate cognitive pretensions, but to instances of those types that pass the tests which are used to distinguish veridical experiences of that type from those which are not veridical. No cognitive claims are being made for the latter.

Finally, the only relevant conflicts are conflicts between propositions which are *immediately* based upon the experiences in question. Claims which are indirectly based upon veridical experiences can be infected with error from other sources. Thus, if I claim that the hat I see in front of me is Jack's, I may be mistaken, not because my visual experience is in error, but because I am wrong in thinking it belongs to Jack. If someone standing nearby says that he sees Tom's hat, then his claim conflicts with mine, but this conflict has no tendency to show that either of our visual experiences is delusive.

Nevertheless, the argument can be reformulated to take account of those objections:

(1) If the criteria which are used to sort out veridical experiences from those which are not veridical are adequate, then all the experiences, which meet those criteria are veridical.
(2) If an experience is veridical, then the claims which are immediately based upon it are true. Therefore,
(3) If the criteria which are used to sort out veridical experiences from those which are not veridical are adequate, then the claims which are immediately based upon an experience which meets those criteria are true. (From 1 and 2.) Therefore,

[3] John Hospers offers an argument of this kind in *An Introduction to Philosophical Analysis*, 2nd ed, Englewood Cliffs, New Jersey, 1967, pp 444–8.

(4) If the criteria which are used to sort out veridical mystical or numinous experiences from those which are not veridical are adequate, then the claims which are immediately based upon an experience which meets those criteria are true. (From 3.)

(5) Conflicting claims are immediately based upon mystical and numinous experiences which meet the criteria that are used to sort out veridical experiences of that type from those which are not veridical. (Among these claims are the claim that God exists and is the supreme reality, the claim that Nibbāna is the supreme reality, and so on.) Therefore,

(6) If the criteria which are used to sort out veridical mystical and numinous experiences from those which are not veridical are adequate, then conflicting claims are true. (From 4 and 5.)

(7) Conflicting claims cannot be true. Therefore,

(8) The criteria which are used to sort out veridical mystical and numinous experiences from those which are not veridical cannot be adequate. (From 6 and 7.)

(8) has significant implications for the cognitive status of mystical consciousness and numinous feeling, for if the criteria of validity which are actually used *cannot* be adequate, one suspects that

(9) Adequate criteria cannot be provided.

But it is plausible to suppose that

(10) For any cognitive mode of experience, there are (adequate) criteria for distinguishing veridical instances of that mode of experience from those which are not veridical. Hence,

(11) Mystical consciousness and numinous feeling are not cognitive modes of experience. (From 9 and 10.)

Although one might question (10), this line of response is not particularly promising, since the only type of cognitive experience for which there seem to be no criteria of this sort is the immediate awareness of some of our own mental states. For example, while there are criteria for determining whether others are in pain, our awareness of our own pain is self-certifying; there are no criteria by which we distinguish those cases in which we really feel pain from those in which we only think we do. As we have seen, the mystic's claims are not private and they are not self-certifying. There is therefore no reason to suppose that they constitute an exception to the general rule.

However, it is by no means clear that (5) is true. We must remember that the only relevant conflicts are conflicts between claims which are *immediately* supported by religious experience. Many of the conflicting claims which people try to support by appealing to mystical or numinous experience are not *immediately* supported by it. For example, that God (as defined by Anselm) exists, or that the Ātman-Brahman is the ground of being, or that Nibbāna is real. None of these propositions would appear to be immediately warranted by the religious experiences upon which they are (partly) based. If all the conflicting claims which people attempt to support by appealing to mystical experience or numinous feeling fall into this category, then premise (5) is false.

It is true that nature mysticism, monistic mysticism, theistic mysticism and numinous experience (immediately?) support *different* claims—that nature is one and sacred, that there is an undifferentiated unity transcending space and time, that an overwhelming loving consciousness exists, that there is a holy Other. But it is not clear that these claims *conflict*. (Monistic and theistic experiences might be experiences of different objects, for example.) In order to establish (5), one must show that claims immediately supported by mystical experience or numinous feeling are not only different but incompatible, and it is by no means clear that this can be done.

I therefore conclude that the objection from conflicting religious experiences or intuitions is inconclusive.

C

The similarity between mystical experiences and certain psychotic experiences have led some to dismiss mystical experience as delusive. There are, of course, differences between mystics and psychotics. Thus, as Kenneth Wapnick points out,[4] although both mystical experience and schizophrenia involve a withdrawal from social reality, the mystic is able to maintain a certain amount of control over this process while the schizophrenic is not. Furthermore, the mystic is able to integrate his special experiences with his normal experiences, and to function successfully in society. The schizophrenic is not able to do this, but lives in his own private universe. Wapnick believes that these differences can be partly attributed to the tradition and training of the mystic which enables him to handle his experiences when they occur.

While there is truth in Wapnick's observations, they are not entirely satisfactory. Nature mysticism is usually spontaneous, not consciously induced, and many nature mystics belong to no tradition. Nevertheless, cosmic consciousness does not normally interfere with the mystic's ability to function socially, and the nature mystic is frequently able to integrate his mystical experience and his other experiences. (Bucke is a case in point.) Control and training are not sufficient to explain the difference between mysticism and schizophrenia.

But there is a more important point. Wapnick speaks as if the essential difference between mystics and schizophrenics was not a difference in their states, but a difference in the effects of their states, and the ways in which they handle them. This is misleading. Wapnick, for example, focuses on the case of Lara Jefferson, but the experience in which she abandoned control and allowed what she called 'Madness' to rage through her, did not, as Wapnick admits, involve an experience of unity. It was thus significantly unlike mystical experience. William James speaks in a similarly misleading fashion. According to James, 'diabolical mysticism' or 'mysticism turned upside down' involves 'the same sense of ineffable importance

[4] Kenneth Wapnick, 'Mysticism and Schizophrenia,' *The Highest State of Consciousness*, ed by John White, Garden City, New York, 1972. (The article originally appeared in the *Journal of Transpersonal Psychology*, 1 (1969), pp 49–67).

in the smallest events, the same texts and words coming with new meaning, the same voices and visions and leadings and missions, the same controlling by extraneous powers; only this time the emotion is pessimistic: instead of consolations we have desolations; the meanings are dreadful; and the powers are enemies to life.'[5] These remarks are misleading because the experiences which James has described are not the obverse of mystical experience, but the obverse of visionary and occult experiences.

Nevertheless, psychotic mysticism is a genuine phenomenon. In his manic periods, John Custance appears to have enjoyed extrovertive mystical consciousness. He experienced a sense of well-being that was 'sometimes ecstatic.' His 'sense of reality' was 'heightened.' For example, lights seemed 'deeper, more intense,' and the taste of strawberries or raspberries gave 'ecstatic sensations.' The experience included a 'sense of communion' extending 'to all fellow-creatures,' and a feeling of expansion. Thus, in describing these states, Custance says 'in a sense I am God . . . I am utterly and completely immortal; I am even male and female. The whole universe . . . is within me . . . I reconcile Good and Evil and create light, darkness, worlds, universes.' His consciousness was infused with 'a sense of ineffable revelation.'[6]

In his depressive periods, Custance suffered from extrovertive states which parodied states of cosmic consciousness. In these experiences everything appeared as phantasmagoric and potentially evil, and, instead of expanding, his soul contracted; it 'turned into nothingness—except unending pain,' 'an almost infinitesimal point of abject misery, disgust, pain and fear.'[7]

Psychotic 'mysticism' is thus a genuine phenomenon: it appears to be of two sorts. Some psychotic states seem to be phenomenologically identical with normal mystical states. Custance's manic experiences are an example. One of E. W. Anderson's cases reported merging 'into everything . . . [and] an intense consciousness of power and absolute ecstasy,' and went on to say 'things appear more real . . . The whole being expands . . . I notice everything I haven't seen before, lights and sounds . . . Everything is absolutely new . . . I seemed above time and yet it was intensified in some way . . . It seemed like something which served a purpose, which was used to divide, to limit something, but not real.'[8] Other psychotic experiences bear a family resemblance to mystical experiences but contain components which are in some sense the opposite of components in normal mystical experience. For example, they may involve a sense of unreality instead of a sense of heightened reality.

> The world now looks remote, strange, sinister, uncanny. Its colour is gone, its breath is cold, there is no speculation in the eyes it glares with. 'It is as if I lived in another

[5] William James, *Varieties of Religious Experience*, New York, 1936, p 417.

[6] John Custance, *Wisdom, Madness and Folly: The Philosophy of a Lunatic*, New York, c 1952. The quoted passages occur between pp 30 and 52. Sexual inhibitions were also relaxed. This is of some interest in view of the contention that nature mysticism is amoral.

[7] *Ibid* pp 73 and 79.

[8] Quoted in Carney Landis, *Varieties of Psychopathological Experience*, New York (etc.), 1964, p 290. I am not aware of any instances in which a psychopath experienced states that were phenomenologically *identical* with those of (normal) monistic or theistic mystics.

century,' says one asylum patient. 'I see everything through a cloud,' says another. 'I see,' says a third, 'I touch, but the things do not come near me, a thick veil alters the hue and look of everything,' 'Persons move like shadows, and sounds seem to come from a distant world.'—'There is no longer any past for me. . . . it is as if I could not see any reality, as if I were in a theatre; as if people were actors, and everything were scenery . . . Everything floats before my eyes, but leaves no impression.'—'I weep false tears, I have unreal hands: the things I see are not real things.'[9]

Rather than a living presence, nature seems dead. 'The immobility became more immobile, the silence more silent, things and people, their gestures and their noises, more artificial, detached one from the other, unreal, without life.'[10] Instead of expansion, a psychotic 'mystic' like Custance experiences contraction. Instead of joy, the dominant emotion is fear and horror.

What implications do these facts have for the cognitive status of mystical experience? As we have seen, some psychotic 'mysticism' is aberrant, but some is not. Custance's manic experiences appear to have been genuine cases of extrovertive mystical consciousness. These cases should not trouble us. The fact that psychotics sometimes have extrovertive mystical experiences is no more disturbing than the fact that psychotics sometimes see physical objects in a perfectly normal way, or hear and understand correctly. If most of the people who had mystical experiences were psychotic, it would perhaps be reasonable to dismiss their experiences as delusive, but they are not.

The aberrant experiences present a different problem. These experiences bear a family resemblance to normal mystical experiences, but are essentially restricted to psychotics. It would be generally agreed that these experiences are delusive. 'Horrorific' visions fail to meet at least five of the six tests described in the first part of this chapter. (They *might* meet the third test; the content of these experiences is not silly or insignificant, though it is hardly 'sweet.') Even people who are suspicious of the tests would dismiss horrific visions as delusive. (There seem to be essentially two reasons for this. First, our assumption that, in the long run, men and women who see things as they really are will lead happier and better lives than those who do not. Second, our assumption that truth is coherent—that, in the long run, valid insights will be seen to cohere, or at least not conflict. The lives of those afflicted by the horrific vision are morally and spiritually wretched, and their 'insights' conflict with the insights of others, and the insights of their own lucid and manic moments.)

Does the occurrence of these delusive parodies of mysticism cast doubt upon the cognitive validity of mystical experience? I believe that it does not. Hallucinations bear a family resemblance to normal sense experience, and some philosophers have suggested that the occurrence of experiences of this type casts doubt on the cognitive validity of sense experience. Their argument is essentially this:

(1) The existence of sensory illusions and hallucinations shows that it is possible for an apparently veridical sense experience to be delusive. But if
(2) Delusion is possible in any given case, then

---

[9] William James, *op cit*, p 149.

[10] Quoted in Landis, *op cit*, p 252.

(3) It is possible in all cases. Therefore,

(4) The cognitive pretensions of sense experience are suspect.

Each step in this argument is questionable. (2) does not entail (3). (The inference from a proposition of the form 'for every x, it is possible that x is Ø' to a proposition of the form 'It is possible that every x is Ø' is invalid. For example, while for any logically contingent proposition, it is possible that it is true, it is not possible that every contingent proposition is true.) (1) implies (2) if and only if there are no relevant differences between the illusions and hallucinations referred to in (1) and other instances of sense experience. But of course there are, viz, the presence of precisely those features which led us to classify them as illusions or hallucinations (viz, their failure to cohere with the rest of the subject's experience and with the experience of others). Neither (2) nor (3) implies (4). Even if (2) or (3) are true, their truth should not bother us unless we have reason to suspect that the possibilities to which they allude are actually realised. The bare possibility of error is not disconcerting; what is disconcerting are special reasons (for example, the lack of agreement) for thinking that the experiences in question are cognitively defective.

The point is clear. The existence of aberrant parodies of mystical experience should bother us only if the reasons which led us to dismiss them as delusive are present in normal cases. The principle reason, viz, their correlation with psychosis or insanity, is not. . . .

III

A pramāṇa is a 'source or means of acquiring new knowledge.'[11] For example, sense perception, yogic intuition, inference and testimony are pramāṇas. According to Advaita Vedānta, all pramāṇas are 'intrinsically valid.' Ideas, judgments and experiences are to be accepted as valid except where they are called into question by other ideas, judgments or experiences. (As our (apparent) experience of a snake is called into question by the experience which is obtained when we examine the object more closely and discover that it is only a rope.) To suppose that an apparent cognition must be justified before it is accepted commits one to the necessity of an infinite regress. An apparent cognition, C_1, can only be justified by another apparent cognition, C_2. Given our supposition, C_2 must itself be justified, and this requires yet another apparent cognition, C_3, and so on. Only Brahman-knowledge (jñāna) is self-certifying in the sense that there are no conceivable circumstances in which the presumption of its validity could be overridden, but all apparent cognitions are 'self-luminous' in the sense that they are presumptively valid.

Advaitins believe that Brahman-knowledge is self-certifying because it is an experience of undifferentiated unity. Since the experience has no content or object, it is impossible to show that its content or object is defective. Hence, the experience cannot be shown to be in error. This is not altogether convincing. As we have seen, it is not clear that monistic mystical experiences have no 'object'

[11] Ninian Smart, *Doctrine and Argument in Indian Philosophy*, London, 1964, p 220.

or 'content'. Nor is it clear that the only way in which an apparent cognition can be shown to be in error is by cancelling or 'sublating' its content. (As the content of the snake experience is cancelled when we look at the object more closely and see that it is only a rope.) For example, regardless of their content, we reject experiences on the basis of their causes when we have reason to believe that apparent cognitions with those causes are invalid.

Nevertheless, I would suggest that the Advaitin doctrine contains an important truth. If there is no type of apparent cognition which is presumptively valid, then it is impossible to avoid an infinite regress. Furthermore, to suppose that one type of apparent cognition is presumtively valid while another is not is arbitrary. It follows that any type of apparent cognition is presumptively valid, and should be accepted in the absence of adequate reasons for doubting its validity.

The argument of this chapter should be placed within the framework of these considerations. Part I attempted to show that various types of mystical experience are presumptively valid apparent cognitions. Part II examined the most important attempts to defeat the presumption of their validity. Since there appears to be a presumption in favour of the cognitive validity of mystical experience, and since attempts to defeat that presumption are unsuccessful, mystical experience should be accepted as a valid means of knowledge.

Suggestions for Further Reading

The classical treatment of mysticism and religious experience is that of William James, *The Varieties of Religious Experience* (Modern Library, 1929). Rudolf Otto examines what he terms "the numinous" in his influential *The Idea of the Holy* (Oxford University Press, 1923). Two influential and still relevant philosophical treatments of mysticism are R. C. Zaehner, *Mysticism, Sacred and Profane* (Oxford University Press, 1961), and W. T. Stace, *Mysticism and Philosophy* (first published by Humanities Press, 1960; J. P. Tarcher, 1987).

A more recent treatment of mysticism can be found in W. J. Wainwright's *Mysticism* (University of Wisconsin Press, 1981). Peter Donovan's *Interpreting Religious Experience* (Seabury, 1975) is an accessible examination of religious experience. C. R. Brakenhielm's *Problems of Religious Experience* (distributed by Coronet Press, 1985) is a good philosophical analysis of religious experience. One version of the argument from religious experience can be found in Gary Gutting's *Religious Belief and Religious Skepticism* (University of Notre Dame Press, 1982). Two other notable works on this subject are Wayne Proudfoot, *Religious Experience* (University of California Press, 1985), and Alister Hardy, *The Spiritual Nature of Man* (Clarendon Press, 1979). The first is a philosophical treatment of various issues having to do with religious experience. The second is a compilation of contemporary cases of religious experiences analyzed from a psychological perspective.

Concerning the issue of drug-induced religious experiences, see Huston Smith, "Do Drugs Have Religious Import?" *The Journal of Philosophy* 61 (1964). See also R. C. Zaehner, *Zen, Drugs and Mysticism* (Pantheon, 1973), and Robert Oakes, "Biochemistry and Theistic Mysticism" *Sophia* 15 (1976).

FAITH
AND
MIRACLES

VI

There are at least two ways of understanding faith and revelation. According to the classical view, God or some other divine being communicates true propositions that cannot be discovered (or at least not easily) by natural reason. Faith is the belief that these propositions have been divinely communicated and are therefore true. The selection from Aquinas provides an example of this position. A commonly held modern view is that revelation is God's self-manifestation. God doesn't reveal propositions; He reveals *Himself*. Faith is devotion—trust in, and commitment to, the one who has graciously disclosed Himself. In this view, faith is not a belief *that* certain propositions are true (those of the Bible, or the Qurān, for example) but a belief *in* the God who has unveiled Himself.

The difference between these views should not be exaggerated. "Believing in" implies "believing that." Belief in a friend, for example, presupposes the belief that he exists, has a certain character, and will respond to our needs in certain ways. Similarly, a faithful response to God's self-disclosure presupposes the belief that He exists, has revealed Himself, and is worthy of our trust and commitment. The second form of faith thus involves at least some propositional believing.

Nor do traditionalists make propositions the object of their faith rather than God. They endorse certain propositions because they believe God has communicated them. Their endorsement is thus grounded in a belief in God's reality and trustworthiness and a conviction that it is good or fitting to believe. Furthermore, in believing revealed propositions, the object of the traditionalists' faith is not the propositions *as such* but the divine reality the propositions express. While traditional faith involves believing that the words of the Bible, the Qurān, or some other sacred teaching are true, its ultimate object is the God these truths are about.

But is faith *legitimate*? Classical, and most modern, accounts of faith and revelation imply that we may, and indeed should, believe some things that we cannot establish by reason. Is this permissible?

In sorting out the issues, it is helpful to distinguish between evidentialism, foundationalism, and classical foundationalism. Evidentialists are committed to two claims. First, religious assertions require evidence. Second, if a proposition requires evidence, we are entitled to believe it only if we have the evidence. Evidentialism does not imply that religion is false but does imply that we should not hold religious beliefs that we cannot support by evidence. Evidentialists are usually foundationalists. Most have been classical foundationalists.

What is foundationalism? A belief is basic if it is accepted without evidence. It is *properly* basic if it is basic and we are rationally entitled to it. Foundationalists think that, in an ideally structured system of beliefs, beliefs are either properly basic or legitimately inferred from properly basic beliefs. In other words, beliefs are either properly basic *or based on evidence*.

Classical foundationalists are foundationalists who think that the only properly basic beliefs are self-evident beliefs, incorrigible beliefs like a belief that we are or are not in pain, or (according to some classical foundationalists) ordinary perceptual beliefs such as "There is a table in front of me."

It is easy to see the connection between evidentialism and classical foundationalism. A belief like "God exists" is neither self-evident nor incorrigible. Nor is it evident to the senses. Thus, if classical foundationalism is true, it is not properly basic and so requires evidence. Hence, it will not be included in an ideally structured system of beliefs unless it is supported by evidence. If we are entitled only to beliefs that meet this ideal, evidentialism follows.

Classical foundationalists are not always evidentialists. For example, Aquinas was a classical foundationalist. Nevertheless, he thought we should believe some things about God that are not properly basic and are not supported by evidence. We should do so because God has revealed them. (The issue is complicated by the fact that Aquinas believed there is evidence that God has revealed Himself in scripture. However, he also thought this evidence will only convince those whom God has assisted by grace.)

William Clifford is a foundationalist who is also an evidentialist. In his opinion, one's religious beliefs should be no stronger than the evidence warrants.

William James and Alvin Plantinga attack evidentialism in different ways. James implicitly concedes that religious beliefs are neither properly basic nor supported by adequate evidence. He argues, however, that we may still be entitled to them. Two related claims lie at the heart of his position. First, the demand for evidence is sometimes unreasonable; there are cases in which the truth of a belief could be established only by evidence but also in which it is irrational to refuse to believe until the evidence is available. Second, our beliefs should be shaped by both intellectual *and* "passional" demands. They must meet standards of consistency, allow us to accurately predict the future, and so on. But they must also enable us to act effectively and adjust satisfactorily to the world we live in. To do this, a system of beliefs must provide life with meaning and make significant action possible. If religious beliefs perform this function (and James thinks they do), we are entitled to hold them even though their truth is "intellectually undecidable." If James is correct, then, the second of the evidentialist's two claims is false.

Alvin Plantinga, on the other hand, suggests that some religious beliefs *are* properly basic. Plantinga thinks there are "characteristic circumstances" in which, for example, we spontaneously form the belief that a tree is in front of us, or the belief that we had breakfast this morning. These beliefs are not based on evidence but are nonetheless reasonable. In the same way, there are characteristic circumstances in which some of us find ourselves spontaneously believing that God has forgiven us, or has created the heavens, or something else of the sort. Since they are not based on evidence, these beliefs are basic. Plantinga thinks they are also *properly* basic and thus as rational as our perceptual beliefs or our memory beliefs. If (some) religious beliefs are properly basic, then they do not require evidence, and the first of the evidentialist's two claims is false.

Much of what James and Plantinga have to say is persuasive. There are cases in which it seems unreasonable to demand evidence before believing, and Plantinga may be right in insisting that classical foundationalism is flawed. Other aspects of their positions are more problematic.

James is sometimes unfairly accused of licensing wishful thinking. But James thinks we have no right to believe when the weight of evidence is *against* a belief, and even when an issue is "intellectually undecidable," we have no right to choose arbitrarily. We are entitled to exercise our right to believe only when an issue is important and cannot be decided on evidential grounds, and the belief we choose must meet our practical demands and satisfy our "passional nature." But serious questions remain. Is the fact that a view provides life with meaning, or makes significant action possible, a reliable indication of its *truth*? And if it is not, *is* it really legitimate to believe it?

The problems with Plantinga's view are different. As Stephen Wykstra points out, theistic propositions *seem* to be the kinds of propositions that require evidence. That is, they seem more like scientific or metaphysical propositions than memory reports or perceptual judgments. If so, they are not properly basic.

Gary Gutting has called attention to another problem.[1] Many people *do not* find themselves spontaneously forming theistic beliefs when reading the Bible or gazing at the starry heavens. Others find themselves spontaneously forming beliefs that seem *inconsistent* with theism. For example, an Advaitin, upon reading the Upanishads, may spontaneously form the belief that they are an expression of the impersonal Brahman. Don't these facts count against the claim that some theistic beliefs are properly basic? Plantinga thinks not. In his opinion, a person whose cognitive faculties are in proper working order will spontaneously form theistic beliefs in the circumstances he describes. The cognitive equipment of those who do not, or who spontaneously form beliefs inconsistent with theism, is defective. Plantinga's claims are plausible, however, only if theistic metaphysics is true.

Two important philosophical questions are connected with the topic of miracles: Are they possible? How should the evidence for them be assessed?

Some philosophers think that miracles are not *logically* possible. "e is a miracle" entails "e violates natural law." It is not possible, however, for e, or any other event, to do so. In saying that e violates a natural law, we imply that it is a law of nature (and thus true) that events like e do not occur in the circumstances in which e occurred, and yet e did occur in those circumstances.

This objection misconstrues what theists mean when they say that a miraculous event, e, violates natural law. A more accurate analysis might be "*Apart from divine intervention*, events like e do not occur in the circumstances in which e occurred, and yet e occurred." This is not logically impossible since God *may* have intervened. Or perhaps we should follow Richard Swinburne and construe the claim as "e is a non-repeatable counterinstance to a law of nature."

But even if miracles are logically possible, the world could be constituted in such a way that they are not *really* possible. For example, if miracles are defined as "a transgression of a law of nature by a particular volition of the Deity, or by the interposition of some invisible agent" (David Hume), and there *are* no invisible agents, then miracles are not really possible. Again, many theists deny that God performs miracles. Some of them think that traditional miracles are ad hoc interventions designed to correct imperfections in the created order. They thus imply that God's original workmanship was defective. Others think that miracles

---

[1] Gary Gutting, *Religious Belief and Religious Skepticism* (Notre Dame: University of Notre Dame Press, 1982), Chapter 3, Section 1.

are arbitrary or irrational interferences with the orderly processes of nature. In either case, God would not perform them. If God would not perform them, however, miracles are not really possible.

None of these arguments is compelling. We cannot simply assume that there aren't any invisible agents without begging the question against theism. Again, only some traditional miracles are remedies for evils. Others reveal God's glory, or attest to the authority of a teacher. Furthermore, in the traditional view, miracles *are not* ad hoc additions to creation; they are essential parts of it. The occurrence of a miracle has been determined from the beginning of time and is as much a part of creation's plan as are events that obey natural laws. Finally, that miracles have no *natural* explanation does not imply that they have *no* explanation or that they are irrational or arbitrary. They are explained by the fact that God performs them, and traditional theists believe God has good reasons for doing so. A miracle is no more inexplicable, arbitrary, or irrational than any other free and purposive act.

But even if miracles are possible, is it reasonable to believe in them? Reports of miracles are fairly common. How should we evaluate them? Hume argues that the general reliability of human testimony should be weighed against humanity's love of wonders and against the fact that the witnesses to alleged miracles are usually few in number, comparatively uneducated, and gullible. More important, it should be weighed against the fact that the whole course of human experience points to the empirical impossibility of these events. Experience shows, for example, that corpses do not rise from the dead, and physiology explains why this does not happen. The improbability of the witnesses being in error must be compared with the improbability of the reported event. In Hume's opinion, the latter will always outweigh the former.

Whether Hume is right depends partly on the truth of theism. If traditional theism is true, it is reasonable to think that some miracles will occur. Since their antecedent probability is not that low, the evidence for a miracle's occurrence need not be stronger than the evidence for any other unusual and extraordinary but genuinely possible event. If traditional religious views are false, however, the antecedent likelihood of a miracle's occurring is almost infinitesimally low. In that case, it is doubtful whether any testimony could be strong enough to be convincing.

Because of these difficulties, some modern theologians define "miracle" in such a way that some scientifically explicable events can be called miraculous. For example, Paul Tillich defines a miracle as an astonishing event that points to the Ultimate and is ecstatically experienced as doing so. Definitions like this allow us to speak of miracles while accommodating ourselves to science. The question is whether redefinitions of this kind retain all the religious significance of the traditional notion.

W. J. W.

FAITH AND THE NEED FOR EVIDENCE

ST. THOMAS AQUINAS
Reason and Revelation

CHAPTER III.   ON THE WAY IN WHICH DIVINE TRUTH IS TO BE MADE KNOWN

(1) The way of making truth known is not always the same, and, as the Philosopher has very well said, "it belongs to an educated man to seek such certitude in each thing as the nature of that thing allows." [1] The remark is also introduced by Boethius. [2] But, since such is the case, we must first show what way is open to us in order that we may make known the truth which is our object.

(2) There is a twofold mode of truth in what we profess about God. Some truths about God exceed all the ability of the human reason. Such is the truth that God is triune. But there are some truths which the natural reason also is able to reach. Such are that God exists, that He is one, and the like. In fact, such truths about God have been proved demonstratively by the philosophers, guided by the light of the natural reason.

(3) That there are certain truths about God that totally surpass man's ability appears with the greatest evidence. Since, indeed, the principle of all knowledge that the reason perceives about some thing is the understanding of the very substance of that being (for according to Aristotle "what a thing is" is the principle of demonstration), [3] it is necessary that the way in which we understand the substance of a thing determines the way in which we know what belongs to it. Hence, if

REASON AND REVELATION   From *On the Truth of the Catholic Faith: Summa Contra Gentiles*, Book I, by St. Thomas Aquinas, translated by Anton C. Pegis. Copyright © 1955 by Doubleday & Company, Inc. Reprinted by permission of the publisher.

[1] Aristotle, *Nicomachean Ethics*, I, 3 (1094b 24).

[2] Boethius, *De Trinitate*, II, (PL, 64, col. 1250).

[3] Aristotle, *Posterior Analytics*, II, 3 (90b 31).

the human intellect comprehends the substance of some thing, for example, that of a stone or of a triangle, no intelligible characteristic belonging to that thing surpasses the grasp of the human reason. But this does not happen to us in the case of God. For the human intellect is not able to reach a comprehension of the divine substance through its natural power. For, according to its manner of knowing in the present life, the intellect depends on the senses for the origin of knowledge; and so those things that do not fall under the senses cannot be grasped by the human intellect except in so far as the knowledge of them is gathered from sensible things. Now, sensible things cannot lead the human intellect to the point of seeing in them the nature of the divine substance; for sensible things are effects that fall short of the power of their cause. Yet, beginning with sensible things, our intellect is led to the point of knowing about God that He exists, and other such characteristics that must be attributed to the First Principle. There are, consequently, some intelligible truths about God that are open to the human reason; but there are others that absolutely surpass its power.

(4) We may easily see the same point from the gradation of intellects. Consider the case of two persons of whom one has a more penetrating grasp of a thing by his intellect than does the other. He who has the superior intellect understands many things that the other cannot grasp at all. Such is the case with a very simple person who cannot at all grasp the subtle speculations of philosophy. But the intellect of an angel surpasses the human intellect much more than the intellect of the greatest philosopher surpasses the intellect of the most uncultivated simple person; for the distance between the best philosopher and a simple person is contained within the limits of the human species, which the angelic intellect surpasses. For the angel knows God on the basis of a more noble effect than does man; and this by as much as the substance of an angel, through which the angel in his natural knowledge is led to the knowledge of God, is nobler than sensible things and even than the soul itself, through which the human intellect mounts to the knowledge of God. The divine intellect surpasses the angelic intellect much more than the angelic surpasses the human. For the divine intellect is in its capacity equal to its substance, and therefore it understands fully what it is, including all its intelligible attributes. But by his natural knowledge the angel does not know what God is, since the substance itself of the angel, through which he is led to the knowledge of God, is an effect that is not equal to the power of its cause. Hence, the angel is not able, by means of his natural knowledge, to grasp all the things that God understands in Himself; nor is the human reason sufficient to grasp all the things that the angel understands through his own natural power. Just as, therefore, it would be the height of folly for a simple person to assert that what a philosopher proposes is false on the ground that he himself cannot understand it, so (and even more so) it is the acme of stupidity for a man to suspect as false what is divinely revealed through the ministry of the angels simply because it cannot be investigated by reason.

(5) The same thing, moreover, appears quite clearly from the defect that we experience every day in our knowledge of things. We do not know a great many of the properties of sensible things, and in most cases we are not able to discover fully the natures of those properties that we apprehend by the sense. Much more

is it the case, therefore, that the human reason is not equal to the task of investigating all the intelligible characteristics of that most excellent substance.

(6) The remark of Aristotle likewise agrees with this conclusion. He says that "our intellect is related to the prime beings, which are most evident in their nature, as the eye of an owl is related to the sun."[4]

(7) Sacred Scripture also gives testimony to this truth. We read in Job: "Peradventure thou wilt comprehend the steps of God, and wilt find out the Almighty perfectly?" (11:7). And again: "Behold, God is great, exceeding our knowledge" (Job 36:26). And St. Paul: "We know in part" (I Cor. 13:9).

(8) We should not, therefore, immediately reject as false, following the opinion of the Manicheans and many unbelievers, everything that is said about God even though it cannot be investigated by reason.

CHAPTER IV.   THAT THE TRUTH ABOUT GOD TO WHICH THE NATURAL REASON REACHES IS FITTINGLY PROPOSED TO MEN FOR BELIEF

(1) Since, therefore, there exists a twofold truth concerning the divine being, one to which the inquiry of the reason can reach, the other which surpasses the whole ability of the human reason, it is fitting that both of these truths be proposed to man divinely for belief. This point must first be shown concerning the truth that is open to the inquiry of the reason; otherwise, it might perhaps seem to someone that, since such a truth can be known by the reason, it was uselessly given to men through a supernatural inspiration as an object of belief.

(2) Yet, if this truth were left solely as a matter of inquiry for the human reason, three awkward consequences would follow.

(3) The first is that few men would possess the knowledge of God. For there are three reasons why most men are cut off from the fruit of diligent inquiry which is the discovery of truth. Some do not have the physical disposition for such work. As a result, there are many who are naturally not fitted to pursue knowledge; and so, however much they tried, they would be unable to reach the highest level of human knowledge which consists in knowing God. Others are cut off from pursuing this truth by the necessities imposed upon them by their daily lives. For some men must devote themselves to taking care of temporal matters. Such men would not be able to give so much time to the leisure of contemplative inquiry as to reach the highest peak at which human investigation can arrive, namely, the knowledge of God. Finally, there are some who are cut off by indolence. In order to know the things that the reason can investigate concerning God, a knowledge of many things must already be possessed. For almost all of philosophy is directed towards the knowledge of God, and that is why metaphysics, which deals with divine things, is the last part of philosophy to be learned. This means that we are able to arrive at the inquiry concerning the aforementioned truth only on the basis of a great deal of labor spent in study. Now, those who wish to undergo such a labor for the mere love of knowledge are few, even though God has inserted into the minds of men a natural appetite for knowledge.

---

[4] Aristotle, *Metaphysics*, Ia, 1 (993b 9).

(4) The second awkward effect is that those who would come to discover the abovementioned truth would barely reach it after a great deal of time. The reasons are several. There is the profundity of this truth, which the human intellect is made capable of grasping by natural inquiry only after a long training. Then, there are many things that must be presupposed, as we have said. There is also the fact that, in youth, when the soul is swayed by the various movements of the passions, it is not in a suitable state for the knowledge of such lofty truth. On the contrary, "one becomes wise and knowing in repose," as it is said in the *Physics*.[5] The result is this. If the only way open to us for the knowledge of God were solely that of the reason, the human race would remain in the blackest shadows of ignorance. For then the knowledge of God, which especially renders men perfect and good, would come to be possessed only by a few, and these few would require a great deal of time in order to reach it.

(5) The third awkward effect is this. The investigation of the human reason for the most part has falsity present within it, and this is due partly to the weakness of our intellect in judgment, and partly to the admixture of images. The result is that many, remaining ignorant of the power of demonstration, would hold in doubt those things that have been most truly demonstrated. This would be particularly the case since they see that, among those who are reputed to be wise men, each one teaches his own brand of doctrine. Furthermore, with the many truths that are demonstrated, there sometimes is mingled something that is false, which is not demonstrated but rather asserted on the basis of some probable or sophistical argument, which yet has the credit of being a demonstration. That is why it was necessary that the unshakeable certitude and pure truth concerning divine things should be presented to men by way of faith.[6]

(6) Beneficially, therefore, did the divine Mercy provide that it should instruct us to hold by faith even those truths that the human reason is able to investigate. In this way, all men would easily be able to have a share in the knowledge of God, and this without uncertainty and error.

(7) Hence it is written: "Henceforward you walk not as also the Gentiles walk in the vanity of their mind, having their understanding darkened" (Eph. 4:17–18). And again: "All thy children shall be taught of the Lord" (Isa. 54:13).

CHAPTER V.   THAT THE TRUTHS THE HUMAN REASON IS NOT ABLE TO INVESTIGATE ARE FITTINGLY PROPOSED TO MEN FOR BELIEF

(1) Now, perhaps some will think that men should not be asked to believe what the reason is not adequate to investigate, since the divine Wisdom provides in the case of each thing according to the mode of its nature. We must therefore prove

---

[5] Aristotle, *Physics*, VII, 3 (247b 9).

[6] Although St. Thomas does not name Maimonides or his *Guide for the Perplexed* (*Dux neutrorum*), there are evident points of contact between the Catholic and the Jewish theologian. On the reasons for revelation given here, on our knowledge of God, on creation and the eternity of the world, and on Aristotelianism in general, St. Thomas has Maimonides in mind both to agree and to disagree with him. By way of background for *SCG*, I, the reader can usefully consult the references to Maimonides in E. Gilson, *History of Christian Philosophy in the Middle Ages* (New York, 1955), pp. 649–651.

that it is necessary for man to receive from God as objects of belief even those truths that are above the human reason.

(2) No one tends with desire and zeal towards something that is not already known to him. But, as we shall examine later on in this work, men are ordained by the divine Providence towards a higher good than human fragility can experience in the present life.[7] That is why it was necessary for the human mind to be called to something higher than the human reason here and now can reach, so that it would thus learn to desire something and with zeal tend towards something that surpasses the whole state of the present life. This belongs especially to the Christian religion, which in a unique way promises spiritual and eternal goods. And so there are many things proposed to men in it that transcend human sense. The Old Law, on the other hand, whose promises were of a temporal character, contained very few proposals that transcended the inquiry of the human reason. Following this same direction, the philosophers themselves, in order that they might lead men from the pleasure of sensible things to virtue, were concerned to show that there were in existence other goods of a higher nature than these things of sense, and that those who gave themselves to the active or contemplative virtues would find much sweeter enjoyment in the taste of these higher goods.

(3) It is also necessary that such truth be proposed to men for belief so that they may have a truer knowledge of God. For then only do we know God truly when we believe Him to be above everything that it is possible for man to think about Him; for, as we have shown,[8] the divine substance surpasses the natural knowledge of which man is capable. Hence, by the fact that some things about God are proposed to man that surpass his reason, there is strengthened in man the view that God is something above what he can think.

(4) Another benefit that comes from the revelation to men of truths that exceed the reason is the curbing of presumption, which is the mother of error. For there are some who have such a presumptuous opinion of their own ability that they deem themselves able to measure the nature of everything; I mean to say that, in their estimation, everything is true that seems to them so, and everything is false that does not. So that the human mind, therefore, might be freed from this presumption and come to a humble inquiry after truth, it was necessary that some things should be proposed to man by God that would completely surpass his intellect.

(5) A still further benefit may also be seen in what Aristotle says in the *Ethics*.[9] There was a certain Simonides who exhorted people to put aside the knowledge of divine things and to apply their talents to human occupations. He said that "he who is a man should know human things, and he who is mortal, things that are mortal." Against Simonides Aristotle says that "man should draw himself towards what is immortal and divine as much as he can." And so he says in the *De animalibus* that, although what we know of the higher substances is very little, yet that little is loved and desired more than all the knowledge that we have about

---

[7] *SCG*, III, ch. 48.

[8] See above, ch. 3.

[9] Aristotle, *Nicomachean Ethics*, X, 7 (1177b 31).

less noble substances.[10] He also says in the *De caelo et mundo* that when questions about the heavenly bodies can be given even a modest and merely plausible solution, he who hears this experiences intense joy.[11] From all these considerations it is clear that even the most imperfect knowledge about the most noble realities brings the greatest perfection to the soul. Therefore, although the human reason cannot grasp fully the truths that are above it, yet, if it somehow holds these truths at least by faith, it acquires great perfection for itself.

(6) Therefore it is written: "For many things are shown to thee above the understanding of men" (Ecclus. 3:25). Again, "So the things that are of God no man knoweth but the Spirit of God. But to us God hath revealed them by His Spirit" (I Cor. 2:11, 10).

CHAPTER VI.   THAT TO GIVE ASSENT TO THE TRUTHS OF FAITH IS NOT FOOLISHNESS EVEN THOUGH THEY ARE ABOVE REASON

(1) Those who place their faith in this truth, however, "for which the human reason offers no experimental evidence,"[12] do not believe foolishly, as though "following artificial fables" (II Peter 1:16). For these "secrets of divine Wisdom" (Job 11:6) the divine Wisdom itself, which knows all things to the full, has deigned to reveal to men. It reveals its own presence, as well as the truth of its teaching and inspiration, by fitting arguments; and in order to confirm those truths that exceed natural knowledge, it gives visible manifestation to works that surpass the ability of all nature. Thus, there are the wonderful cures of illnesses, there is the raising of the dead, and the wonderful immutation in the heavenly bodies; and what is more wonderful, there is the inspiration given to human minds, so that simple and untutored persons, filled with the gift of the Holy Spirit, come to possess instantaneously the highest wisdom and the readiest eloquence. When these arguments were examined, through the efficacy of the above-mentioned proof, and not the violent assault of arms or the promise of pleasures, and (what is most wonderful of all) in the midst of the tyranny of the persecutors, an innumerable throng of people, both simple and most learned, flocked to the Christian faith. In this faith there are truths preached that surpass every human intellect; the pleasures of the flesh are curbed; it is taught that the things of the world should be spurned. Now, for the minds of mortal men to assent to these things is the greatest of miracles, just as it is a manifest work of divine inspiration that, spurning visible things, men should seek only what is invisible. Now, that this has happened neither without preparation nor by chance, but as a result of the disposition of God, is clear from the fact that through many pronouncements of the ancient prophets God had foretold that He would do this. The books of these prophets are held in veneration among us Christians, since they give witness to our faith.

(2) The manner of this confirmation is touched on by St. Paul: "Which," that

[10] Aristotle, *De partibus animalium*, I, 5 (644b 32).

[11] Aristotle, *De caelo et mundo*, II, 12 (291b 26).

[12] St. Gregory, *Homiliae in evangelia*, II, hom. 26, i (PL, 76, col. 1197).

is, human salvation, "having begun to be declared by the Lord, was confirmed unto us by them that hear Him: God also bearing them witness of signs, and wonders, and divers miracles, and distributions of the Holy Ghost" (Heb. 2:3–4).

(3) This wonderful conversion of the world to the Christian faith is the clearest witness of the signs given in the past; so that it is not necessary that they should be further repeated, since they appear most clearly in their effect. For it would be truly more wonderful than all signs if the world had been led by simple and humble men to believe such lofty truths, to accomplish such difficult actions, and to have such high hopes. Yet it is also a fact that, even in our own time, God does not cease to work miracles through His saints for the confirmation of the faith.

(4) On the other hand, those who founded sects committed to erroneous doctrines proceeded in a way that is opposite to this. The point is clear in the case of Mohammed. He seduced the people by promises of carnal pleasure to which the concupiscence of the flesh goads us. His teaching also contained precepts that were in conformity with his promises, and he gave free rein to carnal pleasure. In all this, as is not unexpected, he was obeyed by carnal men. As for proofs of the truth of his doctrine, he brought forward only such as could be grasped by the natural ability of anyone with a very modest wisdom. Indeed, the truths that he taught he mingled with many fables and with doctrines of the greatest falsity. He did not bring forth any signs produced in a supernatural way, which alone fittingly gives witness to divine inspiration; for a visible action that can be only divine reveals an invisibly inspired teacher of truth. On the contrary, Mohammed said that he was sent in the power of his arms—which are signs not lacking even to robbers and tyrants. What is more, no wise men, men trained in things divine and human, believed in him from the beginning. Those who believed in him were brutal men and desert wanderers, utterly ignorant of all divine teaching, through whose numbers Mohammed forced others to become his followers by the violence of his arms. Nor do divine pronouncements on the part of preceding prophets offer him any witness. On the contrary, he perverts almost all the testimonies of the Old and New Testaments by making them into fabrications of his own, as can be seen by anyone who examines his law. It was, therefore, a shrewd decision on his part to forbid his followers to read the Old and New Testaments, lest these books convict him of falsity. It is thus clear that those who place any faith in his words believe foolishly.

CHAPTER VII.   THAT THE TRUTH OF REASON IS NOT OPPOSED TO THE TRUTH OF THE CHRISTIAN FAITH

(1) Now, although the truth of the Christian faith which we have discussed surpasses the capacity of the reason, nevertheless that truth that the human reason is naturally endowed to know cannot be opposed to the truth of the Christian faith. For that with which the human reason is naturally endowed is clearly most true; so much so, that it is impossible for us to think of such truths as false. Nor is it permissible to believe as false that which we hold by faith, since this is confirmed in a way that is so clearly divine. Since, therefore, only the false is opposed to the

true, as is clearly evident from an examination of their definitions, it is impossible that the truth of faith should be opposed to those principles that the human reason knows naturally.

(2) Furthermore, that which is introduced into the soul of the student by the teacher is contained in the knowledge of the teacher—unless his teaching is fictitious, which it is improper to say of God. Now, the knowledge of the principles that are known to us naturally has been implanted in us by God; for God is the Author of our nature. These principles, therefore, are also contained by the divine Wisdom. Hence, whatever is opposed to them is opposed to the divine Wisdom, and, therefore, cannot come from God. That which we hold by faith as divinely revealed, therefore, cannot be contrary to our natural knowledge.

(3) Again. In the presence of contrary arguments our intellect is chained, so that it cannot proceed to the knowledge of the truth. If, therefore, contrary knowledges were implanted in us by God, our intellect would be hindered from knowing truth by this very fact. Now, such an effect cannot come from God.

(4) And again. What is natural cannot change as long as nature does not. Now, it is impossible that contrary opinions should exist in the same knowing subject at the same time. No opinion or belief, therefore, is implanted in man by God which is contrary to man's natural knowledge.

(5) Therefore, the Apostle says: "The word is nigh thee, even in thy mouth and in thy heart. This is the word of faith, which we preach" (Rom. 10:8). But because it overcomes reason, there are some who think that it is opposed to it: which is impossible.

(6) The authority of St. Augustine also agrees with this. He writes as follows: "That which truth will reveal cannot in any way be opposed to the sacred books of the Old and the New Testament." [13]

(7) From this we evidently gather the following conclusion: whatever arguments are brought forward against the doctrines of faith are conclusions incorrectly derived from the first and self-evident principles imbedded in nature. Such conclusions do not have the force of demonstration; they are arguments that are either probable or sophistical. And so, there exists the possibility to answer them.

CHAPTER VIII.   HOW THE HUMAN REASON IS RELATED TO THE TRUTH OF FAITH

(1) There is also a further consideration. Sensible things, from which the human reason takes the origin of its knowledge, retain within themselves some sort of trace of a likeness to God. This is so imperfect, however, that it is absolutely inadequate to manifest the substance of God. For effects bear within themselves, in their own way, the likeness of their causes, since an agent produces its like; yet an effect does not always reach to the full likeness of its cause. Now, the human reason is related to the knowledge of the truth of faith (a truth which can be most evident only to those who see the divine substance) in such a way that it can gather certain likenesses of it, which are yet not sufficient so that the truth of faith may be comprehended as being understood demonstratively or through itself. Yet

[13] St. Augustine, *De genesi ad litteram*, II, c. 18 (PL, 34, col. 280).

it is useful for the human reason to exercise itself in such arguments, however weak they may be, provided only that there be present no presumption to comprehend or to demonstrate. For to be able to see something of the loftiest realities, however thin and weak the sight may be, is, as our previous remarks indicate, a cause of the greatest joy.

(2) The testimony of Hilary agrees with this. Speaking of this same truth, he writes as follows in his *De Trinitate*: "Enter these truths by believing, press forward, persevere. And though I may know that you will not arrive at an end, yet I will congratulate you in your progress. For, though he who pursues the infinite with reverence will never finally reach the end, yet he will always progress by pressing onward. But do not intrude yourself into the divine secret, do not, presuming to comprehend the sum total of intelligence, plunge yourself into the mystery of the unending nativity; rather, understand that these things are incomprehensible."[14]

W. K. CLIFFORD
The Ethics of Belief

I.   THE DUTY OF INQUIRY

A shipowner was about to send to sea an emigrant ship. He knew that she was old, and not overwell built at the first; that she had seen many seas and climes, and often had needed repairs. Doubts had been suggested to him that possibly she was not seaworthy. These doubts preyed upon his mind, and made him unhappy; he thought that perhaps he ought to have her thoroughly overhauled and refitted, even though this should put him to great expense. Before the ship sailed, however, he succeeded in overcoming these melancholy reflections. He said to himself that she had gone safely through so many voyages and weathered so many storms, that it was idle to suppose that she would not come safely home from this trip also. He would put his trust in Providence, which could hardly fail to protect all these unhappy families that were leaving their fatherland to seek for better times elsewhere. He would dismiss from his mind all ungenerous suspicions about

William K. Clifford (1845–1879) was educated as a mathematician at Cambridge and taught for eight years at University College, London. Clifford published essays in literature, philosophy, and mathematics.

THE ETHICS OF BELIEF   From *Lectures and Essays* by William K. Clifford (New York: Macmillan, 1874).

[14] St. Hilary, *De Trinitate*, II, 10, ii (*PL*, 10, coll. 58–59).

the honesty of builders and contractors. In such ways he acquired a sincere and comfortable conviction that his vessel was thoroughly safe and seaworthy; he watched her departure with a light heart, and benevolent wishes for the success of the exiles in their strange new home that was to be; and he got his insurance money when she went down in mid-ocean and told no tales.

What shall we say of him? Surely this, that he was verily guilty of the death of those men. It is admitted that he did sincerely believe in the soundness of his ship; but the sincerity of his conviction can in nowise help him, because *he had no right to believe on such evidence as was before him.* He had acquired his belief not by honestly earning it in patient investigation, but by stifling his doubts. And although in the end he may have felt so sure about it that he could not think otherwise, yet inasmuch as he had knowingly and willingly worked himself into that frame of mind, he must be held responsible for it.

Let us alter the case a little, and suppose that the ship was not unsound after all; that she made her voyage safely, and many others after it. Will that diminish the guilt of her owner? Not one jot. When an action is once done, it is right or wrong forever; no accidental failure of its good or evil fruits can possibly alter that. The man would not have been innocent; he would only have been not found out. The question of right or wrong has to do with the origin of his belief, not the matter of it; not what it was, but how he got it; not whether it turned out to be true or false, but whether he had a right to believe on such evidence as was before him.

There was once an island in which some of the inhabitants professed a religion teaching neither the doctrine of original sin nor that of eternal punishment. A suspicion got abroad that the professors of this religion had made use of unfair means to get their doctrines taught to children. They were accused of wresting the laws of their country in such a way as to remove children from the care of the natural and legal guardians; and even of stealing them away and keeping them concealed from their friends and relations. A certain number of men formed themselves into a society for the purpose of agitating the public about this matter. They published grave accusations against individual citizens of the highest position and character, and did all in their power to injure these citizens in the exercise of their professions. So great was the noise they made, that a Commission was appointed to investigate the facts; but after the Commission had carefully inquired into all the evidence that could be got, it appeared that the accused were innocent. Not only had they been accused on insufficient evidence, but the evidence of their innocence was such as the agitators might easily have obtained, if they had attempted a fair inquiry. After these disclosures the inhabitants of that country looked upon the members of the agitating society, not only as persons whose judgment was to be distrusted, but also as no longer to be counted honorable men. For although they had sincerely and "conscientiously" believed in the charges they had made, yet *they had no right to believe on such evidence as was before them.* Their sincere convictions, instead of being honestly earned by patient inquiring, were stolen by listening to the voice of prejudice and passion.

Let us vary this case also, and suppose, other things remaining as before, that a still more accurate investigation proved the accused to have been really guilty. Would this make any difference in the guilt of the accusers? Clearly not; the question is not whether their belief was true or false, but whether they entertained it on wrong grounds. They would no doubt say, "Now you see that we were right after all; next time perhaps you will believe us." And they might be believed, but they would not thereby become honorable men. They would not be innocent, they would only be not found out. Every one of them, if he chose to examine himself *in foro conscientiæ*,[1] would know that he had acquired and nourished a belief, when he had no right to believe on such evidence as was before him; and therein he would know that he had done a wrong thing.

It may be said, however, that in both of these supposed cases it is not the belief which is judged to be wrong, but the action following upon it. The shipowner might say, "I am perfectly certain that my ship is sound, but still I feel it is my duty to have her examined, before trusting the lives of so many people to her." And it might be said to the agitator, "However convinced you were of the justice of your cause and the truth of your convictions, you ought not to have made a public attack upon any man's character until you had examined the evidence on both sides with the utmost patience and care."

In the first place, let us admit that, so far as it goes, this view of the case is right and necessary; right, because even when a man's belief is so fixed that he cannot think otherwise, he still has a choice in regard to the action suggested by it, and so cannot escape the duty of investigating on the ground of the strength of his convictions; and necessary, because those who are not yet capable of controlling their feelings and thoughts must have a plain rule dealing with overt acts.

But this being premised as necessary, it becomes clear that it is not sufficient, and that our previous judgment is required to supplement it. For it is not possible so to sever the faith from the action it suggests as to condemn the one without condemning the other. No man holding a strong belief on one side of a question, or even wishing to hold a belief on one side, can investigate it with such fairness and completeness as if he were really in doubt and unbiased; so that the existence of a belief, not founded on fair inquiry, unfits a man for the performance of this necessary duty.

Nor is that truly a belief at all which has not some influence upon the actions of him who holds it. He who truly believes that which prompts him to an action has looked upon the action to lust after it; he has committed it already in his heart. If a belief is not realized immediately in open deeds, it is stored up for the guidance of the future. It goes to make a part of that aggregate of beliefs which is the link between sensation and action at every moment of all our lives, and which is so organized and compacted together that no part of it can be isolated from the rest, but every new addition modifies the structure of the whole. No real belief, however trifling and fragmentary it may seem, is ever truly insignificant; it prepares us to receive more of its like, confirms those which resembled it before, and weakens others; and so gradually it lays a stealthy train in our inmost thoughts,

[1] Before the tribunal of his conscience.—*Editors.*

which may some day explode into overt action, and leave its stamp upon our character forever.

And no one man's belief is in any case a private matter which concerns himself alone. Our lives are guided by that general conception of the course of things which has been created by society for social purposes. Our words, our phrases, our forms and processes and modes of thought, are common property, fashioned and perfected from age to age; an heirloom, which every succeeding generation inherits as a precious deposit and a sacred trust, to be handed on to the next one, not unchanged, but enlarged and purified, with some clear marks of its proper handiwork. Into this, for good or ill, is woven every belief of every man who has speech of his fellows. An awful privilege, and an awful responsibility, that we should help to create the world in which posterity will live.

In the two supposed cases which have been considered, it has been judged wrong to believe on insufficient evidence, or to nourish belief by suppressing doubts and avoiding investigation. The reason of this judgment is not far to seek; it is that in both these cases the belief held by one man was of great importance to other men. But forasmuch as no belief held by one man, however seemingly trivial the belief, and however obscure the believer, is ever actually insignificant or without its effect on the fate of mankind, we have no choice but to extend our judgment to all cases of belief whatever. Belief, that sacred faculty, which prompts the decisions of our will, and knits into harmonious working all the compacted energies of our being, is ours not for ourselves but for humanity. It is rightly used on truths which have been established by long tradition and waiting toil, and which have stood in the fierce light of free and fearless questioning. Then it helps to bind men together, and to strengthen and direct their common action. It is desecrated when given to unproved and unquestioned statements, for the solace and private pleasure of the believer; to add a tinsel splendor to the plain, straight road of our life, and display a bright mirage beyond it; or even to drown the common sorrows of our kind by a self-deception which allows them not only to cast down, but also to degrade us. Whoso would deserve well of his fellows in this matter will guard the purity of his belief with a very fanaticism of jealous care, lest at any time it should rest on an unworthy object, and catch a stain which can never be wiped away.

It is not only the leader of men, statesman, philosopher, or poet, that owes this bounden duty to mankind. Every rustic who delivers in the village alehouse his slow infrequent sentences, may help to kill or keep alive the fatal superstitions which clog his race. Every hard-worked wife of an artisan may transmit to her children beliefs which shall knit society together, or rend it in pieces. No simplicity of mind, no obscurity of station, can escape the universal duty of questioning all that we believe.

It is true that this duty is a hard one, and the doubt which comes out of it is often a very bitter thing. It leaves us bare and powerless where we thought that we were safe and strong. To know all about anything is to know how to deal with it under all circumstances. We feel much happier and more secure when we think we know precisely what we do, no matter what happens, than when we have lost our way and do not know where to turn. And if we have supposed ourselves to know all about anything, and to be capable of doing what is fit in regard to it, we naturally do not like to find that we are really ignorant and powerless, that we have to begin again at the beginning, and try to learn what the thing is and how it is to be dealt with—if indeed anything can be learned about it. It is the sense of power attached to a sense of knowledge that makes men desirous of believing, and afraid of doubting.

This sense of power is the highest and best of pleasures when the belief on which it is founded is a true belief, and has been fairly earned by investigation. For then we may justly feel that it is common property, and holds good for others as well as for ourselves. Then we may be glad, not that *I* have learned secrets by which I am safer and stronger, but that *we men* have got mastery over more of the world; and we shall be strong, not for ourselves, but in the name of Man and in his strength. But if the belief has been accepted on insufficient evidence, the pleasure is a stolen one. Not only does it deceive ourselves by giving us a sense of power which we do not really possess, but it is sinful, because it is stolen in defiance of our duty to mankind. That duty is, to guard ourselves from such beliefs as from a pestilence, which may shortly master our own body and then spread to the rest of the town. What would be thought of one who, for the sake of a sweet fruit, should deliberately run the risk of bringing a plague upon his family and his neighbors?

And, as in other such cases, it is not the risk only which has to be considered; for a bad action is always bad at the time when it is done, no matter what happens afterwards. Every time we let ourselves believe for unworthy reasons, we weaken our powers of self-control, of doubting, of judicially and fairly weighing evidence. We all suffer severely enough from the maintenance and support of false beliefs and the fatally wrong actions which they lead to, and the evil born when one such belief is entertained is great and wide. But a greater and wider evil arises when the credulous character is maintained and supported, when a habit of believing for unworthy reasons is fostered and made permanent. If I steal money from any person, there may be no harm done by the mere transfer of possession; he may not feel the loss, or it may prevent him from using the money badly. But I cannot help doing this great wrong towards Man, that I make myself dishonest. What hurts society is not that it should lose its property, but that it should become a den of thieves; for then it must cease to be society. This is why we ought not to do evil that good may come; for at any rate this great evil has come, that we have done evil and are made wicked thereby. In like manner, if I let myself believe anything on insufficient evidence, there may be no great harm done by the mere belief; it may be true after all, or I may never have occasion to exhibit it in outward acts. But I cannot help doing this great wrong towards Man, that I make myself credulous. The danger to society is not merely that it should believe wrong things, though that is great enough; but that it should become credulous, and lose the habit of testing things and inquiring into them; for then it must sink back into savagery.

The harm which is done by credulity in a man is not confined to the fostering of a credulous character in others, and consequent support of false beliefs. Habitual want of care about what I believe leads to habitual want of care in others about the truth of what is told to me. Men speak the truth to one another when each reveres the truth in his own mind and in the other's mind but how shall my friend revere the truth in my mind when I myself am careless about it, when I believe things because I want to believe them, and because they are comforting and pleasant? Will he not learn to cry, "Peace," to me, when there is no peace? By such a course I shall surround myself with a thick atmosphere of falsehood and fraud, and in that I must live. It may matter little to me, in my cloud-castle of sweet illusions and darling lies; but it matters much to Man that I have made my neighbors ready to deceive. The credulous man is father to the liar and the cheat; he lives in the bosom of this his family, and it is no marvel if he should become even as they are. So closely are our duties knit together, that whoso shall keep the whole law, and yet offend in one point, he is guilty of all.

To sum up: it is wrong always, everywhere, and for any one, to believe anything upon insufficient evidence.

If a man, holding a belief which he was taught in childhood or persuaded of afterwards, keeps down and pushes away any doubts which arise about it in his mind, purposely avoids the reading of books and the company of men that call in question or discuss it, and regards as impious those questions which cannot easily be asked without disturbing it; the life of that man is one long sin against mankind.

If this judgment seems harsh when applied to those simple souls who have never known better, who have been brought up from the cradle with a horror of doubt, and taught that their eternal welfare depends on *what* they believe; then it leads to the very serious question, *Who hath made Israel to sin?*

It may be permitted me to fortify this judgment with the sentence of Milton [2]:—

"A man may be a heretic in the truth; and if he believe things only because his pastor says so, or the assembly so determine, without knowing other reason, though his belief be true, yet the very truth he holds becomes his heresy."

And with the famous aphorism of Coleridge [3]:—

"He who begins by loving Christianity better than Truth, will proceed by loving his own sect or Church better than Christianity, and end in loving himself better than all."

Inquiry into the evidence of a doctrine is not to be made once for all, and then taken as finally settled. It is never lawful to stifle a doubt; for either it can be honestly answered by means of the inquiry already made, or else it proves that the inquiry was not complete.

"But," says one, "I am a busy man; I have no time for the long course of study which would be necessary to make me in any degree a competent judge of certain questions, or even able to understand the nature of the arguments." Then he should have no time to believe.

[2] *Areopagitica.*

[3] *Aids to Reflection.*

WILLIAM JAMES
The Will to Believe[1]

I

Let us give the name of *hypothesis* to anything that may be proposed to our belief;
and just as the electricians speak of live and dead wires, let us speak of any hypothesis as either *live* or *dead*. A live hypothesis is one which appeals as a real
possibility to him to whom it is proposed. If I ask you to believe in the Mahdi,
the notion makes no electric connection with your nature,—it refuses to scintillate
with any credibility at all. As an hypothesis it is completely dead. To an Arab,
however (even if he be not one of the Mahdi's followers), the hypothesis is among
the mind's possibilities: it is alive. This shows that deadness and liveness in an
hypothesis are not intrinsic properties, but relations to the individual thinker. They
are measured by his willingness to act. The maximum of liveness in an hypothesis
means willingness to act irrevocably. Practically, that means belief; but there is
some believing tendency wherever there is willingness to act at all.

Next, let us call the decision between two hypotheses an *option*. Options may
be of several kinds. They may be—1, *living* or *dead*; 2, *forced* or *avoidable*; 3,
momentous or *trivial*; and for our purposes we may call an option a *genuine*
option when it is of the forced, living, and momentous kind.

(1) A living option is one in which both hypotheses are live ones. If I say to
you: "Be a theosophist or be a Mohammedan," it is probably a dead option,
because for you neither hypothesis is likely to be alive. But if I say: "Be an agnostic or be a Christian," it is otherwise: trained as you are, each hypothesis makes
some appeal, however small, to your belief.

(2) Next, if I say to you: "Choose between going out with your umbrella or
without it," I do not offer you a genuine option, for it is not forced. You can
easily avoid it by not going out at all. Similarly, if I say, "Either love me or hate
me," "Either call my theory true or call it false," your option is avoidable. You
may remain indifferent to me, neither loving nor hating, and you may decline to
offer any judgment as to my theory. But if I say, "Either accept this truth or go
without it," I put on you a forced option, for there is no standing place outside of
the alternative. Every dilemma based on a complete logical disjunction, with no
possibility of not choosing, is an option of this forced kind.

(3) Finally, if I were Dr. Nansen and proposed to you to join my North Pole
expedition, your option would be momentous; for this would probably be your

William James (1842–1910) was one of the outstanding figures in the philosophical movement known
as Pragmatism; he was a notable psychologist as well. His major works include *Principles of Psychology,
Pragmatism: A New Name for Some Old Ways of Thinking,* and *The Varieties of Religious Experience.*

THE WILL TO BELIEVE   From *The Will to Believe and Other Essays in Popular Philosophy* by William
James. Copyright 1896 by William James.

[1] An Address to the Philosophical Clubs of Yale and Brown Universities. Published in the New World,
June, 1896.

only similar opportunity, and your choice now would either exclude you from the North Pole sort of immortality altogether or put at least the chance of it into your hands. He who refuses to embrace a unique opportunity loses the prize as surely as if he tried and failed. *Per contra*, the option is trivial when the opportunity is not unique, when the stake is insignificant, or when the decision is reversible if it later prove unwise. Such trivial options abound in the scientific life. A chemist finds an hypothesis live enough to spend a year in its verification: he believes in it to that extent. But if his experiments prove inconclusive either way, he is quit for his loss of time, no vital harm being done.

It will facilitate our discussion if we keep all these distinctions well in mind.

II

The next matter to consider is the actual psychology of human opinion. When we look at certain facts, it seems as if our passional and volitional nature lay at the root of all our convictions. When we look at others, it seems as if they could do nothing when the intellect had once said its say. Let us take the latter facts up first.

Does it not seem preposterous on the very face of it to talk of our opinions being modifiable at will? Can our will either help or hinder our intellect in its perceptions of truth? Can we, by just willing it, believe that Abraham Lincoln's existence is a myth, and that the portraits of him in *McClure's Magazine* are all of someone else? Can we, by any effort of our will, or by any strength of wish that it were true, believe ourselves well and about when we are roaring with rheumatism in bed, or feel certain that the sum of the two one-dollar bills in our pocket must be a hundred dollars? We can *say* any of these things, but we are absolutely impotent to believe them; and of just such things is the whole fabric of the truths that we do believe in made up,—matters of fact, immediate or remote, as Hume said, and relations between ideas, which are either there or not there for us if we see them so, and which if not there cannot be put there by any action of our own.

In Pascal's *Thoughts* there is a celebrated passage known in literature as Pascal's wager. In it he tries to force us into Christianity by reasoning as if our concern with truth resembled our concern with the stakes in a game of chance. Translated freely his words are these: You must either believe or not believe that God is— which will you do? Your human reason cannot say. A game is going on between you and the nature of things which at the day of judgment will bring out either heads or tails. Weigh what your gains and your losses would be if you should stake all you have on heads, or God's existence: if you win in such case, you gain eternal beatitude; if you lose, you lose nothing at all. If there were an infinity of chances, and only one for God in this wager, still you ought to stake your all on God; for though you surely risk a finite loss by this procedure, any finite loss is reasonable, even a certain one is reasonable, if there is but the possibility of infinite gain. Go, then, and take holy water, and have masses said; belief will come and stupefy your scruples,—*Cela vous fera croire et vous abêtira.* Why should you not? At bottom, what have you to lose?

You probably feel that when religious faith expresses itself thus, in the language of the gaming table, it is put to its last trumps. Surely Pascal's own personal belief in masses and holy water had far other springs; and this celebrated page of his is but an argument for others, a last desperate snatch at a weapon against the hardness of the unbelieving heart. We feel that a faith in masses and holy water adopted wilfully after such a mechanical calculation would lack the inner soul of faith's reality; and if we were ourselves in the place of the Deity, we should probably take particular pleasure in cutting off believers of this pattern from their infinite reward. It is evident that unless there be some pre-existing tendency to believe in masses and holy water, the option offered to the will by Pascal is not a living option. Certainly no Turk ever took to masses and holy water on its account; and even to us Protestants these means of salvation seem such foregone impossibilities that Pascal's logic, invoked for them specifically, leaves us unmoved. As well might the Mahdi write to us, saying, "I am the Expected One whom God has created in his effulgence. You shall be infinitely happy if you confess me; otherwise you shall be cut off from the light of the sun. Weigh, then, your infinite gain if I am genuine against your finite sacrifice if I am not!" His logic would be that of Pascal; but he would vainly use it on us, for the hypothesis he offers us is dead. No tendency to act on it exists in us to any degree.

The talk of believing by our volition seems, then, from one point of view, simply silly. From another point of view it is worse than silly, it is vile. When one turns to the magnificent edifice of the physical sciences, and sees how it was reared; what thousands of disinterested moral lives of men lie buried in its mere foundation; what patience and postponement, what choking down of preference, what submission to the icy laws of outer fact are wrought into its very stones and mortar; how absolutely impersonal it stands in its vast augustness,—then how besotted and contemptible seems every little sentimentalist who comes blowing his voluntary smoke-wreaths, and pretending to decide things from out of his private dream! Can we wonder if those bred in the rugged and manly school of science should feel like spewing such subjectivism out of their mouths? The whole system of loyalties which grow up in the schools of science go dead against its toleration; so that it is only natural that those who have caught the scientific fever should pass over to the opposite extreme, and write sometimes as if the incorruptibly truthful intellect ought positively to prefer bitterness and unacceptableness to the heart in its cup.

> It fortifies my soul to know
> That, though I perish, Truth is so—

sings Clough, while Huxley exclaims: "My only consolation lies in the reflection that, however bad our posterity may become, so far as they hold by the plain rule of not pretending to believe what they have no reason to believe, because it may be to their advantage so to pretend [the word 'pretend' is surely here redundant], they will not have reached the lowest depth of immorality." And that delicious *enfant terrible* Clifford writes: "Belief is desecrated when given to unproved and unquestioned statements for the solace and private pleasure of the believer. . . .

Whoso would deserve well of his fellows in this matter will guard the purity of his belief with a very fanaticism of jealous care, lest at any time it should rest on an unworthy object, and catch a stain which can never be wiped away. . . . If [a] belief has been accepted on insufficient evidence [even though the belief be true, as Clifford on the same page explains] the pleasure is a stolen one. . . . It is sinful because it is stolen in defiance of our duty to mankind. That duty is to guard ourselves from such beliefs as from a pestilence which may shortly master our own body and then spread to the rest of the town. . . . It is wrong always, everywhere, and for every one, to believe anything upon insufficient evidence."

III

All this strikes one as healthy, even when expressed, as by Clifford, with somewhat too much of robustious pathos in the voice. Free-will and simple wishing do seem, in the matter of our credences, to be only fifth wheels to the coach. Yet if any one should thereupon assume that intellectual insight is what remains after wish and will and sentimental preference have taken wing, or that pure reason is what then settles our opinions, he would fly quite as directly in the teeth of the facts.

It is only our already dead hypotheses that our willing nature is unable to bring to life again. But what has made them dead for us is for the most part a previous action of our willing nature of an antagonistic kind. When I say 'willing nature,' I do not mean only such deliberate volitions as may have set up habits of belief that we cannot now escape from,—I mean all such factors of belief as fear and hope, prejudice and passion, imitation and partisanship, the circumpressure of our caste and set. As a matter of fact we find our selves believing, we hardly know how or why. Mr. Balfour gives the name of 'authority' to all those influences, born of the intellectual climate, that make hypotheses possible or impossible for us, alive or dead. Here in this room, we all of us believe in molecules and the conservation of energy, in democracy and necessary progress, in Protestant Christianity and the duty of fighting for 'the doctrine of the immortal Monroe,' all for no reasons worthy of the name. We see into these matters with no more inner clearness, and probably with much less, than any disbeliever in them might possess. His unconventionality would probably have some grounds to show for its conclusions; but for us, not insight, but the *prestige* of the opinions, is what makes the spark shoot from them and light up our sleeping magazines of faith. Our reason is quite satisfied, in nine hundred and ninety-nine cases out of every thousand of us, if it can find a few arguments that will do to recite in case our credulity is criticised by someone else. Our faith is faith in some one else's faith, and in the greatest matters this is most the case. Our belief in truth itself, for instance, that there is a truth, and that our minds and it are made for each other,—what is it but a passionate affirmation of desire, in which our social system backs us up? We want to have a truth; we want to believe that our experiments and studies and discussions must put us in a continually better and better position towards it; and on this line we agree to fight out our thinking lives. But if a pyrrhonistic sceptic asks us *how we know* all this, can our logic find a reply? No! certainly it cannot.

It is just one volition against another,—we willing to go in for life upon a trust or assumption which he, for his part, does not care to make.[2]

As a rule we disbelieve all facts and theories for which we have no use. Clifford's cosmic emotions find no use for Christian feelings. Huxley belabors the bishops because there is no use for sacerdotalism in his scheme of life. Newman, on the contrary, goes over to Romanism, and finds all sorts of reasons good for staying there, because a priestly system is for him an organic need and delight. Why do so few 'scientists' even look at the evidence for telepathy, so called? Because they think, as a leading biologist, now dead, once said to me, that even if such a thing were true, scientists ought to band together to keep it suppressed and concealed. It would undo the uniformity of Nature and all sorts of other things without which scientists cannot carry on their pursuits. But if this very man had been shown something which as a scientist he might *do* with telepathy, he might not only have examined the evidence, but even have found it good enough. This very law which the logicians would impose upon us—if I may give the name of logicians to those who would rule out our willing nature here—is based on nothing but their own natural wish to exclude all elements for which they, in their professional quality of logicians, can find no use.

Evidently, then, our non-intellectual nature does influence our convictions. There are passional tendencies and volitions which run before and others which come after belief, and it is only the latter that are too late for the fair; and they are not too late when the previous passional work has been already in their own direction. Pascal's argument, instead of being powerless, then seems a regular clincher, and is the last stroke needed to make our faith in masses and holy water complete. The state of things is evidently far from simple; and pure insight and logic, whatever they might do ideally, are not the only things that really do produce our creeds.

IV

Our next duty, having recognized this mixed-up state of affairs, is to ask whether it be simply reprehensible and pathological, or whether, on the contrary, we must treat it as a normal element in making up our minds. The thesis I defend is, briefly stated, this: *Our passional nature not only lawfully may, but must, decide an option between propositions, whenever it is a genuine option that cannot by its nature be decided on intellectual grounds; for to say, under such circumstances, "Do not decide, but leave the question open," is itself a passional decision, —just like deciding yes or no,—and is attended with the same risk of losing the truth. . . .*

VII

One more point, small but important, and our preliminaries are done. There are two ways of looking at our duty in the matter of opinion,—ways entirely different,

---

[2]Compare the admirable page 310 in S. H. Hodgson's "Time and Space," London, 1865.

and yet ways about whose difference the theory of knowledge seems hitherto to have shown very little concern. *We must know the truth;* and *we must avoid error,*—these are our first and great commandments as would be knowers; but they are not two ways of stating an identical commandment, they are two separable laws. Although it may indeed happen that when we believe the truth A, we escape as an incidental consequence from believing the falsehood B, it hardly ever happens that by merely disbelieving B we necessarily believe A. We may in escaping B fall into believing other falsehoods, C or D, just as bad as B: or we may escape B by not believing anything at all, not even A.

Believe truth! Shun error!—these, we see, are two materially different laws; and by choosing between them we may end, coloring differently our whole intellectual life. We may regard the chase for truth as paramount, and the avoidance of error as secondary; or we may, on the other hand, treat the avoidance of error as more imperative, and let truth take its chance. Clifford, in the instructive passage which I have quoted, exhorts us to the latter course. Believe nothing, he tells us, keep your mind in suspense forever, rather than by closing it on insufficient evidence incur the awful risk of believing lies. You, on the other hand, may think that the risk of being in error is a very small matter when compared with the blessings of real knowledge, and be ready to be duped many times in your investigation rather than postpone indefinitely the chance of guessing true. I myself find it impossible to go with Clifford. We must remember that these feelings of our duty about either truth or error are in any case only expressions of our passional life. Biologically considered, our minds are as ready to grind out falsehood as veracity, and he who says, "Better go without belief forever than believe a lie!" merely shows his own preponderant private horror of becoming a dupe. He may be critical of many of his desires and fears, but this fear he slavishly obeys. He cannot imagine any one questioning its binding force. For my own part, I have also a horror of being duped; but I can believe that worse things than being duped may happen to a man in this world: so Clifford's exhortation has to my ears a thoroughly fantastic sound. It is like a general informing his soldiers that it is better to keep out of battle forever than to risk a single wound. Not so are victories either over enemies or over nature gained. Our errors are surely not such awfully solemn things. In a world where we are so certain to incur them in spite of all our caution, a certain lightness of heart seems healthier than this excessive nervousness on their behalf. At any rate, it seems the fittest thing for the empiricist philosopher.

VIII

And now, after all this introduction, let us go straight at our question. I have said, and now repeat it, that not only as a matter of fact do we find our passional nature influencing us in our opinions, but that there are some options between opinions in which this influence must be regarded both as an inevitable and as a lawful determinant of our choice.

I fear here that some of you my hearers will begin to scent danger, and lend an inhospitable ear. Two first steps of passion you have indeed had to admit as necessary,—we must think so as to avoid dupery, and we must think so as to gain truth; but the surest path to those ideal consummations, you will probably consider, is from now onwards to take no further passional step.

Well, of course, I agree as far as the facts will allow. Wherever the option between losing truth and gaining it is not momentous, we can throw the chance of *gaining truth* away, and at any rate save ourselves from any chance of *believing falsehood*, by not making up our minds at all till objective evidence has come. In scientific questions, this is almost always the case; and even in human affairs in general, the need of acting is seldom so urgent that a false belief to act on is better than no belief at all. Law courts, indeed, have to decide on the best evidence attainable for the moment, because a judge's duty is to make law as well as to ascertain it, and (as a learned judge once said to me) few cases are worth spending much time over: the great thing is to have them decided on *any* acceptable principle, and got out of the way. But in our dealings with objective nature we obviously are recorders, not makers, of the truth; and decisions for the mere sake of deciding promptly and getting on to the next business would be wholly out of place. Throughout the breadth of physical nature facts are what they are quite independently of us, and seldom is there any such hurry about them that the risks of being duped by believing a premature theory need be faced. The questions here are always trivial options, the hypotheses are hardly living (at any rate not living for us spectators), the choice between believing truth or falsehood is seldom forced. The attitude of sceptical balance is therefore the absolutely wise one if we would escape mistakes. What difference, indeed, does it make to most of us whether we have or have not a theory of the Röntgen rays, whether we believe or not in mind-stuff, or have a conviction about the causality of conscious states? It makes no difference. Such options are not forced on us. On every account it is better not to make them, but still keep weighing reasons *pro et contra* with an indifferent hand.

I speak, of course, here of the purely judging mind. For purposes of discovery such indifference is to be less highly recommended, and science would be far less advanced than she is if the passionate desires of individuals to get their own faiths confirmed had been kept out of the game. See for example the sagacity which Spencer and Weismann now display. On the other hand, if you want an absolute duffer in an investigation, you must, after all, take the man who has no interest whatever in its results: he is the warranted incapable, the positive fool. The most useful investigator, because the most sensitive observer, is always he whose eager interest in one side of the question is balanced by an equally keen nervousness lest he become deceived.[3] Science has organized this nervousness into a regular *technique*, her so-called method of verification; and she has fallen so deeply in love with the method that one may even say she has ceased to care for truth by itself at all. It is only truth as technically verified that interests her. The truth of truths might come in merely affirmative form, and she would decline to touch it. Such truth as that, she might repeat with Clifford, would be stolen in defiance of her duty to mankind. Human passions, however, are stronger than

[3] Compare Wilfrid Ward's essay, "The Wish to Believe," in his *Witnesses to the Unseen*, Macmillan & Co., 1893.

technical rules. "Le cœur a ses raisons," as Pascal says, "que la raison ne connaît pas;" and however indifferent to all but the bare rules of the game the umpire, the abstract intellect, may be, the concrete players who furnish him the materials to judge of are usually, each one of them, in love with some pet 'live hypothesis' of his own. Let us agree, however, that wherever there is no forced option, the dispassionately judicial intellect with no pet hypothesis, saving us, as it does, from dupery at any rate, ought to be our ideal.

The question next arises: Are there not somewhere forced options in our speculative questions, and can we (as men who may be interested at least as much in positively gaining truth as in merely escaping dupery) always wait with impunity till the coercive evidence shall have arrived? It seems *a priori* improbable that the truth should be so nicely adjusted to our needs and powers as that. In the great boarding-house of nature, the cakes and the butter and the syrup seldom come out so even and leave the plates so clean. Indeed, we should view them with scientific suspicion if they did.

IX

Moral questions immediately present themselves as questions whose solution cannot wait for sensible proof. A moral question is a question not of what sensibly exists, but of what is good, or would be good if it did exist. Science can tell us what exists; but to compare the *worths*, both of what exists and of what does not exist, we must consult not science, but what Pascal calls our heart. Science herself consults her heart when she lays it down that the infinite ascertainment of fact and correction of false belief are the supreme goods for man. Challenge the statement, and science can only repeat it oracularly, or else prove it by showing that such ascertainment and correction bring man all sorts of other goods which man's heart in turn declares. The question of having moral beliefs at all or not having them is decided by our will. Are our moral preferences true or false, or are they only odd biological phenomena, making things good or bad for *us*, but in themselves indifferent? How can your pure intellect decide? If your heart does not *want* a world of moral reality, your head will assuredly never make you believe in one. Mephistophelian scepticism, indeed, will satisfy the head's play-instincts much better than any rigorous idealism can. Some men (even at the student age) are so naturally cool-hearted that the moralistic hypothesis never has for them any pungent life, and in their supercilious presence the hot young moralist always feels strangely ill at ease. The appearance of knowingness is on their side, of *naïveté* and gullibility on his. Yet, in the inarticulate heart of him, he clings to it that he is not a dupe, and that there is a realm in which (as Emerson says) all their wit and intellectual superiority is no better than the cunning of a fox. Moral scepticism can no more be refuted or proved by logic than intellectual scepticism can. When we stick to it that there *is* truth (be it of either kind), we do so with our whole nature, and resolve to stand or fall by the results. The sceptic with his whole nature adopts the doubting attitude; but which of us is the wiser, Omniscience only knows.

Turn now from these wide questions of good to a certain class of questions of fact, questions concerning personal relations, states of mind between one man and another. *Do you like me or not?*—for example. Whether you do or not depends, in countless instances, on whether I meet you half-way, am willing to assume that you must like me, and show you trust and expectation. The previous faith on my part in your liking's existence is in such cases what makes your liking come. But if I stand aloof, and refuse to budge an inch until I have objective evidence, until you shall have done something apt, as the absolutists say, *ad extorquendum assensum meum,* ten to one your liking never comes. How many women's hearts are vanquished by the mere sanguine insistence of some man that they *must* love him! he will not consent to the hypothesis that they cannot. The desire for a certain kind of truth here brings about that special truth's existence; and so it is in innumerable cases of other sorts. Who gains promotions, boons, appointments, but the man in whose life they are seen to play the part of live hypotheses, who discounts them, sacrifices other things for their sake before they have come, and takes risks for them in advance? His faith acts on the powers above him as a claim, and creates its own verification.

A social organism of any sort whatever, large or small, is what it is because each member proceeds to his own duty with a trust that the other members will simultaneously do theirs. Wherever a desired result is achieved by the cooperation of many independent persons, its existence as a fact is a pure consequence of the precursive faith in one another of those immediately concerned. A government, an army, a commercial system, a ship, a college, an athletic team, all exist on this condition, without which not only is nothing achieved, but nothing is even attempted. A whole train of passengers (individually brave enough) will be looted by a few highwaymen, simply because the latter can count on one another, while each passenger fears that if he makes a movement of resistance, he will be shot before any one else backs him up. If we believed that the whole car-full would rise at once with us, we should each severally rise, and train-robbing would never even be attempted. There are, then, cases where a fact cannot come at all unless a preliminary faith exists in its coming. *And where faith in a fact can help create the fact,* that would be an insane logic which should say that faith running ahead of scientific evidence is the 'lowest kind of immorality' into which a thinking being can fall. Yet such is the logic by which our scientific absolutists pretend to regulate our lives!

X

In truths dependent on our personal action, then, faith based on desire is certainly a lawful and possibly an indispensable thing.

But now, it will be said, these are all childish human cases, and have nothing to do with great cosmical matters, like the question of religious faith. Let us then pass on to that. Religions differ so much in their accidents that in discussing the religious question we must make it very generic and broad. What then do we now mean by the religious hypothesis? Science says things are; morality says some things are better than other things; and religion says essentially two things.

First, she says that the best things are the more eternal things, the overlapping things, the things in the universe that throw the last stone, so to speak, and say the final word. "Perfection is eternal,"—this phrase of Charles Secrétan seems a good way of putting this first affirmation of religion, an affirmation which obviously cannot yet be verified scientifically at all.

The second affirmation of religion is that we are better off even now if we believe her first affirmation to be true.

Now, let us consider what the logical elements of this situation are *in case the religious hypothesis in both its branches be really true.* (Of course, we must admit that possibility at the outset. If we are to discuss the question at all, it must involve a living option. If for any of you religion be a hypothesis that cannot, by any living possibility be true, then you need go no farther. I speak to the 'saving remnant' alone.) So proceeding, we see, first, that religion offers itself as a *momentous* option. We are supposed to gain, even now, by our belief, and to lose by our nonbelief, a certain vital good. Secondly, religion is a *forced* option, so far as that good goes. We cannot escape the issue by remaining sceptical and waiting for more light, because, although we do avoid error in that way *if religion be untrue,* we lose the good, *if it be true,* just as certainly as if we positively chose to disbelieve. It is as if a man should hesitate indefinitely to ask a certain woman to marry him because he was not perfectly sure that she would prove an angel after he brought her home. Would he not cut himself off from that particular angel-possibility as decisively as if he went and married some one else? Scepticism, then, is not avoidance of option; it is option of a certain particular kind of risk. *Better risk loss of truth than chance of error,*—that is your faith-vetoer's exact position. He is actively playing his stake as much as the believer is; he is backing the field against the religious hypothesis, just as the believer is backing the religious hypothesis against the field. To preach scepticism to us as a duty until 'sufficient evidence' for religion be found, is tantamount therefore to telling us, when in presence of the religious hypothesis, that to yield to our fear of its being error is wiser and better than to yield to our hope that it may be true. It is not intellect against all passions, then; it is only intellect with one passion laying down its law. And by what, forsooth, is the supreme wisdom of this passion warranted? Dupery for dupery, what proof is there that dupery through hope is so much worse than dupery through fear? I, for one, can see no proof; and I simply refuse obedience to the scientist's command to imitate his kind of option, in a case where my own stake is important enough to give me the right to choose my own form of risk. If religion be true and the evidence for it be still insufficient, I do not wish, by putting your extinguisher upon my nature (which feels to me as if it had after all some business in this matter), to forfeit my sole chance in life of getting upon the winning side,—that chance depending, of course, on my willingness to run the risk of acting as if my passional need of taking the world religiously might be prophetic and right.

All this is on the supposition that it really may be prophetic and right, and that, even to us who are discussing the matter, religion is a live hypothesis which may be true. Now, to most of us religion comes in a still further way that makes a veto on our active faith even more illogical. The more perfect and more eternal aspect of the universe is represented in our religions as having personal form. The universe is no longer a mere *It* to us, but a *Thou*, if we are religious; and any relation that may be possible from person to person might be possible here. For instance, although in one sense we are passive portions of the universe, in another we show a curious autonomy, as if we were small active centres on our own account. We feel, too, as if the appeal of religion to us were made to our own active good-will, as if evidence might be forever withheld from us unless we met the hypothesis half-way. To take a trivial illustration: just as a man who in a company of gentlemen made no advances, asked a warrant for every concession, and believed no one's word without proof, would cut himself off by such churlishness from all the social rewards that a more trusting spirit would earn,— so here, one who should shut himself up in snarling logicality and try to make the gods extort his recognition willy-nilly, or not get it at all, might cut himself off forever from his only opportunity of making the gods' acquaintance. This feeling, forced on us we know not whence, that by obstinately believing that there are gods (although not to do so would be so easy both for our logic and our life) we are doing the universe the deepest service we can, seems part of the living essence of the religious hypothesis. If the hypothesis *were* true in all its parts, including this one, then pure intellectualism, with its veto on our making willing advances, would be an absurdity; and some participation of our sympathetic nature would be logically required. I, therefore, for one, cannot see my way to accepting the agnostic rules for truth-seeking, or wilfully agree to keep my willing nature out of the game. I cannot do so for this plain reason, that *a rule of thinking which would absolutely prevent me from acknowledging certain kinds of truth if those kinds of truth were really there, would be an irrational rule.* That for me is the long and short of the formal logic of the situation, no matter what the kinds of truth might materially be.

I confess I do not see how this logic can be escaped. But sad experience makes me fear that some of you may still shrink from radically saying with me, *in abstracto*, that we have the right to believe at our own risk any hypothesis that is live enough to tempt our will. I suspect, however, that if this is so, it is because you have got away from the abstract logical point of view altogether, and are thinking (perhaps without realizing it) of some particular religious hypothesis which for you is dead. The freedom to 'believe what we will' you apply to the case of some patent superstition; and the faith you think of is the faith defined by the schoolboy when he said, "Faith is when you believe something that you know ain't true." I can only repeat that this is misapprehension. *In concreto*, the freedom to believe can only cover living options which the intellect of the individual cannot by itself resolve; and living options never seem absurdities to him who has them to consider. When I look at the religious question as it really puts itself to concrete men, and when I think of all the possibilities which both practically and theoretically it involves, then this command that we shall put a stopper on our heart, instincts, and courage, and *wait*—acting of course meanwhile more or less as if religion were *not* true[4]—till doomsday, or till such time as our intellect and senses working together may have raked in evidence enough,—this command, I say, seems to me the queerest idol ever manufactured in the philosophic cave. Were we scholastic absolutists, there might be more excuse. If we had an infallible intellect with its objective certitudes, we might feel ourselves disloyal to such a perfect organ of knowledge in not trusting to it exclusively, in not waiting for its releasing word. But if we are empiricists, if we believe that no bell in us tolls to let us know for certain when truth is in our grasp, then it seems a piece of idle fantasticality to preach so solemnly our duty of waiting for the bell. Indeed we *may* wait if we will,—I hope you do not think that I am denying that,—but if we do so, we do so at our peril as much as if we believed. In either case we *act*, taking our life in our hands. . . .

ALVIN PLANTINGA
Is Belief in God Properly Basic?

Many philosophers have urged the *evidentialist* objection to theistic belief; they have argued that belief in God is irrational or unreasonable or not rationally acceptable or intellectually irresponsible or noetically substandard, because, as they say, there is insufficient evidence for it.[1] Many other philosophers and theologians—in particular, those in the great tradition of natural theology—have claimed that belief in God is intellectually acceptable, but only because the fact is there is sufficient evidence for it. These two groups unite in holding that theistic belief is rationally acceptable only if there is sufficient evidence for it. More exactly, they hold that a person is rational or reasonable in accepting theistic belief only if she has sufficient evidence for it—only if, that is, she knows or rationally believes some *other* propositions which support the one in question, and believes the latter on the basis of the former. In [4] I argued that the evidentialist objection is rooted

IS BELIEF IN GOD PROPERLY BASIC?   From *Nous*, vol. 15, no. 1 (March 1981). Copyright © 1981 by Indiana University. Reprinted by permission of the publisher.

[4]Since belief is measured by action, he who forbids us to believe religion to be true, necessarily also forbids us to act as we should if we did believe it to be true. The whole defence of religious faith hinges upon action. If the action required or inspired by the religious hypothesis is in no way different from that dictated by the naturalistic hypothesis, then religious faith is a pure superfluity, better pruned away, and controversy about its legitimacy is a piece of idle trifling, unworthy of serious minds. I myself believe, of course, that the religious hypothesis gives to the world an expression which specifically determines our reactions, and makes them in a large part unlike what they might be on a purely naturalistic scheme of belief.

[1]See, for example [1], pp. 400 ff, [2], pp. 345 ff, [3], p. 22, [6], pp. 3 ff. and [7], pp. 87 ff. In [4] I consider and reject the evidentialist objection to the theistic belief.

in *classical foundationalism*, an enormously popular picture or total way of looking at faith, knowledge, justified belief, rationality and allied topics. This picture
has been widely accepted ever since the days of Plato and Aristotle; its near relatives, perhaps, remain the dominant ways of thinking about these topics. We may
think of the classical foundationalist as beginning with the observation that some
of one's beliefs may be *based upon* others; it may be that there are a pair of
propositions A and B such that I believe A *on the basis of B*. Although this relation isn't easy to characterize in a revealing and non-trivial fashion, it is nonetheless familiar. I believe that the word 'umbrageous' is spelled u-m-b-r-a-g-e-o-u-s:
this belief is based on another belief of mine: the belief that that's how the dictio-
nary says it's spelled. I believe that $72 \times 71 = 5112$. This belief is based upon
several other beliefs I hold: that $1 \times 72 = 72$; $7 \times 2 = 14$; $7 \times 7 = 49$; $49 + 1 = 50$; and
others. Some of my beliefs, however, I accept but don't accept on the basis of any
other beliefs. Call these beliefs *basic*. I believe that $2 + 1 = 3$, for example, and
don't believe it on the basis of other propositions. I also believe that I am seated
at my desk, and that there is a mild pain in my right knee. These too are basic to
me; I don't believe them on the basis of any other propositions. According to the
classical foundationalist, some propositions are *properly* or *rightly* basic for a person and some are not. Those that are not, are rationally accepted only on the
basis of *evidence*, where the evidence must trace back, ultimately, to what is properly basic. The existence of God, furthermore, is not among the propositions that
are properly basic; hence a person is rational in accepting theistic belief only if he
has evidence for it.

Now many Reformed thinkers and theologians[2] have rejected *natural theology*
(thought of as the attempt to provide proofs or arguments for the existence of
God). They have held not merely that the proffered arguments are unsuccessful,
but that the whole enterprise is in some way radically misguided. In [5], I argue
that the reformed rejection of natural theology is best construed as an inchoate
and unfocused rejection of classical foundationalism. What these Reformed thinkers really mean to hold, I think, is that belief in God need not be based on
argument or evidence from other propositions at all. They mean to hold that the
believer is entirely within his intellectual rights in believing as he does even if he
doesn't know of any good theistic argument (deductive or inductive), even if he
doesn't believe that there is any such argument, and even if in fact no such
argument exists. They hold that it is perfectly rational to accept belief in God
without accepting it on the basis of any other beliefs or propositions at all. In a
word, they hold that *belief in God is properly basic*. In this paper I shall try to
develop and defend this position.

But first we must achieve a deeper understanding of the evidentialist objection.
It is important to see that this contention is a *normative* contention. The evidentialist objector holds that one who accepts theistic belief is in some way irrational
or noetically substandard. Here 'rational' and 'irrational' are to be taken as normative or evaluative terms; according to the objector, the theist fails to measure
up to a standard he ought to conform to. There is a right way and a wrong way

---

[2] A Reformed thinker or theologian is one whose intellectual sympathies lie with the Protestant
tradition going back to John Calvin (not someone who was formerly a theologian and has since seen
the light).

with respect to belief as with respect to actions; we have duties, responsibilities, obligations with respect to the former just as with respect to the latter. So Professor Blanshard:

> . . . everywhere and always belief has an ethical aspect. There is such a thing as a general ethics of the intellect. The main principle of that ethic I hold to be the same inside and outside religion. This principle is simple and sweeping: Equate your assent to the evidence. [1] p. 401.

This "ethics of the intellect" can be construed variously; many fascinating issues—issues we must here forebear to enter—arise when we try to state more exactly the various options the evidentialist may mean to adopt. Initially it looks as if he holds that there is a duty or obligation of some sort not to accept without evidence such propositions as that God exists—a duty flouted by the theist who has no evidence. If he has no evidence, then it is his duty to cease believing. But there is an oft remarked difficulty: one's beliefs, for the most part, are not directly under one's control. Most of those who believe in God could not divest themselves of that belief just by trying to do so, just as they could not in that way rid themselves of the belief that the world has existed for a very long time. So perhaps the relevant obligation is not that of divesting myself of theistic belief if I have no evidence, (that is beyond my power) but to try to cultivate the sorts of intellectual habits that will tend (we hope) to issue in my accepting as basic only propositions that are properly basic.

Perhaps this obligation is to be thought of *teleologically*: it is a moral obligation arising out of a connection between certain intrinsic goods and evils and the way in which our beliefs are formed and held. (This seems to be W. K. Clifford's way of construing the matter.) Perhaps it is to be thought of *aretetically*: there are valuable noetic or intellectual states (whether intrinsically or extrinsically valuable); there are also corresponding intellectual virtues, habits of acting so as to promote and enhance those valuable states. Among one's obligations, then, is the duty to try to foster and cultivate these virtues in oneself or others. Or perhaps it is to be thought of *deontologically*: this obligation attaches to us just by virtue of our having the sort of noetic equipment human beings do in fact display; it does not arise out of a connection with valuable states of affairs. Such an obligation, furthermore, could be a special sort of moral obligation; on the other hand, perhaps it is a *sui generis* non-moral obligation.

Still further, perhaps the evidentialist need not speak of duty or obligation here at all. Consider someone who believes that Venus is smaller than Mercury, not because he has evidence of any sort, but because he finds it amusing to hold a belief no one else does—or consider someone who holds this belief on the basis of some outrageously bad argument. Perhaps there isn't any obligation he has failed to meet. Nevertheless his intellectual condition is deficient in some way; or perhaps alternatively there is a commonly achieved excellence he fails to display. And the evidentialist objection to theistic belief, then, might be understood, as the claim, not that the theist without evidence has failed to meet an obligation, but that he suffers from a certain sort of intellectual deficiency (so that the proper attitude toward him would be sympathy rather than censure).

These are some of the ways, then, in which the evidentialist objection could be developed; and of course there are still other possibilities. For ease of exposition, let us take the claim deontologically; what I shall say will apply *mutatis mutandis* if we take it one of the other ways. The evidentialist objection, therefore, presupposes some view as to what sorts of propositions are correctly, or rightly, or justifiably taken as basic; it presupposes a view as to what is *properly* basic. And the minimally relevant claim for the evidentialist objector is that belief in God is *not* properly basic. Typically this objection has been rooted in some form of *classical foundationalism*, according to which a proposition *p* is properly basic for a person *S* if and only if *p* is either self-evident or incorrigible for *S* (modern foundationalism) or either self-evident or 'evident to the senses' for *S* (ancient and medieval foundationalism). In [4] I argued that both forms of foundationalism are self referentially incoherent and must therefore be rejected.

Insofar as the evidentialist objection is rooted in classical foundationalism, it is poorly rooted indeed: and so far as I know, no one had developed and articulated any other reason for supposing that belief in God is not properly basic. Of course it doesn't follow that it *is* properly basic; perhaps the class of properly basic propositions is broader than classical foundationalists think, but still not broad enough to admit belief in God. But why think so? What might be the objections to the Reformed view that belief in God is properly basic?

I've heard it argued that if I have no evidence for the existence of God, then if I accept that proposition, my belief will be groundless, or gratuitous, or arbitrary. I think this is an error; let me explain.

Suppose we consider perceptual beliefs, memory beliefs, and beliefs which ascribe mental states to other persons: such beliefs as

(1) I see a tree,
(2) I had breakfast this morning,

and

(3) That person is angry.

Although beliefs of this sort are typically and properly taken as basic, it would be a mistake to describe them as *groundless*. Upon having experience of a certain sort, I believe that I am perceiving a tree. In the typical case I do not hold this belief on the basis of other beliefs; it is nonetheless not groundless. My having that characteristic sort of experience—to use Professor Chisolm's language, my being appeared treely to—plays a crucial role in the formation and justification of that belief. We might say this experience, together, perhaps, with other circumstances, is what *justifies* me in holding it; this is the *ground* of my justification, and, by extension, the ground for the belief itself.

If I see someone displaying typical pain behavior, I take it that he or she is in pain. Again, I don't take the displayed behavior as *evidence* for that belief; I don't infer that belief from others I hold; I don't accept it on the basis of other beliefs. Still, my perceiving the pain behavior plays a unique role in the formation and justification of that belief; as in the previous case, it forms the ground of my justification for the belief in question. The same holds for memory beliefs. I seem to remember having breakfast this morning; that is, I have an inclination to believe the proposition that I had breakfast, along with a certain past-tinged experience that is familiar to all but hard to describe. Perhaps we should say that I am appeared to pastly; but perhaps this insufficiently distinguishes the experience in question from that accompanying beliefs about the past not grounded in my own memory. The phenomonology of memory is a rich and unexplored realm; here I have no time to explore it. In this case as in the others, however, there is a justifying circumstance present, a condition that forms the ground of my justification for accepting the memory belief in question.

In each of these cases, a belief is taken as basic, and in each case properly taken as basic. In each case there is some circumstance or condition that confers justification; there is a circumstance that serves as the *ground* of justification. So in each case there will be some true proposition of the sort

(4) In condition C, S is justified in taking *p* as basic.

Of course C will vary with *p*. For a perceptual judgment such as

(5) I see a rose colored wall before me,

C will include my being appeared to in a certain fashion. No doubt C will include more. If I'm appeared to in the familiar fashion but know that I'm wearing rose colored glasses, or that I am suffering from a disease that causes me to be thus appeared to, no matter what the color of the nearby objects, then I'm not justified in taking (5) as basic. Similarly for memory. Suppose I know that my memory is unreliable; it often plays me tricks. In particular, when I seem to remember having breakfast, then, more often than not, I *haven't* had breakfast. Under these conditions I am not justified in taking it as basic that I had breakfast, even though I seem to remember that I did.

So being appropriately appeared to, in the perceptual case, is not sufficient for justification; some further condition—a condition hard to state in detail—is clearly necessary. The central point, here, however, is that a belief is properly basic only in certain conditions; these conditions are, we might say, the ground of its justification and, by extension, the ground of the belief itself. In this sense, basic beliefs are not, or are not necessarily, *groundless* beliefs.

Now similar things may be said about belief in God. When the Reformers claim that this belief is properly basic, they do not mean to say, of course, that there are no justifying circumstances for it, or that it is in that sense groundless or gratuitous. Quite the contrary. Calvin holds that God "reveals and daily discloses himself to the whole workmanship of the universe," and the divine art "reveals itself in the innumerable and yet distinct and well ordered variety of the heavenly host." God has so created us that we have a tendency or disposition to see his hand in the world about us. More precisely, there is in us a disposition to believe propositions of the sort *this flower was created by God* or *this vast and intricate universe was created by God* when we contemplate the flower or behold the starry heavens or think about the vast reaches of the universe.

Calvin recognizes, at least implicitly, that other sorts of conditions may trigger this disposition. Upon reading the Bible, one may be impressed with a deep sense that God is speaking to him. Upon having done what I knew is cheap, or wrong, or wicked I may feel guilty in God's sight and form the belief *God disapproves of what I've done.* Upon confession and repentence, I may feel forgiven, forming the belief *God forgives me for what I've done.* A person in grave danger may turn to God, asking for his protection and help; and of course he or she then forms the belief that God is indeed able to hear and help if he sees fit. When life is sweet and satisfying, a spontaneous sense of gratitude may well up within the soul; someone in this condition may thank and praise the Lord for his goodness, and will of course form the accompanying belief that indeed the Lord is to be thanked and praised.

There are therefore many conditions and circumstances that call forth belief in God: guilt, gratitude, danger, a sense of God's presence, a sense that he speaks, perception of various parts of the universe. A complete job would explore the phenomenology of all these conditions and of more besides. This is a large and important topic; but here I can only point to the existence of these conditions.

Of course none of the beliefs I mentioned a moment ago is the simple belief that God exists. What we have instead are such beliefs as

(6) God is speaking to me,
(7) God has created all this,
(8) God disapproves of what I have done,
(9) God forgives me,

and

(10) God is to be thanked and praised.

These propositions are properly basic in the right circumstances. But it is quite consistent with this to suppose that the proposition *there is such a person as God* is neither properly basic nor taken as basic by those who believe in God. Perhaps what they take as basic are such propositions as (6)–(10), believing in the existence of God on the basis of propositions such as those. From this point of view, it isn't exactly right to say that it is belief in God that is properly basic; more exactly, what are properly basic are such propositions as (6)–(10), each of which self-evidently entails that God exists. It isn't the relatively high level and general proposition *God exists* that is properly basic, but instead propositions detailing some of his attributes or actions.

Suppose we return to the analogy between belief in God and belief in the existence of perceptual objects, other persons, and the past. Here too it is relatively specific and concrete propositions rather than their more general and abstract colleagues that are properly basic. Perhaps such items as

(11) There are trees,
(12) There are other persons,

and

(13) The world has existed for more than 5 minutes,

are not in fact properly basic; it is instead such propositions as

(14) I see a tree,
(15) that person is pleased,

and

(16) I had breakfast more than an hour ago,

that deserve that accolade. Of course propositions of the latter sort immediately and self-evidently entail propositions of the former sort; and perhaps there is thus no harm in speaking of the former as properly basic, even though so to speak is to speak a bit loosely.

The same must be said about belief in God. We may say, speaking loosely, that belief in God is properly basic; strictly speaking, however, it is probably not that proposition but such propositions as (6)–(10) that enjoy that status. But the main point, here, is that belief in God or (6)–(10), are properly basic; to say so, however, is not to deny that there are justifying conditions for these beliefs, or conditions that confer justification on one who accepts them as basic. They are therefore not groundless or gratuitous.

A second objection I've often heard: if belief in God is properly basic, why can't *just any* belief be properly basic? Couldn't we say the same for any bizarre aberration we can think of? What about voodoo or astrology? What about the belief that the Great Pumpkin returns every Halloween? Could I properly take *that* as basic? And if I can't, why can I properly take belief in God as basic? Suppose I believe that if I flap my arms with sufficient vigor, I can take off and fly about the room; could I defend myself against the charge of irrationality by claiming this belief is basic? If we say that belief in God is properly basic, won't we be committed to holding that just anything, or nearly anything, can properly be taken as basic, thus throwing wide the gates to irrationalism and superstitution?

Certainly not. What might lead one to think the Reformed epistemologist is in this kind of trouble? The fact that he rejects the criteria for proper basicality purveyed by classical foundationalism? But why should *that* be thought to commit him to such tolerance of irrationality? Consider an analogy. In the palmy days of positivism, the positivists went about confidently wielding their verifiability criterion and declaring meaningless much that was obviously meaningful. Now suppose someone rejected a formulation of that criterion—the one to be found in the second edition of A. J. Ayer's *Language, Truth and Logic*, for example. Would that mean she was committed to holding that

(17) Twas brillig; and the slithy toves did gyre and gymble in the wabe

contrary to appearances, makes good sense? Of course not. But then the same goes for the Reformed epistemologist; the fact that he rejects the Classical Foundationalist's criterion of properly basicality does not mean that he is committed to supposing just anything is properly basic.

But what then is the problem? Is it that the Reformed epistemologist not only rejects those criteria for proper basicality, but seems in no hurry to produce what he takes to be a better substitute? If he has no such criterion, how can he fairly reject belief in the Great Pumpkin as properly basic?

This objection betrays an important misconception. How do we rightly arrive at or develop criteria for meaningfulness, or justified belief, or proper basicality? Where do they come from? Must one have such a criterion before one can sensibly make any judgments—positive or negative—about proper basicality? Surely not. Suppose I don't know of a satisfactory substitute for the criteria proposed by classical foundationalism; I am nevertheless entirely within my rights in holding that certain propositions are not properly basic in certain conditions. Some propositions seem self-evident when in fact they are not; that is the lesson of some of the Russell paradoxes. Nevertheless it would be irrational to take as basic the denial of a proposition that seems self-evident to you. Similarly, suppose it seems to you that you see a tree; you would then be irrational in taking as basic the proposition that you don't see a tree, or that there aren't any trees. In the same way, even if I don't know of some illuminating criterion of meaning, I can quite properly declare (17) meaningless.

And this raises an important question—one Roderick Chisholm has taught us to ask. What is the status of criteria for knowledge, or proper basicality, or justified belief? Typically, these are universal statements. The modern foundationalist's criterion for proper basicality, for example, is doubly universal:

(18) For any proposition A and person S, A is properly basic for S if and only if A is incorrigible for S or self-evident to S.

But how could one know a thing like that? What are its credentials? Clearly enough, (18) isn't self-evident or just obviously true. But if it isn't, how does one arrive at it? What sorts of arguments would be appropriate? Of course a foundationalist might find (18) so appealing, he simply takes it to be true, neither offering argument for it, nor accepting it on the basis of other things he believes. If he does so, however, his noetic structure will be self-referentially incoherent. (18) itself is neither self-evident nor incorrigible; hence in accepting (18) as basic, the modern foundationalist violates the condition of proper basicality he himself lays down in accepting it. On the other hand, perhaps the foundationalist will try to produce some argument for it from premises that are self-evident or incorrigible: it is exceedingly hard to see, however, what such an argument might be like. And until he has produced such arguments, what shall the rest of us do—we who do not find (18) at all obvious or compelling? How could he use (18) to show us that belief in God, for example, is not properly basic? Why should we believe (18), or pay it any attention?

The fact is, I think, that neither (18) nor any other revealing necessary and sufficient condition for proper basicality follows from clearly self-evident premisses by clearly acceptable arguments. And hence the proper way to arrive at such a criterion is, broadly speaking, *inductive*. We must assemble examples of beliefs and conditions such that the former are obviously properly basic in the latter, and examples of beliefs and conditions such that the former are obviously *not* properly basic in the latter. We must then frame hypotheses as to the necessary and sufficient conditions of proper basicality and test these hypotheses by reference to those examples. Under the right conditions, for example, it is clearly rational to believe that you see a human person before you: a being who has thoughts and feelings, who knows and believes things, who makes decisions and acts. It is clear, furthermore, that you are under no obligation to reason to this belief from others you hold; under those conditions that belief is properly basic for you. But then (18) must be mistaken; the belief in question, under those circumstances, is properly basic, though neither self-evident nor incorrigible for you. Similarly, you may seem to remember that you had breakfast this morning, and perhaps you know of no reason to suppose your memory is playing you tricks. If so, you are entirely justified in taking that belief as basic. Of course it isn't properly basic on the criteria offered by classical foundationalists; but that fact counts not against you but against those criteria.

Accordingly, criteria for proper basicality must be reached from below rather than above; they should not be presented as *ex Cathedra*, but argued to and tested by a relevant set of examples. But there is no reason to assume, in advance, that everyone will agree on the examples. The Christian will of course suppose that belief in God is entirely proper and rational; if he doesn't accept this belief on the basis of other propositions, he will conclude that it is basic for him and quite properly so. Followers of Bertrand Russell and Madelyn Murray O'Hare may disagree, but how is that relevant? Must my criteria, or those of the Christian community, conform to their examples? Surely not. The Christian community is responsible to *its* set of examples, not to theirs.

Accordingly, the Reformed epistemologist can properly hold that belief in the Great Pumpkin is not properly basic, even though he holds that belief in God is properly basic and even if he has no full fledged criterion of proper basicality. Of course he is committed to supposing that there is a relevant *difference* between belief in God and belief in the Great Pumpkin, if he holds that the former but not the latter is properly basic. But this should prove no great embarrassment; there are plenty of candidates. These candidates are to be found in the neighborhood of the conditions I mentioned in the last section that justify and ground belief in God. Thus, for example, the Reformed epistemologist may concur with Calvin in holding that God has implanted in us a natural tendency to see his hand in the world around us; the same cannot be said for the Great Pumpkin, there being no Great Pumpkin and no natural tendency to accept beliefs about the Great Pumpkin.

By way of conclusion then: being self-evident, or incorrigible, or evident to the senses is not a necessary condition of proper basicality. Furthermore, one who holds that belief in God *is* properly basic is not thereby committed to the idea that belief in God is groundless or gratuitous or without justifying circumstances. And even if he lacks a general criterion of proper basicality, he is not obliged to suppose that just any or nearly any belief—belief in the Great Pumpkin, for example—is properly basic. Like everyone should, he begins with examples; and he may take belief in the Great Pumpkin as a paradigm of irrational basic belief.

REFERENCES

[1] Blanshard, Brand, *Reason and Belief* (London: Allen & Unwin, 1974).

[2] Clifford, W. K., "The Ethics of Belief," in *Lectures and Essays* (London: Macmillan, 1879).

[3] Flew, A. G. N., *The Presumption of Atheism* (London: Pemberton Publishing Co., 1976).

[4] Plantinga, A., "Is Belief in God Rational?" in *Rationality and Religious Belief*, ed. C. Delaney (Notre Dame: University of Notre Dame Press, 1979).

[5] ———, "The Reformed Objection to Natural Theology," *Proceedings of the American Catholic Philosophical Association*, 1980.

[6] Russell, Bertrand, "Why I Am Not a Christian," in *Why I Am Not a Christian* (New York: Simon & Schuster, 1957).

[7] Scrivin, Michael, *Primary Philosophy* (New York: McGraw-Hill, 1966).

STEPHEN J. WYKSTRA
Toward a Sensible Evidentialism: On the Notion of "Needing Evidence"

In recent years, Alvin Plantinga has been attacking something he calls evidentialism. A number of philosophers have sided with Plantinga, developing what I shall call his "Calvinian view"; others have risen to the defence of evidentialism. The philosophical world has again been alvinized into debate.[1]

But what is this "evidentialism" under debate? Or, put another way, what is

Stephen Wykstra (1949–   ), Associate Professor of Philosophy at Calvin College, received his Ph.D. from the University of Pittsburgh in 1978. He has published articles in both philosophy of science and philosophy of religion.

TOWARD A SENSIBLE EVIDENTIALISM   This article was written specifically for this volume and appears here for the first time.

[1] For the Calvinian view see *Faith and Rationality*, ed. Alvin Plantinga and Nicholas Wolterstorff (University of Notre Dame Press, 1983). For evidentialist replies see Anthony Kenny, *Faith and Reason* (Columbia University Press, 1984) and Gary Gutting, *Religious Faith and Religious Skepticism* (University of Notre Dame Press, 1982), Ch. 2. Daniel Dennett's irreverent *Philosophical Lexicon* defines "alvinize" as "to stimulate protracted discussion by making a bizarre claim."

the issue dividing evidentialists and Calvinians? Stated intuitively, we shall see, the dividing issue is whether belief in God *needs evidence*: evidentialists claim that it does; Calvinians deny this. But what does it mean to claim (or deny) that something "needs evidence"? To explicate this, Plantinga reformulates the dividing issue in more technical terms. The issue, he says, is really whether belief in God can be *properly basic*. Evidentialism, as he then construes it, answers "No." This formulation of the dividing issue and this construal of evidentialism have been widely accepted by both sides in the current debate.

My aim in this essay is not to resolve this issue but to relocate it, so as to construe evidentialism more sensibly and deepen our understanding of the opposing perspectives. Section I examines the current formulation, arguing that it makes evidentialism an extravagant position and the Calvinian denial of it a banality. Seeking a more sensible evidentialism, Section II examines the way in which we take other beliefs (e.g., that electrons exist) to "need evidence." I locate the sense in which we take such beliefs to be *evidence essential* and propose that the real dividing issue is whether theistic belief is similarly evidence essential: construed as opposing answers to this issue, evidentialism is more sensible and Calvinianism more interesting. Section III defuses one of the Calvinian's main charges: exploiting an insight of Thomas Reid, I give evidentialism a rationale that has plausibility for theists and non-theists alike.

I.   THE CURRENT EXPLICATION: PROPER BASICALITY AND EXTRAVAGANT EVIDENTIALISM

As Plantinga observes, many non-believers charge not that there is strong evidence against theism, but that there is insufficient evidence *for* it. Thoughtful believers often respond by adducing evidence for theism, but Plantinga's way is different. As he sees it, such critics and defenders of theism often share a common supposition: they both suppose that theistic belief *needs evidence*, disagreeing only about whether it has the evidence needed. Plantinga calls this supposition "evidentialism." Against all evidentialists, believers and non-believers alike, he urges that "it is entirely right, reasonable, rational, and proper to believe in God without any evidence or argument at all."[2]

To a first approximation, then, the issue dividing evidentialists and Calvinians seems to be this: does theistic belief need evidence? I shall call this the "Pre-Analytic Formulation" of the dividing issue, for at least three things cry out for analysis:

(Q1) What sort of thing is this "evidence" which evidentialists aver (and Calvinians deny) theism needs?

(Q2) What *relation* to this evidence is it that evidentialists aver (and Calvinians deny) theistic belief needs to have?

(Q3) *For the sake of what* do evidentialists aver (and Calvinians deny) that theism needs this relation to evidence?

---

[2]"Reason and Belief in God," in *Faith and Rationality, p. 17.*

Because the Pre-Analytic Formulation is vague about these things, it is vague about what divides Calvinians and evidentialists—and hence about what these positions *are*.

As noted above, Plantinga remedies such vagueness by reformulating the issue thus: can theistic belief be *properly basic*? Because this formulation has been widely accepted, I shall call it the "Current Explication" of the dividing issue. It is an "explication" because, by using the technical notion of "properly basic" belief, it reduces vagueness; it does so by, in effect, specifying certain answers to Q1–3. Let us look at *how* it does this; we can then ask if it reduces the vagueness in the *right* way.

First, the Current Explication invokes a distinction between "basic" and "non-basic" beliefs. Plantinga explains this by examples. My belief that $15 \times 24 = 360$ is non-basic, for I believe it by way of more or less *conscious inference* from other propositions I believe. (When justifying a belief inferred from them, we might call such propositions "inferential justifiers.") In contrast, my beliefs that $1 + 1 = 2$, or that a bird is outside my window, are *basic* beliefs: I hold them not by inferring them from other beliefs, but in a *non-inferential* way. But they are not, Plantinga stresses, groundless: typically, a basic belief is formed when an experience "triggers" some faculty or belief-producing disposition. My basic belief that *a bird is on my window sill* is produced when a particular sensory experience triggers a complex belief-forming mechanism we call "vision." Basic beliefs are produced by many other mechanisms—memory, for example, or spontaneous trust in the testimony of others—when triggered by specific circumstances or experiences. (Such experiences, when justifying the beliefs they trigger, might be called "non-inferential justifiers.")

The basic/non-basic distinction, we can now see, enables the Current Explication to answer Q1: what is "evidence"? Here the Pre-Analytic Formulation is handicapped by an ambiguity, for sometimes "evidence" is used in a narrow sense of *inferential* evidence (e.g., inductive or deductive arguments), while other times it is used in a wider sense that includes non-inferential justifiers (as when we speak of "the evidence of the senses"). The Current Explication in effect specifies that, in his Pre-Analytic Formulation, Plantinga intends the *narrower* sense: the dividing issue, he means to say, is whether theistic belief needs *inferential* evidence. Plantinga consistently uses the term "evidence" in this sense, reserving the special term *grounds* for non-inferential justifiers. (I shall follow his usage.) And he allows—indeed stresses—that non-inferential grounds play a vital role in justifying theistic belief. Contemplating a flower, he says, may trigger in us a disposition to believe *this flower was created by God*; feeling guilty at having done something cheap or wrong or wicked may trigger a belief like *God disapproves of what I've done*. If there is a God, Plantinga suggests, it is by such grounds as these that He, in Calvin's words, "reveals and daily discloses Himself." Plantinga recognizes that such grounds do not trigger belief in everyone. (Perhaps, as Calvin taught, sin often suppresses such dispositions, rendering these grounds inefficacious.) But the dividing issue is whether such grounds, when they are efficacious, can be *enough*. Calvinians think they can be. Evidentialists deny this, insisting that something inferential is required.

By the basic/non-basic distinction, the Current Explication also specifies an answer to Q2. The Current Explication, we have seen, takes evidentialism to be claiming that theistic belief cannot be properly basic—or, equivalently, that theistic belief can be proper only if it is non-basic. Now whether a belief is non-basic depends upon how the individual holding the belief does so: a belief is non-basic only if the individual holding it does so on the basis of that *individual's* inference of it from other beliefs held by *that individual.* So, on the Current Explication the dividing issue is whether each theist's belief in God must, in order to be proper, have this very "individualistic" relation to inferential evidence.

". . . in order to be proper." Here the Current Explication specifies an answer to Q3: *for the sake of what* do evidentialists think theism needs evidence? Evidentialists admit that theistic belief often is basic; they insist (in the Current Explication) only that such belief cannot be *"proper."* Plantinga identifies this proper/improper distinction with the distinction between rational and irrational beliefs. With evidentialists, he agrees that there are *norms* that apply to our believings: to call a person's belief "irrational" is to say that the person's believing does not meet these norms. Plantinga canvasses various options for understanding such norms, showing how these affect whether we regard irrational beliefs as derelictions of duty deserving blame or as non-culpable handicaps deserving sympathy. But in any of these options, to call a person's belief irrational is to diagnose some sort of cognitive failure or malfunction *within the belief-forming processes of the subject.* In the Current Explication, the dividing issue is thus whether a person can believe in God in a basic way and yet be free from this failure or malfunction called *irrationality.* Evidentialism is construed as answering "No" to this issue.

Now it seems to me that Calvinians are right in rejecting evidentialism so construed. Consider Plantinga's example of a 14-year-old theist brought up to believe theism in a community where everyone so believes:

> This 14-year-old theist, we may suppose, doesn't believe in God on the basis of evidence. He has never heard of the cosmological, teleological, or ontological arguments; in fact no one has ever presented him with any evidence at all. And although he has often been told about God, he doesn't take that testimony as evidence; he doesn't reason thus: everyone around here says that God loves us and cares for us; most of what everyone around here says is true; so probably *that's* true. Instead, he simply believes what he's taught.[3]

This youth's belief in God is, in Plantinga's sense, "basic." Is it thereby irrational? Here we might recall that most of us acquired most of our beliefs about scientific matters—that the sun is larger than the moon, say, or that electrons exist—in a similar "basic" way, when our grade school teachers taught us these things, and we trustingly believed them. Were we irrational in so doing? Surely not. But if we allow that it can (under certain conditions) be rational to believe in a basic way in electrons, must we not also allow that it can be rational to

---

[3] *Faith and Rationality,* p. 33. Plantinga gives this example against evidentialism taken as a claim concerning "all things considered" duties; he then construes evidentialism as a claim about *prima facie* duties. For reasons I cannot rehearse here, I think this construal makes evidentialism into an innocuous truism and hence fails.

believe in a basic way in God? To claim the contrary—as does evidentialism on the current construal—seems utterly extravagant. Is this really what evidentialists mean to claim? Or is there, perhaps, some other way of explicating the dividing issue, yielding some more sensible construal—or retrenchment—of evidentialism?

II.   RELOCATING THE ISSUE: EVIDENCE ESSENTIALITY AND SENSIBLE EVIDENTIALISM

In seeking a more sensible evidentialism, I shall make two assumptions. The first is that theism is not the *only* belief evidentialists think "needs evidence": what evidentialists want to say about theism they also want to say about many *other* beliefs—our belief that electrons exist, for example. The second is that, about many of these other beliefs, virtually all of us want to say the same thing as evidentialists—even if we are Calvinians who do not think it should be said of theism. Almost all of us, for example, are "evidentialists" about electrons: we take it that belief in electrons in some sense "needs evidence." To understand what evidentialists want to say about theistic belief, then, we might begin by trying to clarify what *we* want to say about some of these other beliefs.

One thing we do not want to say: in taking, say, electron belief to need evidence, we do *not* mean that it cannot be properly basic. For as noted above, we allow that one can properly believe in electrons through spontaneous trust in the say-so of school teachers. But although person A might so believe by trusting the say-so of person B, and B by similarly trusting C, we take it that this chain of testimony is, *somewhere in the community*, anchored in something other than testimony. And for electrons, we take this "something other" to be an *evidential* case for electrons. Thus, though we may not know what the scientific evidence for electrons is, we take it that such evidence is *available* to us the *community* of electron believers. The role of epistemic community is vital, for the evidence might be inaccessible to you or me as individuals: perhaps we both have such an ineptitude for mathematics that we haven't a hope of ever comprehending the equations ingredient in the case. So it is in some *communitarian* sense—not "individualistically"—that we take evidence to be available for our electron belief.

Not only do we take it that evidence for electrons *is* available in this sense; we also take it as *essential* that it be available. "Essential" in what sense? We can get initial bearings from a hypothetical situation. Suppose we were to discover that no evidential case is available for electrons—say, that the entire presumed case for electrons was a fraud propogated by clever con-men in Copenhagen in the 1920s. Would we, in this event, shrug our shoulders and continue unvexedly believing in electrons? Hardly. We would instead regard our electron belief as being in jeopardy, in epistemic hot water, in (let us put it) big doxastic trouble. Of course not all beliefs are like this: consider our beliefs in perceptual objects like dogs. To be sure, some of us may think an inferential case is available for such beliefs: maybe we endorse Descartes' argument, for example. But we do not take this as essential: if we discovered that some flaw (some vicious circularity, say) rendered Descartes' case worthless, we would not consider our confidence that dogs exist to be in big doxastic trouble. As convenient shorthand, let us put this by saying that we take electron belief (but not dog belief) to be *evidence essential*.

For more clarity about evidence essential beliefs, we must press two questions. First, *what* is essential for such a belief: that an evidential case be *in fact* available, or that the believer *take* (and perhaps justifiably take) it to be available? Second, *for the sake of what* is it essential that evidence be (or be taken to be) available for such belief? We must disentangle two very different ways of answering these questions.

We might, following the Current Explication, assume that it is the *rationality* of belief that is at stake. This would no doubt incline us to say that what is essential is that the believer *take* evidence to be available for his belief. For consider the thousands of young people who have properly believed in electrons on the say-so of their grade school teachers. If the rationality of each of these youth's belief depended upon a case for electrons being in fact available, then were we to discover that the case for electrons is a fraud, we would have to reverse our judgment, deeming each youth irrational. But surely such a discovery would not, in itself, be cause to reverse our judgment; therefore, what is essential to the rationality of their belief is not that the evidential case in fact be available. If something is essential here, one is inclined to say it is that the *subject*, the person holding the belief, take (and perhaps justifiably take) such evidence to be available. When this is essential, let us say that the belief is "*subjectively* evidence essential."[4]

Now some beliefs do seem subjectively evidence essential: some beliefs are such that, to be rational in holding them, one must take it that there is evidence available for them (while perhaps not knowing what this evidence is). But this notion is not, I shall argue, the notion we are seeking. For, typically, whether a given belief of a person is subjectively evidence essential will depend upon that person's second-order view *about* whether this belief "needs evidence" in a different and more fundamental sense.

To see this, it will be helpful to consider a case in which thinkers have disagreed about whether some belief needs evidence. The history of geometry provides one example. Around 300 B.C., Euclid proved a large number of interesting geometrical theorems from five simple postulates—postulates like "between any two points exists one straight line." Now Euclid held the belief—call it "Euclidean belief"—that these five postulates are true. But, in addition, he held a view—call it "the Euclidean meta-view"—about how the truth of such postulates should be determined: the appropriate postulates of geometry, he thought, should be *self-evident*—so simple and clear that any rational person who understands them can see, without any proof at all, that they *must* be true. This view went unchallenged for over two thousand years. To be sure, various early critics doubted whether one of Euclid's postulates (the fifth "parallel thesis") *was* self-evident. But these critics meant to say that the parallel thesis needs to be proven as a theorem instead of

---

[4]This notion of "subjectively evidence essential" beliefs is closely allied to what Robert Audi calls "evidentially dependent" beliefs. See his "Direct Justification, Evidential Dependence, and Theistic Belief," in *Rationality, Religious Belief, and Moral Commitment*, ed. R. Audi and W. Wainwright (Cornell University Press, 1986).

accepted as a postulate—which shows that they accepted Euclid's meta-view that the *appropriate* postulates of geometry are self-evident. Not until the nineteenth century was this metaview challenged, by (among others) the brilliant mathematician Carl Freidrich Gauss. As Gauss came to view it, Euclid's postulates define a physical theory which, as such, *needs evidence*: its truth or falsity must be inferred from delicate experimental tests—tests which, as Gauss knew, had not been done. Euclid's meta-view that geometrical postulates could be known by their "self-evident" quality was, Gauss allowed, a very natural one, and earlier thinkers may have been eminently reasonable in holding it; but it was, as Gauss saw it, utterly false.[5]

Now in seeing it this way (rightly or wrongly), what is Gauss claiming? Is he claiming that Euclid's postulates are *subjectively* evidence essential—i.e., that any person, to be rational in believing them, must *take* evidence to be available for them? Surely not. For, as noted above, Gauss allowed that many past thinkers were eminently reasonable (though mistaken) in holding the meta-view that we can know the truth of certain postulates by their self-evident character. Since he allows this, he may surely also allow that such thinkers were reasonable in believing the postulates without taking inferential evidence to be even available for them. But while regarding these thinkers as entirely rational, it is clear that he would also regard something as deeply defective in their believing as they do. For if their Euclidean beliefs turn out to be true, it is only by luck: as Gauss sees it, the "self-evident" quality of such postulates is an epistemic illusion which, so far as putting one in touch with the truth goes, is of no objective value whatever. We might put it this way: what Gauss means to say is that his predecessors' Euclidean beliefs, even if entirely rational (and true), are *epistemically inadequate*, or *deeply epistemically defective*.

What exactly is "epistemic defectiveness" (or its correlative, "epistemic adequacy")? This is not easy to answer. But our task here is to *locate* this concept, which is, as often in philosophy, distinct from the more arduous task of *explicating* the concept. We can locate the concept of epistemic defectiveness by reflecting on specific cases—on what we would want to say of widespread belief in electrons or (if we are Gaussians) Euclidean geometry if there were in fact no evidence available for these beliefs. Such cases make clear that beliefs can be found wanting in two very different ways (or families of ways). Beliefs can be found wanting in *rationality*, in which case we are diagnosing, as remarked above, a failure or malfunction on the part of the person forming the belief. But beliefs can also be found wanting because they are formed in a *noetic environment* which we judge somehow misleading, deceptive, or glitched. In such an environment, a person may form beliefs in a way we judge to be entirely rational, but nevertheless completely unreliable, so far as giving the person access to the way things are.

---

[5] The Gaussian episode opened fascinating issues concerning the relation of geometry and physics which must here be set aside. For clear introductions see Albert Einstein's "Geometry and Experience," in *Readings in the Philosophy of Science*, ed. H. Feigl and M. Brodbeck (Appleton-Century-Crofts, 1953), pp. 189–94, or, more fully, Part III of Rudolf Carnap's *Introduction to the Philosophy of Science* (Basic Books, 1966).

Beliefs which are entirely rational may thus be sorely lacking in epistemic adequacy; they may be deeply epistemically defective.[6]

Gauss means to claim, then, that Euclidean belief needs evidence for the sake of *epistemic adequacy* and that, for this, an evidential case must be *in fact* available for it. Gauss's claim, let us put it, is that Euclidean belief is an *objectively evidence essential* belief: if no evidential case is in fact available to the community for it, then those holding it have a deeply epistemically defective belief. In claiming this, Gauss is not saying that most people are in a position to *see* that Euclidean belief needs evidence in this sense. After all, the noetic environment is here a very "glitchy" one: the postulates might (Gauss could allow) have a halo of "self-evidentness" so compelling (though illusory) that believing the postulates without proof was the only rational course open to his predecessors. These are peripheral matters; Gaus's only claim—his revolutionary claim—is that however these matters turn out, Euclidean belief is *objectively* evidence essential—it needs an available case in order to be epistemically adequate, or free from deep epistemic defect. It is in this sense that Gauss is an evidentialist about Euclidean belief. In this sense, too, we are evidentialists about electron belief: we take belief in electrons to be *objectively evidence essential*. Since this sense has turned out to be the relevant one, I shall hereafter drop the adjective "objectively," shortening "objectively evidence essential" to "evidence essential."

We can now, on the two working assumptions with which I began this section, better understand what evidentialists want to say about theistic belief. The issue dividing evidentialists and Calvinians, I propose, is whether theistic belief is evidence essential. Evidentialists answer "Yes": their fundamental claim is that if theistic belief is to be free of deep epistemic defectiveness, it is essential that an evidential case for it be available to the theistic community. So construed, evidentialism does not extravagantly entail that individual theists need always base their theistic belief on their own inference from this evidence, or even that they need to know what the evidence is. And because such evidentialism is a claim about epistemic adequacy, it does not even entail that all theists must, to be *rational* in their belief, take such evidence to be available. Since evidentialism so construed avoids these extravagances, I shall call it "sensible evidentialism."

Sensible evidentialism is not, however, so modest as to be insipid. For on the issue of whether theism is *evidence essential*, the evidentialist's "Yes" will be deeply opposed by a Calvinian "No". Calvinians will insist that there does not need to be an evidential case available for theistic belief in order for it to be epistemically adequate. Indeed, I believe that it is only by so relocating the issue—by seeing the dividing issue as concerning not proper basicality but evidence essentiality—that we get at the heart of the Calvinian position. The claim that belief in God can be properly basic is, after all, rather innocuous: even electron belief, as we have seen, can be properly basic. What Calvinians really want to say is that belief

---

[6] Irrationality, I mean to claim, is not the *only* kind of epistemic defectiveness. A full account of epistemic defectiveness requires, I believe, adjudicating the current standoff between internalist and externalist theories of knowledge. See William Alston's "Internalism and Externalism in Epistemology," *Philosophical Topics* 14 (1986), pp. 179–220.

in God (*unlike* belief in electrons) is evidence *non*-essential: even if no evidential case is available for it, theistic belief suffers no epistemic defectiveness and should not be seen as being in big (or little) doxastic trouble. Relocating the issue, as so far proposed, thus does not reduce the disagreement between evidentialists and Calvinians. It rather illuminates the disagreement, deepening our understanding of the divide between the two sides.

III. ESPECIALLY SENSIBLE EVIDENTIALISM

In claiming that theistic belief needs evidence, then, the sensible evidentialist means that theistic belief is "evidence essential." But why should anyone suppose this about belief in God? To be sure, such evidentialism is sensible about things like electrons. But this is because we have no non-inferential access to electrons (we cannot just perceive them); electron belief hence needs inferential support from things we can perceive. But why should we suppose that humans have no non-inferential access to God? The traditional theistic religions teach, after all, that God made us with a faculty—what Calvin calls a *Sensus Divinitatis*—by which we can, under suitable conditions, "sense" God's presence, character, and activity in our lives. To rule out such non-inferential access to God thus presupposes that God (as traditionally presented) does not exist. Non-believing evidentialists cannot, without begging the question, begin by supposing this; theistic evidentialists cannot, without contradicting their own tradition, even *end* by supposing it. What rationale can there be, then, for evidentialism? Calvinians charge that evidentialism is rooted in a bankrupt "classical foundationalism." I shall here propose a better rationale.

Evidentialists hold that theistic belief needs inferential evidence. But what, we must now ask, is "inferential evidence"? One answer stems from what I shall call the derivational picture of inference. In this picture, humans have what we might call basic faculties (the senses, memory, logical intuition, and the like) which allow us to secure certain beliefs non-inferentially; it is by inference that we derive, from these, further truths to which our basic faculties give no access. Thus, in geometry (as understood before Gauss) we secure certain postulates by their self-evident character; once this is done, deductive inference allows us to derive from them further theorems which are not self-evident. Similarly, in science (as traditionally understood) we secure certain truths by sense observation; from these, scientific inference then allows us to justify theories about things we cannot observe. This derivational picture has had tremendous influence, and it cannot be all wrong: inference sometimes is derivational in character. But I want to argue, taking cues from Thomas Reid, that it blinkers us to a very different function of inference.

Consider Reid's discussion of our disposition to trust testimony—our credulity disposition, we may call it. As Reid sees it, testimony has "a native and intrinsic authority," for "the Wise Author of Nature hath implanted in the human mind a propensity to rely upon human testimony before we can give a reason for doing so." This propensity to trust testimony, Reid says, is "unlimited in children, until they meet with instances of deceit and falsehood." Such instances do not extinguish the credulity disposition, but instead lead to its *refinement*: we learn to *discriminate*, giving little credence to some kinds of testimony while believing other kinds more strongly than ever. And of special significance is this: this refining process, as Reid sees it, is one in which *Reason* interacts with our credulity disposition. Reid writes:

> When brought to maturity by proper culture . . . Reason learns to suspect testimony in some cases, and to disbelieve it in others . . . But still, to the end of life, she finds a necessity of borrowing light from testimony . . . And as, in many cases, reason even in her maturity, borrows aid from testimony, so in others she mutually gives aid to it, and strengthens its authority. For, as we find good reason to reject testimony in some cases, so in others we find good reason to rely upon it with perfect security . . . The character, the number, and the disinterestedness of the witnesses, the impossibility of collusion, may give an irresistible strength to testimony, compared to which its native and intrinsic authority is very inconsiderable.[7]

As Reid sees it, the process by which our credulity disposition is refined has an *inferential* component: we learn, he says, to "find good reasons" in some cases for disbelieving testimony while in others for trusting it more securely than ever. Because Reid spotlights such cases of inferential discrimination, let us call them "Reidian cases."

Reidian cases, I want to argue, do not fit the derivational picture in two respects. The first concerns *why* inferential evidence is needed. On the derivational picture, propositions (e.g., that electrons exist) typically need inferential evidence because our "basic faculties" give no access at all to their truth. In Reidian cases, in contrast, propositions come to need inferential evidence because our basic faculties give us, as it were, conflicting signals about their truth. Suppose, for example, that my mother tells me one thing and my father the contrary. Had I only my mother's testimony, my basic disposition to trust testimony would instantly and properly carry my belief in what she says. So also for my father. But I, alas, have both testimonies: since they are contrary I cannot believe them both; but because they are ostensibly on par with each other, I cannot without arbitrariness believe one over the other. I thus face a problem of, let us call it, "ostensible epistemic parity." We might envision this problem as blocking the flow of my credulity disposition, so that instead of carrying my belief in its usual forceful way, this disposition swirls, as it were, in useless eddies. And it is not hard to think of cases in which parity problems similarly block the flow of basic faculties of memory, sense perception, and the like.[8]

What is the function of what Reid calls "good reasons" in resolving such parity problems? Here, too, the derivational picture is unhelpful. In that picture, our basic faculties and inference work at different stages: our basic faculties, on their own, produce certain beliefs; from such beliefs inference then derives further,

[7] Quotations are from Reid's *Inquiry into the Human Mind*, VI, 24.

[8] See Wolterstorff's insightful discussion in "Can Belief in God Be Rational if It Has No Foundations?" in *Faith and Rationality*, pp. 148–55. But Wolterstorff glosses the refining process as a matter of "operant conditioning," which may not do justice to its inferential dimension.

quite different truths. But in Reidian cases, inference and a basic faculty are intimate co-workers in producing one and the same belief. In the above case, I may realize on reflection that my father has no motive for dissembling to me on this particular matter, while my mother does. But if, finding some such "good reason" for taking one testimony over the other, I come to believe my father, I need not be relying on this evidence *instead* of my native credulity disposition. The evidence may instead resolve the ostensible parity by functioning as a discriminating feature; this, so to speak, cuts a channel for my credulity disposition, which itself then forcefully carries my belief toward trusting my father. So, also, when parity problems block the flow of memory, perception, or other basic faculties: in resolving such problems by appeal to "good reasons," our evidence discriminates, as it were, a *direction* for one's believing, while one's basic faculty continues to provide the *force*.

We must, then, distinguish two kinds of inferential evidence—one derivational, the other discriminational. How parity problems create a need for—and are resolved by—discriminational evidence requires far more analysis. For example, parity problems occur in a continuum of contexts, to very different effects. If the testimony of my parents conflicts only on isolated occasions, and I lack any way to discriminate between them, I may simply suspend belief on those occasions while continuing generally to rely on their word. But if the conflicts become more regular and I still find no procedures for evidential discrimination, this will (or should) put in a much more far-reaching crisis my propensity to trust them. A whole territory here deserves philosophical exploration.

Even our brief forray, however, opens an important option for sensible evidentialists. Some evidentialists may suppose that theistic belief needs evidence, because they think that to God, as to electrons, we can have no non-inferential access at all: belief in God, they hence think, needs *derivational* evidence. For reasons noted above, it may not be so sensible for non-theists to begin from such an evidentialism, nor for theists to end with it. But there is also a second way to be a sensible evidentialist. One might think evidence is essential because one sees religious experience as riddled with problems of ostensible epistemic parity. Antony Flew thus argues that religious experiences need "credentials" because from culture to culture such experiences "are enormously varied, ostensibly authenticating innumerable beliefs many of which are in contradiction with one another." John Locke finds similar problems within one culture: reflecting on the "enthusiasts" of his own time, Locke notes that if we trust every "inner light" of ostensibly Christian experience, then "contrary opinions may have the same title to be inspirations, and God will be the Father of opposite and contrary lights." For this reason, thought Locke, "the holy men of old, who had Revelations from God, had something else besides that internal light of assurance, to testify to them, that it was from God."[9]

Whether Flew and Locke are right about the *extent* of such parity problems is an important question for, as noted earlier, isolated parity problems need not

---

[9] See Flew's *God and Philosophy* (Harcourt Brace and World, 1966), p. 126, and Locke's *Essay Concerning Human Understanding*, Book IV, Ch. 19. For a contrasting view, see Richard Swinburne's discussion of defeaters in *The Existence of God* (Oxford University Press, 1979), pp. 265–67.

undermine general reliance on a basic faculty. But insofar as such parity problems are pervasive, there is reason to regard experiential religious beliefs as needing evidence of (at least) the *discriminational* kind. And because the function of such evidence is to refine (not to replace) our basic dispositions, regarding such evidence as essential to theistic belief is not tantamount to denying that there is a God who has given us a *Sensus Divinitatis*. Non-theists can thus begin from such evidentialism without begging the question; theists can end with it without contradicting an important part of their own traditions.

It might be thought that such evidentialism, while perhaps not contradicting theism, is still not very harmonious with it. If theism is true, and God himself has given humans a *Sensus Divinitatis*, is it not odd that our experiential religious beliefs should need so much evidential refining? Here we might ask why our credulity disposition needs as much evidential refinement as it does. Clearly it would need far less if human beings never lied, flattered, spread rumors, or held irresponsible opinions. But in our world, we painfully learn, these glitches are endemic. Does human religiosity face anything like this? The Jew or Christian may here recall that the Biblical prophets reserve their strongest words not for non-belief but for an idolatrous mis-belief, by which even the religious "speak visions from their own minds, not from the mouth of the Lord" (Jer. 23:16). In this view our fallenness depraves (as Calvin put it) not just part but the totality of our nature: it corrupts even our spiritualities, distorting (not just suppressing) our dispositions to form experiential beliefs about God. The claim that theistic belief needs discriminational evidence is, I conclude, both philosophically plausible and harmonious with Judeo-Christian teaching. I submit it as *especially* sensible evidentialism.

MIRACLES

DAVID HUME
Of Miracles

Though experience be our only guide in reasoning concerning matters of fact; it must be acknowledged, that this guide is not altogether infallible, but in some cases is apt to lead us into errors. One, who in our climate, should expect better weather in any week of JUNE than in one of DECEMBER, would reason justly, and conformably to experience; but it is certain, that he may happen, in the event, to find himself mistaken. However, we may observe, that, in such a case, he would have no cause to complain of experience; because it commonly informs us beforehand of the uncertainty, by that contrariety of events, which we may learn from a diligent observation. All effects follow not with like certainty from their supposed causes. Some events are found, in all countries and all ages, to have been constantly conjoined together: Others are found to have been more variable, and sometimes to disappoint our expectations; so that, in our reasonings concerning matter of fact, there are all imaginable degrees of assurance, from the highest certainty to the lowest species of moral evidence.

A wise man, therefore, proportions his belief to the evidence. In such conclusions as are founded on an infallible experience, he expects the event with the last degree of assurance, and regards his past experience as a full *proof* of the future existence of that event. In other cases, he proceeds with more caution: He weighs the opposite experiments: He considers which side is supported by the greater number of experiments: To that side he inclines, with doubt and hesitation; and when at last he fixes his judgment, the evidence exceeds not what we properly call *probability*. All probability, then, supposes an opposition of experiments and observations, where the one side is found to overbalance the other, and to produce a degree of evidence, proportioned to the superiority. A hundred

OF MIRACLES From "An Enquiry Concerning Human Understanding" in *Essays, Moral, Political and Literary* by David Hume, edited with preliminary dissertations and notes, by T. H. Green and T. H. Grose. Volume II. London, Longmans, Green, and Co., 1875.

instances or experiments on one side, and fifty on another, afford a doubtful expectation of any event; though a hundred uniform experiments with only one that is contradictory, reasonably beget a pretty strong degree of assurance. In all cases, we must balance the opposite experiments, where they are opposite, and deduct the smaller number from the greater in order to know the exact force of the superior evidence.

To apply these principles to a particular instance; we may observe, that there is no species of reasoning more common, more useful, and even necessary to human life, than that which is derived from the testimony of men, and the reports of eye-witnesses and spectators. This species of reasoning, perhaps, one may deny to be founded on the relation of cause and effect. I shall not dispute about a word. It will be sufficient to observe, that our assurance in any argument of this kind is derived from no other principle than our observation of the variety of human testimony, and of the usual conformity of facts to the reports of witnesses. It being a general maxim, that no objects have any discoverable connexion together, and that all the inferences, which we can draw from one to another, are founded merely on our experience of their constant and regular conjunction, it is evident, that we ought not to make an exception to this maxim in favour of human testimony, whose connexion with any event seems, in itself, as little necessary as any other. Were not the memory tenacious to a certain degree; had not men commonly an inclination to truth and a principle of probity; were they not sensible to shame, when detected in a falsehood: Were not these, I say, discovered by *experience* to be qualities, inherent in human nature, we should never repose the least confidence in human testimony. A man delirious, or noted for falsehood and villany, has no manner of authority with us.

And as the evidence, derived from witnesses and human testimony, is founded on past experience, so it varies with the experience, and is regarded either as a *proof* or a *probability*, according as the conjunction between any particular kind of report and any kind of object has been found to be constant or variable. There are a number of circumstances to be taken into consideration in all judgments of this kind; and the ultimate standard, by which we determine all disputes, that may arise concerning them, is always derived from experience and observation. Where the experience is not entirely uniform on any side, it is attended with an unavoidable contrariety in our judgments, and with the same opposition and mutual destruction of argument as in every other kind of evidence. We frequently hesitate concerning the reports of others. We balance the opposite circumstances, which cause any doubt or uncertainty; and when we discover a superiority on any side, we incline to it; but still with a diminution of assurance, in proportion to the force of its antagonist.

This contrariety of evidence, in the present case, may be derived from several different causes; from the opposition of contrary testimony; from the character or number of the witnesses; from the manner of their delivering their testimony; or from the union of all these circumstances. We entertain a suspicion concerning any matter of fact, when the witnesses contradict each other; when they are but few, or of a doubtful character; when they have an interest in what they affirm;

when they deliver their testimony with hesitation, or on the contrary, with too violent asseverations. There are many other particulars of the same kind, which may diminish or destroy the force of any argument, derived from human testimony.

Suppose, for instance, that the fact, which the testimony endeavours to establish, partakes of the extraordinary and the marvellous; in that case, the evidence, resulting from the testimony, admits of a diminution, greater or less, in proportion as the fact is more or less unusual. The reason, why we place any credit in witnesses and historians, is not derived from any *connexion*, which we perceive *a priori*, between testimony and reality, but because we are accustomed to find a conformity between them. But when the fact attested is such a one as has seldom fallen under our observation, here is a contest of two opposite experiences; of which the one destroys the other, as far as its force goes, and the superior can only operate on the mind by the force, which remains. The very same principle of experience, which gives us a certain degree of assurance in the testimony of witnesses, gives us also, in this case, another degree of assurance against the fact, which they endeavour to establish; from which contradiction there necessarily arises a counterpoise, and mutual destruction of belief and authority. . . .

But in order to increase the probability against the testimony of witnesses, let us suppose, that the fact, which they affirm, instead of being only marvellous, is really miraculous; and suppose also, that the testimony, considered apart and in itself, amounts to an entire proof; in that case, there is proof against proof, of which the strongest must prevail, but still with a diminution of its force, in proportion to that of its antagonist.

A miracle is a violation of the laws of nature; and as a firm and unalterable experience has established these laws, the proof against a miracle, from the very nature of the fact, is as entire as any argument from experience can possibly be imagined. Why is it more than probable, that all men must die; that lead cannot, of itself, remain suspended in the air; that fire consumes wood, and is extinguished by water; unless it be, that these events are found agreeable to the laws of nature, and there is required a violation of these laws, or in other words, a miracle to prevent them? Nothing is esteemed a miracle, if it ever happen in the common course of nature. It is no miracle that a man, seemingly in good health, should die on a sudden: because such a kind of death, though more unusual than any other, has yet been frequently observed to happen. But it is a miracle, that a dead man should come to life; because that has never been observed, in any age or country. There must, therefore, be a uniform experience against every miraculous event, otherwise the event would not merit that appellation. And as an uniform experience amounts to a proof, there is here a direct and full *proof*, from the nature of the fact, against the existence of any miracle; nor can such a proof be destroyed, or the miracle rendered credible, but by an opposite proof, which is superior.[1]

---

[1] Sometimes an event may not, *in* itself, *seem* to be contrary to the laws of nature, and yet, if it were real, it might, by reason of some circumstances, be denominated a miracle; because, in fact, it is contrary to these laws. Thus if a person, claiming a divine authority, should command a sick person to be well, a healthful man to fall down dead, the clouds to pour rain, the winds to blow, in short,

The plain consequence is (and it is a general maxim worthy of our attention), 'That no testimony is sufficient to establish a miracle, unless the testimony be of such a kind, that its falsehood would be more miraculous, than the fact, which it endeavours to establish: And even in that case there is a mutual destruction of arguments, and the superior only gives us an assurance suitable to that degree of force, which remains, after deducting the inferior.' When any one tells me, that he saw a dead man restored to life, I immediately consider with myself, whether it be more probable, that this person should either deceive or be deceived, or that the fact, which he relates, should really have happened. I weigh the one miracle against the other; and according to the superiority, which I discover, I pronounce my decision, and always reject the greater miracle. If the falsehood of his testimony would be more miraculous, than the event which he relates; then, and not till then, can he pretend to command my belief or opinion.

PART II

In the foregoing reasoning we have supposed, that the testimony, upon which a miracle is founded, may possibly amount to an entire proof, and that the falsehood of that testimony would be a real prodigy: But it is easy to shew, that we have been a great deal too liberal in our concession, and that there never was a miraculous event established on so full an evidence.

For *first*, there is not to be found in all history, any miracle attested by a sufficient number of men, of such unquestioned good-sense, education, and learning, as to secure us against all delusion in themselves; of such undoubted integrity, as to place them beyond all suspicion of any design to deceive others; of such credit and reputation in the eyes of mankind, as to have a great deal to lose in case of their being detected in any falsehood; and at the same time, attesting facts, performed in such a public manner, and in so celebrated a part of the world, as to render the detection unavoidable: All which circumstances are requisite to give us a full assurance in the testimony of men.

Secondly. We may observe in human nature a principle, which, if strictly examined, will be found to diminish extremely the assurance, which we might, from human testimony, have, in any kind of prodigy. The maxim, by which we commonly conduct ourselves in our reasonings, is, that the objects, of which we have no experience, resemble those, of which we have; that what we have found to be most usual is always most probable; and that where there is an opposition of

should order many natural events which immediately follow upon his command; these might justly be esteemed miracles, because they are really, in this case, contrary to the laws of nature. For if any suspicion remain, that the event and command concurred by accident, there is no miracle and no transgression of the laws of nature. If this suspicion be removed, there is evidently a miracle, and a transgression of these laws; because nothing can be more contrary to nature than that the voice or command of a man should have such an influence. A miracle may be accurately defined, *a transgression of a law of nature by a particular volition of the Deity, or by the interposition of some invisible agent.* A miracle may either be discoverable by men or not. This alters not its nature and essence. The raising of a house or ship into the air is a visible miracle. The raising of a feather, when the wind wants ever so little of a force requisite for that purpose, is as real a miracle, though not so sensible with regard to us.

arguments, we ought to give the preference to such as are founded on the greatest number of past observations. But though, in proceeding by this rule, we readily reject any fact which is unusual and incredible in an ordinary degree; yet in advancing farther, the mind observes not always the same rule; but when anything is affirmed utterly absurd and miraculous, it rather the more readily admits of such a fact, upon account of that very circumstance, which ought to destroy all its authority. The passion of *surprize* and *wonder*, arising from miracles, being an agreeable emotion, gives a sensible tendency towards the belief of those events, from which it is derived. And this goes so far, that even those who cannot enjoy this pleasure immediately, nor can believe those miraculous events, of which they are informed, yet love to partake of the satisfaction at second-hand or by rebound, and place a pride and delight in exciting the admiration of others.

With what greediness are the miraculous accounts of travellers received, their descriptions of sea and land monsters, their relations of wonderful adventures, strange men, and uncouth manners? But if the spirit of religion join itself to the love of wonder, there is an end of common sense; and human testimony, in these circumstances, loses all pretensions to authority. A religionist may be an enthusiast, and imagine he sees what has no reality: He may know his narrative to be false, and yet persevere in it, with the best intentions in the world, for the sake of promoting so holy a cause: Or even where this delusion has not place, vanity, excited by so strong a temptation, operates on him more powerfully than on the rest of mankind in any other circumstances; and self-interest with equal force. His auditors may not have, and commonly have not, sufficient judgment to canvass his evidence: What judgment they have, they renounce by principle, in these sublime and mysterious subjects: Or if they were ever so willing to employ it, passion and a heated imagination disturb the regularity of its operations. Their credulity increases his impudence: And his impudence overpowers their credulity. . . .

Thirdly. It forms a strong presumption against all supernatural and miraculous relations, that they are observed chiefly to abound among ignorant and barbarous nations; or if a civilized people has ever given admission to any of them, that people will be found to have received them from ignorant and barbarous ancestors, who transmitted them with that inviolable sanction and authority, which always attend received opinions. When we peruse the first histories of all nations, we are apt to imagine ourselves transported into some new world; where the whole frame of nature is disjointed, and every element performs its operations in a different manner, from what it does at present. Battles, revolutions, pestilence, famine, and death, are never the effect of those natural causes, which we experience. Prodigies, omens, oracles, judgments, quite obscure the few natural events, that are intermingled with them. But as the former grow thinner every page, in proportion as we advance nearer the enlightened ages, we soon learn, that there is nothing mysterious or supernatural in the case, but that all proceeds from the usual propensity of mankind towards the marvellous, and that, though this inclination may at intervals receive a check from sense and learning, it can never be thoroughly extirpated from human nature. . . .

I may add as a *fourth* reason, which diminishes the authority of prodigies, that there is no testimony for any, even those which have not been expressly detected, that is not opposed by an infinite number of witnesses; so that not only the miracle destroys the credit of testimony, but the testimony destroys itself. To make this the better understood, let us consider, that, in matters of religion, whatever is different is contrary; and that it is impossible the religions of ancient ROME, of TURKEY, of SIAM, and of CHINA should, all of them, be established on any solid foundation. Every miracle, therefore, pretended to have been wrought in any of these religions (and all of them abound in miracles), as its direct scope is to establish the particular system to which it is attributed; so has it the same force, though more indirectly, to overthrow every other system. In destroying a rival system, it likewise destroys the credit of those miracles, on which that system was established; so that all the prodigies of different religions are to be regarded as contrary facts, and the evidences of these prodigies, whether weak or strong, as opposite to each other. According to this method of reasoning, when we believe any miracle of MAHOMET or his successors, we have for our warrant the testimony of a few barbarous ARABIANS: And on the other hand, we are to regard the authority of TITUS LIVIUS, PLUTARCH, TACITUS, and in short, of all the authors and witnesses, GRECIAN, CHINESE, and ROMAN CATHOLIC, who have related any miracle in their particular religion; I say, we are to regard their testimony in the same light as if they had mentioned that MAHOMETAN miracle, and had in express terms contradicted it, with the same certainty as they have for the miracle they relate. This argument may appear over subtile and refined; but is not in reality different from the reasoning of a judge, who supposes, that the credit of two witnesses, maintaining a crime against any one, is destroyed by the testimony of two others, who affirm him to have been two hundred leagues distant, at the same instant when the crime is said to have been committed. . . .

Upon the whole, then, it appears, that no testimony for any kind of miracle has ever amounted to a probability, much less to a proof; and that, even supposing it amounted to a proof, it would be opposed by another proof; derived from the very nature of the fact, which it would endeavour to establish. It is experience only, which gives authority to human testimony; and it is the same experience, which assures us of the laws of nature. When, therefore, these two kinds of experience are contrary, we have nothing to do but substract the one from the other, and embrace an opinion, either on one side or the other, with that assurance which arises from the remainder. But according to the principle here explained, this substraction, with regard to all popular religions, amounts to an entire annihilation; and therefore we may establish it as a maxim, that no human testimony can have such force as to prove a miracle, and make it a just foundation for any such system of religion.

I beg the limitations here made may be remarked, when I say, that a miracle can never be proved, so as to be the foundation of a system of religion. For I own, that otherwise, there may possibly be miracles, or violations of the usual course of nature, of such a kind as to admit of proof from human testimony; though, perhaps, it will be impossible to find any such in all the records of history. Thus, suppose, all authors, in all languages, agree, that, from the first of JANUARY 1600, there was a total darkness over the whole earth for eight days:

Suppose that the tradition of this extraordinary event is still strong and lively among the people: That all travellers, who return from foreign countries, bring us accounts of the same tradition, without the least variation or contradiction: It is evident, that our present philosophers, instead of doubting the fact, ought to receive it as certain, and ought to search for the causes whence it might be derived. The decay, corruption, and dissolution of nature, is an event rendered probable by so many analogies, that any phænomenon, which seems to have a tendency towards that catastrophe, comes within the reach of human testimony, if that testimony be very extensive and uniform.

But suppose, that all the historians who treat of ENGLAND, should agree, that, on the first of JANUARY 1600, QUEEN ELIZABETH died; that both before and after her death she was seen by her physicians and the whole court, as is usual with persons of her rank; that her successor was acknowledged and proclaimed by the parliament; and that, after being interred a month, she again appeared, resumed the throne, and governed ENGLAND for three years: I must confess that I should be surprized at the occurrence of so many odd circumstances, but should not have the least inclination to believe so miraculous an event. I should not doubt of her pretended death, and of those other public circumstances that followed it: I should only assert it to have been pretended, and that it neither was, nor possibly could be real. You would in vain object to me the difficulty, and almost impossibility of deceiving the world in an affair of such consequence; the wisdom and solid judgment of that renowned queen; with the little or no advantage which she could reap from so poor an artifice: All this might astonish me; but I would still reply, that the knavery and folly of men are such common phænomena, that I should rather believe the most extraordinary events to arise from their concurrence, than admit of so signal a violation of the laws of nature.

But should this miracle be ascribed to any new system of religion; men, in all ages, have been so much imposed on by ridiculous stories of that kind, that this very circumstance would be a full proof of a cheat, and sufficient, with all men of sense, not only to make them reject the fact, but reject it without farther examination. Though the Being to whom the miracle is ascribed, be, in this case, Almighty, it does not, upon that account, become a whit more probable; since it is impossible for us to know the attributes or actions of such a Being, otherwise than from the experience which we have of his productions, in the usual course of nature. This still reduces us to past observation, and obliges us to compare the instances of the violation of truth in the testimony of men, with those of the violation of the laws of nature by miracles, in order to judge which of them is most likely and probable. As the violations of truth are more common in the testimony concerning religious miracles, than in that concerning any other matter of fact; this must diminish very much the authority of the former testimony, and make us form a general resolution, never to lend any attention to it, with whatever specious pretence it may be covered. . . .

I am the better pleased with the method of reasoning here delivered, as I think it may serve to confound those dangerous friends or disguised enemies to the *Christian Religion*, who have undertaken to defend it by the principles of human reason. Our most holy religion is founded on *Faith*, not on reason; and it is a sure method of exposing it to put it to such a trial as it is, by no means, fitted to endure. To make this more evident, let us examine those miracles, related in scripture; and not to lose ourselves in too wide a field, let us confine ourselves to such as we find in the *Pentateuch*, which we shall examine, according to the principles of those pretended Christians, not as the word or testimony of God himself, but as the production of a mere human writer and historian. Here then we are first to consider a book, presented to us by a barbarous and ignorant people, written in an age when they were still more barbarous, and in all probability long after the facts which it relates, corroborated by no concurring testimony, and resembling those fabulous accounts, which every nation gives of its origin. Upon reading this book, we find it full of prodigies and miracles. It gives an account of a state of the world and of human nature entirely different from the present: Of our fall from that state: Of the age of man, extended to near a thousand years: Of the destruction of the world by a deluge: Of the arbitrary choice of one people, as the favourites of heaven; and that people the countrymen of the author: Of their deliverance from bondage by prodigies the most astonishing imaginable: I desire any one to lay his hand upon his heart, and after a serious consideration declare, whether he thinks that the falsehood of such a book, supported by such a testimony, would be more extraordinary and miraculous than all the miracles it relates; which is, however, necessary to make it to be received, according to the measures of probability above established.

What we have said of miracles may be applied, without any variation, to prophecies; and indeed, all prophecies are real miracles, and as such only, can be admitted as proofs of any revelation. If it did not exceed the capacity of human nature to foretell future events, it would be absurd to employ any prophecy as an argument for a divine mission or authority from heaven. So that, upon the whole, we may conclude, that the *Christian Religion* not only was at first attended with miracles, but even at this day cannot be believed by any reasonable person without one. Mere reason is insufficient to convince us of its veracity: And whoever is moved by *Faith* to assent to it, is conscious of a continued miracle in his own person, which subverts all the principles of his understanding, and gives him a determination to believe what is most contrary to custom and experience.

R. G. SWINBURNE
Miracles[1]

In this article I wish to investigate whether there could be strong historical evidence for the occurrence of miracles, and contrary to much writing which has derived from Hume's celebrated chapter "Of Miracles", I shall argue that there could be. I understand by a miracle a violation of a law of Nature by a god, that is, a very powerful rational being who is not a material object (viz., is invisible and intangible). My definition of a miracle is thus approximately the same as Hume's: "a transgression of a law of nature by a particular volition of the Deity or by the interposition of some invisible agent".[2] It has been questioned by many biblical scholars whether this is what the biblical writers understood by the terms translated into English 'miracle'. I do not propose to enter into this controversy. Suffice it to say that many subsequent Christian theologians have understood by 'miracle' roughly what I understand by the term and that much medieval and modern apologetic which appeals to purported miracles as evidence of the truth of the Christian revelation has had a similar understanding of miracle to mine.

I shall take the question in two parts. I shall enquire first whether there could be evidence that a law of nature has been violated, and secondly, if there can be such evidence, whether there could be evidence that the violation was due to a god.

First, then, can there be evidence that a law of nature has been violated? It seems natural to understand, as Ninian Smart[3] does, by a violation of a law of nature, an occurrence of a non-repeatable counter-instance to a law of nature. Clearly, as Hume admitted, events contrary to predictions of formulae which we had good reason to believe to be laws of nature often occur. But if we have good reason to believe that they have occurred and good reason to believe that similar events would occur in similar circumstances, then we have good reason to believe that the formulae which we previously believed to be the laws of nature were not in fact such laws. Repeatable counter-instances do not violate laws of nature, they just show propositions purporting to state laws of nature to be false. But if we have good reason to believe that an event E has occurred contrary to predictions of a formula L which we have good reason to believe to be a law of nature, and we have good reason to believe that events similar to E would not occur in

R. G. Swinburne (1934–   ) is Nolloth Professor of Philosophy of Religion at Oxford University. He is the author of An Introduction to Confirmation Theory, The Coherence of Theism, The Existence of God, and Faith and Reason.

MIRACLES   From The Philosophical Quarterly, Vol. 18, No. 73, October 1968. Reprinted by permission of the author and The Philosophical Quarterly.

[1] I am most grateful to Edgar Page and Christopher Williams for their helpful criticisms of an earlier version of this paper.

[2] David Hume, An Enquiry Concerning Human Understanding, ed. L. A. Selby-Bigge (Oxford, 2nd ed., 1902), p. 115, footnote [in Philosophy of Religion: Selected Readings, 2nd ed., page 441].

[3] Ninian Smart, Philosophers and Religious Truth (London, 1964), Ch. II.

circumstances as similar as we like in any respect to those of the original occurrence, then we do not have reason to believe that L is not a law of nature. For any modified formula which allowed us to predict E would allow us to predict similar events in similar circumstances and hence, we have good reason to believe, would give false predictions. Whereas if we leave the formula L unmodified, it will, we have good reason to believe, give correct predictions in all other conceivable circumstances. Hence if we are to say that any law of nature is operative in the field in question we must say that it is L. This seems a natural thing to say rather than to say that no law of nature operates in the field. Yet E is contrary to the predictions of L. Hence, for want of a better expression, we say that E has violated the law of nature L. If the use of the word 'violated' suggests too close an analogy between laws of nature and civil or moral laws, that is unfortunate. Once we have explained, as above, what is meant by a violation of a law of nature, no subsequent confusion need arise.

The crucial question, not adequately discussed by Smart, however, is what would be good reason for believing that an event E, if it occurred, was a nonrepeatable as opposed to a repeatable counter-instance to a formula L which we have on all other evidence good reason to believe to be a law of nature. The evidence that E is a repeatable counter-instance would be that a new formula L^1 fairly well confirmed by the data as a law of nature can be set up. A formula is confirmed by data, if the data obtained so far are predicted by the formula, if new predictions are successful and if the formula is a simple and coherent one relative to the collection of the data.

Compatible with any finite set of data, there will always be an infinite number of possible formulae from which the data can be predicted. We can rule out many by further tests, but however many tests we make we shall still have only a finite number of data and hence an infinite number of formulae compatible with them.

But some of these formulae will be highly complex relative to the data, so that no scientist would consider that the data were evidence that those formulae were true laws of nature. Others are very simple formulae such that the data can be said to provide evidence that they are true laws of nature. Thus suppose the scientist's task is to find a formula accounting for marks on a graph, observed at (1, 1), (2, 2), (3, 3), and (4, 4), the first number of each pair being the x co-ordinate and the second the y co-ordinate. One formula which would predict these marks is $x = y$. Another one is $(x-1)(x-2)(x-3)(x-4) + x = y$. But clearly we would not regard the data as supporting the second formula. It is too clumsy a formula to explain four observations. Among simple formulae supported by the data, the simplest is the best supported and regarded, provisionally, as correct. If the formula survives further tests, that increases the evidence in its favour as a true law.

Now if for E and for all other relevant data we can construct a formula L^1 from which the data can be derived and which either makes successful predictions in other circumstances where L makes bad predictions, or is a fairly simple formula, so that from the fact that it can predict E, and L cannot, we have reason to believe that its predictions, if tested, would be better than those of L in other circumstances, then we have good reason to believe that L^1 is the true law in the field. The formula will indicate under what circumstances divergencies from L similar to E will occur. The evidence thus indicates that they will occur under these circumstances and hence that E is a repeatable counter-instance to the original formula L.

Suppose, however, that for E and all the other data of the field we can construct no new formula L^1 which yields more successful predictions than L in other examined circumstances, nor one which is fairly simple relative to the data; but for all the other data except E the simple formula L does yield good predictions. And suppose that as the data continue to accumulate, L remains a completely successful predictor and there remains no reason to suppose that a simple formula L^1 from which all the other data and E can be derived can be constructed. The evidence then indicates that the divergence from L will not be repeated and hence that E is a non-repeatable counter-instance to a law of nature L.

Here is an example. Suppose E to be the levitation (viz., rising into the air and remaining floating on it) of a certain holy person. E is a counterinstance to otherwise well substantiated laws of mechanics L. We could show E to be a repeatable counter-instance if we could construct a formula L^1 which predicted E and also successfully predicted other divergences from L, as well as all other tested predictions of L; or if we could construct L^1 which was comparatively simple relative to the data and predicted E and all the other tested predictions of L, but predicted divergences from L which had not yet been tested. L^1 might differ from L in that, according to it, under certain circumstances bodies exercise a gravitational repulsion on each other, and the circumstance in which E occurred was one of those circumstances. If L^1 satisfied either of the above two conditions, we would adopt it, and we would then say that under certain circumstances people do levitate and so E was not a counter-instance to a law of nature. However, it might be that any modification which we made to the laws of mechanics to allow them to predict E might not yield any more successful predictions than L and they [might] be so clumsy that there [would be] no reason to believe that their predictions not yet tested would be successful. Under these circumstances we would have good reasons to believe that the levitation of the holy person violated the laws of nature.

If the laws of nature are statistical and not deterministic, it is not in all cases so clear what counts as a counter-instance to them. How improbable does an event have to be to constitute a counter-instance to a statistical law? But this problem is a general one in the philosophy of science and does not raise any issues peculiar to the topic of miracles.

It is clear that all claims about what does or does not violate the laws of nature are corrigible. New scientific knowledge may force us to revise any such claims. But all claims to knowledge about matters of fact are corrigible, and we must reach provisional conclusions about them on the evidence available to us. We have to some extent good evidence about what are the laws of nature, and some of them are so well established and account for so many data that any modifications to them which we could suggest to account for the odd counter-instance would be so clumsy and *ad hoc* as to upset the whole structure of science. In such cases the evidence is strong that if the purported counter-instance occurred it was a violation of the laws of nature. There is good reason to believe that the following events, if they occurred, would be violations of the laws of nature: levitation; resurrection from the dead in full health of a man whose heart has not been beating for twenty-four hours and who was, by other criteria also, dead; water turning into wine without the assistance of chemical apparatus or catalysts; a man getting better from polio in a minute.

So then we could have the evidence that an event E if it occurred was a non-repeatable counter-instance to a true law of nature L. But Hume's argument here runs as follows. The evidence, which *ex hypothesi* is good evidence, that L is a true law of nature is evidence that E did not occur. We have certain other evidence that E did occur. In such circumstances, writes Hume, the wise man "weighs the opposite experiments. He considers which side is supported by the greater number of experiments."[4] Since he supposes that the evidence that E occurred would be that of testimony, Hume concludes "that no testimony is sufficient to establish a miracle, unless the testimony be of such a kind, that its falsehood would be more miraculous, than the fact which it endeavours to establish."[5] He considers that this condition is not in fact satisfied by any purported miracle, though he seems at times to allow that it is logically possible that it might be.

One wonders here at Hume's scale of evidence. Suppose two hundred witnesses claiming to have observed some event E, an event which, if it occurred, would be a non-repeatable counter-instance to a law of nature. Suppose these to be witnesses able and anxious to show that E did not occur if there were grounds for doing so. Would not their combined evidence give us good reason to believe that E occurred? Hume's answer which we can see from his discussion of two apparently equally well authenticated miracles is—No. But then, one is inclined to say, is not Hume just being bigoted, refusing to face facts? It would be virtually impossible to draw up a table showing how many witnesses and of what kind we need to establish the occurrence of an event which, if it occurred, would be a non-repeatable counter-instance to a law of nature. Each purported instance has to be considered on its merits. But certainly one feels that Hume's standards of evidence are too high. What, one wonders, would Hume himself say if he saw such an event?

But behind Hume's excessively stringent demands on evidence there may be a philosophical point which he has not fully brought out. This is a point made by Flew in justification of Hume's standards of evidence: "The justification for giving the 'scientific' this ultimate precedence here over the 'historical' lies in the nature of the propositions concerned and in the evidence which can be displayed to sustain them . . . the candidate historical proposition will be particular, often singular, and in the past tense. . . . But just by reason of this very pastness and particularity it is no longer possible for anyone to examine the subject directly for himself . . . the law of nature will, unlike the candidate historical proposition,

[4]*Op. cit.*, p. 111 [in *Philosophy of Religion: Selected Readings*, 2nd ed., p. 438].

[5]*Op. cit.*, p. 116 [in *Philosophy of Religion: Selected Readings*, 2nd ed., p. 441].

be a general nomological. It can thus in theory, though obviously not always in practice, be tested at any time by any person".[6]

Flew's contrast is, however, mistaken. Particular experiments on particular occasions only give a certain and far from conclusive support to claims that a purported scientific law is true. Any person can test for the truth of a purported scientific law, but a positive result to one test will only give limited support to the claim. Exactly the same holds for purported historical truths. Anyone can examine the evidence, but a particular piece of evidence only gives limited support to the claim that the historical proposition is true. But in the historical as in the scientific case, there is no limit to the amount of evidence. We can go on and on testing for the truth of historical as well as scientific propositions. We can look for more and more data which can only be explained as effects of some specified past event, and data incompatible with its occurrence, just as we can look for more and more data for or against the truth of some physical law. Hence the truth of the historical proposition can also "be tested at any time by any person".

What Hume seems to suppose is that the only evidence about whether an event E happened is the written or verbal testimony of those who would have been in a position to witness it, had it occurred. And as there will be only a finite number of such pieces of testimony, the evidence about whether or not E happened would be finite. But this is not the only testimony which is relevant—we need testimony about the character and competence of the original witnesses. Nor is testimony the only type of evidence. All effects of what happened at the time of the alleged occurrence of E are also relevant. Far more than in Hume's day we are today often in a position to assess what occurred by studying the physical traces of the event. Hume had never met Sherlock Holmes with his ability to assess what happened in the room from the way in which the furniture lay, or where the witness was yesterday from the mud on his boot. As the effects of what happened at the time of the occurrence of E are always with us in some form, we can always go on examining them yet more carefully. Further, we need to investigate whether E, if it did occur, would in fact have brought about the present effects, and whether any other cause could have brought about just these effects. To investigate these issues involves investigating which scientific laws operate (other than the law L of which it is claimed that E was a violation), and this involves doing experiments *ad lib.* Hence there is no end to the amount of new evidence which can be had. The evidence that the event E occurred can go on mounting up in the way that evidence that L is a law of nature can do. The wise man in these circumstances will surely say that he has good reason to believe that E occurred, but also that L is a true law of nature and so that E was a violation of it.

So we could have good reason to believe that a law of nature has been violated. But for a violation of a law of nature to be a miracle, it has to be caused by a god, that is, a very powerful rational being who is not a material object. What could be evidence that it was?

To explain an event as brought about by a rational agent with intentions and

[6] Antony Flew, *Hume's Philosophy of Belief* (London, 1961), pp. 207 ff.

purposes is to give an entirely different kind of explanation of its occurrence from an explanation by scientific laws acting on precedent causes. Our normal grounds for attributing an event to the agency of an embodied rational agent A is that we or others perceived A bringing it about *or* that it is the sort of event that A typically brings about and that A, and no one else of whom we have knowledge, was in a position to bring it about. The second kind of ground is only applicable when we have prior knowledge of the existence of A. In considering evidence for a violation E of a law of nature being due to the agency of a god, I will distinguish two cases, one where we have good reason on grounds other than the occurrence of violations of laws of nature to believe that there exists at least one god, and one where we do not.

Let us take the second case first. Suppose we have no other good reason for believing that a god exists, but an event E then occurs which, our evidence indicates, is a non-repeatable counter-instance to a true law of nature. Now we cannot attribute E to the agency of a god by seeing the god's body bring E about, for gods do not have bodies. But suppose that E occurs in ways and circumstances C strongly analogous to those in which occur events brought about by human agents, and that other violations occur in such circumstances. We would then be justified in claiming that E and other such violations are, like effects of human actions, brought about by agents, but ones unlike men in not being material objects. This inference would be justified because, if an analogy between effects is strong enough, we are always justified in postulating slight difference in causes to account for slight difference in effects. Thus if because of its other observable behaviour we say that light is a disturbance in a medium, then the fact that the medium, if it exists, does not, like other media, slow down material bodies passing through it, is not by itself (viz., if there are no other disanalogies) a reason for saying that the light is not a disturbance in a medium, but only for saying that the medium in which light is a disturbance has the peculiar property of not resisting the passage of material bodies. So if, because of very strong similarity between the ways and circumstances of the occurrence of E and other violations of laws of nature to the ways and circumstances in which effects are produced by human agents, we postulate a similar cause—a rational agent, the fact that there are certain disanalogies (viz., we cannot point to the agent, say where his body is) does not mean that our explanation is wrong. It only means that the agent is unlike humans in not having a body. But this move is only justified if the similarities are otherwise strong. Nineteenth-century scientists eventually concluded that for light the similarities were not strong enough to outweigh the dissimilarities and justify postulating the medium with the peculiar property.

Now what similarities in the ways and circumstances C of their occurrence could there be between E (and other violations of laws of nature) and the effects of human actions to justify the postulation of similar causes? Suppose that E occurred in answer to a request. Thus E might be an explosion in my room, totally inexplicable by the laws of nature, when at the time of its occurrence there were in a room on the other side of the corridor men in turbans chanting "O God of the Sikhs, may there be an explosion in Swinburne's room". Suppose, too, that when E occurs a voice, but not the voice of an embodied agent, is heard giving reasonable reasons for granting the request. When the explosion occurs in my room, a voice emanating from no man or animal or man-made machine is heard saying "Your request is granted. He deserves a lesson". Would not all this be good reason for postulating a rational agent other than a material object who brought about E and the other violations, an agent powerful enough to change instantaneously by intervention the properties of things, viz., a god? Clearly if the analogy were strong enough between the ways and circumstances in which violations of laws of nature and effects of human action occur, it would be. If furthermore the prayers which were answered by miracles were prayers for certain kinds of events (e.g., relief of suffering, punishment of ill-doers) and those which were not answered by miracles were for events of different kinds, then this would show something about the character of the god. Normally, of course, the evidence adduced by theists for the occurrence of miracles is not as strong as I have indicated that very strong evidence would be. Violations are often reported as occurring subsequent to prayer for them to occur, and seldom otherwise; but voices giving reasons for answering such a request are rare indeed. Whether in cases where voices are not heard but the occurrence of a violation E and of prayer for its occurrence were both well confirmed, we would be justified in concluding that the existence of a god who brought E about is a matter of whether the analogy is strong enough as it stands. The question of exactly when an analogy is strong enough to justify an inference based on it is a difficult one. But my only point here is that if the analogy were strong enough, the inference would be justified.

Suppose now that we have other evidence for the existence of a god. Then if E occurs in the circumstances C, previously described, that E is due to the activity of a god is more adequately substantiated, and the occurrence of E gives further support to the evidence for the existence of a god. But if we already have reason to believe in the existence of a god, the occurrence of E not under circumstances as similar as C to those under which human agents often bring about results, could nevertheless sometimes be justifiably attributed to his activity. Thus, if the occurrence of E is the sort of thing that the only god of whose existence we have evidence would wish to bring about if he has the character suggested by the other evidence for his existence, we can reasonably hold him responsible for the occurrence of E which would otherwise be unexplained. The healing of a faithful blind Christian contrary to the laws of nature could reasonably be attributed to the God of the Christians, if there were other evidence for his existence, whether or not the blind man or other Christians had ever prayed for that result.

For these reasons I conclude that we can have good reason to believe that a violation of a law of nature was caused by a god, and so was a miracle.

I would like to make two final points, one to tidy up the argument and the other to meet a further argument put forward by Hume which I have not previously discussed.

Entia non sunt multiplicanda praeter necessitatem.—Unless we have good reason to do so we ought not to postulate the existence of more than one god, but to suppose that the same being answers all prayers. But there could be good reason to postulate the existence of more than one god, and evidence to this effect could be provided by miracles. One way in which this could happen is that prayers for a certain kind of result, for example, shipwreck, which began "O, Neptune" were often answered, and also prayers for a different kind of result, for example, success in love, which began "O, Venus" were also often answered, but prayers for a result of the first kind beginning "O, Venus", and for a result of the second kind beginning "O, Neptune" were never answered. Evidence for the existence of one god would in general support, not oppose, evidence for the existence of a second one since, by suggesting that there is one rational being other than those whom we can see, it makes more reasonable the postulation of another one.

The second point is that there is no reason at all to suppose that Hume is in general right to claim that "every miracle . . . pretended to have been wrought in any . . . (religion) . . . as its direct scope is to establish the particular system to which it is attributed; so has it the same force, though more indirectly, to overthrow every other system. In destroying a rival system it likewise destroys the credit of those miracles on which that system was established".[7] If Hume were right to claim that evidence for the miracles of one religion was evidence against the miracles of any other, then indeed evidence for miracles in each would be poor. But in fact evidence for a miracle "wrought in one religion" is only evidence against the occurrence of a miracle "wrought in another religion" if the two miracles, if they occurred, would be evidence for propositions of the two religious systems incompatible with each other. It is hard to think of pairs of alleged miracles of this type. If there were evidence for a Roman Catholic miracle which was evidence for the doctrine of transubstantiation and evidence for a Protestant miracle which was evidence against it, here we would have a case of the conflict of evidence which, Hume claims, occurs generally with alleged miracles. But it is enough to give this example to see that most alleged miracles do not give rise to conflicts of this kind. Most alleged miracles, if they occurred, would only show the power of god or gods and their concern for the needs of men, and little else.

My main conclusion, to repeat it, is that there are no logical difficulties in supposing that there could be strong historical evidence for the occurrence of miracles. Whether there is such evidence is, of course, another matter.

[7] *Op. cit.*, pp. 121 ff [in *Philosophy of Religion: Selected Readings*, 2nd ed., p. 443].

PAUL TILLICH
Revelation and Miracle

The word "miracle," according to the ordinary definition, designates a happening that contradicts the laws of nature. This definition and the innumerable unverified miracle stories in all religions have rendered the term misleading and dangerous for theological use. But a word which expresses a genuine experience can only be dropped if a substitute is at hand, and it does not seem that such a substitute has been found. The New Testament often uses the Greek word *sē-meion*, "sign," pointing to the religious meaning of the miracles. But the word "sign" without a qualifying addition cannot express this religious meaning. It would be more accurate to add the word "event" to "sign" and to speak of *sign-events*. The original meaning of miracle, "that which produces astonishment," is quite adequate for describing the "giving side" of a revelatory experience. But this connotation has been swallowed by the bad connotation of a supranatural interference which destroys the natural structure of events. The bad connotation is avoided in the word "sign" and the phrase "sign-event."

While the original naïve religious consciousness accepts astounding stories in connection with divine manifestations without elaborating a supranaturalistic theory of miracles, rationalistic periods make the negation of natural laws the main point in miracle stories. A kind of irrationalist rationalism develops in which the degree of absurdity in a miracle story becomes the measure of its religious value. The more impossible, the more revelatory! Already in the New Testament one can observe that, the later the tradition, the more the antinatural element is emphasized over against the sign element. In the postapostolic period, when the apocryphal Gospels were produced, there were no checks against absurdity. Pagans and Christians alike were not so much interested in the presence of the divine in shaking and sign-giving events as they were in the sensation produced in their rationalistic minds by antirational happenings. This rationalistic antirationalism infected later Christianity, and it is still a burden for the life of the church and for theology.

The manifestation of the mystery of being does not destroy the structure of being in which it becomes manifest. The ecstasy in which the mystery is received does not destroy the rational structure of the mind by which it is received. The sign-event which gives the mystery of revelation does not destroy the rational structure

Paul Tillich (1886–1965) was born and educated in Germany, where he pursued a successful academic career until 1933. Dismissed by Hitler, he came to the United States, taught for many years at the Union Theological Seminary in New York, and later at Harvard and the University of Chicago. Tillich has perhaps had more influence on the development of theology in the United States over the past thirty years than any other single figure. Among his most important works are *Systematic Theology*, *Dynamics of Faith*, and *The Courage to Be*.

of the reality in which it appears. If these criteria are applied, a meaningful doctrine of sign-events or miracles can be stated.

One should not use the word "miracle" for events which create astonishment for a certain time as scientific discoveries, technical creations, impressive works of art or politics, personal achievements, etc. These cease to produce astonishment after one has become accustomed to them, although a profound admiration of them may remain and even increase. Nor are the structures of reality, the *Gestalten*, the qualities, the inner *teloi* of things miracles, although they always will be objects of admiration. There is an element of astonishment in admiration, but it is not a numinous astonishment; it does not point to a miracle.

As ecstasy presupposes the shock of nonbeing in the mind, so sign-events presuppose the stigma of nonbeing in the reality. In shock and stigma, which are strictly correlated, the negative side of the mystery of being appears. The word "stigma" points to marks of disgrace, for example, in the case of a criminal, and to marks of grace, for example, in the case of a saint; in both instances, however, it indicates something negative. There is a stigma that appears on everything, the stigma of finitude, or implicit and inescapable nonbeing. It is striking that in many miracle stories there is a description of the "numinous" dread which grasps those who participate in the miraculous events. There is the feeling that the solid ground of ordinary reality is taken "out from under" their feet. The correlative experience of the stigma of nonbeing in the reality and the shock of nonbeing in the mind produces this feeling, which, although not revelatory in itself, accompanies every genuine revelatory experience.

Miracles cannot be interpreted in terms of a supranatural interference in natural processes. If such an interpretation were true, the manifestation of the ground of being would destroy the structure of being; God would be split within himself, as religious dualism has asserted. It would be more adequate to call such a miracle "demonic," not because it is produced by "demons," but because it discloses a "structure of destruction" (see Part IV, Sec. I). It corresponds with the state of "being possessed" in the mind and could be called "sorcery." The supranaturalistic theory of miracles makes God a sorcerer and a cause of "possession"; it confuses God with demonic structures in the mind and in reality. There are such structures, based on a distortion of genuine manifestations of the mystery of being. A supranaturalistic theology which employs patterns derived from the structure of possession and sorcery for the sake of describing the nature of revelation in terms of the destruction of the subjective as well as of objective reason is certainly intolerable.

The sign-events in which the mystery of being gives itself consist in special constellations of elements of reality in correlation with special constellations of elements of the mind. A genuine miracle is first of all an event which is astonishing, unusual, shaking, without contradicting the rational structure of reality. In the second place, it is an event which points to the mystery of being, expressing its relation to us in a definite way. In the third place, it is an occurrence which is received as a sign-event in an ecstatic experience. Only if these three conditions are fulfilled can one speak of a genuine miracle. That which does not shake one by its astonishing character has no revelatory power. That which shakes one without pointing to the mystery of being is not miracle but sorcery. That which is not received in ecstasy is a report about the belief in a miracle, not an actual miracle. This is emphasized in the synoptic records of the miracles of Jesus. Miracles are given only to those for whom they are sign-events, to those who receive them in faith. Jesus refuses to perform "objective" miracles. They are a contradiction in terms. This strict correlation makes it possible to exchange the words describing miracles and those describing ecstasy. One can say that ecstasy is the miracle of the mind and that miracle is the ecstasy of reality.

Since neither ecstasy nor miracle destroys the structure of cognitive reason, scientific analysis, psychological and physical, as well as historical investigation are possible and necessary. Research can and must proceed without restriction. It can undercut the superstitions and demonic interpretations of revelation, ecstasy, and miracle. Science, psychology, and history are allies of theology in the fight against the supranaturalistic distortions of genuine revelation. Scientific explanation and historical criticism protect revelation; they cannot dissolve it, for revelation belongs to a dimension of reality for which scientific and historical analysis are inadequate. Revelation is the manifestation of the depth of reason and the ground of being. It points to the mystery of existence and to our ultimate concern. It is independent of what science and history say about the conditions in which it appears; and it cannot make science and history dependent on itself. No conflict between different dimensions of reality is possible. Reason receives revelation in ecstasy and miracles; but reason is not destroyed by revelation, just as revelation is not emptied by reason.

Suggestions for Further Reading

An excellent survey of the views of various thinkers concerning the nature of faith and belief is *Religious Belief and the Will* by Louis P. Pojman (Routledge & Kegan Paul, 1986). Other excellent treatments concerning the relationship of faith and reason are Anthony Kenny's *Faith and Reason* (Columbia University Press, 1983) and Richard Swinburne's *Faith and Reason* (Oxford University Press, 1981). Stephan T. Davis's *Faith, Skepticism and Evidence* (Bucknell University Press, 1978), examines faith, evidence, William James's "The Will to Believe," and epistemic justification.

The anthology *Faith and Rationality: Reason and Belief in God*, ed. Alvin Plantinga and Nicholas Wolterstorff (University of Notre Dame Press, 1983), contains several essays that examine the epistemic relation between religious belief and evidence. Four other works ought to be examined: George Mavrodes's *Belief in God* (University Press of America, 1985); Paul Helm's *The Varieties of Belief* (Humanities Press, 1973); Terence Penelhum's *God and Skepticism* (D. Reidel, 1983); and Gerald D. McCarthy's *The Ethics of Belief Debate* (Scholars Press, 1986). The first is a short but incisive philosophical analysis of experience, justification, and religious belief. The second includes an interesting historical exposition of the views of Locke, Calvin, Kant, and others. The third is a historical and philosophical examination of skepticism and fideism. The fourth is a collection of attacks on, and defenses of, evidentialism.

A good historical treatment of the seventeenth- and eighteenth-century debate on miracles is found in *The Great Debate on Miracles* by R. M. Burns (Bucknell University Press, 1981). A good philosophical analysis of the concept of miracles is Richard Swinburne's *The Concept of Miracle* (St. Martin's Press, 1970). The article "Miracles and God's Existence" by J. C. Thornton, *Philosophy* 59 (1984), examines Hume's account of miracles. J. L. Mackie updates Hume's account in Chapter 1 of his *The Miracle of Theism* (Oxford University Press, 1981). An accessible treatment of the case for the rationality of a belief in miracles is C. S. Lewis's *Miracles* (Macmillan, 1978).

DEATH
AND
IMMORTALITY

VII

S ince the dawn of civilization people have thought and wondered about whether there is life after death. From the various religions there have emerged several different conceptions of the afterlife. Among the ones that emphasize the continued existence of the *individual*, we can distinguish at least three views: (1) disembodied existence of the soul after the death of the body; (2) reincarnation of the soul after bodily death, and (3) the reuniting of the soul with its resurrected body. And among these, the two that have been dominant in western culture are the Platonic version (1), in which the person is basically the soul that survives bodily death, and the Christian view (3), in which the person is a unity of soul and body and survives death by means of the reuniting of its soul with its resurrected body. Underlying both of these views is a common conviction: *the human person exists and has experiences after the death of his or her body.*

There are two questions that need to be raised concerning the conviction that the person survives the death of his or her body. There is the *conceptual* question: is the conviction meaningful? And there is the *factual* question: is the conviction true?

Why should anyone think that there is some logical or conceptual difficulty in the idea that a person survives bodily death? Some would argue that a person is something that acts, has thoughts, memories, perceptions, emotions, and certain physical characteristics (height, coloring, shape, weight). But bodily death would do away with physical characteristics, and perhaps perceptions and actions as well. So some philosophers have genuine doubts that the idea of a human person in the absence of a human body makes any sense at all.

Anthony Quinton discusses another facet of the conceptual problem: what is it that constitutes something to be the *same person*? Again, a number of philosophers would argue that it is the identity of the body through time that is essential to a later thing being the same person as an earlier thing. If so, then a person could not survive bodily destruction since the continuing thing, lacking a body, could not be identical with the earlier embodied person. Quinton raises some important objections to this view and develops the theory that continuity of character and memory, not bodily identity, constitutes something to be the same person. If Quinton is correct, the continued existence of a person does not logically require the continued existence of a *particular* body. But, as he notes, this doesn't establish the possibility that a person can exist without any body whatever. Concerning the factual question, Quinton gives a qualified answer. He thinks that the person does depend on the continued existence of the brain.

Suppose that the conceptual problem can be solved in favor of the possibility of the person surviving bodily death. What reasons are there on each side of the factual question? Perhaps the strongest reason on the positive side derives from whatever reasons we have to believe that the theistic God exists. For according to theism, God has created finite persons to exist in fellowship with Himself. But if this is true then it seems to contradict His own purpose if He allows them to perish completely when His purpose for them remains unfulfilled.

Another reason that has been given for human survival of bodily death is the results of the scientific investigation of the phenomena of mental mediumship.

H. H. Price examines these results and suggests that the simplest hypothesis to explain the facts is that of human survival. The only other hypothesis that might account for the facts, the Super-ESP hypothesis, involves imputing quite extraordinary powers to mediums, powers we have no good reason to think they possess. Price draws back from fully endorsing this argument for survival, being content with the advice, "Do not be too sure that you will *not* continue to exist as a person after your physical organism has died."

Bertrand Russell briefly presents the basic argument against the view that we continue to think and have experiences after bodily death. The central point in this argument is that the evidence we have indicates that our mental life is *dependent* on certain bodily processes, particularly those associated with the brain. We know, for example, that damage to various parts of the brain results in the cessation of certain kinds of conscious states—memories, thought processes, and the like. It seems eminently reasonable to infer from this that consciousness is dependent for its existence on the existence and proper functioning of the human brain. When at death the brain ceases to function, the reasonable inference is that our mental life ceases as well. J. M. E. McTaggart suggests, however, that all the argument really shows is that *while we have a body* the self is dependent on the proper functioning of the brain.

It is worth noting that those theories that emphasize that the person is simply a soul and affirm the continued existence of the person (soul) after the death of the body are more subject to the objections to survival than are theories that emphasize that the person is a composite of soul and body and affirm that genuine life after death is possible only with a resurrected or reconstituted body.

W. L. R.

ANTHONY QUINTON
The Soul

1.   THE SOUL AND SPIRITUAL SUBSTANCE

Philosophers in recent times have had very little to say about the soul. The word, perhaps, has uncomfortably ecclesiastical associations, and the idea seems to be bound up with a number of discredited or at any rate generally disregarded theories. In the history of philosophy the soul has been used for two distinct purposes: first, as an explanation of the vitality that distinguishes human beings, and also animals and plants, from the broad mass of material objects, and, secondly, as the seat of consciousness. The first of these, which sees the soul as an ethereal but nonetheless physical entity, a volatile collection of fire-atoms or a stream of animal spirits, on some views dissipated with the dissolution of the body, on others absorbed at death into the cosmic soul, and on others again as capable of independent existence, need not detain us. The second, however, the soul of Plato and Descartes, deserves a closer examination than it now usually receives. For it tends to be identified with the view that in each person there is to be found a spiritual substance which is the subject of his mental states and the bearer of his personal identity. But on its widest interpretation, as the nonphysical aspect of a person, its acceptance need not involve either the existence of a spiritual substance over and above the mental states that make up a person's inner, conscious life or the proposition that this spiritual substance is what ultimately determines a person's identity through time. When philosophers dismiss the soul it is usually because they reject one or both of these supposed consequences of belief in it.

It is worth insisting, furthermore, that the existence of a spiritual substance is logically distinct from its being the criterion of personal identity. So the strong, and indeed fatal, arguments against the substance theory of personal identity do not at the same time refute the proposition, self-evident to Berkeley and many others, that there can be no conscious state that is not the state of some subject.

As a criterion of identity spiritual substance has three main weaknesses. First, it is regressive in just the same way as is an account of the identity of a material object through time in terms of its physical components. No general account of the identity of a kind of individual thing can be given which finds that identity in the presence of another individual thing within it. For the question immediately arises, how is the identity through time of the supposed identifier to be established? It, like the thing it is supposed to identify, can present itself at any one time only as it is at that time. However alike its temporally separate phases may be, they still require to be identified as parts of the same, continuing thing. In practice we do identify some wholes through their parts, normally where the parts

Anthony Quinton (1925–   ) was educated at Oxford and has been President of Trinity College, Oxford, since 1978. Quinton has published works in metaphysics and ethical theory.

THE SOUL   From *The Journal of Philosophy* vol. 59, no. 15 (July 19, 1962), pp. 393–409. Reprinted by permission of *The Journal of Philosophy* and the author.

are more stable and persistent unities than the wholes they compose and where, in consequence, the parts are more readily identifiable, as, for example, when we pick out one person's bundle of laundry from the bundles of others after the labels have been lost. But this can be only a practical expedient, not a theoretical solution.

A second difficulty is to find any observable mental entity that can effectively serve as a criterion in this case. The only plausible candidate is that dim, inchoate background, largely composed of organic sensations, which envelops the mental states occupying the focus of attention. This organic background is a relatively unchanging environment for the more dramatic episodes of conscious life to stand out against. But both the fixity and the peripheral status of this background are only relative. It does change, and it, or its parts, can come or be brought into the focus of attention. Even if its comparatively undisturbed persistence of character suggests it as a criterion, its vagueness makes it even less accessible to public application than the general run of mental criteria and leaves it with little power to distinguish between one person and another. The organic background is, of course, as regressive a criterion as any other part of a person's mental life. Its only virtues are that it is observable and that it does seem to be a universal constituent of the momentary cross sections of a person's experience. In this last respect it is preferable to most distinguishable features of a person's mental life. For, generally speaking, the parts of a complex and enduring thing are not necessary to the identity of that thing. Just as a cathedral is still the same cathedral if a piece has been knocked off it, whatever the piece may be, so a person is the same person if he ceases to have a particular belief or emotion, whatever that belief or emotion may be.

Finally, if it is held that the spiritual substance is nevertheless a permanent and unaltering constituent of a person's conscious life, it follows that it must be unobservable and so useless for purposes of identification. Suppose that from its very first stirrings my consciousness has contained a continuous whistling sound of wholly unvarying character. I should clearly never notice it, for I can only notice what varies independently of my consciousness—the whistles that start and stop at times other than those at which I wake up and fall asleep. It is this fact that ensured from the outset that Hume's search for a self over and above his particular perceptions was bound to fail. The unobservability of spiritual substance, and its consequent inapplicability as a criterion, can also be held to follow directly from taking its status as substance seriously, as an uncharacterized substratum for qualities and relations to inhere in with no recognizable features of its own.

But to admit that spiritual substance cannot possibly be the criterion of a person's identity and that it cannot be identified with any straightforwardly observable part of a person's mental life does not mean that it does not exist. It has seemed self-evident to many philosophers that every mental state must have an owner. To believe this is not to commit oneself to the existence of something utterly unobservable. If it is true, although both subjects and mental states are unobservable in isolation, each can be observed in conjuction with the other. There is a comparison here with the relations and observability of the positions and qualities of material things. One cannot be aware of a color except as present at some place and at some time or of a position except as the place and time where some discernible characteristics are manifested. So it might be argued that one can be aware of a conscious subject only as in some mental state or other and of a mental state only as belonging to some subject or other. Critics of the Berkeleyan principle sometimes suggest that it is no more than a faulty inference from the subject-object structure of the sentences in which mental facts are reported. It would certainly be a mistake to infer that a conscious subject is something entirely distinct from all its states from the linguistic fact that we commonly assign mental states to owners. We say of a chair that it has a back, a seat, arms, and legs, but this should not and does not lead us to conclude that the chair is something over and above the parts that it has, appropriately arranged. A more usual argument for the principle starts from the premise that mental states are acts that cannot be conceived without an agent in the same way as there cannot be a blow without a striker or a journey without a traveler. The premise of this argument has been much criticized by recent philosophers. A feeling of depression or a belief in the trustworthiness of a friend is not a precisely datable occurrence but a more or less persisting dispositional state. Nor is it an instance of agency in the sense of being the intentional execution of a decision. But these mistaken implications do not affect the validity of the argument under consideration. A disposition requires a possessor as much as an act requires an agent, and the blow I get from a swinging door still presupposes the existence of the door even though it did not mean to hit me.

The strength of the argument lies in the fact that we can assert the existence of some mental state, a feeling of anger let us say, only when we are in a position to assert either that we ourselves are angry or that somebody else is. We have given no sense to the words "discovering the existence of a mental state that is not my own or anyone else's." The nearest we come to speaking in this way is when we say, for example, "there is a sadness about the place," when walking about some ruins in a contemplative frame of mind. What we mean in this case is that the place inclines us to feel sad and might well give rise to the same inclination in others. And this capacity for producing sad feelings in myself and others, as a disposition, has its own substance, so to speak: the broken columns and collapsed walls with which it is bound up.

The subject in this rather thin and formal sense is not borne down in the ruin of that concept of spiritual substance in which it is proposed as the determinant of personal identity. It could be argued that it is a loose way of referring to the related series of other mental states or to the body or both with which any given mental state is universally associated by our manner of reporting such states. If it is something distinct from both of these, as it has traditionally been believed to be, it is not properly to be called the soul. It could not exist without any states at all, and even if it could it would be an emotionally useless form of survival of bodily death. Its existence, in fact, is irrelevant to the problem of the soul, which is that of whether a person is essentially mental in character and so distinct from his body, a connected sequence of mental states and not a physical object. It is irrelevant whether the sequence of mental states composing a person on this theory presupposes a distinguishable subject or not.

Spiritual substance cannot be the criterion of personal identity, and it may or may not be presupposed by the existence of conscious mental states. Whether as part or presupposition of our mental life, it should not be identified with the soul when this is conceived as the nonbodily aspect of a person. The well-founded conviction that there is no spiritual substance in the first sense and widespread doubts as to its existence in the second should not be allowed to obscure the issue of whether there is a unitary nonbodily aspect to a person and, if there is, whether it is the fundamental and more important aspect. Locke saw that spiritual substance could not account for personal identity and, although he believed in its existence, speculated whether it might not have been possible for God to endow a material substance with the power of thinking. Yet he clearly believed in the soul as the connected sequence of a person's conscious states, regarded this sequence as what a person essentially was, and held it to be capable of existing independently of the body. I want to consider whether an empirical concept of the soul, which, like Locke's, interprets it as a sequence of mental states logically distinct from the body and is neutral with regard to the problem of the subject, can be constructed.

2.   THE EMPIRICAL CONCEPT OF THE SOUL

It will be admitted that among all the facts that involve a person there is a class that can be described as mental in some sense or other. Is it enough to define the soul as the temporally extended totality of mental states and events that belong to a person? It will not be enough to provide a concept of the soul as something logically distinct from the body if the idea of the series of a person's mental states involves some reference to the particular human body that he possesses. In the first place, therefore, a nonbodily criterion of personal identity must be produced. For if the soul were the series of mental states associated with a given body, in the sense of being publicly reported by it and being manifested by its behavior, two temporally separate mental states could belong to the history of the same soul only if they were in fact associated with one and the same human body. This notion of the soul could have no application to mental states that were not associated with bodies. The soul must, then, be a series of mental states that is identified through time in virtue of the properties and relations of these mental states themselves. Both the elements of the complex and the relations that make an identifiable persisting thing out of them must be mental. To establish the possibility of such a mental criterion of identity will be the hardest part of the undertaking.

Locke's criterion of memory has been much criticized, and it is certainly untenable in some of the interpretations it has been given. It will not do to say that two mental states belong to the same soul if and only if whoever has the later one can recollect the earlier one if the possibility of recollection involved is factual and not formal. For people forget things, and the paradox of the gallant officer is generated in which he is revealed as identical with both his childish and his senile selves while these are not identical with each other. However, a more plausible criterion can be offered in terms of continuity of character and memory. Two soul-phases belong to the same soul, on this view, if they are connected by a continuous character and memory path. A soul-phase is a set of contemporaneous mental states belonging to the same momentary consciousness. Two soul-phases are directly continuous if they are temporally juxtaposed, if the character revealed by the constituents of each is closely similar, and if the later contains recollections of some elements of the earlier. Two soul-phases are indirectly continuous and connected by a continuous character and memory path if there is a series of soul-phases all of whose members are directly continuous with their immediate pre-decessors and successors in the series and if the original soul-phases are the two end points of the series. There is a clear analogy between this criterion and the one by means of which material objects, including human bodies, are identified. Two object-phases belong to the same object if they are connected by a continuous quality and position path. Direct continuity in this case obtains between two temporally juxtaposed object-phases which are closely similar in qualities and are in the same position or in closely neighboring positions. Indirect continuity is once again the ancestral of direct continuity. There is no limit to the amount of difference in position allowed by the criterion to two indirectly continuous object-phases, but in normal discourse a limit is set to the amount of qualitative differ-ence allowed by the requirement that the two phases be of objects of the same kind. Character in the mental case corresponds to quality in the physical and memory to spatial position. The soul, then, can be defined empirically as a series of mental states connected by continuity of character and memory.

Now there is an objection to the idea that memory can be any sort of funda-mental criterion of identity which rests on the view that a memory criterion pre-supposes a bodily criterion. I shall defer the consideration of this issue, however, until two less serious difficulties have been met. These are that the construction suggested requires an exploded Cartesian dualism about the nature of mental states and, arising out of this, that a person's character is not clearly distinguishable from his body. The former, Rylean, objection can be met without difficulty. Even if the most extreme and reductive version of logical behaviorism were correct, even if a person's mental states were simply and solely behavioral dispositions, actual or potential, his character a complex property of these dispositions, and his memory a particular disposition to make first-person statements in the past tense without inference or reliance on testimony, the empirical concept of the soul would still apply to something distinct from any particular human body, though some body or other, not necessarily human perhaps, would be required to mani-fest the appropriate dispositions in its behavior and speech. In other words, an extreme, reductive, logical behaviorism is perfectly compatible with reincarnation, with the manifestation by one body of the character and memories that were previously manifested by another body that no longer exists. The second objection is that the soul as here defined and the body cannot be clearly distinguished, since the possession of some sorts of character trait requires the possession of an appro-priate sort of body. I do not see that there is much empirical foundation for this to start with. It would be odd for a six-year-old girl to display the character of Winston Churchill, odd indeed to the point of outrageousness, but it is not utterly inconceivable. At first, no doubt, the girl's display of dogged endurance, a world-historical comprehensiveness of outlook, and so forth, would strike one as distasteful and pretentious in so young a child. But if she kept it up the impression would wear off. We do not, after all, find the story of Christ disputing with the doctors in the temple literally unintelligible. And a very large number of character traits seem to presume nothing about the age, sex, build, and general physical condition of their host. However, even if this were an empirically well-founded point, it would not be a relevant one. It would merely show that the possession of a given trait of character required the possession of an appropriate *kind* of body, a large one or a male one or an old one, and not the possession of a *particular* body. As things are, characters can survive large and even emotionally disastrous alterations to the physical type of a person's body, and these changes may have the effect of making it hard to others to recognize the continuity of character that there is. But courage, for example, can perfectly well persist even though the bodily conditions for its more obvious manifestations do not.

3.   MENTAL AND BODILY CRITERIA OF IDENTITY

In recent philosophy there have been two apparently independent aspects to the view that the mind is logically dependent on the body. On the one hand, there are the doctrines that hold mental states either to be or necessarily to involve bodily states, whether bodily movement and dispositions thereto or neural events and configurations. With these doctrines, I have argued, the empirical concept of the soul can be reconciled. On the other hand, many philosophers have insisted that the basic and indispensable criterion of personal identity is bodily. Even mind-body dualists like Ayer, who have accepted the existence of a categorially clear-cut class of mental events, have sometimes taken this position. In his first treatment of the problem he appears at first to give a mental account of the concept of a person as being a series of experiences. But the relation that connects them in his theory involves an indispensable reference to a particular persisting human body. A person is made up of those total mental states which contain organic sensations belonging to one particular human body, presumably to be identified itself in terms of continuity of qualities and spatial position. Ayer draws the conclusion that properly follows from this and from any other account of personal identity that involves reference to a particular human body, namely that the notion of a person's disembodied existence is a self-contradictory one and, further, that even the association of a personality with different bodies at different times is inconceivable. These conclusions may well seem to constitute a reductio ad absurdum of the bodily criterion of personal identity rather than a disproof of the possibility of a person's survival of death. To explore them a little further will help to present the claims of mental as against bodily criteria in a clearer light.

At the outset it must be admitted that the theory of a bodily criterion has a number of virtues. It has, first, the theoretical attraction of simplicity, in that it requires only one mode of treatment for the identification through time of all enduring things, treating human beings as just one variety of concrete objects.

Second, it has a practical appeal, in that its application yields uncontentiously correct answers in the very great majority of the actual cases of personal identification with which we are called upon to deal. Finally, it has the merit of realism, for it is, in fact, the procedure of identification that we do most commonly apply. Even where, for lack of relevant evidence, it is inapplicable, as in the case of the Tichborne claimant, it would not be supposed that the result of applying other criteria such as memory would conflict with what the bodily evidence would have shown if it had been forthcoming. Is there anything better to set against these powerful recommendations in favor of a bodily criterion than that it entails that things many people have wanted very deeply to say about the survival of death are inconsistent? A supporter of the bodily criterion might argue that it was so much the worse for them, that their inconsistent assertions arose from attempting to assert and deny at the same time that a person no longer existed.

It does seem strange, all the same, to say that all statements about disembodied or reincarnated persons are self-contradictory. Is it really at all plausible to say this about such familiar things as the simpler type of classical ghost story? It may be argued that there are plenty of stories which are really self-contradictory and yet which can be, in a way, understood and enjoyed, stories about time machines, for example. To try to settle the case we had better consider some concrete instances. Suppose I am walking on the beach with my friend A. He walks off a fair distance, treads on a large mine that someone has forgotten to remove, and is physically demolished in front of my eyes. Others, attracted by the noise, draw near and help to collect the scattered remains of A for burial. That night, alone in my room, I hear A's voice and see a luminous but intangible object, of very much the shape and size of A, standing in the corner. The remarks that come from it are in A's characteristic style and refer to matters that only A could have known about. Suspecting a hallucination, I photograph it and call in witnesses who hear and see what I do. The apparition returns afterwards and tells of where it has been and what it has seen. It would be very peculiar to insist, in these circumstances, that A no longer existed, even though his body no longer exists except as stains on the rocks and in a small box in the mortuary. It is not essential for the argument that the luminous object look like A or that it speaks in A's voice. If it were a featureless cylinder and spoke like a talking weighing machine we should simply take longer becoming convinced that it really was A. But if continuity of character and memory were manifested with normal amplitude, we surely should be convinced.

Consider a slightly different case. I know two men B and C. B is a dark, tall, thin, puritanical Scotsman of sardonic temperament with whom I have gone on bird-watching expeditions. C is a fair, short, plump, apolaustic Pole of indestructible enterprise and optimism with whom I have made a number of more urban outings. One day I come into a room where both appear to be, and the dark, tall, thin man suggests that he and I pursue tonight some acquaintances I made with C, though he says it was with him, a couple of nights ago. The short, fair, plump, cheerful-looking man reminds me in a strong Polish accent of a promise I had made to B, though he says it was to him, and which I had forgotten about, to go in search of owls on this very night. At first I suspect a conspiracy, but the thing continues far beyond any sort of joke, for good perhaps, and is accompanied by suitable amazement on their part at each other's appearance, their own reflections in the mirror, and so forth.

Now what would it be reasonable to say in these circumstances: that B and C have changed bodies (the consequence of a mental criterion), that they have switched character and memories (the consequence of a bodily criterion), or neither? It seems to me quite clear that we should not say that B and C had switched characters and memories. And if this is correct, it follows that bodily identity is not a logically complete criterion of personal identity; at best it could be a necessary condition of personal identity. Of the other alternatives, that of refusing to identify either of the psychophysical hybrids before us with B or C may seem the most scrupulous and proper. But the refusal might take a number of different forms. It might be a categorical denial that either of the hybrids is B or C. It might, more sophisticatedly be an assertion that the concept of personal identity had broken down and that there was no correct answer, affirmative or negative, to the question: which of these two is B and which C? It might, uninterestingly, be a state of amazed and inarticulate confusion.

What support is there for the conclusion required by the empirical concept of the soul, that B and C have substituted bodies? First of all, the rather weak evidence of imaginative literature. In F. Anstey's story *Vice Versa* the corpulent and repressive Mr. Bultitude and his athletic and impulsive schoolboy son are the victims of a similar rearrangement. The author shows not the smallest trace of hesitation in calling the thing with the father's character and memories the father and the thing with the father's body the son. (Cf. also Conan Doyle's *Keinplatz Experiment*.) A solider support is to be found by reflecting on the probable attitude after the switch of those who are most concerned with our original pair, B and C, as persons, those who have the greatest interest in answering the question of their personal identity: their parents, their wives, their children, their closest friends. Would they say that B and C had ceased to exist, that they had exchanged characters and memories or that they had exchanged bodies? It is surely plain that if the character and memories of B and C really survived intact in their new bodily surroundings those closely concerned with them would say that the two had exchanged bodies, that the original persons were where the characters and memories were. For why, after all, do we bother to identify people so carefully? What is unique about individual people that is important enough for us to call them by individual proper names? In our general relations with other human beings their bodies are for the most part intrinsically unimportant. We use them as convenient recognition devices enabling us to locate without difficulty the persisting character and memory complexes in which we are interested, which we love or like. It would be upsetting if a complex with which we were emotionally involved came to have a monstrous or repulsive physical appearance, it would be socially embarrassing if it kept shifting from body to body while most such complexes stayed put, and it would be confusing and tiresome if such shifting around were generally widespread, for it would be a laborious business finding out where one's friends and family were. But that our concern and affection would follow the character and memory complex and not its original bodily associate is surely clear. In the case of general shifting about we should be in the position of people trying to find their intimates in the dark. If the shifts were both frequent and spatially radical we should no doubt give up the attempt to identify individual people, the whole character of relations between people would change, and human life would be like an unending sequence of shortish ocean trips. But, as long as the transfers did not involve large movements in space, the character and memory complexes we are concerned with could be kept track of through their audible identification of themselves. And there is no reason to doubt that the victim of such a bodily transfer would regard himself as the person whom he seems to remember himself as being. I conclude, then, that although, as things stand, our concept of a person is not called upon to withstand these strains and, therefore, that in the face of a psychophysical transfer we might at first not know what to say, we should not identify the people in question as those who now have the bodies they used to have and that it would be the natural thing to extend our concept of a person, given the purposes for which it has been constructed, so as to identify anyone present to us now with whoever it was who used to have the same character and memories as he has. In other words the soul, defined as a series of mental states connected by continuity of character and memory, is the essential constituent of personality. The soul, therefore, is not only logically distinct from any particular human body with which it is associated; it is also what a person fundamentally is.

It may be objected to the extension of the concept of personal identity that I have argued for that it rests on an incorrect and even sentimental view of the nature of personal relations. There are, it may be said, personal relationships which are of an exclusively bodily character and which would not survive a change of body but which would perfectly well survive a change of soul. Relations of a rather unmitigatedly sexual type might be instanced and also those where the first party to the relationship has violent racial feelings. It can easily be shown that these objections are without substance. In the first place, even the most tired of entrepreneurs is going to take some note of the character and memories of the companion of his later nights at work. He will want her to be docile and quiet, perhaps, and to remember that he takes two parts of water to one of scotch, and no ice. If she ceases to be plump and red-headed and vigorous he may lose interest in and abandon her, but he would have done so anyway in response to the analogous effects of the aging process. If he has any idea of her as a person at all, it will be as a unique cluster of character traits and recollections. As a body, she is simply an instrument of a particular type, no more and no less interesting to him than a physically identical twin. In the case of a purely sexual relationship no particular human body is required, only one of a more or less precisely demarcated kind. Where concern with the soul is wholly absent there is no interest in individual identity at all, only in identity of type. It may be said that this argument cuts both ways: that parents and children are concerned only that they should have round them children and parents with the same sort of character and memories as the children and parents they were with yesterday. But this is doubly incorrect. First, the memories of individual persons cannot be exactly similar, since even the closest of identical twins must see things from slightly different angles; they cannot be in the same place at the same time. More seriously, if more contingently, individual memories, even of identical twins, are seldom, if ever, closely similar. To put the point crudely, the people I want to be with are the people who remember me and the experiences we have shared, not those who remember someone more or less like me with whom they have shared more or less similar experiences. The relevant complexity of the memories of an individual person is of an altogether different order of magnitude from that of the bodily properties of an entrepreneur's lady friend. The lady friend's bodily type is simply enough defined for it to have a large number of instances. It is barely conceivable that two individual memories should be similar enough to be emotionally adequate substitutes for each other. There is the case of the absolutely identical twins who go everywhere together, side by side, and always have done so. Our tendency here would be to treat the pair as a physically dual single person. There would be no point in distinguishing one from the other. As soon as their ways parted sufficiently for the question of which was which to arise, the condition of different memories required for individuation would be satisfied.

It may be felt that the absolutely identical twins present a certain difficulty for the empirical concept of the soul. For suppose their characters and memories to be totally indistinguishable and their thoughts and feelings to have been precisely the same since the first dawning of consciousness in them. Won't the later phases of one of the twins be as continuous in respect of character and memory with the earlier phases of the other as they are with his own earlier phases? Should we even say that there are two persons there at all? The positional differences of the two bodies provides an answer to the second question. Although they are always excited and gloomy together, the thrills and pangs are manifested in distinct bodies and are conceivable as existing separately. We might ignore the duality of their mental states, but we should be able in principle to assert it. As to the matter of continuity, the environment of the two will be inevitably asymmetrical, each will at various times be nearer something than the other, each will block some things from the other's field of vision or touch; so there will always be some, perhaps trivial, difference in the memories of the two. But even if trivial, the difference will be enough to allow the application in this special case of a criterion that normally relies on radical and serious differences. However alike the character and memories of twin no. 1 on Tuesday and twin no. 2 on Wednesday, they will inevitably be less continuous than those of twin no. 2 on the two days.

4.   MEMORY AND BODILY IDENTITY

I must now return to the serious objection to the use of memory as a criterion of personal identity whose consideration was postponed earlier. This has been advanced in an original and interesting article on personal identity recently published by Sydney S. Shoemaker in this JOURNAL.[1] He argues that memory could not be the sole or fundamental criterion for the identity of other people, because in order to establish what the memories of other people are I have to be able to identify them in a bodily way. I cannot accept sentences offered by other people

---

[1] *Personal Identity and Memory*, vol. 56, no. 22 (Oct. 22, 1959), p. 868.

beginning with the words "I remember" quite uncritically. I must be assured, first, that these utterances really are memory claims, that the speaker understands the meaning of the sentences he is using, and, secondly, that his memory claims are reliable. Mr. Shoemaker contends that it is essential, if either of these requirements is to be satisfied, for me to be able to identify the maker of the apparent memory claims in an independent, bodily way. In order to be sure that his remarks really are intended as memory claims, I have to see that he generally uses the form of words in question in connection with antecedent states of affairs of which he has been a witness. And to do this I must be assured that he is at one time uttering a memory sentence and at another, earlier, time is a witness of the event he purports to describe; in other words I must be able to identify him at different times without taking his apparent memories into account. The point is enforced by the second requirement about the conditions under which I can take his memory claims as trustworthy. To do this I must be able to establish at least that he was physically present at and, thus, in a position to observe the state of affairs he now claims to recollect.

There is a good deal of force in these arguments, but I do not think they are sufficient to prove that the soul is not logically distinct from the particular body with which it happens to be associated at any given time. In the first place, the doubt about the significance of someone's current memory claims is not one that I must positively have laid to rest before taking these claims as evidence of his identity. The doubt could seriously arise only in very special and singular circumstances. If someone now says to me, "I remember the battle of Hastings," I will presume him to be slightly misusing the words, since I have good reasons for thinking that no one now alive was present at that remote event. I shall probably take him to be saying that he remembers that there was such a thing as the battle of Hastings, having learnt of it at school, or that it took place in 1066, that Harold was killed at it, that it was the crucial military factor in the Norman conquest, and so forth. But if, on being questioned, he says that these reinterpretations distort the meaning he intended, that he remembers the battle of Hastings in the same way as he remembers having breakfast this morning, if perhaps a little more dimly, then I cannot reasonably suppose that he doesn't understand the meaning of his remark though I may well think that it is false, whether deliberately or not. Mr. Shoemaker admits that in a case of apparent bodily transfer the significance of a person's memory claims could be established by considering the way in which he used memory sentences after the transfer had taken place. So at best this part of his argument could prove that in order to identify people we need to be able to make at least local applications of the criterion of bodily identity. They must be continuous in a bodily way for a period of time sufficient to enable us to establish that they are using memory sentences correctly. But in view of the somewhat strained and artificial character of the doubt in question, I am inclined to reject even this modest conclusion. At best it is a practical requirement: people must be sufficiently stable in a bodily way for me to be able to accumulate a large enough mass of apparent memory claims that are prima facie there to infer from the coherence of these apparent claims that they really are memory claims and not senseless noises.

The reliability of the memory claims of others is a more substantial issue. For, unlike significance, it is a feature of apparent memory claims that we commonly do have serious reason to doubt. It must be admitted, further, that if I have independent reasons for believing that Jones's body was physically present at an event that Jones now claims to remember, I have a piece of strong evidence in support of the correctness of his claim. It is not, of course, conclusive. Even if he were looking in the direction at the time, he might have been in a condition of day-dreaming inattentiveness. The question is, however: is it in any sense a necessary condition for the correctness of my acceptance of a man's present memory claim that I should be able, in principle, to discover that the very same body from which the claim under examination now emerges was actually present at the event now purportedly remembered? I cannot see that it is. To revert to the example of a radical psychophysical exchange between B and C. Suppose that from B's body memory claims emerge about a lot of what I have hitherto confidently taken to be C's experiences. I may have good reason to believe that C's body was present at the events apparently recalled. If the claims are very numerous and detailed, if they involve the recollection of things I didn't know B had seen although I can now establish that they were really present for C to observe, and if the emission of apparent C memories from B's body and vice versa keeps up for a fair period, it would be unreasonable not to conclude that the memory claims emerging from B's body were in fact correct, that they were the memory claims of C not of B, and that therefore the person with B's body was in fact not now B but C. Here again a measure of local bodily continuity seems required. I shall not say that C inhabits B's body at all unless he seems to do so in a fairly substantial way and over a fair period of time. But as long as the possibility of psychophysical exchange is established by some salient cases in which the requirement of local bodily continuity is satisfied I can reasonably conjecture that such exchange has taken place in other cases where the translocation of memory claims is pretty short-lived. At any rate it is only the necessity of local bodily continuity that is established, not the necessary association of a person with one particular body for the whole duration of either. Bodily continuity with a witness is a test of the reliability of someone's memory claims, and it is an important one, but it is not a logically indispensable one.

5.   THE PROBLEM OF DISEMBODIMENT

Nothing that I have said so far has any direct bearing on the question whether the soul can exist in an entirely disembodied state. All I have tried to show is that there is no necessary connection between the soul as a series of mental states linked by character and memory and any particular continuing human body. The question now arises: must the soul be associated with some human body? The apparent intelligibility of my crude ghost story might seem to suggest that not even a body is required, let alone a human one. And the same point appears to be made by the intelligibility of stories in which trees, toadstools, pieces of furniture, and so on are endowed with personal characteristics. But a good deal of caution is needed here. In the first place, even where these personal characteristics are not associated with any sort of body in the physiological sense, they are associated with a body in the epistemological sense; in other words, it is an essential part of the story that the soul in question have physical manifestations. Only in our own case does it seem that strictly disembodied existence is conceivable, in the sense that we can conceive circumstances in which there would be some good reason to claim that a soul existed in a disembodied state. Now how tenuous and non-human could these physical manifestations be? To take a fairly mild example, discussed by Professor Malcolm, could we regard a tree as another person? He maintains with great firmness that we could not, on the rather flimsy ground that trees haven't got mouths and, therefore, could not be said to speak or communicate with us or make memory claims. But if a knothole in a tree trunk physically emitted sounds in the form of speech, why should we not call it a mouth? We may presume that ventriloquism, hidden record-players and microphones, dwarfs concealed in the foliage, and so forth have all been ruled out. If the remarks of the tree were coherent and appropriate to its situation and exhibited the type of continuity that the remarks of persons normally do exhibit, why shouldn't we regard the tree as a person? The point is that we might, by a serious conceptual effort, allow this in the case of one tree or even several trees or even a great many nonhuman physical things. But the sense of our attribution of personality to them would be logically parasitic on our attributions of personality to ordinary human bodies. It is from their utterances and behavior that we derive our concept of personality, and this concept would be applicable to nonhuman things only by more or less far-fetched analogy. That trees should be personal presupposes, then, the personality of human beings. The same considerations hold in the extreme case of absolutely minimal embodiment, as when a recurrent and localized voice of a recognizable tone is heard to make publicly audible remarks. The voice might give evidence of qualitative and positional continuity sufficient to treat it as an identifiable body, even if of an excessively diaphanous kind. The possibility of this procedure, however, is contingent on there being persons in the standard, humanly embodied sense to provide a clear basis for the acquisition of the concept that is being more or less speculatively applied to the voice.

Whatever the logic of the matter, it might be argued, the causal facts of the situation make the whole inquiry into the possibility of a soul's humanly or totally disembodied existence an entirely fantastic one. That people have the memories and characters that they do, that they have memories and characters at all, has as its causally necessary condition the relatively undisturbed persistence of a particular bit of physiological apparatus. One can admit this without concluding that the inquiry is altogether without practical point. For the bit of physiological apparatus in question is not the human body as a whole, but the brain. Certainly lavish changes in the noncerebral parts of the human body often affect the character and perhaps even to some extent the memories of the person whose body it is. But there is no strict relationship here. Now it is sometimes said that the last bit of the body to wear out is the brain, that the brain takes the first and lion's share of the body's nourishment, and that the brains of people who have starved to death are often found in perfectly good structural order. It is already possible to graft bits of one human body on to another, corneas, fingers, and, even, I believe, legs. Might it not be possible to remove the brain from an otherwise worn-out human body and replace it either in a manufactured human body or in a cerebrally untenanted one? In this case we should have a causally conceivable analogue of reincarnation. If this were to become possible and if the resultant creatures appeared in a coherent way to exhibit the character and memories previously associated with the brain that had been fitted into them, we could say that the original person was still in existence even though only a relatively minute part of its original mass and volume was present in the new physical whole. Yet if strict bodily identity is a necessary condition of personal identity, such a description of the outcome would be ruled out as self-contradictory. I conclude, therefore, not only that a logically adequate concept of the soul is constructible but that the construction has some possible utility even in the light of our knowledge of the causal conditions of human life.

H. H. PRICE
The Problem of Life After Death

May I first say, Mr. Chairman,[1] that I regard it as a great honour to have been invited to take part in this Conference? I speak to you as a philosopher who happens to be interested both in religion and in psychical research (like the Neoplatonists long ago). But I am afraid I am going to discuss some questions which it is 'not done' to talk about.

Some of you may have heard a story about Frederick Myers, the most celebrated, perhaps, of all psychical researchers. At a dinner party he asked his neighbour 'What do you think will happen to you after death?' The reply was 'Oh, I suppose I shall inherit eternal bliss; but I do wish you would not talk about such a depressing subject'. The modern reply to such an inquiry would be rather different. Nowadays the subject of life after death is not merely a depressing one. It is something worse. It is a topic which arouses such strong and uncomfortable emotions that we prefer not to mention it at all. Therefore I address you this afternoon with no little fear and trembling. I am going to talk about what psychical researchers call 'the Problem of Survival'.

H. H. Price (1899–1984) was the Wykeham Professor of Logic at Oxford from 1935 until 1959. Although most of Price's work was in the area of epistemology, he also published several essays in philosophy of religion. Price gave the Gifford Lectures in 1960, published as *Belief*.

THE PROBLEM OF LIFE AFTER DEATH   From *Religions Studies*, vol. 3, (April 1968). Copyright © 1968 Cambridge University Press. Reprinted by permission.

[1] This paper was first read to a meeting of The Society for the Study of Theology at a conference at Nottingham in April 1967, with H. D. Lewis in the Chair.

In the past 80 years or so, a good deal of evidence has accumulated which is relevant to this problem. Most of it comes from mediumistic communications. Some apparitional phenomena may be relevant as well, and also some of the strange experiences which psychical researchers call 'out-of-the-body experiences'. But I shall talk mainly about mediumistic communications. I shall not say anything about *physical* mediumship, in which such phenomena as telekinesis and materialisation purport to occur. I shall only talk about *mental* mediumship, the sort in which verbal communications are given, either orally or in the form of automatic writing. These communications can be divided roughly into two kinds. First, there are those which claim to give us evidence for survival, that is, for the continued existence of human personality after bodily death. And secondly, there are those which claim to give us descriptions of 'the other world' (or worlds) in which surviving personalities are alleged to live. Both sorts of communications raise problems which are relevant to the philosophy of religion. And the second sort, the descriptive ones, are very unwelcome to many religious people. If I have time to say anything about them in this paper or in the discussion afterwards, my fear and trembling will be greater than ever. But obviously one must consider the evidential communications first, because you might very well ask why we should pay any attention to mediumistic communications at all.

EXTRA-SENSORY PERCEPTIONS

In order to understand what is happening in the very strange phenomena of mental mediumship one must first consider what is called 'extra-sensory perception' (ESP for short)—telepathy, clairvoyance, precognition and retrocognition. Extrasensory perception is the best-established of all paranormal phenomena. I confess I don't think it is really very like perception, and should prefer the more non-committal phrase 'paranormal cognition'. But the term ESP is now so familiar that I shall go on using it.

It has not been possible, so far, to explain ESP by any kind of radiation hypothesis, and I doubt whether it ever will be possible unless we first modify our views of physical space and time in a pretty drastic manner.

We can, however, say a little about the psychology of ESP. There seem to be two distinguishable stages in the ESP process. The first may be called 'reception' and the second 'emergence'. It would seem that ESP impressions are first received at an *unconscious* level of the subject's mind, and that some sort of barrier or censorship has to be surmounted or circumvented before they can emerge into consciousness. Consequently, they often emerge 'in an oblique manner' as my SPR colleague Mrs. Rosalind Heywood has put it. The paranormally acquired information may only manage to 'get through' in a symbolic form. Or it itself does not get through, though some idea closely associated with it does. Or it is mixed in among other items which have a normal as opposed to a paranormal origin (as a traveller might elude the vigilance of the customs officials by mixing in some prohibited articles among a lot of other innocent ones). Or again, the paranormally acquired bit of information manages to slip into the margin of consciousness but not into the focus, and therefore is easily overlooked and quickly forgotten. Sometimes, again, it emerges in the form of bodily behaviour, as in automatic writing or the semi-automatic speech which occurs in some forms of the mediumistic trance. If as we manage to solve the problem of bringing our ESP powers under voluntary control (for I suspect that we all have them in some degree) I think we shall have to do it by 'smoothing the passage', as it were, between the unconscious level of our personalities and the conscious level. The curious practices which diviners and other psychic persons in all ages have used were probably designed for this purpose and may not be quite so silly as they look.

I hope that these sketchy remarks about the nature of ESP, and especially about its two-stage character (first unconscious reception and then emergence) may throw some light on the difficult problems which we now have to discuss.

CONTROLS AND COMMUNICATORS

The phenomena of mental mediumship are both puzzling and complex. They also vary considerably from one medium to another; for instance, some go into a deep trance, while others are only in a slightly dissociated state, not very far removed from normal waking consciousness.

But most trance mediums purport to have a 'controlling spirit', usually called 'a control' for short, and some have more than one. It is important to distinguish between the control on the one hand, and the communicators on the other. The control is a kind of master of ceremonies, whose function is to introduce the communicators and to look after the medium. It is his task to open the séance and to bring it to an end when the medium has had enough. The control usually claims to be the 'spirit' of a deceased human being, but seldom or never gives much evidence to support this claim. It seems very likely that the control is a secondary personality of the medium herself, some part or stratum of her personality which is repressed in waking life. Word-association tests give some support to this view. It may also be significant that controls sometimes give themselves high sounding foreign names (Mrs Garrett for example has two: Urani and Abdul Latif) and that they sometimes have a rather childish character, for example Mrs Leonard's control Feda.

The mediumistic evidence for survival, whatever weight you may attach to it, is provided by the communicators and not by the control, who seems to be just a psychologically helpful part of the machinery of communication.

Next we must notice that the communicators present themselves in two quite different ways. Usually the medium claims to be seeing them or listening to them. She describes what they look like, and then passes on the information which they give her. She says 'he is showing me such and such a thing' or 'he is telling me so and so'. But with some mediums the communicators occasionally takes a more dramatic form, sometimes called 'the direct voice'. It is as if the medium were *possessed* by an alien personality quite different from her normal one, who is somehow able to use her body and speak through her lips. There may even be a succession of such alien personalities. Each possesses the medium's body for a time and then gives way to another quite different one.

I myself have witnessed this phenomenon only once (the medium in this case was a male, a Mr Flint). I will mention two of these 'possessing' personalities. The first announced that he had been a London street-Arab in earthly life. He then proceeded to give a long theological discourse, uttered with almost incredible rapidity. It was an exposition of Adoptionist Christology, exceedingly fluent but not at all convincing. I think I have never listened to a more boring sermon in my life.

Then another quite different personality took over, and for some reason he took a special interest in me. At any rate, he walked over to the place where I was sitting and had a short conversation with me. I say 'he' did so, because that was how it felt at the time. Though the physical organism which walked across the room was of course the medium's own, and the lips through which the words came were his, it never struck me at the time that the person talking to me was Mr Flint himself. On the contrary, it was like meeting a rather friendly stranger whom one had never met before. The first thing he said to me was 'You know, some of your theories are quite wrong'. I replied that this might well be true. Then he said 'your spectacles are broken'. I opened my spectacle case and showed him that they were not. But an hour or so later, while I was waiting for my train at Paddington, I happened to meet an Oxford colleague of mine, who told me that he had broken *his* spectacles. He was much concerned about it, and on the way back to Oxford we spent a considerable time trying to repair them with pipe-cleaners.

I mention this to show how very life-like these 'possessing' personalities can be and how they can apparently have telepathic or precognitive capacities. For though my own spectacles were not broken, a quite unexpected incident concerning broken spectacles did happen to me shortly afterwards. But however impressive this 'possessive' type of mediumship can be, just as a phenomenon, from the *evidential* point of view it is neither better nor worse than the more usual type, in which the medium merely claims to be passing on what he or she has been told (or shown) by the communicator. From the evidential point of view, the crucial question is just this: do we ever find, in either sort of communication, that verifiable information is given concerning the earthly life of the alleged communicator, information which is sufficient to *identify* him with a particular deceased human being?

But first we must make sure that the medium could not have acquired the information in any normal manner (for instance by looking up an old copy of *Who's Who*). We must also make sure that the sitters do not give anything away, either orally or otherwise. For example, it would be unfortunate if one of them were wearing widow's weeds. To avoid such difficulties, we can make use of 'proxy' sitters who were not personally acquainted with the deceased person. Or again, if someone is 'booking' a sitting with a medium, he himself can give an assumed name instead of his real one.

But even though verifiable information is quite often given concerning the earthly career of a particular deceased person, and even though we can often be sure that the medium has not acquired this information in any normal manner, might she not have acquired it by means of her own powers of extra-sensory perception? *Some* paranormal hypothesis seems to be needed, if we are to explain the facts. But need it be the survival hypothesis? This is the most important question we have to ask when we consider the phenomena of mental mediumship, and it is a very difficult question indeed.

To show how difficult it is, I shall make a few remarks about a celebrated case, called the Edgar Vandy case. You will find a full account of it in Professor C. D. Broad's *Lectures on Psychical Research* ch. 15, and a briefer and more popular one in a recent book by Mr. Andrew Mackenzie called *The Unexplained*, Ch. 11.

THE EDGAR VANDY CASE

A young man called Edgar Vandy died in a drowning accident in August 1933. It was not clear how exactly the accident had happened. So his brother George Vandy had a number of sittings with several mediums in the hope of finding out. (When he arranged the sittings he gave himself a false name and also a false address.) The mystery was never completely cleared up, but some interesting information was given. For instance, at one of the sittings the medium said 'I get the letter H. He is wearing something belonging to your brother who has passed over'. She added 'He (the communicator) is persistent about it. Check it up'. So George Vandy did so; and it turned out that another brother, Harold Vandy, had inadvertently taken and worn Edgar's hat a day or two after Edgar's death.

On another occasion, the medium said that Edgar was showing her a cigarette case, and added 'And that's funny, because he did not smoke'. It was true that Edgar did not smoke, and therefore it seemed very unlikely that he possessed a cigarette case. But the medium gave directions about the place where the cigarette case was. A search was made in the place she described (a certain chest of drawers) and right at the bottom of a drawer, underneath some folded clothes, there was 'a new aluminium box which when held in the hand looked exactly like a metal cigarette case'.

We do have to admit that verifiable information is quite often given in such communications, and we do have to admit (as in the Vandy case which I have just quoted) that it is quite often information which the medium could not have acquired in any normal manner.

How are we to explain such communications? The Survival Hypothesis is one way of explaining them. If the personality of Edgar Vandy did continue to exist after his death he might have found out about the hat in some telepathic or clairvoyant manner, and he might remember about the aluminium box at the bottom of the drawer. He also gave particulars about a drawing of a complicated machine designed by himself, which the medium could not understand at all. If he did survive death, he might be expected to remember about this too.

As I have said, the mystery about his death was never completely cleared up, though several different mediums were consulted. But in a way this apparent failure is consistent with the survival hypothesis and even supports it. At one of the earlier sittings the medium had said 'He is not terribly keen on this enquiry. He does not want you to enquire too closely into the cause of his death'. At a later sitting the medium said 'He was not alone—there was somebody near him who swam away and did not want to help him.' And according to the medium, Edgar added 'I do not altogether blame him'. This suggests that the surviving personality of Edgar Vandy *was* communicating and was trying to shield this other person and save him from getting into trouble.

THE SUPER-ESP HYPOTHESIS

But there is an alternative hypothesis. It is sometimes called the Super-ESP hypothesis. A medium, on this view, is not a person who is capable of getting in touch with inhabitants of another world. She is a person who has very extensive powers of extra-sensory perception. After all, anything which is verifiable in her communications must from the nature of the case be concerned with facts about *this* world. The ostensible communicator may also tell us about the kind of life he claims to be living in the next world and what sort of a world it is. Indeed, we are told a good deal on this subject in some mediumistic communications, both in spoken communications and in automatic scripts. But surely it is obvious that we have no way of 'checking' communications of this other-worldly kind? We can neither verify them nor falsify them. Therefore (it is argued) we must just disregard them altogether, on the ground that they are 'non-evidential'. At the most, they can only throw light on the psychology of the medium in the way that dreams and fantasies do. So we must fix our attention on the evidential communications, those which concern events in *this* world, whether past, present or future.

Since some of them are in fact verified and the information cannot have been acquired in any normal manner, we must try to explain how they come to be made. This is what the Super-ESP hypothesis undertakes to do. (Some continental writers call it 'the Animistic hypothesis'. I find this terminology confusing, since the word 'Animism' also has another, quite different sense. The term has long been used to denote the belief—alleged to be held by primitive peoples—that inorganic objects, such as stones or rivers, are alive or 'have souls'.)

Indeed, the Super-ESP hypothesis offers us a complete theory of mediumship, and a very plausible one. We know from other evidence (including experimental evidence) that paranormal cognitive capacities—telepathy, clairvoyance, precognition and retrocognition—do exist in a number of human beings. All the verifiable information which a medium gives us, about the earthly life of a particular deceased person, and also sometimes about the affairs of his still-living relatives, including things which are going to happen to them in the future—all this information might conceivably have been acquired by means of the ESP powers of the medium herself. Let us assume that it *was* acquired in that way, at an unconscious level of the medium's mind. The only other assumption we need is that the information acquired is then (as it were) 'worked up' by a process of unconscious imaginative dramatisation, and is presented to the sitters in the form of a more or less plausible impersonation of the deceased relative or friend about whom they are enquiring.

But indeed it is not just an assumption that the human mind has these powers of imaginative dramatisation. We may have to suppose that mediums are more gifted in this respect than most of us. But such powers of imaginative dramatisation are shown in all of us when we are dreaming (also, to a lesser extent, in our waking fantasies).

I think we do not sufficiently consider what an extraordinary phenomenon dreaming is. Even the most commonplace and matter-of-fact person shows an astonishing power of imaginative dramatisation in his dreams. And it seems to me that there really is a close analogy between mediumistic phenomena and dreaming. The medium is as it were 'dreaming aloud' when she utters her communications. We must remember in this connection that spontaneous cases of telepathy occur sometimes in dreams. Indeed, the telepathic dream is perhaps the best known of all types of paranormal phenomena. Dreams are sometimes precognitive too.

If the paranormal cognitive powers of the medium are extensive and her powers of imaginative dramatisation are sufficiently great, there is no reason why she should not present to us a quite recognisable 'impersonation' of a particular deceased person whom we know. We can do this for ourselves when we dream about him. But we get the materials for our imaginative construct from our own memories, whereas she gets them by means of her ESP powers.

PSEUDO-COMMUNICATORS

The Super-ESP hypothesis is also able to explain an awkward fact which I have not hitherto mentioned. There are cases of psuedo-communicators. The most famous example is a purely fictitious character who called himself 'John Ferguson' and purported to give communications about his earthly life. The sitter was the well-known psychical researcher Dr S. G. Soal.

Moreover there is another case, also reported by Dr Soal, which is even more peculiar. A man called Gordon Davis had been a friend of Dr Soal's in his youth and Soal believed him to be dead, having heard that he was killed in the first world war. At a sitting in 1922, Gordon Davis was the communicator. He gave a number of correct details about his schooldays and also about the period when he and Soal had been cadets in the army. Moreover, he spoke with a voice and accent resembling Davis's (it was what is called a 'direct-voice' seance). But it turned out later that Gordon Davis was still alive and was practising as an estate agent in Southend. At the time of the sitting he was interviewing a client.

A believer of the Survival Hypothesis might point out that there are *apparitions* of the living as well as of the dead. But if this analogy is valid, one would expect that mediumistic communications from the living would be more frequent than they are. There are a good many cases of apparitions of the living: but the Gordon Davis case is almost if not quite unique.

You will remember that at an earlier stage of the discussion I distinguished between 'controls' and 'communicators'; and I suggested, in agreement with the majority of psychical researchers, that the control is not a discarnate entity (though it usually claims to be) but is a second personality of the medium herself. Its habitat, so to speak, is not the next world, but some unconscious stratum of the medium's own mind. But according to the Super-ESP hypothesis, communicators have much the same status as controls have. Both alike are imaginative constructs.

The difference between them, according to the super ESP hypothesis, is only this:—the materials out of which a communicator is constructed get *into* the medium's unconscious in a telepathic or clairvoyant or precognitive manner; whereas the materials out of which a control is constructed are just repressed and perhaps childish wishes, memories and thoughts of her own.

This is the one point on which the Super-ESP theory of mediumship agrees with the Spiritualist theory. For the Spiritualists too assign the same status to the control and the communicators: they hold that both alike are discarnate spirits. It is a curious meeting of extremes.

SUPER-ESP VERSUS SURVIVAL

How are we to decide between the Super-ESP hypothesis and the survival hypothesis? *Is* there any way of deciding between them? Well, we can say this at any rate. If we accept the Super-ESP hypothesis we do have to suppose that some living human beings have ESP powers of almost unlimited scope—telepathic, clairvoyant, precognitive and retrocognitive capacities much greater than our *other* evidence about those capacities would suggest.

Let us consider a sitting at which information is requested concerning a particular deceased person Mr A. And let us suppose that it is a proxy sitting: that is, no person who is present at the sitting is a relation or friend or even acquaintance of the late Mr A. All the medium is told is Mr A's name, and the date and possibly also the place of his death.

No doubt there are living human beings who know a number of facts about the earthly career of the late Mr A. There may also be *documentary* evidence of various kinds about him (for example, letters which he wrote when alive, obituary notices about him in newspapers). But how does the medium—or her unconscious—manage to get in touch with just these people among all the millions of living human beings that there are? Or if she is to exercise her clairvoyant powers upon those letters or other documents, how is she to *select* them from among the tons and tons of written material which exist? Does she, so to speak, follow a telepathic link from the sitter, who is just a proxy, to the absent friends or relatives of the late Mr A, and then proceed to 'tap' those memories of this deceased person, and also perhaps their memories concerning the whereabouts of documents written by him or about him? I do not think we have much other evidence to suggest that this sort of thing can be done even by very gifted ESP subjects; and it will of course have to be done unconsciously if the Super-ESP hypothesis is correct.

COSMIC MEMORY

Similar difficulties arise if we try to bolster up the Super-ESP hypothesis by postulating a 'cosmic memory' in which every event (or every human event) which ever happens is somehow retained: something like the 'Great Book' which we are told of in traditional descriptions of the Day of Judgement. (You will recall the splendid stanzas about it in the hymn *Dies Irae*.) For here too the medium suffers from a kind of *embarras de richesse*. The Great Book may, somehow, be available to her, but how is she to find the right page and the right paragraph? It is a very voluminous work indeed!

Moreover, much of what is said about imaginative dramatisation in the Super-ESP hypothesis could quite well be accepted by a believer in the Survival Hypothesis. On either of these two hypotheses, we can admit that information acquired in a telepathic manner, at some unconscious level of the medium's mind, *presents* itself in a dramatised form in her utterances. Her remarks 'he is telling me this' 'he is showing me that' need not be taken to mean that 'he' is literally there beside her. She may indeed have interior mental images—visual images—which make it natural for her to speak in this way. But we may quite well suppose (as I have suggested already) that she is dreaming aloud, as it were—experiencing something like a dream and describing it while she has it.

The important question is, where do the *materials* of this dream come from, since in the course of her dreaming aloud she manages to give correct information which she could not have acquired in any normal manner. If she got them by telepathy, who was the telepathic agent? In the Gordon Davis case he turned out to be a living and physically embodied human being. When the communicator is wholly fictitious, as in the John Ferguson case, the telepathic agent was presumably the sitter, Dr Soal. It is not at all uncommon for a medium to 'pick up' thoughts from the minds of the sitters.

Or if the word 'agent' is misleading (because it may suggest that telepathy is a more conscious and more voluntary process than it actually is) let us ask, who or what was the source of this telepathically acquired information? Once the medium has got the information, she herself (or her unconscious) may proceed to use it as material for a piece of elaborate imaginative dramatisation. But where did she get the information from? This question still remains on our hands, even though we accept all that has been suggested concerning the part which imaginative dramatisation plays in mediumship. And it seems to me that in some cases (the Edgar Vandy case, for instance) much the simplest answer is that she gets the information from the surviving mind of some physically deceased person, and that some part, at least, of his personality does continue to exist after his physical organism is dead.

The communicator, as he presents himself to us through the medium's utterances, might still be wholly or partly a 'construct' produced by the medium's own mind. And yet telepathy from a discarnate source might provide some, or much, or even most of the materials out of which this imaginative construct is built up. Professor Hornell Hart has used the analogy of a historical novel to illustrate this idea. A historical novel is a product of imaginative dramatisation (and much of the work of composing it may well be done at an unconscious level of the writer's mind). Yet quite a lot of perfectly good historical fact enters into this imaginative construct. Some of the characters in the book are wholly fictitious. But others are not. They really existed and really did, or said, or suffered the things the novelist describes. And some parts of the story are betwixt and between. For instance in Scott's picture of King James I in *The Fortunes of Nigel* there is much genuine historical material; but some of the incidents and most of the conversations were the products of the writer's own imaginative powers.

SURVIVAL OF MEMORIES ONLY?

But even though we do think that the Survival hypothesis is the simplest explanation of some mediumistic communications, what kind of survival do they point
to? Is it personal survival? Or does the evidence only suggest that some or many
of the late Mr A's memories continue to exist after his physical organism had
died? In that case, what survives would be something less than a person. It was
said of the Bourbons that they had 'learned nothing and forgotten nothing' during
their period of exile after the French Revolution. If this had been a complete
description of their mental life in that period, they must have ceased to be *persons*
for 24 years or so, and only began to be persons again when they returned to
France in 1814. (This may suggest a rather repulsive version of the Reincarnation
theory, which I leave to you to work out for yourselves.) For genuinely personal
survival, we need evidence of something more than mere survival of memories.
We need evidence of continuing mental activity of a purposive kind.

Do we get it? On the face of it, we sometimes do. In the Edgar Vandy case
already quoted, it looks as if the communicator was trying to produce evidence
which would identify him. Moreover (and more important perhaps) it looks as if
he was trying to prevent his relatives from finding out just why he was not res-
cued, and trying—successfully—to shield or protect the person responsible. As
you will remember, he was represented as saying 'He does not want you to enquire too closely into the causes of his death'.

I will now mention another case, a non-mediumistic one, which seems to
show evidence of purpose. It is the Chaffin Will case. Mr Chaffin, a farmer in
North Carolina, died in 1921. He left a will, dated 1905, in which the whole of
his property was left to one of his four sons, Marshall Chaffin. Some four years
later another son, James, began to have vivid dreams in which his father appeared
at his bedside and spoke to him. In one of these (it is not quite clear whether it
was a dream or a half-waking vision) his father was dressed in an old black overcoat and said 'You will find my will in my overcoat pocket'. James found the
overcoat and looked inside the pocket which had been sewn up. Inside was a piece
of paper on which was written 'Read the 27th chapter of *Genesis* in my daddie's
old bible'. (This is the chapter describing how Jacob supplanted Esau.) James
found the old bible in a drawer and between the pages containing *Genesis* ch. 27
there was another will dated 1919, 14 years later than the first one. In this the
testator said that after reading Genesis ch. 27, he wished his property to be divided
equally between his four sons. This will, though unattested by witnesses, was valid
by the laws of North Carolina, and its provisions were accordingly carried out.
Here we do seem to have evidence of *post mortem* purposive activity.

THE CROSS-CORRESPONDENCES

Moreover, we sometimes seem to have evidence of something more, not
only purpose but also of a quite elaborate intelligent desire. The best-known examples of this are the Cross Correspondence cases investigated by the Society for
Psychical Research in the first quarter of this century. The story is exceedingly

complicated. You will find an excellent presentation of it in Mr W. H. Salter's book *Zoar*, pp. 169–208. I shall just give you a very brief sketch of the kind of thing which happened. Most of the material came in the form of automatic writing. A number of automatic writers began to produce scripts independently of each other. The scripts contained many rather recondite literary allusions, mostly to the Greek and Latin classics; and when any one script was read by itself, it was impossible to see what the point of the allusions was. But when several scripts were considered together, it was found that those cryptic allusions made sense. What automatist A had written referred to something which automatist B had written independently. Sometimes *directions* were actually given in the script of one automatist A, telling her to send her script to another automatist B, someone she had never met.

It does look as if there were evidence of *post mortem* design here (a very ingenious design too) and it was eventually claimed in the scripts themselves that the author of the design was Frederick Myers, who had died shortly before the Cross-Correspondences began and was himself a very accomplished classical scholar. If we reject this explanation, we shall have to suppose that a great deal of elaborate and ingenious planning went on in the mind of one of the automatists, though none of them had any conscious awareness of any such planning. There must have been a great deal of unconscious telepathy too, whereby the arch-planner revealed little bits of the plan (but not too much) to each of the other participants.

Here we have another illustration of a point which I tried to make earlier. One may put it like this:—the more you *deflate* the survival hypothesis, the more you have to *inflate* the powers of the human unconscious—the unconscious stratum or level of the minds of physically embodied human beings. We have already seen how much they have to be inflated in the Super-ESP hypothesis. And we have to inflate them still more when we consider the special sort of evidence presented to us in the Cross-Correspondence cases.

COMMUNICATIONS DESCRIBING 'OTHER WORLDS'

Finally, there is one other point which has to be considered if we are inclined to think that the mediumistic evidence for survival will only establish (at the most) the survival of a set of memories, something much less than the survival of a complete personality.

There are mediumistic communications which purport to describe 'the other world' and the kind of life which the communicator is living in his *post mortem* condition. As I have said already, some psychical researchers maintain that communications of this purely descriptive kind should be ignored altogether, on the ground that they are 'non-evidential'. It is of course true that we have no way of verifying them or falsifying them; and it is not much good to reply 'just wait till you are dead, and then you will be able to see for yourself whether they are correct or not', since this obviously begs the question in favour of the Survival Hypothesis. All the same, this recommendation, that communications of this other-world-describing kind should just be ignored altogether, seems to me altogether *too* positivistic and puritanical.

May I remind you of my point about the Bourbons, who were said to have learned nothing and forgotten nothing? These so-called non-evidential communications do suggest that the communicators *have* learned something since they died. We 'live and learn'. Or rather we do not live in a personal way unless we continue to have experiences—new experiences, and not just memories of old ones. Let me put it this way: if the Survival Hypothesis is true, there *ought* to be communications of this purely descriptive kind, describing 'other worlds' and the kind of life which is alleged to be lived in them. And if such descriptive communications never occurred, that would be a very serious objection to the Survival Hypothesis. In fact, however, communications of this other-world-describing kind are very abundant, almost embarrassingly so. Some of these descriptions (not all of them) are tolerably clear and coherent and have at any rate the kind of interest which traveller's tales have. My own knowledge of this kind of mediumistic literature is pretty slight and superficial. All the same I wish I had time to say a little about it, because these other-world-describing communications do raise theological problems. Some of them are very repugnant to religious people (and not without reason). I am afraid there are the beginnings of a kind of conflict between psychical research and religion here; and this distresses me, because I happen to have a foot in both camps.

CONCLUSION

Obviously I have not time to discuss these other-world-descriptions now (I will try to say something about them in the discussion afterwards, if any of you are interested). But now I must try to sum up the main argument of this lecture.

My aim was to show that some mediumistic communications do provide us with *evidence* for the continued existence of human personality after death. I am very far from claiming that this evidence is conclusive. But I think it is strong enough to justify the following piece of advice: 'Do not be too sure that you will *not* continue to exist as a person after your physical organism has died'. And even though we cannot go farther than that, the investigation of mental mediumship has taught us something which is quite important.

BERTRAND RUSSELL
An Argument Against Immortality

Before we can profitably discuss whether we shall continue to exist after death, it is well to be clear as to the sense in which a man is the same person as he was yesterday. Philosophers used to think that there were definite substances, the soul and the body, that each lasted on from day to day, that a soul, once created, continued to exist throughout all future time, whereas a body ceased temporarily from death till the resurrection of the body.

The part of this doctrine which concerns the present life is pretty certainly false. The matter of the body is continually changing by processes of nutriment and wastage. Even if it were not, atoms in physics are no longer supposed to have continuous existence; there is no sense in saying: this is the same atom as the one that existed a few minutes ago. The continuity of a human body is a matter of appearance and behavior, not of substance.

The same thing applies to the mind. We think and feel and act, but there is not, in addition to thoughts and feelings and actions, a bare entity, the mind or the soul, which does or suffers these occurrences. The mental continuity of a person is a continuity of habit and memory: there was yesterday one person whose feelings I can remember, and that person I regard as myself of yesterday; but, in fact, myself of yesterday was only certain mental occurrences which are now re-membered and are regarded as part of the person who now recollects them. All that constitutes a person is a series of experiences connected by memory and by certain similarities of the sort we call habit.

If, therefore, we are to believe that a person survives death, we must believe that the memories and habits which constitute the person will continue to be exhibited in a new set of occurrences.

No one can prove that this will not happen. But it is easy to see that it is very unlikely. Our memories and habits are bound up with the structure of the brain, in much the same way in which a river is connected with the riverbed. The water in the river is always changing, but it keeps to the same course because previous rains have worn a channel. In like manner, previous events have worn a channel in the brain, and our thoughts flow along this channel. This is the cause of memory and mental habits. But the brain, as a structure, is dissolved at death, and memory therefore may be expected to be also dissolved. There is no more reason to think otherwise than to expect a river to persist in its old course after an earthquake has raised a mountain where a valley used to be.

All memory, and therefore (one may say) all minds, depend upon a property which is very noticeable in certain kinds of material structures but exists little if

Bertrand Russell (1872–1970) was a prolific and influential English philosopher who studied mathe-matics and philosophy at Trinity College, Cambridge. Russell taught at various British and American universities. In 1950 he received the Nobel Prize for Literature.

at all in other kinds. This is the property of forming habits as a result of frequent similar occurrences. For example: a bright light makes the pupils of the eyes contract; and if you repeatedly flash a light in a man's eyes and beat a gong at the same time, the gong alone will, in the end, cause his pupils to contract. This is a fact about the brain and nervous system—that is to say, about a certain material structure. It will be found that exactly similar facts explain our response to language and our use of it, our memories and the emotions they arouse, our moral or immoral habits of behavior, and indeed everything that constitutes our mental personality, except the part determined by heredity. The part determined by heredity is handed on to our posterity but cannot, in the individual, survive the disintegration of the body. Thus both the hereditary and the acquired parts of a personality are, so far as our experience goes, bound up with the characteristics of certain bodily structures. We all know that memory may be obliterated by an injury to the brain, that a virtuous person may be rendered vicious by encephalitis lethargica, and that a clever child can be turned into an idiot by lack of iodine. In view of such familiar facts, it seems scarcely probable that the mind survives the total destruction of brain structure which occurs at death.

It is not rational arguments but emotions that cause belief in a future life.

The most important of these emotions is fear of death, which is instinctive and biologically useful. If we genuinely and wholeheartedly believed in the future life, we should cease completely to fear death. The effects would be curious, and probably such as most of us would deplore. But our human and subhuman ancestors have fought and exterminated their enemies throughout many geological ages and have profited by courage; it is therefore an advantage to the victors in the struggle for life to be able, on occasion, to overcome the natural fear of death. Among animals and savages, instinctive pugnacity suffices for this purpose; but at a certain stage of development, as the Mohammedans first proved, belief in Paradise has considerable military value as reinforcing natural pugnacity. We should therefore admit that militarists are wise in encouraging the belief in immortality, always supposing that this belief does not become so profound as to produce indifference to the affairs of the world.

J. M. E. McTAGGART
The Dependency Argument

. . . 79. We must now pass on to our second question. My self cannot be a form of the activity of my body. But it is still possible that the nature of my self makes the possession of my present body essential to it. Granted that the body could not exist except for knowledge, it may be that the knowledge of my body, by myself or other selves, is a necessary condition of the existence of my self. In that case it would be an inevitable inference that when my body dissolves, and ceases to be known as a body at all, my self must have ceased also. If A, whenever it exists, is necessarily accompanied by B, then the cessation of B is a sure sign of the cessation of A.

What evidence is there in favour of such a view? In the first place, while we have plenty of experience of selves who possess bodies, we have no indubitable experience of selves who exist without bodies, or after their bodies have ceased to exist. Besides this, the existence of a self seems to involve the experience of sensations. Without them, the self would have no material for thought, will, or feeling, and it is only in these that the self exists. Now there seems good reason to suppose that sensations never occur in our minds at present without some corresponding modifications of the body. This is certainly the case with normal sensations. And, even if the evidence for clairvoyance and thought-transference were beyond dispute, it could never prove the possibility of sensation without bodily accompaniments. For it could not exclude—indeed, it seems rather to suggest—the existence of bodily accompaniments of an obscure and unusual kind.

80. But, after all, these considerations would, at the most, go to show that *some* body was necessary to my self, and not that its present body was necessary. Have we, after the results already reached, any reason to suppose that the death of the body must indicate anything more than that the self had transferred its manifestations to a new body, and had, therefore, passed from the knowledge of the survivors, who had only known it through the old body? The apparent improbability of this lies, I think, simply in our instinctive recurrence to the theory that the self is an activity of the body. In that case, no doubt, it would be impossible that it should be successively connected with two bodies. But that theory we have seen to be untenable. The most that a body can be is an essential accompaniment of the self. And then the supposition that the self has another body would fit the facts quite as well as the supposition that the self has ceased to exist.

There seems no reason why such a change should not be instantaneous. But even if it were not so, no additional difficulty would be created. If a body is essential to the action of a self, the self would be in a state of suspended animation

J. M. E. McTaggart (1866–1925) was an idealist philosopher who studied and taught at Cambridge University. Although he denied the existence of the traditional theistic God, McTaggart defended the concept of immortality.

THE DEPENDENCY ARGUMENT   From *Some Dogmas of Religion* (London: Edward Arnold, 1906; reprinted, New York: Greenwood Press, 1968).

in the interval between its possession of its two bodies—a state which we might almost call one of temporary non-existence. But this is nothing more than what happens, as far as we can observe, in every case of dreamless sleep. During such a sleep the self, so far as we know, is unconscious—as unconscious as it could be without a body. Yet this does not prevent its being the same man who went to sleep and who woke up again. Why should the difficulty be greater in a change of bodies?

81. And then, have we any reason, after all, to suppose that a body is essential to a self? It seems to me that the facts only support a very different proposition— namely, that, *while a self has a body*, that body is essentially connected with the self's mental life.

For example, no self can be conceived as conscious unless it has sufficient data for its mental activity. This material is only given, as far as our observations can go, in the form of sensations, and sensations again, as far as our observations can go, seem invariably connected with changes in a body. But it does not follow, because a self which has a body cannot get its data except in connexion with that body, that it would be impossible for a self without a body to get data in some other way. It may be just the existence of the body which makes these other ways impossible at present. If a man is shut up in a house, the transparency of the windows is an essential condition of his seeing the sky. But it would not be prudent to infer that, if he walked out of the house, he could not see the sky because there was no longer any glass through which he might see it.

With regard to the connexion of the brain with thought, the chief evidence for it appears to be that diseases or mutilations of the brain affect the course of thought. But this does not prove that, even while a man has a brain, his thoughts are directly connected with it. Many things are capable of disturbing thought, which are not essential to its existence. For example, a sufficiently severe attack of toothache may render all consecutive abstract thought impossible. But if the tooth was extracted, I should still be able to think. And, in the same way, the fact that an abnormal state of the brain may affect our thoughts does not prove that the normal states of the brain are necessary for thought.

Even if the brain is essential to thought while we have bodies, it would not follow that when we ceased to have brains we could not think without them. The same argument applies here as with the organs of sense. It might be that the present inability of the self to think except in connexion with the body was a limitation which was imposed by the presence of the body, and which vanished with it. . . .

Suggestions for Further Reading

A wide-ranging and interesting work is John Hick's *Death and Eternal Life* (Harper & Row, 1976). *Survival and Disembodied Existence* by Terence Penelhum (Humanities Press, 1970) is a good philosophical analysis of the notion of afterlife. Peter Geach examines reincarnation and immortality in his *God and the Soul* (Routledge and Kegan Paul, 1969). Antony Flew argues against the plausibility of survival after death in *God, Freedom and Immortality* (Prometheus Books, 1984). Flew also argues against the notion of personal survival, in *The Logic of Mortality* (Basil Blackwell, 1987). The problem of identity with regard to the idea of resurrection is examined in R. T. Herbert, *Paradox and Identity in Theology* (Cornell University Press, 1979).

Ray Anderson's *Theology, Death and Dying* (Basil Blackwell, 1987) examines the notion of afterlife from a theological perspective. Oscar Cullmann examines the role of the notions of immortality and resurrection in the early Christian movement in his *Immortality of the Soul or Resurrection of the Dead?* (Epworth, 1958). The work *Survival?* by David Lorimer (Routledge & Kegan Paul, 1984) examines the relevance of psychic experiences for the notion of afterlife. C. D. Broad's *Lectures on Psychical Research* (Humanities Press, 1962) is still a helpful work on this subject. Robert Kastenbaum, *Is There Life After Death?* (Prentice Hall, 1984), is a work that looks at the question of the evidence for afterlife from perspectives both pro and con. The notion of afterlife is examined from what some have called a "Wittgensteinian Fideistic" perspective in D. Z. Phillips, *Death and Immortality* (St. Martin's Press, 1970). Two other worthwhile works on this subject are *Immortality or Extinction?* (Barnes & Noble, 1981), by Paul Badham and Linda Badham, and *Is Man the Phoenix? A Study of Immortality* (University Press of America, 1983) by Bruce Reichenbach.

B
C
D   1
E   2
F   3
G   4
H   5
I   6
J   7